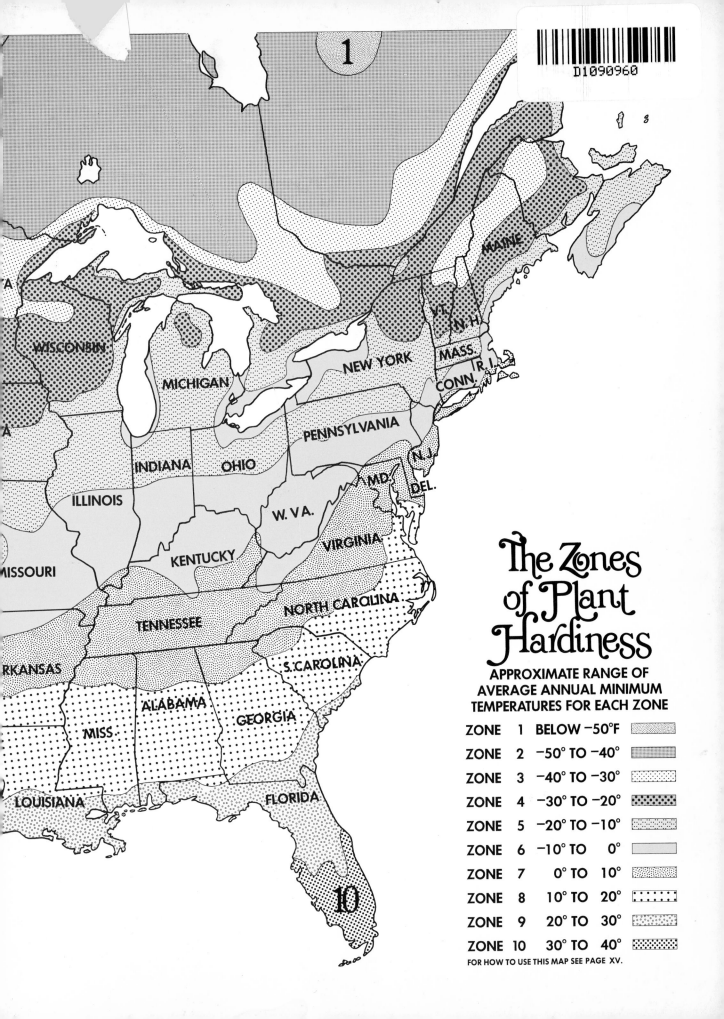

THE
COMPLETE GARDENER

THE
COMPLETE GARDENER

A LIVELY PRACTICAL GUIDE WHEREVER YOU LIVE

by

LOIS WILSON

with special contributions by regional experts

A Helen Van Pelt Wilson Book

Hawthorn Books, Inc.
Publishers
New York

Book design	*GENE ALIMAN*
Jacket photography	*Gene Aliman*
Editors	*Joan Weatherseed and Daniel T. Walden*
Drawings	*Jerry Lazare, Lewis Parker and Gabe D'Aoust (page 93)*
Photography	*Malak; Normunds Berzins; Ivan Kotulsky; Gene Aliman; Clive Webster; Bio-Graphic Unit, Canada Department of Agriculture; John Beaton; Ray Halward; J. I. Thompson; J. H. Eddie; Henry Fry; Royal Botanical Gardens, Hamilton, Ontario; University of Saskatchewan, Saskatoon; Cliff Wright; George Taloumis; M. E. Warren; Rudi Rada; Gretchen Harshbarger; and Lois Wilson*

THE COMPLETE GARDENER

Library of Congress Catalog Card Number: 77-179112
ISBN: 0-8015-1662-5

2 3 4 5 6 7 8 9 10

The Complete Gardener *is a fully revised and enlarged edition of* Chatelaine's Gardening Book.

CREDO

A garden can be many lovely things. It can enhance the house it surrounds.

It can enhance the lives of the people who live in the house.

It can visually stimulate the community.

It can add a new dimension of beauty to the total landscape.

But I believe that it can also be

a place where the magic and mystery of growth refresh and replenish the spirit,

and that refreshing and replenishing can make of the gardener a person who sees the world –

and comes to know it well –

as an exciting place where, by his own hand, miracles can and do happen.

lois wilson

EDITOR'S FOREWORD

How delightful to read a book whose author's voice comes through as clearly as if she were by your side, a person in your own garden. All her sound advice, her know-how, whether she is helping you to design a patio or to plant an airy balcony, is given here in such a lively style that Lois Wilson becomes your friend and adviser from the first page on. You soon find out that she is practical and has broad interests; a wife and mother, she can make a garden for the whole family, including plans for a generous sandbox for "tads" and game-plans for teen-agers. You discover that you can depend on her as a specialist to help you grow better roses, lilies, petunias, fruits or vegetables — all the garden plants you can think of. Warm and understanding, often humorous as she is, Mrs. Wilson is not superficial, though. Obviously, she herself *works* at gardening (I remember her winter-heated cold frame of white violets); she stresses that a satisfactory planting comes with thinking and doing, not just with wishing.

In her own suburban garden — shaded by a two-hundred-year-old oak tree — azaleas, prim-roses, wild trilliums, ferns, magnolias and hundreds of spring bulbs flower as though they belonged there. Feeders are alive with wild birds winter and summer as they splash in a small pool that reflects the blue of the sky. I marvel at how she has kept work to a mini-mum while achieving a handsome year-round effect. The "garden for all seasons," illus-trated on the first page of color in this book, is her own; so, too, are the antique fountain and the "Will o' the Wisp" sculpture in the color section following page 112, for she likes to introduce other arts into her garden.

The great value of *The Complete Gardener* is that it is equivalent to a multivolume ency-clopedia. You don't need to crowd your shelves with a dozen garden books — it's all here in one. If I were giving advice on what would make a basic household reference library, I'd recommend a modern Bible, an unabridged dictionary, a one-volume encyclopedia, a biographical dictionary and *The Complete Gardener*.

Helen Van Pelt Wilson

AUTHOR'S NOTE

It would have been impossible to write a book of this scope
for a country so vast without the help of a great many people.
This we have been fortunate to have.

Our consultants are all experts in their own fields, and they have
responded to the needs of the home gardener in today's world
with help and advice in a warmly human, practical way.
They have been a delight to work with, and their very great
contribution to this book will, I know, be appreciated
by all gardeners everywhere in America.

Lois Wilson

CONSULTANTS

REGIONAL

Dr. Gordon P. DeWolf, Jr., Horticulturist,
The Arnold Arboretum of Harvard University,
Jamaica Plain, Massachusetts

Barbara H. Emerson, Consulting Horticulturist,
Gwynedd Valley, Pennsylvania

Sam L. Fairchild, Garden Consultant,
Reidsville, North Carolina

F. A. C. McCulla, Editor, *The Yardner*,
Men's Garden Club of Houston, Texas

Victor H. Ries, Professor Emeritus, Horticulture,
Ohio State University, Columbus, Ohio

Dr. John Philip Baumgardt, Garden Consultant,
Kansas City, Missouri

Dr. Edward R. Hasselkus, Associate Professor,
College of Agricultural and Life Sciences,
University of Wisconsin, Madison, Wisconsin

Dr. Fred B. Widmoyer, Professor and Head,
Department of Horticulture,
New Mexico State University, Las Cruces, New Mexico

Dr. F. L. Steve O'Rourke, Associate Professor of Horticulture,
Colorado State University, Fort Collins, Colorado

Joseph A. Witt, Associate Director,
University of Washington Arboretum,
Seattle, Washington

Dr. R. B. Streets, Sr., Plant Pathologist Emeritus,
University of Arizona, Tucson, Arizona

SPECIAL

Children's Outdoor Play Equipment . . . . Cornelia Hahn Oberlander

Garden Lighting, Indoor Light Units . . . . General Electric Company
Mrs. Leni Forsdike

Vegetables, Fruit and Nuts . . . . U.S. Department of Agriculture:
Dr. Howard A. Brooks
Dr. August E. Kehr
University of Connecticut:
Richard A. Ashley
David A. Kollas
Connecticut Cooperative Extension Service:
Joseph J. Maisano, Jr.
Canada Department of Agriculture:
V. W. Nuttall
Robert Keith, C.B.C. Gardener of the Air

PLANT SOCIETIES AND ADVISERS

GROWERS AND SUPPLIERS

The Avant Gardener, Vol. 3, No. 3, November 15, 1970

CONTENTS

Part I

WHAT IS YOUR KIND OF GARDEN?

Part II

OF PRACTICAL HELP

Part III
THE FINE POINTS OF GROWING GOOD GARDEN PLANTS WELL

Part IV
THE FUN OF GARDENING INDOORS

Part V
GUIDES TO GARDENING IN ELEVEN REGIONS OF THE UNITED STATES

ILLUSTRATIONS
IN THE TEXT

HOW TO USE
THE ENDPAPER MAP

When specific trees and shrubs are mentioned in the text, you will find a number (in parentheses) following each. This relates to the zones on the endpaper map and indicates, for Parts I-IV, the coldest range in the United States and Canada where this plant is reasonably hardy.

For Part V, which is concerned with specific regions of the United States, the zone number following any tree or shrub indicates the lowest zone *in that region* in which the plant is hardy. You can also expect that plant to grow well in warmer zones as far as Zone 9, which is too warm for a few northern plants and beyond which (Zone 10) the subtropical vegetation takes over.

The designation *a* following a zone number indicates the colder (more northerly or more mountainous) part of that zone; the designation *b* indicates the milder part of the zone.

PART I

WHAT
IS
YOUR
KIND
OF GARDEN?

1 A GARDEN OF ALL-YEAR BEAUTY

Through the whole twelve months of the year, a garden's beauty offers a tonic impact beyond measuring. Tonic for its bracing effect on your spirit; impact for its impressions to be recognized and enjoyed.

Sometimes this impact is subtle, like the appearance of the first tiny snowdrop in spring; sometimes it is spectacular, like a six-foot spire of delphinium spearing the blue of the sky.

Sometimes it is beauty in its season, like the fresh fragrance of lilacs in spring; or it is a delight because of the time of day or night of its happening, like a white birch in moonlight.

Sometimes it's to do with flowers — like a balcony window box tumbling with red geraniums and white petunias; sometimes with leaves, like a cool green tree in summer.

Sometimes it's to do with color shouting like a blazing red climbing rose on a white wall, sometimes a whisper like the brushstrokes of a purple pansy.

But always it's a tonic, always there asking to be recognized and enjoyed. Some of it you can deliberately plan for, some will be unexpected magic. Whichever way it happens in your garden, let the dishes pile up in the sink, the snow lie deep on the drive, the leaves on the lawn and enjoy it!

WINTER BEAUTY IN YOUR GARDEN

Winter's main delight isn't flowers, although a few lucky gardeners in the more temperate parts of the country can coax a Christmas or Lenten rose into bloom and the Pacific Northwest gardener has, in what he calls a "normal" winter, his ice pansies, his camellias, the glistening lively green of rain-wet mosses and ferns.

But for most of us in this country, winter's delight is bare, muscled strength in tree trunks, the leafless black tracery of their twigged branches against a late-day turquoise sky. It's the surprising brightness of bark on many trees and shrubs — gold in the willow, red in shrubby dogwood, shiny bronze-purple in cherry, grey in beech, and dozens of others. Where they're hardy, it's the glossy green of broad-leaved plants — the rhododendrons, mahonias, firethorn, wintercreeper and ivy on a wall. It's a high bush-cranberry hung with puckered, ruby-jewelled fruit. And of course, everywhere, it's evergreens, feathery and deceptively soft — and in dozens of shapes and shades of green.

As well, and especially in winter, it's being aware of those fast-fingered apprentices of the garden — the sun that casts bright blue shadows on sparkling white snow; the rain that, freezing, turns every tree, every twig, every needle, into a magical glitter of glass; the great bowl of the sky; the birds that visit your garden. To me, it's always a miracle that something as tiny a bundle of feathers as a chickadee can survive our winter cold, sometimes, birders in Alaska report, 60° below.

Planning for this liveliness and beauty in your garden precedes delight.

If you haven't already one large tree to act the flexing wrestler in winter, plant one and experience the pleasure of watching it grow. If you haven't already used evergreens as a major part of your garden design, rethink your planning, because just about every kind of evergreen grows well and looks well in all gardens, large and small. Well placed, their fine shape and texture in winter is more clearly seen when it is not blurred by trees and bushes in leaf around them.

Consider a Christmas-tree-shaped one where its mature conical height will be cleanly outlined against the winter sky. Use groups and clumps of bushy ones near a feeder where their friendly shelter will comfort wild birds. Feather a bank with horizontal juniper or yew to catch a frosting of snow. Think of an evergreen hedge as an all-year faithful blocker of an unattractive view.

When you come to choose leafy bushes and trees, check their winter effect not only of shape and bark but for bright fruit. While you are installing services in your garden, plan for the dramatic effect of night lighting. There is nothing, absolutely nothing, so thrilling as a storm of crystal snowflakes teetering down in the floodlit black of night. Put up feeders and connect a warmed drinking pan to draw in the birds.

If you live where sweeping wind is a familiar part of winter — in the Midwest, by any of our great lakes or wide rivers, by the sea — plant a shelterbelt of both deciduous and evergreen trees to break the thrust of the wind. And if you live on that ocean-warmed part of our favored Pacific coast where everything grows with such abandon, choose some of your plants from those with special winter beauty of foliage and flower.

(For detailed help in choosing trees and shrubs for winter effect and for windbarriers see your region's special lists in Part V; CHAPTER 20, Trees; CHAPTER 21, Shrubs; for attracting wild birds to your garden, CHAPTER 10, directions for installing garden lights, CHAPTER 4.)

THE WORD FOR SPRING IS PROMISE

Spring can be as exciting in its promise of coming as in its arrival.

Some late-winter noonday when you're longing for it to appear, try stepping into the hot sun in the garden. Perhaps you'll hear a crow caw or a cardinal throwing his lariat of song, a running trickle of water under the snow at the edge of a path, see how the ice is shrinking at the edge of a pool. If you've had the forethought to plant a pussywillow, look up and see its furry buds fattening. It may already be in yellow-whiskered flower and drawing the honeybees from miles away.

Seek out the little sun traps where snow melts first and where you have thought to plant snowdrops or early crocuses. Let yourself be amazed at the fantastic force of a tiny winter aconite snapping its buttercup-yellow head up out of the barely unfrozen earth. If you have a tall tree, think how high the sap must go to reach its top. (Have you ever wondered what message in a seed tells one plant to be a 6-inch pansy, another a 50-foot tree?) All these small signs will help you to exult in the *promise* of spring even before it actually comes.

When it does come in all its bursting glory — and glory is the only word for it — be prepared by wise planning, done months before, to enjoy what the whole world would agree is a "garden." Flowers everywhere against the clean dark earth — weedless and other-plantless as it will not be again till this time next year.

First come the little bulbs, those I have mentioned and, as well, spurts of crocus, the bluest early scillas nodding in the warming wind, that little beauty, glory-of-the-snow, and a dozen others. Later the taller and splashier daffodils, tulips and hyacinths, many fragrant, all stunning. And planted among them, the earliest-to-bloom perennials — Virginia bluebells, the pink and purple flowered pulmonaria (pretty in spite of a name that sounds like a bad cold), white trilliums, the lovely gold daisies of doronicums; all these give weeks of bloom.

If you plan to have a rock garden, now is its high-flower time. Carpets of blossoming rock plants, flowery dwarf shrubs like the yellow brooms and the fragrant daphnes, small-scale flowering trees like the pink and white Sargent crab apple. All of these are planted early in spring and, with care, bloom for years.

Up in the air, there are more spectacular flowers in shrubs and trees. The big pink and white cups of magnolias and golden stars on forsythia, both in bloom before their leaves; in many states, clouds of flowering dogwood; on the plains and in the east, white froth on May Day trees, Manchu cherries, serviceberries and shadblow. And everyone's favorites, everywhere, lilacs to scent the air with their heavenly perfume, and crab apples — some hardy in nearly every zone of our country — with beautiful flowers in spring, bright fruit for the birds in summer and jelly for us in the fall.

While all this brilliance of flowers goes on, the trees are first a faint haze, then gradually become greener. White birches and balm of Gileads hang with catkin earrings. Horse chestnuts and beeches unpleat their leaves. The poplars are shiny and new. And the haze becomes, in a few weeks, a leafy canopy.

If you have done your homework on proper lawn care and if the fearful fungi that causes snow mold and brown dead patches have *not* done theirs, the grass by now is greening well. Ferns uncurl their fiddleheads and the new green tips on the evergreens make this their handsomest time of the year.

In some parts of the country, a heat wave with temperature in the 80s sometimes interrupts this pleasant progression of cool-loving flowers and grass. When this happens in my garden, I always remember a transplanted Englishman, who said, during one of them, "Spring in America, more often than not, is just an audible click between winter and summer."

Equally, though, a long cool spring often prolongs the loveliness of all spring flowers. This is the happy kind of weather so often part of the pattern of the Pacific coast. There spring begins months earlier than in the rest of the country and every flower lasts weeks longer. A true gardener's heaven. It's here that the showy rhododendrons and azaleas take over the spotlight. If cultivars are chosen for sequence of bloom, they flower dramatically for three months or more.

Now follows a green pause. This is the time when inexperienced Sunday School Superintendents inevitably plan to have Flower Sunday and to take the massed beauty to the nearest hospital. Sadly all they get is a parade of shining faces and hot little hands bringing their gifts of wilted dandelions, a late lilac or two or a very early peony, the flowers off the geraniums their mother has just bought for her garden, or a sticky, wet early iris. Set the date for a spring Flower Sunday when the congregation's gardens are at their mid-spring best, not during the green pause that inevitably follows two weeks later.

LATE SPRING BEAUTY

Iris, either the luminous tall beardeds or the butterfly-flowered Siberians (particularly hardy), break the green spell and begin the parade of handsome perennials which every year can make a breathtaking place of your garden. Peonies come next. Then the big poppies, which are the photographer's delight for their prickled buds, ferny foliage and huge tissue-chiffon flowers, are fascinating backlit with sunlight or a hidden spot.

If you haven't thought about vines for this time, think now. The large flowered clematis takes almost no space, is easy to grow, is delicately graceful and in most gardens has some bloom all summer, even into early fall.

Among the flowery shrubs and small trees, two of the best are the Japanese tree lilac — much later blooming than other lilacs — and the sweet-smelling mock oranges.

Then come the roses. Fragrant, poetically beautiful, capable of making a dedicated gardener out of a man who can't tell a dandelion from a buttercup. Their first flush of bloom comes at this time, then with many kinds there is another, sometimes of better quality, in fall. And by now, it's

Oriental poppy

HIGH SUMMER

Leading the show are the stately, elegant lilies; the radiant, exclamation points of delphiniums; the free-flowering, easy-to-grow day lilies; the exuberant bouncy blooms of phlox; the dahlias, soup plate to teacup size; gorgeous gladiolus and dozens of others. You don't have to be especially aware to enjoy these beauties. There is nothing subtle about their clamor for your attention. But what may intrigue you is the wonder of how anything as lovely as a lily could come from such a fusty brown bulb; anything as statuesque as a 6-foot delphinium grow from such a tiny seed, or anything as ordered and adaptable as a day lily from such a seemingly unorganized chunk of lumpy root. (For details of these plants, see CHAPTER 27, PERENNIALS, and CHAPTER 28, BULBS, CORMS AND TUBERS.)

While all these prima donnas are performing, the annuals — and I count the sun-loving geraniums and marguerites and the shade-loving patience, fuchsia and coleus among them — are tossing their brilliant colors all over the garden. Bright yellow and orange marigolds as tall as a hedge or as low as your shoe; petunias with ruffles and frills; zinnias tip-turned to the sun; white embroidered carpets of sweet alyssum. And all the less well-known beauty of hundreds of others. Probably the most unexpected delight of annuals is how easy most of them are to grow. You can, for early bloom, start them indoors about 6 weeks before they go into the garden; you can buy little prestarted plants from your nurseryman or you can, with many, sow the seed directly in the ground. (For details, see CHAPTER 29.)

Flowering shrubs in summer are rarer than in spring but the hydrangeas — both the white Snowhill and the pinkening PG — are favorites all over the country. The hazy purple fruiting of the smoke tree begins in midsummer and goes on till October wind blows it away. Especially recommended for the Midwest because of their winter hardiness are the plumy cream spikes and cut leaves of the Ural false-spirea which I've seen naturalized over a great outcropping of granite in way-below-zero country and the sister spireas, one short, one a little taller (*S. bumalda* 'Anthony Waterer' and 'Froebelii'), both with hot pink flowers that bloom for a long time if you keep the spent heads cut off.

For the west coast, good summer-flowering shrubs are the pink glossy abelia, an excellent hedge plant; the white New Zealand daisy bush; the fragrant eucryphia, hardy only in the mildest areas and the Irish-born hybrids of escallonia. (For details for growing these shrubs, see CHAPTER 21.)

AND FOR AUTUMN BEAUTY

Summer doesn't turn into autumn, it slides into it. You only know fall has really come when, over the back fence, you smell your neighbor's chili sauce cooking, when the quarterbacks in your family go back to school and when your lawn suddenly stops looking as though a herd of elephants had been having a picnic on it.

Most summer annuals, if you keep their flowers cut off to prevent seed setting, will bloom till frost. With very flowery ones like petunias and alyssum, where you couldn't possibly catch up with every dead flower, you just clip the whole plant back about half in midsummer.

When to this continuing bloom you add all the very special beauty of the autumn prima donnas, the growing part of the year ends with a triumphant chorale, not a long-drawn-out sigh. Michaelmas daisies — and the 'Royal Gem' series are particularly fine — begin as early as mid-August and go on to the end of September. Hardy chrysanthemums in gold and scarlet, rose and white will, in many places, bloom for more than two months — in fact, right past the first few frosts if you cover them at night.

But the real stars of autumn are the bright-berried trees and shrubs, the leaves that turn a glowing yellow, scarlet, cerise or rose. Tops for berries or fruit — many also for coloring in leaves — are the mountain-ashes, the hawthorns, the red and yellow crabs, the white snowberries, the cotoneasters. As well, hardy only in mild regions, there are scarlet skimmia, dogwood and holly and the strange orange, strawberry-like fruit of the madrona tree.

In leaves, nothing is more golden or more a favorite garden tree than white birch, although in some parts of the Midwest poplar runs it a close second. Among large trees, it's hands down in the east for the yellow, orange and red of the sugar maple. For the same brilliance in small trees, the Amur maple. On the west coast, the new hybrid dogwood shows spectacular color and the smaller vine maple turns to a brilliant scarlet.

Of the shrubs, the spindletree is both strange and beautiful. Its stems are oddly flanged, its tiny fruit like burst cerise balloons with bright orange seed within. As if that wasn't enough, its fall color is a show-stopping, shouting cerise. Witch hazel is a delight, its yellow tassels in bloom as the leaves are falling.

A few jewel-like flowers bloom in fall and seem all the more precious because they are few. Where it is hardy, the spikey red-purple flowers of the fall flowering bush clover on 8-16-foot stems are an unusual color for your September garden. I can never decide which of its two botanical names I like best — the newer one, *Lespedeza thunbergii* which to me sounds like a highly trained white horse galloping around a show ring, or its older name, *Desmodium penduliflorum*, a lovely name for a flower because it makes me think of a leading lady in a Greek tragedy, hanging in a dying swoon over a balcony rail. This perennial shrub frequently does die to the ground every year, but like all the best Greek tragediennes, appears alive and well on stage again the next. And luckily blooms on new wood. Another species, *L. bicolor*, is a little hardier and starts to bloom in July. The Japanese anemone is a delicate, dainty flower, a delight to grow and the autumn crocus, looking completely off cycle, spurts a spring-like shoot of mauve-purple leafless flowers. In the Northwest, the dogwood is blooming for the second time and many of the gardens are covered with rosy heather. Lawns are an exuberant green.

Of the vines, the sweet autumn clematis will have begun its fragrant frothing in late summer and, if the weather is cool, will continue into early fall. The large-flowered clematis too continues to bloom and the bittersweet, if you've been thoughtful enough to make it a co-educational planting of two vines, throws its tangles and twists studded with orange berries over anything that will let it roam over it.

Thus we complete the cycle of a garden of year-round beauty. The fallen leaves are scratching dry on the paving stones, there's an icy rime on the grass by morning and a few last courageous roses and pansies bloom alone. The tree trunks are bare again and the evergreens dark once more against the cold sky. Winter is on its way.

SPRING

The Little Bulbs:
Winter Aconite, *Eranthis*
Snowdrop, *Galanthus*
Crocus
Scilla, *S. sibirica*
Glory-of-the-Snow, *Chionodoxa*
Grape Hyacinth, *Muscari*
Species Tulip, *Tulipa*

Perennials:
Lungwort, Bethlehem Sage, *Pulmonaria saccharata*
Virginia Bluebell, *Mertensia virginica*
Doronicum
Bleeding Heart, *Dicentra*
Rock Plants, selections

Wild Flowers:

Hepatica	Bloodroot
Trillium	Jack-in-the-Pulpit
Violet	Columbine
Ferns	Mertensia
Marsh Marigold	Blue Phlox
Shooting Star	Trout-Lily

FLOWERING TREES AND SHRUBS:

Native:
Pussy Willow, *Salix discolor*, Zone 3.
Serviceberry, *Amelanchier alnifolia*, Zone 1;
    Midwest and North.
Shadblow, *Amelanchier canadensis*, Zone 4; east.
May Day tree, *Prunus padus commutata*, Zone 2.

Cultivated:
Magnolia, selections; Zone 5.
Flowering Dogwood, selections, *Cornus*, Zone 6.
Bridalwreath, *Spiraea x vanhouttei*, Zone 4.
Viburnum, selections, Zone 2.
Forsythia, selections, Zone 4.
Flowering Crab Apple, selections, *Malus*, Zone 4.
Flowering Japanese Cherry, *Prunus serrulata*, Zone 5b.
Lilac, selections, *Syringa*, **Zone 2.**
Azalea and Rhododendron, *Rhododendron*
    Species, **Zone 2.**
    Cultivars, Zones 5-8.
Broom, selections, *Cytisus*, Zone **2.**
Goldenchain Tree, *Laburnum*, Zone **6b.**

The Taller Bulbs:
Daffodil and Narcissus
Tulip

LATE SPRING OR EARLY SUMMER,
Call It What Pleases You Most!

Perennials:
Iris, Tall Bearded and Siberian
Peony, *Paeonia*
Poppy (perennial), *Papaver*

Vines and Climbers:
Clematis, Large Flowering Hybrids
Honeysuckle, *Lonicera*
Rose, Climbing, *Rosa*

Prestarted Plants (either your own or greenhouse):
Begonia, Fibrous, *B. semperflorens*
Coleus
Fuchsia, *F. magellanica*
Geranium, *Pelargonium*
Impatience, *Impatiens*
Pansy and Viola, *Viola*

Rose, *Rosa:* Hybrid Tea, Grandiflora, Polyanthus and
    Miniature

Small Flowering Trees and Shrubs:
Japanese Tree Lilac, *Syringa amurensis japonica*, Zone 2.
Mock Orange, selections, *Philadelphus*, Zone 3.
Shrub Rose, *Rosa rugosa*, Zone 3.

MIDSUMMER

Annuals:
 All the annuals, particularly
 Petunia
 Marigold
 Salvia
 Zinnia

Perennials:
 Lily, *Lilium*
 Day Lily, *Hemerocallis*
 Delphinium
 Phlox, *P. paniculata*
 Torch Lily, *Kniphofia*

Bulbs, corms and tubers:
 Tuberous Begonia, *B. tuberhybrida*
 Dahlia
 Gladiolus
 Canna

Small Flowering Trees and Shrubs:
 Snowhill Hydrangea, *H. arborescens* 'Grandiflora', Zone 3b.
 Peegee Hydrangea, *H. paniculata* 'Grandiflora', Zone 3b.
 Shrubby Cinquefoil, selections, *Potentilla fruticosa*, Zone 1.
 Bottlebrush, *Aesculus parviflora*, Zone 4b.

LATE SUMMER INTO FALL

Annuals:
 Still all the annuals

Perennials:
 Michaelmas Daisy, *Aster novi-belgii*
 Chrysanthemum
 Japanese Anemone, *A. japonica*

Flowering Shrubs:
 Rose of Sharon, *Hibiscus syriacus*, Zone 5.
 Butterfly Bush, *Buddleia davidii*, Zone 5b.
 Bush-clover, selections, *Lespedeza*, Zone 4b.
 Late Blooming Heather and Heath, *Calluna, Erica*, Zone 5;
  mainly west coast.

Vines:
 Silver-Lace Vine, *Polygonum aubertii*, Zone 6.
 Sweet Autumn Clematis, *C. paniculata*, Zone 2.

For Berries and Fruit:
 Mountain Ash, selections, *Sorbus*, Zone 2.
 Hawthorn, selections, *Crataegus*, Zone 2.
 Flowering Dogwood, *Cornus*, Zone 6.
 Crab Apple, *Malus*, Zone 2b.
 Bittersweet, *Celastrus scandens*, Zone 4b.
 European High Bush-cranberry, *Viburnum opulus*, Zone 2b.
 Snowberry, *Symphoricarpos albus*, Zone 2.
 Firethorn, *Pyracantha coccinea*, Zone 4b.

FOR BRIGHT FALL COLOR

Small Trees and Shrubs:
 Serviceberry, *Amelanchier alnifolia*, Zone 1.
 Amur Maple, *Acer ginnala*, Zone 2.
 Smoke Tree, *Cotinus coggygria*, Zone 4b.
 Spindletree, *Euonymus alata*, Zone 3.
 Staghorn Sumac, *Rhus typhina*, Zone 3.
 Witch-hazel, *Hamamelis virginiana*, Zone 4.

Vines:
 Boston Ivy, *Parthenocissus tricuspidata*, Zone 5.
 Virginia Creeper, *Parthenocissus quinquefolia*, Zone 2b.

2

AN ALL-ROUND FAMILY GARDEN

CAST OF CHARACTERS

Tads who love sandboxes and swings
Next-size-Small-Fry who love playing house and building things
Teens who whack balls and love to barbecue
Mother who loves growing flowers and a few herbs for the kitchen
Dad who likes to practise his golf swing and do the minimum in upkeep

The backdrop is a garden that is pretty to look at, fun to play in and not costing too much in time or money. It may sometimes be weedy and the grass in need of cutting. There'll be bare spots under the swings to prove that small feet push there to ride high, high up in the sky, and thin bits in the lawn on either side of a deck-tennis net. More than likely, if there's a young boy in the family, there'll be a pile of boxes and boards in one corner that look like junk to visitors, but to the budding astronaut who put them there they're a space-ship to the moon. The flowers, once planted, pretty much look after themselves and if their color combinations and design are not the most sophisticated in the world it doesn't matter because they're the ones Mother likes best — probably pink petunias.

A hundred combinations of a hundred ideas are possible. Here are some to help you choose what you and your family will enjoy most.

FOR THE WHOLE FAMILY

Your garden should, first of all, be a private place, a place to have what *you* think is pleasure in, by yourself, when you feel like it; a haven from life's hurly-burly; comfortable chairs or a hammock in which to sit and read or dream or snooze in the shade of a summer day; to play soft music in on a moonlit night; to walk barefoot in the dew of early morning; to get a late winter or early spring suntan in; to build things in and, if you're really small fry, to play that best of all games, "Let's Pretend."

You get this kind of a garden by planning for screening from neighbors and the street, by putting sitting places in sun and shade at the right time of year and by creating play areas to take full advantage of the site and your family's idea of fun. To help you with this, see CHAPTER 13, DESIGN AND DECORATION.

Your garden should be planned for easy entertaining, whether it's a birthday party with Drop-the-Handkerchief — nobody has to sweep up crumbs or mop up spilled milk — a barbecue for young and old; a joyful wedding party with a dance floor and a fiddler; a patio supper party with good friends, or maybe a nutsy winter picnic with a campfire and a cookout in the snow.

It's a place to learn about the fascinating things that go on in gardens, like feeding wild birds, putting up nesting boxes and watching the baby birds hatch, identifying them by name and learning about their habits. It's a marvelous place to learn the wonder of stars and the life cycles of insects, or what a simple earthworm can do to enrich the soil.

It's a place to practise skills besides gardening that you'll use all your life, like building a playhouse or a picnic table, making a wind chime or learning to swim if you have a pool.

And, of course, best of all it's a place to find for yourself the joy in growing plants, whether you are a small tad with a row of radishes, a teenager who likes fresh corn-on-the-cob, Mother who loves sweet peas or Dad who thinks red salvia is the most beautiful flower in the world.

FOR MOTHER AND THE GARDENERS IN THE FAMILY
The greatest pleasure for the gardeners will be flowers, not great swashes of them necessarily, but small plantings planned so that there is something exciting to see all year, even if it's only for glancing delight out the window.

For spring:
a few snowdrops snugged up against a
 warming rock
a cluster of pale yellow waterlily tulips or early
 daffodils, a fuzzy mat of pasque flower
just one glorious forsythia bush (Zone 4b)
 glowing yellow in sun or shadow
in the far South, a glossy camellia (Zone 8b);
 for the northern plains, a fluffy
 white saskatoon (Zone 1)
for later, one of the fragrant pink and white
 viburnums (Zone 5a) with rosy lily-flowered
 tulips at its base and a patch of crisp white
 perennial candytuft low down in front.

For late spring, early summer:
one gorgeous clump of tall bearded pink iris
 or a butterfly-flowered azalea. My favorite is
 Rhododendron schlippenbachii because it is
 easy to grow in my garden (Zone 6a), a
 heavenly pale pink in flower and lovely red
 foliage in fall, but there are many others
 equally good

a lavender-blue starry clematis vine — 'Nelly
 Moser' is a beauty — trained on the house
 and dipping a little over a window so that it
 can be easily seen from inside.

For summer:
a trio of pink climbing rose, a deep blue
 delphinium and two or three stalks of
 white trumpet lilies
a clump of lime-yellow day lilies by the door
a big pot on the patio, filled with a tumble of
 white petunias, salmon pink geraniums and
 a china blue cascading lobelia
hot yellow marigolds with scarlet salvia and a
 few spectacular zinnias for a bright spot in the
 sun; the jazzy colors of coleus for a shady
 place
for early frost areas like the valleys in
 northern mountains, a planting of orange
 and cream-yellow African daisy,
 Dimorphotheca, which goes merrily on
 blooming even when nipped.

For late summer, early fall:
a heavenly blue morning glory vine climbing up
  to a bedroom window for a bright good
  morning
a cerise-rose, berried, burning bush, *Euonymus
  alata* (Zone 3)
a white birch (Zone 2) turning golden yellow
  in the autumn sun
a plant or two of michaelmas daisies or bronze
  shaggy 'mums in front of a frosty-blue juniper
a fragrant, pure white buddleia (Zone 4b)
  dancing with butterflies, perhaps some of them
  Monarchs on their way to winter in Mexico.

For winter:
the soft sureness of any of the hardy evergreens
  carrying a white dusting of snow
the bright red bark of dogwoods (Zone 1b);
  the berries of holly (Zone 6) on the west coast
  or the native winterberry (Zone 3b) or high
  bush-cranberry (Zone 2) for the colder
  parts of the country.

For forcing branches into flower indoors:
pussy willow, forsythia, flowering quince,
flowering dogwood, prairie almond, apple, plum,
cherry, peach and pear and the earliest of the
viburnums.

**For flowers to cut for spring and summer time
bouquets:**
daffodils and other spring bulbs, pansies, violas,
arabis, doronicums, peonies, shasta daisies,
sweet peas, gladiolus, green flowers like the
zinnia 'Envy' and nicotine 'Limelight',
marguerites, roses, snapdragons, all foliages,
especially those streaked with white, and
evergreen branches for Christmas.

For good eating:
a few herbs — chives, parsley, sage, rosemary;
some salad fixings — lettuce, radishes, a few
tomato plants; for tasty cooking — garden peas,
green beans, if you have the space for it, corn;
for fruit — a couple of dwarf apple or pear
trees, a berry patch.

ESPECIALLY FOR DAD

The garden should be a handsome setting for his house and increase both its
monetary value and his pride and pleasure in it. And be:

designed for easy maintenance both in man
  hours and money, see Chapter 15
equipped with good tools that are a pleasure to
  work with, see Chapter 18
be thoughtfully planned with easy paths for
  getting garbage cans to their pick-up spot, a
  driveway that provides safe entry and exit from
the street, smooth walks and steady steps for
  deliveries to prevent accidents and perhaps
  lawsuits, handy storage for garden materials
  with a lock-cupboard for poisonous sprays;
  convenient water and electric outlets in
  waterproof boxes, see Chapter 14.

Maybe too, Dad should have the fun of an artificial lighting unit in the
basement to grow seedlings and cuttings economically, see CHAPTER 31, and a
generous open space in the garden for practising his putting if he golfs, fly
casting if he fishes.

And a good hammock!

ESPECIALLY FOR CHILDREN

Whatever is planned for youngsters should have supersafety built in. No sharp
corners, no metal to rust or scratch, rungs on ladders and ropes on swings
tested often, a pail of water and a dipper at hand when you barbecue, to douse
unexpected flames, and strict rules, if you have a pool, swimming or otherwise.
While children are small, it's a good idea for play equipment to be where you
can see it easily from indoors.

PLAY PEN:

set in sunshine on cool days, and in sky shine — that is open to the sky but not in direct sun — on hot ones. Set it up off the ground if ants or other insects are a problem. Net against flies or mosquitoes if the child is small.

SWINGS:

can be to sit on, everybody knows this one;
to sit in, an old rubber tire is good;
to stand on, a log; or
to hang on, make rings from an old hose and string up with rope.

A life-long, safe sturdy swing: secondhand telephone-pole uprights, J bolts with nuts and washers, a metal thimble inside clamped loops of rope.

For young children, four holes in the seat are safer than two.

For small fry who are not always able to control the direction of their swing, frames that stand out in the open garden are best and available by mail order and at department and sporting goods stores. For older children, a sturdier one that lasts much longer can be made from heavy poles set in the ground with a cross bar at the top, or hung from a strong beam between two trees, or from a large branch. Sitting swings should be hung so that the child's whole foot is flat on the ground when he's still, and made shorter as he grows (about 12 inches at first, up to 20-22 inches). A climbing rope with spaced knots is a useful rig to tie up into a good strong tree. Spread wood chips, sawdust or shredded bark beneath both swing and rope for soft landings.

SANDBOX:

can be bought but usually too small for real adventure. It's much better to make your own. Cornelia Hahn Oberlander, a well-known expert in play equipment, recommends that, if you can spare the space, a large sand pit up to 14 feet square is not too big. Boys will use one like this for years. Dig out to a depth of 2-3 feet, backfill with 12-18 inches of gravel, then add sand. Curb it with concrete, preservative-treated wood, or make the frame of a naturally long-lasting lumber like cedar, setting this 3-6 inches above the ground. If you want to finish the top with a level board, this makes a handy seat or a shelf for building on. Have a hose bibb nearby for water supply and dam building. Older boys will have great fun with loose rocks (too big for throwing, but just right for pushing around), some boards for building and pieces of plastic sheeting for lining pools and river beds.

SLIDES:

these are tricky equipment for a home garden. If wood, they must be examined often for splintering. If metal, they must be rustproof and have no jagged bits. They'll be hot in sunny weather, very cold in cold. They must have a safe place for landing on at the bottom. Mrs. Oberlander only recommends them for gardens where supervision can be given.

OTHER IDEAS:

a tree house or a play house; a place to pitch a pup tent (this can be something as handy-dandy as a cedar hedge planted in informal wiggles rather than a precise line, leaving hidden places just big enough for a little tent in behind); hopscotch marked out on a paved drive; paved paths for trikes, wagons and roller skates; a rabbit hutch and a lettuce patch for both children and rabbit; and for plants, a pussywillow tree (look up, in Rutherford Platt's book *The River of Life*, the fascinating story of how one honeybee tells the rest of the hive where he has found a pussywillow tree in bloom); snapdragons with their yawning jaws; those self-seeders, the forget-me-nots that go on willy-nilly year after year — all sorts of flowers and trees with intriguing habits and names.

13

ESPECIALLY FOR TEENAGERS

These are the years for more organized games played with rules and sometimes needing special equipment. Remember that most can be simplified and played more casually than the bona fide space and rules state and still be good fun.

shuffleboard (46′ x 6′), marked out on a hard surface. Good for grown-ups too.

a backboard and basketball ring set over the garage door, the driveway used for the court; a portable hockey goal set up in front of the door.

deck tennis and badminton (40′ x 18′) on any level surface — grass or paved.

bucket cricket (a circle 40′ in diameter) — this one is hard to play because everyone laughs so much. You play it like cricket, with a bat, which can be a real one or a sawed-off old broom, but the batter has to stand on an upturned bucket. Any member of the opposing team, standing outside the circle, can throw the ball at the bucket and the batter tries to hit it. He's out when the bucket is hit. The score is two runs every time a hit ball isn't caught and one every time the ball misses the bucket.

tetherball (a 14′ pole, 4′ of which is set in the ground with a 7½′ rope attached to the top and a tennis ball in a strong twine net tied to the free end). Two people, standing on opposite sides, take turns to bat the ball with tennis racquets, trying to wind it around the pole so that the other fellow can't get it off.

clock golf (a circle 20′-24′ in diameter), with cans sunk where the numbers of a clock would be. You try to put a golf ball from the middle into each.

And when your children are themselves too old for these games, it won't be long till they will need to go back to the beginning of the list to plan for their own garden fun and your grandchildren's fun.

(For other games and rules of play see *The Complete Book of Games* by Wood and Goddard.)

14

3 BALCONIES AND PATIOS

An apartment balcony or roof top, high in the sky, is a heavenly place to make a garden. Flowers in boxes, flowers in baskets, little trees in tubs — perhaps a big one if you have a generous roof — bubbling fountains are not only possible but they have a closeup excitement about them that ground-bound gardeners never know.

More than this, such gardens, with clever plotting of furniture and fixings, can become an intimate summery extension of a living room, a suntrap for an early tan or a romantic spot for a moonlight date. They can even, in winter, be fascinating places of snowdrifted miniature evergreens, sparkling Christmas decorations and, in certain locations, a lively centre for feeding wild birds.

If you like the idea of a high-rise winter greenhouse, it's also possible to glass in your balcony. Delightful little garden settings can be made in this way. Depending on your exposure and the conditions required by the plants you wish to grow — orchids, begonias, primroses, geraniums or a mixed flowery bag of a little of everything — you set it up with the necessary plug-in electric heaters, light units if you want them and humidity equipment. You will probably need permission from the owner of the building to do this and he will require that the same company do the work for all tenants wanting such glassed-in balconies so that, from the outside, the effect is consistent.

The tenant pays for the installation and, although the glass panels are always put in so that they can be easily taken out when summer comes, some find that their balcony is so much cleaner, quieter, with the temperature easier to control and their garden just as flowery, that they keep the panels in place all year.

15

First, decide what kind of a garden will give *you* the most pleasure. Elegant and sensitive? Buxom and bursting with giddy flowers? Are you away in the day most of the week, and more than anything else would you like a pale and fragrant garden for after dark?

Next consider how much you can spend — perhaps planning for major costs like furniture and carpet to be made over two or three years. Whatever the pattern of your life, whatever gives you the most pleasure, whatever your budget, thoughtful planning must come first, for there just isn't room on balconies and roof tops to make mistakes.

FIRST, A SIMPLE CHART

Begin by measuring your space and drawing it in scale on a piece of paper, indicating windows, sills and doorway. Make cardboard cutouts of the shapes of basic furniture you want — a lounge chair, a couple of sidechairs, a small table or gaily painted little chest to double as table and storage for tools and supplies. If you have enough space and like to picnic outside, be sure to cut a pattern for a small pedestal or four-legged table and a couple of sidechairs. Plan to keep all as small and simple as possible. To get exact measurements and know what is available, scout with your tapemeasure in the stores. Avoid the over-ornate, extra twists and twirls that would take up valuable space, fat cushions when a skinny one would do. Next move your patterns around on the scaled drawing until you have the groupings you want and know what to buy.

One simple and effective arrangement for a narrow long balcony with a door in the middle — many are like this — is to put the table and storage area at one end, the relaxing area at the other, tying them together as a design with something like bright matching cushions on all the chairs, or carpet that covers the whole floor. Easily available, felt-like floor coverings stay outdoors happily through rain, snow and sleet, are inexpensive and come in smashing colors. Using it will do more to make your garden look glamorous than anything else you can do.

Thin-legged chairs and a table with clean open lines — perhaps wrought iron or cast aluminum and glass — will look better than heavily-based ones. For shelter from wind and close neighbors, plan screens. Pierced, to let the wind sift *through*, are better than solid design which are more likely to blow over. These give you both privacy and shelter. Keep the view clear to the front for this dimension of horizon is one of the great assets of a high-in-the-sky garden.

Plan to light it at night with concealed floods or spots. The same electrical connection will take power to a fountain — simply made with a small pump, a pool which holds water that is used over and over. Reproductions of old English lead pieces are available, or a piece of traditional or contemporary sculpture can be handsome outdoors in summer, indoors in winter.

For the right situation — a balcony no higher than the third floor, the top of a garage roof, or higher if there are big trees nearby to act as an aerial bridge — a birdfeeder bolted to the rail, kept filled with seed and blocks of suet, is a constant winter joy.

When you have the scene set, the furniture and ornament chosen, then plan the flowers and plants that will bring your garden to life.

A garden for all seasons

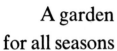

How intriguing and exotic that sounds. Yet it's practical and possible if you choose your plants knowingly, place them skillfully and, most important of all, train yourself to see them sensitively. The great chorale of spring is easily masterminded if you plant early-flowering trees and shrubs, and, during the fall before, some of the best spring-blooming bulbs. The lush loveliness of summer is easier still with handsome perennials and swashes of easy-to-grow annuals. Fall takes more thought for, although leaves and berries turn their brilliant crimsons and yellows without any help from you, to have flowers freshly blooming takes foresight. But it's winter that will make a true artist of you. Here it's subtle beauty in color and texture of bark, the softness of broody evergreens fat puffed with sparkling snow, a lively ballet of wild birds at your feeder.

A garden for all seasons — practical, possible magic.

*A garden in four seasons:
the freshest green of spring;
filled with flowers in summer;
burnished gold in fall;
white-frosted in winter.*

Summertime bloom in a country garden
with every annual grown from seed
and skillfully placed to show its best.

Early snow catches yellow Hillier crab apples with
leaves still green on the trees.

'Rosy Wings' tulips beneath a white-blossoming cherry
tree — a perfect picture of spring.

The frilly, lovely double petunia 'Lyric'.

Flowers of the saucer magnolia, delicate pink-and-white porcelain cups on dove-grey branches, appear before its leaves in early spring. The tree is equally beautiful in winter with its pointed furry buds.

A beloved favorite and award winner over the years — the ethereal 'Dainty Bess' rose, single petaled, with the quality of finest suede; perfect for bouquets.

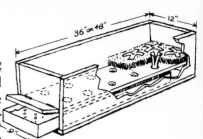
Self-watering window box.

FLOWERS IN BOXES

Flower boxes on railings or sills are intimate and cheery; the pattern for making them and the growing medium used in them convenient and easy. Best material is wood — cedar and redwood last longest — well-fitted, fastened at the corners with non-rusting screws.

I grew exuberant, luxuriant jungles for many years in two such boxes, designed to be self-watering (see drawing). The box is doublebottomed, a hinged door at one side or end, and in the lower space is a metal pan kept filled all the time with a dilute, water-soluble fertilizer solution. Drainage holes, 1½ inches in diameter, are drilled in the bottom of the upper box, 6 inches apart, and wicks of fibreglass, nylon or simple cotton lamp wicking — some people use old nylon stockings — their ends in the solution, drawn up through these holes and laid out on the growing medium. Cut each wick about 9 inches long, put 4 inches in the water and pull 5 inches through the hole, splitting it in four to spread out. If the boxes are to face into hot sun, the outside should be made of double wood with moist peat or fibreglass packed in the space between. This keeps the plant roots on that side from cooking and drying out, a common cause of poor bloom.

My favorite growing medium is peatlite, developed by Cornell University, and now widely used by nurserymen and greenhouses. It is available in bags through your garden supplier. It uses no soil and is therefore clean and light-weight, and it's so effective to grow things in you'll have to pinch and prune your flowers constantly. If you want to mix your own (see page 153 for the formula) it's neither tricky nor difficult.

DIRECTIONS FOR SETTING UP SELF-WATERING BOXES

Fill bottom pan with solution, pre-wet wicks and place in lower pan, lay 1 inch of damp peatlite in bottom of upper pan, drawing wicks through holes and peatlite and spreading out to cover well. Add more peatlite to within 1 inch of top. Knock plants and seedlings from their pots (or cut individual seedlings with a block of earth if growing in a tray) and insert in the peatlite. Water lightly with the same solution as in the pan, shade for a day or so and that's it.

PLANTING

When plotting your planting, be lush rather than lean. Nothing looks more mournful than skimpy window boxes. Here is a guide for minimum quantities needed for a 3-foot box: 6 geraniums, 5 cascade or balcony petunias, 2 trailing plants, such as German ivy or vinca.

If you want to cover a long space with such boxes, better to build several, no longer than 3 feet each, rather than one long one. They are easier to service, easier to move if you wish to, and stronger. Properly made by a good carpenter and tinsmith, they will last for years. Paint them a gay color outside, or stain with any non-creosote material.

INSTALLATION

Be careful and secure with your fastenings — your building superintendent could be irritable if your flower boxes go crashing to the ground, even if they don't hit anybody. Some apartment houses do not allow boxes to hang outside

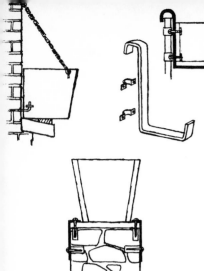

Three types of window-box fastenings: hanging bracket, for a coping, for a sloping windowsill.

railings, but if it is permitted you will have a more spacious garden. Alternatively, they can be hung inwards and still be effective, or, if you have a parapet or wall, put them on the coping. Whatever the position, they *must be bolted securely* to something fixed. (For how to do this, see drawings.)

Boxes may also be fastened on windowsills. If there is no wide overhang above, they can be planted with the same sun-loving flowers you would use on a railing box; if there is an overhang, then choose plants that bloom well in shade. (For lists, see page 20.)

PLANT BICYCLE BASKETS FOR A BUDGET BALCONY

Bicycle baskets, handily one-sided, make ingenious planters along a rail. Old-fashioned wicker ones are still about, or inexpensive molded plastic ones are available in bicycle stores. Lash them to the rail with brightly colored, plastic-covered clothesline. Line each with sheet moss from your florist, then a piece of burlap to keep water from running through too quickly and fill with peat-lite. Knock plants out of pots or pans and insert in peatlite.

And here's a handy trick for a party. Since your plants will have more bloom on the *outside* because of the light, snip some off and, inserting the stems in old toothbrush tubes, plastic bags or plastic picks filled with water, tuck them into the *inside* of your box for a more flowery face where it will be seen. Sneaky, but good.

HANGING FLOWERS

Since you need every clear square inch of floor space you can get to make your garden appear spacious, hanging and suspended plants are ideal. Hanging baskets can be a burst of flowers and bouncing with color.

If there is a ceiling above to imbed a hammock hook securely in, this is fine. Often the tenant above you will give you permission to fasten a chain around the base of the railing post above, to hang a basket on. However, since buffeting wind is usually a factor in this situation, you may rather hang your basket on a sturdy bracket fastened into the back main wall. Whatever you use, have a clip within easy reach to detach the basket so that you can bring it down for a thorough soaking and draining once a week.

Plastic and wire baskets are available at greenhouses. Make up as for bicycle baskets (above) and choose plants with a graceful, cascading habit — vines, spreading carpeters like lobelia and alyssum, and a few flowery uprights (see list page 20). Imaginative handcrafted hanging pots are tops for showing off one elegant plant — a delicate pendulous fuchsia, a spider plant (*Chlorophytum*) that can double for winter decoration too, or a fragrant yellow begonia. One of the most fascinating balcony planters you could have is a handsome birdcage on a stand, filled with a tumble of flowers. For real pizzazz, paint it black.

Individual metal rings with hangers that hold one pot are in many stores. Attach them either to the wall or to a firmly fixed screen. Buy your potted plant — salmon pink geraniums in turquoise pots are lovely for this — one size smaller than the pot that fits the ring. Double potting, with moist peatlite between, keeps the inside pot cool and moist, better for growing.

CONTAINERS: FREESTANDING POTS AND TUBS

For a budget balcony, roof or terrace on the ground, less than a dollar will buy a specially treated large papier-mâché pot in textured, dull brownish-red. Another few cents will buy a packet of annual vine seed — heavenly blue or cerise morning glories, nasturtiums, canary vine, cup and saucer vine or, for both eating and enjoying, scarlet runner beans.

Stand some tall branch-twigs in the pot for twining on, fill with peatlite, plant your seeds and have a flowery conversation piece for a corner. Be sure to move the pot into the sun for part of each day and give it a quarter turn once a week to develop bloom and leaves all round.

Contemporary containers in asbestos fibre or plastic are available in smart shops, and in many sizes. Although usually they are soft grey or white, you can paint them any color you wish. They take well to something simple and inexpensive like a marigold tree. Buy a packet of seed of the hedge-type Golden Jubilee, or, my favorite after many years of marigold growing, the lemon yellow Glitters. Put half a dozen seeds in the pot, thinning out to three when they sprout. As they grow upwards, pinch off sideshoots, letting the leader grow till it is about 2½′ tall, then let sideshoots develop to a tidy standard tree shape. Coleus also makes a marvelous tropical burst, especially if you pick up the dominant color of the leaves in paint for the container. If you are a gourmet, try cherry or pear tomato vines staked up to a firmly set post. Do not allow the soil to dry out, and fertilize once every two weeks, and you will have the most magical flowers or fruit where no one would believe you could grow them.

For an elegant balcony, a standard tree, as one so often sees in the well-tended gardens of Europe, can be a theme setter. Buy directly from a greenhouse, or with patience and time grow your own. Roses, geraniums, lantana, genista are all good, but most beautiful of all is fuchsia, with its graceful flowery earrings. These plants deserve a handsome outside pot to stand in — an antique urn, a terra cotta pot, a contemporary bowl.

Tubbed evergreens and some deciduous trees — small willows or a flowering cherry — behave amazingly well in roof gardens or on capacious balconies. But remember to check the strength of your floor before you decide to use them — they must have a tub of soil at least 2 x 2 x 2 feet, a heavy load, manoeuvrable only by two men. And be sure to have castors put on the base so that you can later push it around to get the best light on all sides.

When planting, use a layer of fibreglass over 2 inches of drainage material, such as broken-up flower pots or crushed tile, in the bottom of the tub, and add soil above that. The fibreglass allows excess water to drain out but holds back the soil.

TOOLS

In your tool kit you will need a trowel, a watering can with a long thin spout, clippers, a set of measuring spoons, a spray and a small wash tub if you have hanging baskets or free standing pots that will need deep soaking once a week.

SUPPLIES

For supplies, green paper-wrapped wires are handy for tying things up or green string and some small stakes will do as well. A heavy sheet of poly-ethylene about 4 feet square from the dime or hardware store is useful to work on, with some lighter-weight plastic or burlap to line baskets; a quantity of ready-mixed peatlite or soil, a spray bomb insecticide and a can or bottle of water-soluble fertilizer completes the list.

CARE

The care of such gardens is easy. Water as the plants need it — your touch will tell you when the soil is dry. If you use self-watering window boxes, you can easily check the pans to see when they need refilling. About every second time, add the recommended dose of soluble fertilizer to the water in the pan.

For hanging pots, soak for 1-2 hours in a tub of water, once a week, adding general purpose fertilizer every second week. Plantings that do not get rainfall need a shower bath or top spray once a week to dust them off and keep them clean.

Large containers, sitting where drip on your neighbor below could be a nuisance (to put it mildly) or they could stain your floor, should be set on trays or saucers deep enough to catch the overflow.

Dead flowers should be picked off promptly and straggly growth trimmed back to neatness. Insects, unless brought in with purchased plants, seldom bother a balcony or roof garden. If they do appear, rout them with an aerosol insecticide.

Flowering annuals are finished when winter comes. House plants vacationing on the balcony should be moved indoors gradually as the weather cools — out in the day, indoors at night. Before freezing frost, they should be inside all the time. Valued standards can come indoors or board in a greenhouse till spring. Tubbed evergreens and deciduous trees should be sprayed with an anti-desiccant and in temperate zones, and if kept watered, can remain out-doors safely all winter.

When Christmas comes, lash as big a tree as you can to your railing and sparkle it with lights. It will give everybody who sees it — many more than if it were inside — a truly merry feeling of Christmas.

SUITABLE PLANTS FOR WINDOW BOXES, HANGING BASKETS AND CONTAINERS

For best looks, combine erect, compact and trailing plants — suggestions to consider are listed below. Where a name has an (S) after it, the plant is suitable for a north or east exposure where there is shade most of the day.

ERECT	COMPACT	TRAILING & SPILLING	STANDARDS	VINES FOR TRAINING UPWARDS
Mignonette	Portulaca	Thunbergia	Roses	Morning Glory
Dwarf Nicotine (S)	Sweet Alyssum	Morning Glory	Lantana	Cup and Saucer
Dwarf Snapdragon	Ageratum	Cup and Saucer	Geranium	Nasturtium
Cornflower	Nierembergia	Balcony & Cascade Petunia	Genista	Thunbergia
Geranium	Lobelia (S)	Lobelia (S)	Fuchsia	Canary Vine
Dianthus	Pansies (S)	Ivy-leaved Geranium		Scarlet Runner Bean
Vinca rosea	Torenia (S)	English Ivy (S)		Moonflower
Browallia (S)	Dwarf Marigold	Vinca Major (S)		
Patience (S)	Fibrous Begonia (S)	Trailing Begonia (S)		
Marigold		Fuchsia (S)		
Balsam		Lantana (S)		
Fuchsia		Sweet Alyssum		
		German Ivy (S)		
		Wandering Jew (S)		

4 A NIGHT GARDEN

Velvet night as a backdrop, a ceiling pricked with stars, the surprising magic of familiar plants lit by a silver moon and cleverly concealed lighting sound like a set for a glamorous movie — but it can be your garden, your garden any night of the year.

Lost in the dark are distracting views over the fence, the confusion of detail, the weeds, the buggy leaves. Instead, you see the gleam of pale flowers, fascinating texture and depth in deep-shadowed trees and leafy plants. With wise choice of what you grow and artificial light to supplement the moon, only what you choose to be seen is seen — your favorites, the stars of the garden after dark.

I'm suggesting first some plants you might choose for highlights in this kind of a garden, other decorative uses for light in pools and fountains, to accent ornament and sculpture, then what fixtures to choose and how to install them.

TREES FOR NIGHT BEAUTY

Easily the prima donna, and hardy for most of the country, dramatic all year but especially a knockout in spring in its pale leafy green, is the white trunked birch, *Betula* (Zone 2b). Then, for bold beauty, the upturned pale cups of the saucer magnolia, *Magnolia x soulangiana* (Zone 5b), flowering before its leaves emerge. White and pink-flowered crab apples are good, especially *Malus* 'Hillieri' (Zone 2b). And particularly at home in the plains, the white blossoming cherries, the Amur chokecherry, *Prunus maacki* (Zone 2b) and the Shubert chokecherry, *P. virginiana* 'Shubert' (Zone 2). In mild parts of the country, nothing surpasses the delicate lace of the flowering dogwood, *Cornus florida* (Zone 5).

For planting beds under the trees, choose from the dozens of white and pale narcissus, hyacinths and tulips, and somewhere in your garden, near enough to the windows to catch its heavenly fragrance on a soft May evening, plant a white lilac — *Syringa vulgaris* 'Maude Notcutt', 'Vestale', or 'Mme Lemoine' (Zone 2b).

Lit from the bottom, pearlbush, *Exochorda* 'The Bride' (Zone 5a), with its dainty, drippy earrings of flowers, is a lovely sight and later in the year white bouquets of flowers cover the catalpa tree, *C. speciosa* (Zone 5b).

SHRUBS

Where they are hardy, the great flowery bursts of white and pale pink rhododendrons are stunning, and so also are the crisp, clustered blossoms of the azaleas — some notably fragrant.

The white and pale pink-flowered viburnums, spireas, mock orange, beauty-bush and golden arches of forsythia are all good and white clouds of shadbush are an early, early beauty.

PERENNIALS

A little light on a clump of white columbine, *Aquilegia hybrida*, makes it look like a gathering of moths in the night, and later in the summer a fragrant white buddleia, *B. davidii* 'Peace', will draw real moths — the big fluttering Sphinx. White delphiniums, the Pacific Hybrid 'Galahad', are flowery exclamation points for early summer; snakeroot, *Cimicifuga racemosa*, for late. But watch these late-season bloomers for most need a long dark night to flower and artificial light on them may delay it. It also may delay hardening-off in fall and leave the plant open to winterkill. The effect of interrupted dark on long-night flowering plants is under study now but no results have yet been published. Lilies are truly one of the flowers made to be lit — elegant, regal in the way they hold their heads up-tilted or out-trumpeting. The annual datura is a trumpeter too.

ANNUALS, CORMS AND TUBERS

Petunias are the showiest of the annuals for nighttime. 'White Cascade', an exuberant tumbler, teamed with pink or red geraniums and variegated green and white vinca for trailing delicacy, in a white asbestos planter, lit with a flood from above, is a joy. White nicotine, intensely fragrant, will flower from early July to frost, and even seed itself for another year.

The form of the tall bearded iris takes on a new beauty in night light, and the spotlight handsomeness of a big cactus dahlia looks as though you had deliberately put it there. Hanging baskets of the palest of the Pacific Giant pendulous begonias are stunning on a porch or balcony and will flower till frost nips them.

VINES

The aerial impact of flowering vines at night is fascinating. The big white clematis, 'Henryi', or the tucked and pleated, sweetly fragrant 'Duchess of Edinburgh' should be planted near a window or patio and softly lit. Another white one, the moonflower, *Calonyction aculeatum* is, as its name suggests, a natural for night time. For the look of a frothy wave breaking over a fence,

Moonflower vine.

grow silver lace vine — fleece vine on the west coast — *Polygonum aubertii*, and light it from the side.

FOR LEAF AND BARK INTEREST

All leaves look lovely floodlit, especially from the back. Ferns become almost transparent and a feathery pale green; high trees, like oak and maple, a cool canopy; variegated leaves, particularly the boldly margined green and white hosta, *H.* 'Thomas Hogg', are sharp and clearly outlined in the darkness.

The shaggier the bark, the rougher the texture, the more interesting trunks and branches become in night light. For most telling effect, the beam should be set off to the side just to graze the surface. The muscled strength of a great oak is a real thrill revealed in winter by hidden lights at the base, one on the trunk, another shooting up into the tree; evergreens fatly puffed with snow, especially if it is still softly falling, are spectacular in winter lights.

LIGHT IN POOLS AND FOUNTAINS

Pools take on mystery lit at night. For a dark pool, this is startlingly effective if a white-flowering plant on the rim is floodlit and reflected in the black water — a sweetly scented white mock orange, the starry *Philadelphus x virginalis* 'Minnesota Snowflake' (Zone 4b) is a beauty, or an arching bridal-wreath spirea *S. x vanhoutteii* (Zone 4). In the fall, leafless branches of white snowberries, *Symphoricarpos albus* (Zone 2) can lean out over the black water, or the pale gold leaves of a turning white birch (Zone 2). For a pool with water lilies, a spotlight on the cultivar 'Missouri' in bloom, backed by dark water, is a sight no one will forget.

LIGHT IN THE WATER

Light installed in the water to create an undersea glow is possible, but unless your pool is regularly washed and cleaned — I am speaking here of decorative pools, not swimming pools — you may, with this kind of lighting, reveal only what you would rather keep hidden.

Swimming pools, which are necessarily cleaned often, can be enthrallingly lit under water. For this, lighting experts recommend submersible fixtures and 110-120 volt power with a control that immediately disconnects the power if there is a short. Your system should be installed by a licensed electrician and be regularly checked by him for worn or loose connections.

Light can be well used too in fountains, which look their sparkliest when a soft beam is shot *through* the spray, rather than *at* it.

LIGHTING ORNAMENTS AND SCULPTURE

For garden figures, ornament of all kinds, sculpture, experimenting with light from various angles is the only sure way to find what is most effective. Usually, gentle light from one side and stronger light from above or the other side is good. Try different kinds of light — floods and spots — to be certain to find the most pleasing picture.

CHOOSING AND INSTALLING FIXTURES

The secret of a superbly lit garden is restraint, simplicity, hidden sources of light and, I think, natural color, although many gardeners like soft pinks, some red and some luminous green lights. Whatever you choose, you can, with the equipment now on the market and new appliances coming along every year, do it easily and economically.

First, consult your electrician. Have him check your present house service to determine whether it will carry the extra load you plan. Check local building codes to find out what you may do and if you need a permit for outdoor lighting installation. Unless you are qualified to do so, have the electrician put in the necessary connections. *Don't, under any circumstances, let an amateur do the job.*

Underground cables must be weatherproof, lead-sheathed in watertight conduit. In some areas, chemically coated cable, with no conduit, is permissible. Special care must be taken at the points where the cable enters and leaves the ground to install it for safe performance.

If possible, lay cable before walks, lawns and plantings are put in. Bury it at least 18 inches underground, to avoid cutting when digging to plant. It is advisable, as a double precaution, to staple the cable to a 1 x 3 inch board, laying it board side up.

Install more outlets than the number you will need for the lights you plan so that the system will take care of electric garden equipment like hedge clippers, barbecue spit, fountain pump, Christmas decorations. Outlets should all be grounded to minimize hazard — three-hole outlets are recommended and cords with three-prong plugs to three-wire cords. Outlet boxes should be waterproof with spring-shut covers.

Once outlets are in place, experiment, using extension cords and clip-on portable lights on stakes, moving them around till you get the effect you want. If you are considering lights mounted high up in open branching trees, get someone with a long extension ladder to try different installations and angles with you looking on from the ground. Don't hurry at this job, experiment for a whole year of changing seasons if need be. Locate your final outlet positions so that two or more fairly short cords can run from one outlet, rather than long ones. Install boxes on sturdy places — a wall, the trunk of a tree, a strong fencepost or a stake driven deeply into the ground.

For light fixtures just above the ground — and a socket screwed or clipped to a movable stake is one of the most satisfactory ways to light different features at different times of the year — be sure to leave extra cable so that it can be moved about freely. Also, if any cord must be attached around a tree, do it loosely to allow for growth.

TYPES OF LIGHTS

For different kinds of fixtures available, consult your electrician's catalogue. For bulbs, consider whether you want spots to pick out special detail, or floods for general illumination. Clip-on filters in different colors are available too. Bulbs should be weatherproof so that cold rain or snow falling on the hot surface will not break them. About twice a year, disconnect the system and clean out bugs and debris that may have collected in the sockets of any upturned fixtures.

Light shooting from far away gives a more mysterious effect in the garden than close up and the source is often easier to conceal — a real must. Be careful, when hiding the fixture, to set it far enough away from plants near it so that the heat of the bulb does not scorch flowers and foliage, and check this as the plants around the light grow and change position.

Switching can be manual, but it is far better to put the system on a timer which you can set to come on at dark and turn off when you want it to — or which you can turn off completely if you are going to be away. Photoelectric cells are also available to turn the lights on and off at dark and dawn. Many householders also have a master switch installed by their bed so that the garden lighting can be turned on in the middle of the night if there is any suspicious noise in the garden.

LOW VOLTAGE LIGHTING

Twelve-volt lighting, rather than the customary 120 volts, makes good sense in some installations. In many ways it is safer than the higher voltage. A child can poke his finger in a 12-volt socket without receiving a dangerous shock; and in digging, if you inadvertently cut the cable with your spade, the lower voltage may spark but that's all.

Low voltage garden lights and connections can usually be bought through hardware stores. They need a sealed, step-down transformer to reduce 110-120 volts to 12, and you may require more lights for the same effect.

Since fragrance is a second subtle charm of gardens at night, you might also like to read CHAPTER 9, A FRAGRANT GARDEN. CHAPTER 14, PERMANENT FEATURES, gives further directions for outdoor lighting.

5 SMALL, INNER-CITY GARDENS

A green oasis in a desert of brick and dirty pavement — is this what you long for? A flowery, leafy signal of the seasons, a quiet place for a change of pace in the clamor of the city? A near-at-hand spot for a calm drink by yourself on a hot summer evening or a cheerful party for fifty? If you have the makings and the wish for such a garden, your back yard can become an elegant feature where before it was a mess.

There will undoubtedly be problems, but usually none that, with a little know-how, can't be solved. Here are the common ones:

1. You're only renting, therefore you don't want to spend a fortune fixing it up. You own the property, but you're not sure it's worth the cost of fixing it up.

2. You have a feeling of being hemmed in by high relentless buildings and of people in them peeking down at you. (Of course, if you're young, beautiful and lonely, we might have to leave this one as is.)

3. Your yard has a dirty, dark, dingy look — all city gardens usually begin like this.

4. Your space seems too small to bother with.

5. You don't know what plants will grow in polluted city air (when you're a plant all city air is polluted).

Now, in that order, here are the solutions.

YOU DON'T OWN THE PROPERTY

To begin with, a wise and intelligent landlord will often share the cost of improvements that will make his property more valuable. To sell him on the idea, have a plan made and an attractive drawing of the best feature in it to show him. Unless you have a talent for this yourself, employ a landscape architect or garden designer to do one for you, to your specifications. This is *always* money well spent, especially for small gardens where every inch counts. If the landlord won't share the whole cost, suggest that he pay for the immovable parts, such as gravel or heavy, built-in pavings, and design the rest to move with you if you leave.

Privacy screens, a pool and fountain, sculpture and ornament, a trellis — even prefabricated paving stones — can all be installed so that they can be taken out, although you may find that the following tenant will like the look of what you have done and want to buy the whole kit and caboodle from you. **Movable paving slabs** can be preformed flat blocks, plain or patterned, laid on a bed of 4-6 inches of sand with a layer of plastic sheeting between the bottom and upper half of the sand to prevent weeds from growing through. Consider, too, outdoor carpeting in one of many heavenly colors which might, for you, be a better answer than hard surface pavings. Kinds are available that withstand years of rain, dirt, treading on, and even snow, slush and ice. This you could roll up and relay in another garden as easily as falling off a log.

Trellises, fences and screens can be designed in easily dismantled sections, held upright by bolting to steel plates set in concrete (see drawing). The plates you would have to leave behind if you moved.

Pre-fabricated pools and detachable fountain heads are movable and sculpture, lighting and ornament can be as easily taken with you as your furniture. **Plants**, in some cases and at some times of the year, can be safely moved but you might better count on leaving them as a legacy for the next tenant. Their cost will depend on your taste and pocketbook, but for a small garden this should not be a major expense. Flowery annuals can be grown in handsome contemporary pots or containers and be easy to care for and easy to move, besides being excellent design features. All kinds of containers are available at garden suppliers — most are strong, versatile and light weight.

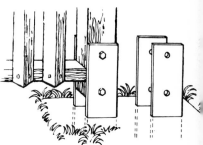

Fence post bolted to steel plates set in concrete.

YOU OWN THE PROPERTY but you're not sure a garden on it makes sense

The hardheaded view of spending money and time to make a gem of a garden on your property is that it appreciably enhances its real estate value.

The softheaded view is that a garden in a city has all the elements that people — especially city-harried people — cherish. It's unexpectedly lovely, it's a fascinating contrast of textures and greens, of flowers and foliages, of delicate fragility and timeless strength; it's a challenge; it's constantly changing and often a miraculous surprise; it's something everyone enjoys even if he doesn't know a dandelion from a buttercup. Besides all that, you can take care of it with inexpensive, small-scale equipment in a few minutes, when you want to and by yourself. More you could hardly ask of a small patch of backyard dirt.

A FEELING OF BEING HEMMED IN, a dark and dingy look, a small and crampy space

All these can be overcome with clever design.

First, analyse the immediate problem of what you already, unchangeably have. Neighboring abutting walls or buildings in a mishmash of materials and patterns should, if possible, be painted all one light color. This opens up your space, and adds an ordered, serene quality to the whole garden. Alternatively, if you can't paint, grow a tracery of vines over them or hide them with lattice and plants or well designed screens. Install trellises and lattices at least 6 inches out from the wall to allow for good air circulation.

An ugly view in the distance can be hidden by growing a tree in front of it. If it's a *big, wide* ugly view, don't try to block it out with a whole forest of trees — use one handsome one and thus shift the emphasis of where to look. An attracting focal point at ground level — a flowering vine on a fence, a splashing fountain — will draw your eye away from a poor view.

Thoughtful placement of where you will sit can divert your glance too. The most convenient sitting area will almost certainly be nearest the house, but, if there is no way to avoid looking at something unpleasant if you sit there, put your patio at the rear of the garden looking back at your own house. This view you can control and make smashing with giddy flowery window boxes, a bright awning and good planting at ground level.

Don't let the design get busy. Restraint and continuity in the use of plant material and an overall theme that repeats the kinds you use will add to a spacious feeling. Keep the centre clear, the most dominant interest at the back of the garden, using the lines of planting beds at the sides to carry your eye back. These lines should be straight or only gently curving, not wiggling restlessly in and out. Use the brightest colors in flowers — yellow and orange marigolds, scarlet zinnias and geraniums, hot pink petunias, tulips and daffodils planted every year then discarded, pots of chrysanthemums in the fall, exotic tuberous begonias all summer if your garden is shady.

To break the neighbor's view from above, put a roof over your sitting space, but let it be light and airy — an open trellis with a grapevine perhaps, fragrant in the spring, leafy all summer and the grapes tops for treading in the fall. Or make use of a shady tree, which could be one you plant or an overgrown weedy one you inherited with the garden and cleverly pruned out.

Most small gardens can accommodate only one tree. If you have more, either prune them drastically or cut down all but one. Even this one should probably be pruned. Opening up the garden to the sky will go far to correct the dark look. Get a professional tree man to do this — it can be very expensive and sometimes painful, if you knock down a power line or your neighbor's fence, or land on your own head.

Correction for the dingy look is as simple as this: use brightly colored, gaily patterned, weatherproof materials in sun-umbrellas, bright awnings and removable chair coverings. Decorate side walls with mosaics, murals or tiles, or grow on them an all-summer-flowering vine like purple clematis; or hang cascading, variegated green and white ivy in a china lavabo, or any one of a dozen dress-up ideas. Floodlight the garden at night. Make a pool of fibreglass with a brilliant turquoise lining. For a party, use kerosene torchères, Japanese lanterns strung through the garden, or my favorite more-brains-than-money-idea, cheap prayer candles in large paper bags with a simple flower-cut-out on the side and set along the edges of the paths.

To make the garden look larger, less cramped, the most important rule is

Paper bag lights for party paths.

to choose everything you put in it — permanent features, decorations, furniture and plants — to a small compact scale. The plants, the only things whose shape and size will change every year, should be chosen from those that grow slowly.

Keep walls, screens and fences as low as the view beyond dictates and yet allow you privacy. For instance, a 4-5 foot wall will hide you when you sit yet not prevent your seeing beyond the garden when you stand. For more privacy, make the wall 5-6 feet; higher than that cuts off air circulation.

Changes in level will add interest and a feeling of spaciousness. A trellised roof over a terrace or patio that opens out to a high tree or the sky is good. A floor of a terrace on a level lower than the rest of the garden or, at the back of the garden, raised up is intriguing. Raised planting beds not only add interest with a change of level, but provide a perfect way to supply the best soil to your plants. They can be built of whatever material best goes with your garden — block, bricks, stone, wood — and some of the most economical and good looking are made of old railroad ties which have the advantage of built-in long life because they are already impregnated with preservative. If you can't buy old railroad ties, you may be able to buy new ones and still, in comparison with the cost of other materials, save money. If you use wood of any kind, face the top with a wide board that can double as a fine finish and seating for a party. Less expensive, and useful for heights of 3-4 inches of raised bed, is preformed aluminum or plastic stripping.

Use dominant features — a bold sculpture, a dramatic tree like the huge flowered saucer magnolia, *M. soulangiana* — as far away as you can place them to enhance the feeling of distance. If this strikes your fancy, reflect the whole garden or part of it in a mirror installed in the side or back fencing; this gives an on-and-on look.

WHERE TO GET SKILLED HELP?
Landscape architects are available in most cities and large garden contractors have designers on staff. (See CHAPTER 13, DESIGN AND DECORATION, for more information.)

Tree experts, maintenance services, suppliers of garden furniture and ornament are also listed in the phone book. Catalogues of plants are available from nurseries and good specialist garden books through your public library.

Once planted, there is a good chance you will want to take over the ongoing care of the garden yourself. Use all the short cuts you can find or invent: premixed, bagged soil; balanced chemical fertilizers (foliar fertilizers are especially good for they wash as well as feed); insecticides and fungicides in bombs; early and easy rather than late and complicated pruning; ground covers and mulches to reduce need for weeding and watering; flowering plants that hold themselves firmly up without staking and those that need minimum care; handy ground-level storage for a few tools and for furniture and cushions. In fact, to reduce the need for washing down the furniture often, it's a good idea to have a storage box designed just to keep loose covers and chair pads in. Pop these, all clean and fresh, onto the chairs when you use the garden and put them away between times.

WHAT PLANTS WILL GROW IN POLLUTED CITY AIR?

The list of city tolerant plants is surprisingly long. To get on it, plants must be able to thrive in moderate to dense shade; soil that is nearly always acid, slower than more exposed gardens to freeze in fall and quicker to thaw in spring, slow to dry and therefore moist most of the time; air that is unusually still and often smoggy and with a heavy concentration of fallout dust and chemicals. To offset these disadvantages city gardens usually have less drying wind and smashing gales, less bitter cold, and their very compactness and size make them easier to care for.

Leaf trees are a safer choice than needle evergreens, but a few cultivars of yew do well in city air and some cedars, pine and spruce can be tried with good hope of success if they can get a minimum of 6 hours of sun daily. Both needle and broad-leaved evergreens benefit from weekly syringing during the growing season to wash off dirt. Old trees and shrubs may sometimes be kept if they are growing where you want them, but it is wiser to buy new ones than to try to move them to a new spot.

Consider fall planting if this fits your schedule. The later coming of winter to city gardens gives a longer time for plants to become established before freeze-up. A few trees — birch, cherry, magnolia are some — do not transplant well in fall. They should be moved in as soon as ground has thawed in spring. Look for plants already growing in containers to move in at any time of the year, for instant effect. Do not crowd plants; movement of air around them is important for good health and insurance against disease.

Soil improvement is usually an absolute necessity. Do one of three things:

excavate, break up subsoil and replace with good earth (6-8 inches for ground covers, 12-18 inches for small shrubs and flower beds, 24-36 inches for trees)

break up and improve existing soil by digging in large quantities of leaf mold, good topsoil, coarse sand, compost or peat and adding recommended quantities of inorganic chemical fertilizers, or

make raised beds by first spading existing soil then building retaining walls and backfilling with new soil. I like this one best.

FOR NEW TREES CONSIDER THESE
(bracketed numbers indicate zones)

Open leafy types:
> any of the honey locusts, *Gleditsia triacanthos* (4)
> maidenhair tree, *Ginkgo biloba* (4)
> any of the flowering crab apples, *Malus* (4)
> the weedy but lovely, much maligned Tree of Heaven, *Ailanthus altissima* (5b), which would rather grow in a dirty, dingy city than open sunny suburbia

The fascinating fastigiate trees, which are tapering and conical, and columnar trees, which are narrow and vertical; both types are good for exclamation point accents. Some to think about:
> maple, *Acer rubrum* 'Columnare' (4b)
>   *saccharum* 'Temple's Upright' (4b)
> hornbeam, *Carpinus betulus* 'Fastigiata' (5b)
> beech, *Fagus sylvatica* 'Fastigiata' (5b)

> poplar, *Populus alba* 'Pyramidalis' (4)
> oak, *Quercus robur* 'Fastigiata' (4b)

Weeping trees:
> birch, *Betula verrucosa* 'Gracilis' (2), 'Youngii' (2b)
> Camperdown elm, *Ulmus glabra* 'Pendula' (4a)

Dwarf trees, with their small and delicate flowers, especially:
> flowering almond, *Prunus triloba* 'Multiplex' (2b)

SHRUBS

Compact dwarf shrubs are ideal. For evergreens:
> Korean box, *Buxus microphylla koreana* (4b); makes a neat hedge.
> yew, *Taxus cuspidata* 'Nana' (4), is a highly tolerant, small-needle evergreen.
> rose daphne, *D. cneorum* (2b), is dainty and fragrant.

euonymus, *E. fortunei* 'Silver Gem' and 'Goldtip'
(5b), one silver-grey and pink, the other
chartreuse-yellow and green, are showstoppers.

azaleas: if you live in Zones 5-9 and have acid
soil, nothing is prettier.

Deciduous dwarf shrubs:

mock orange, *Philadelphus* 'Silver Showers' (4)

potentilla, *P. parvifolia* 'Farreri' (2), or any of the
shrubby ones, which flower from early summer
to frost.

VINES

Because they lie flat against walls, vines are especially
good:

silver lace, *Polygonum aubertii* (6a) grows quickly
and blooms a creamy froth in fall.

Dropmore scarlet trumpet honeysuckle, *Lonicera
x brownii* 'Dropmore Scarlet Trumpet' (3b) was
developed for the midwest and similar climates.

Dutchman's pipe, *Aristolochia durior* (4b) makes a
marvellous dense screen.

firethorn, *Pyrancantha coccinea* (5b), a semi-
evergreen, is hung with clusters of brilliant orange
berries in late fall and winter.

HERBS

Grow a few herbs for the fun of it and to surprise
your supper guests when you go into-the-garden-Maud
to snip a bit of fresh chives for the Vichyssoise. And
one pot of rosemary will do things to fried
chicken you wouldn't believe.

GROUND COVERS

Low ground covers are perfect substitutes for grass
and high-care flowering plants:

periwinkle, *Vinca minor* (3), blue, white or purple
flowers.

Canby pachistima, *P. canbyii* (2b).

cotoneaster, *C. dammeri* 'Skogholm' (4)

English ivy, *Hedera helix* (5b), many cultivars.

All these are delightful and low-maintenance plants.

PERENNIALS

Choice of which of these plants to grow depends on
your taste and the light in your garden. If you have
little sun, consult lists in CHAPTER 6, The Shady
Garden; for a continuous calendar of bloom, CHAPTER
1, A Garden of All-Year Beauty. For lists of
good perennials and how to grow them, CHAPTER 27.

BULBS, RHIZOMES, CORMS, TUBERS

Spring bulbs — crocus, snowdrops, daffodils, tulips, —
planted in fall are surefire gardening. Although many
will, given the right culture, bloom for some years
if left in the ground, I suggest that for a small city
garden you stretch your budget to buy new ones each
year and thus be sure of consistent showy flowering.

For the best summer flowering bulbs, rhizomes,
corms, and tubers — gladiolus, iris, lilies, tuberous
begonias, dahlias are the most familiar ones —
consult your garden supply catalogue. These can be
kept from year to year without needing too much
ongoing care. (See CHAPTER 28, for recommended
kinds and culture.)

ANNUALS

For one year shots-in-the-arm, nothing beats annuals
and I class the prestarted geraniums, fibrous begonias
and impatiens in this group too. (See CHAPTER 29 for
lists.)

INNER CITY FRONT GARDENS

Space between housewall and street is mostly minimal
and is more a construction and design problem
than a horticultural one.

Any plantings used should be neat; pavings of
gravel or river bed stones, rather than lawn grass,
well curbed to hold the material securely in place.
Evergreen ground cover is useful if it will not catch
debris blowing along the street. Plants should be
chosen for their architectural quality — a potted
standard fuchsia or lantana in an elegant urn (which
you should probably chain to an embedded iron ring
or buried log to prevent stealing) or a small
geometrical bed centred by a standard planted tree.
Euonymus, *E. fortunei vegeta* (5b) is a good
evergreen; for a deciduous flowery burst there's the
well-loved and well-known PeeGee hydrangea, *H.
paniculata* 'Grandiflora' (3b) or forsythia, *F.
intermedia* 'Spectabilis' (5b).

USEFUL FURTHER READING:

CHAPTER 4: A NIGHT GARDEN

CHAPTER 9: A FRAGRANT GARDEN

CHAPTER 13: DESIGN AND DECORATION

CHAPTER 14: PERMANENT FEATURES

CHAPTER 15: ECONOMY AND EASY MAINTENANCE

CHAPTER 19: THE CONTROL OF COMMON PESTS AND
DISEASES

PART V: GUIDES TO GARDENING IN ELEVEN REGIONS
OF THE UNITED STATES

6 THE SHADY GARDEN

Gardening in the shade can be either an exasperating frustration or a delight so surprising you can hardly believe that you were the magician who caused it to happen. Good preliminary planning is a must, faithful preparation of the site and the soil is absolutely necessary and accurate knowledge of the habits of shade-tolerant plants will promise success.

DIFFERENT KINDS OF SHADE

First, analyse the quality of shade you have.

Is it cast by high leafy trees that are bare in winter and spring, then dapple the ground with sun and shadow in summer and fall?

Is it from heavy thick evergreens that cast darkness all year?

Is it from solid buildings, fences or walls that let not a smidgen of sunlight creep through their shadows?

Is it perhaps half time, not full time, of any of these?

If you are not sure which of these conditions you have, take time to chart your problem. Watch not only where full sun and shade lie during the growing months of the year, but observe the moving angle of the sun in all the different seasons. The choice of what you can grow successfully in dappled light from high leafy trees — that is, places where there is strong winter sun and soft summer shade — is fairly wide: the choice of what you can grow in *sky* shine rather than *sun*shine is about the same, but what you can grow in constant, heavy full shade — as exists close against a tall building standing to the south — is limited.

CONSIDER THE BUILDING OF ARCHITECTURAL FEATURES

While you are in this first planning phase, consider whether it might be wise to build an architectural feature of some kind on part or all of your shady area, using plants only as accents.

One of the happiest answers to meagre straggly growth in shade around a north-facing front door is to extend the steps sideways and forward to create a small stage for a show of portable pots of standard fuchsias or white wire stands packed with bright begonias, both of which do beautifully in sky shine.

A dank spot in a city garden, constantly shadowed by tall buildings, can be dramatic and less gloomy with a cedar-framed, ground-level bed of large white pebbles with a big well-shaped rock, a piece of sculpture or a birdbath pool as a focus point. And repeat the white of the pebbles with accenting plants — like a delicate white shadbush for early spring, a collar of white patience plants at the base of the birdbath for summer, or a lacy border of fragrant sweet alyssum to flower till frost.

If you have children, a shady place in your garden could become a pitch for a teepee and a council ring, or a playhouse with some wild flowers which the children could collect and grow themselves.

The answer to an untidy bald patch under a tree in the back garden, where grass refuses to grow, could be a flagstone or wood terrace for barbecue suppers and near it pots of rosemary, a wonderful herb to chop over frying chicken, and some chives to clip for tasty hamburgers.

Another good idea is to replace a scruffy flower bed in shade with a shimmering shallow pool, and flag it with bright blue irises to match the reflected summer sky.

SPECIAL FLOWER PLANTINGS

Whether you build such features into the picture or not, you can still plan to make exciting stagecraft with special plantings — things such as a sunbeam piercing tree shadow to highlight some specially chosen plant, or a small wild flower dell to spill early spring flowers over the ground while the trees are still only a haze of green — starry white trilliums, bending arches of belled Solomon's seal and purple sweeps of sweet violets; under a pink and white apple tree a carpet of heavenly blue scillas and dancing yellow daffodils with a ground cover of glistening periwinkle; or stretching white birches with an underplanting of feathery ferns and rose-pink bleeding hearts.

For a flower border in shade, try fragrant white mock orange as a backdrop for 5-foot, rose-spired foxgloves or a jazzy pattern of red and burgundy coleus, orange, cerise and salmon patience plants and scarlet fibrous begonias with bronze leaves.

For planters and window boxes facing north or east, use huge camellia-petalled tuberous begonias in yellow, white, pink, apricot and scarlet.

All these and a thousand more equally exciting combinations will change gloom to glamour in the shady places of your garden. Your local nurseryman or government station will also be able to add to the lists of plants we give you on pages 36-38 and be sure to observe successful shady gardens in your neighborhood, noting what plants do well in them.

THE NEXT STEP, CHECK YOUR SOIL

Half the battle of successful growing in shade is won with good soil and just about all the battle is lost with poor soil. So dig down about 9 inches in each different shaded place in your garden and examine the soil. Often it is bone dry under greedy big trees. If so, whatever you plant there will die, not from lack of sun but from lack of moisture. Less likely, but sometimes the cause of straggly limp growth in shade, is ground too wet and soggy. In either case, your first problem is to improve growing conditions.

Ground that is too dry needs humus — moisture-holding material — added to it. Dig out the area to a depth of 2 feet and into the dug-out soil mix a shovelful of moist peat, leaf mold or rotted compost for each shovelful of earth. While you are about it, add fertilizer too — a shovelful of rotted manure or dehydrated commercial manure in quantities according to the directions on the bag, and also a general garden chemical fertilizer in quantities recommended by the manufacturer.

Finish off the level about 6 inches higher than the surrounding ground to allow for settling, and water well. If a tangle of tree roots makes it impossible to do this thoroughly, dig out and replace what you can, then build up a 12-inch bed of good mix on top of and all over the old level. It often helps to contain this good mix with a low wall of stone or brick, sawed-off butts of cedar post or old railway ties standing snugly side by side. Continue to fertilize this special area at least twice a year with garden chemical fertilizer, mulch it every season with more peat, leaf mold or compost and add, at least once every two years if you can get it, a top dressing of rotted manure. This part of your garden, with that kind of care, will never backslide into poverty again and whatever you plant there will grow luxuriantly.

If your shaded ground is too wet — and this can vary from real muck to consistently spongy wetness that produces moss, weak grass and poor growth — you have a choice of action. If it is really wet all year, take advantage of it and make a bog garden, a little stream or a pool by deepening the grade, and plant it with material that likes wet feet — golden marsh marigolds, for instance, are glorious beside a small dark pool in the early spring. If you would rather have the ground drained to be of more average moisture content, dig a small dry well 2-3 feet deep at the lowest point, backfill it with gravel for 12 inches, lay weeping tile underground through the wet area, sloping it into the dry well, add more gravel, cover with heavy polyethylene and fill up with good earth mix. Again leave the finished grade 6 inches higher than the surrounding ground.

SOIL IN HEAVY SHADE

Where solid, constant shade is cast by tall buildings, fences or walls, again dig out a sample of soil and examine it for good growth factors. If you do not feel competent to do this analysis yourself, your nearest agricultural college or experimental station will do a professional job for you or tell you who will, but elementary good garden soil is not hard to recognize. It will not be so hard that it cracks open in dry hot weather, it will not be so sandy that it runs through your fingers, it will have a pleasant earthy smell, it will squeeze together into a soft patty in your hand.

Ground close to buildings and walls is usually sharply drained and desperately in need of humus to make it more moisture-retentive. Chemical fertilizer should also be added, for what might originally have been there will have leeched out because of the sharp drainage. If you find this condition, improve the earth as recommended for too dry areas.

NEXT, LOOK UP

Large trees are such treasures in a garden you naturally hesitate to cut them down, yet allowed to develop without wise care they can throw shade so dense it is impossible to have a lovely garden under or near them. It is seldom necessary to cut a big tree down completely — very often the situation can be corrected by skillful pruning to let more light through to ground level. This should be done by a trained tree man who will go up through the tree and lighten the branches all over. For the tree's sake and for the pruner's, this is not a job for an amateur, for it takes strength, skill and the proper tools. If you have a multiple, medium-height stand of trees, it is usually best to open it out by taking some out entirely and pruning the remainder. This job, if you are handy with tools, you can do yourself. (For instructions see page 154.)

NEXT, LOOK OVER

Where shade falls on your garden from trees growing in your neighbor's garden or the public domain, check with your lawyer or city government to learn what rights you have to prune them back, thin out or remove entirely. In some cities, you have the right to do anything you wish to any part of the tree that overhangs your property, but take time to make your decision carefully, for chopping off an offending limb at your lot line could be drastic for the scenery, or the health of the tree, to say nothing of friendly relations with your neighbor. A professional thinning might be all that is needed to create light below, followed by an intelligent choice of plant material to grow there.

LAWNS IN SHADE

High thinning of large trees and cutting off low branches up 10 feet also make it possible to grow lawn grass, where it has hitherto been thin and scruffy, by allowing more light to reach ground level. Wise choice of grass seed also helps. Your seedsman will help you find the proper formula for your special situation.

Ground cover and daffodils.

Healthy thick turf of most grass mixtures needs at least 6 hours of sunlight every day. If you have less sun than this it may be wiser for you to plan something other than a lawn for shady places in your garden.

ALTERNATIVES

Ground covers: Most successful, with the least care, are low-growing, leafy plants that spread sideways and cover the ground. (See CHAPTER 24.) Prepare the soil to a depth of at least 12 inches and set the plants on 8- or 12-inch centres. Mulch the ground after watering and give good care to the planting for the first 2-3 years until well established.

Interplantings of bright spring bulbs — tulips, crocus, early daffodils — can be made through the ground cover, but avoid using summer annuals; competition for food and light will result in scrawny growth of the ground cover.

Pavings: Pavings of flagstone, slate or any one of the handsome precast concrete slabs on the market — you can also make your own — are a good solution, and low, shade-loving plants such as stonecrop or thymes can be planted in the cracks. One of the true delights of a shady garden are the patterns of shadow and light thrown by tree trunks and branches onto the ground, and this pattern is sharpest on the smooth paving. Marble chips, pebbles or wood chips are also good as surface cover and if laid with care will require minimum maintenance. A frame of metal, wood or brick projecting a few inches above the surface of the ground is useful to keep them from scattering, and a layer of heavy polyethylene laid underneath discourages weeds.

WHAT TO PLANT

When you have the best possible soil conditions, the best possible intensity of light, and have built a special architectural feature (if you have decided to have one), the next step is to study plant lists of recommended trees, shrubs, flowers and bulbs to decide what you wish to grow. If you are not sure what will do well for you, experiment for the first two or three years; then, when you know what you like, increase your plantings. Instead of a few primroses have a carpet of them, instead of one hesitant azalea a whole pink cloud. When your shady garden passes its fifth birthday, you will have to thin the plants out and trim up into the trees again, and probably every five years thereafter. Experiment with new plants and be perceptive about what grows successfully in other shady gardens that you might wish to copy for your own.

A Selected List of Plants to Choose From for Your Shady Garden

All that we recommend will do well in dappled light under trees, places where sunshine falls one or two hours a day and places of full early-spring sun and summer-to-fall shade. Those with an asterisk are the only plants to consider for constant solid shade such as that cast by buildings, fences, walls or close to dense evergreens.

EVERGREEN TREES AND SHRUBS

*Hemlock, *Tsuga canadensis* (Zone 4) : fits well into the scale of a home garden if clipped to size ; can stand alone, in a clump or as a hedge, although its minimum need for 6-8 feet base width at maturity makes it a pretty fat hedge for the average garden.

Juniper, *Juniperus* (Zone 2) :
Andorra, *J. horizontalis* 'Plumosa', a low-spreading, graceful shrub, blue-green in summer, purple in winter; recommended for shade in the Midwest.

Savin, *J. sabina* 'Arcadia' and 'Skandia', low and compact, especially useful in Midwest.

*Yew, *Taxus cuspidata* (Zone 4) : without doubt the most versatile ; grows well in city fumes and dirt ; comes in a variety of shapes and looks lovely when new bright green tips the dark green mature foliage in spring.

8 BROAD-LEAVED EVERGREENS: VINES, SHRUBS AND GROUND COVERS

These plants hold their leaves all winter.

*English Ivy, *Hedera helix* 'Baltica' (Zone 5b) : glossy vine or ground cover.

Euonymus, many (Zone 4) : can be grown as a vine, a shrub or small hedge ; leathery leaves all year ; orangey fruits in fall; one of the best.

Holly, American, *Ilex opaca* (Zone 6) : glossy leaves, our familiar Christmas red-berried holly.
English, *Ilex aquifolium* (Zone 7): larger berries. Oregon & South.

*Japanese Spurge, *Pachysandra terminalis* (Zone 3) : an excellent ground cover under trees and as a green carpet for bulb plantings ; hides ripening foliage of bulbs.

Mountain Laurel, *Kalmia latifolia* (Zone 4) : a shrub, dainty parasols of pink and white flowers in spring.

Oregon Grape, *Mahonia aquifolium* (Zone 5): a shiny, holly-leaved shrub, yellow flowers and blue fruit, much happier in shade than sun.

Pachistima, *P. canbyii* (Zone 3) : a fine-leaved ground cover.

Periwinkle, *Vinca minor* (Zone 3) : shining green and trailing ground cover, lovely blue, white or purple flowers in spring, excellent where grass will not flourish.

Rhododendrons and azaleas in variety (reliably hardy only to Zone **5a** and up) ; showstoppers in flower ; new hardier cultivars being developed.

---

6 FLOWERING TREES

Flowering trees in shade are usually drifting with blossom rather than thick with it, but the contrast of fragile bloom against dark shadow is breathtaking.

Carolina Silverbell, *Halesia carolina* (Zone 5) : branches a-dangle with little white bells in spring.

Cornelian Cherry, *Cornus mas* (Zone 4b) : a yellow mist in spring when covered with tiny flowers.

Flowering Dogwood, *Cornus florida* (Zone 5b) : flowers like white suede in spring ; outstanding.

Redbud, *Cercis canadensis* (Zone 5b) : completely covered in spring with pink flowers ; hardy a little farther north than dogwood, but not much.

Saskatoon, *Amelanchier alnifolia* (Zone 1) : particularly fine for the Mountain States.

Shadbush, *Amelanchier canadensis* or *A. grandiflora* (Zone 4) : a cloud of white in early spring ; hardy ; bird-beloved fruits in summer.

---

10 SATISFACTORY SHRUBS FOR SHADE

(T for tall ; M for medium height ; S for small)

Alpine currant, *Ribes alpinum*, M (Zone 2) : a fine deciduous shrub for clipped hedges in shade ; also good for informal bushy plantings ; leafs out first thing in spring and holds till late fall.

Dwarf European, High Bush-Cranberry, *Viburnum opulus* 'Nanum', T (Zone 2b) : lovely white flowers, followed by bright red, very bitter fruit.

*Elder, *Sambucus canadensis* 'Aurea', T (Zone 3) : flat creamy heads of flowers in summer, golden foliage, followed by purple-black fruit.

Forsythia, many, mostly T (Zone 4) : comet's tails of bright yellow stars in early spring ; easy to grow.

*Hydrangea, *H. arborescens* and *H. grandiflora*, M (Zone 3b) : the first has green-white flower heads in mid-summer ; the second, pink bloom in late summer.

*Kerria, *K. japonica*, M (Zone 4) : bright green with yellow flowers in spring ; bark bright green in winter.

Mock Orange, many, *Philadelphus*, MT (Zone 3) : one of the showiest and most fragrant shrubs ; single and double white flowers.

Prairie Almond, *Prunus pedunculata* x *P. triloba*, M (Zone 2) : graceful, pink, semi-double, redeyed flowers (not from weeping) that come before the leaves ; especially good for the northern plains.

Pygmy Caragana, *C. aurantiaca*, M (Zone 2) : makes an excellent dwarf hedge.

*Silverleaf Dogwood, *Cornus alba* 'Argenteo-marginata', M (Zone 2) : its foliage is silver-green edged with white ; good where you want an airy look.

---

12 PERENNIALS AND BIENNIALS

*Ajuga, *A. reptans*, S : a glossy, easy ground cover or rock garden plant ; flowers blue, leaves green, variegated or bronze.

Astilbe, M : feathery spikes of crimson, red, lilac pink and white ; needs moist soil.

*Bergenia, *B. cordifolia*, M : big-leaved, loose heads of rose flowers in spring, needs moisture.

Bleeding Heart, *Dicentra spectabilis*, M : one of the loveliest plants for shade ; ferny cut foliage and drips of rose hearts in late spring ; foliage disappears in summer so mark clearly, then plant to cover, if in a prominent place.

Columbine, *Aquilegia*, M : delicate, flying-dove flowers ; plant where you can see it at close range.

Doronicum, *D. caucasicum magnificum*, M : bright yellow daisies that last for weeks in early spring.

Foxglove, *Digitalis*, T : with really fertile soil this spectacular flower rises 5-8 feet ; white, pink and cerise spikes in early summer ; a biennial, so after flowering it dies ; new plants should be set each year to bloom the next.

*Lily of the Valley, *Convallaria majalis* S : for patches of ground cover ; tur-

quoisey-green leaves and stems of fragrant tiny white bells ; late spring.

Lungwort, *Pulmonaria saccharata*, S ; speckled leaves with stems of pink-rose to blue bells in earliest spring.

*Plantain Lily, many, *Hosta*, M : handsome foliage plants that truly love shade ; some leaves deep green, some glaucous, some rimmed spectacularly in white ; flowers not showy, but *H. plantaginea* 'Grandiflora' has large white sweet-scented flowers in late summer.

Primroses, many *Primula*, S ; all are tops for shady gardens ; need moist, cool soil, bloom in spring.

Virginia Bluebell, *Mertensia virginica*, M ; pale blue, pink-blue and purple flowers in early spring ; a dell of it would be lovely, then follow with ferns and flowering tobacco for the bluebell leaves disappear in summer.

---

4 VINES FOR SHADE

*Boston Ivy, *Parthenocissus tricuspidata* and *P. quinquefolia* Engelmannii : the first is the familiar, big-leaved Boston Ivy, rambling and rampant and a gorgeous scarlet in the fall ; the second is a miniature of the first with foliage like wild Virginia creeper.

*Clematis, large-flowered varieties in white, mauve and purple are our most showy shady garden vine ; likes a little sun in the morning, shade from noon on ; delicate and graceful ; other kinds, *C. paniculata*, the sweet autumn clematis, and *C. virginiana*, the virgin's bower, both frothy and lovely.

*Climbing Hydrangea, *H. petiolaris* : slow to establish but one of the best ; flat, lacy white flower heads in early summer ; a strong muscled pattern of stems all year.

*Dutchman's Pipe, *Aristolochia durior;* leaves are big green hearts, a favorite for veranda screening.

---

6 ANNUALS FOR SHADE

*Begonias, *B. semperflorens*, S ; the giddy little Tizzie-Lizzies that cover themselves with glistening blooms all summer—pink, red and white ; foliage green, silver or dark red ; can be grown from seed but easiest to buy.

Browallia, S : white or royal blue stars, fine and delicate, blooms all summer if started as plants.

*Coleus, M: grown for its brilliant foliage; untidy flower spikes should be clipped off; new Japanese hybrids with frilled edges on leaves; can grow from seed but faster if bought as plants; good all summer.

*Flowering Tobacco, *Nicotiana,* TM: delightful for summer evening garden, open and fragrant at night; some new cultivars open also in daytime; moths love it; white the best, but also comes in green and cerise; all summer; seed or plants.

Forget-me-not, *Cynoglossum* and *Myosotis,* S: everybody knows forget-me-nots, but not everyone knows that if you plant them in moist loose soil they will seed themselves; spring and summer; blue, sometimes also pink and white.

*Impatience and Balsam, *Impatiens sultani* and *I. balsamina,* MS: successful in shade, particularly in good moist soil under trees; pink, orange, scarlet and white; all summer; best buy as plants or keep cuttings over winter for following year.

BULBS AND CORMS FOR SHADE

For the early spring garden and through ground covers under trees, plant winter aconite, snowdrops, crocus, scilla, glory-of-the-snow, grape hyacinths, fritillaria — both the big stunning crown imperial and the little spotted guinea hen flower — early daffodils and the sturdy small species tulips, camassias. For late spring and early summer, plant lily-of-the-valley, iris, lilies. For foliage like sheer silk, plant after all danger of frost is past and the ground warm, caladiums in green and white, pink, or red and white; buy as plants or start indoors in early spring.

For the real showstoppers of summer, plant tuberous begonias; often each flower is 5-6 inches across; many-petalled in white, pink, apricot, orange and scarlet; big and heavy, especially after a rain, so best plant up off the ground — perhaps in a window box or a raised planter — so that you look *into* the face of the flower, not down on the back of its neck.

WILD FLOWERS FOR SHADE

Most bloom before tree leaves are fully out in the spring. For detailed information on culture see Chapter 8.
Bloodroot; Blue flag; Blue phlox; Bouncing Bet; Bunchberry; Cardinal flower; Claytonia; Clintonia; Columbine; Corydalis; Creeping snowberry; Dog's-tooth violet; Dutchman's breeches; Evening primrose; Foamflower; Foxglove; Gentian; Goldthread; Hepatica; Jack-in-the-Pulpit; Lady's slipper; May apple; Meadow rue; Mint; Moccasin flower; Orchis; Partridge berry; Pipsissewa; Shinleaf; Shooting star; Solomon's seal; Squirrel corn; Stonecrop; Trailing arbutus; Trillium; Twinflower; Violet; Virginia bluebell; and Ferns of all kinds.

FOR POOLSIDES IN SHADE

Cardinal flower; Cinnamon and Royal fern; Forget-me-not; Marsh marigold; Mint; Primula; Virginia bluebell; Water iris.

WATER PLANTS FOR SHADE

Cattail; Ostrich fern; Papyrus; Umbrella plant; Water iris.

For details of how to grow, see PART III.
For how to build permanent features, see CHAPTER 14.
For techniques of improving soil, planting, etc., see CHAPTER 18.

7 ROCK AND WALL GARDENS

Rocks in your garden should look as though they have been there forever. Outcroppings — either naturally revealed or cleverly man-made — pushing strongly out of the land; blocky chunks stepping firmly down a hillside; sturdy stone walls curtained with flowers, buttressing a slope; a great beautiful hunk as a piece of freestanding sculpture — all or any can add a handsome immortal look to your garden.

More permanent than people, rocks also give a sense of timeless calm to a garden. They don't need constant care — no watering, feeding or staking against wind or winter snows. Bugs don't bother them. But they do need careful planning and careful handling. Setting them in place is heavy work, usually a job for more than one strong man. But I do know one dainty lady gardener who, with a Dr. Seuss bent for clever invention, manhandled alone, with planks and pipes as rollers, a half dozen morsels of a Precambrian outcrop into a sensitive, fern-frilled rock garden-cum-pool. Each stone weighed between one quarter and 2 tons.

MAKING A ROCK GARDEN

The best rock gardens fit the site as though they belonged there. If you have been lucky enough to inherit natural outcroppings with your land, all you need do is design your garden to show them off. This may begin with scraping them bare of overgrowth to be more fully seen. A good rock garden is one-half to one-third visible rock. Then go on to enhance them with complementary planting.

If you have not inherited rock and yearn for such a garden, make trips through the countryside looking at outcroppings and the way they lie. Visit other good rock gardens in your area. Buy some modelling clay at a hobby shop and bits of sponge or moss for plants, and make a model of the garden you want. Then, with the help and advice of a good stone man, choose the rock you will use. If you want the outcrop look, on gently rolling land, pick stone with a horizontal rhythm and set its striations running all in the same direction. If you want the chunky look for a steep slope — a kind of abandoned quarry — then choose block stone that will lie in a cubist pattern. Avoid, if you can, the raw look of newly-quarried stone and be sure to choose the same kind of stone for the whole garden. The best will look already weatherworn, be patterned with moss and lichen and fit in right from the beginning.

KINDS OF STONE

Limestone, especially the worn pocked kind, and sandstone are both good materials. Granite, being extremely hard, is difficult because it doesn't crevice or crack and therefore does not easily cradle plants. But if granite is all you have, then ask your stonemason to crack it after it is in place and to pry it apart to make channeled niches to pack with soil for plantings. If you can, choose stone with the topside roughly level: building with this shape is easier, design cleaner. Avoid boulders and cobbles — they make a lumpy, unpretty garden.

CHOOSING THE SITE

Full sun all day, sharp drainage and freely moving air over it are musts if your rock garden is to be a flowery picture all the growing year. If you have cool summers, it can face east, west or south. For warm summer areas, choose east, northeast or northwest. Full south or west exposures are good only if you can give the garden light shade — like a leafy tree sited to filter the sun during the hottest part of the day.

You can build a fully shaded rock garden if you will be content with ferns (see CHAPTER 8) and leafy wild plants. Drainage for them is not so urgent a problem and the air above such a garden can be calm and still.

In the sunny rock garden, drainage must be sharp because mat and tuft plants — the chief charmers — will rot easily in waterlogged soil. Good insurance against this trouble is gritty soil and a site that slopes. Heavy rains that would normally wash down the slope from above can be diverted by digging a ditch just behind the crest and running it crosswise to the slope. Water that would otherwise collect at the bottom of the site can be carried away by similar ditching.

A WATER FEATURE

Water deliberately planned as part of the design, however, is delightful. It can be a small stream that wanders and splashes downhill into a series of small pools; a silvery cascade falling off a rocky shelf, or a still dark pool mirroring the plants on its rim. Low horsepower, small, submersible pumps, plastic pipe and connections placed out of sight make it possible to use the same water over and over. Pools should have an overflow, an outlet for draining to clean and sloping sides to prevent pressure-cracking in winter. Stream bed and pool can be inexpensively lined with two thicknesses of heavy-ply black plastic sheeting anchored on the edges with soil and flat stones projecting over the water bed. Alternatively, concrete, although more expensive, is more permanent and if used should be painted or stained dark brown or black to make it appear deeper and hide sediment. (See page 47.)

BUILDING

Rocks in different sizes should be set at different levels and roughly parallel to the land at the base of the garden. Begin by setting the largest at the bottom, then spreading out sideways, following the natural contour of the land. Most important, set one-half to two-thirds of each rock *into* the ground so it will look surely placed and secure. Make the most level side the top, the longest edge out and tip back so that rain and melting snow will run *into* the soil behind. Never set rocks on end in such a garden and never, as the excellent handbook, *Rock Gardens*, published by the Brooklyn Botanic Garden, warns, so that they look like a penitentiary rockpile, a giant's lost dentures, neglected tombstones or the rock collector's pride.

Let paths or steps wander diagonally on a gentle slope, widening out here and there to a small level viewing plateau. Keep path surfaces below the level of the edging rocks on either side so that fragile plants growing on the edge of the steps will be silhouetted against the rocks, and those on top easily seen. Make risers of steps low, treads wide.

Plan paths so that you can comfortably reach all plants to look after them. If possible, set plants in place as you build.

SOIL

Good sandy loam, 1 foot deep, will be right for the average creeping rock plant. A few of the most prized dwarf specimens — rhododendrons, azaleas, heaths and heathers, the underground-rooting wintergreen and bearberry — require acid soil. True alpines — more difficult to grow but the collector's challenge — will need a grittier mix — one part humus, one good garden soil, one sand and five parts of ¼″ crushed limestone.

Stamp the soil firmly under and behind the rocks as they are laid, to eliminate air pockets. Add a little extra the first year to allow for settling but make the final surface of the plant pockets almost level with or a little lower than the rock in front, so that soil will not wash out in heavy rains. Wedge smaller rocks between large ones and pack the crevices behind with more soil.

FERTILIZER

Feeding rock plants is only necessary — and this seldom — when you want luxuriant growth. Since hugging the ground, growing slowly and remaining dwarf are desirable characteristics you want to retain, most such plants will respond well if only a fresh top dressing of soil or a stone chip mulch is used in spring. Avoid manure like the plague. The weed seeds it carries will be a deep-rooting headache haunting you for years. If your plants are growing poorly, and you decide it would be wise to fertilize, use an inorganic chemical one, and never feed after early summer; this encourages late-season growth which is sensitive to winterkill.

CHOOSING ROCK GARDEN PLANTS

Choose perennials (repeat-bloomers) depending on the kind of rock garden you want and the climate where you live (see pages 46-47). Small plants are rated as 1-8 inches high; average 1 foot, and large up to 2 feet. Native plants will always grow successfully if you reproduce the conditions they originally grew in. Favorite low-growing and creeping ordinary garden plants hardy for your zones should also do well. But the true dyed-in-the-wool rock gardeners eventually want to grow true alpines. Gardens in Victoria, B.C., make this city the centre of rock gardening in North America. Here plants that grow wild at altitudes of 4,000-12,000 feet have been persuaded to grow happily at sea level or very little higher. A true challenge and so successfully met.

Being sure to use a variety of shape, habit, color and texture is the first maxim to follow. Trailers or prostrate forms such as the soft-grey-leaved white-flowering arabis, *A. alpina*, or the shiny green, red-berried cotoneaster, *C. adpressa*, should flow over the ground. Tufted plants like the tiny early yellow-starred draba, *D. aizoides*, and moundy ones like 'Silver Mound' artemisia, *A. Schmidtiana* 'Silver Mound', nestle snug against the stone and as they grow spread over it. Creepers and sturdy joint-rooters like thyme, *Thymus serpyllum*, probe deep into fissures then stretch flat over the surrounding stone.

Shrubs and small evergreens — and be sure to buy with the *mature* size in mind — give variety of shape, color and texture especially; the small rose daphne, D. *cneorum*, has sweetly fragrant pink flowers; the small 'Silver Gem' euonymus, fascinating grey, green, cream and pink leaves all year; the dwarf mountain pine, *Pinus mugo mughus* 'Pumilio', mates superbly with rocks.

For the most tender flowering, and therefore the most intriguing contrast with the dark brooding strength of the rocks, are the plants whose delicate flowers catch the glancing light — the dainty columbines, *Aquilegia*; the shooting star, *Dodecatheon alpinum*, a native of the west coast; the delicate bellflowers, *Campanula*; the tiny cyclamens, *C. neapolitanum*, which is the last of the bulbs to bloom in fall and, of course, all the lovely small bulbs of spring from the earliest snowdrops, *Galanthus nivalis*, through the miniature 2-inch daffodils, *Narcissus minimus*, and the spectacular species tulips, *Tulipa*, to the later-blooming bluebells, *Scilla campanulata*.

Beware of nuisance plants whose quick cover-up quality may seem like a wonderful idea in the beginning. Within a few years, you will be frustrated beyond belief trying to control them. My list would include, bugleweed, *Ajuga reptans*; snow-in-summer, *Cerastium tomentosum*; some of the sedums, *S. kamtschaticum*, particularly; ivy, *Helix*; Virginia creeper, *Parthenocissus quinquefolia*; grandmother's bluebell, *Campanula rapunculoides*; violets of all kinds, *Viola*; goutweed, *Aegopodium podagraria* (a real devil this one); forget-me-nots, *Myosotis*, and creeping charlie or creeping jennie, *Lysimachia nummularia*, depending on which sex you think can be the most nuisance. Some of these may not behave rampantly in *your* garden and there may be others you would put on the list. But be suspicious of any recommended rock plant that sounds easy to grow, and any that a generous neighbor can pull tufts of from his garden to give you.

Annuals fill a useful role by adding flowers for summer, filling gaps left by ripened bulbs or plants that have succumbed to winter. Again choose the low ones — portulaca, small marigolds or zinnias, fibrous begonias, sweet alyssum, lobelia. Shear each plant back about one third every two weeks to keep low bloom coming on.

ONGOING CARE

Set plants in spring and/or early fall, if your climate encourages it. Putting the rocks in place can go on at other times of the year, if it is easier for you to do it then, and the plants can be added at the appropriate time. Most gardeners, however, find it easier and better to design their rock garden and plant as they build, which implies doing all in spring or fall.

Water planting holes with starter solution of water-soluble fertilizer, set plants, water again, add soil and a 1-2 inch chipped stone mulch. Shade for the first week. Thereafter soak thoroughly when watering, never sprinkle. Once-a-week watering is usually needed for the first year unless there has been regular rainfall. Screes must often be watered daily during the growing season if rainfall is light and weather warm.

Prune and train constantly, snipping off bits going off in the wrong direction while they are still small, cutting back to keep the bold line of rocks revealed, pressing trailing rooters into the earth, cutting new shoots of conifers and broad-leaved evergreens in half to keep them compact and dwarf. Shear heathers lightly after blooming.

Pick off dead flowers before they can seed unless you want them to. Penstemon and columbine, the waterside *Primula japonica*, will self-seed delightfully, often defying the sparseness of the soil where they choose to grow. I once had a dainty McKana hybrid columbine with flowers like white butterflies grow apparently straight out of a granite boulder and it even had the sensitivity to choose the one spot in the garden where a sunbeam shone through the great oak above and fingered it lightly every morning.

Pull weeds when these usurpers are still small — easiest after a rain or watering. If weeds become tangled in your garden plants, put your left hand (or right if you're a southpaw) on the plant you want to keep, press down, then with your other hand, wiggle the weed out. *Rock gardens, because of the need for constant weeding, are high maintenance plantings and no one should build one unless he enjoys being on his knees.* A new herbicide-impregnated fibre that can be laid around the plant just under the surface of the soil to prevent weed growth is being tested in the United States, and may go far to eliminating this high care of rock gardens.

For winter protection, when the garden is frozen hard lay evergreen branches over the tenderest plants to prevent late-winter sun from burning them, then remove branches gradually as spring comes in. Press winter-heaved plants back into the ground as it thaws. Top dress in spring with fresh gritty soil and stone chips.

Dividing and transplanting perennial plants about every 3 years in the spring is wise. Your rock garden, even with the best of care, will also probably need a complete re-do every 10-15 years. Some gardeners do a major overhaul of one section of the mature garden each of three or four years, rather than all at once. In this way, the upset of re-planting is not so noticeable.

WALL GARDENS

Buttress a terrace, a grade change between you and your neighbor, a house that sits too high out of the ground, a sidewalk or drive much below grade, with a dry stone wall (meaning unmortared). They are clean, handsome and, when dressed with flowery plants, a treat to look at. A well-planned and planted wall garden is easy maintenance after the initial laying and has a lifetime of 25 to 50 years before it needs to be rebuilt. There is, in fact, a good chance that the wall may outlast you.

A dry wall needs no deep foundation as a mortared wall does. Up to a height of 2 feet can be built directly on firm ground; up to 4 feet with one layer of large rocks set, as a base, beneath the surface.

CHOOSING ROCK

Rock should be slabs, all the same kind, of whatever stone is most easily available and therefore least expensive. Most are limestone, but it is possible to make a good rock wall out of random cut granite, discarded stepping stones, or (less good-looking but utilitarian) cracked-up road paving or sidewalk. These last two need lots of curtaining plants.

For small walls up to 2 feet high, rock should be approximately 10-12 inches long and wide, 1-3 inches thick. A larger wall needs larger rock — a 4-foot wall, for instance, looks best with rocks 18 inches long and wide and proportionately thick.

BUILDING

The whole wall should slope backwards (known as the 'batter'), in the proportion of 1 inch to each foot of height and each stone should tip inwards and down ¼-½ inch, to drain melting snow and rain (see page 108).

Place stones so that joints are not directly above one another. Leave spaces only large enough to hold the plants, which are easiest set in place while the wall is being built. If you must add them later, wash off loose earth, wrap roots in wet sphagnum moss, tie lightly with string, soak in starter solution and then chink them into the wall with a stick or the handle of a wooden spoon.

SOIL

Equal parts of good garden loam, sand and peat, well mixed, should be tamped behind and between the stones as they are laid, the same mix should be used for a planting bed you will probably want across the top of wall. This bed can be approximately 1-4 feet wide, 10-12 inches deep. If you have space and would like it, a similar bed can be built along the bottom of the wall, but remember that you are going to have to step into it to tend the plants growing in the wall.

PLANTS FOR ROCK WALLS

Cascading forms of perennial garden plants — the thymes; stiff-starched white candytuft, *Iberis sempervirens*; the moss pinks, *Phlox subulata*; the greeny-grey catnip, *Nepeta x faassenii* are all good. Sempervivums, known as "live forevers"; sedums, whose name means to sit, and the saxifrages, the "stone breakers," are at home in cracks and crevices and their bold pattern striking against the rocks. The little plant called living mortar in Europe, in America, Kenilworth ivy, *Cymbalaria muralis*, seeds itself often in the most incredibly tiny bit of soil, and roots at every node. Small ferns are gracefully green and grow well if you have some dappled shade.

Do not try to grow evergreens or bulbs in rock walls. Instead, plant them in a bed along the top and bottom of the wall, using low prostrate forms to feather out and downwards. Think twice before you plant running rooters like ivy in your wall garden — they are almost impossible to keep in bounds.

(For lists of recommended plants, see pages 46-47. For recommended ferns, see CHAPTER 8.)

CARE OF ROCK WALLS

The usual care — watering in dry weather, shearing off faded flowers, replacing plants that die — is all that a wall garden needs except for pruning. Once plants have grown to the size you like best, trim them to stay that way. Leave plenty of rock face clear. Don't let one plant run over into others around it. Give each a solo performance.

ROCKS AS SCULPTURE

Rocks standing alone, or in a deliberately planned grouping, can be as forceful, as decorative as well-chosen sculpture. America has learned this appreciation from the highly sensitive and symbolic use of rock in Japanese gardens. A single stone, with minimal planting of an architectural quality to marry it to the ground, can be everlasting beauty. As companions for a single stone, this could be one feathery evergreen, low to one side, and a cluster of ferns in its shadow. For a pair of flat-topped limestones at the turn of a path or beside a pool use a clump of sword-leaved yellow iris, for a bold boulder that finishes a low stone wall a small festoon of Virginia creeper trailed over its shoulder.

To eliminate the need for picky, close-trimming of grass around these sculpture stones, set them on a bed of stone chips or pebbles, with a layer of black plastic beneath to prevent growth of weeds.

Choosing and placing such rocks is a matter of personal taste, but one word of warning for all who do it. Always set rocks well into the ground and brace them firmly against toppling. Otherwise they will look as though a dump truck had bounced them into your garden willy-nilly, or they will be in danger of falling over on someone, maybe you.

IMPORTED AND SYNTHETIC STONE

A very lightweight stone that can be cut, carved and generally handled much more easily than native heavy materials is available. It comes in different shades of grey and is said to stand up to the vicissitudes of northern winters. One caution — it is terribly sharp and therefore must be handled with coated gloves and is not recommended for gardens where small children play.

For details of building stone steps, pavings, retaining walls, see CHAPTER 14.
For the use of stone as a mulch, see CHAPTER 18.
For wild flowers and ferns suitable for rock gardens, see CHAPTER 8.

PERENNIAL PLANTS THAT ARE EASY TO GROW

COMMON NAME	BOTANICAL NAME
Aster, Alpine	*A. alpinus*
Aubrietia, several	
Bellflower, Carpathian	*Campanula carpatica*
Bleeding Heart, Western	*Dicentra formosa*
Candytuft, Evergreen	*Iberis sempervirens*
Draba, Creeping	*D. repens*
Twisted	*incana*
Goldentuft (not for prairies)	*Alyssum saxatile*
Harebell	*Campanula garganica*
	rotundifolia
House-leek, several	*Sempervivum*
Iris, Dwarf	*I. pumila*
Pasque-flower, European,	*Anemone pulsatilla patens*
Prairie-crocus	
Rock-cress, several	*Arabis albida*
Saxifrage, Tufted	*Saxifraga caespitosa*
Star-moss, Gold-moss	*Sedum acre*
Violet, several	*Viola*

11 EASY TO GROW ANNUALS FOR ROCK GARDENS

Very often an annual tucked in here and there
will keep your rock garden looking flowery all
summer and well into fall.

Ageratum
Cupflower, *Nierembergia*
Fibrous Begonia, *B. semperflorens*
Lobelia, *L. erinus*
Marigold, dwarf and compact types, *Tagetes*
Nasturtium, *Tropaeolum*
Petunia
Portulaca, *P. grandiflora*
Sweet Alyssum, *Lobularia maritima*
Verbena
Zinnia, the compact types

5 PLANTS FOR WALKS AND STEPPING

COMMON NAME	BOTANICAL NAME
Cushion Pink, Moss Campion	*Silene acaulis*
Mother-of-Thyme	*Thymus serpyllum*
Pink, Cheddar	*Dianthus gratianopolitanus*
Maiden	*deltoides*
Speedwell, Common	*Veronica officinalis*
Creeping	*repens*
Thrift, Mountain	*Armeria montana alpina*

ALPINES THAT ARE EASY TO GROW

COMMON NAME	BOTANICAL NAME
Bellflower, Dalmatian	*Campanula portenschlagiana*
Rainer	*raineri*
Singlenod	*caespitosa*
Swiss	*cenisia*
Bluets	*Houstonia coerulea*
Cress, Alpine	*Hutchinsia alpina*

Cushion Pink, Moss Campion	*Silene acaulis*
Draba, Whitlow-grass	*D. aizoon*
Gentian	*Gentiana septemfida*
Lewisia, Columbia	*L. columbiana*
Liver-balsam, Alpine	*Erinus alpinus*
Mixedflower, Limecleft	*Phyteuma comosum*
Weakstem	*scheuchzeri*
Pink, Alpine	*Dianthus alpinus*
Granite	*graniticus*
Zoned	*callizonus*
Poppy, Alpine	*Papaver alpinum*
Rock-jasmine, Dwarf	*Androsace*
Saxifrage, Aizoon	*Saxifraga aizoon*
Burser	*burseriana*
Mossy	*muscoides*
Soldanella	*S. alpina*
Stone-cress, Persian	*Aethionema grandiflorum*
	'Warley Rose'
Thrift, Prickly	*Acantholimon glumaceum*
Toad-flax, Alpine	*Linaria alpina*

8 DWARF SHRUBS

COMMON NAME	BOTANICAL NAME
Arborvitae, Globe	*Thuja occidentalis* 'Globosa'
Daphne, Rose, Garland Flower	*D. cneorum*
Euonymus, Dwarf	*E. nana*
Juniper, Andorra	*Juniperus horizontalis*
	'Plumosa'
Bar Harbor	'Glauca'
Common	*communis*
	'Depressa'
Sargent	*chinensis* 'Sargentii'
Savin	*sabina*
	'Tamariscifolia'
Pine, Dwarf mountain	*Pinus mugo mughus* 'Pumilio'
Potentilla, several	
Spirea, 'Anthony Waterer'	*Spiraea x bumalda*
	Anthony Waterer'
Yew, Dwarf Japanese	*Taxus cuspidata* 'Nana'

9 BULBS FOR THE ROCK GARDEN

COMMON NAME	BOTANICAL NAME
Anemone	*A. blanda*
Crocus	
Daffodil, Dwarf	*Narcissus*, dwarf
Glory-of-the-Snow	*Chionodoxa luciliae*
Hyacinth, Grape	*Muscari* species
species	*Hyacinthus amethystinus*
Snowdrop	*Galanthus*
Squill, Siberian	*Scilla sibirica*
Tulip	*Tulipa*, dwarf types
Winter Aconite	*Eranthis*

12 PLANTS FOR DRY-STONE WALLS

COMMON NAME	BOTANICAL NAME
Aubrietia, several	*A. deltoidea*
Bellflower	*Campanula portenschlagiana*
Catnip	*Nepeta x faassenii*

Cheddar Pink	Dianthus gratianopolitanus
Double Wall Rock-cress	Arabis albida 'Flore Pleno'
Evergreen Candytuft	Iberis sempervirens
Gold Dust	Alyssum saxatile
Ground-Pink, Moss-Pink, several	Phlox subulata
House-leek, several	Sempervivum, most species and cultivars
Mother-of-Thyme	Thymus serpyllum
Potentilla	P. tormentillo-formosa
Saxifrage, several	Saxifraga aizoon
	caespitosa
	oppositifolia

6 PLANTS TO GROW IN SHADE

COMMON NAME	BOTANICAL NAME
Anemone	A. blanda
Bugleweed	Ajuga reptans
Cotula	C. squalida
Epimedium	
Primrose, several	Primula
Shooting Star	Dodecatheon alpinum

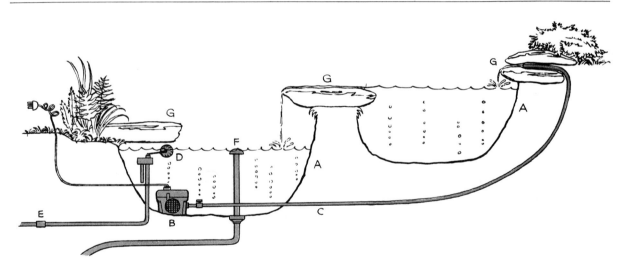

Cross section of a two-pool waterfall:

A *Pools lined with black polyethylene or dark-stained concrete, sloped sides prevent cracking in winter.*

B *Low horsepower, submersible pump, with three-prong, grounded connection, pushes water in lower pool back up to upper one.*

C *Plastic hose.*

D *Float valve (like those in toilet cisterns) connected to house water supply opens and refills pool if level drops.*

E *Check valve, to prevent pool water from flowing back into the house system should pressure drop there.*

F *Strainer-topped drain leads overflow to a dry well (see page 108) and, lifted out, empties lower pool for cleaning.*

G *Flat rocks camouflage edges and hide equipment.*

8 WILD FLOWERS AND FERNS

Wild flowers attract gardeners as apple blossoms attract bees. It's love at first sight and forever after.

The quest is pure pleasure; the identification and delving into their history and habit a challenge; the wish to grow them a natural next step.

Today this is possible as it has never been before. Nurseries propagate and sell wild flower plants; a dozen or more companies sell seeds; methods for collecting and transplanting successfully have been simplified. A few — the pink lady's slipper is one — still need conditions that elude even the most experienced, but there are hundreds of others that are easy to grow and wonderfully rewarding.

Without going more than a few steps into your garden, you could see the excitement of a drift of Virginia bluebells as they would grow in a country birch wood; a furry mat of prairie crocus as they carpet the ground in the Midwest; a spectacular purple-pink shooting star, native of the Pacific coast. This kind of treasure is possible not only this year in your garden, but next year and the one after that too because most of the recommended wild plants in our lists are perennial. Once planted they go happily on, even increasing in numbers.

And the fact they're free is always a fillip. Free that is, if you don't count the depreciation on your car, the gas, your tools, the anti-bug spray and the cost of your picnic.

If you grow your own wild flowers from seed, as many do, there is the added excitement of seeing a speck the size of a grain of pepper grow, with your help and know-how, into something as spectacular as a 6-foot glistening spire of white foxglove. I think you'll agree, if you try it, this is real miracle making.

Tame
the wild ones

Treasure, pure treasure, are wildings in a cultivated garden. Give them a friendly site and proper soil, their own measure of light and moisture and they can be your most cherished plants. Not only will they contribute their own tender beauty but, as each blooms, you will see again in your mind's eye the shadowed woods, the sunny fields, the little brook from which they came.

Be thoughtful about where and how you get them. Gather a few seeds, learn how to grow a whole lovely plant from a snippet of root or a twiggy cutting, or buy from a specializing nursery that propagates from its own stock. Gardeners, of all people, must lead in following wise conservation practices if the natural beauty of the land they love is to be kept.

Stars of the northwoods spring: white trilliums, easy to grow and in bloom for at least two or three weeks.

The dainty shooting star of the Northwest: small purple-tailed comets held high above the leaves, especially lovely in rock gardens.

green-tipped waxy bells in spring.

The pasque flower, South Dakota's floral emblem, greets the warm winds of spring with fuzzy-stemmed flowers.

The glossy, evergreen, blue-berried Oregon grape of the Pacific coast.

The joyous bounty of high summer: white daisies, black-eyed Susans, grandmother's bluebells, Queen Anne's lace.

The glorious June-flowering western red lily, not easy to grow, but a treasure when it does well.

One of the glories of spring: the spilling gold of marsh marigolds beside a brook.

Endearing purple violets: dainty, early flowering and easy to grow.

BUT DON'T BE A PIRATE

Understand that in painting this glowing picture of wild flower growing, I am *not* recommending indiscriminate, careless digging or picking. I would like to have been able to give you a list of plants you could gather in abundance, more you could collect sparingly and those so precious and temperamental you should never pick nor transplant them. But this is impossible because this is so vast a country, its wild flowers and their incidence so varied.

Your own awareness and sense of responsibility for the continuing beauty of the land must guide you when you collect. Know conservation laws for your area. Learn all you can about the habits of wild plants. Observe them intelligently. For instance, if you learn that trailing arbutus is difficult to transplant and grow successfully in a cultivated garden — which is so — leave it where you find it. If you come upon half an acre of white trilliums blowing in the soft spring wind, move a single plant to your garden and propagate more from that. If you find only one rare clump in the woods, leave it where it is and instead buy nursery plants or seed to grow your own.

PLANT THEM TO LOOK AS THOUGH THEY HAD ALWAYS BEEN THERE

Woodland wild plants grow best in a setting that looks like the forest. High deciduous trees, barebranched and letting through sun in late winter, then leafing out to create cool shadow by summer are ideal for hepaticas, Dutchman's breeches, trilliums, Solomon's seal, dog-tooth violets, Virginia bluebells. Let the grade of the ground roll gently and unevenly. Add the feathery light green of ferns — and, for the west coast, the gleam of Oregon grape and salal — and settle the roots in moist soil beneath a crisp carpet of dried leaves.

A dark-watered brook, real or man-made, spilling waves of golden marsh-marigolds down its banks is a springtime delight you will never forget. If you can't raise a brook, then make a reflecting pool with a leaky side so the earth there will be soft and wet and welcoming for damp-foots like marsh-marigolds. Follow with blue forget-me-nots which will self-seed from year to year, wild blue flags and, in late summer, the bright red sentinels of cardinal flowers. (For how to build a pool, see page 47.)

Make a casual grouping of stones such as you would find on a sunny rocky hillside to cradle some shiny, creeping bearberry, textured mats of golden stonecrop, blueberry bushes, entrancing in flower, fruit and foliage. To age new rocks fill their crevices with fine sandy soil and encourage bits of lichen to grow in them. Be sure to set any new rocks in your garden well down with their bulk at least half below the ground, like a well-balanced iceberg. On a king-size one in dappled shade, think of growing a ruff of polypody fern, one of the oldest, loveliest and most amenable little wild plants.

A half-buried, half-rotten stump or log makes a fine setting for plants that grow well in humus and peat. Plant it with Virginia bluebells, more and fancier ferns and for close up delight, the delicate twinflower or creeping snowberry. Yellow lady's-slippers grow happily against a peaty log too.

Don't overlook the graceful charm of wild vines to climb over fences or up a scraggly tree. Virginia creeper is lovely all summer and turns to a gorgeous burgundy red in fall; bittersweet is a rhythmic tangle of twisted branches and orange fruits to cut for indoors in winter; the silky seed heads of wild clematis catch the light in late summer. Wild grape, one of the most useful, has a haunting fragrance in flower, flavory leaves for wrapping around hamburgers and marvelous fruit for gourmet jelly and jam.

If you live where such plants are not officially classified as noxious weeds* and you have no weed-chasing farmer friends with low boiling points, you might try planting white daisies on a patch of gravelly soil — they bloom for 3 weeks in early summer — or a hedge of feathery goldenrod as it is so handsomely grown in show gardens in Switzerland. A plant or two of the biennial Queen Anne's lace makes treasure picking for the house, fresh or dried. Easy-to-grow blackeyed susans make a nice giddy centrepiece for a patio supper and last for ages in the garden, besides drying well for winter bouquets. To prevent wayward spread, be sure to cut flower heads off all these weedy beauties before they go to seed.

BE OBSERVANT

Success in growing wild plants depends on whether you can reproduce in your garden the same conditions they thrive on in the wild. When you find a plant you want to collect, observe particularly these things:

the light it grows in. This may be full sun all day, half sun, light or heavy shade. If you can't match this exactly in your garden, you can often get more sun at ground level by judiciously pruning out high existing trees and shrubs. If you need more shade, you will have to plant tall material and wait for it to grow.

the soil it prefers. This may be sandy, rocky or very high in humus content. If necessary, adjust yours by adding sand, bringing in gravel or rocks, mixing in more humus or compost. Some of our most cherished wild flowers also need acid soil. This you can make, even in an alkaline area, by adding peat moss, oak leaf or pine needle compost and ammonium sulphate according to manufacturer's directions. An alternative and easier way to grow one acid-loving beauty is to take a small tin wash tub, punch a couple of holes in the bottom for drainage, put a bit of broken flower pot over each, or a pebble, to keep them from becoming plugged, and fill with soil dug from the spot where you collect the plant. Water only with rain water if your hose supply is alkaline.

the moisture content of the ground. This can be under water, boggy, damp, meadowy or dry. To match this in your own garden, you can make artificial pools, bogs or damp ground; meadow or dry soil, where it is now too damp, by draining or raising the level of the ground.

GROUND RULES FOR COLLECTORS

Good manners and good sense are the best rules for collectors of wild plants, and if you live where there are laws governing what you may gather know what they are and observe them. No one is going to mind if you dig a daisy from a wayside or a horny bit of violet root from dozens in a ditch, but on private property always ask the owner — even if you have to hunt for him — for permission to collect plants from his land. Learn how, with the rare

* A noxious weed — daisies, goldenrod, Queen Anne's lace, kochia are some — is a plant listed by a municipal, county, state or provincial government as harmful to crops. The uncontrolled growing of it, where it can seed into cultivated land, is prohibited.

ones, to take the smallest piece that will grow into a new plant. This is sometimes a division of the root, sometimes a cutting from a branch, sometimes the seed.

Be wary of collecting from roadsides that have been sprayed with chemical brushkills. Plants that survive this — and surprisingly many do — are easy to see in these cleared spaces and would seem to be easy to collect, but harmful chemical residues on the debris could rub off on bare legs or hands. Also, although the plants may look perky when you find them, in my experience they do not transplant nor grow as well as those gathered from unsprayed areas.

Know the poisonous plants — mainly poison ivy, oak and sumac — and learn to recognize them in all their phases. The president of one of the largest and most knowledgeable garden clubs in America once transplanted a dozen plants with fascinating chartreuse berries and later found to her horror that they were poison ivy. Her hands and arms were a mass of itchy blisters for weeks. Her red face lasted even longer.

Don't hesitate to gather wildlings where bulldozers are about to crunch through — in new subdivisions, where there is clearing for industrial sites, widening of highways. Here you are supporting wise conservation if you save such wild plants from destruction.

Poison ivy.

TOOLS

Carry in the trunk of your car a trowel; a sharp small spade — the one sold as a lady's spade is just right — and an old bread knife for cutting off a small piece of tough root such as the blue flag or Solomon's seal; a supply of different sizes of plastic bags and twist-ties to close them and a couple of apple baskets or large plastic garbage bags. For taking cuttings you will need a good pair of clippers; for gathering seed some envelopes, a marking pencil and, in case you have to go back later in the year, some bright cotton or plastic ties to help you to find the plant.

THE BUSINESS OF TRANSPLANTING

Most wild flowers can be transplanted at any time of the year, providing you take a big enough earthball and get them quickly into your own garden. Wild trees and shrubs are best moved in early spring before they leaf out or in late fall after leaves have dropped. Cuttings can be taken, with most hope for success, in early summer or late fall. Seed is best gathered just when it becomes ripe, although you can pick it just before it's fully ripe and dry it in a warm place indoors (the birds may eat it if you put it outdoors).

Moving Plants: when you find the plant you want and get permission to dig a bit of it, make a sharp cut straight down with your spade, all around, and dig it out with as much earth as you can carry. Slide it into a small plastic bag, tie it snugly over the earth ball allowing the top of the plant to stick out the top of the bag. If there is water nearby, pour some over the rootball before you tie the bag up. Then stack the bag, standing upright, in the apple basket or on the spread-out plastic garbage bag. If the plant must remain in your car more than a few hours, see that it is kept as cool and airy as possible and plant it in your garden as soon as you can.

For holding plants over while you prepare a site for them, have a small nursery bed in an out-of-the-way shady corner of your garden. An easy one can be made by setting four planks on edge, braced at the corners, and filling with light, moist, peaty garden soil.

DIVISIONS, CUTTINGS, SEEDS

Divisions of wild flower plants — pieces of growing root with a leafy shoot — I have moved most successfully just as the plant is coming into bloom. Since biennials — foxgloves, Queen Anne's lace, some of the blackeyed susans are in this category — take 2 years to flower and then they die, collect seed of these rather than take a division, or look for small one-year-old seedlings growing nearby.

Cuttings of woody shrubs and trees are wrapped in damp tissue and popped into a small plastic bag to take home. Then follow procedure for rooting as outlined in CHAPTER 18.

Seed should be tapped into an envelope, marked with the name of the plant, the date, and the conditions it grows in. If there is time to grow a sizeable plant before winter, sow it right away (for how to, see CHAPTER 18). Pulpy seeds like jack-in-the-pulpit or trilliums should be soaked in water until you can rub the pulp off, then planted. If seed is gathered too late in the year to plant, store it in a covered jar in the refrigerator until about 3 months before spring. Then put it in a sterile mix of damp but not wet peat moss and vermiculite or perlite in a closed plastic bag, and put it back in the refrigerator until you can sow it in the garden — a sneaky way to fool the seeds into thinking they have wintered outdoors.

PLANTS AND SEED BOUGHT FROM NURSERIES

Wild plants grown and sold by nurseries — mainly flowers and ferns — should be handled as you do those you collect yourself, except that, because they have been out of the ground longer, you should soak them in a starter solution of special water-soluble fertilizer and water for 1-2 hours before planting.

Seed bought from suppliers can be sown directly in the open ground or indoors. If it arrives during the winter, follow the same procedure as outlined for storing in the refrigerator.

NURSERIES SELLING WILD FLOWER PLANTS

The United States:

EDELWEISS GARDENS, Box 66, Robbinsville, N.J., 08691. (*ferns; do mail order; catalogue 25 cents*)

HIGHLANDS NURSERY, Boxford, Massachusetts, 01921

LESLIE'S WILD FLOWER NURSERY, 30 Summer St., Methuen, Massachusetts, 01844 (*catalogue 25 cents*)

EUGENE MINCEMOYER, Route 5, Box 329, Jackson, New Jersey, 08527 (*catalogue 10 cents*)

ORCHID GARDENS, Route 3, Box 224, Grand Rapids, Minnesota 55744 (*catalogue 25 cents*)

PUTNEY NURSERY INC., Putney, Vermont, 05346 (*catalogue 25 cents*)

SKY-CLEFT GARDENS, Barre, Vermont, 05641 (*catalogue, plants shipped to U.S. only*)

THE WILD GARDEN, 8243 N. E. 119th, Kirkland, Washington, 98033 (*catalogue $1, deductible from order*)

Canada:

ALPENGLOW GARDENS, 13328 Trans-Canada Highway, North Surrey, New Westminster, B.C. (*mainly alpines*)

C. A. CRUICKSHANK LTD., 1015 Mount Pleasant Rd., Toronto 315 (*wild flowers and ferns*)

E. H. LOHBRUNNER, 1101 Lohbrunner Rd., R.R. #4, Victoria, B.C. (*mainly alpines*)

KEITH SOMERS, 10 Tillson Avenue, Tillsonburg, Ontario (*wild flowers, native trees*)

U.S. nurseries selling wild flower seeds:

CLAUDE A. BARR, PRAIRIE GEM RANCH, Smithwick, South Dakota, 57782, (*annual list*)

LESLIE'S WILDFLOWER NURSERY, 30 Summer St., Methuen, Mass. 01844 (*catalogue, 20 cents*)

CLYDE ROBIN, P.O. Box 2091, Castro Valley, California, 95012

FRANK H. ROSE, 1020 Poplar St., Missoula, Montana, 59801

HARRY E. SAIER, Dimondale, Michigan, 48821 (*catalogue, 50 cents*)

THURMAN'S GARDENS, Route 2, Box 259, Spokane, Washington, 99200

MIDWEST WILD FLOWERS, Box 664A, Rockton, Illinois, 61072

RECOMMENDED WILD FLOWERS FOR YOUR GARDEN

FOR THE EAST:

Blackeyed Susan, *Rudbeckia hirta,* easy to grow in poor soil, move plants or grow from seed, good for cutting; orange-yellow, bronze-black centre; medium height; summer.

Bloodroot, *Sanguinaria canadensis,* white, small and early, followed by large leaves; a double form that's particularly lovely.

Bluebell, Virginia, *Mertensia virginica,* pink to blue little clusters of bells; medium height; spring bloom; foliage disappears in summer, so best move early, and mark where it grows.

Columbine, *Aquilegia canadensis,* a dainty, graceful little plant of thin soil, rocky places; flowers orange-red and yellow; easy to transplant or grow from seed; excellent teamed with rock; medium height; late spring.

Daisy, *Chrysanthemum leucanthemum,* the white and gold he-loves-me, he-loves-me-not flower of summer gravelly roadsides and dryish fields; moves easily; medium; classified as a noxious weed in some areas.

Dog's-Tooth-Violet, *Erythronium americanum,* early, low-growing, yellow bell standing well above the leaves; difficult to move because bulblet so deep, so dig *way* down.

Golden-rod, *Solidago,* there are many kinds of this fall-blooming wild flower, but all are golden-yellow and feathery in bloom, some medium, some tall; easy; a noxious weed in some areas.

Hepatica, *Hepatica americana,* small and low blooming first thing in spring; white, pink or lavender blue; easy to move as a plant; likes to be undisturbed in garden.

Jack-in-the-pulpit, *Arisaema triphyllum,* strange hooded pulpit in purple or green, can grow 1-3 feet in rich soil; set root deeply in the garden; can move plant anytime or grow from seed; late spring.

Lady's-slipper, Yellow, *Cypripedium calceolus* var. *pubescens,* the only one of the native lady's-slippers I would recommend for home gardens; medium height, slipper held high; buy or move as plant into good garden earth, top dress annually with leaf mold, likes semi-shade; late spring.

Lilies, *Lilium canadense,* the meadow lily, grows to 4 feet, varies from yellow to orange, spotted brown; loved by bees and butterflies; set bulbs 4-5 inches deep in moist fertile loam, well drained; summer.

Lilium philadelphicum, the wood lily, flaming orange-scarlet, uptilted, can grow to 3 feet; difficult to move; needs acid soil, sun or part shade; a bulb; summer.

Lilium michiganense, colonies of these lovely little lilies appear in moist areas of the prairies in early summer; red-orange, spotted, borne singly.

Marsh-marigolds, *Caltha palustris.* Golden, shiny-leaved beauties blooming in early spring in or right beside water; move early, keep wet till planted; one of the best; medium height.

Milkweed, *Asclepias syriaca,* fragrant tall (3 feet) roadside plant of early summer, intriguing seedpods filled with silky parachutes in fall; seed or small plants; the favorite food and hatching ground of the monarch butterfly larva.

Queen Anne's Lace, *Daucus carota,* a beauty of midsummer, likes dry poor soil, its white delicate flowers excellent for bouquets and to dry for winter; medium height; summer; cut before it seeds to prevent spread.

Trillium, *Trillium grandiflorum,* this is the easiest and showiest of the trilliums; white, starry, in bloom for three weeks, early spring; move in one plant, grow in good garden soil and you will have a dozen in a few years; medium height.

Ferns, see below.
Vines, see Chapter 25.

FOR THE MIDWEST

Anemone, *Anemone canadensis,* white-flowered, 1-2 feet, early summer, likes moist meadowy soil, a bit of a wanderer in the garden.

Avens, *Geum triflorum,* three pink or yellowish flowers, lovely leaves; medium; early summer.

Beard Tongue, Smooth Blue, *Penstemon nitidus,* funnel-shaped blue flowers; medium; summer; whitish bloom on leaves.

Blazing Star, Dotted, *Liatris punctata,* dense spikes of rosy-purple flowers; medium; summer.

Blue Violet, Early, *Viola adunca,* tufty plants of dark purple or blue flowers; early; small; likes poor soil; easy.

Coneflower, *Ratibida columnifera,* dark upstanding cone of purple-black with yellow petals around base; medium; summer.

Gaillardia, Great Flowered, *Gaillardia aristata,* daisy-like, yellow petalled flowers, disk purplish; medium; summer.

Gumbo Evening Primrose, *Oenothera caespitosa,* low-growing plant with 3-inch white flowers; early summer; excellent for rock gardens.

Harebell, *Campanula rotundifolia,* dainty light blue bells on wiry stems; 6-12 inches.

Prairie Crocus, *Anemone patens,* Manitoba's floral emblem; one of the first signs of spring; low, light-lavender flowers centred yellow, hairy leaves; silky seed heads give its common name of "prairie smoke."

Purple Cactus, *Mammillaria vivipara,* purplish flowers on spiny plants; low; early summer; grows singly or in a mound.

Wood Lily, *Lilium philadelphicum,* orange-red, dark spotted flowers up to 3 inches wide; 2-3 feet; summer; needs acid soil.

Ferns, see below.
Vines, see Chapter 25.

FOR THE WEST COAST

Beard Tongue, *Penstemon scouleri,* downy low shrub; 2-inch lilac flowers.

Bleeding Heart, *Dicentra formosa,* medium; spring; nodding little hearts of rose purple.

Blue-eyed Grass, *Sisyrinchium,* just what it sounds like, a bright-blue-eyed flower in grassy foliage; summer; medium.

False - Solomon's - Seal, *Smilacina amplexicaulis,* tall and graceful, racemes of greenish white flowers; spring; makes a good colony.

Lupines, *Lupinus,* medium to tall; spikes of blue, sometimes pink or white flowers; fingery leaves; downy stems; summer; wonderfully showy.

Saxifrage, *Saxifraga integrifolia,* medium, flowers white, small and in panicles; good for rockeries; early summer.

Shooting Star, *Dodecatheon,* a delightful rock garden plant; 1 foot; flower stalk rising from rosette of leaves; lilac-purple; spring.

Western Columbine, *Aquilegia formosa,* medium to tall, red and yellow dainty flowers, nodding; late spring.

Western Dog's-Tooth Violet, *Erythronium grandiflorum,* bright yellow flowers, recurved, plain green leaves; medium; spring.

Wild Tiger Lily, *Lilium parviflorum,* or *L. columbianum,* tall; early summer; bright reddish-orange flowers thickly spotted with purple; a bulb.

Ferns, see below.
Vines, see Chapter 25.

WILD FERNS

Some of the most beautiful grace notes for a wild garden are ferns. Varying in size from a few inches to a few feet, in lovely cool-glade shades of green, some evergreen, they are delicate, feathery, light-catching and a knockout back-lit at night. Most prefer shade, some make excellent ground covers, and a few of the daintiest are fragile companions for stern rocks. All are easy to move (if you cut widespreading roots sharply with a spade) except in spring, when the fiddleheads are beginning to grow. Here is a list of some of the best:

Christmas Fern, Dagger Fern, *Polystichum acrostichoides:* hardy, evergreen, one of the first to appear in spring; grows to 1-2 feet in deep woodsy soil; mainly likes high shade but tolerates some sun if soil moist.

Cinnamon Fern, *Osmunda cinnamomea:* 2-3 feet; yellow to deep green; likes swampy ground; its fertile fronds wither early, then the sterile fronds follow and remain green all summer; needs constantly damp, acid soil.

Crested Shield Fern, Narrow Swamp Fern, *Dryopteris cristata:* tall, narrow leaves, dark green and leathery; hardy; grows to 2-2½ feet; breaks easily so protect from wind; needs a cool place, in shade, moist, slightly acid soil.

Goldie's Fern, also known as the **Giant Wood Fern,** *Dryopteris Goldiana:* a large rare deciduous fern, sometimes to 4 feet; it needs shade, soil deep in humus and a mulch of rotting leaves in early summer; if the weather gets hot and it looks limp, spray lightly.

Hay-Scented Fern, *Dennstaedtia punctilobula:* a versatile fern that spreads extensively if not controlled with a barrier; deep shade or full sun, wet or dry soil; makes fascinating ground cover under trees or on a slope; it does smell like new-mown hay if you lie down on it—and what is better to do on a fine summer day?

Holly Fern, *Polystichum lonchitis:* hardy, evergreen; common on the Bruce Peninsula of Ontario; 2 feet long.

Intermediate Shield Fern, Fancy Fern, Intermediate Fern, *Dryopteris spinulosa intermedia:* about 2½ feet; deep green fronds, common and easy to grow; prefers deep rocky sites, lots of humus, neutral to slightly acid soil; grows mainly in deep shade but tolerates some sun if air is cool.

Interrupted Fern, *Osmunda claytoniana:* in perfect growing conditions—highly acid, constantly wet soil in shade—this is a large (3-4 feet) fern; it adapts to less than ideal conditions, but does not grow to full size; leathery, yellow to dark green.

Lady Fern, *Athyrium filix-femina:* easy to grow and if kept watered produces new leaves all summer; yellow to medium green, 1-2 feet; prefers neutral to slightly acid soil.

Maidenhair Fern, *Adiantum pedatum:* loveliest of all to grow in your garden; dainty flat fans of leaves growing on black wiry stems, 1-2 feet high; needs rich loose soil, well-drained; some shade.

Marginal Shield Fern, Marginal Wood Fern, Evergreen Wood Fern, Leather Wood Fern, *Dryopteris marginalis:* 15-20 inches long; strong and leathery, evergreen; handsome beside a boulder; likes deep stony soil, mulch with well-rotted leaves; grows in shade but takes some sun.

New York Fern, Tapering Fern, *Thelypteris noveboracensis:* tapering fronds of yellow to medium green, 1-2 feet; browns early in the summer and needs to be controlled; likes deep soil, rich in humus.

Ostrich Fern, Fiddlehead Fern, *Matteuccia struthiopteris:* deep green and leathery, about 3-4 feet high; the edible fiddleheads are a great treat; the sterile ferny leaves get brown and shabby in late summer—I cut them off then—and the later feather-shaped fertile leaves make marvelous indoor decorations; likes marshy ground but will grow in high-humus garden earth; spreads easily so should be controlled.

Royal Fern, Flowering Fern, Locust Fern, Buckthorn Fern, Ditch Fern, Snake Fern, all alias *Osmunda regalis var. spectabilis:* looks different from the average fern—more like a locust leaf fastened to the end of a 2½-3 foot stem, and with a fruiting spike on the end; leaves are red-green when young, changing to deep green; needs high acid, very wet soil, open shade; grows in sun if the air is cool.

Spinulose Shield Fern, Toothed Wood Fern, Fancy Fern, Florist's Fern, *Dryopteris spinulosa:* almost evergreen, in many parts; grows to 1½ feet in deep soil with plenty of humus, neutral to slightly acid; mulch in summer; makes a delightful frilly planting for a stump.

ESPECIALLY FOR THE WEST COAST, where I'm sure all good ferns go when they die everywhere else

---

Parsley Fern, *Cryptogramma crispa arostichoides:* an 8-inch dwarf, growing in tufts; especially good tucked into crevices and around rocks.

Western Sword Fern, Giant Holly Fern, *Polystichum munitum:* sharp-pointed, about 3 feet tall; will take some sun; evergreen; and in this part of the world you don't need to be reminded to keep the soil moist and rich with humus.

SMALLER FERNS, MAINLY USED IN ROCK PLANTING
Transplant first to pots, then, when growing well, move into the garden.

Bulblet Bladder Fern, *Cystopteris bulbifera:* long (2½ feet) tapering fronds that look best if the plant is pressed into a crevice high on the rock, where both soil and rock can be kept damp most of the time; a delicate beauty.

Cliffbrake, Purple, *Pellaea atropurpurea:* hardy, 1 foot; likes to grow on limestone; takes sun once established.

Ebony Spleenwort, *Asplenium platyneuron:* an erect, small (8-12 inches) hardy fern.

Fragile Bladder Fern, Brittle Fern, *Cystopteris fragilis:* grey-green, 10 inches; looks well at the base of stones.

Maidenhair Spleenwort, *Asplenium Trichomanes:* likes a steep crack; hardy; evergreen; to 4 inches.

Polypody, American Wall Fern, *Polypodium virginianum:* an ancient and delightful little fern, given to cresting big granite boulders; curls up in dry weather and in winter; I have had a seedling on my kitchen window sill, growing in a damp piece of wood, under an ordinary jelly jar, for 6 years; it makes new little green leaves every so often, but the whole plant and its wood base is never more than 2 inches high; in the woods, it grows to 6-8 inches; high shade.

Walking Fern, *Camptosorus rhizophyllus:* hardy; roots at the tips—hence the "walking" name; evergreen; to 9 inches; plant in humus in a crevice in rocks.

Woodsia, Blunt-nosed, Common, *Woodsia obtusa:* grows in tufts in cool shade beside a big stone; 15 inches.

Rusty, *Woodsia ilvensis:* takes sun and wind; plant in rock cracks; 10 inches.

WILD PLANTS FOR REGIONS NOT LISTED HERE WILL BE FOUND IN PART V.

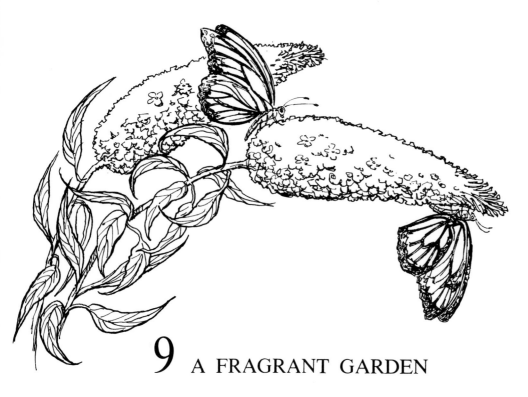

9 A FRAGRANT GARDEN

Fragrance in your garden is a sometime thing. Some cherish it, some don't. For those who do, it opens up a whole new dimension of delight. Memory gets mixed up in it, like my sudden recollection, every time I smell sweet peas, of happy holidays at my grandmother's house on the Saint John River in New Brunswick — real sweet pea country — where her garden was filled, all summer long, with their heady fragrance.

Magic is part of it, for you can't help being mystified by the power of a tiny apple blossom to throw its lovely scent so far. And just the way it makes you feel gets mixed up in it too, for a sweet smell, especially an unexpected sweet smell, can give you a sense of alert well-being as few things in this world will.

It's easy to mastermind this kind of experience in your own garden, but don't count on it happening always precisely as you plan. Factors you will not be able to control come into the picture too, sometimes to enhance, sometimes to destroy fragrance. The temperature of the air, the time of day, for instance, has bearing on how fragrant roses smell — they're headiest on a warm noonday, least fragrant in early morning, late evening. The time of year — sweet alyssum is sweetest just after a flick of frost in fall — makes a fantastic difference in the strength of a smell. Weather can intensify it or carry it completely away on a rainy wind. Most of all, the kind of nose you have can make one fragrance either a pleasure (my favorite is mock orange on a cool June morning) or something you can't stand (the famous English boxwood of Virginia smells to me like old, never-washed tomcats) or something that just doesn't exist at all. This one for me is, unbelievably, mignonette, even though my family swears I have a sense of smell that would make a hungry lion pale with jealousy and mignonette is near the top of everybody else's list of fragrant garden plants. What it all comes down to is that fragrance is an intensely personal thing, a sometime thing and you are going to have to make your plans for fragrant planting *your* garden with *your* nose.

WHAT KINDS OF FRAGRANCE?

Fragrance can be subtle or strong, heady or sweet, dry and musky, pungent, fruity or a mysterious blend of many odors. It can blow down the wind till it fills whole valleys, as often happens when lilacs are in bloom in Des Moines or Rochester in May, or it can be as personal and contained as a tiny white violet held to your nose for a second only. It can be something you smell at high noon when a ground cover patch of wild strawberries is in fruit, or on a midsummer midnight when the white nicotine is in bloom.

With wise planning, it can be a special pleasure the whole growing year, from the delicate scents of early spring, through the heady airs of summer, to the crisp dry smells of autumn.

CLASSIFICATION OF FRAGRANCES

Perfume manufacturers long ago classified scents in technical words, but the most useful information for home gardeners is, I believe, the original, imaginative and accurate listing given in *The Fragrant Year* by Helen Van Pelt Wilson and Leonie Bell (Barrows), a whole book on fragrant plant gardening indoors and out. They list them thus:

BALSAMIC:- found in leaves that contain essential oils, such as mints.

SPICY:- found in leaves or flowers, often blended with a balsamic, such as carnations.

HEAVY:- a free and penetrating perfume, such as lilies.

SWEET:- found in many flowers, some grasses and ferns, such as heliotrope.

HONEYED:- the largest group, divided into
(a) dry, such as hawthorn, *Crataegus oxyacanthoides* (some haws smell terrible, but not this one)
(b) yeasty, such as broom
(c) musky, such as the beautiful Bechtel's crab apple.

FRUITY:- found in either flowers or foliage
(a) grapelike, such as mignonette
(b) pineapple-orange, such as the polyanthus narcissus
(c) plum, peach, apricot, such as hybrid tea roses
(d) lemon, orange, such as lemon verbena

VIOLET:- such as sweet violets, *Viola odorata*.

ROSE:- all roses do not contain this scent, but some do, see list of fragrant hybrid teas, page 59. Also peony.

UNIQUE:- such as lily-of-the-valley.

To help you to decide what scent appeals to you most, take your nose to a nursery when the plants are in flower. Pick out those that please you most right then and there. If they are growing in containers, you can bring them home and plant immediately. If not, leave an order *for that very plant*, for delivery at the proper time for transplanting.

WHERE TO PLANT EFFECTIVELY, AND SOME IDEAS FOR WHAT TO CHOOSE

Think first of the places where you and your family most frequently are — going in and out of doorways, sleeping near open bedroom windows, eating in the dining room (when even one flower can scent the whole room), sitting on a patio, even something as humdrum as coming and going between kitchen and outdoor garbage box. Then plan so that you have, in these spots, a sequence of scent all season.

For near doorways, think of a few hyacinths or jonquils in the spring, a peony

Wisteria.

nearby for bloom in early summer, and be sure to cut one to float on a big glass plate for the dinner table. Then, to follow the peony, make a planting of petunias and sweet alyssum to go on till frost.

Near windows that will often be open, plant one of the carnation-scented viburnums — the early *V. farreri*; the later and more spectacular *V. carlesii* or *V. x carlcephalum*; or if you live in the midwest, the lovely May Day tree of the prairies, *Prunus padus commutata*. A wisteria vine will climb with its perfume to second floors and lilacs beneath a bedroom window send their heavenly scent upwards too. Follow with one of the mock oranges — *Philadelphus* x *virginalis* 'Minnesota Snowflake' is a beauty, or a shrubby rose — *Rosa rugosa* 'Hansa' has a true rose smell. Then move into one of the pervasive summer plants — heliotrope perhaps, or a clump of summer phlox.

For patio plantings, bulbs in the spring — narcissus are fresh and sweet and the scent will follow you all over the garden. As summer comes in, plant sweet william and tea roses, a small clump of the beloved old-fashioned lemon lily, *Hemerocallis flava*, a few of the best-scented true lilies — not all are fragrant. For annuals, consider night-scented stock — just a few plants will fill your whole garden — or mignonette.

For treading scent underfoot near garbage box or between stones of pavings, plant thyme or one of the mints, and, for brushing by, a rose-scented or woolly peppermint geranium. For squeezing in your hand as you gather them for your cooking, a soft velvet sage leaf or some summer savory.

Plantings of any of these flowers in other parts of your garden, down the side borders, at the back, near the street, can bring pleasure of fragrance to neighbors and passersby. For other plants, see lists.

One word of warning. Use restraint in the number of fragrant plants you use in intimate places in the garden. You don't want to swoon in perfume. Remember the magic of the unexpected — the most intriguing fragrances will be whiffs wafted on the wind, quickly come, quickly gone.

SOME FRAGRANT PLANTS TO CHOOSE FROM

These recommended plants are from the source list used in planning The Fragrant Garden for the Blind, Canadian National Institute for the Blind, Toronto. This delightful and thoughtfully planned one acre garden is planted with flowers, trees and shrubs to give the pleasure of fragrance, touch and sound to blind people. To this list have been added names of fragrant plants that will grow well in the much milder climates of Zones 7, 8 and 9. For others, see Part V.

TREES AND SHRUBS
(in the approximate order of their blooming)

COMMON NAME	BOTANICAL NAME	ZONE
Witch-Hazel, Chinese	*Hamamelis mollis*	6
February Daphne	*D. mezereum*	3
Rose Daphne	*cneorum*	2b
Winter Daphne	*odora*	7
Tea Olive	*Osmanthus delavayi*	7
Fragrant Guelder Rose	*Viburnum farreri*	5
Korean Spice Viburnum	*V. carlesii*	5
Burkwood Viburnum	*x burkwoodii*	5b
Fragrant Snowball	*x carlcephalum*	5b
Laurestinus	*tinus*	7
Japanese Pieris	*P. japonica*	5
Flowering Crab Apples, several	*Malus*	4
Buffalo Currant	*Ribes odoratum*	2

COMMON NAME	BOTANICAL NAME	ZONE
Lilacs, most	*Syringa*, especially good are:	2
	x prestoniae 'Elinor'	
	vulgaris 'Lamartine'	
	'Ellen Willmott'	
	'Congo'	
	'Leon Gambetta'	
	'President Lincoln'	
	'St. Joan'	
Flowering Cherry	*Prunus serrulata* 'Amanogawa'	5b
Yoshino Cherry	*x yedoensis*	7a
Mexican Orange	*Choisya ternata*	8
Azaleas	*Rhododendron schlippenbachi*	4
	luteum hybrids	
	Exbury and	5b
	Knap Hill	
	hybrids	

COMMON NAME	BOTANICAL NAME	ZONE
Rhododendrons	*R. falconeri*	Hardy to **5**
	fortunei	Hardy to **5**
	decorum	Hardy to **5**
	moupinense	Hardy to **5**
Mock Orange, most, especially	*Philadelphus* 'Galahad'	**3**
	'Mont Blanc'	**4**
	'Purity'	**4**
	'Avalanche'	**4**
	x virginalis	
	'Minnesota Snowflake'	**4**
Roses in Variety	*Rosa* **'Mrs. John Laing'**	**4**
	'Dr. Merkeley'	**3**
	eglanteria 'Magnifica'	**4**
	'La Noblesse'	**4**
	rugosa 'Hansa'	**3**
	'Mme. George Bryant'	**3**
	'Schneezwerg'	**3**
	'Therese Bugnet'	**2**
Littleleaf Linden	*Tilia cordata*	**3**
Silverberry	*Elaeagnus commutata*	**2**
Thorny Elaeagnus	*pungens*	**7**
Broom (sometimes a pest on the west coast)	*Cytisus scoparius*	**7**
Carolina Allspice	*Calycanthus floridus*	**5**
Summersweet	*Clethra alnifolia*	**5**
Butterfly Bush	*Buddleia davidii*	**5**
Escallonia	*E. rubra*	**8**
Abelia	*A. x grandiflora*	**7**
Rosy Jasmine	*Jasminum beesianum*	**8**
Jasmine	*parkeri*	**8**

VINES AND CLIMBERS

Honeysuckle, Early Dutch	*Lonicera periclymenum*	
	'Belgica'	**2b**
	fragrantissima	**8**
	caprifolium	**8**
	japonica 'Halliana'	**6**
	pileata	**8**
Wisteria	*W. sinensis*	**6**
Climbing Roses	*Rosa* 'Dr. J. H. Nicolas'	
	'American Beauty'	
	'Heidelberg'	

BULBS AND CORMS

Iris	*I. reticulata*
Hyacinth	*Hyacinthus*
Narcissus and Daffodils	*Narcissus*
Tulip	*Tulipa* 'Bellona'
	'De Wet'
	'Gudoshnik'
Lily-of-the-Valley	*Convallaria*
Lilies	*Lilium auratum,* and hybrids
	regale
	pumilum
Mexican Tuberose	*Polianthes tuberosa*

WILD FLOWERS

Sweet White Violet	*Viola blanda*
Blue Wood Phlox	*Phlox divaricata*
Sweet Rocket	*Hesperis matronalis*
Milkweed	*Asclepias*
Meadowsweet	*Spiraea alba*

BRUISING FRAGRANCES

COMMON NAME	BOTANICAL NAME
Artemisia	
Tips of Balsam-Fir	*Abies balsamea*
Hay-Scented Fern	*Dennstaedtia punctilobula*
Lavender	*Lavandula officinalis*
Lemon Verbena	*Lippia citriodora*
Mints	*Mentha*
Cooking Herbs, most	
Scented Geraniums, all	*Pelargonium*
Thymes, all	*Thymus*

PERENNIALS

Violets, several	*Viola*
Pinks, several	*Dianthus*
Day Lilies, especially Lemon Lily	*Hemerocallis flava*
Heliotrope	*Heliotropium*
Garden Heliotrope	*Valeriana officinalis*
Bee-Balm	*Monarda*
Summer Phlox	*P. paniculata*
Plantain Lily	*Hosta plantaginea*
Chrysanthemum, several	

ANNUALS

Candytuft	*Iberis*
Mignonette	*Reseda*
Nasturtium	*Tropaeolum majus*
Nicotine	*Nicotiana alata* 'Grandiflora'
Night-Scented Stock	*Mathiola bicornis*
Petunia	
Sweet Alyssum	*Lobularia maritima*
Sweet Peas	*Lathyrus odoratus*
Verbena	

25 FRAGRANT HYBRID TEA ROSES

Anne Letts	*pale pink*
Charlotte Armstrong	*deep carmine*
Chrysler Imperial	*deep crimson*
Crimson Glory	*deep crimson*
Diamond Jubilee	*cream, orange buff*
Duet	*pink, deeper reverse*
Dr. F. Debat	*clear, rose-pink*
Ena Harkness	*bright crimson-violet*
Fragrant Cloud	*vermilion-scarlet*
Gail Borden	*rose-pink, cream reverse*
Hawaii	*coral-red*
Helen Traubel	*pale salmon-pink*
Josephine Bruce	*deep velvety scarlet-crimson*
King's Ransom	*pure golden yellow*
Mirandy	*dark red*
Mojave	*orange red*
Mr. Lincoln	*deep crimson*
Pink Peace	*medium pink*
Prima Ballerina	*cherry pink*
Show Girl	*deep rose pink*
Sterling Silver	*silvery lilac*
Sutter's Gold	*golden yellow with pink*
Tiffany	*pink, gold base*
Tropicana	*light vermilion*
Tzigane	*scarlet, yellow reverse*

59

10 A GARDEN TO LURE BIRDS

Luring wild birds to your garden brings a new delight in sight and sound right outside your window. A fair guess is that more than 10,000,000 people in North America are feeding wild birds every winter. Leading suppliers of wild bird seed report their sales at more than 30,000,000 pounds yearly and this, as the chickadee said to the nuthatch, isn't all peanuts.

Provide a few simple facilities — food, shelter and water — and your garden is bound to be a lively frieze of feathered friends you would never otherwise see. While you are mine-hosting them, they help you, not only by looking chirpy and decorative, but by eating fantastic quantities of troublesome insects and larvae that would otherwise play hob with your flowers and lawn. Even, in the case of purple martins who eat mosquitoes, by eating bugs that could play hob with you.

EUROPEAN OR AMERICAN PLAN?

You can plump for a whole program of à la carte items like cookies and cake for chickadees, sunflower seeds for cardinals, bits of apple for robins, suet puddings for woodpeckers and sapsuckers, stale doughnuts from somebody's lunch box, saskatoons and blueberries picked all juicy and warm on a summer day then deepfrozen and set out on the feeder for a tasty treat at Christmas. Or you can install a feeder or two in your garden, keep it filled with commercial bird food, which you buy in almost any supermarket, hardware or dime store, and still have lots of fascinating visitors.

You can attract birds with specially chosen trees, shrubs and flowers — things with tasty berries like mountain ash, or honeysuckle, or the sweetnectared plants such as monarda for such winged jewels as the hummingbirds — and be sure that somewhere near your feeders there is a thickety clump of needled evergreens for take-offs and perching out of the wind.

You can put up special nesting boxes — this works well for the little wrens whose warbling is, without doubt, one of the loveliest songs in the world — and you can plug in ingenious gadgets to provide deluxe warm bath and drinking water all winter. Or you can leave housing and wassail to the neighborhood trees and puddles.

WHAT'S THE MENU?

Food for birds can be something you provide or something you plant. In the provision category, it is a matter of setting up feeding stations that will attract birds.

This means that they should be open on the lee side of the wind, the food kept dry, and be set up near perching sites because birds prefer to approach a feeder warily.

Open trays on windowsills or stumps cater to the first-come, first-served. They can be simple wooden shelves with a low ridge around the edge to keep seed from blowing off. Some also have clear glass or plastic sides and roof so that you can see the birds feeding.

Snow- or rain-wet seed should be brushed off to keep it from becoming moldy — this can make a bird ill. Better to put out a small quantity of fresh seed often than to try to stock the feeder with a lot at one time. This is best done at night — birds usually begin feeding before you wake.

Small enclosed feeders can be hung in trees with a funnel fastened upside down on the hanging line to discourage squirrels. The light weight of this type of feeder tips heavy voracious starlings and grackles off yet lets desirable little nuthatches feed easily. Bird authorities, by the way, say that birds are not naturally greedy, but they have such a high metabolism rate they must eat constantly to survive.

If you are just beginning to feed the birds and they are shy about coming near the house, put a feeder on a pulley line to a tree or post at the back of the garden, starting with it as far back as it will go, then gradually move it a little closer to the house every few days. Eventually the birds will come right up to the windows.

WHAT KIND OF A FEEDER?

Large feeders are available in many designs. The best have gravity bins which refill the feeding trays with dry fresh food as the birds eat it away. A roof over the trays keeps them clear of snow and rain. They stand about 6 feet high on a metal pole, inserted firmly in the ground, and have a metal hood about two thirds of the way up to keep out marauding squirrels.

A highly popular model, which looks like an airborne ranch bungalow, features pigeon-proofing (although why a pigeon eating should be less desirable to look at than a blue jay stuffing his face would make an interesting psychological study). This is accomplished by setting a fence of small wooden dowels around the rim of the platforms. The dowels are spaced just far enough apart to let "U" birds like cardinals and blue jays reach the food, but not far

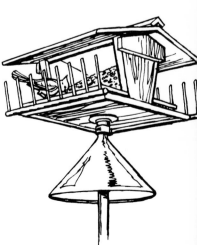

Gravity bin feeder with pigeon proofing and squirrel guard.

enough to let "non-U" pigeons in. However, a flip young pigeon in my garden did find a way to beat this barrier. By standing and stretching on his tiptoes and hunching his shoulders he could make himself thin enough to get through between the dowels. But greed done him in. He ate himself so fat and paunchy he eventually could not get through.

Another excellent feeder on the market is a roofed and boxed-in platform with a weathervane on the sides. The wind swings the feeder so that the entrance is always in the lee of the wind. Even a non-birder will understand, I'm sure, how much more comfortable it must be for a hungry bird to feed in the lee of the wind than have a gale ignominiously upend his tail section just as he is reaching for a morsel of millet.

All feeders should be set close enough to the house for easy viewing and with trees — if possible, evergreens — nearby yet not so close that squirrels can jump from them to the feeder.

Thus far, all feeders I have described have been for seed — sunflower, peanuts, cracked corn and all the grains. You can buy them already mixed or make up your own. A little snooping will sometimes turn up bargain sources for this — sunflower seed at vegetable oil co-ops, grain screenings at elevators, peanut hearts from local manufacturers of peanut butter.

Suet log feeder.

Also tasty, if you're a bird, is beef suet served up plain in a netted bag such as onions come in, or a plastic-coated-wire cage, or melted to a pudding and laced with seed. The pudding can be packed into a log drilled with 2-inch holes here and there, and hung from a branch. Spare refills can be made up at the same time the original is made, poured into little paper cups the same size as the holes and put in the freezer. These filled suet logs can also be bought commercially and some stores have a refill service.

Special treats are raisins, currants, bits of apple, banana and orange. Mocking birds eat cheese; robins like cake or old pie crust; and Roger Tory Peterson, the famous bird artist, feeds his wild models on cooked spaghetti. In the Midwest, bird fans put out the rack of the Christmas turkey and freeze cranberries and choke cherries for the winter visits of the spectacular yellow, black and white evening grosbeaks and the sleek, crested cedar waxwings. In Alaska, magpies and ravens often share a dog's food outdoors, and black-capped chickadees are a common sight on feeders when the air is 60 below.

All seed-eaters like peanut butter and cornmeal smeared on sunflower seed-heads. Bird experts warn that peanut butter, although a favorite food of many winter birds, should always be mixed with something coarse like cornmeal, small seeds or breadcrumbs so that it will not catch in a glob in birds' throats and choke them.

Don't be discouraged if the birds seem to disdain your food. It sometimes takes a little while for them to catch on to its availability, but once they do they are your friends for ever. You, on your part, must not begin feeding birds in winter and then stop. If you go away have someone restock your feeders regularly for you.

For those who live near wild land, or even on big city ravines or park fringes, feeding game birds on the ground in winter can be fascinating. Pheasants are common, quail and woodcock rarer.

Small birds like juncos and sparrows and the gentle, pink-footed mourning dove also prefer to feed on the ground. Brush deep snow off to a firm base, spread out small seed and many birds too nervous to attempt a station in the air will feed there. And don't disdain the sparrows. Nosy and noisy as they are, their interest in you and your food leads rarer birds into your garden.

You can feed birds all year, but most people do it just in winter when natural food is scarce. Begin about Labor Day before all summer visitors have migrated and when birds from north of you are beginning to migrate south. Stopping off to enjoy your fare may induce them to stay.

Hummingbirds, though, those swift, brilliant flashes of gorgeous color, are summer visitors only and can be coaxed into sight by putting out inexpensive glass-tube feeders on stakes among your flowers. The bait is red-colored sugar water. Baltimore orioles too have been known to find this easy sweetness and to settle down for a season of bliss. To prevent ants from climbing the stakes to steal the syrup, fasten a little tray filled with grease and kerosene halfway up the stake.

AND WHAT SHALL YOU PLANT FOR BIRDS?

Although nearly all fruiting trees are attractive to birds, two of the most decorative are mountain-ash and any of the fruiting thorns. Russian olive, planted in groups, is a favorite everywhere. On the west coast, cotoneaster attracts robins and cedar waxwings. The native flowering dogwood and wax berry are also there. In northern states, the box-elder is a favorite with evening grosbeaks, but I cannot recommend it as a garden tree in the more temperate parts of the country. In the east it has become the practice of many bird-loving gardeners to leave all of their late seeded annuals standing. Seeded celosia is also a favorite with white throat and white crowned sparrows in the Midwest. On the Atlantic coast, as in all other parts of the country where they will grow, multiflora roses supply quantities of fruits. Mulberry and crab apples are fine for fruit too. In fact, four robins of my acquaintance spent a stormy below-zero winter once in a heavily laden crab apple tree, fed, and doubtless warmed to a happy haze, by the fermented frozen apples.

For summertime ambrosia for hummingbirds, plant all kinds of bright flowers — morning glories, balsam, monarda, columbine, scarlet sage, nasturtiums. And for all birds, choose trees and shrubs with twiggy thorn or thick needle growth to use as nesting sites and shelter from their enemies.

HOUSING PROGRAM

Birds can often be persuaded to settle in your garden by providing them with nesting boxes — wrens, kingbirds, phoebes, chickadees, flickers, starlings if you want them, screech owls and, on the west coast, violet green swallows. All nesting boxes should be hinged front or bottom for cleaning out yearly before the new pair nests. They should be placed in the shade to keep from baking the baby birds and on poles in preference to trees to keep off cats and other marauders. All should have a perch just outside the entrance for the bird to pause on.

Various ways can be devised to keep out undesirables. A clever birder in

Wren house.

Vermont keeps cheeky English sparrows from moving into his boxes for later-arriving tree swallows by cutting an oval, rather than a circular opening in them. It is 2½ inches wide and only 15/16 of an inch high. An equally smart man in the west reports that sparrows are reluctant to enter tree-swallow nesting boxes in his garden if he puts an old hat — straw, fedora or peak cap — on top of the box. Probably the pregnant grandmother of all present English sparrows was once frightened by a bowler-hatted scarecrow.

Robins prefer to nest on a shelf or drainpipe against an eave or roof out of the rain, and will come back year after year to the same place.

The most spectacular of all nesting probably is the apartment house set up for purple martins. Choose a clear space in the garden, for they must have lots of space for gliding and flying in great swoops. Set the house 10-15 feet above the ground on a telescopic pole for easy raising and lowering to clean it out each year. There should be no fewer than 6 compartments, 6 x 6 x 6 inches, with a 2⅛-inch entry hole. The bottom should be removable for cleaning and so that you can leave it out till the first martin scouts arrive in the spring, thus preventing other less desirable birds from getting in first. Ready-made aluminum houses, which stay cool in summer, are available and they come with porches and guardrails to keep the fledglings from falling out. These are not only practical, they are good-looking too.

Gardeners who set up nesting boxes should not become discouraged if they are not occupied immediately by the appropriate birds. It sometimes takes two or three years for them to discover and occupy them, but once in use there is every good chance that the same pair of birds will return year after year.

WATER!

Birds need water summer and winter. Summer birdbaths can often be more ornamental than practical unless they are shallow enough for the birds to stand in about 1 inch of water and on a surface rough enough not to slip.

Many birds, particularly robins, will use high freestanding birdbaths, but small timid birds, like the brightly colored warblers, prefer a shallow puddly pool on the ground both to bathe in and to drink from. Too deep a bath can be made practical by setting some flat-topped stones in the water, too slippery a one can be painted and coarse sand dusted on it while the paint is still tacky.

Midwest bird fans say that in summer it is more important to supply drinking and bathing water to wild birds than food.

Various commercial products and some inventive amateur ones are available to keep water in baths from freezing in winter. One good one is a thermostatic poultry water warmer plugged into a weatherproof outdoor socket and set in a dish of water: the water is kept just above freezing. Another is an outdoor hotbed heating cable laid in sand and a birdbath set above it. This too keeps the water thawed out.

Give us another ten years of this merry coddling and we will be into electric blankets for the nesting boxes, automatic dispensers of perfumed oil for the bath water and Scotch and soda ready-mixed for a pick-me-up before a tasty dinner of toasted suet and sunflower seeds 'sous cloche.' The way things are going, you might even wake up some morning and see a long-legged pink Florida flamingo on your bird feeder!

11 VEGETABLES AND HERBS

The prize in vegetable gardening is not how lovely the plants look, but how they taste when you eat them. Yet the prospect pleases, for just gazing at green peas swelling on the vine or tomatoes ripening in the sun tickles your taste buds in anticipation. What you grow, how you grow it and where you grow it depends on your family's likes, the space in your garden for vegetables and the length of your growing season.

Such gardens, even with the best work-saving techniques, take a fair amount of care. They also must have exposure to full sunshine at least six hours a day — eight is better; they should not be crowded by roots of trees or shrubs, and should have good soil and drainage and enough space to grow the crops you want. It also helps if you can site them in a protected place that warms up early in the spring, but you should avoid low ground where late and early frosts gather.

Steep slopes where soil can wash away in heavy rains are not good, but a slight slope will work if you plant the rows across it. On level ground, run rows north and south for maximum exposure to the sun and choose a site near your hose outlets for easy watering in dry weather. If your soil is poor and will take a lot of fuss to make it fertile, consider building raised beds of 2 × 12-inch planking and bring in good earth to fill them. This makes a neat, easily controlled garden. For the most economical use of a small space, grow everything you can upwards, on a trellis or some kind of support, rather than sideways — cucumbers, tomatoes, pole beans, runner beans, peas, New Zealand spinach, are a few that work well this way.

For tasty summer treats, stick to salad plants like lettuce, tomatoes, and herbs and add a few of the vegetables that your family likes best — snap beans, carrots (youngsters all seem to love raw carrots), spinach and/or chard (these taste best cooked and eaten together), beets (boil when small with their own leaves, add a few drops of lemon, some butter and a pinch of nutmeg), perhaps a plant or two of rhubarb to pull early for pies.

If you have the space and time to look after them, grow asparagus — a delicious treat every spring — peas, corn, squash, cucumbers, pumpkins for your own Thanksgiving pies and Halloween jack-o'-lanterns.

If you have a streak of squirrel in you and you like to stash away good things for winter, choose good freezing varieties of asparagus, broccoli, cauliflower, peas, beans, corn (see pages 70-74); and those that make savory pickles and relishes — tomatoes, peppers, corn, cucumbers. If you live where keeping vegetables over winter is important and you can provide cool (32-40°F) storage facilities, grow turnips, parsnips, carrots, beets, onions, cabbage. Catherine Parr Traill, advising "females" emigrating from Britain to Canada 100 years ago, urged them to bring cabbage seed to the new land, for this vegetable was one of the best winter keepers and a staple in the diet of early settlers. A modern note on this same vegetable is that, in experimental test plots in the Far North where extreme day-length, low evening and warm day temperatures create fantastic growing conditions, cabbages sometimes weigh 30 pounds! And at the Alaska State Fair they have a class for cabbages weighing more than 50 pounds with always some exhibitors each year.

People who live in apartments, or who have only patio space for growing plants, should think of growing some of the little red and yellow pear and cherry tomatoes in planters. Scarlet runner beans make an edible screen too. Plant them in a 10-12 inches wide, 8-10 inches deep container, in good soil. Stake at planting time. Fertilize with 4-12-10 every two weeks and water daily. Top spray if weather hot. With beans, pick when young and tender. Don't let any mature and they will produce until frost.

SOIL

You will want fertile, friable soil, free of stones and rubble, prepared to a depth of 10-12 inches (see How to Improve Soil, CHAPTER 18). If you can, spade or rototill in the fall, mixing in compost for moisture retention and both organic and inorganic fertilizers recommended for vegetables (4-12-10, 3 pounds to 100 square feet is a good general purpose fertilizer). Leave the ground roughly turned to expose the earth to the beneficial action of the frost and snow. In the following spring, rake level and prepare for seeds or transplants (see CHAPTER 18). If you cannot prepare ground in fall, wait to do it in spring when the soil is no longer sticky and wet — *never* work wet soil. It will be ready when it is crumbly, when you can pick up a handful, squeeze it, have it hold its shape for a second, then break.

Some gardeners, to prepare a vegetable plot, deliberately pile garden trash — grass clippings, straw, hay, seaweed if they have it, dead flowers and leaves — over the turned-up ground until it is 2 feet deep, and leave it there till spring. What has not rotted down by then is raked off and put on the compost pile. Worms will have carried their castings up through the soil beneath the trash and it will be in fine, clear tilth for planting top crops like lettuce. For growing root vegetables, it may take one or two more years of piling garden debris on the same spot to make it really fertile to the desired depth.

PLANNING

Begin modestly with a few of your favorites, and enlarge your garden only when you find you can manage more.

Plan successive plantings of such things as beans, beets, corn, carrots, lettuce, peas and radishes which hold tenderness for a relatively short time. In this way, you will have fresh supplies at just the right degree of flavor over a a long period. You can extend crops of such vegetables as corn by planting early, mid-season and late varieties all at the same time.

Intercrop early maturers like radishes and lettuce among cabbage and corn. They will be finished before the late ones need the space. Follow early-finish cool-weather crops, such as peas, with beans or beets, which grow best later when the weather is warm. Or plant prestarted cauliflower or cabbage when the peas are over. Tomatoes can follow early onions and radishes, cabbage early carrots. If double cropping, be sure to fertilize a second time.

Plan spacing of rows according to growth habits. Lettuce, radishes, carrots, take little space. Vines of cucumbers, melons, squash and tomatoes sprawl, but can be grown in less space if staked up on poles or supports. Corn, because it grows tall (although the midget varieties are not as tall as the regular ones) should be planted on the north of your plot where it will not shade other plants and in a two- or three-row block, rather than a single line, for best pollination and production of ears.

Rotate crops so that you do not grow the same vegetable in the same place two years running, to avoid a build-up of pests and diseases that especially attack one kind of vegetable.

Perennial vegetables that come up every year — asparagus, rhubarb, and horseradish — should be planted to one side of the garden so that they need not be disturbed by the care and cropping of annual vegetables.

Leave space to walk and work between the rows in a small garden — you can still plant double rows and reach them easily from different sides. In a large vegetable garden, make paths and turn-arounds at the ends of the rows wide enough for a mechanical cultivator.

PLANTING

For recommended varieties, zones, planting dates, depth to plant and spacing, see chart, pages 70-74. This is intended only as a guide. Many other varieties are available — and new ones every year — and I urge you most strongly to get pamphlets from your federal or state government service and catalogues from seedmen who specialize in the best varieties for your area. Even if you do not order all they list, it will make your mouth water just to read about them!

To jump the season, start seeds indoors or in hotbeds outdoors 4-8 weeks before the last frost-free date in the spring, or buy prestarted plants from a greenhouse. Best for this are broccoli, cabbage, cauliflower, tomato (gardeners in Alaska also prestart head lettuce, celery, corn and kale). You can experiment with other prestarted seeds if you can't wait till the regular time for a taste of them; one year our family had succulent corn on the cob in early July by doing this. Put two or three seeds in a pot in good earth, or the handy expandable compressed peat planter, then when the weather is right transplant into the ground, making sure that earth and pot are both well-soaked beforehand with a dilute solution of water-soluble fertilizer.

For seeding directly in the garden, some vegetables prefer cool soil and cool weather. Lettuce, cabbage, cauliflower, broccoli, chard, carrots, beets, peas, radishes, onions, spinach, turnips, potatoes and parsnips can be planted 4-6 weeks before the last frost-free date. Others prefer warm soil and warm air and should be planted when all danger of frost is over — snap and lima beans, New Zealand spinach, squash, cucumbers, corn, eggplant, peppers, melon, and, for a late-season crop, tomatoes. Wherever possible, buy disease-resistant strains. F_1 hybrids are more costly, but worth it. To make them go farther, plant these one seed to a pot.

CULTURE

To protect small new plants from unexpected frosts, use small waxed paper tents you can get from your garden supplier. Use as you buy them at first. Then as the sun gets hotter, snip a small slice off near the top and place this side to the lee of the wind; when hot sun hits them, this little airhole will act as a ventilator. As the plant pushes through the opening, widen the tent into a collar for protection from cutworms and slugs. If your exposed plants do get caught with a freeze, turn a fine, cold-water mist on them and keep it going till the temperature is again above freezing. This works down to 19°F. If you garden where cold weather comes early in the season, be sure to buy early-ripening varieties of vegetables. Research and experimental stations in colder parts of the country and Canada are now working on developing early-ripening strains of tomatoes, and others will be available in the future.

Thinning is essential after first seeding is up and growing well — usually when plants are about 2 inches high. (Check pages 72-74 for distances that plants and rows should be apart.) Take away from the garden small plants you pull out — use bits of lettuce and green onions in salads — do not leave them on the ground to attract pests and disease.

Sufficient water is also necessary for good growth and flavor. Soak, do not sprinkle, every week or 10 days if rain is scant. An old wive's tale handed down by champion pumpkin growers recommends a milk-dampened piece of yarn threaded through the stem, the end of it kept in a dish of milk beside the pumpkin. Another trick, supported by a radish prizewinner, is to insert another radish seed into a slit in the side of a growing radish. They say the impregnated radish grows to unbelievable bragging size. You are on your own with these. I have no personal experience with them, but it sounds like an easy way to fame, to grow a Cinderella coach-size pumpkin or the biggest radish in the world.

Mulches of hay, straw, peat moss, seaweed, plastic, building paper or asphalt shingles, laid on the ground around plants after they are growing well, conserve moisture, discourage weeds and keep the soil cooler. You can also lay plastic on the ground when you plant the seed, slitting it crosswise where you see the seed germinate. Fertilize and water the ground before planting the seed, then lay the plastic and weight the edges with soil to keep it from blowing away. In temperate parts of the country, this plastic should be black polyethylene sheeting. In the Far North, it should be clear, to build up and hold warmth.

Weeds take valuable nourishment from the soil which might better go into your vegetables, so be faithful with the hoe, herbicides or use mulches to reduce them. Bugs and disease also weaken plants, so check them too as soon as they appear. Frequent and shallow cultivation discourages both weeds and pests. Be especially careful to observe the recommended lapse between spraying with certain chemicals and harvest so that harmful residues are not present when you pick them to eat and store.

For common pests and diseases and what to do about them, see pages 75-78.

VEGETABLES FOR BOYS AND GIRLS TO GROW

Cherry and Pear Tomatoes: Are handy for popping from vine to mouth.

Carrots: Good eaten on the hoof too.

Peanuts: Must have a long season, warm, sandy soil to mature, but great fun when they do. Dig up in the fall and leave plants in piles to mature before removing the nuts. Have to be roasted before being eaten — they taste terrible raw.

Pumpkins: The smile on the Hallowe'en pumpkin will be a real one when the youngster who carves it grew it himself.

Radishes: They germinate quickly for impatient small gardeners and will even survive if dug up to see if they are sprouting and then planted again. I know, we have.

Lettuce: Encourages salad eating and just as good for bunnies as boys.

Midget Corn: Nobody can resist their own corn-on-the-cob, straight from the garden to the pot, to the tooth. Run an electric extension to the corn patch and string Christmas tree lights, and light at night, if you have trouble with marauding raccoons.

28 FAVORITE VEGETABLES TO GROW IN YOUR GARDEN

Recommended varieties for certain zones are indications only. You may well find that you can grow others not listed for your zone by providing favorable, more temperate areas within your own garden, others that your family may find tastier than those we list.

Also, keep abreast of *current* vegetable introductions through your government department of agriculture, garden columnists and broadcasters.

KINDS	ZONE	USE	SEEDING TIMES		DEPTH TO PLANT SEED	SPACING		REMARKS
			INDOORS	OUTDOORS		BETWEEN PLANTS	BETWEEN ROWS	
ASPARAGUS		Spring				18"	3'-4'	Set plants 6" deep in trench, cover with 1" soil; as they grow, fill in soil; do not cut till 2nd year then only for 2 weeks; 3rd year and thereafter, crop for 6 weeks; follow with weeding and fertilizing (3 lbs. per 100 sq. ft.)
Mary Washington	1	F	Set plants in early spring					
Waltham Washington	1	F						
BEANS (BUSH)		Summer	For early crop 4 weeks before soil and air are warm outdoors	After last frost when soil and air are warm (see corn)	1"-2"	2"	18"-24"	Your own beans are one of the best treats of summer; make successive plantings 3 weeks apart; do not walk through rows when wet, or let pets there (this could spread disease)
Yellow: Pencil Pod	1	F						
Black Wax	1	F						
Bountiful	1	F						
Green:								
Tendergreen	1	F						
Tendercrop	1	F						
BEANS (POLE)		Summer		After frost is past and soil and air are warm (see corn)	Plant 3"-4" Thin to 10" -12"	Between poles 4'		Train on a tripod of poles, fence or netting, allowing for an eventual height of 6'-8'; harvest all pods as soon as ready, to prolong production
Green: Kentucky								
Wonder	1	F						
Blue Lake	1	F						
Yellow: Kentucky								
Wonder Wax	1	F						
BEANS (LIMA)		Summer		When soil is really warm (see corn)	1"-1½"	2"-3"	20"-24"	Need a long growing season to produce a usable crop; coat seed with disinfectant, see page 175
Fordhook 242								
Thaxter	5	F						
Thorogreen Bush (Baby)	4	F						
BEETS		Summer & Winter		Sow early— as soon as ground can be worked	½"	1"	15"-18"	Make successive plantings 4 weeks apart; for winter storage, plant end of June or early July
Detroit Dark Red	1	S 32°F						
Ruby Queen	1	S 32°F						
BROCCOLI		Late Summer	6 weeks before setting out	mid-May	¼"-½"	Thin to 18"-24"	20"-24"	For fall crop, plant middle to end of June
Green Mountain	1	F						
Cleopatra (F₁)	1	F						
BRUSSELS SPROUTS		Late Summer	4 weeks before outdoors	2nd-3rd week of May	¼"	30"	2½'-3'	Start picking as soon as sprouts are firm and well-formed
Long Island (Catskill)	1	Fall						
Jade Cross (F₁)	1							
CABBAGE		Early and Late	6 weeks before outdoors	as soon as ground can be worked— transplant 4-5 weeks	½"	15"-18"	24"-30"	Cabbage is one of our most useful vegetables; you can start it indoors, or outdoors, and transplant directly to where it is to grow; heavy feeder; do not sow late where season is short
Golden Acre (strains)	1							
Danish Ballhead	1	S 32°						
Mammoth Red Rock	1	S 32°						
Chieftain Savoy	1	S 32°						

F marks varieties suitable for freezing
S marks varieties suitable for storage

KINDS	ZONE	USE	SEEDING TIMES		DEPTH	SPACING		REMARKS
			INDOORS	OUTDOORS	TO PLANT SEED	BETWEEN PLANTS	BETWEEN ROWS	
CARROT		Summer & Winter S 32°		As soon as ground can be worked. Mid-June for fall crop	½″	Thin to 1″	18″-20″	If you're fond of carrots, make successive sowings; there is a special miniature carrot—'Baby Finger Nantes' that matures in 50 days
Royal Chatenay	1							
Imperator	1							
Nantes Coreless	1							
CAULIFLOWER		All Season F	for early crop 6 weeks before putting out late-April to mid-May	for late crop sow early June	¼″-½″	18″-24″	2½′	When heads start to form, tie leaves together over the top to keep head white
Early or Super Snowball	1							
Snowdrift type	1	F						
Snowball Y	1	F						
CORN			for early crop 4 weeks before planting out	Soil must be warm. Zones 6b-9 early May Zones 5a-6a mid-May Zones 3a-4b last of May and early June Zones 1a-2a early June	½″-1″	Early: 8″-10″ Late: 10″-12″	Early: 2½′ Late: 3′	Plant 2-3 rows adjacent rather than a long, single row for better pollination and more ears; even though it takes up a lot of space proportionately, sweet corn, picked fresh, boiled in salted water for 8 mins. (NO MORE!) and served with butter is truly food for gourmet gods; ears should be picked when kernels well-rounded and yield milky juice when punctured with your thumbnail; for freezing whole cobs, cook 8 mins., then cool quickly and freeze; for cut kernels, cook whole cob and cool similarly then slice off and freeze immediately at 0°F.
Early:								
Earliking (Y)	3							
Golden Beauty (Y)	3							
Xtra Early Sweet Hybrid (Y)	3							
Golden Midget (Y)	3							
Seneca Golden (Y)	3							
North Star (Y)	3							
Midseason:				Follow same zone dates for beans, cukes, squash and melons	1″-1½″	Early: 8″-10″ Late: 10″-12″	Early: 2½′ Late: 3′	
Aristogold Bantam Evergreen (Y)	5							
Golden Cross Bantam (Y)	5							
Ioana (Y)	5							
Seneca Chief (Y)	5							
Late:								
Iochief (Y)	5							
Silver Queen (W)	5							
Country Gentleman (W)	5							
(Y):-Yellow (W):-White								
CUCUMBER			4 weeks before planting out in warm soil and warm air	When weather warm and no danger of frost	1″	Sow 2″-3″ thin to 1′-2′. In hills sow 6-8 seeds in each, thin to 3 plants per hill	4′-5′	Spartan Valor is an All-America winner. If space is at a premium, train on strong trellis
Slicing: Spartan Valor (F₁)	3	Summer						
Burpless Hybrid	3							
Ashley	1			for zone dates, see corn, may be sown 2 wks. earlier if Hotkaps used				
Spartan Valor (F₁)	1							
Pickling: Wisconsin SMR 18	1	Fall						
National Pickling	1							
Gherkin	1							

F marks varieties suitable for freezing
S marks varieties suitable for storage

| KINDS | ZONE | USE | SEEDING TIMES | | DEPTH | SPACING | | REMARKS |
			INDOORS	OUTDOORS	TO PLANT SEED	BETWEEN PLANTS	BETWEEN ROWS	
LETTUCE (HEAD)		Summer to Fall	6-8 weeks before planting outside	as soon as soil fit to work, spring & fall plantings 10 days apart give continuous crops	¼″	8″-12″	15″-18″	Encourage to grow quickly for best flavor, so water if no rain, feed with high nitrogen fertilizer; will take a little shade; mulch prevents rain spatter. If rabbits are a problem, fence with 2′ chicken wire.
Buttercrunch (Bibb type)	1							
Butter King (Boston type)	1							
Great Lakes (Crisp Head)	1							
LETTUCE (LEAF)						6″		
Salad Bowl	1							
Grand Rapids	1							
MUSKMELON, CANTALOUPE		Summer	4 weeks before planting in warm ground outside	When soil and air both warm. For zones, see corn. 2 weeks earlier if Hotkaps used	1″	Sow 6-8 seeds, thin to 2 plants	4′-5′	Buy resistant seed, keep soil well watered, but do not wet leaves; harvest when melon will pull easily from stem, and when skin below netting has changed from dark to light yellowish green. 'Harper Hybrid' is especially resistant to fusarium wilt.
Delicious 51	4							
Far North	1							
Harper Hybrid	5						3′	
Iroquois	5							
Samson (F₁)	5							
ONIONS		Summer and Fall		as soon as ground can be worked	½″	Thin to 1″-2″		Use thinnings for green onions.
White or Yellow Bermuda	1	S	8 weeks before ground can be worked outside					
Early Yellow Globe	1	S						Clip back indoor seedlings to 4″; harden seedlings before transplanting to permanent place.
Spanish type— **Crystal White Wax**	1	short term				4″-5″	18″	
Sweet Spanish	1	S						Sweet Spanish requires a long season for good sized bulbs to mature before frost; start indoors.
Southport Red Globe	1	S						
ONION SETS	1	Spring & Summer		as soon as ground can be worked	1″	for green onions, touching each other; for large: 2″-3″	18″	
PARSNIP		Fall and Winter S 32°F		as soon as ground can be worked	¼″-½″	4″	18″	Use fresh seed and protectant; harvest after cold weather chills ground; can be left in ground all winter and dug as soil thaws.
Hollow Crown Improved	1							
PEAS		Summer		as soon as ground can be worked	1″	1″-2″	1½′-2′	Dwarf peas need no support, but tall ones should be trained on brush netting fence or string from time they are 4″-6″ high; peas will not grow well in hot weather, harvest when young and tender, picking those nearest to ground first; sever carefully with thumbnail or clippers; Supersweet seedlings survived freezing temperatures that destroyed other kinds at Brandon, Man.
Alderman (Tall)	1	F						
Lincoln (Med. Tall)	1	F						
Little Marvel (Dwarf)	1	F						
Thos. Laxton (Med. Tall)	1	F						
Super Sweet (Dwarf)	1	F						
PEAS (EDIBLE POD)								
Mammoth Melting Sugar	1							
PEPPERS		Summer	6-8 weeks before when plant outdoors after last frost		1″	15″-18″	20″-24″	Needs rich soil, warm site; plastic mulch good; go lightly with nitrogen fertilizers.
Early Calwonder	3	F						
Bell Boy Hybrid	1	F						

F marks varieties suitable for freezing
S marks varieties suitable for storage

KINDS	ZONE	USE	SEEDING TIMES INDOORS	SEEDING TIMES OUTDOORS	DEPTH TO PLANT SEED	SPACING BETWEEN PLANTS	SPACING BETWEEN ROWS	REMARKS
POTATOES		Summer & Winter		Zones 6-9 end of April early May	4"-5"	1	2½'-3'	Use certified seed potatoes or eyes from certified seed; in open trench 4"-5" deep, set chunk of potato with 1-3 eyes (most satisfactory size 1½-2½ oz.) and cover; for the average potato this means cutting into 3-4 pieces; use a 4-8-10 fertilizer, but do not let it touch seed; harvest as foliage begins to die, late varieties when it is dead; let dry in sun for one day before storing; plastic mulch is effective. In cold soils, seed is planted on ridges covered with about ½" of soil; Norgold Russet is early, and not knobby; scab resistant.
Early: Irish Cobbler	1	S 40°F		Zone 5, 2nd -3rd week May				
Mid: Cherokee	1	S 40°F						
Late: Kennebec	1	S 40°F						
Late: Katahdin	3	S 40°F		Zone 1-2 last week May first June				
Russet Burbank	1	S 40°F						
Sebago	3	S 40°F						
Especially for the coldest areas:				about May 20	1½"-2"	12"	3'-3½	
Norgold Russet	1	S 40°F						
RADISH		Summer to Fall		first thing in spring and successive sowings every 2 wks. till Aug. 1	½"	1"	12"-15"	Tastiest in spring; quick to germinate; can intercrop with other slower vegetables; will produce till snow flies; for a continuous supply, sow seed every 2 weeks.
Cherry Belle	1							
Comet	1							
RHUBARB		Spring		Set roots as early as ground can be worked		3'-4'	4'	Pull, do not cut, stalks; eat only stems, leaves are highly poisonous; do not pull first year, only a few stalks second year and thereafter only till July to allow plants to develop crowns for next year; divide every 3 years; a heavy feeder—fertilize well.
McDonald	1	F						
Canada Red	1	F						
SPINACH		Late Spring & Fall		early in spring successive sowings 2-3 weeks till early June	¾"	thin to 3"	15"-18"	A cool-weather crop; needs water if no rain; harvest when tender—goes to seed quickly; does not grow well in acid soil; use lime if necessary
America	3	F						
Dixie Market	3							
Hybrid #7	3							
New Zealand	1	Summer		when soil and air warm		thin to 1'-1½		Will grow on trellis
SQUASH				when soil and air warm	1"	Bush: 3'	Bush: 4'	Use summer squash while small and tender, before rind hardens, and while skin can still be punctued with your fingernail; pick Hybrid Zucchini when 6"-8" long, keeping plants stripped to obtain maximum yield; harvest winter squash when rind hard and flesh mature.
Summer: Hybrid Zucchini	1	Summer				Vining: 2'-3'	Vining: 6'-8'	
Summer Crookneck	1	Summer				Hills: sow 6-8 seeds per hill, thin to 2-3	Hills: 5'-6'	
Winter: (Vining)								
Buttercup	1	WinterSF						
Butter Nut	3	SF 50°F						
Hubbard (various)	3	SF 50°F						

F marks varieties suitable for freezing
S marks varieties suitable for storage

| KINDS | ZONE | USE | SEEDING TIMES | | DEPTH TO PLANT | SPACING | | REMARKS |
			INDOORS	OUTDOORS		BETWEEN PLANTS	BETWEEN ROWS	
SWISS CHARD Fordhook Giant	1	Summer		when ground can be worked	½″	8″-12″	2	A relative of beets, but grown for leaves which are best cooked with some spinach; water and feed well; harvest outside leaves while young and tender.
TOMATO (BUSH, NON-STAKING) Fireball Harbon New Yorker Variant Veecrop Veeset Vision **TOMATO (ADAPTABLE FOR STAKING)** Campbell 1327 Early Hybrid (F₁) Early Giant Hybrid (F₁) Stokesdale Viceroy Vendor Supersonic Spring Giant		Late Summer & Fall	Plant 4-6 weeks before last frost in peat pots	Transplant Zone 6-9 2nd-4th week May Zone 5 last week May or first June Zone 3-4 1st-2nd wk. June Zone 1-2 3rd week June 2 weeks earlier if Hotkaps used	½″	$2\frac{1}{2}'$ Large varieties: $3\frac{1}{2}'$ $1\frac{1}{2}'$-2	3' 4' 3	Everybody's favorite—there is nothing more luscious than a sun-ripened tomato from your own garden; buy prestarted plants or grow your own; staked plants take up less space and fruit is cleaner; set 6′ stake 1′ in ground at time of planting; tie with soft twine or strips of cloth so as not to injure stems; pinch side shoots out as they appear; water if no rain; some gardeners sink large perforated fruit juice can beside each plant and if weather dry, they fill the can, which gradually soaks soil; fertilizer (4-8-10) can be fed this way or sprinkled 6″ from main stem on ground; put a spadeful of ashes or sand around plants to discourage snails, slug and cutworms; paper collars good too; cut down on watering as fruit comes into final ripening stage.
TURNIP Tokyo Cross (F₁) Shogoin (especially for the South) **RUTABAGA**	1	Summer		as soon as ground can be worked	¼″	Thin to 3″	18″	Harvest when root approximately 2″ in diameter; cook with a little brown sugar; tops may be eaten as greens.
American Purple Top	1	Fall & Winter S		Middle to end of June	¼″	Thin to 6″-8″	2'	Excellent for winter storage; wax to prevent shrinking and to retain quality.

F marks varieties suitable for freezing
S marks varieties suitable for storage

Pest and Disease Control for Vegetables

PESTS: considered here to be insects, mites, slugs, millipedes, sowbugs, etc.

DISEASE: covers disorders caused by fungi, bacteria, viruses and nematodes.

Insecticides: are applied either by spraying or dusting, usually to kill pests which you know are on your plants or, as some gardeners do when they use an all-purpose spray or dust, to prevent pests from getting started. The ideal way is to control only the pest you know is present, with a chemical just for that pest, but small home gardens are often more conveniently and just as effectively treated with an all-purpose material that combines a control for a number of pests and a fungicide too.

Fungicides: which you apply either as a spray or a dust, are used *preventively* before trouble starts. Experienced gardeners will recognize the kind of weather that breeds fungus and apply the correct control at that time. Others would be wise to carry on a regular program during the whole growing season, in case such protection might be needed.

New improved insecticides and fungicides are constantly replacing those already in use and more experienced assessments of some of the older chemicals are taking them off the approved list. *All* gardeners would be wise to:

keep up with current information on recommended chemicals through their federal and state departments of agriculture. Most issue pamphlets and charts for a small charge or free.

consult these agencies if a particular unknown trouble develops.

learn, in the case of vegetables and fruit, the safe number of days between the last spraying or dusting and harvesting so that there will be no danger of harmful residue.

check CHAPTER 19, Pests and Diseases, for precautions in handling *all* insecticides and fungicides.

Pests

APHIDS Common, but particularly fond of potatoes, peppers, tomatoes, cabbage, cauliflower, squash, cucumbers.

Trouble: Curled, stunted leaves and shoots, caused by sap-sucking, soft, tiny, green, red or black insects (over 200 kinds are listed in technical texts). Gourmet fare for ladybugs, milk cows for ants, transmitters of disease.

Control: First make sure, by watching for a few days, that beneficial insects are not already controlling the population explosion with a little first-class murder of the enemy. If not, then spray or dust with insecticide. It will probably take more than one application.

LEAFHOPPERS on beans, potatoes, lettuce.

Trouble: Browning, stunting and curling of leaves caused by small, sucking, Olympic-medal-calibre green jumpers.

Control: Spray or dust insecticide when hoppers first noticed on underside of leaves.

CUCUMBER BEETLES on cucumbers, squash, pumpkins, melon, and others.

Trouble: Chewed leaves; serious also because infects host (or hostess?) with virus and bacterial wilt. Yellow beetle with black stripes or spots.

Control: Spray or dust insecticide when first seen and thereafter as necessary.

POTATO BEETLES on potatoes, peppers, eggplant, tomatoes.

Trouble: Shot-like holes in leaves caused by tiny shiny black flea beetles. Larger chunks eaten by your old friend the potato bug, officially the Colorado beetle — black-striped yellow, big enough to see easily and a dandy source of income for youngsters hand-picking into a jar of kerosene.

Control if no youngsters handy: Spray or dust insecticide when first seen.

ROOT MAGGOTS cabbage maggots, which attack cabbage, cauliflower, broccoli, Brussels sprouts, radishes, turnips, rutabaga; onion maggots which attack onions; carrot rust fly, which attack carrot, celery, parsnip; seed corn maggots that attack cabbage, cauliflower, broccoli, Brussels sprouts, turnips, radishes, onions, carrots, beans in the ground.

Trouble: Underground roots and stems tunneled by small white legless maggots after plants appear above ground or when transplants set out.

Control: Use granular insecticide in furrow when planting seed or aboveground immediately after planting. With beans, buy seed treated for maggot and shallow plant.

SLUGS common, and thoroughly nasty bits of business.

Trouble: Holes chewed in leaves by grey slimy legless horned shell-less snail-like creatures that leave a shiny trail just to tell you — as though you wouldn't know by the cutwork — that they've been by that way.

Control: Keep garden free of debris, which slugs need for shade during day — they would dry up if they got sunburned. Circle susceptible plants with lime or cinders, for they don't like to have their tummy tickled, or put out slug bait. For the safety of small children, pets and birds, cover bait with a shingle or a metal lid propped up on a couple of small stones.

WIREWORMS common.

Trouble: Destroyed underground vegetables, seed, stems and roots. Caused by shiny, dark yellow, wiry worms.

Control: Granular insecticide applied to soil and dug in, or sprinkled along rows, not more than once every 4 years.

CUTWORMS common.

Trouble: Succulent seedlings cut off at or just below the surface. Caused by nasty, greasy, grey night-feeders.

Control: A cardboard or foil collar, or a small frozen-juice can with both ends cut out, set around the new plant, pushed well into the ground; or insecticide dusted or sprayed along row, at base of plants.

ASPARAGUS BEETLES on asparagus.

Trouble: Chewed young shoots, followed by distorted spears and later damaged leaves. Caused by small bluish-black and red-with-black-spots beetles. Larvae also destructive.

Control: During cutting season, spray or dust with insecticide observing short period of being safe to use before harvest. Repeat after cropping if leaves being bitten.

CORN BORER, EUROPEAN chiefly on corn, but sometimes peppers and others.

Trouble: Wormy cobs and stalks, broken tassels. Caused by dirty-white with pinkish or brown stripes, ¾-1-inch worms boring through plant parts.

Control: Spray with insecticide when first tassel shows and thereafter 3 times at 5-day intervals, twice if only early and second-early cultivars are grown. Interval can be longer if infestation not too severe.

CORN EARWORM on corn, sometimes tomatoes.

Trouble: Wormy, moldy tip of cob (burrows into green tomatoes at stem). Caused by large 1½-2-inch light-green to dark-striped caterpillars.

Control: Mother Nature is on your side because earworms are really cannibals at heart and frequently eat each other; but if this fails, when 50% showing, cover silk of tassel thoroughly with spray or dust insecticide, and repeat in 7 days.

CABBAGE WORMS on cabbage, cauliflower, Brussels sprouts, broccoli.

Trouble: Bitten holes in leaves. Caused by green caterpillars.

Control: Examine plants before heads form and if worms are seen, dust (rather than spray) with insecticide, especially checking for safe interval between treatment and harvest.

Diseases

BLACK ROT affects cabbages, cauliflower, collard, turnips, broccoli, Brussels sprouts, Kohl-rabi, others.

Trouble: Yellowed leaves, beginning at tips, and blackening veins; cross section of stalk shows black ring; seedlings killed or seriously checked; in older plants, heads do not form. Bacteria that follow cause bad odor. Happens most often when weather very warm and moist. Disease seed-borne and may persist in soil.

Control: Hot-water treat seed, see page 78. Practise long rotation of different crops. Destroy infected plants. Don't work in garden nor let your pets romp there when plants are wet, you or they could be the culprit spreading the disease.

CLUB ROOT affects cabbages, cauliflower, radishes, turnip, rutabaga, others.

Trouble: Leaves yellow, wilt on hot days, examination shows round or spindle-shaped swellings on roots or base of stem which can become large and irregular. Discolored insides and bad odor. Common in acid soil and can live there for years.

Control: Apply enough lime to soil 6 weeks before planting, to give pH 7.2. Work in thoroughly. Don't plant same crop where soil known to be infected. Eliminate cruciferous weeds (mustard, penny cress, shepherd's purse, etc.). When transplanting, water with soil fungicide.

YELLOWS a fungus which affects cabbages, particularly in summer.

Trouble: Seedlings wilt and die, older plants are stunted, leaves turn yellow, wilt and drop. Plants may look one-sided. Fungus survives in soil for many years. Disease most often serious in summer when soil temperature and moisture high.

Control: Plant resistant varieties, such as Resistant Golden Acre, Marion Market, Badger Market, Badger Ballhead.

DAMPING OFF affects most vegetables, especially peas, spinach, beets, lettuce, carrots, cucumbers.

Trouble: Seed rots in soil, and seedlings rot at ground level, caused by a soil-borne fungus.

Control: Dust seed with fungicide, see CHAPTER 19, page 175. If disease appears on your seedlings, immediately water with fungicide and thereafter 2 or 3 times at weekly intervals.

EARLY AND LATE BLIGHTS affect celery.

Trouble: Severely spots and yellows foliage, dead places appear on stalks (late blight lesions are usually smaller and covered with tiny black fungus). These diseases are seed-borne and live over in debris or soil.

Control: Use 3-year-old, or hot-water treated seed, see page 178. Spray or dust with fungicides when seedlings about 2 inches high, repeating every 10-14 days.

ASTER YELLOWS affects celery, carrots, lettuce, endive, salsify.

Trouble: Leaves yellow, twisted and stunted. Virus causing disease is carried by leafhoppers.

Control: Eradicate weeds in early spring because leafhoppers can carry disease from them to crops. Control leafhoppers with insecticide.

SMUT affects sweet corn on stalks, tassels and ears; onions, leeks, shallots, garlic on leaves.

Trouble: White swellings appear on corn; on the others, swellings are filled with black powdery spores, dark streaks appear within the tissue of leaves or bulbs, filled with brown powder dust.

Control: Keep a clean garden and rotate crops. With corn, remove swellings, with the others use fungicide on seed, see CHAPTER 19, page 175.

DOWNY MILDEW affects peas, lettuce, onions.

Trouble: On peas, grey-brown growth on undersurface of leaves and pods. Pods often have no seeds. Growth checked.

On lettuce, yellow spots on upper leaf-surface, grey-white growth on lower surface.

On onions, purple growth on stems and leaves, followed by yellowing and death of affected leaves.

On all these vegetables, disease will be most severe during moist weather and fungus may remain in soil or debris from one season to another.

Control: Rotate crops, eliminate weeds, destroy infected refuse. Spray fungicide at 14-day intervals, but on lettuce *no less* than one week before harvest.

POWDERY MILDEW affects cucumbers, cantaloupes, pumpkins, squash, watermelons, others.

Trouble: a whitish, powdery growth on leaves, which finally dry and die.

Control: Spray with fungicide at 14-day intervals as soon as mildew appears. Buy resistant seed or plants where possible.

ANTHRACNOSE affects beans.

Trouble: Pods have irregular, sunken brown spots covered with mold. Most severe in moist weather. May also attack leaves and stems. Disease is seed-borne and may be carried over in refuse or soil.

Control: Buy disease-free seed. Don't work in your plants or allow pets to roam through when they're wet. Rotate crops over at least 3 years.

BACTERIAL BLIGHTS affects beans.

Trouble: Dead spots on foliage and spots on pods, infected stems may be girdled and wilted. Disease seed-borne and possibly carried in debris.

Control: Buy disease-free seed; don't work when plants wet; rotate crops for at least 3 years.

BACTERIAL WILT affects cucumbers, melons, others.

Trouble: Young or old vines may completely collapse and die. Disease is not seed-borne, it winters in cucumber beetles and is spread by them.

Control: Dust or spray cucumber beetles with insecticide when plants emerging and for following 3-4 weeks. Rotenone is satisfactory and may be applied when bees working in garden, when other insecticides would be fatal to them. Look for wilt-resistant seed.

VERTICILLIUM WILT affects peppers, eggplant, tomatoes, potatoes, others.

Trouble: Leaves turn yellow and die from base of plant up; roots seem normal. Occurs in cool weather; fungus persists in soil.

Control: Do not plant in soil known to be infected. Rotate with unrelated crops. Use resistant varieties if possible, and certified *seed* potatoes.

FUSARIUM WILT affects watermelons, tomatoes, cucumbers, melons, others.

Trouble: Plants wilt and show internal discoloration in stems; in some, disease shows more on one side than the other. Prevalent in hot weather. Persists in soil for years.

Control: Avoid planting in infected soil, buy good seed or plants. Practice long rotation, destroy affected plants. Grow fusarium-resistant muskmelon.

COMMON SCAB affects potatoes.

Trouble: Rough, scabby, raised or pitted areas on tubers. Fungus carried on tubers and lives in soil.

Control: Choose varieties with degree of resistance such as Cherokee, Keswick or Sebago. Plant clean tubers in acid soil. Do not grow potatoes where scab has occurred before. Do not use lime or wood ashes in soil.

LATE BLIGHT affects potatoes, tomatoes.

Trouble: Dark, water-soaked spots on leaves and stems. Infected potatoes may rot in storage. Spots on tomatoes turn brown. Disease worst in cool, moist weather. Fungus carried on potato tubers.

Control: Be sure to plant clean potato tubers, healthy tomato transplants. Grow blight-resistant potatoes such as Sebago, Kennebec. Destroy any culls and plants that develop from potatoes left over in the ground from the year before. Spray with fungicide when disease appears.

VIRUSES (mosaics, leaf roll streak, yellows) affect potatoes, tomatoes, cucumber, pepper, others.

Trouble: Mottled, crinkled, rolled leaves; dwarfed, spindled plants; mottled, distorted fruits, in other words, **Trouble.** Spread by insects some also by plant handlers.

Control: Use certified seed potatoes, clean seed. Where few plants affected, remove and destroy. Wash hands thoroughly after handling diseased plants. Eliminate weeds and debris.

ROOT KNOT affects tomatoes, melons, celery, carrots, many others.

Trouble: Stunted plants that wilt and turn yellow; roots may have tiny or very large rotten galls. Disease lives in soil over long periods, caused by an almost invisible nematode.

Control: Examine seedlings for galls when planting and discard if found. Destroy infected plants; cultivate as little as possible. Do not plant highly susceptible plants such as cucumbers, melons, tomatoes, in garden where this disease has previously occurred.

ROOT ROT affects most vegetables.

Trouble: Roots wholly or partly decayed, plants look unhealthy, leaves yellow, wilt and fall. Caused by a number of fungi that overwinter from season to season.

Control: Follow good garden practice, check and improve drainage. Use fungicide on seed, see page 175.

Hot water treatment for vegetable seeds to prevent disease

Some seed may be purchased already treated. The directions on the packet will indicate this.

The method: Place seed in thin cloth bag and then in water at recommended temperature, maintaining that temperature throughout the treatment. Use a candy thermometer. (Tomato seed only should be given a cold water bath following the hot one.) Spread seed out to dry indoors (the birds will eat it outdoors), then dust with fungicide as a protectant. Be careful not to over-heat or treat overlong — this could reduce germination.

Time and temperature recommended:

cabbage, Brussels sprouts, peppers and eggplant at 122°F. for 25 minutes
cauliflower, Kohl-rabi, kale and turnip at 122°F. for 15 minutes
celery at 118°F. for 30 minutes
tomato at 130°F. for 25 minutes

HERBS

If you have a lively interest in good food, the growing of culinary herbs is a must. Nothing rates you faster as *cordon bleu* cook than a mysterious, enhancing flavor in something familiar — a snippet of basil over fried tomatoes at breakfast, a faint hint of rosemary on broiled chicken, the delicious taste of dill in potato salad (make it as the superb Mennonite cooks do, with a coating of melted bacon fat over the potatoes before you add the mayonnaise or boiled dressing), sweet parsley butter on a piece of trout or boned chicken breasts with a dusting of tarragon and cooked in white wine. This last makes a rave party menu.

All these herbs can be bought, but to get top rating grow your own. They are handier and have fresher flavor. A few herbs grown near the kitchen door will flavor your summertime meals and pro-vide plenty to harvest for winter. Although this is not a cookbook, we cannot resist giving you directions for storing and some ideas for using good herbs, but first we tell you what to grow and how to grow it.

Dill, to stay the hiccough and strengthen the brain.

THE FAVORITES

Parsley: *Petroselinum crispum*: 8 inches: too often it's used to decorate a dish and never eaten; chopped into salads, with melted butter or margarine on grilled fish, or as parsley butter on chops, it has a characteristic flavor of its own. Add it to stock in soups and to sauces too. Plants take 2 years to set seed in the garden, but, since it is the leaves you use not the seeds, treat it as an annual and grow from seed or buy started plants. The curly kind is the most flavorful. Slow to germinate. Prestart seed indoors.

Chives: *Allium schoenoprasum*: 10 inches: best buy a potted plant to get started, but can be grown from seed. A perennial. Clumps should be divided when the plant becomes thick and crowded. A mild onion flavor, try mixing it with sour cream for crisp-skinned baked potatoes and sprinkled on iced vichyssoise — both food for particularly appreciative gods.

Dill: *Anethum graveolens*: 2-3 feet: an annual, sow seeds when the ground is warm, where it is to grow. Thin to 12 inches apart if they come up thicker. Grow for seeds and feathery bouquets of blue-greenery indoors. Seeds perfect for dill pickles and a gourmet's delight in mayonnaise for smoked salmon; the fresh green leaves in melted butter over grilled lamb chops, in lamb stew, fish sauces and tomato soup.

Mint: *Mentha spicata* (spearmint): 18 inches: *Mentha piperita* (peppermint): 2 feet: a perennial, in fact, sometimes a rampagious perennial, so contain it in a large pot sunk in the garden or let it run wild in a dull corner where you will enjoy its fresh fragrant greenness. Spearmint the favorite, but peppermint nice if you are having your old auntie to tea. Use leaves, which are at their best just before flowering begins. Mint sauce for roast lamb and sprigs for juleps are musts, but use it too chopped over cucumbers in a thin, fresh-bread sandwich or pop a pinch into fresh peas as they cook.

Summer Savory: *Satureja hortensis*: 18 inches: an annual, grow from seed. Pick the top 6-8 inches of the plant, just as it comes into flower. Dry and rub off leaves and buds. Just the thing to lift dressing in roast chicken and pork tenderloin to the superb.

Sage: *Salvia officinalis*: 2 feet; a perennial, grow from prestarted plants, seed or cuttings. Gets woody so new plants should be set out every 3-4 years. Velvety grey leaves are the part you use and they look as fascinating as they taste. Particularly good in sausages and cheese fondue and for dressing in duck.

Thyme: *Thymus vulgaris*: 6-10 inches: buy plants or start seed indoors. Since it is the leafy tops of the stems and the just-opening flowers you want, cut back plants each spring to induce new shoots. Lifts carrots out of the humdrum.

Sweet Basil: *Ocimum basilicum*: 18 inches: pretty as well as useful. An annual; one with purple leaves, 'Dark Opal', is interesting as a flowerbed edging and the best of several cultivars for flavoring food. Leaves should be picked just before flowering — you can prolong this period by nipping off the flowers. Wonderful with all tomato dishes, but especially good if you sprinkle it on sliced tomatoes in a casserole, add a little white wine and olive oil and a dusting of Parmesan cheese.

Tarragon: *Artemisia dracunculus*: 2 feet: a perennial, buy plants, divide clumps every 2-3 years. Will do well with a little shade, but must have perfect drainage at the roots. Cover with evergreen branches after the first hard freeze in winter, put in à frame, or take indoors. Superlative with scrambled eggs, duck, shellfish, chicken and artichokes. Makes excellent herb vinegar for salads.

Chervil: *Anthriscus cerefolium*: 2 feet: annual, use fresh leaves, likes a little shade. Sow two crops a few weeks apart for a continuous supply. Use as you would parsley, particularly good in soup.

Rosemary: *Rosmarinus officinalis*: 3-6 feet: a tender perennial that must be taken indoors in winter in most of the country. Best to begin by buying a plant. Prune back each spring for more leafy

shoots. Tuck leaves into slits in roast pork; mix with a pinch of thyme and marjoram for an omelette; finely pulverized, add to tea biscuits — really subtle.

Sweet Marjoram: *Marjorana hortensis*: 8-12 inches: treat as an annual, fragrant and popular. Soak seeds for 24 hours before planting. And try this for a lift to an ordinary meal: mix with a little butter, 2 tablespoons olive oil, 1 clove of garlic, 1 green onion and cook for 10 minutes. Add 4 rounds of zucchini with the peel left on, 1 teaspoon each fresh marjoram and parsley (½ teaspoon if dried), ⅓ cup bouillon, cover and cook 10 minutes more, serve with a dusting of Parmesan cheese.

Fennel: *Foeniculum officinalis*: 3-4 feet: an annual, grows easily from seed. Tall, use seeds for flavoring, leaves for faint licorice taste. Crush seeds into butter for topping salmon or halibut steaks or add to lemon juice and oil as dressing for cucumber to be served with lobster or trout.

OTHERS TO TRY:

Caraway: *Carum carvi*: 30 inches: a biennial and since you will want the seeds, grow where it can stay for 2 years. Use in cakes and cookies.

Anise: *Pimpinella anisum*: 1½-2 feet: an annual, leaves in salads, seeds for cakes and cookies, licorice-like.

Borage: *Borago officinalis*: annual, coarse leaves but beautiful blue flowers to float in summer drinks. Cucumbery. Never dried. In old folklore, it was "borage for courage"!

Coriander: *Coriandrum sativum*: 2 feet: annual, don't use leaves. Seeds deliciously perfumed. Particularly good in gingerbread or in stuffing for wild game.

Lemon verbena: *Lippia citriodora*: 2 feet: take indoors in winter.

Lemon balm: *Melissa officinalis*: 2 feet: perennial.

Camomile: *Matricaria chamomilla*: annual.

These last 3 make tasty tea.

Lavender: *Lavandula officinalis*: 1½-3 feet: use flower and seed heads for scenting the linen cupboard and bureau drawers.

WHERE TO PLANT A HERB GARDEN

Near the kitchen door, for handy snipping, is the place for your herb garden. Hot sun and dryish soil develop more flavor in all but tarragon and chervil, which will take a little shade and extra moisture. The mints like moist soil too. Any good garden soil will do for the growing.

For a pleasing design, make a pattern of bricks and tiles. Or, for least fuss, grow your plants in rows, the taller ones at the back, the perennials in one bed; the annuals, which improve with a little cultivating, in another.

A few of these flavor herbs are good looking enough to grow with other plants in the garden — the purple-leaved 'Dark Opal' basil is one, thyme another. Many enhance and do well in a rockery. Parsley is a magnificent green in such a site, tarragon appreciates the sharp drainage of being planted among rocks. Rosemary is at home among roses; thymes are a spilling fragrance growing in the cracks of stepping stones; chives make wonderful early spurts of green, then, with a severe cutting-back, a feeding of bone meal and a little new soil around the roots, come back strong again for the autumn and to face the winter.

Herb buffs are divided on whether to fertilize the ground or not. Some say yes but never with manure, only with chemical inorganics. Others say only with well-rotted manure. Still others — the real purists — say no fertilizer at all. One thing is certain — that strength of flavor is enhanced with sparse growing conditions. For the rest you will have to experiment to find what is best for you.

PLANTING

For correct planting techniques for seeds, cuttings, divisions, bulblets, see CHAPTER 18.

Tender herbs like rosemary and lemon verbena, which cannot survive most northern winters outdoors, can be grown in pots sunk in the ground or tended on a terrace, then moved into a greenhouse or cool indoor porch for the winter.

HARVESTING FOR SUMMER USE

Cut stems and remove leaves just as plants come into bloom on a fine sunny morning when the dew has dried but the sun is not yet high. Wash quickly by swishing through ice cold water and lay loosely on paper towels to dry, turning often.

DRYING FOR WINTER USE

Herb leaves, to dry for winter, need a dark, dry, warm, airy place, not necessarily very hot. One method is to hang stems in loose bunches in a dark closet or in brown paper bags open at bottom. Turn on a fan to move the air if necessary. An alternative, and some think the best way with large-leaved plants like sage, mint or basil, is to lay single leaves on screens in a warm but not sunny, airy place, turning occasionally until they are fully dry. Small-leaved herbs such as thyme and marjoram need not be stripped from stems but should also be dried on screens.

When dry, remove leaves from stems and store loose in sealed jars in the dark — slide them into paper bags to cut off the light if you have to. Do not crush leaves till you are going to use them. Upend large containers two or three times in the first month so that leaves will not pack down and perhaps mold. Seeds can be stored in tight-topped bottles or wrapped in foil. All should be labelled.

FREEZING FOR WINTER USE

Wash in cold water as for regular drying, do *not* blanch with boiling water as you do vegetables for freezing. With leaves, lay a single layer between two pieces of kitchen plastic or waxed paper — about as many as you would use at one time. Cut up chives and parsley and wrap. Lay the little parcels flat in plastic bags or wrap in a piece of foil, or alternatively pack loosely in shallow plastic refrigerator dishes, dipping out a little as you need it. Herbs defrost quickly — but use immediately for best flavor. And don't forget to label your parcels for the freezer!

HERBS INDOORS IN WINTER

In late summer or early fall, take cuttings or divisions and grow them on. Alternatively, pot up the whole plant if it is not too big, and adjust to your house temperature by gradually moving it in at night and outdoors during the day for two weeks. Before frost, bring it in to a sunny, cool window to stay. Chives, parsley, chervil, mint and rosemary dress up many a winter meal handled like this.

AMOUNTS TO USE

To 1 pint of liquid (in stews and so on) add ¼ teaspoon dried, ½ teaspoon fresh, for the last hour of cooking. For vegetable juice or cold sauce, the same amount for one hour overnight. For salad dressing, the same amount for half an hour at room temperature. Freezing makes herb flavors stronger and you may wish to change recommended quantities to suit your own taste.

12 YOUR OWN FRUIT

Sun-warm fruit, ripe to perfection, grown in your own garden is luscious beyond belief. Juicy sweet strawberries, raspberries with a tang to tickle your tongue, red currants for jelly with toast and hot biscuits, all the bounty of cherries and apples, pears and plums, peaches and apricots, and in the Midwest and Far North, the delectable saskatoons — all are a treat and a triumph for the home gardener.

Growing fruit, however, is not just a matter of planting a small tree or bush in the ground and stepping back out of the way to let it grow. You need the necessary space and the absolute must of sun all day. And you need time to give your fruit regular and skillful care if you are to grow it superbly. Nothing less is worth the effort. A crop of wormy apples, for instance, is more ruin than relish: apart from the disappointment, somebody must pick them up and dispose of them. But it is possible for those same apples to reach maturity wormless and glowing, if they are frequently sprayed and properly cared for. These and other techniques for successful production take time and you must be able to give it them.

You need to be wily too. Your otherwise-welcome friends, the birds and the squirrels, know a tasty treat when they see one and will steal your pride and joy right from under your nose. I have learned that, in a cultivated garden, it is possible to trap squirrels humanely. Then I drive them out to the country and let them go — to live in the fruitless woods and fields. Netted enclosures, or one large fruit net drawn over the tree or plantings, will discourage birds like the boat-tailed grackle, who love raspberries and pears; trunks wrapped before winter with foil or wire mesh will keep rabbits and

A large net drawn over fruit trees will discourage birds

mice from snicking the lower twigs and nibbling the bark. For how to control other predators, see CHAPTER 18.

HELPFUL KNOW-HOW

Space: although a generous plot is needed to grow a full orchard, it is possible to plant fruit trees and such leafy beauties as strawberries in much smaller space — in your flower borders, for instance. Nothing is prettier in the springtime garden than a white froth of cherry tree in bloom with a skirting of early pink tulips or golden daffodils; nothing more interesting than the leaves of strawberries used as an edging and fruit for dessert. But if you wish to go seriously into the production of your own fruit, more space and more plants will be needed.

Apples, crabs, pears, apricots and sweet cherries should be at least 25 feet apart each way; plums and peaches 20 feet; cherry-plum and sour cherries 15 feet; serviceberries 8 feet (these measurements may have to be adjusted upwards if you use a tractor for cultivating between rows). In areas where wind-gust is a factor, plant your trees to the lee of a shelterbelt and 40 feet away from it.

Dwarf fruit trees, where they are hardy (mainly Zones 6-9), are a joy for home gardeners. They vary from 1/10 to 3/4 the size of a standard tree and need only 10-20 feet between. They are easier to care for in every way because you work at them standing on the ground. Specially grafted dwarf trees, with as many as 4 cultivars, all different yet growing from one trunk, are also offered by a number of nurseries. Their space needs are similar to the regular dwarfs. Apart from making you feel smarter than Mother Nature herself, those pomological believe-it-or-nots make wonderful conversation for parties.

Sunlight: all fruit needs full sun, all day. If your garden is shady, give up the thought of growing it.

Good garden soil, well drained, will grow fruit well. For how to improve yours, see CHAPTER 18. Blueberries are about the only homegrown fruit needing special soil. They need acid soil with a rating of pH 4.5, see under *Blueberries* for how to make this if your soil does not have it now.

Favorable climate is needed for successful growth and ripening of fruit before frosts. Winterkill occurs when temperatures go too low, wind dries out bark (chinook winds are particularly noted for this in the west) and when alternate freezing and thawing strains the plant. Late spring frosts can nip buds and flowers; killing frosts too early in the fall can injure the whole plant before it is fully dormant for winter. High summer temperatures are less hazardous. Fruit trees can withstand temperatures up to 100°F., if they have sufficient water at the roots. Some of these factors are beyond your control, others you can modify. Damage from spring frosts after the plants are in leaf and flower can often be prevented by spraying the frozen plants with a cold-water fine mist from the hose before the sun hits them and continuing this treatment until temperatures are again above freezing. Withholding extra water and fertilizer in late summer and fall will encourage timely dormancy. Supplementary watering during droughts, especially in late spring and early summer, will help to set good crops and develop tasty fruit.

Choosing cultivars recommended as hardy for your zone is the most important step in preventing disappointment. See pages 86-87 for suggestions and consult your government services and local nurseryman for others. And do experiment! This is half the fun of gardening.

Make a study of your own garden conditions. It is often possible to make use of a small area of more favorable climate within your garden and to grow there tree and bush fruits that would not normally be hardy for your zone. For instance:

Plant fruit trees on a gentle slope if you can, frosty air will flow downward to the bottom past the trees.

Avoid steep slopes. They are difficult to cultivate and drain too quickly. A north or east slope is best for several reasons — trees are exposed to less freezing and thawing in late winter and spring; the earth stays cool longer after the winter, delaying premature development of flower buds, and trunks of trees are less likely to be burned by late winter sun.

Avoid sites where the wind sweeps through.

Plant shelterbelts to reduce the force of the wind in both winter and summer and to catch snow for welcome moisture. Even a couple of rows of corn or sunflowers left standing will protect a planting of young trees. Older trees need a full-size shelterbelt, see CHAPTER 20.

Do not plant too close to each other or to other trees — free air circulation will reduce the chance of fungus disease and rot.

Break out your Sherlock Holmes deerstalker and deduce other such clever moves for yourself.

Purchase: send for catalogues of nurseries specializing in fruit for your zone and put your order in early for spring delivery (fall is just as good in the coastal West and the South), or if you want to purchase in the fall, heel in the plants, see CHAPTER 18, and plant as soon as the ground can be worked in spring.

Specify, in your order, the cultivar wanted and ask for virus-free or virus-resistant stock if it is available.

Check whether you will need two or more plants to effect successful pollinization and whether the cultivar you have chosen bears every year or every second year, which is the case with some apples and pears. Different cultivars of the same fruit, ripening at different times — early, mid-season and late — may be chosen to prolong the season for cropping.

Examine plants carefully on arrival and make sure they are not dried out. If they are borderline, give them a good soaking under water for 24 hours. If you cannot plant immediately, heel them in and plant in their permanent site as soon as possible. Do *not* let them dry out.

Planting: in most parts of the country, this is done before buds swell in spring; in milder parts of the West and the South, also in fall, after the leaves have dropped.

Choose a site that does not compete with other trees or shrubs for light or ground, that is weed-free, moist but not soggy. Fruit trees will not survive in soaking wet soil. Do not plant strawberries, raspberries, or sweet cherries for 3-4 years where potatoes, tomatoes, eggplant or peppers have grown. Soil here may be infected with a fungus that could injure them.

Plant as for other trees and bushes, see CHAPTER 18, setting 1-2 year old trees at the same depth as in the nursery or a shade lower; but with dwarf trees see that the graft union — a bump low on the stem — is at least 4-5 inches *above* soil level; it is not strong. Berry bushes and grapes are planted at the same depth as in the nursery.

Place a sturdy stake in the planting hole before the tree is in place and tie the whip securely to it with a piece of wire through a rubber hose, an old nylon stocking or anything that will not bruise the bark as the tree blows in the wind. Plan to remove this tie for good in 3-4 years, but with dwarf trees simply retie it, for they need such support all their lives.

Correct planting of a dwarf tree: graft 4-5 inches above ground.

Burning and consequent splitting of the bark on the trunk, vertically, is a common injury caused by late winter sun. It can be prevented by wrapping the trunk with foil, heavy paper or sacking. Authorities in the North suggest that fruit trees be allowed to multi-branch low down, as a bush would, to avoid this scald and also to prevent injury from the prevailing high winds there.

Moisture: For general directions on how to water, see CHAPTER 18. Adequate water is important not only for the current season's crop but also for future development, especially of currants, gooseberries and raspberries, where vigorous new shoots are needed for bearing fruit next year. Where rain is scant as blossoms are forming and again as fruit fills out, supplementary watering should be done by running the hose slowly on the ground (not on the plants) to soak deeply.

For strawberries, 1 inch of water should be applied 9 inches out on each side of the rows; for cane fruit, 2 inches out 2 feet on each side; and for young trees, 2 feet as far out as the branches extend. Established trees can usually manage, except in extreme drought, with good mulching, see CHAPTER 18, herbicides and cultivation to control the weeds. Keep the mulch back from the trunk of the tree to a diameter of 12 inches so mice and moles will not use it for cover as they nibble the bark.

Cultivation: the surface soil should be shallow and cultivated just enough to kill weeds, encourage good aeration and expose pupae of injurious insect pests to the birds and destroying winter cold; discontinue after midsummer to allow growth to slow down and the trees to harden up for winter; hoe out root sprouts and suckers from below the graft as soon as they appear.

Pruning: cut back 1-2 year old trees ¼-⅓ when planting; thereafter prune to develop the tree or bush to maximum strength and bearing capacity to carry a heavy load of fruit and to let plenty of sunlight into the centre of the tree.

Remove suckers and branches that are weak, rub against one another or cross. Do this pruning 6-8 weeks before the ground thaws in spring.

With canefruit, take out any weak shoots when plants are young. **Red raspberries** increase by sucker growth — in fact they come up all over the place — therefore allow them to increase freely the second year, then prune to keep them in rows about 18-24 inches wide thereafter. Take out old canes each year after fruiting.

Black and purple raspberries rarely ramble. Top these if they grow higher than 36 inches; toward the end of the first season, each new cane throws out side branches; fruit is borne on the smaller branches that develop from these laterals; these bearing branches should be pruned back in spring before growth starts, to two buds each on slim canes, up to six buds on sturdy ones.

With currants, reduce the length of side branches and cut out completely all canes more than 3 years old; the ideal plant has 9-12 shoots (3-4 each of 1 year, 2-year and 3-year-old wood); trim laterals to 2-3 buds.

Grapes are pruned in late winter when vines are dormant; cut back at end of first season to 1-2 buds; if trained on a fence or the traditional two-wire horizontal support, tie to a stake and carry the upright to the top; pinch this off and lead two laterals out at the top, in either direction, fastening them to a wire or a fence; next season, cut off all but two of the buds on the main stem and train these, one on each side, along the lower level; fruit is borne on shoots of the previous year's wood. When the vine is fully grown, rub off all but 50-60 buds each year for best production of fruit.

APPLES (*Malus*)*:* always a favorite and with good reason. A bouquet of fragile pink and white in the spring buzzing with honeybees, bending with fruit in the fall, fruit which with careful storage peps up meals and snacks for months. Apple betty, apple strudel, apple pancakes, applesauce, apple jelly, apple juice, apple cider, apple champagne or just a great big red apple for the teacher—all are winners.

		Zone
'Battleford,'	'Brooks #27,'	
	'Heyer #12'	**1-4**
'Haralson,'	'Breakey,'	
	'Goodland'	**3-4**
'McIntosh,'	'Northern Spy,'	
'Red Delicious,'	**'Red Melba'**	**4-9**
'Golden Delicious,'	'Lobo,'	
	'Wealthy'	**5-9**

Crab Apples

'Osman,'	'Robin'	**1-2**
'Columbia'		**1-4**
'Dolgo'		**1-9**
'Florence'		**3-4**
'Hyslop'		**4-9**
'Kerr,'	'Renown,'	
	'Rescue'	**1-4**
'Trail'		**3-4**

PLUMS (*Prunus*)*:* the dewy bloom on a plum matches the exotic taste within —plum dowdy, plum jam, plum chutney, a staunch fruit for the first settlers in our land and still good now.

		Zone
'Bounty,'	'Dandy,'	
	'Northern'	**1-4**
'Assiniboine'		**1-4**
'Ivanovka,'	'Pembina'	**3-4**
'Grenville,'	'Redcoat,'	
	'Redglow'	**3-4**
'Burbank,'	'Damson,'	
'Early Golden,'	**'Italian,'**	
'Prune,'		
'Lombard,'	'Reine Claude,'	
'Shiro,'	'Stanley'	**5-9**

Cherry-Plum:

'Opata,'	'Dura,'	'Manor'	**1-4**

CHERRIES (*Prunus*)*:* Can she bake a cherry pie, Billy Boy?

		Zone
'Mongolian,'	'Nanking,'	
'Northern Limits,'	'Drilea'	**1-4**
Sweet Cherries: 'Bing,'	**'Lambeth,'**	
'Van,'	**'Sam,'** **'Napoleon'**	**5-9**
Sour Cherries: 'Montmorency'		**5-9**
Sand Cherries: 'Brooks,'		
	'Manmoor'	**1-4**
All will freeze.		

PEARS (*Pyrus*)*:* at home with a partridge in each tree, ambrosia when grown well. The leaves a glorious red in fall.

		Zone
'Pioneer'		**1-4**
'John,'	'Golden Spice'	
'Bartlett,'	'Bosc,'	**3-4**
	'Clapp's Favorite'	**5-9**

For areas where fire blight, a bacterial disease, is a problem: 'Moonglow,' 'Magness,' 'Dawn,' 'Maxine'

Never plant a pear tree by itself—always use two varieties for sure, successful pollination.

STRAWBERRIES (*Fragaria*)*:* the first and most delectable fruit of the year and grows well even in the northernmost parts of our land. In fact, here strawberries often do not even need winter protection because of early, persistent and deep snow cover, and, once established, often produce well for many years. In the more temperate zones they are best grown as a biennial planted one year to crop the next. The first year, pick off all blossoms and, if grown in hills, cut runners out, except from everbearing cultivars, which can safely have a small bounty of berries the first fall. If growing in matted rows, allow runners roughly 4 inches apart to develop between plants. Choose a spot with well-drained, light soil. Avoid low, frost-gathering places that will be a hazard to very early blossoms. Purchase certified plants if possible. In spring, set 2 feet apart, in rows 3 feet apart, dusting each planting hole first with chlordane to kill root weevil, grubs and wireworms; or plant in hills, 2-3 inches deep, the crown level with the ground, and shallow ditches in the earth on either side for watering. Fertilize at planting with a starter solution and mulch with straw, hay or plastic to keep the berries clean and free of disease (see Chapter 19). For winter protection in most parts of the country, lay evergreen branches or straw (wheat straw is the most free of weed seeds) over the plants after the ground is frozen hard.

Regular strains (those marked F especially good for freezing):

		Zone
'Sparkle' F		**1-2**
'Senator Dunlap'		**1-4**
'Bodgerbelle'		**1-9**
'Catskill' F,		
'Midway,'	'Surecrop,'	
'Fletcher,'	'Garnet'	**3-9**
'Earlidawn,'		
'Raritan,'	'Gala'	**4-9**

Everbearing (which means mainly a crop in spring, another in fall):

		Zone
'Gem,'	'Ogallala'	**1-4**
'Geneva,'		
'Red Rich,'	'Ozark Beauty'	**1-9**

Additional cultivars especially good for the northwest coast:

		Zone
'Puget Beauty,'	'Northwest'	**6-9**

Currants, Red (those marked F especially good for freezing):

		Zone
'Prince Albert,'	'Red Lake,' F	
'Stephens #9' F		**1-9**
'Cascade,'	'Fay's Prolific,'	
'Red Perfection' F		**3-9**

Recommended especially for the North: 'Red Cross,' 'Ruby Castle,' 'Victoria'

Currants, White (all good for freezing)

'Large White,'	'White Grape,'	
'White Imperial'		**1-9**

RASPBERRIES (*Rubus*): are the most subtle of bush fruits, a true delicacy. Buy certified stock if possible; plant in spring, setting crown 3 inches below the surface, 2 feet apart, in rows 6-8 feet apart; deep rooted, so prepare soil well down. Need moisture at all times, so water if no rain. Control weeds with herbicide before emergence, but only in established plantings, thereafter cultivate by hand or machine. For winter protection, in severe climates, bend over and weight down with poles or earth.

Raspberries, Red (those marked F good for freezing):

	Zone
'Chief' F, 'Latham' F, 'Citadel,' 'Madawaska,' 'Taylor,' 'Southland'	1-9
'Newburgh,' 'September' F, 'Williamette,' 'Heritage'	4-9

Raspberries, Black

	Zone
'Bristol 'F, 'Cumberland,' 'Morrison'F	4-9
'Munger'	5-9

Raspberries, Purple

	Zone
'Clyde,' 'Marion,' 'Sodus'F	4-9

BLACKBERRY (all will freeze)

	Zone
'Darrow,' 'Raven,' 'Lowden'	4-9
'Cascade,' 'Marion, 'Thorntree' (recommended for northwest coast, especially good for pies and jam)	5-9

BOYSENBERRIES and LOGAN-BERRIES: suitable only for northwest coast and mildest areas in other parts of the country. Check with your nurseryman.

GOOSEBERRIES (*Ribes*):

	Zone
'Abundance'	1-2
'Pixwell'	1-9
'Clark,' 'Oregon Champion'	3-9
'Captivator,' 'Fredonia,' 'Poorman'	4-9
America,' 'English,' 'Leveler' (recommended especially for west coast)	5-9

GRAPES (*Vitis*): a handsome vine as well as fruit, fragrant in blossom, intriguing pattern of sun and shade if used to roof a trellis; trained to a single stem when used as an ornamental or, where winter climate is severe, as a fan that can be bent to the ground for protection. Deep rooted, needs warmth, ample humus. Buy 2-year-old plants and cut back to 2 buds. Drive in a 4-foot stake when planting for support.

	Zone
'Beta'	1-5
'Fredonia,' 'Concord,' 'Niagara'	3-9
'Delaware,' 'Ontario'	4-9

SERVICEBERRIES (*Amelanchier alnifolia*): native to southern Yukon, Northwest Territories, all the Canadian prairie and northern provinces, and the northern plains of the United States. So good that Canada's Department of Agriculture Research Station at Beaverlodge, northern Alberta, is searching to find the best strains for cultivation. Fruit, which is borne on previous year's growth and old wood of 2-4-year-old trees, is sweet both raw and cooked, in pies, for wine and jelly.

	Zone
'Smoky,' 'Pembina,' 'Forestburg,' 'Northline' All will freeze.	1-4

BLUEBERRIES (*Vaccinium*): a true north-country berry, beloved wild by people, bears, chipmunks, birds. A gourmet's delight in pies and puddings (blueberry grunt is a favorite pudding on the east coast), muffins, pancakes. Cultivated blueberries must have acid soil (pH 4.52) organically rich, open, porous, well-drained. If you have slightly alkaline soil and wish to grow blueberries, it can be modified with ½ cup of dusting sulphur to 9 square feet and additives of acid peat, pine needles, leaf mold from oak or beech mixed thoroughly into the soil. If soil is highly alkaline, better not to try blueberries. Need full sun, a mulch to keep roots cool. Foliage turns glowing red in fall. Fruit may need to be netted against predators.

	Zone
'Bluecrop,' 'Blueray,' 'Darrow,' 'Earliblue,' 'Berkeley,' 'Herbert'. All will freeze.	4-9

APRICOTS (*Prunus*):

	Zone
'Perfection,' 'Blenheim Royal,' 'Tilton'	5-9

PEACHES (*Prunus*): probably the most luscious of all fruits

	Zone
'Red Haven,' 'Red Globe,' 'Loring,' 'Redskin,' 'Elberta,' 'J.H. Hale.' All will freeze.	5-9

NUT TREES

The few edible nut trees recommended for our part of the world are grown as other trees are, with one exception. Squirrels like nuts too, and winning the crop from them can be a lively pastime. For those who would like to try this game, or to leave a legacy of a nut plantation to their great-grandchildren, here is the list:

Butternut: *Juglans cinerea* (Zone 3)
Chestnut: Chinese — *Castanea mollissima* (Zone 5b)
Sweet — *Castanea dentata* (Zone 4b) should be planted only in the extreme east and west of the country where crippling disease is not already present.
(You must plant two chestnuts for effective cross-pollination, or have one in a nearby garden to mate with yours. New hybrids, presently being developed in Connecticut to be resistant to disease, should be on the market in a few years.)

Hazelnut, Filbert: *Corylus avellana* (Zone 5a) (You need two trees for successful cross-pollination.)
Heartnut: *Juglans ailanthifolia cordiformis* (Zone 4b)
Hickory: Shagbark: *Carya ovata* (Zone 4b)
Pecan: *Carya illinoensis* (Zone 7b)
Walnut, Carpathian: *Juglans* 'Carpathian' (Zone 4)
English: *Juglans regia* (Zone 7a)
Black: *Juglans nigra* 'Thomas' (Zone 3b)

FRUIT PESTS AND DISEASES

PESTS: are insects, grubs, caterpillars, moths, etc.

DISEASES: covers disorders caused by fungi, bacteria, viruses.

Follow rules for good garden practice, and to obtain perfect fruit follow a regular spray program as well, noting particularly, on the label of the material you use, the safe interval before last spraying and harvesting.

Keep up with current information on controls through your federal or state department of agriculture; new ones are constantly coming on the market and more experienced assessment of those already in use sometimes necessitates their withdrawal from the recommended list.

Home garden mixes, containing fungicides to prevent disease and insecticides to kill pests, are available at your garden supply store. If you need only a small quantity these may be more convenient and just as effective as single chemicals designed for one purpose only.

Whatever you use, follow manufacturer's recommendations on the label *to the letter*. These materials are poisons. Also, before using, read precautions in CHAPTER 19.

Dusts, easier to use than sprays, do not adhere as well and must be used oftener for comparable control. Always cover the whole plant with spray or dust, including undersides of leaves and stems.

On dwarf fruit trees, some gardeners eliminate the need for chemical sprays after fruit has formed by slipping a transparent plastic sleeve, open top and bottom, over each piece of fruit on the tree.

Aluminum foil spread on the ground under strawberries repels aphids and some other insects. Plastic sheeting on the ground also protects strawberries from some insects and soil splash.

The principal pests of fruit trees in home gardens are codling moth and apple maggot on apple; plum curculio on all tree fruits and cherry fruit flies (their maggots) on cherries. Apple maggot and plum curculio do not occur on the west coast. All other apple trees within 300 yards of *your* tree must be properly sprayed also to ensure perfect apples for you.

Sprays or dusts for fruit trees should include an insecticide for pests and a fungicide for diseases, especially in the early growing season. Controls sometimes vary in different regions, depending on climate and on pests or diseases which occur at different times. Consult your nearest government department of agriculture for special help. Most have pamphlets on this subject for the home gardener.

Control of fruit tree pests

EARLY FEEDING INSECTS affect apples
Trouble: caterpillars and plant bugs damage leaves and blossom buds.
Control: Spray with combined insecticide and fungicide after leaf buds open but *before* blossoms open. Repeat if weather wet.

CODLING MOTH affects apples
Trouble: large holes filled with brown castings, in fruit, which drops early. Caused by white or pinkish worm about ¾ inch long.
Control: spray with insecticide
  1. when petals fall
  2. 10 days after petal-fall
  3. during first 2 weeks of July
  4. third week of July
  5. every 10 days thereafter to mid-August, but no closer to harvest than the safe period stated on the package label.

APPLE MAGGOT affects apples
Trouble: white legless maggots about ⅕ inch long, tunnel through fruit. Worst attack in July. Infected apples drop early.
Control: same as the July and August sprays for codling moth (see above).

PLUM CURCULIO affects all fruit
Trouble: Crescent or D-shaped scar on fruit where eggs laid by brown beetle early in season. Grub feeds in fruit causing early drop of injured plums, peaches and apricots.
Control: Spray with insecticide when petals fall and again 10 days after.

CHERRY FRUIT FLIES (Their maggots) affect cherries
Trouble: White maggots feed on flesh near pit, ruining fruit. Caused by black flies with banded wings laying eggs which hatch into maggots.
Control: Spray with insecticide, sweet cherry only when buds are bursting; all cherries when petals fall; again 10 days later. Combine with a fungicide for disease control at the same time.

Small fruit pest control

Currants, Gooseberries, Grapes, Saskatoons
All benefit from applications of a home garden mixture (fungicide and insecticide in one material) sprayed on just before bloom appears and again immediately after fruit forms. Check the label for the safe time between last spray and harvest.

Raspberries, Blackberries, Loganberries, Boysenberries
Watch for borers and girdlers of canes — sometimes first sign is wilting of tips. Cut out and burn all canes showing swellings, holes or tunnels.

Diseases that commonly affect garden fruit

SCAB affects apple

Trouble: Olive-black spots appear on leaves, fruit and young fruit stems. Heavy fruit and leaf drop may occur. Early infection often results in deformed, cracked fruit. Heavy foliage infection weakens trees and reduces future crops. Fungus overwinters in old leaves, infects expanding leaves in spring. Degree of infection varies with temperature and length of time leaves remain wet from rain or dew.

Control: Spray trees with fungicide from *greentip* stage to *calyx* period. Once fungus suppressed through this time, disease may be kept in check with additional cover sprays at 10-14-day intervals. Number of sprays will vary, since they may be left out when weather hot and dry and if less susceptible varieties are grown (for these, consult your nurseryman when you buy).

SCAB affects pear

Trouble: Appears as dark, circular, sooty spots on both leaves and fruit. Later, spots on fruit become roughened and corky. Can cause serious defoliation and loss in yield where spring rainfall heavy. Disease caused by a fungus similar to apple scab, but differs in host preference.

Control: As buds show white, apply fungicide. Also spray trees with fungicide after petals have fallen.

FIRE BLIGHT affects pear, apple, quince

Trouble: First appears as infected blossoms, leaves turn brown to black and cling to tree, as though a flame had seared them. Infection may spread to trunk and main limbs, producing cankers in which bacteria overwinter and become a source of infection for next year. Bacteria is spread by bees and other insects visiting blossoms.

Control: Remove all diseased wood while dormant. Disinfect pruning tools with 20% Javex or rubbing alcohol between each cut. Remove all suckers and water sprouts. Do not fertilize heavily. Spray during bloom and postbloom period with streptomycin antibiotic. To reduce spread of blight on twigs apply fungicide during hot, humid weather and after removal of infected twigs.

POWDERY MILDEW affects apple, cherry, raspberry, grape, gooseberry, others

Trouble: Small, indistinct white patches appear on upper leaf surface, later becoming powdery or mealy. Severely attacked leaves have tendency to curl upward during hot, dry weather. On some crops, blossoms are attacked and may wither and drop. Terminal leaves decrease in size and twig growth may be shortened. Infected grape berries drop off. Spends winter in buds of many plant species.

Control: Reasonable control usually with fungicide sprays. Apply 3 or 4 times — when new growth 4-6 inches long; before bloom; two cover sprays at 2 week intervals after fruit set. Avoid planting in poorly drained soil or where aeration poor.

VERTICILLIUM WILT affects raspberries, strawberries, sweet cherries

Trouble: With raspberry, leaves shrivel and drop from bottom to top of cane until only few left at tip. Cane usually becomes dark blue or purple. Favored by cool, wet weather and poor soil drainage. Black raspberries highly susceptible. Fungus invades roots. With strawberry, leaves become pale, wilt, turn reddish. Severe when moisture low. Later, affected leaves dry out, turn brown and die. Plants may die quickly or gradually. Symptoms sometimes mistaken for fertilizer burning.

Control: Do not plant where tomatoes, potatoes, peppers, eggplant have been growing for previous 3-4 years. Choose a well-drained site for your plantings. Carefully dig out and destroy infected plants. Plant healthy stock, certified if available.

ANTHRACNOSE affects raspberries

Trouble: Symptoms may occur on all above-ground parts but most common on canes. Numerous small, greyish spots with purple borders, varying in size, run together, bark may crack. On leaves spots are purple, later brown and may drop out. Infected green fruit fails to mature and dries up.

Control: Keep rows wide and well pruned to let air circulate. Spray with fungicide while dormant or just as buds begin to break; spray again immediately after harvest.

BROWN ROT affects peach, cherries, plums, apricots

Trouble: Small brown spots increasing in size until entire fruit becomes brown, soft and rotten. Often covered with powdery light-brown or grey fungus, which spends winter in mummified fruits. Loss most severe during hot, humid weather at harvest time.

Control: Start spraying with fungicide when blooms open. Repeat at 7-day intervals through blossoming if weather wet, then again 2-3 weeks before harvest. Control insects that puncture fruit with insecticides.

LEAF SPOT affects cherries

Trouble: Minute purple spots on upper surface of leaves which enlarge but may remain quite small if infection heavy. Later, area in centre of spot may die and fall out, giving a shot-hole effect. Many leaves turn yellow before falling — usually early in the season — and vigor of tree is reduced. Most wild and cultivated species of *Prunus* are infected including apricot, but not peach. Winters in dead leaves. When temperature nears 60°F. in spring, fungus begins to spread. May continue from before bloom to 2 months later.

Control: Spray fungicide at petal-fall and thereafter as needed with an application immediately after harvest.

LEAF SPOT affects currants, raspberries, loganberries, strawberries, others

Trouble: Numerous small circular red-brown spots on leaves which often turn yellow and drop prematurely. Frequent rain or heavy dew before bloom favors outbreak of this disease.

Control: Spray with fungicide once at prebloom period and again post-bloom.

BLACK ROT affects grapes

Trouble: Appears on fruit as a light area surrounded by a brownish line later. Berries become hard, black and shrivelled. Fungus overwinters in old leaves.

Control: Spray with fungicide just before blossoming and immediately again after bloom is over.

GREY MOLD affects strawberries, raspberries, others

Trouble: Appears first as small water-soaked spot on fruit which may increase in size and involve entire fruit with soft, watery rot, usually covered with grey fungus. Most prevalent on mature fruit in excessively moist weather conditions.

Control: Apply 1-2 sprays fungicide after bloom.

ROOT ROT affects strawberries, raspberries, others

Trouble: Crown and roots discolor, plants become stunted and die. Caused by various soil fungi. Poor drainage makes plants susceptible.

Control: Avoid planting on heavy poorly-drained soil. Use disease-free plants and protect from winter injury.

VIRUSES (mosaic, leaf, curl, ring spot) affect strawberries, raspberries, others

Trouble: Leaves mottled, misshapen, dwarfed, curled on tip; leaflets abnormally green or rolled at margins, yellow-green rings or wavy patterns. Plants stunted. Many viruses carried by insects. Most survive in perennial crops and weeds.

Control: Buy certified plants if possible. Destroy infected plants that could start new infections. Control virus-carrying insects. Eliminate weeds.

PART II

OF
PRACTICAL
HELP

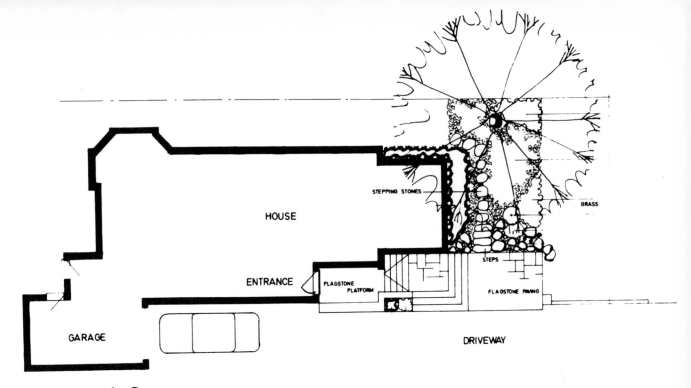

Labels in figure: HOUSE, GARAGE, ENTRANCE, DRIVEWAY, STEPPING STONES, GRASS, FLAGSTONE PLATFORM, STEPS, FLAGSTONE PAVING

13 DESIGN AND DECORATION

Design in a garden, as the great landscape architect Humphrey Repton said 200 years ago, is ultimately poetry. It should draw from you a personal, pleasurable, emotional response — a tingle down your spine; an appreciative pause; if you feel like it, a Swan Lake leap in the air in your bare feet on a dewy morning — whatever is *your* way of feeling delight.

It comes with the sensitive handling of line, form, balance, color, rhythm, perspective, scale and, most of all, space. Some people seem to have this instinctively, others have the pleasure of learning it little by little.

FIRST THINGS

Note first that good garden design is often the result of an amalgam of opposites. It should give you at one time a sense of calm and repose, at another, excitement and stimulation. There should be a feeling of sanctuary close about you, yet an exhilarating view of limitless sky. There should be beauty thoughtfully planned, yet always the possibility for surprise; the tonic of timeless strength in rocks and trees, yet also the precious fragility of flowers; a feeling of distance which often, by measure, is not actually there. In other words, your garden should be designed so that it is a place to draw from you an emotional response whatever the time of day, whatever the season.

To begin with, think of it as an open-air extension of your house. The front garden is the entry, the sides are hallways, the back garden is a living and family room for everyone to enjoy.

YOUR FRONT GARDEN IS YOUR PUBLIC FACE

The pleasant response you want to create is that your house is attractive and well-set; that you, the people who live in it, are the welcoming, safe-harboring kind.

To do this, design a generous walk to the front door; keep plantings, walls or fences low and in correct scale so that your house is well seen. Use good-looking fixtures for outdoor service lighting for steps and entry ways and, if you can, hide the source of the light. Place trees that will eventually grow large well out at the sides to frame rather than block the windows. If they get too big, replace them. Choose foundation plants whose habit is low and spreading. Keep lawn areas horizontal or only gently sloping and uninterrupted with flower beds.

If the grade drops sharply within a short distance between house and street, build a wall and top it with a flat terrace rather than have an awkward steep slope of grass or a fussy-care rock garden.

Use ground covers or a stone mulch with a containing curb instead of grass where street trees overhang your lawn, for their light-cutting foliage and greedy roots will make it impossible to grow good grass there.

If you plant a vine on the front of your house, never let it upholster the whole facade. Use bright flowers in neat, controlled ways — a pair of tubs or urns to frame the front door, narrow flowery borders up the walk, cascades of bloom tumbling out of window boxes. Keep them fresh and vigorous all the growing year and substitute small evergreens for winter.

Choose specimen plants for your front garden for their architectural quality — a broad-leaved evergreen wintercreeper to twist up a chimney; a pair of blue-green pyramidal junipers to flank the front door; an exotic clump of devil's-walking-stick to stand beside a wall; a climbing rose to festoon a side-door trellis; one dramatic rhubarb plant beside a step.

While you're working these things out, check how your house looks from all approaches. Take black and white snapshots from different angles and in all seasons to see the bones of what you're doing without color to divert your eye. Adjust and improve from year to year — you're working here with constantly changing materials.

THE SIDE GARDENS ARE HALLWAYS

Most side gardens are simply walkways from front to back. Make the path itself direct, smooth, hard-surfaced and wide enough to take garden equipment such as wheelbarrows and mowers without squeezing. If the space is narrow, don't attempt to grow grass there, rather use stone or pebble mulches to border the walk. If you have to pick up a change in grade from front to back, do it with ramps rather than steps for easier handling of equipment.

Keep plants in these spaces to a minimum. Choose trees of tall, thin habit (listed in nursery catalogues as columnar or fastigiate) and vines that lie flat against the wall, as ivy does. For the boundary, you'll find that fences take less space than a hedge. A trellis over the walk with a leafy vine trained over it — a climbing hydrangea? a wild grape? — makes an intriguing feature because of the sudden pleased response to the high ceiling of the sky when you step out from under it. For a finished look, nothing is so good-looking as gates to close the space between your house and those on either side. And a "look-through" of something as ingenious as an old black iron hot-air register is clever expertise in a gate.

Be aware that open spaces will be as important as things you put in them: that a suggestion of mystery — perhaps a path leading out of sight behind a tree — is delightful: that privacy from neighbors and street is always pure pleasure: that interesting, colorful plants all the year round are bound to draw a happy response from everyone. Then go on to plan your back garden design in terms of what you would do with a living room indoors. What will you put on the floor? the walls? the ceiling? Think of furniture as flowers and especially chosen plants, and the ornaments you put in the garden as its final, fine-touch decoration.

The floor can be green plantings, applied loose materials such as stone chips, pavings; or, if the grade is very steep, wood decking makes a marvelous design feature. Lawn grass, the finest green flooring of all, is flattering for any garden but it must be laid on well-drained ground and get a minimum of 6 hours of sunshine daily. Ground covers can be successfully used where grass would grow poorly. The most popular are broad-leaved and evergreen — periwinkle, pachysandra, ivy. They take about 2-3 years of weeding and pinning down of new runners before they really cover the ground, but from then on are lovely to look at and easy to care for. They're also a glossy background for plantings of spring bulbs and a handy hideaway for unpretty leaves of ripening bulbs. (For others, and their special culture, see CHAPTER 24: GROUND COVERS.)

Applied loose materials can be stone or wood chips, pebbles or cobbles, trap rock, crushed tile or gravel. They won't bind firmly together, so if you expect to walk on them often plan to lay a path through them of flagstone or precast stones.

Large areas of pavings, especially useful for patios and sitting terraces because they're smooth and dry quickly, can be flagstone, precast stone of various kinds and patterns, brick or poured concrete with a textured finish of tiny aggregate pebbles or a roughly-brushed surface. Make the size generous, the placement convenient to the house, with a variety of sun and shade for different times of the year, and a beckoning view even if you must create it with thoughtful planting.

If you happen to be blessed with a small forest of tall trees in your back garden, a thoroughly lovely and low-maintenance design can be done with the whole floor in flagstone paving, laid dry, interspersed with beds of low, shade-loving evergreens, dwarf flowering shrubs and ground covers and the trees pruned and thinned to a high leafy canopy. Without the trees, this design would be too hot for comfort.

Wood decking is wonderful for steep, drop-away land where, to have any level floor at all in your garden, you must build it. Natural sites for this treatment are craggy rocks that overhang the sea, a lake or a river; a rim of a valley; a high, steep hill. Again, make the space generous, the material — cedar or redwood is best — as long-lasting as possible. Grow flowers in wooden boxes or lightweight containers and be sure that your deck is built to carry their weight.

Think too of water as a possible garden floor. A dark reflecting pool covering part of the ground can be one of the most exciting features you can possibly design — a mirror of all that's lovely above it when it's still, a swiftly shifting pattern of riffles on a windy day, a glassy pond on an icy one, a hospitable bath for hundreds of wild birds to splash in. There's never a moment when a pool like this is not pure joy. And to a small boy, well . . . For best viewing, design it to be below eye level. For best reflections, choose plants for the far side that are graceful and delicate in color. Swirl part of its rim with ferns, pierce it with a planting of water iris, dart it with a carp or two.

THE WALLS

The walls of your garden are the fences, screens, and plantings that give you protection and privacy and a backdrop to set off your plants. To establish the line of your property, landscape architects advise that you set or plant precisely on the surveyed line even if, to create the impression of greater distance, you also make a second more free-line boundary inside the first one.

Fence and wall heights must often comply with municipal bylaws, but the design can be anything you choose. Open patterns are best for they give a sense of lightness and airiness. Screens, freestanding or attached to the house, give protection from side sun glare and wind. They're much the best way to hide an unsightly view or to achieve privacy for a patio.

As the walls of your garden, plantings can be many things — a row of columnar trees, a variety of trees and shrubs, an informal or formal hedge. For faithful, constant beauty, summer and winter, and gentle sifting of wind, needle evergreens are tops. Their broody darkness is also a stunning foil for the delicate grace of smaller trees and flowering shrubs planted in front of them.

Where neighboring buildings are the walls of your garden, try to get permission to paint them a pale color. If you can't paint, plant a vine to conceal them.

If you have a neighboring view too big and ugly to screen completely, clever design plants one large tree to partially block it then places an outstanding feature somewhere else in the garden to divert the eye — a pool with a bubbling jet, a birdhouse, a figure of St. Francis, the patron saint of gardens, a translucent fibreglass screen with a weeping cherry tree trained over it, a fluttering mobile, perhaps your own personal totem pole.

St. Francis, patron saint of gardens.

THE CEILING

The ceiling of your garden can be sky or trees or perhaps a roofed trellis with a leafy vine. My only advice is never to let it become completely closed in. No matter how much you love a forest, no matter how much it hurts to cut down a tree or prune a vine, for your own soul's sake, always keep open a place where you can see the sky.

From a design point of view, high trees usually need skillful pruning to reveal their trunk and stretching arms and, if leaf growth is thick and dark, to let dappling light filter through to the plants below. This is a job for experts.

If your garden faces south and a big tree stands at the rear between you and the sun, where its shadow falls lay a surface of smooth paving or lawn. When the tree is bare its massive, bony, silent, moving shadow can be eerily thrilling on a sunny winter day, a true tingler in moonlight on snow.

If you don't have such trees and must plant them to get such excitement, check with your nurseryman about sizes available, eventual mature height and possible growth per year. Some trees grow more quickly than others; some, too, are more suitable as canopy cover.

Sunshades and patio roofs of various materials are instant snap-up for garden design. One of the best is natural fibreglass framed in cedar or metal bars. It has a translucent, soap-bubble look, is light, strong and intriguing with vines growing over it. Wood beams with climbing plants trained over them also make a good open trellis roof. Canvas, eyeletted around its rim and laced to a pipe frame, comes in wonderfully giddy colors and has the advantage of casting shade in summer and being removable to let sun through in winter.

THE FURNITURE (nonsitting)

Plants, to be fine furniture in your garden, should be hardy for your area (see PARTS III and V) and deliberately chosen to create interest at different times of the year. Use them with restraint, setting each to be individually seen.

For longest beauty, choose those notable for their flowers, fruit and foliage and, if trees or shrubs, for their winter frame of trunk and branch, their often fascinating bark. Learn their idiosyncrasies — for instance, that the light-filtering habit of honey locust is good if you want to grow grass under it, that the fruit-dropping of some crab apples, mulberries and thorns makes them messy over patios or paths. (See CHAPTER 20: TREES.)

Think of trees as an accent standing alone, or planted in groups or rows. Plant a pendulous one for its grace and flowing movement in the wind. Choose an oddball to spark party talk — a contorted willow or hazel that looks as though a mean witch had cast a spell on it, the strange upside-downness of a Camperdown elm, the historical oddity of a ginkgo or a dawn redwood.

Use shrubs, dramatic flowering perennials and annuals for their color, form and line. Repeat large clumps of one color and one plant in different parts of the garden rather than a mixture of many. Add interest by choosing them for different textures, for wind-drifting or pinching fragrance, for grace of shape. Put the earliest blooming ones where they will be seen from indoors, the smallest where you'll be near them often; at the height of its bloom light each at night.

THE FURNITURE (for sitting and setting upon)

Chairs and tables to furnish your garden should be simple, practical and good looking. The best so far are molded aluminum with a long-lasting finish. They're light to move about, yet not so light that they blow around. They're easy to clean and wonderfully comfortable to sit or lie on. Unfortunately they're relatively expensive. Some day perhaps there'll be finely designed garden furniture that will be both practical and reasonable in cost.

Patio and terrace walls that are designed to be sat on are dandy for extra seating for parties. If they can be built for storage as well, they can hold toys and games equipment and a batch of bright cushions.

ORNAMENT

The decoration of your outdoor living room — its ornament — should be what you like best. If you're not sure what this is, begin by observing good garden ornament in other places — public and private gardens, art galleries, exhibitions, garden supply stores, books and magazines, catalogues of garden ornament suppliers. Teach yourself to have a seeing eye so that you recognize possibilities in what some people would call junk — a fragment of iron or stone from the wreckers, a big green glass Italian wine bottle — all kinds of everyday things.

A few basic rules fit the choosing of all decoration for your garden:

It should look, when it's in place, as though it belonged there. Materials should match or blend, in substance and color, with your house or be in sharp contrast to it. A pair of black cast-iron ducks standing beside a pool, for instance, will look more belonging in our part of the world than a pink plastic flamingo. Yet when you plan an awning for a terrace, you may want to plunk for the most way-out pattern and color you can find: this then, doesn't fit in, it deliberately stands out.

It must be in scale with people, with your house, with its own setting and with your garden. Something too big will look as though it should never be there at all: something too small will never be seen.

If it is to stay outdoors all winter, it must be in a material, finish and construction to stand freezing without breaking. If you have a smoggy city garden, it should be cleanable. This doesn't mean that you must only use pieces that stand up to these conditions, but be prepared to move breakable ones indoors in winter and to give some finishes extra care. Sculptured stone can be left to weather. Bronze is indestructible. Iron or steel must be painted or deliberately left to rust. Terra cotta and pottery must be taken indoors.

It should look neither cute nor coy. Gnomes and plaster rabbits are fine for a little girl's playhouse garden but they downgrade a grown-up one.

The most intriguing pieces play a second role — wind chimes to add the faint tinkle of faraway bells, a sundial to tell the time, a fountain to splash, sparkle and spill, a handsome container that enhances the plants growing in it.

PLANT CONTAINERS

Just about anything that will hold a quart to a bushel of earth will hold a growing plant; but you want something of good design, of interesting material and practical to care for.

Premolded planters in asbestos fibre and cement, fibreglass or plastic are strong and lightweight. Wood boxes and tubs — the best are redwood or cedar — can be bought or made to your own specifications and finished to match the trim of your house. Improvised ones can be made from old barrels or kegs cut in half, drilled for drainage and reinforced at the top with an extra hoop of binder wire. Wooden butter boxes, drilled, stained and painted, make a good blocky grouping and small pickled herring buckets set to one side of steps or sills can hold a vivid plant or two.

Various gimmicks can be used to catch overflow water if your containers are not sitting directly on earth. Clay saucers, shallow galvanized iron boxes, small pots, metal or glass pie-plates painted to match the container are handy and inexpensive. If you want to be able to move a heavy container around to encourage even growth on all sides, a dolly of an inconspicuous wood platform and castors can be made to fit the base.

Iron urns give a most distinguished air to a doorway, but it's a good idea to grow the plants for them in clay pots to slip into the urns. In sun, the metal becomes so hot, roots in direct contact are burned and killed. Fibreglass copies — a much better buy though sometimes more expensive — do not get so hot. Cast aluminum reproductions of Victorian urns are also on the market and have the advantage of being lighter than iron to handle but they too get very hot in sun. Precast concrete pieces, some of better design than others, are also available.

Self-watering boxes, built on the same principles as the window box illustrated in CHAPTER 3, are a joy to look after. Flowers bloom exuberantly in them and care is minimal. Syrup pots, coal scuttles, copper kettles, all make imaginative containers for plants but if they have no holes drilled in the bottom watering must be done carefully. A standard tree in a handsome container can do wondrous things for a patio — the tree can be a swish fuchsia, a lantana with its bright embroidered flowers, a geranium or, most appealing of all, a tree rose.

Strawberry jars capture the fancy of many gardeners and one of the prettiest is a sky-blue jar filled with bronze-leaved, pink-flowered begonias. There's a trick to the planting. You must tamp the soil down hard as you put each layer in place, then lay the plant with its crown barely out of the hole, add more soil and tamp some more until the jar is full. If the soil is only loosely put in, it settles downward, pulls the plants back into the jar, and, in effect, strangles them. A dreadful fate for the begonias and no flowers for all your trouble.

PLANT DESIGN IN CONTAINERS

Freestanding containers that you want to look like flowery islands are best designed with tall plants in the middle, medium height next, with trailers and cascades around the rim (see lists with CHAPTER 3). Containers whose back will be against a wall need be planted on three sides only, or even with just one exuberant vine, such as a giant rose-pink morning glory, and a frill of white sweet alyssum at its base.

If your container is to be in shade — particularly the heavy shade of a patio roof — choose shade-loving flowers (see CHAPTER 6) or use plantings of all green — ferns, foliage houseplants outdoors on vacation, trailing ivies. These can be stunning in white pots.

MINIATURE GARDENS

A whole hobby in itself, and an absorbing one, is the growing of miniatures. A decorative one too if a large planter or, as is often seen in England, an old sink or cattle trough is used to hold a tiny but diverse garden of these plants. Dwarf evergreens, rock plants, true miniatures of larger ones like the tiny ½-inch roses or a water lily that could comfortably sit on a shirt button, can all be planted as though in a full-scale garden. Care is mainly a manicuring job and placing should be where it can be closely seen and enjoyed. (See page 345 for recommended books for this special kind of gardening.)

BONSAI

As decoration in your garden design, a good collection of bonsai is a showstopper. Again, their miniature beauty calls for an intimate setting. One of the best is a shelf for each small tree, fastened against a high wood screen with an open trellis or lath roof overhead to break the strongest heat of the sun. Another is a table-height platform with various sizes of blocks to hold the containers so that the individual beauty of each small tree is fully shown.

ARCHITECTURAL ORNAMENT

The fine finish of the design of a garden is often small architectural details. For ideas for these look in books and magazines in your public library. There are graceful finials for walls and gateposts in pictures of the gardens of Colonial Williamsburg, intriguing details in iron, stone and wood in illustrations of French, English, Italian and, in particular, Japanese gardens. There's good contemporary design in modern books and magazines.

And don't overlook the wrecker's yard in your own city. Many an old building being torn down has produced, almost for pickings, an interesting piece of carving to hold up a plant shelf on an outside wall of a terrace, a pedestal for a house fern on holiday on the porch, an old weathervane to mount on a martin house. Old filigree iron makes handsome gates and fences.

SCULPTURE

I think of sculpture in a garden as any beautiful in-scale shape added for the purpose of ornament. It can be a piece of driftwood, carved into rhythmic twists and turns by wind and storms and set on a flat stone at the base of steps; a massive hunk of stone — perhaps from your own excavation — with a feathery juniper or a sword-leaved yucca at its base; an abstract form in steel or iron; a contemporary figure in stone; something as traditional as a bronze fairy riding a dragonfly over the riffle of a pool; something as small and inconsequential (but fascinating) as a cast brass butterfly for a tap head. These and a hundred others can be found for the looking.

Each piece must be assessed by you. No one else can make the decision of whether it's right or wrong for *your* garden. If in time any seem wrong, send them off to a rummage sale. If they're right, the personal, pleasurable, emotional response will always be there.

As that famous philosopher Charlie Brown says, "Happiness is walking in the grass in your bare feet, climbing a tree, a pile of leaves, three friends in a sandbox and no fighting."* Perhaps for you in your garden happiness will be a psychedelic fountain, a cote of cooing doves, or a sculpture of three warriors forever fighting. The choice is yours.

For further help: PART I: What is your kind of Garden? CHAPTER 16: Making a new garden on new land, and CHAPTER 17: The remake of an old garden, PART III: The fine points of growing good garden plants well.

---

*From *Happiness is a Warm Puppy* by Charles M. Schultz © 1962 United Feature Syndicate.

WHERE TO GET EXPERT HELP
WITH THE DESIGN OF YOUR GARDEN

Landscape architect

Look in the yellow pages of your telephone directory for listings. Landscape architects visit your garden, discuss your wishes and your budget, basing their charge for this on an hourly fee. If you decide to proceed, they will then draw up plans and specifications, basing the fee for this, which is fixed by the American or Canadian Society of Landscape Architects, on a percentage of the cost of the contract. You may then send these plans out for bidding and go on to supervise the job yourself. Or — and by my measure this is money well spent — you may retain the architect not only to draw plans and specifications but also to call for tenders and supervise the whole job while it is being done, making sure that you get the best possible building and material. All landscape architects are happy to draw up plans that may be accomplished in stages, over a period of years.

Garden designer

Sometimes a free lance, sometimes on staff in a retail nursery. Again, check the yellow pages of the directory. If free lance, the fee is based on a percentage of the contract; discuss this in your first conversation so that all is clear. If employed by a nursery, designer's fees are usually part of the contract for the whole construction and planting of the garden.

Landscape contractor

Usually a builder and planter who comes in after plans are made, but many will advise clients who wish their help. Some have garden designers on staff.

Government and education

Many government departments of agriculture and universities have publications to help the home gardener to plan his garden. For lists, write to yours.

Public libraries, Garden Centres, Garden Clubs and Horticultural Societies are all excellent sources of help.

FOR A SPECIAL
TOUCH OF MAGIC

Camouflage the boundary by informal planting in front of it.

Create the illusion of distance in a small garden with a mirror set in the fence, angled to reflect the best view; in a large garden by dividing it with a wall or hedge opening to a view beyond.

Overcome an ugly view and deepen distance by building a double fence and planting a tree or trees between.

Place an eye-catching feature at the end of your longest vista.

Plant small-leaved plants farthest away, large-leaved ones close at hand. Use soft grey plants — Russian olive is ideal — to add the out-of-focus fuzziness of distance.

Use line skillfully. For your garden to appear larger, design paths, lawn, and edges of beds on a diagonal line, lengthwise of the garden, starting from the point where you usually view it. For a serene, fluid look, make these lines flow rhythmically between two obvious points — the house to a pool, a clump of trees to a large boulder or planter, a corner of a wall to a piece of sculpture. If you prefer a symmetrical, evenly-balanced plan with straight rather than curved lines — and this is often the best design for a very small garden — deliberately make the lines of the side plantings converge at the farthest point. Viewers will then think the garden much deeper than it really is.

Increase the third dimension of a naturally flat garden by changing the level of the ground — make the middle near the house lower, then slope up towards the rear.

Double the view of the sky by reflecting it in still water.

Use color with ingenuity — blue to repeat the sky in chairs, umbrellas, screens, on the wall and ceiling of an overlooking porch: dark brown, green or black as the base of a shallow reflecting pool to make it seem deeper, or as the color of pole supports for patio roofing to make it seem airy and floating.

Open up a good view of the distance, if you have one, by skillful pruning; remember that plants grow and change, so check regularly and correct as necessary.

14 PERMANENT FEATURES

A sense of well-being fills the air in a garden with wisely planned features. Walks and paths beckon. Fences and walls have a sheltering look, firmly closing out noise and intrusion. Steps are in right places and generously fit your foot. A pool mirrors the sky or is a gay burble, a setting for a gorgeous water lily, a spilling silver sheet or a place for a warm sun bath or a cool swim. A patio or terrace is comfortable and used. Flowers in raised or framed beds look, at one and the same time, contained yet spilling over, neat yet not too neat.

Essential services — hose connections and watering systems, electric waterproof plugs, compost heap, trash storage, delivery access are there. Extras such as a cold frame or hotbed, tool storage and work area (some gardeners would list this with essentials), a dry space for a woodpile, a small salad and herb garden by the kitchen door, posts for a line to hang drip-dry curtains in the sun — these are where you choose to have them, there are enough of them and they're in the right places. Your garden has an all's-right-with-the-world look.

It begins with thoughtful planning. Visit other people's gardens, go on garden tours, read books on how to build and look at pictures in magazines, visit lumber yards, stone and brickyards, and find out what materials are suitable, durable and available. Match what you can spend to the estimated cost of what you plan, remembering that many constructed items can have a high original cost but low maintenance both in money and time. Consult experts. Take into account that you and your family's habits will change. Some day you may want a swimming pool that you cannot afford now. Allow for it in the beginning — for a place to put it, a way to get a bulldozer or earth digger in to excavate it at less expense than by men with shovels and wheelbarrows. Your small fry may need a sandpile for only a few years, so make it a shape that can later become a reflecting pool or a flowery bed for a treasured plant collection.

WALKS AND PATHS (I use the words interchangeably)

All essential paths should have a smooth surface for safe walking and easy snow-shovelling. They should be graded (1 foot in 50 feet), with a slight hump in the middle, to drain and dry quickly after a rain, be non-slip, firmly made and almost level. This is no place for wiggly stones, puddle-collecting spots, nor soft or loose material into which you can sink.

At the beginning, they should be set slightly above the level of the ground on each side, for it will be only a matter of time until accumulated top dressings or grass clippings lift the ground even with then higher than the path. It will be doubly important then to have the path properly drained so that it does not become a canal or a skating rink. (After all, it is a champion gardener you want to be, not Hans Brinker on his silver skates, or the man who, with both arms and legs in plaster casts, could prune a rose with his teeth.)

The surface should be hard permanent material unless you want a wandering, woodsy path through a wild flower planting when pine needles, wood chips or shredded bark make the right topping. Materials commonly used for working paths are flagstone, brick, precast concrete or exposed aggregate (small, smooth-surfaced stones embedded in concrete). All can be installed dry.

This means on a well-drained sand bed without mortar. Alternatively they can be set on a poured concrete slab and mortared at the joints. This is more permanent and expensive than the first way and should be done by a builder, unless you are especially skilled at this work. Do not mortar stones laid dry without a concrete base. They will heave and the mortar will crack. But do, if you like the idea, grow creeping plants such as thyme in the crevices of a dry-set path for stepping fragrance.

Formula for setting flagstones, precast stones and bricks dry in sand

First make sure the area you plan to path is well drained. If it is not, lay drainage tile through it to a dry well. Excavate to 7 inches, lay 3-inch layer of gravel, spreading and tamping well. Follow with 1 inch of sand, again tamping. Place flags, slabs or bricks and fill crevices with more sand, pouring it into cracks, over the walk and brushing in. Water lightly and add more sand till spaces between the stones are filled. Check your work with a spirit level as you go along.

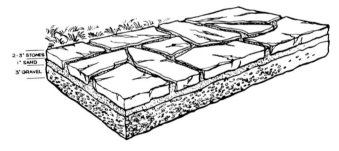

Correct width is a must. Walks 50 feet or less in length should ideally be a minimum of 4 feet wide. A lesser width may be used if space is limited and if such a measurement is in scale with other details in the design. For every extra 50 feet, add another 6 inches to the width. Two people walking side by side — what you expect when guests come — need a minimum of 5 feet in width.

Curve a path when there is an immovable object — a 200-year-old oak perhaps — or if it fits into the general design. If a path must climb a steep slope, take it on the diagonal with a gradual rise. The recommended grade is 8 percent, or about 1 foot in 12½ feet.

THE FRONT WALK

The approach to your house should say "Welcome!" The recipe is a generous walk, a wide entry, good night lighting and, if possible, a canopy, so that guests wait out of the rain. If you need steps, three or more is a safer number than two. One is so dangerous it's never recommended. Electric light shining on them at night is a thoughtful courtesy.

If the walk comes from a driveway at the side, across the front of the house, keep it well forward so that eaves will not drip on it to make it wet or slippery. A slight trough in the soil filled with gravel or pebbles, between walk and house, is a good way to control the collecting of drip. (For construction and materials for walks, see preceding section.)

ACCESS WALKS TO SIDE, AND REAR

Smooth and level is the ticket, and a convenient width for a wheelbarrow to go through without scraping your hands on walls at the sides — a minimum of 3½ feet. If there are slopes, ramps will be more useful than steps. Keep plantings to vines, narrow trees or bushes so that the path is clear. If it must turn at right angles — perhaps through a gate or round the corner of the house — hard-surface the inside of the turn. Only sergeant majors turn wheelbarrows at right angles, the rest of us cut the corner.

STEPPING STONES

Precast stepping stones.

This is a pleasant, informal way to lead to, or through, the garden, but not businesslike enough for your front walk or access walks. If flagstone, lay by setting stone, usually random-cut or square, on the grass where you want to step. Cut around it, lift, take out sod and replace stone. You may need to add a little sand beneath to set it firmly level.

Other good materials are often available locally. Precast circles or oblongs you lay the same way as flags. Smooth slate has a more sophisticated finish and one handsome kind, a dark blue-grey stone, can be very tidy and tailored if cut precisely and set in a bed of rolled and tamped blue-black trap rock. Plastic sheeting laid under the trap rock keeps it weed free, a work-saver you will constantly bless. Wood rounds are possible as stepping stones, but slippery after a heavy dew or rain, and they rot easily.

DRIVEWAYS

The most direct route from the street to the garage makes sense for the placement of the driveway. Cars need, on the average 12 feet in width for a single drive, 22 feet for a double one. This allows 2 feet of clearance at the side, and for stepping out onto surfacing rather than lawn. Coming from and going out to the street, the corner of the drive and lawn or sidewalk should be slightly curved to make for easy turning.

In building circular drives, a single one needs an inside radius of 18 feet

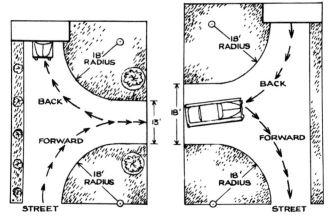

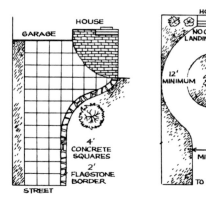

Two U-turn driveways that allow car to enter street going forward.

Left: Combination of drive and walk in concrete slabs and flagstone.

Right: measurements for a single, circular drive.

minimum. For a double one, the inside radius is the same, but you need a width of 22 feet, minimum, for passing at the turn. Make no curve at the landing point at the front door.

Many drivers, for safety's sake, include a Y turn in their driveway layout so that they may always enter the street going forward. (For needed measurements and plan for this and the circular drive, see drawing).

Surfaces for drives should be of materials that are locally practical and of a cost to fit your budget. A gravel drive, draining away from the house, covered with several inches of loose stone chips is both clean and dry but should be curbed to prevent scattering of the stones onto the lawn, street or walks. Such materials are also hard on good shoes and almost too handy for scampy little boys looking for something to throw. Asphalt or black top is commonly used and its dark color partially hides oil stains from parked cars. For a small house with a single drive, making driveway and front walk all in one, of the same material, is pleasing and practical. For this, you might consider exposed aggregate or brushed concrete marked off in 4-foot squares, each bordered with granite setts or flagstone.

Measurements for single and double driveways.

FENCES

Once in a long, long while a group of neighbors will agree to no fences and plan their gardens as a communal park. This rarely works, mainly because every family's idea of what their garden should be is different. Before long, somebody's dog digs up somebody else's pet tulips and one family's boys use the whole place for a football field. And, let's face it, most of us, homing in from the hurtle of the world, like the comforting haven of our own clearly defined territory.

Design You want to know your fences are there yet not have them jump out at you. Better they blend than blare. They should be sturdy, straight and in the right place. If you are sharing costs fifty-fifty with your neighbor, this can be *on* the surveyed line between your two properties. But if you wish to make all the decisions about design and material, put your fence 1 inch *inside* your line and pay for it all yourself. This is sometimes the only way to have a continuous, well-designed look of the same pattern, material and finish all the way around. From a good design point of view, this is extremely desirable.

Before you choose the design and settle on measurements, check the local building laws on allowable heights. Some localities have official Fence Viewers (sounds like a heavenly job!) who will, on request, visit your lot and advise you on your rights. Whatever design you decide to build, begin with a professional survey. Investigate available materials and their cost. Most fences are wood — cedar or redwood have the longest life — and some of the best wood is rough sawn. This makes a light-catching and intriguing texture. Patterns can be one of many. Louvers of 1-inch boards set vertically or horizontally are popular. White pickets come in dozens of designs and look especially well with colonial architecture. Basket weave, ½-inch boards or plywood bent horizontally in and out of uprights, is attractive on both sides. Plank fences are 1-inch boards set with a narrow space between each board. These can be built so that one board is on one side of the stringer and the next on the other, thus making two good sides rather than one good one and one poor one. Board-and-batten fences are 1-inch boards with a pattern of overlaid small strips, usually running vertically. Split-rail fences, reminders of the countryside, are good as boundary indicators and most suitable when used for suburban properties.

You will find other materials and patterns on your local market. Bamboo reeds, for instance, are available in some cities. Bound with wire and framed in cedar 2 × 4s, finished with a clear resin-based preservative, they make an inexpensive attractively textured fence.

Synthetics — fibreglass or Transite — set in panels make low-maintenance, handsome fences that can be sawed, nailed, painted or not. They are also fire and decay proof.

The most utilitarian fences are wire or chain link. Neither are very good-looking and both call for planting in front to screen them, or a festoon of vines to soften their harsh lines.

INSTALLATION AND FINISH

Construction should be carefully done and very strong. Board fences are fastened to stringers between wood posts which should be set 3 feet deep and prepainted with wood preservative. Many builders also saturate the backfill in the hole, to a depth of 1 foot, with creosote. You will not be able to grow anything in this earth and it would be sensible to lay a piece of plastic over it to shed rain which might carry the creosote even farther into the adjoining soil. An alternative would be to creosote the post before you set it in the ground from the bottom to 6 inches *above* ground — 90 percent of wood posts rot first at ground level.

One of the best installations — and I have it in my own garden — is to set in concrete, two iron plates each drilled with two holes, and projecting 8-12 inches above it. Four-inch square upright wood posts are bolted between the plates, leaving 2 inches of clearance between them and the concrete so that the wood is always dry and thus lasts much longer. When posts must be replaced, it is simply a matter of knocking the bolts out of the old one and setting a new one in place. (See drawing page 27).

Green wire makes a short-life, but inexpensive, temporary fence, when strung between painted or stained cedar posts set into holes dug with a post-hole digger, with painted wood two-by-fours used as stringers.

Chain link fences, particularly effective as barriers or security fences, are ugly unless planted with vines or shrubs. They are stretched between metal posts, the wire pulled tight by special equipment — best done by a contractor. Various finishes are available, and a non-rusting one is a must. The type with green or black plastic coated wire is better for home gardens because it is less conspicuous. This fencing can be set very close to the ground if you are bothered by rabbits and other furry friends, but high IQ types among them will find ways to go over or under it, no matter how clever *you* are.

Wood fences can be painted, a necessity for a perky white picket fence, but future cost and labor are a factor to consider here for they must be regularly repainted. Other wood fences can be left to weather, although one coat of a clear, resin-based wood preservative will lengthen their useful lives. They can also be stained any one of a dozen colors — the best will be earth tones. This finish seldom needs redoing.

Paneled fence for a sophisticated city garden; white urn filled with flowers.

A stunning wood fence for a sophisticated city garden can be made with panels of weatherproof plywood painted a dark color — elephant grey or olive green are both good — framed with white posts and finials and the panels traced out, about a foot in from the edge, with white molding. On the ground, in front of where each panel joins the next, set a reproduction stone urn on a pedestal, also painted white. Fill it, for a sunny garden, with a Victorian splurge of dracaena, pink and red geraniums, brilliant pink petunias and masses of drippy green German ivy. If in a shady garden, use different textures of green — frilly fern, smooth variegated peperomia, leathery ivies — all are sophisticated and striking against the dark fence.

With any new fence, paint all parts that will overlap before you nail them together. Use galvanized nails to prevent rust stains on natural finish wood.

WALLS SHOULD LOOK TIMELESS

A wall that is connected to and part of the house, as one often sees in contemporary design, should match it in material. The coping too should blend with other stone or brick in the garden. An alternative is to top it with painted galvanized iron to match eavestroughing and flashing on the house. Such coping is needed to keep rain and melting snow from seeping into the wall, which, in winter, could freeze and burst it.

Walls built as part of the house are usually higher than eye level. They should be sited to create warm areas in cold weather, particularly those border times of the year when a spring sun bath or an hour outdoors at noonday in October can be pure delight. For coolth on hot days, plant a leafy tree between where you sit and the sun.

Freestanding walls in the garden, as boundaries, must often be no higher than the law allows. Be sure to check this before you build. In any case, although you want a sense of enclosure, you do not want to feel boxed in. Four to five feet in height will provide sitting privacy and at the same time let you see trees and sky beyond the wall. A height of 6 feet will give you stand-up privacy, providing your neighbors' gardens are at the same level or below yours, and providing you aren't built to the measurements of the Jolly Green Giant.

Low walls, 1-2 feet high, create a visual break between different parts of the garden. They can also be used on boundaries as a base for an open fence built on top. As an edging for a patio or terrace, they can double as sitting for large parties (numbers, not individuals). A comfortable height for this is 16-20 inches.

Retaining walls, low or high, are a neat and strongly handsome way to handle changes in level. For heights up to 2 feet, they can be laid in dry stone (without mortar), with a large deep flat stone at the base for a footing. Railroad ties and planks are also fine.

Higher than 2 feet, stone can be laid dry, but block and brick must be mortared. Footings, usually concrete, must go below the frost line. Construction must be well done to withstand great earth pressure. Drainage of the ground above by tiles through the wall is needed. As an extra precaution, where there is heavy run off, a line of tile should also be laid behind the base of the wall and lead into a dry well. (For how to make a dry well, see below). Tilt of the wall, known as the 'batter,' should be backwards 1 inch every 6 inches, or 6 inches in 3 feet. (For directions for building a wall garden, see CHAPTER 7.)

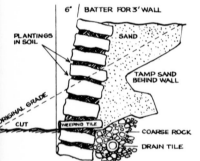

Cross section of a dry wall: stones, on footings of larger stones or concrete, are tilted down at back; fill behind wall is light and sandy, drained by tile through base of wall and, if in a heavy run-off area, also through a parallel line of tile at base.

Formula for a dry well

Choose a spot lower than the area you want to drain where it's easy to dig. Dig a hole 2-4 feet deep, 2-3 feet in diameter, with vertical sides and a flat bottom. Line it with a 30-inch concrete well tile or a steel drum with the top and bottom cut out. (Some dry wells are built with brick walls, laid dry, but they eventually fall in and block drainage.) Fill to within 6-8 inches of the top with stones no larger than 2 inches, loosely packed.

Add a layer of ½-inch small stones, then a batt of rock wool or fibreglass (this will be about 3 inches thick at first, but squash down to about 1 inch). Level up with soil. Connect tile on a downgrade from the line already laid behind the retaining wall, or whatever area you want to drain, bringing it into the upper part of the well.

MATERIAL FOR WALLS

stone: limestone and sandstone are easiest to handle — can be cut either in flat slices (ashlar) or to all shapes and sizes (random).

concrete: looks best with a rough-textured surface brushed on, or rough lumber used for forms — which leaves its imprint.

brick: does not make as strong a wall as the first two and should not be built higher than 3-5 feet without a concrete core, the brick being used only as facing. Even this is tricky.

concrete block or preformed beams: both utilitarian and nondecorative: need plants to soften their harshness.

railroad ties: second hand or new, are excellent for low wood walls, and come already impregnated with preservative.

MORTAR PATTERNS

scooped out between the stones, will make a sharp shadow pattern

rounded, will outline the shape of each stone

back-mortared (that is, out of sight at the back), stones look as though they were laid dry.

Stone that is locally available is best. Brick should be hard-fired, paving or concrete brick. Have the job professionally done unless you have the talent, strength, patience, knowledge and time to do it yourself. Making walls is hard work and takes great skill.

Steps: left, a gentle slope of logs and wood chips; centre, stone steps on the diagonal with easy landings; right, railway ties and stone chips.

STEPS

Steps should relate to the size of the human foot and comfortable lift of a leg. They can suggest a slow, leisurely ascent — a sort of conversational pace; be businesslike and designed to get you there with no nonsense and the least effort; or make you curious about where you are going. No matter how they look or what purpose they serve, one formula of measurement is the rule: for comfort and safety, twice the height of the riser, plus the width of the tread, should equal 26 inches.

This means that an average riser 6 inches high should have a 14-inch tread. For a more leisurely step, a 4½-inch riser with a 17-inch tread. For a minimum tread of 12 inches — and less than this you may not safely build

— make the riser 7 inches high. Steps should tip ⅛-¼ inches to the foot, out and down, to shed water. Break up long flights with generous landings. Take a steep, high slope on the diagonal. For safety, plan no fewer than three or more steps in a group, *never* one, seldom two.

Sloping ramp steps — a staked railroad tie or a cedar log as the riser — backed with a gentle earth slope to the next step, as you might want in the country — are best planned to allow a minimum of 3 stepping paces to each tread.

Building materials in steps should match pavings and walls in the garden. They should be made carefully and repaired at the slightest sign of a wobble. They can be stone, wood, precast, brick or concrete. Although grass is sometimes used as treads with wood risers, the upkeep is fussy and the usefulness limited. It is possible to use small flowering plants in steps, however, by setting them at the back and sides to soften the lines and make a fragile contrast with the strength of the step. (For patterns of steps and construction, see drawing page 109).

POOLS

Nothing so lifts a garden from the prosaic to the sublime as water. A thousand shimmering pictures can be reflected in it if it is a still, dark-bottomed saucer. Birds make a splashing sparkle as they bathe, and if you are lucky a mother raccoon will teach her babies, in moonlight, to wash their paws in it. If you are unlucky it will be a mother skunk. One petal of a porcelain magnolia flower floating on its royal blueness on a spring morning can be a sight you will never forget.

You can make a bubble and quicksilver drip with a fountain, or a little water picture with something as ordinary as a sunken washtub and one gorgeous water lily.

And if you yearn for a swimming pool, that is another story again.

Reflecting pools should be black, dark brown or bottle green on the bottom for best reflection. They can be as shallow as 8 inches, a safe depth for venturing children. If deeper, they can still be made safe by setting a non-rusting metal mesh table in the deep part of the pool. Legs should be long enough to raise the mesh to within 6 inches of the surface and the whole painted dull black. With this treatment and a dark bottom in the pool, the table will never be seen. It will also act as a strainer for leaves and floating debris, and the pool can be cleaned by simply lifting it out. If your pool is so large that one table would be too cumbersome to handle easily, make more than one, each small.

Design the pool with sloping sides to throw off the grip of winter ice, an overflow pipe and drain for cleaning; have a hose nearby to fill it again. A simple form of construction, the floating concrete pad, is neither fussboxey nor expensively impossible to build. (For directions, see drawing).

For best reflections, set the pool below eye level and in a quiet windless place. Fill it to the edge for a wink at the brim and add a little fresh water every day to keep down algae growth. Alternatively, put copper sulphate crystals in a cloth bag (⅛ ounce for 11,000 gallons of water) and swish it through the water, or use permanganate of potash according to manufacturer's

Cross section of floating concrete pad pool.

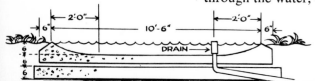

directions. Have goldfish if you wish to — neither of these chemicals, in the correct strength, will harm them. Live scavengers — snails, tadpoles and fresh-water mussels — bought from water plant nurseries will help keep the water clean. A bubbler attached to a small pump will add air to the water and keep it clear. Run it for an hour or two every day, then turn it off for still water. The pump needs an electrical connection and switch, and, if it does not have a strainer on the intake, make one of wire to keep debris from being sucked in. For draining the pool to clean it, build a simple loose-stone, dry well a few feet off, below the level of the pool. (For how to make a dry well, see page 108).

For more temporary construction, and especially useful to try out ideas for size and shape before you build permanently, copy the idea of the plastic-lined farm pond. Scoop out the shape you think you want, making it flat on the bottom and sloping on the sides. Clear out sharp stones and debris. Line it with 2 inches of fine sand if your soil is rough, and on that lay builder's black polyethylene, drawing the edge up and over the side and weighting it down with soil. An alternative to the polyethylene is an asphalt and fibre mat which is relatively inexpensive and looks like dark heavy roofing material. For a large pool or pond in heavy clay soil, a cold-mix asphalt base can be used. A little water may seep through and there will be loss through evaporation. If no natural stream or spring feeds into it, this loss can be made up with a valve and water connection to the house supply or well.

Moving water in streams or spilling pools gives a glint to the garden and a soft plash of sound. Built down the slope of a rock garden, falling into a series of little pools, running over here and there at the edges to wet a patch of candelabra primula or a wild pitcher plant, it can look as though it had always been there. The trick here is to conceal the source at the top with plantings of evergreens or a large stone with trees behind it. A pump, hidden under a flat stone in the pool at the base, pushes the water back up through a con-cealed plastic pipe to start its merry way down again. To replace loss, a float valve, which opens only when the level drops below a certain point, is con-nected to the regular water supply. There should also be a valve at the lowest point for draining the system for winter. For the silver-sheet look in little waterfalls, set a flat stone in the water, the width of the stream bed, *exactly level* and projecting a little over the stone below. Let the water at this point drop over into a kind of basin, then continue on. (See drawing, page 47).

Prefabricated fibreglass spilling bowls with all necessary fittings are also available in sets of three graduated sizes that sit one above the other, a little offside. These look best by themselves on a terrace or patio. Evaporating water here can easily be replaced from a hose.

Wading pools for small fry are also best bought prefabricated, or built into a family-sized swimming pool.

WATER GARDENS
A pool for water plants can be large or small, boggy, or deep water, depend-ing on what you wish to grow. A good material to make them of is waterproof concrete, reinforced with steel rods or wire mesh. The sides should be sloped to push ice upwards in winter thus preventing cracking and breaking of the

concrete. Overflow pipe and drain can be installed as one unit when the concrete is being poured. For growing shallow and deep-water plants in the same pool, build a rock ledge at the edge just under the surface of the water for the shallow rooters. Make planting holes nearer the centre for those needing more water.

Prefabricated fibreglass pools are available also. They have the advantage of needing almost no maintenance. Many are lined with a permanent turquoise blue which is both an asset and a liability — an asset if the water plants are in pots that don't spill mud on the bottom, or if their leaves are so luxurious they cover most of the view of any mud that does collect, mussy and therefore a liability if they don't.

For water lilies, everybody's favorites, the pool must be in full sun most of the day and be 18-24 inches deep. Their roots, usually grown in a box which can be easily lifted, need 12 inches of soil in them and 6-12 inches of water over the crown of the plant — about 8 inches is ideal. In a pool deeper than this, the boxes can be set up on bricks so that there will be the correct depth of water from the crown to surface. In a shallower pool, individual deeper holes can be made for plants when the pool is being built.

For the easiest way to grow a water lily in a small space, sink an ordinary galvanized iron washtub in the ground or paving of your patio. Remember, *full sun*. Plant root in soil in the bottom, hide the blunt edge of the tub with a few flat stones, tuck in some pansies and forget-me-nots around the rim and there is your picture.

Water lilies do best in rich soil with added fertilizer, which can be bought from the nursery supplying your plants. Most gardeners grow them in cedar boxes which they make themselves (15-18 inches square, 10 inches deep, is a good size) or buy from water plant nurseries. They should have openings on sides and bottom, and be filled with soil within a few inches of the top. The roots are set so that the crown is slightly above the soil, then mulched with an inch or two of sand or stones to keep the earth from muddying the water. For hardy varieties, plant in May or June and be careful to have the water at air temperature — fill it a day or two before. Tender varieties — the showy tropical beauties are in this class — should not be put in the pool until weather and water are summertime warm, about 70°. They will make up for the later start by blooming well into the fall.

For winter, drain the pool, lifting your boxes of hardy lily roots into a cool basement where they should be kept damp till put out again the next year. You do not need to completely repot every year. Scraping off the top few inches of soil and replacing with enriched material should be enough, but if plants and flowers are becoming smaller it is time to divide and repot. Tropicals are best treated as annuals and new ones planted each year. If you live in a zone where your pool is not likely to freeze solid in winter, you can leave hardy lilies and water in it, covering the top of the pool with heavy plastic or boards. Over that put a blanket of dry leaves or straw with chicken wire to hold it in place. If your pool does freeze solid, even hardy lilies must be stored indoors.

Caution: when unpacking lily roots from the nursery, have a tub or large pail of air-warm water nearby to pop them into till you are ready to plant

Fine design
and decoration

If anything can give a new gardener the cold shivers, it's suggesting that he can design his garden himself with the flair of a pro. Yet it's as simple as designing the inside of a house. You make it pretty to look at, comfortable to use. Fences, hedges and boundary trees are walls. Lawn, flower beds and ground covers are carpets and floors; paths the hallways, steps the stairs. Planned views are the windows and framing plants — often a tendriled vine — the curtains. A patio is really an outdoor living room, a barbecue just another kitchen. High-canopied trees and the sky are ceiling. Then all the flowery plants — the shrubs, the bulbs, perennials and annuals — are the pictures and decorations that give a final fine finish to it all. But instead of being in one place, looking always the same, as decorations tend to in your house indoors, they change with every season, every day, every whim of weather, every flick of light. Courage, mes amis! It's easy to design a lovely garden.

An antique, cast-iron fountain, complete with cherubs peeking from under its saucers, connected to a handy compact twentieth-century electric pump.

*For an elegant apartment balcony, centre flowers and foliages
with a small lead fountain.*

For low care, think of pavings, raised beds and stone mulches like these.

Fine design at a gate: a planter of geraniums, set on riverbed stones.

Great fun for a budget balcony — geraniums and petunias tumbling from bicycle baskets, a comfortable chair, handy table, stone owls and a screen twined with morning glories.

A good wall to buttress a terrace —
built of random granite, mortared,
set on below-frost-line footings
with grade-level
tiles inserted for drainage.

A water basin you could make yourself
with mosaic tiles,
then set a little terra-cotta figure
behind it and glistening
glass bottles on the rim.

A velvet lawn is at its loveliest when it is traced with shadows.

A beckoning side gate made from an old French-Canadian iron balcony.

A random stone wall on below-frost footings with, for dramatic accent, a Japanese maple planted in front.

A garden for family fun: a pool to sail a boat, lots of space for play.

A Pacific Coast garden that picturesquely marries trees, shrubs, flowers and great sloping rock to the wide sea.

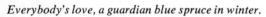

Everybody's love, a guardian blue spruce in winter.

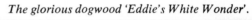

The glorious dogwood 'Eddie's White Wonder'.

Bronze and steel 'Will o' the Wisp' by Gord Smith.

Ferns and hemlock against a grey-stained, split-cedar fence.

*Clever stagecraft—night lighting to dramatize
the beauty of your garden.*

Bold free-form sculpture to focus a fine view, by E. B. Cox.

A ceramic strawberry jar,
bursting with bright-flowered, fibrous begonias;
delightful decoration anywhere.

them — which should be as soon as possible. Handle them carefully, they are brittle and break easily. Those with a tuber-like root are planted horizontally just under the surface, with the growing tip sticking out and a flat stone on top of the tubers to hold them in place. Until new growth starts, brace the box with stones or a brick so that its surface is only 2 or 3 inches below the water, then lower it to the final level. The Marliac strains are set *vertically* in the soil, otherwise treated as above.

Fish can survive in a pool with water lilies but are caught and eaten by raccoons and skunks when there are no lily pads or plants to hide under. Consult your nearest aquarium supplier about kinds and numbers best for you. They will live over winter if your pool does not freeze solid, but not if it does.

RECOMMENDED WATER LILIES AND BOG PLANTS

HARDY WATER LILIES: *Nymphaea*

Yellow:
'Chromatella', large deep rich yellow, blooms from early spring to fall.
'Sunrise', clear yellow with a little green, exceptionally fragrant

Red:
'James Brydon', early, cup-shaped, crimson red
'Attraction', large, garnet red, vigorous, needs a fair space

White:
'Gonnere', dazzling white, fully double, free-blooming
'Marliac Albida', the old-fashioned, fragrant, free-blooming white

Changeable:
these cultivars open one color, then change a little each day:
'Comanche', rich apricot, changing to dark copper bronze streaked with red
'Paul Hariot', light yellow, changing to orange pink then an almost red
'Aurora', a pygmy lily just right for a little tub garden, opens apricot yellow and changes to a deep orange red

Pink:
'Marliac Rosea', deep pink, shading to delicate rose at tips, cuts well, fragrant
'Pink Sensation', rich pink, free-blooming, stays open a long time.

TROPICAL WATER LILIES

Tropical water lilies, not put out until both water and weather are averaging 70° F, can give you 24 hours of flowers if you choose both day and night-blooming cultivars. They are all fragrant and often hold their flowers well up above the water.

DAY BLOOMERS:

Blue:
'Blue Beauty', large deep blue flowers, held high
'Midnight', double-flowered violet blue with darker centre
'August Koch', large wisteria blue-lilac flowers 7-8 inches across, open for 4-6 days

White:
'Mrs. Geo. H. Pring', large fragrant white, sometimes with 13-inch flowers

Pink:
'Mrs. C. W. Ward', deep rose pink, strong flowers 8 inches across
'Golden West', peach pink changing to light apricot

Yellow:
'Yellow Dazzler', double, rich yellow, large

Purple:
'Panama Pacific', rich wine turning to royal purple, blooms a long time

NIGHT BLOOMING TROPICALS

Red:
'Emily Grant Hutchings', large cup-shaped flowers, red pink

Pink:
'Mrs. Geo. C. Hitchock', large rose pink

White:
'Missouri', creamy white flowers, 10-14 inches across

SHALLOW WATER AND BOG PLANTS

Set 6 inches below the water
Azure Hyacinth: *Eichhornia azurea:* a fast-growing trailer, rich purple blue flowers
Floating-Heart, *Nymphoides peltatum:* brilliant yellow flowers
Water-Poppy, *Hydrocleys nymphoides:* pale yellow flowers held above the water

Set 2 inches below the water
Arrowhead, *Sagittaria latifolia:* tall spiked white flowers, arrowhead-shaped leaves
Cattail, *Typha latifolia:* the familiar bulrush or cattail, tall graceful, brown rushes
Flowering-rush, *Butomus umbellatus:* graceful clumps of pink flowers
Iris, Blue, *I. versicolor:* the familiar wild iris of the countryside
Iris, Yellow, *I. pseudacorus:* the fleur-de-lys of France, very tall, golden
Papyrus, *Cyperus papyrus:* the paper plant of the Egyptians, tall stems each topped with a tuft of threadlike leaves

Set 1 inch below the water, or level with it
Calla, Yellow, *Zantedeschia elliottiana:* large, throated flowers of golden yellow, spotted leaves
Imperial Taro, *Colocasia antiquorum illustris:* violet black blotching on leaves which are the shape of elephants' ears

Marsh Marigold, *Caltha palustris:* the most incredibly golden
  yellow of all spring flowers, easy to grow and hardy
Umbrella Palm, *Cyperus alternifolius:* just what it sounds like,
  a little green umbrella on top of each stem

A floater for shallow water
Water Hyacinth, *Eichhornia crassipes major:* likes to float in
  shallow water where its root tips can just reach the soil
  beneath, rose lilac flowers

FOUNTAINS

Fountains can be a thrilling big spurt into the air or they can be tossed patterns of sparkling drops. Using the same water over and over, with a small recirculating pump, they are one of the simplest yet most beautiful garden features to own. Place them if you can, between you and the sun and hide a light behind them for nighttime sparkle. They are far more spectacular when luminous.

The pool at the base of the fountain is the reservoir. You also need to select a pump of the correct horsepower for the size and height of jet you want, the right head for the pattern of spray (aerator jet heads do not splash as much as others), electric cable to the pool for the pump and, at the end of it, a connection you can dismantle in order to bring the pump indoors for winter. Think too of where the spray will drift and don't put your fountain to windward of sitting places in the back garden or the sidewalk in front. Soaked passersby tend to be touchy.

SWIMMING POOLS

A pool really big enough for a good swim is a job for a pro. Choose the man to build your pool by looking at others he has built and talking to his satisfied (???) customers.

Here are some things you should think about beforehand. Swimming pools, except in very large gardens or on unusual sites, become a major item in the design of a garden and practically impossible to screen from other parts of your house. In some cities they require a high fence and self-closing locked gate. They must be carefully sited to be protected from the wind. They are more fun if their borders can catch sun in early spring and late fall, yet be shaded — perhaps with awnings or umbrellas — in the warmest times of summer. Placing them away from trees reduces the number of leaves that must be scooped out of the pool.

Good ones are not only expensive to build originally, they have to be maintained — cleaned regularly and painted, water chlorinated and filtered, drained and sometimes heated.

PAVINGS AND DECKS

Major to the design of the garden year round, pavings can be a simple uninterrupted patio or terrace floor, or spread out to surround the trunk of a big tree or hug a rock. They can also frame flower and planting beds and thus make the whole garden appear more spacious. These surfaces will be warm in summer — and if weather gets very hot where you live they should be shaded with trees or trellis. Fairly expensive, but a great boon to some, radiant heating can be installed below the surface and is especially successful if there is an overhead canopy of awning or leafy tree. Infra red heaters can also be installed in a canopy. The creeping pattern of the shadow of a leafless big tree over smooth paving in winter is both eerie and mysterious, and dry leaves scooting over it in the fall rustle a "winter's coming" tune.

Initial cost is relatively high and continuing maintenance low, although not nonexistent as many think. Pavings laid dry will, after ten or fifteen years, need to be lifted and relaid because of heaving from frost action and roots growing beneath. Those laid on a 6-inch reinforced slab on a 6-inch gravel base should need no further care.

Although the most convenient place for a terrace or patio will be outside your garden door, they can be anywhere in the garden. If the obvious situation for a shady summertime one is at the back of garden, put it there. If your back garden faces the unfriendly north and your front one south, screen the front from the street and put a sitting terrace there.

CONSTRUCTION AND MATERIAL

Laying pavings yourself is possible and pleasurable if you have the back for it, know something about taking levels, mixing concrete and mortar and fitting and laying stone or brick. Some materials are more difficult to lay than others. Most gardeners call in contractors to lay flagstone, which is heavy, exposed aggregate concrete that takes special equipment and skill, and for any material that is going to be laid on a concrete slab.

Flagstone is hard, permanent and comes in colors that weather well. It is, on an average, 1-3 inches thick. Shape can be random or cut in squares or rectangles. It should be laid with a slight pitch away from the house for drainage. The bed can be concrete slab and the stone mortared, or laid dry. In this case, the bed is excavated 9-10 inches, 6 inches of gravel put in the bottom, watered and tamped; then a layer of plastic to discourage weeds; then 2 inches of sand tamped and leveled, the flags fitted snugly and set on that. More sand is brushed into the cracks and lightly watered in till all is level. (See drawing for laying a dry flagstone path, page 103).

Exposed aggregate — concrete with small stones in its surface — can be laid in all sorts of patterns. It is tough and textured, long lasting and for best results should be laid by a craftsman who knows its potentialities. It is poured usually 4 inches thick on a 6-inch base of coarse gravel and marked into squares or oblongs by stone or brick headers. Wood dividers are sometimes recommended but these are seldom satisfactory because of heaving as they age.

Brushed concrete — especially if it is framed and divided with stone or brick — can make an excellent paving. The surface is patterned with a coarse scrub or stable brush, while the concrete is wet.

Brick, a more formal paving than stone or concrete, can be laid in one of many patterns, dry or on concrete. Buy only hard-fired or paving brick, other types shatter eventually. Follow directions for laying flagstones.

Precast slabs are available through many garden suppliers. They come in a variety of handy shapes, sizes and colors and may be laid dry on a level 2-inch sand base or on concrete. The slabs themselves are about 1⅜ inches thick, some have patterns in ⅛-inch relief which makes them both decorative and non-slip.

WOOD DECKS

Wood decks, as so many west coast houses have, are a happy answer where a steep hillside slope and a jutting house make other types of terracing impossible. They are particularly fine for precipitous sites by the sea.

Design, specifications and supervision of building should be done by an architect or landscape architect, who can stress the exhilarating feeling of being projected into space. Useful cupboards can be built into benches or flooring for cushions, hose and other storage, and flowers grown in boxes or portable planters.

RAISED BEDS

A joy to work in, especially because you do not have to bend way down or kneel, and a most dramatic way to set off your plants, raised beds are best made of wood framing. Rough or smooth-sawn lumber, railroad ties, either second hand or new, are all good. The ties have the advantage of being long-lasting because of being impregnated with preservative before you get them, but it is not too big a job to treat lumber yourself. Do it before you nail the frames together so that all surfaces will be coated.

You have almost complete control of the soil mix and moisture content within such beds and can therefore grow all kinds of plants whose temperament and requirements may not normally fit your garden — acid-loving azaleas in an alkaline-soil garden, for instance. Growing flowers on rocky ground is also possible with soil in raised beds. Fewer flowers count for more, for they have a look-at-me-I'm-lovely air about them.

Depth of top soil in beds should be 6 inches over a 2-6-inch batt of fibreglass, for creeping and low plants, 12 inches for annuals and 18-24 inches for shrubs and small trees. To double as seating for parties, make them 14-18 inches above the ground and put a 2-inch plank or boards on top. While you are about it, make some, or all — for you can never have too much storage — into cupboards for extra cushions from the terrace chairs, barbecue supplies, garden tools and fixings. Line with galvanized iron to make water and rodent proof.

Finish can be stain or, if for seating, copper naphthenate is recommended. A soft green, it does not rub off on clothes as stain may. An alternative is a couple of coats of a clear penetrating resin-base preservative.

ESSENTIAL SERVICES

Hose connections and watering systems: the main need is to have enough water outlets so that you never have to pull a hose more than 50 feet. Bibbs should be high enough off the ground to put a pail under them — you would be surprised how many aren't. Fit each line with a turn-off tap inside the house so that you can shut it off before freeze-up, opening the outside tap to drain. The pipe then will not burst in below-zero weather.

Automatic systems, at prices that vary according to the size of your garden, are available for installation by specializing companies or in a simple rig to put in yourself if you know something about plumbing. First check your present water supply to find out whether it can take the extra load. If it can, connect a main valve to it and from that run plastic pipe terminating in brass heads to various parts of the garden. These heads pop up to sprinkle, then drop back out of the way of mowers and foot traffic. To prevent overloading, the system should be set to come on in sequence rather than all at once. Automatic control can be adjusted to do this and to come on at a certain time of day, on a certain day and turn off after a set length of time. Manual systems can be turned on, a section at a time, if there is a tap on each.

Caution: with automatic control, it is important to check the distance that the sprinkler heads throw water and be sure that it does not repeatedly hit painted surfaces that could peel and warp if continuously wetted. Also some trees, notably the mountain-ash, which rot easily resent water repeatedly hitting their trunks. This check should be made at the same time of day or night that the systems will come on. At night, the water pressure will be greater and the stream thrown farther than in the daytime.

Electric plugs: outdoor weatherproof plugs are a convenience for garden equipment — electric hedge clippers and mowers, pump connections; for spits in barbecues; hotbed cables and thermostats; warmers to keep birdbath water from freezing; Christmas decorations and outdoor garden lighting. Cables and connections are best installed when other building is being done, but it is not too difficult to add them later. *Have a licensed electrician do the job, with approved equipment*, and have it checked and repaired if necessary every few years. Be sure to have enough outlets put in, and in convenient places.

Outdoor garden lighting for service areas, walks, and floodlighting for your house as security, are sensible and well worth the money. Many homeowners have a control switch installed in the master bedroom for middle-of-the-night emergencies. Service areas are usually lit from a floodlight attached to the house. Walks can be lit the same way, by small standing fixtures attached to underground cable following the walk, or by inset lights in steps or wall. Floodlighting your house can be accomplished with portable lights staked into the ground from nearby outlets or by fixtures attached to the eaves of the house, shining downwards. Consult your electrician for types of fixtures and safest installation.

Construction for compost heaps: something to screen it from view and dividers for the different bins are usually all the permanent construction needed for a compost heap. The screen can match other fencing in the garden or be something plain and good-looking like framed panels of wood, fibreglass or transite fastened to pipe or heavy posts; or heavy wire — chain link is the most durable. (For how to make compost, see CHAPTER 18, page 141).

Delivery access, trash storage, woodpile: handiness to the back door is involved in all these. A concrete or stone-floor porch with a roof is ideal. For garbage cans, a built-in box with a sturdy lid to keep night-prowling animals out is a real necessity. Wood can be piled for winter fires, bird food stored in a clean, tightly lidded container to be handy for the feeder; delivered parcels and supplies can be safely left on such a porch.

Cold frames or hotbeds: in a warm spot against the house, facing the sun, sheltered from the wind is the place for these. They can be made of lumber or prefabricated metal, set flush with the ground or above it (this type will need insulation). Construction should be done with rustproof nails and the covering sash-framed glass or plastic. Two-inch planks treated with non-creosote wood preservative, which will not harm plants, are recommended for long life. The top board for each end should be cut on the diagonal, 9 inches at the back end, 3 inches at the front. Posts should be of 3×3-inch material. Sash should be fitted snugly to prevent loss of warmth in winter. Two loose pieces of board about 1 foot long, cut down one side in steps, are handy to brace the sash partly open in hot, late winter sun. The total measurement back to front and the length is up to you: a convenient one is 4 feet by 6-10 feet. Handiness to a water outlet for nonfreezing times of the year is convenient and an electric connection for a thermostat and lead-covered heating cable brings violets in January, primroses in December. Portable ½-inch mesh wire screens are handy to keep out marauding squirrels. Seedlings can be brought along, transplants grown to planting-out size in such frames and hotbeds.

Tool storage and work area: any gardener who has ever known the luxury of a tool storage and work area right in the garden will never gracefully go back to the garage wall or a corner in the basement. It need not be elaborate and it can be combined with a flowery accent like a lath house for growing gorgeous basketed hanging begonias and fuchsias and for summer-holidaying house plants. It can be built against a house or garage and have closed storage cupboards for fertilizers, sprays and such similar supplies that should be kept dry and locked up. Racks to hang tools, a metal-topped table to work on, bins with their bottoms slightly above ground to store soil, peat and fertilizers in the dry go here too. And a place to store pots, flats, a pail or two, with water tap and — real luxury — a rain barrel for soft water off the roof will make work in the garden a joy.

A salad and herb garden by the kitchen door: construction here can be neat and precise. Squared wooden frames, prefabricated tiles or raised brick rims, set in a geometric pattern, can each grow a useful kitchen herb or salad green in the kind of soil it likes best. Siting should be in full sun and as near the kitchen door as possible. (For information on herb growing, see pages 78-79).

A small hanging line: it used to be that gardens were designed to include a "utility area" where clotheslines of great length could be strung out to dry the weekly wash. Now that many dry clothes indoors in electric dryers, long lines outdoors are not needed, but it's still a great help to have somewhere to hang biggish drip-dry things like curtains or bedspreads and clothes to be aired. A short line strung handily near the kitchen door between the house and a tree, or a portable rotary line, is usually plenty. If you need posts to hold the line, let them double as supports for hanging suet-packed logs for feeding wild birds in the winter. (See CHAPTER 10).

Supports for vines and climbers
Supports for plants that cling should be strong, easy to adjust and either

unobtrusive or deliberately good-looking. If they must be set against surfaces that are regularly repainted, they should be framed and hinged so that they can be swung away from the wall while this is going on.

For strength, set uprights of freestanding supports deep into the earth or bolt to metal plates set in concrete. (See page 27). Check with your nurseryman the eventual height and possible weight of the mature vine you choose and plan the support to bear this. Wisteria and trumpet vine, for instance, will be both tall and heavy, climbing roses less so, clematis much lighter.

For those that need help to climb a wall — big-leaf wintercreeper, honeysuckle, climbing hydrangea, espaliered trees are some — set nonrusting bolts with hooks and eyes directly into Rawlplugs in the wall. Alternatively, insert blocks of wood into wall to hold bolts. To them fasten a slim wood trellis or strong wire stretched horizontally. Plastic-covered clothesline is good for this, inexpensive and durable. To this trellis or wire, fasten the vine as it grows.

Future tie-ups will be easier if, while you are setting the first bolts, you put in all you may eventually need even though for the first year or two your vine may not climb that high. A coat of paint on bolts, trellis and line will by matching the background make it inconspicuous or by contrasting with it bring out detail.

Set these supports 2-6 inches out from the wall to allow good air circulation behind the plant. This is especially necessary where masonry walls facing south can reflect tremendous heat in late winter sun and, if too close, easily scorch the plant in front.

For supports that can also double as decoration, think of these. For a natural screen, cedar posts set in the ground — allowed to weather or stained — with Virginia creeper trained up and across on wires about a foot apart. They will be twisty and pretty all the growing year, then a vivid splash of scarlet and burgundy red when they change color in fall. Another screen idea for a white house is to paint panels of weatherproof plywood white, their frames turquoise blue, and on horizontal white wires on each train a climbing rose, the deep pink 'Galway Bay' on one panel, a fiery red 'Heidelberg' on the next and so on, alternating for as far as you want your screen to stretch.

For setting off the most graceful of all garden vines, the clematis, make tall narrow panels of opalescent fibreglass, the color the manufacturers call "natural." Frame them with metal or wood painted a pearly grey. Set them facing south or west and on the backside plant 'Nelly Moser' clematis. It has starry flowers of mauve and striped cerise. Train it to come up the back and over the top of the panel to suspend itself delicately down the side you will see. You do this because clematis likes to grow where its roots are cool and shaded, its foliage and flowers in the sun. Another simple and stunning picture with clematis is to plant the huge, white-flowered *C. lawsoniana* 'Henryi' against a dark brown, bottle-green or dull-black fence.

CHANGING GRADE AT THE BASE OF A BIG TREE

A big tree is a treasure. You will not wish to harm it nor shorten its life by one day. Yet a few quick unthinking pushes of a bulldozer grading your ground can do just that. Feeding roots of many trees are so close to the surface that a foot or two of earth scooped off them rips and ruins them. The tree

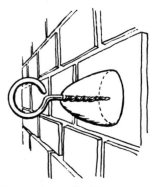

Hanger for a climbing rose: a dab of plastic wood rubbed on the wall, another piece made into a flat-bottomed cone with a screw eye in it, pressed onto the first spot of wood. Allow to dry for 24 hours before using. Can be removed by tapping with a hammer and reused elsewhere.

sickens and, in time, dies. Adding a foot or two of earth over the top of the root-run to raise a grade can be just as serious: it cuts off usual channels of needed air and water with the same fatal result.

To safely lower the grade around a large tree: first feed it — a couple of weeks or a month beforehand — then make a vertical trench as far out under the branch tips as possible, in a circle around the tree and to the depth you intend to lower the ground, plus a footing. If you strike roots, cut them. Build a retaining wall of stone, block or brick against the cut as deep as the trench and as high as the original level of ground. You may have to shore the earth up temporarily while you do this and you will need to add some backfill to the space behind the finished wall to bring it up even. Then cut away the grade outside this wall to the level you want. Give your tree tender loving care thereafter — feeding, spraying, watering, on a regular program.

Alternatively, it is often possible to lower a tree where it stands by digging under one side, tipping over the rootball into the open space, then digging out the other side. This has been successfully done in midsummer without any shock to the tree.

To safely raise the grade: feed the tree two weeks or a month before commencing the work, then, about 1-2 feet out from the trunk, build a wall as high as you intend to raise the grade, to provide the air space around the trunk that it has been accustomed to. Lightly cultivate the ground between the wall and the outside circle of the branch tips, then lay down over it 8-12 inches of large crushed stone. Set fibreglass batts over this and finish the grade with good soil. The purpose of this is to allow air and water to reach the feeding roots of the tree which are just below the surface of the original grade. Covering them without the gravel and fibreglass (which keeps soil from clogging the gravel) would smother them. Here and there through the fill and reaching down to the gravel, sink 6-inch weeping tiles on about 3-foot centres, standing vertically. Supplementary water and food can be fed to the tree through these tiles until the tree becomes adjusted to the change of grade — probably 2-3 years.

If the space enclosed by the wall around the trunk is awkward or hazardous, make a metal or wood grating to fit, or cover it with a circular bench. Be careful not to snug up either too closely to the growing trunk of the tree.

Laying a driveway, path or parking paving over the roots of a big tree: if this is to be solid surfacing, that is, asphalt or concrete rather than loose gravel, plan to cover no more than half the tree roots with the paving and over the other half lay paving brick or flagstone in sand so that water and air can still reach the roots of the tree through the joints. Feed and water the tree on a regular schedule — even with care like this it is growing under difficulties and needs special help to survive.

As a last resort to save a beautiful big tree, consider transplanting it. This is a job for experts, and costly, but if feasible is worth every penny.

15 ECONOMY AND EASY MAINTENANCE

Economy, as I interpret it, is a saving of money. Easy maintenance is a saving of time. Each, in this chapter, is listed separately although some economical ideas are also easy to maintain and *vice versa*. Good advice and planning by a landscape architect, for instance, will result both in economy and easier maintenance. Pavings, although relatively more expensive in the beginning than grass, are less costly to maintain in the long run.

You must also judge the value of each idea in relation to your own life — how much time you have to give to gardening, how much money, what pleases you most and the pattern of other lives that must dovetail with yours. It would be economical, for instance, to seed rather than sod a lawn around a new house, but it takes some weeks, sometimes more than one season, to develop sturdy turf. If, to compensate for the extra cleaning caused by your small fry tracking over your borning lawn and bringing dirt indoors, you must take your wife out to dinner and the theatre each week, you haven't saved a thing.

One of the easy maintenance ideas I recommend is that you should *not* keep your garden meticulously tidy at all times — leave a few leaves on the flower beds, let the sunflower seed hulls pile up under the birdfeeder. If, however, you are a litter-stabber at heart and such casual untidiness bothers you buy yourself an outdoor vacuum sweeper. It is what pleases *you* that will make gardening easy and a pleasure.

An assessment of the kind of time you have for gardening is most necessary. Growing your own annuals from seed has many advantages besides economy, but they do take careful, faithful tending. Unless you can be home sometime almost every day between when you sow them and when you move them into the garden, it makes far more sense to buy more expensive plants already started.

An honest assessment of the present and future pattern of your life is another concern. If, in your later years, you find yourself building a new garden and needing in it a large shade tree, then it is obvious economy and good sense to spend the extra money needed to move in a full-size tree, two-ton rootball and all. You will not want to wait out the years it takes for a small sapling to grow 20 or 50 feet tall.

The ideas that follow are separately listed under ECONOMY AND EASY MAINTENANCE, and then subheaded under ECONOMY WITH PLANTS, ECONOMY WITH THE BUILDING OF PERMANENT FEATURES, ECONOMY IN TECHNIQUE and so on.

---

13 ideas for economy with plants
(and they're all lucky)

Buy the best guaranteed stock you can find, from reliable companies, preferably members of nurserymen's associations. Avoid like the plague fly-by-night operators of street-corner stands and hawkers of supplies who come to your door with dubious supplies.

Buy only those plants recommended as hardy for your zone, or a lower number. You will be more sure of survival with these. (This does not mean that you should never take a flyer on a tricky plant sometimes, but this is advice for economy.)

Buy small and therefore cheaper sizes in trees, shrubs and hedge plants. If you do your part with correct placing and planting, they will grow more quickly in their first years than larger sizes will. By the end of 2 or 3 years, they will be as big or bigger than the larger size you might have bought.

Avoid new introductions. They are always more expensive than older cultivars. In a few years the price will come down and you will have the fun of growing them then.

Look in catalogues for package deals where collections of popular cultivars are sold for less than if you buy each separately. These may not be the biggest and the best stock, but from a reliable dealer they will still be excellent plants. Besides, as the snowdrop said to the lily, who says the biggest is always the best?

Buy and grow seeds rather than plants, of annuals, biennials, perennials.

Keep an eye out for self-seedlings in your garden. Either encourage them to grow where they are or transplant to a better place. Forget-me-not is in this class, *primula japonica*, foxglove, aconite, violas, many others.

Seed a lawn if you have time and the family pattern for it. Sod it if you need a usable surface quickly. Hard pave what you do not want in grass and flower beds and all heavily trafficked areas — constant replacement and repair of grass can be expensive and a nuisance. Make drives wide enough — repairing ruts in lawns can be expensive too.

Use wildlings that you gather in the woods and fields. (See CHAPTER 8: Wild Flowers and Ferns.)

Learn the techniques of propagating — making cuttings, divisions, layering, grafting and so on. (See CHAPTER 18. How to Propagate.) In this way you can increase your own stock of any one plant, perhaps sell or swap some. You can grow bits and pieces which other people give you too.

Put the right plant in the right place in your garden so that it will have every chance to grow well and not need to be replaced.

Do not plant willow or poplar in a small garden where there is a septic tank tile bed. Roots can clog the tiles and eventually the whole system will have to be dug up and cleared. And this blow to your budget could happen the month you planned to buy a mink coat or a new Rolls Royce.

Keep up to date on current information on all garden subjects through your local experts — nurserymen, government horticultural specialists, newspaper columnists and broadcasters, garden clubs, plant societies.

---

8 ideas for economy in building permanent features

Pavings for walks, terraces, patios, steps, curbs, are most economical made with precast blocks or slabs, or with hard-fired or paving brick which you can lay yourself.

Second-hand materials — railroad ties, brick, stone are cheaper than new material. Talk to wrecking companies, railway maintenance departments, keep your eyes open for useful things in buildings being demolished. (Don't buy ordinary building brick for pavings though: it shatters in winter cold.)

Containers for flowers to deck the garden can be low-cost, ingenious and imaginative — beer kegs cut in two, butter boxes, lard pails from bakeries, washtubs, plastic wastebaskets, flue tiles are only a few.

Pools can be lined with polyethylene or mat sheeting instead of more expensive concrete.

A trellis with a grape vine for shade is less expensive than an awning and does not have to be taken down and put up every year.

Cold frames and hotbeds are good economy — they

grow seedlings, cuttings, divisions, overwinter tender plants.

A compost heap produces humus to add to your soil, taking the place of purchased top soil, manure, peat.

Good tools for the job, and good care of them, are an economy. Keep them clean, oiled for winter, blades sharpened. Tattoo a distinctive pattern on the handles so that they cannot be permanently borrowed or lost, or at least so that you can recognize the dastardly culprit when you see them again.

8 ideas for economy of technique

Consult the experts in your area — what they suggest will nearly always pay for itself and save you money in the long run. Most, too, love gardening so much they are happy to help someone else to learn about it.

Unless you are qualified to do it yourself, hire skilled help to do highly technical jobs. Make sure they are insured against injury and that they observe national and local building and wiring codes. Except in very unusual circumstances, it is wise to hire experts to prune and cut down big trees and to plant large ones, to do carpentry, stonemasonry, put up fences, pour concrete and asphalt, make electrical installations, build pools. If you find that you need help with the maintenance of your garden, somebody to cut the grass is the cheapest labor to hire and requires the simplest skill. There are few expert gardeners available for hire. You can usually — and with more economy, efficiency and pleasure — do garden chores needing intelligence and skill yourself.

Plan for easy maintenance. If, for instance, you install mowing strips around the edges of your lawn, a man cutting your grass without the need for hand-trimming the edges can do it in half the time at, presumably, half the cost.

Do maximum soil preparation *before* planting. A healthy, vigorous plant is an economical plant. It does not need special sick-bay care, does not die and have to be replaced.

Buy the best machinery and tools you can afford and keep them in repair.

On wood surfaces, stain is more economical than paint. It seldom needs to be redone, whereas paint must be renewed every few years. Preservative-treated wood, especially with those processes known as Boliden or Wolmanizing, which use waterborne, salt pressured chemicals such as copper chrome arsenate, lasts for years and years. Wood with no finish, allowed to weather, is cheaper still. Cedar is usually recommended for this because of its lovely color, texture and long life.

Buy only the quantity you need in any one growing year of fertilizer, sprays, dusts, etc. Some deteriorate over winter. Some are too poisonous to keep around when you are not using them.

Check content and price of different kinds of supplies. One kind of fertilizer, for instance, can be cheaper to buy than another if there is more actual fertilizing material in it in proportion to filler. Also, all-purpose sprays and fertilizers are more expensive than those made up for one purpose and in buying them you may be paying for something you do not need. But if you only need a small quantity, an all-purpose type may be cheaper.

10 ideas for easy maintenance with plants

Plant the right plant in the right place — a plant growing well will be easier to look after than an ailing one.

Choose low-care plants (see PART III). Some will be easier to grow in the first place, some require less ongoing care, some normally live longer and do not need frequent replacing, some provide more divisions for more new plants. Day lilies and peonies, for instance, are good; roses comparatively are not, for they need constant care to grow beautifully, sometimes don't live very long and for most gardeners produce no replacements. (This doesn't mean that I don't think roses are worth every minute of care they take, but they are not, by my measure, easily maintained plants.)

Trees, shrubs, evergreens, both needled and broad-leaved, some vines, native plants, once they are established, take less care than perennials, bulbs and annuals which must be planted every year.

Avoid nuisance plants. Everybody has their own pet peeves in this division. Mine are goutweed, violets, knotweed, snow-in-summer, grandmother's bluebell, and false dragonhead, which spreads by underground roots and pops up all over the place. You can either not plant them at all, or else contain them in metal rims pushed level with the ground or in submerged pots or tubs (some people control garden mint this way). Be wary, too, of rampant vines — Boston ivy and wisteria are two — and prune to keep them out of your eavestroughs and off the roof, or you will have a major repair job on your hands.

Choose trees that do not add to your work. Avoid summer leaf shedders such as the box-elder, seed producers such as maples, elm, poplar; catkin shedders such as Balm-of-Gilead, twig shedders such as willows, lombardy poplars. Plant crab apples, mulberries, where their fruit will not drop on walks, patios, or driveways. Avoid wild cherry trees because they are the favorite breeding ground of devastating caterpillars. Be wary of the tree-of-heaven for it would rather be busy seeding and suckering than shading angels.

Use ground covers and low-spreading plants in areas where grass grows poorly. Cost is higher to begin with but, once growing well, maintenance will be less.

Check span of blooming time of plants you buy. Some bloom longer than others in any one season and therefore the space they occupy requires less maintenance. Big white trilliums or the yellow daisy-like doronicum, for instance, bloom for a good 3 weeks in spring compared, if the weather is warm, with a few days for daffodils.

Use plants that look well at all stages. This rules out bulbs that have a messy six-week period while their leaves are ripening, but leaves in such beauties as hosta, Solomon's seal, flowering crabs, evergreens, forsythia that look well in all seasons.

Some plants, to continue blooming, must have dead flowers hand-picked before they can go to seed — pansies, sweet peas, marguerites are in this class. Those that don't are naturally more easily maintained — petunias are the outstanding one for this, sweet alyssum is another.

Pruning can be reduced by choosing slow, rather than fast-growing plants for hedges — alpine currant, yew, cotoneaster, for instance, rather than Chinese elm. Although you have to wait longer for the eventual size you want, dwarf plants take less pruning than full-size varieties.

10 ideas for easy maintenance of permanent features

Design your garden simply: no busy little beds cut out of the lawn to be trimmed around, no specimen trees or shrubs standing alone for the same reason, continuous shelter planting along boundaries rather than stop-and-start flower beds. Paths where people habitually walk, otherwise they will wear thin places that will have to be repaired.

Plan curbs and mowing strips around beds and big trees. A soldier course of Roman brick (one brick the size of four normal building bricks) standing on edge in sand as a border for flower beds will hold earth neatly in place and keep grass from creeping in. Butt tightly against it a row of the same brick laid flat and flush with the lawn. The mower will then run with one wheel on the bricks, one on the lawn and no hand-trimming will be necessary. Just one quick sweep after each mowing and everything is shipshape. Precast pavers designed especially to circle the base of large trees will do the same thing.

For a low-care mulch, use chipped stone laid over black plastic sheeting. Then cut a slit in it wherever you want a plant to grow. This is good-looking, weed-free and moisture retaining. Especially useful in a 2-3-foot wide band around the house, where it will also prevent splashing of earth on the foundation wall and be a handy walkway for the screen putter-upper and the window washer. Incidentally it also moves plantings well forward of overhanging eaves where they will grow much better.

Handle steep slopes by building walls and flat terraces rather than having grass on a tilt, which is difficult to grow and awful to mow.

Think twice before you build a feature that takes repetitious care — pools, both swimming and reflecting, need regular draining and cleaning; flower beds mean special care of the plants and weeding (chemicals and mulches can help here); grass must be fed, watered, cut (paving instead is the answer here). Fences and walls call for less maintenance than clipped hedges. New products often cut down work — there is, for instance, a plant food that comes in small perforated bags which when placed beneath the root at planting time, nourishes the plant over a period of 5 years, eliminating the need for two-or-three-times-a-year fertilizing.

If you use loose stone on walks or drives, or as mulch, curb it so that it does not scatter easily into nearby grass and flower beds. If caught and thrown by a mower it could be very dangerous.

Flowers grown in raised beds, window boxes and containers are easier to care for than in open ground-level beds, and they often look more dramatic.

Design your garden so that permanent features and long-life plantings make it lovely to look at even when flowering plants are not in high bloom.

Ramps make for easier maintenance than steps where wheeled equipment must go up and down different levels.

Service features conveniently placed — electric plugs, water outlets, tools and supplies — cut down on temper as well as time.

8 easy maintenance techniques

Take your gardenkeeping casually. Let leaves (but not diseased leaves) collect on flower beds in the fall — they will serve as a mulch. Let bulb leaves ripen where they are, planting summer annuals through them will, in 3 or 4 weeks, hide them. Leave grass clippings on lawn if not too thick. Sweep up sunflower seedhulls under bird feeder at the end of the winter only. Plant an evergreen hedge (cedar is good for this) informally in groups rather than in a soldier-straight line and clip it just enough to keep it from getting thin. Let plants like 'mums sprawl rather than tie them up. And be content with a relaxed look in your garden, rather than a precisely-kept look.

Use mulches to keep down weeds and conserve moisture (see CHAPTER 18, page 148).

In very light sandy soils, where water and fertilizer run through quickly, try a layer of perforated plastic, rock wool batt or shredded newspaper under plantings to retain food and moisture. Use the same technique in hanging baskets, window boxes and planters to reduce need for frequent watering.

Don't cut your grass too short (most varieties should be cut no less than 2 inches), and don't let any maintenance crew do it either. Shaved turf encourages weed seeds like crabgrass to germinate and roots of desirable lawn grasses to dry out and either grow poorly or die. When you must weed your lawn, use chemical herbicides rather than guillotine with the old kitchen carving knife. (An exception to the what-height-to-cut rule is bent grass — it must be kept close.)

Fertilize and water regularly for good growth and healthy plants. Spray to control fungus disease when the weather indicates that conditions are ripe for its appearance and before it does. (See CHAPTER 19: The Control of Common Pests and Diseases.)

Decide whether you want to dust or spray insecticides

and fungicides. Dusting is easier but does not do as good a job. Good cultural control is better still.

Fasten plants that must be supported with plant twists rather than string or raffia — use special rings for peonies, sturdy stakes for tall beauties such as delphinium and dahlias, putting them in place before the heavy blooms come out.

Use power rather than hand tools — mowers, hedge clippers, snow blowers, garden tractors for large areas — wherever you can, and automatic controls for such jobs as watering, turning on and off of lights.

Economy in building a low wall: secondhand streetcar paving blocks, called granite setts, laid without mortar.

Easy edging: a mowing strip of Roman bricks laid flat, butted against an upright soldier course of similar bricks.

Easy design: a band of stone chips around the house under eaves catches drip, moves plants forward where they grow better and prevents mud from splashing on the house.

Easy-care plants — the beautiful day lily.

16 A GARDEN ON NEW LAND

The beginning of a new garden on new land is real adventure — exciting, challenging, creative adventure. Stretching out before you, in your mind's eye, is a lifetime of horticultural bliss. Robust, well-shaped trees cast fascinating shadows over smooth green, weedless lawns. Almost at the snap of your fingers, brilliant flowers of all kinds burst into bloom from earliest spring to frost. Ripening fruit hangs glowing and unbuggy on your trees, succulent vegetables wait for the picking, vines climb at your will.

Your children, the little darlings, all smiles and sweet airs, play happily on their swings while you lie in your lounge chair, relaxed and content, breathing the flowery fragrances wafting on the breeze, admiring your clever handiwork, graciously accepting compliments of visitors on your obvious skill as a gardener.

A dream? Certainly. But it's not an impossible one if you plan intelligently for the good things and accept the fact that some of the time all will not be blissfully perfect. Buds, you will find, can be as beautiful as fully-open flowers. Digging can be more fun — and better for your waistline — than sitting. Beating slugs to the lettuce can make salads a tasty victory. Examining textures of leaves alone is a constant delight. Looking at a velvet smooth lawn is fine, but it's nothing to the lovely feeling of riding or guiding a mower up and down over it on a bright May morning and smelling the freshness of newly-cut grass.

One of the small boys will almost inevitably snap off the heads of your best tulips some year but that fall, when you plant new bulbs, you'll show him how to plant some of his own and he'll never snap tulip heads again. Every experience — not always those you foresee — is part of the exciting adventure.

CHOOSING THE LAND

There is no land that will not grow a garden of some sort, even if you have to do it in beds or pots on top of it. But if you want to specialize in growing plants that demand certain soil conditions, certain exposures — rhododendrons are one — you will have to choose a site that has them. However, factors other than soil usually come first when you buy new land on which to build. The location matters, the community services such as schools, the cost of living there, taxes and so on. But there are some things you should look for, whatever you buy, for they can vitally affect both your house and your garden. They are:

Avoid filled land. It is seldom good soil, can be shifting and unsettled. Very often it is poor to build on, poor to grow a garden in and often packed with rubbish you can't see.

Although a sloping or rolling grade makes a much more interesting garden than flat land, steep drops can be difficult to landscape and may require expensive buttressing.

Trees are a priceless dividend. If there should be too many, it's easy to clear out what you do not want. Those you keep are pure treasure, for it takes years and years to grow a large tree. A variation of this holds for the Northwest coast. Here the high winter water table of the coastal rain forest encourages shallow rooting of large trees. If, to clear space to build a new house on new land, some must be cut down, the ones left standing seldom survive. It is better to clear the land completely, modify the soil, correct drainage if necessary and replant with new material. Growth is so fast on the Pacific coast, it will catch up in no time. Have all work on large trees done by professionals with the proper equipment and skill.

Beware of boggy ground. There may be hidden springs or a watercourse. If it bubbles up in the garden it's an asset because you can design a feature to include it. But if it comes through under your house or patio, the only design for that is a sump pump and nobody ever thought they were beautiful.

Look up and around to the views you'll have, especially from your windows. If possible, choose land with a cheerful vista.

If you enjoy sunbaths in late winter and fall and extra-early and late flowers, pick an exposure that will place the back of your house and the adjoining garden facing south or west into the sun and protected from sharp cold winds.

When you decide on the land you want, have a professional survey made. It's absolutely essential to know where you stop and your neighbors start when fencing, hedging and chasing dogs (theirs).

PRELIMINARY PLANNING

Begin by making a plan so that each step fits into an overall design. Qualified landscape architects to help you to do this are available in most large cities, their fees based on a percentage of the total cost of the work. Garden planners and designers on staffs of nurseries charge a fee depending on the work involved — materials they specify are supplied by their nursery and the total cost included in the final contract. Both architects and planners are happy to schedule a program that you can carry out over two or three years and you will find that their training and experience save you money and heartache in the long run.

Alternatively, you can make a plan yourself. On graph paper draw the outlines of your land to scale — the house, driveway, doors, windows, buildings that abut your garden (such as a neighbor's garage), septic tank and tile bed if you have them, existing features like large trees you intend to keep. Then, thinking of sun and shade, protection from the wind, and what your family wants, draw in what you would like to have. (For suggestions see CHAPTER 13.)

BEFORE THE BUILDING OF THE HOUSE

Trees to be kept should be boarded around the trunk, high up, to prevent bruising and damage by building equipment. If the grade over their root system is to be changed — either higher or lower — special treatment is needed (see CHAPTER 14, Section on Changing Grade at the Base of a Big Tree). If you do not do this, you could lose your tree in a few years.

If your plan calls for the moving of a large tree to the back garden, do it before the excavation of your house is dug and while big trucks and trailers can back directly to the place where it is to be planted. See that it is finally set so that the surface of the root ball will be correct for the finished grade, not the first rough one.

Stockpile large quantities of heavy supplies you may want for construction of features in the back garden — rock for walls, lumber for fences, bricks for a patio — while a truck can still get in all the way.

Build a swimming pool first for the same reason. The cost will be lower if heavy equipment can directly reach the site.

Scrape off all good topsoil and store where it will not be disturbed. Then use it when you make final soil preparation and grading.

After grades are established, incorporate whatever is needed to improve the soil with mechanical equipment like a Rototiller (these can often be rented). Nothing is so important for future vigorous growth as deep and thorough preparation of the soil. It is even wise to spend all your first-year budget for the garden on this if necessary, using inexpensive flowery annuals for plantings in the meantime.

MAKING A NEW GARDEN WHERE THE HOUSE IS ALREADY BUILT, THE GROUND ROUGH-GRADED

Check to be sure that the grade slopes away from the house, that earth has not been piled over large tree roots or cut away without special treatment of the change; if fill has been brought in, see that it is clear of rubbish and weeds.

If sodding or seeding of lawn areas is in your contract with the builder try to hold him off till *you* can do extra special preparation of the base soil. This is the best insurance you can possibly have for a good future lawn. (See CHAPTER 23, LAWNS.)

Check to see if debris from the building of your house is buried anywhere on the site. Trades are often careless with trash left from their work, especially around the open excavation of the foundation. You may not find this deadly garbage till two or three years later when brown patches appear on your lawn or your plants inexplicably die. You then dig down to discover the reason and there it is sitting looking at you — a great lump of old plaster or a barrowload of broken bricks.

If you can watch your house being built, pay someone to cart rubbish away as it collects, or do it yourself. This will be far cheaper than digging it out later, and will keep you from thinking nasty thoughts about the builder. If you cannot catch this during the building, cajole the foreman into telling you where he buried his treasure and get it out before you do anything else.

Install enough hose bibbs by connecting to the house service, so that you will not have to pull a hose more than 50 feet to reach any part of the garden. Consider putting in an automatic watering system. It will be easier to install it at this stage than later (see CHAPTER 14, section on Watering Systems).

Connect any weatherproof outdoor electric outlets you may need — for garden lighting, perhaps a hotbed cable, Christmas decorations, an electric spit for a barbecue (see CHAPTER 14, section on Electric Outlets).

MAKING A NEW GARDEN WHERE THE HOUSE IS BUILT, FINAL GRADING DONE, LAWN SEEDED OR SODDED

Live with your new garden for a year, making notes in all seasons on how you would like to develop it.

Feed and water the grass to give it every chance to become a good lawn. If it does not respond, plow it in for green manure and go back to the beginning (see CHAPTER 23, LAWNS).

Grow annuals for flowers. Do not put in permanent plantings till you know what you want and are sure that the soil is properly prepared for it.

Your soil: See CHAPTER 18, section on How to Improve Soil.

Your new lawn: See CHAPTER 23, LAWNS.

YOUR FIRST PLANTS

Trees: Because they add pleasure to your garden with their cooling shade, value to your house by their handsome look, and take a fair time to grow to good size, plant trees first. Two places with top priority for the first ones are at the front of your house to one side, to give a framing, sheltering look, and on the sunny side of a west or south-facing patio, for shade in summer. On a hot day, a tree can reduce the temperature of the air under it by at least 10 degrees. (For what trees to choose and how to plant see CHAPTER 20).

Air is 10 degrees cooler in the shade of a leafy tree.

Hedges: Because of the wish to create screening quickly, most new gardeners fall into the trap of buying fast-growing hedge material — often Chinese or Siberian elm. Be warned, however, that a hedge that grows quickly upwards can also grow quickly sideways and may need two or three prunings a year to keep it trim. For immediate privacy consider instead a wood or fibreglass screen or, where you want living plants as hedges, choose those which make a moderate yearly growth and therefore demand less maintenance. (For good hedges to plant, see CHAPTER 22, section on HEDGES.)

Foundation plantings: Although formal foundation plantings are not as commonly used now as they once were, some planting is appropriate and good looking to marry the house to the ground. Unless you are in a great hurry to get a finished look, wait a year to do this. Earth fill around the foundation is bound to settle and you yourself need time to assess the effects of exposure, dryness, drip from eaves and so on. In the meantime, annual plants, bulbs, corms and tubers will give you all the flowers and foliage you wish.

129

Flowers for the first-year garden: Flowers are no problem at all — annuals which sprout, grow, flower and set seed all in one season, then die, can be grown either from seed or bought already started from nurseries, greenhouses and supermarkets. Geraniums and pansies already in bloom are available. Simply knock them out of their pots or boxes and set them directly in the garden. Dahlia tubers grow four or five feet in a summer and have flowers big or little. Gladiolus throws a 2-3 foot spike of brilliant color within weeks. Begonias, both small and large, are faithfully flowery in shade.

A Heavenly Blue morning glory vine, costing only a few cents for a packet of seed, will cover a screen 10-15 feet high or scramble up a string of nylon fishing line to a second-floor bedroom window and cover itself with trumpets of sparkling sky blue. Tubs of frilly white petunias can spill ballerina flowers all summer long using less than a dollar's worth of plants to a big tub. You can have hedges, carpets, borders of marigolds from the middle of July till hard frost. Nothing to write home about for fragrance, they are incredibly easy to grow, unbuggy and undemanding of care.

On dry banks and hot rocky places with poor soil, you can grow giddy yellow, orange and magenta portulaca or the hummingbird's favorite, nasturtiums. For a big bold accent there is nothing more spectacular than the pointed, pleated, 10-inch leaves of castor bean which grows 6-7 feet high all in one season. I have seen these plants grow as high as 10 feet in Assiniboine Park in Winnipeg, Manitoba. When I asked the director what he fed them to make them grow to such a fantastic height, he said, "Wild buffalo manure." Sure that he was pulling my leg, I said he could hardly expect me to believe that today a park in the middle of a big city could get wild buffalo manure for their plants. He took me by the arm and along a little path in the castor bean jungle. There, behind a wire fence, in a small zoo enclosure were six wild buffalo. So there you are, gardeners all, wild buffalo manure is the food I recommend to grow 12-foot castor beans. But don't let your children eat the seeds, they are poisonous. Sunflowers are good fun both to look at and as food for winter birds. Plant them to the north of your view in order to see their faces, which always turn to the sun.

There is literally no limit to the flowers you can grow in your garden in its exciting first year. (For others, see CHAPTER 28, BULBS, CORMS, TUBERS, and CHAPTER 29, ANNUALS.)

And to go on with: Keep notes and a scrapbook, lists of plants you see that you like — otherwise by October you may have forgotten the name of the big red tulip you fell for in May (Red Emperor probably, usually is). Visit nurseries, parks, other gardens, to see plants at their best. Join your nearest horticultural society, garden centre or club and become acquainted with the members and their gardens. Subscribe to a good garden magazine. Send for pamphlets from your government extension service. Read gardening sections in newspapers and magazines. Listen to gardeners on the air. Send for catalogues and read them, especially on cold winter nights when your new garden lies deep under a blanket of snow. Make plans for next year and the year after that — it's all part of the exciting, challenging, creative adventure!

17 REMAKING AN OLD GARDEN

To make a silk-purse new garden out of a tired sow's-ear old one is a challenge, and often more difficult than making a brand new garden from scratch. Often, though, it can be a more quickly satisfying project because you are working with mature sizes of plants, often full of character.

With a little magic wand-waving — usually your pruners — you have the chance to reveal beauty that no one would believe was there, beauty that would take years to develop if you were using new, nursery-size plants.

If you are in this business of remaking an old garden, it will be for one of two reasons. Either it is, and has been for a long time, your own garden which you now wish to change: the pattern of your life is different; skillful help is hard to get and you need something that calls for lower maintenance; early plantings have become overgrown and tatty or, because of the age and growth of material, the pattern of sun and shade has changed so radically plants once vigorous are now languid and begging to be replaced.

Or you are remaking somebody else's garden because it is now your garden. If this is the case, begin by checking your official survey to be sure that what appear to be your boundaries really are. Then take a year to see·what you already have. Make a rough scale plan of the garden as it is. Sketch in existing trees, shrubs and plants you can identify, learn names and habits of unknowns. Add others as they appear. Put a good permanent marker where each plant grows to avoid disturbing those you may decide to keep. Do not be too hasty to change what at first seems to be something you do not like; it may be the only thing that will grow there. But discard what you are absolutely sure you don't want.

From here on, my advice is the same to both remakers.

LIKELY PROBLEMS

Plants overgrown, tangled, no clear pattern, too much shade
Pruning to clean out, to thin out, is the answer. Have professionals advise you on removal and repair of big trees. If there are no expert tree services in your area, power or telephone linemen will often help you in their own time. A big tree that looks like a goner can often, with skillful treatment, be rejuvenated. Large trees needing to be completely cut down or drastically pruned are best done with professional equipment and skill.

With the proper tools and techniques, you yourself can prune small trees and shrubs. But a word to the wise. After you have taken out all diseased and old wood, step back and have a long look at what is left. Even wait a few days, a week, a month before you go further. An appetite for drastic and sometimes disastrous pruning develops into a holocaust with some gardeners, so take it slowly. You can always take a branch off, but you can never sew it back on. If you have young children, stop short of being so tidy that there are no places left to hide or a good sturdy branch to hold a tree house. Tatty hedges, with the kind of long bare legs that look well on a heron but poor on a hedge, are usually best cut right to the ground, the stubs should be fed and watered well. As new growth appears, treat it as though it were a new hedge. (See CHAPTER 22). Be sure that there is at least 7 feet of clear air above the hedge and if necessary cut back large branches of overhead trees to get this. If the old hedge does not come back thick and green, consider replacing it with a wood fence or fibreglass screen; these need less maintenance and are an effective barrier sooner.

Foundation plantings: most old foundation plantings are best dug out and discarded; substitute a new planting, using materials in a more contemporary way. Consider individual forms of plants; keep them clear of windows; use pebble mulches against the house; replace steep banks with low walls or a slow slope. (See CHAPTER 13, DESIGN AND DECORATION.)

Poor, dank soil: heavy growth and too much shade, not enough cultivation of the soil, not enough fertilizing can create conditions so discouraging that you may well wonder if anything can improve them — short of digging out deeply, carting it all off to the dump and starting afresh. Once again, it is worth a try for a year. Clear out and prune trees and shrubs to let in more light. Dig deeply — 2-3 feet — and mix in conditioners like peat, leaf mold; nutrients like organic and inorganic fertilizers. Use raised beds filled with fresh, fertile earth over thin scruffy places. Use pavings or stone mulches over some sections and concentrate your intensive care of soil where you especially want plants to grow well. Make compost of your leaves, and dig it and some fertilizer into every new planting hole you make. Turn bare earth up roughly in the fall to expose it to the beneficial action of frost over winter. Grow annual rye wherever you get a vacant space in your vegetable or annual flower garden and turn it under before you plant again. Continue a regular, consistent program of good garden practice.

Patchy, weedy lawns
Check grade to be sure that (a) it drains well, leaving no soggy spots for poor growth and (b) that the ground is modeled the way you want it to be and the levels are best for design and utility. If these things are not satisfactory, plow it up and make a new lawn. If they are, try a remake by spiking the sod, fertilizing with special lawn food and watering regularly (if no rain). Control weeds with herbicide, topdress and seed for one year. If the lawn shows no signs of a comeback, if it is still a weedy patch, then dig it in and begin a new lawn. (See CHAPTER 23, LAWNS.) You will not have lost too much time, and all the good you have put into the old lawn will be waiting to give a shot in the arm to your new seed or sod.

Overgrown old perennials
Lift and divide choked perennial plantings, and replant in improved soil in a different part of the garden. (For how to and when, see CHAPTER 18, TECHNIQUES AND TOOLS.) Consider replacing some with new and better strains — iris, lilies, delphiniums, 'mums, gladiolus, day lilies are only a few that have wonderful new hybrids on the market.

Old twiggy roses
Keep old roses for a year, pruning them back if they have been allowed to grow uncontrolled. Watch their health and strength and the quality of bloom. If it is good, keep them, if not, dig them out and replace them with some of the new spectacular cultivars. (See CHAPTER 26.)

Spring bulbs
Bulbs flowering poorly — single big leaves and no flowers on tulips or striped petals when they should

be plain; too much foliage and too few flowers on daffodils; leaves and no flowers on others. Discard the old and plant new ones. (See CHAPTER 28, section on Bulbs.)

Rampant vines: If vines are overgrown because they have not been controlled, but you like their habit, cut them back. (With deciduous kinds, this is easier to do when they are bare in fall, winter or early spring.) If they are coarse and invasive, as Boston ivy can be, dig them out, rip them off and replace with something more tractable. (See CHAPTER 25, section on Vines.)

To reduce maintenance

Most old gardens have large borders and plantings that, to look well, must be partially or wholly replanted with each season. This involves a tremendous amount of work, costly in both time and money. Consider a change to minimum-care plants and reduce the number needed by setting off those you do use in complementary containers or raised beds. Plan your design with pavings instead of grass which must be cut, brick coursing or wood or metal stripping at the edges to eliminate the need for hand trimming. (For dozens of ideas for easy maintenance, see CHAPTER 15.)

Up-Date the design

Often the biggest lift you can give both yourself and your garden is to redesign it with a patio, terrace or deck, a barbecue, a court for games, or a pool. Before you plan any new construction, however, check foundations and drainage. If there has been paving right up to the house and you want to break it up to do planting or new building, make a small hole first and pour a bucket or two of water into it to see where it will go. If it turns up in your basement, then handle this problem first, for it is a major one. Redesign the grade to slope it away from the house. Also, check with local authorities to see if building permits are needed, if there are regulations about height of fencing, building of pools, and so on. (See CHAPTER 13, DESIGN AND DECORATION and CHAPTER 14, PERMANENT FEATURES.)

Old front gardens

The approach to your house often needs face-lifting as much as the back garden. This can sometimes go hand in hand with redesign of the house itself. Now is the time for new ideas, new materials, something that will give you and your neighborhood a lift. A wider driveway and extra parking, a new walk with good lighting for night, curbing for where lawn meets sidewalk, any one of a dozen things may be needed that will improve the whole view of your house from the street and its value in the real estate market.

(These ideas are developed in CHAPTERS 13 and 14.)

Other sections of value to read:
PART I: What Is Your Kind of Garden?
PART II: Of Practical Help
PART III: The Fine Points of Growing Good Garden Plants Well
PART V: Guides to Gardening in Eleven Regions of the United States

18 TECHNIQUES AND TOOLS

Most people think that a green thumb is a mystical, magical thing to be born with. Perhaps it is, but I believe that the talent so often called a green thumb is really sympathetic observation and intelligent response and that both of these can be learned. If you love plants you are bound to observe them sympathetically. If you take time to learn good gardening techniques, you will respond to their needs intelligently. It's just as simple as that.

This chapter outlines basic responses you will find helpful in all kinds of gardening (specific care of individual plants is given in PART III: The Fine Points of Growing Good Garden Plants Well). We begin with guidelines, then tell you how to:

dig efficiently
improve soil, make acid soil
fertilize
make compost
water properly (not as simple as it sounds)
weed
eliminate stumps
mulch (so that you do not, among other things, have to weed)
plant
transplant
prune

propagate
protect plants
select the tools to use
take special precautions in the use of power mowers

GUIDELINES FOR ALL GARDENING

Take time to prepare your soil well

Soil should be fertile, porous, well-drained yet moist (sites for bog or water plants are the exception). Since most gardeners cannot hope to have the perfect soil mix, and since the very act of growing plants takes nourishment from even the best soils, you can be sure that you are right if, in the beginning, you build for good drainage and yearly thereafter add organic and inorganic fertilizer and soil conditioners such as peat or compost.

Government soil-testing laboratories will test home garden soil on request — some charge a small fee — and recommend materials to improve it. Late summer or fall is the best time to do this. Home soil-testing kits are also available from your garden supplier, but be sure that the material in them is fresh. However, except for growing the few plants that need determined acidity or alkalinity in the soil — rhododendrons and iris are two — an overall program for regular soil improvement will suffice.

Check the drainage

Above all else, check drainage of all parts of your garden. Many good garden plants are lost from too much water rather than not enough. Roots must have air as well as water to grow well. If water fills all air spaces in the soil, plants die. If rain sits for more than an hour on top of your soil, it is not well-drained.

The cure for poor drainage is one of these:

dig soil out of the bed to below planting level, lay 6-8 inches of gravel, then weeping tile, sloping to a deeper dry well, more gravel and finally replace soil; unless this is a familiar task for you, it's a job for a pro
dig out soil to below planting level and lay a 6-8 inch layer of gravel in the bottom, then replace soil
raise the level of the whole bed by adding soil to the top — 6 inches is the usual added height — this is the cure most commonly used
give in and make a pond.

Buying stock

Buy from reputable dealers with established businesses, who give a reasonable guarantee. If possible, choose nurseries whose stock is grown in a similar weather pattern to yours. If you want to import plants from outside the country, you must get a permit to do so from the government. If it is possible, bring in imported stock by air — it will be more expensive than by surface mail but much quicker, with less shock to the plant.

All plants you buy should be free of badly bruised or broken branches and roots; be free of disease; be of good form and have an ample root system in proportion to the total size of the plant. As well:

bark of deciduous trees and shrubs should look fresh, not dried out evergreens should be fresh and supple; a healthy green (this does not always mean *bright* green); with roots in a firm, solid earthball, snugly tied in burlap or container-grown

bulbs, corms and tubers should be plump and firm; show no signs of injury, disease or rot; large and medium-large sizes, except for hyacinths, are a better buy than smaller, cheaper stock

perennials are best bought container-grown or wrapped in damp moss and heavy wax paper; buy vigorous, good-sized plants

roses should have healthy, sturdy green canes and be cultivars recommended for your zone; be well-wrapped with roots in moss and heavy paper, or container-grown; although some gardeners have good luck with imported roses produced in different climates from ours, most prefer those grown in this country

annual seedlings should be bushy, vigorous, not dried out, not leggy, showing only a little bloom, if any; be sure to check the number of plants in a box against the price — what appears to be a bargain may turn out to be two or three fewer plants per box.

Take care

Between buying and planting, keep new plants cool, out of strong and drying wind and hot sun; if bare root, keep them moist and covered; if balled and container-grown, keep them watered; if aquatics, keep in water; also:

take bulbs out of shipping bags or cartons and store in an airy cool (40°-50°F) place till you can plant them

Heeling in: unwrap roots and soak if dried out, lay in shady trench, pile earth over roots, water, plant as soon as possible.

if more than a day or two must elapse between delivery and planting of nursery stock, heel the plants into a shallow ditch in a shady place (see drawing) and move to their permanent site as soon as possible

shade newly planted stock from bright sun for 3-7 days

give extra care in watering, feeding, mulching, staking, guying and winter protection to long-life plants such as trees, shrubs, hedges, during their first vulnerable season.

WHY, WHEN AND HOW TO DIG

Why dig carefully?

Soil, to be fertile, must be porous, moist and hold nutrients in a form that can be absorbed by plants. Careful digging can create and/or improve these conditions by:

breaking up soil to improve drainage where the ground is too wet

improving the texture of the soil by exposing it to sun, rain and frost improving its fertility by mixing in while digging, soil conditioners like peat, compost, leaf mold and organic and inorganic fertilizers

in the Far North, exposing the soil to warmer air temperatures and thus reducing the level of the permafrost below.

When to dig

To allow for settling, site should be dug at least 2 weeks before planting; longer is better and there is a distinct advantage in digging new beds a whole season before they will be needed — in fall for spring because frost action is an excellent conditioner of soil; in spring for fall because a crop of grass can be grown as green manure and turned in before permanently planting.

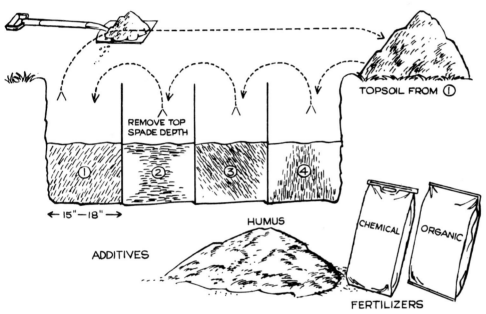

TOPSOIL FROM ①

REMOVE TOP SPADE DEPTH

① ② ③ ④

← 15"-18" →

ADDITIVES

HUMUS

CHEMICAL ORGANIC

FERTILIZERS

How to dig

A large bed: trenching is the most effective method and well worth the time it takes; divide space into sections 15-18 inches wide, take one spade's depth from the top of the first section and pile it beside the last section; in the first hole, turn over another spade's depth, at the same time mixing fertilizer and conditioners into the soil; next, shovel the top of the second section onto the top of the first, again mixing fertilizers and conditioners into the soil as you work; proceed similarly to the end of the bed, one section at a time and at the end add the topsoil from the first section to the top of the last (see drawing).

One planting hole: dig out soil to required depth, reserving the top soil to put on top again when finished; mix fertilizers and conditioner with the soil you have dug out and replace it in the bottom of the hole, add a layer of unfertilized soil that will be in immediate contact with the roots of the plant, set the plant in place, add soil tamping it gently around the roots to eliminate large air spaces, add top soil till the hole is just slightly below the level of the surrounding ground, water deeply; when plant is growing well, add more topsoil till the hole is level with the surrounding ground, or a little above it.

WHY, WHEN AND HOW TO IMPROVE SOIL: HOW TO MAKE ACID SOIL

Why improve soil?

Few garden soils are of perfect tilth (20% sand, 40% clay, 40% humus); most need additives to be fertile.

Clay soils are heavy and hard to work; they hold water (an asset in dry areas but not in wet), are slow to dry out and warm up in spring, and they form a crust in hot summer sun making it difficult for rain and air to enter.

Sandy soils are easier to work and they warm earlier than clay, but water runs through them, they dry out too quickly and nutrients leach out.

HOW AND WHEN TO IMPROVE SOILS

Clay: by digging in each year, to a depth of at least 1 foot, quantities of humus, which may be compost made from your own leaves and garden refuse and/or vegetable scraps, peat moss, sand or ashes, commercial conditioners; at the same time add organic fertilizers, such as manures and bone meal, and inorganic commercial fertilizers; clay soils are best dug up in the fall and left rough — frost will help to break up heavy lumps.

Sandy: dig out bed completely to a depth of 2 feet; on the bottom place either a layer of clay soil, a thickness or two of black polyethylene, fibreglass batts or a 6-8-inch layer of shredded newspaper; replace sandy soil, mixing in the same kinds of humus and fertilizer as for clay soil; work on sandy soils is best done in fall or spring.

To make acid soil

If you want to grow plants that must have acid soil to do well, either test the soil yourself with a home kit (making sure the material in it is fresh), or send samples to your nearest soil-testing service, indicating what you intend to grow in it. (For where to get this help, see Part V.) The laboratory will send you a report indicating the acidity of your soil, measured in pH. Seven is the breaking point of this scale, above that soil is alkaline, below it acid. Acid-soil plants such as rhododendrons and azaleas need a pH of 4.5 to 5.5. If the report indicates that your soil is only slightly acid or slightly alkaline, and you wish to grow these plants, you may be able to adjust it by mild means — adding acid peat or composted oak leaves up to a proportion of 50-50, chemicals such as ferrous sulphate or sulphur at a rate of 2-3 pounds per 100 square feet, and mixing them in thoroughly. If the test shows that your soil is a long way off and you want to grow many plants, you would do better to raise the whole bed, first digging out to a depth of two feet, then replacing with acid soil, raising the final level 6 inches above the surrounding ground. This will have to be checked yearly to be sure that it maintains the proper level of acidity. If it begins to slip, try to bring it back by adding 1 tablespoon of sulphur in the soil around each plant, and an acid mulch of oak leaves, pine needles, or shredded pine bark. If you want to grow only one or two special acid-loving plants in a non-acid soil, you can do this by planting them in a galvanized iron washtub filled with acid soil, with two or three good-sized holes punched in the bottom for drainage. I once saw the most dazzling clump of 3-foot high showy lady's-slippers, *Cypripedium reginae*, growing this way in a garden that, everywhere else, was alkaline. Experts do not recommend planting acid-demanders singly in a hole filled with acid soil in an otherwise alkaline bed — it is impossible to maintain acidity in such a situation and the plant eventually dies.

WHY, WHEN AND HOW TO FERTILIZE

Why

Fertilizers add vital nutrients to your soil and replace those already taken up by plants growing in your garden. A continuous replenishing is necessary. Fertilizers can be either organic or inorganic — good gardeners use both. Inorganic fertilizers with their quick availability are absolutely essential to good growth in the Far North where organic fertilizers are very slow to break down because of cold soil.

The well-fertilized plant not only grows and flowers better, its consequent good health resists and survives disease and insect attack, its vigor reduces fussy care and maintenance.

All fertilizer must be liquified before the plant can absorb it, therefore follow all dry applications with a thorough watering if no immediate rain. Organics must be chemically altered by soil microbes before they can be taken up by plants and should therefore be applied some months before needed.

How and When

Organic fertilizers: the natural organics, manure, green manure, processed sewage, bone meal, fish meal, blood and bone, cottonseed meal and the synthetic organic, urea formaldehyde, are slow-release and some act as soil conditioners and activators of beneficial bacteria as well. Dollar for dollar and hour for hour of your time in applying them, natural organics are not considered to be as effective as a good program of soil conditioning with additives of balanced, inorganic fertilizers; however, many gardeners still swear by them and most still use them in one form or another.

Fresh manure, which is usually applied as a top dressing to planting beds in fall, should never be used in direct contact with plants; rotted or dehydrated manure is mixed with soil during preparation of planting beds and as a mulch; highly concentrated manures such as chicken or pig should be thoroughly mixed with soil before applying. Green manure is the product of growing (usually between other crops — as in a vegetable garden) a grass or other plant that rots rapidly and produces organic fertilizer and humus when turned under in the soil; rye is the most widely grown; seeded early in fall, it makes good growth before winter, stays green and commences to grow quickly in spring; should be turned into the soil before seed heads form.

Processed sewage is spread on top of soil from spring to midsummer and watered in according to directions on bag.

Bone, fish and cottonseed meal, blood and bone, and so on are mixed with soil at planting time in recommended proportions.

Urea-formaldehyde, especially recommended for lawns, is long acting, non-burning and should be used as directed on bag.

Inorganic fertilizers: these are balanced chemical formulas available from garden suppliers; they should be chosen carefully to provide what is needed for your soil and your plants. Too much, the wrong one, or applied at the wrong time, is worse than none at all. Too much will burn the plant, the wrong one will stimulate the wrong type of growth — all leaves, for instance, and no flowers — and applied at the wrong time it could throw the plant off a good growing pattern — as would happen if soft new growth that would later winter-kill formed because fertilizer was applied in late summer or early fall. If you are not sure what to use, consult your provincial or state department of agriculture.

All inorganic fertilizers are nonpoisonous: content and recommended dosages are all clearly marked on their packages. Follow instructions explicitly: an overdose or incorrect application can quickly and seriously injure or kill a plant. Always water in granular fertilizers and never feed a wilting or apparently sick plant: try plain water and shading from the sun first.

The useful contents of general garden chemical fertilizers are primarily:

nitrogen, which promotes leaf growth and, in correct quantities, a rich green color; it also feeds microorganisms during their decomposition of organic materials, a very necessary action in good soil

phosphorus, which stimulates the production of flowers and therefore fruit and seed

potassium, which induces strong stalks and roots and builds resistance to disease and winter damage

By government regulation the percentage of these minerals in each brand of fertilizer is marked on the bag. For instance, 10-6-4 means that the fertilizer contains at least 10% nitrogen, 6% available phosphorus and 4% water-soluble potassium. The rest is filler. Check these percentages against the price and compare with other brands. What may appear to be a cheaper brand may actually be less fertilizer and more filler. Find out from local authorities what is the best formula of inorganic fertilizer for general garden use in your area — some soils, for instance, need no extra potassium.

Minute quantities of such minerals as magnesium, calcium, iron, known as trace elements, are also needed for good growth, but most garden soils have these in sufficient quantities. However, if you have a problem that applications of regular brands of inorganic fertilizers do not correct consult your department of agriculture — it may be that your soil needs extra trace elements.

Inorganic fertilizers come in different forms:

as granules, to be mixed in soil, spread on lawns and around (not touching) plants and then watered in

as crystals, to be dissolved in water and the solution sprayed on foliage (known as foliar feeding), poured on the soil around the base of plants, injected through a root feeder into the ground, or, as a starter solution of fertilizer and water, used to feed seeds and transplants

in various concentrates such as tablets, sticks and perforated, long-lasting plastic packets.

Uses of inorganic fertilizers

For flowers and vegetables: before planting, thoroughly mix granular inorganic fertilizers into the soil, according to manufacturer's recommendations; after planting, before and after flowering add recommended quantities to the top of the soil in a circle around each plant, not touching leaves or stems, and water in. Bulb plantings benefit from an application of fertilizer in the fall, but do not fertilize perennials, trees, shrubs or hedges after midsummer to prevent the formation of tender new growth that could winter-kill. Vegetables in rows should be fertilized by first mixing the granular form into the soil when the bed is being prepared, then adding more (at rates recommended by the manufacturer) up and down the rows, 4 inches away from the plants, when growth first appears, and again just before bloom. Foliar feedings are used as a quick pickup for all leafy plants and are particularly effective as a supplement to granular fertilizers mixed in the soil. Liquid starter solutions are used to damp down seed beds before sowing and to soak planting holes before new plants are set in place.

For deciduous trees and shrubs: in spring work granular fertilizer into the surface of the ground above the roots, which usually spread out as far as the shrub or tree's branches extend outwards above it; or apply liquid feedings through a specially designed feeder to the roots. Dosage is usually half that for flowers, but be sure to check directions on the package.

For evergreens: apply in spring as above, dosage is usually one quarter that for flowers. Some horticulturists believe that, other than an application of a high-phosphorus fertilizer below the root ball at planting time, evergreens do not need extra feeding for the rest of their life.

For lawns: before seeding or sodding, work a balanced lawn fertilizer into the top 3-4 inches of soil. For established lawns, feed with a high-nitrogen fertilizer on the last snow. For both new and old, follow with further feedings in late spring and again in late summer. Always water in if no rain.

For established gardens: where a fertilizing program has been consistently carried out for more than 5 years, use inorganic fertilizers high in phosphorus rather than those high in nitrogen.

For a starter and transplant solution: used to soak new plants before setting in the ground, seed beds before planting seeds, new plantings immediately after putting in place and young seedlings. Make a dilute solution of water soluble fertilizer (20-20-20 is the most commonly used) in proportion of 1 teaspoon to 1 gallon of water and mix well. Can be poured directly on roots and leaves without injuring them.

Inorganic fertilizers combined with other materials
Fertilizers are sometimes combined with insecticides, herbicides and trace elements and have the value, in one application, of feeding the plant, preventing weeds and killing insects, both in the soil and by systemic penetration of the plant. Insecticides in this mix may be poisonous so extreme care should be used in handling them (see Chapter 19 for precautions). When applying, soil should be loose, moist yet dry enough to crumble easily and have all weeds removed. Work the mixture into the top 2-3 inches of soil at time of application and water in immediately. Not recommended for vegetable or edible crops. For correct dosage, read the label.

Where using fertilizers combined with herbicides, to control weeds on lawns, be careful not to apply so much that trees or valuable plantings, whose roots may be below the grass roots, are killed by seepage.

WHY, WHEN AND HOW TO MAKE COMPOST

Compost is homemade humus: a lightener for heavy clay soil, a moisture-holding, spongy additive for sandy ones, a simple way of returning to the earth some of the nourishment that plants must take out of it to grow, bloom and fruit. In other words, a boon, and the making of it great good sense.

Why make it?
for economy; as a soil improver it costs almost nothing to make and the
    ingredients are, for the most part, things you would otherwise have to get
    rid of at some cost or inconvenience — dead leaves, grass clippings, stalks

and flower heads, pulled weeds, old sods, dropped fruit (watch out for wasps with these!), leftovers from the vegetable garden. You can also add kitchen scraps, eggshells and coffee grounds. The other ingredients are inexpensive and easy to come by — some fertilizer and a little lime, air and water

for improving soil by creating conditions for better drainage and better retention of moisture (this isn't as contrary as it sounds because good garden soil needs both)

for encouraging excellent growth of plants by stimulating and supporting development of helpful bacteria in the soil

for increasing good tilth in soil by mixing in when digging new beds and making plantings of all kinds, when adding top dressings and mulches.

When to make compost

Almost any time you have the materials to begin with. Good technique can produce usable compost in temperate parts of the country in a year, in the colder north it may take up to two or three years. But a yearly sequence of making the mix will eventually pay off in constant production, it is just a matter of getting started and keeping at it.

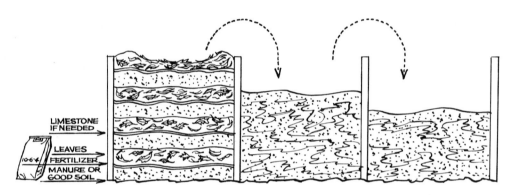

How to make compost

There is more than one good way to make a compost pile, but all have the general characteristics of a large, varied, damp sandwich. If you live in Zone 3 and up, choose a shady, out-of-the-way part of the garden because, except to dyed-in-the-wool conservationists and thrifty gardeners, a compost pile is not a thing of beauty. In Zones 0, 1 & 2, because of the more prolonged deep cold, it's wiser to place a compost pile in a well-drained area in full sun.

Set off an area of three sections, each approximately 4 × 4 feet. Divide them from each other by heavy link fencing set firmly with metal posts, or build low unmortared walls of concrete block laid with its holes horizontal to allow air to penetrate the pile, or take a chance on the sureness of your eye and pile up each section of compost without any support. In number one bin, start with 6 inches of manure or 1 inch of soil. Dust the surface, in proportions of 4-6 ounces per square yard, with a high nitrogen fertilizer. (Nitrogen hastens rotting and the sooner this is complete the sooner your compost is ready to use.) Next, add 8 inches of leaves or other vegetative material, dusting with ground limestone; if you will be using the finished

compost for acid-requiring plants such as rhododendrons omit the limestone. You can also add wood ashes, if you have them, for their high potash content. Then repeat the sequence of layers until the pile is about 4 feet high. Dish the top inwards so that rain will run into not out of the pile, and if weather is dry keep it moist (but not sopping wet) by hosing. (See drawing).

Turn it over at the end of the first month with a digging fork, and as frequently thereafter as your time will allow. The oftener it is turned — up to once a month — the quicker it will decompose. But don't be disheartened if you cannot do it this often. Lots of good compost piles are only turned once or twice a year.

In the Far North, it is best not to enclose the pile with block or fencing because collected rain in the base could freeze into a solid block of ice that might never completely thaw during the summer, thus slowing the whole process. Better build in the open, cover with clear plastic, battening it down snugly with soil. Further watering will not be necessary until the pile is uncovered in 10 weeks, turned, fertilized, watered again and re-covered. (See drawing next page.)

A compost pile for the Far North.

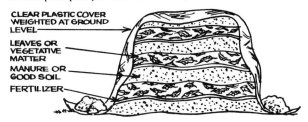

CLEAR PLASTIC COVER
WEIGHTED AT GROUND
LEVEL

LEAVES OR
VEGETATIVE
MATTER

MANURE OR
GOOD SOIL

FERTILIZER

Compost will be ready for use when it is dark, crumbly and of good tilth. Because not all materials decompose at the same rate, it may be necessary to screen the rough material to get soil for special plantings. Rub rough compost against a ½-1-inch mesh screen to get a fine mix for potting soil, seed beds and lawn dressing. What does not go through the screen return to the pile for another year. If making large amounts of compost quickly and effectively is important for you, buy a power-shredder.

At the end of the first period of decomposition, toss the material from bin number one into number two. At the end of the second into number three; use this while repeating the process, starting a new pile each time in the first vacated bin.

WHY, HOW AND WHEN TO WATER

Why

Plants, like people, cannot live without water. Intake of nutrients depends on it and replacement of what transpires into the air is essential if plants are to live and grow. To know how and when to water properly is one of the most useful pieces of knowledge a gardener can have.

How

The how of good watering is that it must get maximum, thorough penetration down to the roots of the plants. Moisture, either from adequate rain or hosing, should soak down 1-2 feet for the average plant; for the very small plants less, for very large ones, such as big trees, more. Skimpy watering — a hand-held sprinkle on your lawn on a balmy evening while you chat with your neighbor, for instance — is worse than no watering at all. By dampening only the top of the soil, roots are drawn into the upper, easily-dried-out surface where they will develop less vigorously and be more quickly killed or stunted. And the same goes for all plants, not just lawn grasses.

Water spreads sideways very little; most goes straight down. Tests have shown that on completely dry, average soil, it soaks down 8 inches in one hour; faster and farther in sandy ones, slower and less far in clay. Since your garden will not be bone dry to begin with, a workable yardstick is to aim, if there has been no rain for 10 days, to lay down 1 inch of water once a week on average soil, the same amount every ten days on clay, a little less twice a week on sandy soil.

Since a permanent workable moisture gauge for home gardeners has yet to be invented, the simplest way to find out how much water your sprinkler delivers is to set out three or four cans at different distances from the head and check the time it takes to collect an inch of water in them. Make a note of this and use it as a guide. If your sprinkler fills the cans unevenly, adjust it, live with it or get a better one. Whatever schedule you follow, let the soil dry out between waterings — this sends plant roots deeper to seek water and thus they develop sturdier growth.

Special situations:

all soil dries out faster in hot windy weather; under heavy surface-rooting trees like elm and maple; on steep slopes, especially if they face south or west; in sharp-drainage, no-rain-or-dew places like those next to house walls under eaves. In these places use plants that prefer these conditions

runoff is faster on slopes, so, if you are making new plantings on such a site, around the outside edge of each plant place a baffle of stone pieces, some wood or a strip of tin to hold water till it can soak into the ground for the roots to use

all new plantings need watering often; on seed and seedlings use a fine spray that will not wash them out of the ground; for their first season (and frequently during their whole life) evergreens should be washed down and top-sprayed frequently to clean them

pots, planters and window boxes need to be watered frequently in place; be self-watering (see page 17), or be lifted into a large tub of water for a thorough soaking as often as necessary, usually once a week at least. Free-standing clay pots can be kept moist more steadily if they are set permanently in a larger pot, with the space between packed with peat, kept moist. Hanging baskets should be lined with moss and a piece of burlap or perforated plastic, before being filled with soil, to keep water from running right through before it can be fully absorbed. Open cracks that develop at the sides of large containers where soil meets pot should be repacked by ramming a sharp stick into the hardened edge of the earth, otherwise all water put on the top will run swiftly through the open crack and out the bottom, completely bypassing the soil and roots

a newly transplanted large tree, or one where a major grade change will pile new earth over established roots, should have clay tiles inserted vertically in the ground around the outside circumference of the branches, the tops of which should be level with the final grade, and these tiles should be filled with water every few days for the first growing season, frequently thereafter until the tree is well established, and always during periods of drought. This is also an effective way to save a big tree where a major part of the root system must be sealed off with a paved driveway or walk. The tiles should be set when the paving is being laid and be deep enough to go through the solid part of the paving to the loose gravel or soil below, where the roots will be.

Tools for watering

an ample, well-balanced watering can with interchangeable nozzles for fine or heavy spraying

hoses of handy lengths: plastic is lighter and cheaper than rubber, but if your water is icy cold it stiffens and is hard to handle, whereas rubber stays more flexible. It is well worth the time, money and muscle saved to install a generous number of outlets when you are building a new house or garden, or to have them put into an old one; a good measure is to have an outlet placed so that you never have to pull more than 50 feet of hose to reach any part of the garden. Water can be dispensed from the hose in many ways. There are dozens of models in sprinkler heads — an oscillating arm is one of the best; long tubes of perforated plastic or canvas are excellent for soaking flower beds and rose plantings, so that the ground can be saturated without wetting the foliage above (wet rose leaves are prone to fungus disease); metal bubblers break the force of the water too, and it is always possible to invent a simple dispenser with an old gunnysack wrapped around the hose end or a board set at an angle to disperse the flow. The idea is to lay the water down at the best rate for maximum absorption without washing out the roots or harming the plants

automatic watering systems: this can be a pro job, or, if you are handy with tools, something you can do yourself. The use of plastic pipe and connections that will not break or burst in freezing weather has made it possible to lay waterlines just under the surface of the ground from a central connection in the house to all parts of the garden. Pop-up heads to spray the water lift when the system is turned on and drop back when it goes off, allowing lawn mowers to move over the top without harm. Valves allow you to water one section of the garden at a time, switches can turn the whole system off if it has rained or if you want to water one part of the garden manually, as you might just after planting a bed of annuals. Such systems now can be connected to the average home water service because they can be set to bring on the sections in sequence. Timers are available to turn each section on and off at a certain time of day or night and on a certain day of the week. Be wary, though, if you install such a system, to preset the throw of the sprinkler heads at a time when water pressure will be the same as when you set the system to come on. I know of one sad tale where a new automatic watering system was installed and the throw of the sprinkler heads was set during the day when the workmen were there. Some three weeks later the happy gardener, who had set his system to begin spraying at three in the morning and finish at six before everybody was up, suddenly realized that something dreadful was happening to his front door — the paint was peeling off and the seams opening alarmingly. The culprit was the new watering system, which at three in the morning was spraying four feet farther than it had been set during the lower pressure time of the day and was regularly soaking the front door. The valve was turned down, the door mended and repainted and everyone was happy again.

When to water

Watering is most effectively done early in the day.

Special situations:

new plantings are the exception to the general rule — they should be watered at any time they are wilting or the soil around them is dried out.

in late summer and early fall, watering should be done only to prevent wilting; withholding it at this time encourages proper hardening of new growth so that it does not winter-kill easily, but one last deep watering of all plants should be given in late fall so that they go into winter with earth at their roots thoroughly moist. This is especially important for evergreens, which continue to transpire all winter, and in parts of the country where extremely variable winter temperatures put great stress on plants.

harmful effects of sudden early frosts can often be overcome by hosing nipped plants very early in the morning before the sun hits them and continuing to hose until they are completely thawed out.

WHY, HOW AND WHEN TO WEED

Gardeners weed to remove plants they do not wish to grow, because they know that uncontrolled weeds strangle and smother good plants, and spoil the planned beauty of the garden. Experienced gardeners also know that it is even more important to remove weeds because they take from the soil valuable nourishment that would otherwise be available to chosen plants.

How and when to weed

You can weed by hand, by instruments, such as one of the many kinds of hoe, or by application of herbicidal chemicals. The last is the easiest.

Weeding by hand: advised mainly for flower beds and ground cover plantings where special care must be taken not to destroy the wrong plant. To make it easy, weed after a rain, or water the ground the day before, preferably when weeds are small and tender. Be sure to pull entire plant.

Weeding with a hoe: a historic method of ridding gardens of unwanted plants, going back years and years. Basically, it is cutting off the main stem of the plant just under the surface of the ground and leaving it to die. Nearly every gardener has his favorite tool for this and his favorite method. The best do a short sharp job with the weed and at the same time scuffle the surface of the soil to create a beneficial dust mulch. It is important not to go too deep and not to hoe when ground is soaking wet.

Weeding with herbicidal chemicals: herbicides are compounded to kill weeds in many different ways:

by destroying germinating weed seed in the ground, as pre-emergent herbicides do. This is prescribed for pesky crabgrass in lawns, an annual which reappears every year from seeds dropped the year before. The correct herbicide applied before these seeds have a chance to germinate eliminates the crop for that year, but since new seed may blow or be tracked in from other untreated areas it may take a regular annual program to keep it under control. If herbicides of this type are used in spring, do not attempt to re-seed desirable lawn grasses until August.

pre-emergent herbicides can also be used in flower beds where plants are already established or where annuals are going to be grown from started plants. For treatment before transplanting, weed, cultivate and water the bed; measure herbicide carefully; sprinkle on soil and mix in thoroughly; transplant seedlings with good earthball; water again. For treatment after transplanting, wait a few days till plants recover; then, using granular or liquid herbicide, measure accurately, apply to soil, being careful not to touch the plants with it, and water in.

by selectively killing foliage and broad-leaved weeds such as ragweed, dandelions, buttercups, chickweed, clover, black medic, creeping charlie, shepherd's purse in lawns, leaving grass unharmed. Spray in spring or early fall, following directions on label. Protect nearby garden plants and work only when air is still, to eliminate drift. Do not soak the ground under trees with herbicide — some may seep down and damage the tree. In these places, you might better weed by hand or selectively, with just a small amount of the solution.

by killing outright such nuisance plants as poison ivy, plants of all kinds in gravel driveways, walks and tennis courts. Spray according to directions; persistent weeds may need more than one application. Again be careful of seepage or drift.

by rotting unwanted stumps left when a tree is cut down. Drill holes in stump and treat according to label. (See below for other ways to banish stumps).

CAUTIONS
Herbicides are believed to be nontoxic to man but still they should be handled carefully

1. Keep equipment for mixing, carrying and applying for this use only — even a slight residue left in a seemingly well-washed watering can and sprayed in error on a sensitive garden plant could be the end of it.
2. Do not let it spill over or seep into ground around valuable plants or vegetables.
3. Do not apply on a breezy day for it may drift onto desirable plants in your or your neighbor's garden.
4. For good penetration, soak weeds with liquid herbicides until they drip, cultivate granular types into ground and immediately water well.

5. If you have a choice of pre-emergent or post-emergent control, choose pre-emergent. Weeds are most susceptible when they are young.

6. Although large commercial growers now use herbicides on vegetable crops — carrots, for instance, are unharmed with specified sprayings of varsol, the common petroleum-base floor cleaner, to eliminate weeds — home gardeners are strongly advised to control weeds in vegetable gardens with mulches of vegetative matter or plastic sheeting, black for the temperate parts of the country, clear for the Far North.

HOW TO KEEP WEEDS FROM GROWING
IN THE FIRST PLACE

use mulches on bare ground under flowering plants and shrubs (See How to Mulch, page 148).
use ground covers of living plants under large trees and in problem areas. (See CHAPTER 24: Ground Covers.)
learn good management of lawns by choosing the correct strains of seed or sod, lay it properly and then follow up with a regular, wise program of feeding, watering and cutting. (See CHAPTER 23: Lawns.)
start control measures as soon as weeds appear, do not let them go to seed to perpetuate themselves.

Dandelion.

HOW TO ELIMINATE STUMPS
1. Cut off below ground, keep any new growth cut off, and eventually it will rot away — it may take a while.
2. Make cuts in the bark of the trunk that is left and in any roots that are above ground; pack with crystals of ammonium sulfamate.
3. Mix 2-4-D and 2-4-T, as manufacturer recommends, in either water, fuel or motor oil; soak stump and sprouts with it.

4. Excavate all round the stump, cutting any roots, then, with a block and tackle, yank it out of the ground.
5. Do what your ancestors did — burn it by drilling, filling the holes with oil and setting fire to it; this could be dangerous and you might have to have a permit from the fire department.
6. Make it into a sculpture — there's a whole block in Montreal with fascinating tree-stump sculpture.
7. Carve it into a garden seat.

WHY, WHEN AND HOW TO MULCH

A mulch is one of many materials spread on the surface of the soil around plants to improve growing conditions.

WHY MULCH?

In spring: as a top dressing for lawns, *to encourage thick turf*; as a fine-textured bed *for new seed*.

In summer: *to save time and labor* by discouraging growth of weeds and providing a clean, porous soil surface

to reduce the need for extra watering by retarding evaporation of moisture from soil below

to keep soil cool, loose and spongy, a condition which encourages:

growth of beneficial bacteria

activity of worms, whose castings have nutrient value

improvement of structure and tilth of soil

improvement in flavor of fruits and vegetables, growth in all plants

to act as a barrier between ground-based infections and plants above

to keep plants clear of soil splash during rains

In fall: *to keep ground unfrozen* for late planting of such things as lilies (so apply before freeze-up)

to encourage root formation of newly planted bulbs for spring blooming

In winter: *to improve tilth* of soil during non-growing months of the year.

to prevent deep penetration of frost and alternate thawing and freezing which can result in damaging or total heaving of plants out of the ground.

WHEN TO MULCH, HOW AND WITH WHAT

In spring: for lawns — rake, aerate, fertilize, water and then apply ¼-½ inch of damp peat, fine compost or soil as a top dressing and favorable surface for new seed (see Chapter 23).

In summer: when plants are growing well and at onset of hot weather; weed, fertilize and water ornamental plants and vegetable gardens, then, on top of the soil around plants, add one of the following:

buckwheat hulls (1-2 inches), especially good for roses, perennials (annuals usually don't need mulching), and tuberous begonias

leaf mold, compost, pine needles (2-3 inches), especially good for wild flowers

pine needles, wood chips or shredded bark (1-2 inches), especially good for rhododendrons, azaleas, but keep back from main branches at base, which may rot if continuously damp

sawdust (1-2 inches), especially good for vegetables, put 1-inch-deep layer in 4-inch-wide bands on either side of rows, applying high-nitrogen fertilizer to the soil first

tree leaves (6-9 inches), especially good for shrubs and small trees,
rhubarb, sweet corn, tomatoes (apply when staking or when first blossoms
appear)

ground corncobs (2-4 inches), not handsome but effective on roses

hay (marsh, salt, field), *eelgrass, kelp, straw* (6-8 inches), especially
good for sandy soil, seaside gardens and fruit trees (keep back from
the trunks to discourage rodents; also set out poison bait under it, or
mound gravel around the base of the trees)

building paper, asphalt shingles, especially good for berry bushes if
laid flat on the ground over the roots

black plastic (polyethylene), available from garden suppliers, especially
good for vegetables that require heat to ripen — tomatoes, peppers,
cucumbers, squash and corn. Lay on the ground before planting, then slit
the plastic just enough to insert each plant. Weight the sides of the plastic
with soil to keep it from blowing away. If applying after plants are in
the ground, lay strips of plastic down the rows on either side of the plantings

In fall:

mulch all new bulb plantings to keep them growing as long as possible
before the ground freezes deeply

to prevent freezing of soil so that late delivered bulbs such as lilies can still
be planted, prepare holes early in the fall, mound topsoil beside them,
or better still, put it in a plastic bag or basket in your garage or in a shed
where it will not freeze, then fill the hole with dry leaves (oak are good),
excelsior, dry peat, hay or straw or place several thicknesses of weighted
newspaper over it. When bulbs arrive, remove mulch, plant, replace topsoil,
mounding it to drain well and to allow for settling, mulch again for the
winter with leaves or evergreen branches.

In winter:

after ground is frozen hard, topdress flower beds, vegetable garden,
new tree plantings, with one or a combination of the following:

manure

leaves, the best are those that do not mat (such as oak)

hay, cornstalks, compost

evergreen branches (cut-up Christmas trees are fine and usually
available at the right time), especially good laid over or up around
tender, flower-budded plants such as heather, azaleas, rhododendrons,
mainly to protect them from burning by late-winter sun

shavings or *sphagnum moss* weighted with branches — a favorite
in northernmost parts of the country.

(For special mulching of rose beds, see CHAPTER 26.)

WHY, WHEN AND HOW TO PLANT

WHY PLANT CAREFULLY?

Because with careful, skillful planting your material will respond with quicker new growth, more beautiful form, flowers and foliage and with better health and vigor all its life.

WHEN TO PLANT

large trees after leaf-drop in fall, with a frozen earthball in winter (this is a job for pros), before budding out in spring. Best of these is spring.

bare-root trees and shrubs, after leaf-drop in fall or before bud-out in spring. Better of these two is spring. Lilacs are an exception — they should be planted in the fall.

new perennials in spring, new divisions of old perennials just after blooming. Exceptions are peonies, which should be planted in fall, poppies in late summer, iris in early summer, roses in either spring or fall.

spring flowering bulbs are planted in the fall, small bulbs such as crocus and all daffodils and narcissus as soon as they can be bought, tulips from October till frost.

gladiolus just as trees are beginning to leaf out.

summer bulbs, corms and tubers such as caladiums, dahlias, begonias, after the ground is warm and there is no danger of a killing frost (for last spring frost dates, see Part V). You can have earlier bloom if bulbs, corms and tubers are started indoors 4-6 weeks before the last spring frost, then planted outdoors.

lily bulbs (which are not harvested till the fall) are planted as soon as you can get delivery of them, except the Madonna lily, *Lilium candidum*, and *L. testaceum*, which are planted in August.

seeds of hardy annuals (California poppy, candytuft, clarkia, cornflower, cosmos, larkspur, love-in-a-mist, pansy, pink, calendula, snapdragon, sweet alyssum, sweet pea) can be planted outdoors in the fall or in the very early spring.

seeds of tender annuals are planted indoors 4-6 weeks before the last predicted spring frost or outdoors after the last spring frost.

Planting balled and burlapped material.

HOW TO PLANT:

Balled and burlapped material (listed in nursery catalogues as B & B)

if unable to plant immediately, heel into the ground or keep covered and damp till planted.

when planting permanently, place in prepared hole, loosening but not unwrapping the burlap.

fill in around the earthball with good soil, packing it tight with your foot.

add more soil to the top but leave a shallow saucer to catch water and lead it to the roots.

if evergreen, during its first year spray the whole plant with water once or twice a week if possible, especially during dry weather. When watering, allow hose to run slowly over the roots and soak deeply; be sure to do this just before the first hard frost so that roots go into the winter moist.

Bare-root shrubs and trees

if plants on arrival are dried out, soak for a couple of days in a starter solution of water and fertilizer. If they are too large to do this, set their roots in the solution and spray the tops.

if unable to plant immediately, heel in and water well — roots must never dry out.

when planting in permanent site, prune out any injured roots, reduce the top growth by one third to compensate for the loss of roots in moving from the nursery, or spray the whole plant with anti-desiccant.

set in the prepared hole, spreading roots gently outwards, backfill with good soil, tamping it gently, and saucer the rim of the hole to catch rain or hose water until the plant is established — usually one growing season.

stake or guy all trees against whipping winter wind, using wood or metal stakes and ties of rope, wire threaded through pieces of hose or old nylon stockings. Examine these ties every few months to be sure they are not chafing the bark or binding the tree too tightly.

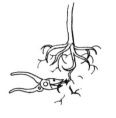

Rampant plants

What may appear, in the beginning, to be a desirable garden plant can sometimes become a rampant nuisance if not controlled. For such plants — snow-in-summer, goutweed and the deeper rooting knotweed are some — press a barrier strip of metal edging into the soil around them. This can be bought from your garden supplier and is similar to that used to keep lawn grass from creeping into flower beds.

Seeds outdoors

plant in a prepared row or bed of finely screened, porous soil, with good drainage, in bright light but not sunshine.

first soak soil with starter solution of fertilizer and water to give the germinated seed a quick sure beginning.

dust fine seed on the surface, do not cover it but press it gently in; press coarse seed into the soil and lightly cover it. Hard-coated seeds like morning glories should be soaked for an hour before planting and lightly nicked on the side to break the hard case. Cup-and-saucer vine seeds should be planted on edge. Beans are planted eye down.

label.

if birds are a nuisance, mix your seed before planting with a camouflage of fine wood ash or sand.

put a thin cover of damp burlap or newspaper over the seed bed, or a piece of glass braced a few inches above it. Remove as soon as the first seed sprouts.

at all times, keep the seed bed moist by fine sprinkling — seedlings will die if they dry out.

(For what to do next, see the section in this chapter on how to transplant).

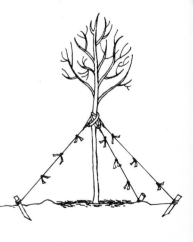

Seeds indoors

containers for indoor planting can be many things — clay pots or bulb pans (old ones should be scrubbed and boiled, new ones soaked overnight in

151

water), seed trays, Jiffy pots made of compressed peat or Jiffy Sevens, which are a mixture of peat and fertilizer in a little net bag, pressed into a small cookie that expands in a few minutes when soaked in water, plastic dishes, ordinary tin cans or aluminum foil dishes. Where necessary, punch holes in the bottom for drainage.

place a piece of broken pot over each hole, then a layer of four thicknesses of wet newspaper and add soil or special mix to within 1 inch of the top. An alternative to the bit of pot and newspaper is a piece of sponge rubber.

the mix can be one of many good things — fine soil, a mixture of soil and vermiculite, peat or perlite, or a soilless mix, such as that developed by Cornell University, called "peatlite" (for formula see page 153). If soil is used, it should be oven sterilized at 180°F for half an hour, then cooled before use. Many good gardeners put a 1-inch layer of sterile milled sphagnum moss on top of the soil as extra insurance against damping-off disease, which is fatal to seedlings.

a further precaution against disease is to dust seed while it is still in its packet with a fungicide or special protectant (see Chapter 19 for how to do this).

sprinkle fine seed on top of the mix and press it in; barely cover coarse seed with a little of the mix or some dampened sphagnum, being careful to plant only one kind to a pot.

water with a fine sprinkler or set the container in water until moisture just shows on the surface of the mix, let it drain and cover with a piece of glass, heavy paper or cardboard.

set in a warm (60°-70°F) place with, if possible, mild bottom heat, or place under fluorescent lights, 4-6 inches away, for 14-16 hours per day.

remove cover as soon as sprouts appear, keep watered and if in window light turn the seed pan a little each day for more even growth, or on the inner side set up a reflector of foil-wrapped cardboard.

if peatlite is used, water with ½ strength, water-soluble fertilizer (20-20-20 fertilizer at the rate of ½ teaspoon to 1 gallon) once weekly for 4 weeks, then a solution of 1 teaspoon to 1 gallon every second week till transplanted outdoors.

(For how to transplant, see page 153).

For Specific Details of How to Plant:

Peatlite mix formula

1 bushel each of shredded peatmoss and horticultural vermiculite #4
10 level tablespoons ground limestone
5 level tablespoons potassium nitrate (saltpetre at your drugstore)
1 teaspoon chelated iron

(Everything but nitrate is available at your garden and building supplier)
To mix: swab table with Javex and water; with clean dustpan, mix 1 gallon warm water into ingredients, mixing thoroughly. Place in plastic bag or clean garbage pail to store. Will keep up to 6 months.

WHY AND HOW TO TRANSPLANT

WHY TRANSPLANT?

The purpose of transplanting is to move a plant from one place to a more desirable one with the least disturbance to its growth cycle. For instance:

a shrub may have become so shaded by a tree above it that it must be moved to a sunnier spot if it is to flower well.

construction may be taking over a site where valuable plants are growing and they must be moved to save them.

your designing eye may wish to move perennials or bulbs to a more picturesque place in the garden scene.

seedlings may need to be moved from their original seedpan or from their first transplant stage to a final blooming site in the garden.

bulbs with unattractive ripening foliage may need to be moved out of the main part of the garden to a less conspicuous one.

HOW TO TRANSPLANT

Some techniques are common to all good transplanting: beforehand water any plant to be moved, trees and shrubs on each of several days before the final one; have new hole ready so that plants need not be kept out of the ground; move as quickly as possible to reduce shock and drying out; when ready to set plant in place, fill the hole with starter solution, let it drain, put the plant in, working soil gently around the roots, press down, backfill with more soil, water again with starter solution and shade from sun till well-established, usually a few days.

SPECIAL TECHNIQUES OF TRANSPLANTING

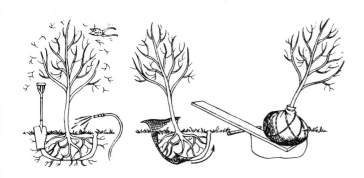

Established trees and shrubs: large heavy trees or shrubs are best moved by professional tree services or cut out and replaced with new nursery-size stock. It is seldom possible for an amateur to move a large old tree or shrub successfully. Smaller sizes are fairly easy to move. Cut all round the roots by driving a sharp spade straight down in a circle about 2 feet out from the trunk or base, dig under half the rootball and roll canvas, heavy burlap or plastic under it, then dig out the other half; tipping the earthball, pull the wrapping material under the second half and fasten it securely around the roots with rope or tie the corners of the wrapping tightly

153

over it; lever the wrapped earthball up and out of the hole and pull it to its new site — sometimes a ramp made of a board or small logs laid on rollers helps with this. Ease it into the new hole, tipping to unwrap half at a time. Prune top growth back one third, and, if weather is hot, use an anti-desiccant spray. Early spring, just before new growth begins, is the most favorable time to make such a move.

Perennials: lift clumps, with as much earth as possible, just as growth begins or just after blooming. Transfer to new site, reduce heavy top growth by pruning. Water with starter solution and shade from sun. (For special techniques with individual plants, see CHAPTER 27).

Annual Seedlings: transplant first seedlings when they show three pairs of leaves by carefully separating them from each other, leaving as much earth on the roots as possible; insert them singly in a pencil-sized hole in a box, flat or peat pot, a little deeper than they were growing before. Press lightly on each side of the seedling to make it firm and water gently with a little starter solution. When it is time to move these transplants to their place in the garden, cut them apart, leaving as much earth as possible with each root and set a little deeper, in prepared bed, outdoors. If in Jiffy pots, soak the pot and root in starter solution, pull off the rim of the pot and plant a little below the level the seedling was growing at in the pot; if in Jiffy Sevens, soak in starter solution and plant. Label; shade till the plant looks perky and is firmly growing again.

Bulbs: transplanted after blooming mainly to ripen their foliage in an inconspicuous place and to produce a flowering-size bulb for the next year. Dig each with a generous earthball; heel into soil at the same depth as it was growing before; feed and label; move back into flower bed at the usual fall bulb-planting time. If you have trouble with squirrels and rabbits eating your bulbs, try planting them in a special bed that can be fenced with chicken wire until they show green in the spring, then transplant them to planned places in the open garden. By that time your four-footed friends are more amorous than hungry and more likely to ignore your bulbs.

Sod for lawns: buy only green, weed-free fresh sod; fertilize and water the prepared soil bed, lay sod, tamp, water again and keep moist until grass roots catch well and start to grow again. Do not allow to dry out the first season. If on a steep slope, stake with wooden pegs or brush until the sod catches well enough to hold by itself.

WHY, WHEN AND HOW TO PRUNE

WHY PRUNE?

Skillful pruning accomplishes many good things:

it enhances the grace and rhythm of your garden

it encourages plants to be healthy and prolongs their lives

it restricts undesirable and promotes desirable growth of hedges so that they become both beautiful and impenetrable

it creates better and larger bloom on flowering plants, better bigger fruit on fruit trees

it repairs damage

it rejuvenates old overgrown trees and shrubs

WHEN AND WHAT TO PRUNE:

All year: For a garden to be at its best, some pruning should go on now and then all year. Make a pruning survey once a month, twice a month in spring, examining all the permanent growth of your garden. Are the walks clear? The vines tidy, not creeping over windows and pruned to show the wall behind in some places? Is the view of your house from the street framed by trees and shrubs, not blocked by them? Can you see pleasant views from all your windows? Do your trees and shrubs show graceful shapes or are they thick lumps of green in the landscape? Do the shapes of all plants in your garden complement each other? If you answer "Yes" to all these questions it's time to find a hammock and a good book. If it's "No," then read on.

Winter: this is a good time to prune deciduous trees because their leafless structure can be clearly seen. If any of your trees are so large you must climb above ladder height to prune them, it's probably better for both you and the tree to hire a professional arborist with the training and proper equipment to do the job. If there are no tree services where you live, try the telephone and hydro service linemen — they will sometimes come on their time off to help you.

Smaller trees that you can prune yourself should have large branches removed by first making a cut from the underside up and halfway through, 12 inches from the trunk; then a similar cut, a little farther out on the branch, halfway through from the top down. This takes off most of the limb. Lastly, make a clean cut, parallel with the trunk, to remove the stub. Smooth any splintery bits with a sharp knife and seal the cut with tree paint. (See drawing). Small branches can be cut off with a pruning saw, a long-handled tree knife, loppers or shears; cuts over an inch in diameter sealed with tree paint.

Do not prune birch or maple after mid-February — the rising sap will bleed from the cuts. Except in extreme cases, never prune out more than a third of a tree or shrub in any one year (fruit trees are the exception). Too heavy pruning can damage the tree's system and expose the bark to sunburn.

Shrubs and vines that bloom in summer on new wood — buddleia, rose-of-sharon, white and P.G. hydrangea, bittersweet, trumpet-vine are some — should be pruned in winter or early spring by cutting out the oldest branches at ground level.

Shrubs and vines that bloom in spring on wood formed the year before should be pruned right after flowering by cutting out the oldest branches at ground level — they are never pruned in spring before they flower. The only exception is that you prune spring-flowering shrubs in late winter when you want to use their branches for forcing indoors — forsythia, pussy willow, wild plum and cherry are in this class.

One of the real joys of the winter garden is to be able to cut your own evergreens for Christmas decorations indoors. This is particularly successful with yew, juniper, euonymus, mahonia, holly, ivy and cedar because they can be cut inconspicuously and will make new growth to fill the gaps. Pine, fir, cypress and spruce can be cut only if the symmetry of the tree will not be spoiled as they will not branch there again.

Fruit trees are pruned in late winter by cutting out one third of all year-old wood and reducing the balance by another third. When pruning fruit trees for high quality production, as commercial growers do, consult your provincial or state department of agriculture: they will have pamphlets on the subject. If you are faced with the problem of what to do with old neglected fruit trees, the consensus of experts is that it's better to replace than attempt to rejuvenate them. (For specific details for pruning different fruits, see CHAPTER 12.)

If ice and winter wind smash your trees, make clean cuts as quickly as possible but leave major repairs till spring. Broken branches should be cut back to the nearest crotch or trunk and sealed with tree paint; splits, if not too serious, can be pulled back together and bolted or bound; bent over trees can

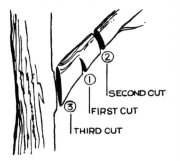

Cutting off a large branch.

SECOND CUT

FIRST CUT

THIRD CUT

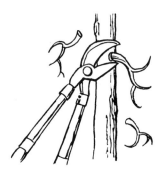

Pruning small branches.

Pruning small evergreens by cutting tips under a side leader.

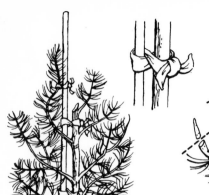

Replace a broken leader by staking up side branch.

Cut new side candles of pine in half in June.

Prune needle evergreens lightly in spring.

Prune out centre of small trees to let light in; take out crossing branches that could rub.

be propped up; broken heads can be cut cleanly off and sealed, then when spring comes, the strongest side branch nearest to the top can be staked upright to make a new leader (see drawing, above).

Spring: When planting new deciduous trees, shrubs, roses and woody vines, cut off any bruised or broken roots and branches and reduce top growth by about one third. When cutting branches, always prune to an outside bud so that new growth will develop away from the centre of the tree.

Cut out winter-kill on needle evergreens and prune lightly for good shape and to keep dense. Cut new growth in half while it is still soft, leaving the end tip of long side branches and the leader at the top a little longer than the others. This is especially necessary for Mugho pine. (See drawing, above).

Prune broad-leaved evergreens — euonymus, mahonia, kalmia, laurel are some — to develop fine shape and to produce better foliage.

Cut off dead wood of all winter-killed plants.

Prune out the oldest branches of bright barked shrubs such as the red-osier dogwood to encourage young growth that will be a brighter color than the old.

Shear lightly bushy ground covers like pachistima, heather that has bloomed; nip the heads out of pachysandra to encourage it to branch; cut verticals or nip the leader of vinca and bend new runners over and pin them to the ground. The purpose of this (and other special techniques you will find in CHAPTER 24) is to keep ground covers spreading sideways and hugging the ground.

Late Spring: Trim hedges so that the top is narrower than the bottom, otherwise they will become leggy and bare at ground level (see CHAPTER 22 for details).

Trim loose pieces of climbing vines; cut back those of rampant growth. Wherever you can reach them, cut off spent flower heads of vines such as wisteria, *Hydrangea petiolaris*, clematis.

Each year after blooming, prune out one or two old branches of early flowering shrubs at ground level (see Chapter 21 for details).

Remove old blooms of flowering broad-leaved evergreens such as rhododendrons and azaleas, before they can set seed.

156

Nip out heads of annuals when planting to develop bushier growth and more bloom.

Summer: Nip annuals wherever a stem gets leggy and shear in midsummer to develop a second bloom.

Cut off spent stalks of perennials such as delphinium, hollyhock and lythrum and they will bloom a second time.

If you want bushy plants with many flowers, prune first shoots of late-summer and fall-blooming perennials such as 'mums, aster, phlox, Michaelmas daisies, golden glow, to leave 5-6 shoots, and again when the side shoots on the first ones are 4-5 inches long. If you prefer a few taller, bigger flowers, nip out all side buds and shoots as they begin to form, leaving only the main shoot to develop.

Prune mature shrubs yearly by cutting out one or two of the oldest branches, at the base. Do not trim shrubs all over like a shaving brush — allow natural form to develop. Always cut just above an outside bud.

HOW TO PRUNE:

Always make clean sharp cuts, leaving no splintery bits. If necessary, smooth the open wound with a knife.

Seal all cuts over an inch in diameter with tree paint, which can be bought as an aerosol bomb or a liquid at a hardware or garden supply store.

When pruning off part of a branch always cut to an outside bud.

Trim bruised bark on trunks of trees to a vertical oval shape to allow for drainage of rain and melting snow.

Always prune out crisscross branches and twigs, those that rub one another, those on the inside of the shrub or tree, and any that are torn or broken.

Go slowly with your pruning. Cut a third of what you plan to take out and live with it for a while, then if the plants will be improved by it take out another third, and so on. Don't cut any shrub like a shaving brush, its branches in even lengths all over the top. Instead, go right to the base and cut out one or two stems of the oldest wood each year. Shorten the new wood unevenly, but only if it needs to be done. Try

to keep the naturally graceful shape of the tree or shrub.

The training of plants in special shapes by pruning:

The sculpturing and training of plants by pruning is an art in itself demanding great patience and study. One of the most ornamental is the espaliered tree or vine trained on a wall or fence to add a decorative pattern to the design of the garden. You will find recommended books on this special technique in the Bibliography at the end of the book.

Tools needed for general pruning:

Hand clippers for small branches and flower stalks

Loppers for thick low branches (buy with handle grips that will bump together before they can blood-blister your fingers)

A pruning saw — the best are curved with teeth on one side

A long-handled tree knife, very handy for cutting long tendrils of vines and high, smallish branches

A pruning knife

Hedge clippers, electric or manual

A bomb or can of tree paint and brush.

WHY, WHEN AND HOW TO PROPAGATE

WHY PROPAGATE?

for economy: you save money because at no cost you use pieces of plants already growing in your garden, or someone else's, to make more

for exact reproduction: plants propagated in these ways are exactly like their parents, something you cannot be sure of with seed

because the plant you want to reproduce is rare: some plants, notably many fine hybrids, are sterile so cannot set seed and the only way to increase them is by propagation

to get a headstart on a new plant: your cutting, division or layer will be larger sooner than if you began with seed or a seedling

to reproduce a notably excellent plant: this can mean one with better color, bigger flowers or more of them, finer foliage or form than the average

for fun: successful propagation, particularly if you have never done it before, makes you feel like a miracle-maker.

WHEN, HOW AND WITH WHAT

Propagation can be done with many kinds of material: softwood and hardwood cuttings, layers, leaf and root cuttings, divisions, runners, bulb divisions and by budding and grafting.

Softwood cuttings are taken from the current season's growth — deciduous trees and shrubs in summer; broad-leaved evergreens and conifers in summer, fall or winter.

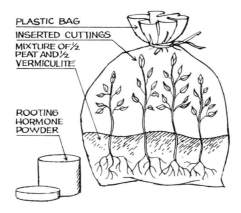

PLASTIC BAG
INSERTED CUTTINGS
MIXTURE OF ½ PEAT AND ½ VERMICULITE
ROOTING HORMONE POWDER

Try to work in the early part of the day, in a cool, shady place.

Cut terminal pieces of branches, 2-6 inches long, at a 45° angle, with a thin, sharp blade, one quarter of an inch below a node (junction of leaf and stem with a bud in it).

Remove one third of the leaves up from the base. If, at this point, you are not able to proceed with the job immediately, keep these cuttings moist in a plastic bag in the refrigerator.

Take off a thin slice of bark, 1-2 inches long, at the base, cutting just deeply enough to expose the cambium layer beneath the bark.

Dip in special hormone powder sold for the purpose (this stimulates rooting) and insert one third to one half of the lower end of the stem in one of the following:

a mixture of clean sharp sand and vermiculite or perlite

a mixture of sand and peat moss

a mixture of sand, peat moss and powdered styrofoam, equal parts (particularly good for broad-leaved evergreens)

All these mixes should be evenly moist.

Containers can be clay pots, pans, flats or boxes, but my favorite is an ordinary plastic bag which, after the cuttings are put into the medium, is blown up and tied tightly at the top and set in a north window, examined only every two weeks or so to see if roots have formed and if more water is needed to keep it moist (it rarely is). (See drawing, page 158). If you use flats or pots, it's still a good idea to slip the whole thing into a large plastic bag with a bent wire coat hanger or other support to hold the plastic up off the cuttings. With this treatment, further watering is seldom needed.

Insert cuttings at a slight angle and far enough apart to allow all leaves to receive light.

Set container in bright light, *not* sunlight; or under a fluorescent light unit (40 watts, cool white, 16 hours daily).

The time it takes to form roots varies, but most cuttings will have rooted and begun to grow in 8-12 weeks.

Take off plastic when growth begins, feed every 2-3 weeks with a solution of 1 teaspoon of 20-20-20 fertilizer in 1 gallon of water. If time is right to plant outdoors, harden off by moving out during the day to a cool shady place and indoors at night, for 5-7 days, then transplant to a frame or shaded bed in the garden. If time not right for planting out, transplant cuttings to individual pots and grow on in a cool (55°-60°F) brightly lit place or fluorescent unit till they can be safely set outdoors, hardening off before doing so.

Give special care for one full season — watering so that soil never dries out, a mulch in hot weather and protection in winter, then transplant to permanent location the following spring.

Hardwood cuttings are not as easy to root as softwood, but they're worth a try if you need a lot of one kind of plant, as you might for a hedge. This is a particularly successful technique with privet, alpine currant, forsythia, spirea, (*Spiraea x bumalda*), mock orange and hydrangea. Take cuttings from current growth or new canes from the base of the plant during the dormant season in fall or winter — they root most easily when taken early.

Cut pieces about lead-pencil size, 6-8 inches long, below a bud, leaving 1 inch of stem above the top bud to protect it from injury.

Dust with fungicide and rooting hormone powder (The Royal Botanical Gardens in Hamilton, Ontario, find that they can root hardwood cuttings successfully by dipping in fungicide alone).

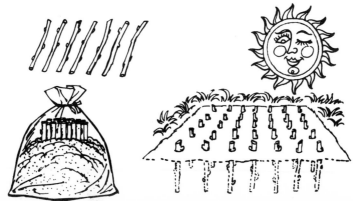

Half fill a plastic bag with moist milled sphagnum moss and push the cuttings into it so that only one quarter of their length sticks out of the moss. Seal and leave for 10 days at 50°-55°F for callus to form, then put in refrigerator at 40°F (not the freezer), or bury in the ground next to your house foundation or other cold place where until spring they will be about 40°F, but not frozen. Some kinds will root during this period, others will only form a heavier callus.

Plant out, 2 inches apart, in spring, exposing only the top two buds, in light soil.

Shade for the first month, keep moist and begin to feed with a solution of 1 teaspoon of 20-20-20 fertilizer in 1 gallon of water when active growth begins and every 2-3 weeks thereafter. Do not feed after July 1.

When buds show a growth of 4-5 inches, remove shade.

Water well just before freeze-up and give a protection of evergreen branches over winter and you should have good-sized hedge plants to move into their permanent location by the following spring.

Root cutting is the best way to propagate many fine perennials and is particularly good practice with bleeding heart, Japanese anemone, Oriental poppy, phlox. Roots of fall-flowering plants should be cut in spring; spring-flowering plants in late summer or just after blooming is finished.

Lift plant gently with a digging fork and wash soil off the roots.

Cut pieces of healthy root, 2-3 inches long, dust with fungicide and plant in a specially prepared nursery bed of fine, friable soil, 1 inch deep.

Water and shade till established.

When well rooted and growing well, transplant to permanent location.

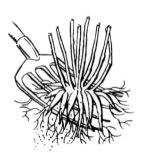

Root cuttings.

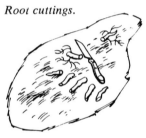

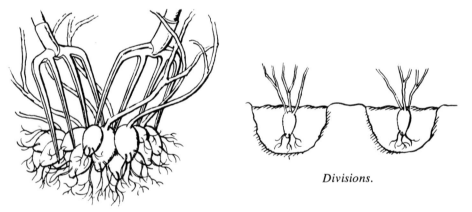

Divisions.

Divisions are a dandy way to propagate very good perennial cultivars and to renew fine old plants. Usually done in spring or right after blooming. This is a recommended technique for chrysanthemums every spring; for perennial asters, bee balm and evening primrose every 2-3 years in spring; for day lilies, phlox and iris as soon as bloom is over every 3-4 years. (For specific details for dividing other perennials, see CHAPTER 27.)

Lift clump gently, wash off earth, pry apart with digging or hand fork.

Discard old roots, usually the centre part of the clump.

Dust open cuts with fungicide.

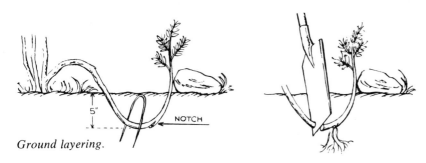

Ground layering.

Replant healthy new sections in prepared permanent spot, water and shade till established and growing well.

Layering is one of the most foolproof methods for propagating trees and large shrubs. It works best with those that have supple low branches that can be bent down to the ground, such as juniper, yew, forsythia, viburnum, azaleas. Do this in spring or summer, using dormant wood, or in late summer using current growth.

Make a notch in a low branch about 18 inches from the tip, rub rooting hormone powder into the cut, twist the branch or, as our grandmothers did, brace the cut open with an oat, which they believed had special powers for rooting.

Lay the branch 5-10 inches deep in soil, the cut in the middle, and peg it in place with wire, a forked stick or lay a stone over it.

Brace the protruding tip up so that it is vertical.

Leave in place till the following spring, inspect for roots. If they have formed, sever the rooted section from the parent plant. If no roots, leave for another year.

Transplant to a nursery area for another season, or move directly into its permanent place in your garden, shading and watering till established.

Runners pegged to the ground around the parent plant are a useful way to propagate ground covers such as vinca, vines such as ivy or wintercreeper, and surface rooting plants such as the lovely spring rock cress.

Simply water the ground well around the plant, then peg runners down with staples — for fine-branched ones ordinary wire hairpins are handy.

Keep plants watered and fertilized, and when roots have formed cut from the parent plant.

Either leave in place to make a larger planting, as you might want to do with ground cover plants, or move to another spot in the garden.

Mound layering is useful with multistemmed plants such as currants, raspberries, hydrangea and shrub roses, and can be done almost anytime.

Choose one or two stems of year-old wood and cut a notch in each a few inches above the base, bracing open the cut with a tiny stick, a pebble or an oat. Rub with rooting powder, mound earth up over the cut and keep damp for one growing season.

Inspect and, if roots have formed, cut from the parent and transplant. If no roots, leave for another season.

Air layering works well with plants that have rigid branches that cannot be layered in the ground, such as lilacs.

Cut notch in current growth about 18 inches from a tip of a branch, prop

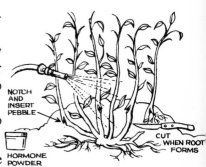

NOTCH AND INSERT PEBBLE

CUT WHEN ROOT FORMS

HORMONE POWDER

Mound layering.

Air layering.

open, rub with rooting hormone powder.

Wrap with a handful of wet, squeezed-out sphagnum moss, cover with a piece of plastic, and tape it closed above and below the moss.

After the first good rain, inspect the parcel to see if water has collected inside it. If it has, pierce the bottom of the plastic to allow it to drain.

Watch for root development — it won't hurt to open the plastic — and when it appears, cut the rooted branch from the parent plant and transplant to a nursery bed, shading and watering till established.

After one season move to a permanent place in your garden.

Bulbs, Corms and Tubers form small new ones each year around the mother bulb. After bloom is over, these may be dug up, separated and replanted in a nursery bed where they will grow to full size in 2-5 years.

Hyacinths will develop more bulblets if in August the mother bulb is scored with several diagonal cuts or the base lightly scooped out. Keep in a warm, light, dry place and plant in October; dig up the following summer, separate the bulblets and replant.

Lilies can be propagated by detaching scales from the mother bulb, dusting each with fungicide and planting them in a prepared nursery bed or cold frame. They should grow to blooming size in 1-4 years.

Grafting and Budding is the skillful placing of a small piece of twig or bud of a desirable cultivar onto a closely related plant that furnishes the root. By placing and holding the actively growing tissue of the twig or bud against the actively growing tissue of the root plant, they unite, sap passes from the root-stock to the scion (the piece you cut), the junction heals and the twig or bud then grows, retaining its own characteristics of flower, foliage and fruit. This is especially useful where tender-root twig or bud stock is grafted to a hardier rootstock or where a desirable cultivar is grown to useful size more quickly. Budding is used extensively in the commercial production of roses, grafting in the production of fruit trees. Choose related plants such as rose on a rose, crab apple or apple on apple, cherry on cherry and so on.

Grafting: scion should be from the previous year's growth and taken in late winter or early spring, ¼ inch in diameter, showing a dormant bud at the base of the leaf and be about 3 buds long.

There are three ways to shape and fit the tip of the scion to the rootstock, by splice, saddle or cleft grafting. In the *splice graft*, the scion must match the rootstock in size, and both be cut with matching slants; the *saddle graft* splits the scion upwards and points the rootstock to fit into it; *the cleft*, the most common, is used for grafting scions much smaller than the rootstock — the size, for instance, of a twig as big as a pencil — into the butt of a large branch

Cleft grafting.

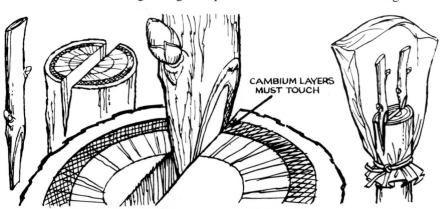

CAMBIUM LAYERS MUST TOUCH

of a tree. With this method, the scion is cut with a long sloping stroke on both sides, the edges slightly beveled; the cut off top of the rootstock is smoothed with a sharp knife and split down the middle; the scions are inserted into a tight fit, one on either side of the split, with the bottom bud on each becoming the outside bud just above the cut surface of the stock. To be successful, the cambium layers must touch.

In all types of grafting, scions and rootstocks are bound firmly and open wounds sealed with grafting wax; many place a plastic bag overall.

Examine binding to be sure it is not constricting the bark — it should deteriorate and disappear in six weeks. If, as in a cleft graft, both scions catch, allow both to grow for three years, then remove the poorer one. Keep all growth of the rootstock cut off so that all the strength of the limb will go into growing the new scion. (See drawing, page 162).

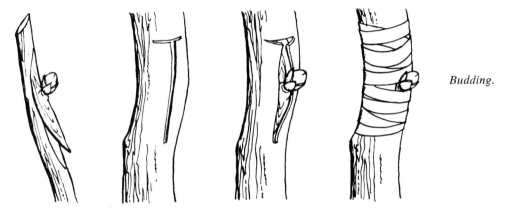

Budding.

Budding: a bud is taken from the current year's growth in late July or August and set into the bark of a seedling planted the previous spring or on suckers or sprouts of older trees. It is essential that the bark of the rootstock peel easily and sometimes this can be helped along by watering the plant thoroughly for a week before budding.

choose scions of pencil size, remove leaves (there will be a dormant bud in each axil) leaving a bit of the stem of the leaf to hold on to. Keep fresh and moist till used; cut from this stick a bud with a small shield of wood from the main stem with it.

make a T cut in the bark of the rootstock, loosen bark, insert bud under bark and slip it snugly down till it fits; wrap and wax

early the following spring, cut off the twig or branch of the rootstock above the bud and remove wrapping; if it is to be a shrub, cut rootstock just above the T-cut; if for a tree, leave 6 inches of rootstock branch to tie the elongating bud to so that it will grow straight up; take off all suckers on rootstock.

Repair grafting: every spring when the snow melts thousands of garden and orchard trees show girdling by mice, rabbits and other rodents. Provided the damage does not completely circle the tree and is not too wide, the tree will eventually heal over if the damaged area is trimmed back to tight live bark and sealed with tree paint. If the damage is more extensive, then bridge grafting or inarching may save the tree. If you cherish your tree, it's worth a try.

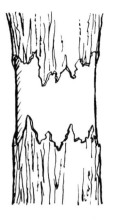 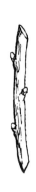 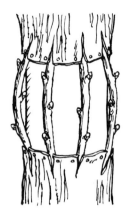

Bridge grafting: trim injured area of loose and frayed bark — smooth surfaces heal faster and more successfully discourage pests and diseases.

choose scions from 1-year shoots of the same type of tree, during dormancy (you may have to work quickly) and long enough to bridge the injury

make one-sided sloping cuts at both ends of scion, lay over sound bark below and above trimmed area and with a sharp point trace the shape and size of the tips of the scion on the bark, to use as a pattern

cut flap of bark of rootstock to match the tracing, insert scion and fasten in place with small nails, placing such a bridge every 2 inches around the tree.

seal with wax all grafts, injured areas, buds and scion and wrap a thick layer of newspaper over all for extra protection from strong light and drying wind. In the future, protect your trees before they get chewed by such unwelcome pests, see how to protect plants, page 167.

Inarching: generally used when damage is near or at ground level; the principle is that a young growing whip is grafted into the injured tree above the damage to take over the duties of the root; if a young tree or sucker is not already growing close to the injured tree, one can be moved in and immediately grafted. Make a cut similar to bridge grafting above the wound and proceed similarly, wax and wrap.

HOW TO PROTECT PLANTS

AGAINST WINTER DAMAGE

Most frequent causes of winter damage are:

very low or very high temperatures, or a combination of both
sun scald, especially in late winter
weight of snow or ice

Avoid trouble in the first place by choosing plants recommended as hardy for your area, then by practising one or more of the following sly devices:

all new plants and known tender plants should be mulched after the ground

164

is frozen, with evergreen branches (old Christmas trees are fine for this and usually available at just the right time); hay or straw; excelsior or dry leaves such as oak held in place with wire netting or branches. Plants with crowns, like foxgloves, should have leaves tucked in around the crown, not over it. Also being tested is a three-sided, double plastic bag held over the plant by three stakes set as a tripod; each side of the bag is partially filled with water, which freezes and thaws as the temperature goes up and down, but the air temperature inside the bag is always higher than the minimum outside and lower than the maximum, and the plant therefore does not have to survive as great extremes as if it were not protected in this way. There are other useful removable covers made of heavy paper, glass and styrofoam on the market.

Winter protection in deep-snow areas.

very tender plants — in many parts of the country 'mums are in this class — can be protected by moving them into cold frames and mulching with hay or straw, or into hotbeds.

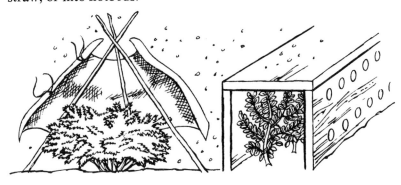

Left, protection against salt spray; right, against sunburn and too-early thawing.

low evergreens in deep-snow areas should have fat puffs of snow knocked off while it is still soft or have a cover. This can be a burlap teepee, a box or small canopy to go over the top (this should be drilled with air holes to keep the inside ventilated and cool). Do not wrap in plastic, it burns.

evergreens exposed to salt-spray drift from roads or the sea should have a screen of burlap, board or plastic erected between the plant and the direction of the spray; but do not cover completely.

broad-leaved evergreens burn easily in late-winter sun. To prevent this, spray with anti-desiccant and circle with a snow or wire fence to the depth of the plant and backfill with dry leaves.

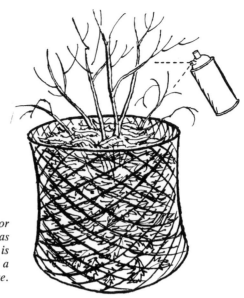

Winter protection for tender shrubs such as azaleas in some zones is anti-desiccant spray and a leaf-filled wire enclosure.

unexpected early or late frosts can damage many plants. Since moist earth is warmer than dry earth in cold weather, keep your garden well watered in late spring and early fall. If frost does strike, thaw above-ground parts of plants with a cold water spray before the sun touches them.

For special information on the winter protection of individual plants see:
Roses, CHAPTER 26
Perennials and biennials, CHAPTER 27
Water lilies, CHAPTER 14

AGAINST WIND

High winds can loosen roots of newly planted trees and shrubs, dry out plants, especially bark, and break tall beauties like delphiniums right over. Prevention is wise:

stake or guy newly planted trees in three directions, being careful that the binding around the tree will not bruise the bark

stake all tall-growing heavy-headed perennials; delphiniums, dahlias, gladiolus and, although they are not as tall but have very heavy flowers, peonies

plant shelterbelts in gardens in exposed areas

build fences or screens to brake the wind. Open patterns are best for this because they sift rather than block the wind, preventing it from coming down on the inside with even greater force.

AGAINST ANIMALS AND BIRDS

Pets are fine in moderation but when your own or your neighbors' destroy your garden and kill too many songbirds, it's time to act firmly. As for wild furred and feathered friends, they too are fine to a point, but when they damage trees, dig up and eat your bulbs, tunnel lawns, eat fruit on your trees and litter your garden with garbage, it's time to do something about them too.

Dogs by nature bury bones and flower beds are dandy bone-burying sites, so make a special fenced run for your own dog and fence and gate your garden to keep out your neighbor's. In front gardens, which are seldom completely fenced, a handy gadget is to cut the crossbar of some wire coathangers, bend the two cut pieces outwards and hook the top of the hanger around the outermost branch of the shrub or tree that projects farthest out into the garden. Dogs, who take things the easy way, will water the coathanger, not your plants. There are also a number of very effective dog repellents on the market, some more fragrant than others.

Cats by nature stalk and sometimes kill desirable birds. Tie a bell around the cat's neck if it's your own and try to persuade your neighbors to bell their cats also. If they are reluctant to do this, you might take them the dead birds their cats kill, suitably gift-wrapped.

Rabbits, mice and moles can really wreak havoc in a garden. In winter, they nibble the bark of trees, sometimes completely girdling them. To prevent this, paint or spray a special repellent on the bark in the fall, or set a collar of fine-mesh wire into the ground, covering the base of the tree well above the possible snow line. Rabbits also nibble tender new growth of plants, especially tulips. The cure for this is to spray the plants with a chemical repellent available at your garden suppliers. Moles that tunnel through lawns can be eliminated by setting poison bait in their tunnels. A Be-Kind-To-Mole Note: moles are often blamed for damaging bark on trees, but they are, I'm told, guiltless of this. It's Mouse using Mole's tunnel for a freeway who does the damage.

Squirrels eat flower buds of trees like magnolia and apple; dig up and eat tulip bulbs, crocus and others (never daffodils; somehow they know they're poisonous); eat ripening fruit and steal birdfood from a feeder. The prevention for bulb trouble is to plant them in wire baskets made of 1 inch mesh or grow them in a wire-fenced enclosure and move them into your garden just as the buds begin to show. Mothballs and naphthalene flakes are frequently recommended, to be spread on the ground over bulb plantings, but I have found them ineffective, smelly and a danger to small children because they're poison. Bird feeders can be designed with squirrel guards (see Chapter 10) but the only cure I know for stealing fruit and eating flower buds is to trap them in a specially designed humane trap that does not harm them in any way and cart them out to a nice big patch of woods in the country. This can be a lifetime hobby, for new squirrels move into your recently vacated property, but in the meantime your plants do have a chance to grow and flower without harm.

Skunks and raccoons mainly dig up lawns hunting for tasty grubs. The cure is to spray the lawn with an insecticide that kills the grubs. Raccoons also eat fish in garden pools. The cure for this is to build a non-rusting wire-mesh table that will sit just below the surface of the pool, be practically invisible if you paint it black and prevent night-fishing poachers from having any luck. Or you can plant water lilies, whose leaves make good hiding places for the fish. Prevention for skunks and raccoons getting into your garbage is to build a sturdy box with a heavy lid and use cans with a tight snap lock.

The gardening world, like every other department of life's activities, is filled with necessary tools, useful equipment and dinky gadgets. Some are basic and a must, some are just very handy to have, others fill a special need and the rest make it easy for your family to think they know exactly what to give you for your birthday. Our classification will not be the same for everybody, but here are the recommended basics:

2 square-ended digging spades, one regular size, the other what the trade politely calls a lady's spade because it is smaller, although I have often thought that calling it a lady's and small gentleman's spade would be fairer; both spades are essential for digging and planting, the smaller one is particularly handy for putting in smaller plants in already snug spots. Both should be kept razor sharp — watch your feet — for it makes the job ten times easier

1 digging fork for turning over earth, compost and other such jobs

1 flexible, fan-shaped metal leaf rake for fall and spring cleanup, picking up grass clippings and so on

1 rigid metal-toothed rake for smoothing soil, cleaning up

hoses, nozzles, sprinkler heads and soakers as needed; a root feeder for deep watering; a good watering can

a variety of stakes for tying things to

a work basket to hold handy small things — the best trowel and clippers you can buy, a rubber pad for kneeling, twist-ties for fastening, a can or bottle of fast-acting water-soluble 20-20-20 fertilizer for quick plant pickups and a measuring spoon, a can of pellets of slug bait and anything else you fancy. Hand cream? A cake of soap for your fingernails? A small bottle of smelling salts or brandy? A good cigar?

And these tools we recommend for special jobs:

for lawns: a mower, either power (gasoline or electricity) that you guide or ride, or a hand mower you push; a spiker for aerating and a spreader for fertilizing the lawn — these can often be rented from your garden supplier; an edger to keep grass borders trim, although I hope you design your garden to eliminate these as much as possible — it's a fussy-no-fun job

for preparing large areas of ground: a power Rototiller (this too can often be rented)

for hedges: a pair of good clippers, either hand or power

for pruning: hand pruners, loppers for shrubs, a tree knife and pruning saw, all kept sharp; tree paint either as a bomb or paint; work gloves for handling prickly plants like roses

for weeding and cultivation, if you're a bear for punishment and ignore our advice about herbicides and mulches: a hoe

for spraying insects and controlling fungus disease: small aerosol cans if you have little to cover or want to catch the beginning of trouble with a short sharp spray: for larger jobs, attachments for your hose, tanks or packs for carrying around the garden, with a long applying wand and a nozzle that can be adjusted to get under as well as over foliage

for chewing up garden refuse if you make a lot of compost: a mechanical shredder.

Design a special paint pattern to identify your tools from your neighbors' — perhaps red and white barber pole stripes around the handles — and take the time to paint it on each new piece; it's the best insurance I know against loss or permanent borrowing.

WHAT YOU SHOULD KNOW ABOUT BUYING, USING AND TAKING CARE OF A POWER MOWER

WHEN YOU BUY

Go to a reputable dealer who will stand behind what he sells you.

Look for a well-built, solid piece of equipment made by a manufacturer who specializes in this kind of machinery.

Consider whether you want a gas-powered engine or an electric one. The electric one is quieter, but using it on a large lawn with interruptive plantings that catch the cord can be frustrating. Also, there is danger of inadvertently cutting the cord with the mower. For these reasons, most home gardeners prefer gas-powered machines.

Consider whether you want a reel or a rotary type. The reel cuts with blades turning against a bar, the rotary chops the grass with a whirling blade. Rotaries are generally a little cheaper. A well-kept rotary power mower will last from 5-10 years, a reel one 10-15 years. Blades of either are easily replaced by a competent serviceman — what usually ends a mower's life is poor care and/or lack of maintenance.

Be sure to buy a type with some feature that deflects or catches bits the mower may pick up and throw out. A nail, a dog bone, a piece of wire, a stone can come flying out at you or someone near you with the force of a bullet if it is not diverted.

Other useful features:

electric key starting, powered by a replaceable battery, instead of the pull-string recoil start. The manufacturers, with tongue in cheek, recommend this for lady and elderly gardeners. They overlook the fact that if anybody is Mr. Atlas in a household today, it's the Little Woman; that if anybody loves pushing buttons, it's the Little Man; that if anybody loves instant starting power it's The Young.

a safety shield across the back, to protect your feet from unidentified flying objects

all controls on the handle, to make things both safer and easier

large wheels, because this makes the mower easier to push. Some kinds come with 5-inch wheels but the better ones are 7-inch.

WHAT YOU SHOULD DO BEFORE YOU USE YOUR MOWER

Read the owner's manual that comes with the machine. In particular, learn how to stop the engine quickly in an emergency.

Clear the lawn, before you begin, of all debris — sticks, wire, stones, etc. Place large movable things like tricycles and toys where you won't step back and trip over them.

If you're using a gas-powered machine, see that the tank is full. Never add fuel when the engine is running or hot, and always use an approved container or funnel for the filling.

Tie up the dog, put your pet elephant back on its chain in the compound, send your youngsters off for an ice cream cone — 150 feet is the safe distance for anybody but the operator to come near a running mower.

Check to be sure that any blade and drive clutches are disengaged before starting. If the engine does not start easily, have it checked by a competent serviceman. Mow only in daylight and never when the grass is wet. Never mow in bare feet; in fact, you'd be wise to wear hard-toed or special safety shoes.

Do not start the mower when it's standing in high grass, on a slope, or on a loose surface.

With an electric mower, use a UL-approved, outdoor, three-wire safety cord, plugged into a grounded outlet. Connect cord to the power source first, making sure the switch on the mower is "off," then connect cord to it, tying it once around the handle of the mower to keep it from pulling out when you don't want it to.

HOW YOU SHOULD USE YOUR MOWER

Don't let anyone run the mower without knowing how and never let young children run it even if they think they know how.

Keep your feet away from the blades when you start it, and start it in the open where fumes will blow away. If you're running it for a check in a closed space, such as the garage, have lots of fresh air moving through so that dangerous fumes can not build up.

Whenever you leave the mower — to get a beer, to talk to a neighbor — turn off the engine. And don't let anybody come up to talk to you while it's running.

When crossing paving or gravel driveways, walks, roads, turn off the engine and wait till the blade stops turning.

Watch for loose things in the grass that could be picked up and shot out.

Always push the mower away from you. Don't move or steer the mower with your foot.

Never lift the machine off the ground or carry it while the blade is turning.

Never run while mowing; and push, don't pull.

On slopes, mow across, not up and down. Be steady on your feet. When mowing on rough surfaces, or in high grass, set the machine for its highest cutting to minimize chances of hitting something hidden.

If the mower does hit something, switch it off, disconnect cord if electric, and examine mower carefully for damage. If you're not sure how to do this, have a serviceman do it.

When checking the motor, always stop the engine and disconnect the spark wire first. If it's an electric one, unplug the cord.

Never leave an impulse starter in a cocked position.

If you have a riding mower, use extreme caution on slopes — it can turn over on you if not driven properly. Also, don't let any little guys hitch rides with you.

Run the mower at the speed it's set for — altering settings overspeeds the engine and shortens the mower's life.

Ongoing care of both electric and gasoline mowers includes frequent checking of the handle mounting and assembly to make sure they're secure; the blade mounting; the blades for damage; all nuts and bolts for tightness; and, in the electric mower, the cord for cuts, nicks or insulation defects.

HOW TO STORE YOUR MOWER FOR THE WINTER

Don't just give your lawn one last cut and let the mower sit in the garage or your basement till spring. Give it the care any good piece of machinery deserves. Either take it to a mower service centre for this, or do it yourself. If you do it yourself, here's how:

drain tank, fuel lines and carburetor of all gas. Do this by starting the motor at half speed and letting it run till it's completely out of gas. To clean out the last drop, with a small stick push an absorbent piece of cloth into the bottom of the tank through the opening and let it absorb the last of the gas. Pull it out and be careful to discard it safely.

while the engine is warm from the draining, take out the crank case plug and let all the oil drain out. Refill with fresh oil, as specified by the manufacturer.

disconnect spark-plug wire carefully so as not to let debris fall into the opening and pour 2-3 spoonfuls of oil down through the hole, hand-turning the engine by pulling slowly on the starter rope. Replace spark plug, but leave the wire disconnected to prevent anyone from starting the machine when they shouldn't.

clean the outside by scraping off clippings and dirt, rinse the screening of the air cleaner on top of the engine in gasoline and clean out any sediment in the oil cup at the bottom of the filter. Replace and add a little clean oil to the filter and cup.

on reel mowers, remove grass wrapped around reel ends and clean drive chains, pulleys and belts. Coat chains and drive sprockets with oil and lubricate all moving parts. Rotary mowers should be turned over and the underside of the housing cleaned and repainted to prevent rusting.

clean and check blades to see if they need sharpening. On reel mowers, hold a piece of paper between the knife blade and the reel and slowly turn the reel by hand. If it's properly sharp and adjusted, each blade should cut the paper along its entire length. If not, the blades need adjusting and possibly sharpening. For both reel and rotary mowers, have only a serviceman take out and replace blades, unless you're qualified yourself.

store for winter up on blocks so that the machine is supported by the frame and the tires are clear of the ground. Wrap loosely in plastic to keep out dust and moisture.

19 PESTS AND DISEASES

Pests, in this chapter, are insects, mites, slugs, millipedes, sowbugs, etc., and are commonly controlled by insecticides. For information on how to protect your plants from such pests as rabbits, mice, dogs, etc., see CHAPTER 18.

Disease, in this chapter, covers disorders caused by bacteria, which are controlled by bactericides, nematodes controlled by nematicides usually applied by professional services, fungi, commonly controlled by fungicides, and viruses, which are controlled in the home garden by the use of insecticide to kill the insects which transmit viruses.

The gardening world is divided between those who, at any cost, want a disease- and pest-free garden; those who, deeply concerned about harm to man, wild- life and beneficial insects, prefer to live with a certain amount of trouble with their plants rather than use toxic materials; and that happy-go-lucky band who, with no particular penchant for worry, go merrily on with their garden- ing, ignoring all bugs and blights.

Whichever group you belong to, I believe all home gardeners have an urgent responsibility to do these things:

to carry on wise, intelligent garden practices that will, as far as possible, create a climate for a healthy garden and thus reduce the need for use of insecticides and fungicides;

that when some chemical must be used for control, first choice should be one that research and experience have shown will do the job without high hazard to other things;

that when a chemical known to be highly toxic is indicated, the home gardener either decides to live with his trouble or uses that chemical with the UTMOST CAUTION and the fullest sense of his responsibility to himself, his family, his community.

You will notice that I have used the designation "home gardener." Opinion on the wide use of chemicals on commercially grown crops is not the province of this book.

WISE, INTELLIGENT GARDEN PRACTICE

Keep your garden fed, pruned and watered. A healthy plant is a strong plant.

Keep it weeded by hand, by hoeing or with herbicides.

Keep it clean. Dispose of debris, cut off dead flowers and foliage and bury in compost heap or, if diseased, burn or wrap for garbage collection.

Seal pruning cuts over 1 inch in diameter with tree paint. After cutting out the disease known as fire blight, disinfect tools by wiping with rubbing alcohol.

Don't work in plants when they are wet, nor let pets run through them at this time — this could spread disease.

As far as possible, buy resistant or certified seed and plants, or treat them with chemical protectants (see page 175).

Give each plant the kind of growing conditions it is known to do well in.

Rotate yearly plantings so that the same kind do not grow in the same place every year. If a plant dies or must be replaced, put in a different kind.

Know your plants. Some are more susceptible to trouble than others. Some, called alternate hosts, can contract one stage of a disease, then pass it on to another plant which develops it in a second stage. For instance, do not plant crab apples near red cedar, Douglas fir near blue spruce, currants or gooseberries near white pine.

Do not crowd plants. Freely moving air around them reduces the build-up of excessive moisture and decreases the chance of fungus attack. For the same reason don't water your garden late in the evening.

Use simple methods for control whenever you can — paper collars or open-ended tin cans around the base of plants to block cutworms; sand and ashes or bait for slugs; handpick white grubs under damaged sods on lawn if it is not too heavily infested; examine your garden by day and night and handpick any large feeding insects. Drop them into a can of kerosene or squash them underfoot.

If aphids appear — little bugs on tender growth of new shoots or buds — watch for a couple of days to see if they are really increasing in numbers. Spray with insecticides only if they are. Otherwise you might, by spraying too soon, destroy beneficial insects such as lady bugs or praying mantis that are actually keeping them under control.

The ideal program is to spray or dust for pests only *after* you find and identify them; to spray or dust for disease *before* it occurs and when conditions are ripe for its appearance. This system naturally takes time to learn and involves a certain amount of time-consuming careful application. Multi-purpose mixtures that contain both an insecticide and a fungicide are, on the other hand, easier to use. For many gardeners needing only small amounts, they are both convenient and effective. They should be applied as you would a fungicide alone, that is, before trouble starts.

When you spray or dust, be sure to cover the entire surface of leaves on both sides, and all stems. Fungicides are generally more effective when applied before rain rather than after, because disease spores germinate and spread most during this time.

Feed and water wild birds in your garden: they eat hundreds of insects every day of the year.

Some gardeners put great store by companion planting — marigolds with roses, nasturtiums with cucumbers, garlic with many things. They believe that one protects the other from infestation. Here you are on your own; there is no scientific support for this theory, it's pure green thumbery!

Accept gift plants from friends warily: quarantine them first if you are uncertain about their good health.

Buy only from reliable growers whose plants you can expect to be disease-free.

Abide by the laws of plant immigration, obtaining a permit from the government to import. *Never* smuggle plants; you might unwittingly bring a serious pest or disease into the country that was not here before.

HOW TO DEAL WITH TROUBLE

To begin with, realize that the world — and your garden — is full of insects and disease and that most have been around longer than you have. As an instance of this, Dr. A. M. Harper, of the Canada Department of Agriculture Research Station at Lethbridge, Alberta, reports that an aphid was recently found embedded in clear amber in the tailings of an open-pit coal mine near Medicine Hat, and it was determined radiometrically that the bentonite that overlaid the amber-bearing coal was approximately 72,000,000 years old, which is quite a while ago.

A few plants are more prone to trouble than others and these you should find out about — for example, roses to blackspot, peonies to botrytis, lilacs and phlox to mildew, snowball bushes and nasturtiums to aphids, iris to borer and so on. (See chart for details of especially susceptible plants, how to identify and what to use for control, pages 176-178).

Chemicals, dosages and techniques for handling the problem of pests and disease change often. Keep up with current information on this subject through your provincial or state department of agriculture. Pamphlets are also available from The Queen's Printer, Ottawa, Ontario, and the Superintendent of Documents, Government Printing Office, Washington, D.C. 20402.

PRECAUTIONS IN THE USE OF INSECTICIDES AND FUNGICIDES

Read the label: it gives content, recommended doses, cautions and, frequently, when *not* to use and what *not* to use it on, and what it is and is not effective for. For instance, do not use toxic sprays on a windy day, someone might inhale them. Be sure to allow a safe interval to elapse between the application of any systemic insecticide and the handling of any plant or soil you may have used it on — *most are highly poisonous.*

174

Be careful, when treating flowers and trees with toxic materials, *not* to let any of the chemicals get on nearby vegetables or fruit — and this includes runoff that could reach them above or below the ground.

Keep chemicals in a closed locked cupboard away from children and food supplies.

Buy only in small quantities. Keep in the original container with its original label so that you will always know the contents. Discard carefully at the end of the season by pouring on a gravel path or drive, leaving no puddles; or wrap or tie in several thicknesses of newspaper and put in your garbage for collection.

When using in the garden, cover pools with fish in them, birds in cages, pets and their dishes, birdhouses, feeders and baths. Do not spray flowering trees when bees are gathering honey from their blossoms. One veterinarian also warns dog and cat owners to keep their pets off lawns and out of shrubbery that have been treated until rain or hosing dispels it, for they can pick up a toxic dose on their feet or coat.

Keep appliances *only* for the use of spraying or dusting. Clean thoroughly after use according to manufacturer's directions. *Do not* apply herbicides with your insect and disease control equipment. Even residual traces of herbicides which you may have used to kill weeds could seriously injure good plants. Mark your sprayers and dusters so that you will recognize what they have been used for.

For yourself, try to prevent spilling on bare skin or clothing. If any does, wash with soap and water immediately and change your clothes. Do not eat any food with your fingers, rub your mouth or eyes, or light a cigarette without washing your hands first. Many gardeners wear rubber or dry cotton gloves. After spraying or dusting, change your clothes and be sure that they are washed *separately* before you wear them again. Do not work in a wind and be careful not to inhale any spray or dust.

RECOMMENDED EQUIPMENT
Since thoroughness of application is essential, it is important to have good equipment and to keep it in good condition.

Sprayers
Aerosol bombs are useful when only small quantities are needed, expensive otherwise.
Hand atomizers useful for small areas. Buy only one that throws a continuous spray and has an adjustable nozzle so that both upper and underside of leaves can be thoroughly covered. Nozzle and container should be made of noncorrosive material, easily cleaned.

Compressed-air sprayer with capacity of 1-5 gallons is most satisfactory for home gardens. If not equipped with agitator, shake frequently to keep the material in suspension.
Dusters
Plunge type, with adjustable tube and nozzle for dusting underside of leaves as well as upper.
Fan type, more efficient and durable than other kinds.

HOW TO TREAT SEEDS TO RESIST DECAY
Various fungicides dusted on seeds as a protectant can reduce diseases that cause decay and damping off (killing of seedlings). If not already treated when you purchase them, you can do this yourself.

For a small quantity: Tear off corner of seed package. Pick up a little fungicide dust on tip of a small knife and drop into package. Fold down corner and shake thoroughly. When finished, wash knife carefully.

For a large quantity: Check label on fungicide for correct amount to use. Place dust and seed in a closed metal or glass container and shake for 1-2 minutes.

Proper recognition of diseases and pest damage is important so that correct controls can be used. If in doubt, consult your provincial or state department of agriculture or nearest agricultural college.

Care in preparing specimens will help to get prompt, accurate service:

if possible send several stages of the development of the trouble but do not send old, dead plants

if plant is small, place entire specimen in plastic bag without any moist packaging, or wrap loosely in wax paper (diseased samples sealed in airtight containers decay quickly). If specimen is large, send piece of the worst part in its various stages

enclose in a strong, light box and mail or express promptly with a letter giving the following particulars:

species of plant affected, whether growing in shade or sun, and condition of soil

appearance of disease or pest in garden

date first noticed

whether it is on many kinds of plants or one only, and difference of severity on each

what sprays, if any, have already been used.

Controls for pests and diseases of flowers, ornamental trees and shrubs

These are the *common* pests and diseases that attack your ornamental garden plants. Should they become infected with something you cannot identify, take or send samples of the damaged plant (see above for how to prepare) to your federal or state department of agriculture. Remember, too, that good garden practice can often prevent the need for chemical controls and that if you do need them *use caution*. My consultants and I recommend that you wait till you *see* pest damage before moving in with chemical control, but that you follow a *preventive* program for disease.

Because of new products coming on the market and more experienced assessments of those already in use, there are frequent changes in chemicals recommended for control of garden pests and disease. Be sure to seek current information on correct materials. Most provincial and state departments of agriculture print up-to-date pamphlets with this information and make them available free or at a small charge.

Common pests of flowers, ornamental trees, shrubs

APHIDS (little flies) Common, especially on snowball bush, spirea, nasturtium, roses, sweet pea.

Trouble: Sticky "honeydew" on plant, later black with mold. Caused by tiny, green, black, red or white flies that suck juice of plant and sometimes transmit disease.

Control: Spray or dust with insecticide when seen and at 7-day intervals till controlled; ants very often are responsible for spreading root aphids, and where they appear should be controlled.

LEAFHOPPERS Common, especially on Virginia creeper, rose, aster, dahlia, sweet pea.

Trouble: Stunted tips, curling and browning leaves. Caused by small green sucking insects on undersides of leaves. Jump when startled.

Control: Spray or dust with insecticide when first seen.

CATERPILLARS AND BEETLES Common.

Trouble: Chewed leaves and flowers. Caused by cankerworms, webworms, elm and willow leaf beetles and others.

Control: Spray or dust with insecticide when first seen.

CUTWORMS Common, see chart for vegetable pests, CHAPTER 11.

BORERS Common, especially on locust, birch, mountain ash, willow, lilac, iris.

Trouble: Tunnels through main stems and trunks which weakens plants. Caused by caterpillars or grubs. Sometimes you can spot them by little piles of sawdust at entrance hole.

Control: Tricky to catch them with ordinary insecticides

because it must be timed when they are on outside of plant. Check with your federal or state department of agriculture for correct timing for your area and recommended insecticide.

TARNISHED PLANT BUG affects aster, dahlia, zinnia, chrysanthemum, others. Also many weeds.

Trouble: Deformed buds and blooms. Caused by shiny, wingless ¼-inch bugs and yellow-green nymphs that suck sap.

Control: Spray or dust with insecticide when bugs seen, usually July and August.

GLADIOLUS THRIPS affect gladiolus.

Trouble: Leaves silver-spotted and flowers flecked and blotchy. Caused by slender, brownish-black insects $\frac{1}{16}$-inch long and yellow-green nymphs.

Control: Spray with insecticide when first seen and every 10 days thereafter. Treat corms before storing in fall with multipurpose dust.

BLACK VINE WEEVIL affects yew.

Trouble: Chewed bark and foliage, bush eventually dies. Caused by shiny black ⅜-inch beetles that feed on bush and long white ¼-inch larvae feeding on roots.

Control: Spray lower branches of plant with insecticide during last week of June and weekly thereafter twice to catch beetle as it emerges from the ground. Granular insecticide can be spread on ground under bush and watered in to control grub, but spraying of bush usually controls.

CLAY COLORED WEEVIL (west coast) affects rhodo-

More brains
than money

Imagination and ingenuity when you're making a garden can often be handier than gold in the bank. Many's the old cast-iron hot-air register from the wrecker's that's made a perfect see-through for a good-looking gate. Many's the old telephone pole that now braces a swing for a little guy to safely ride the sky, or a retired railway tie that now strongly buttresses a bank or braces a sturdy step. Clever tricks such as these are a dime a dozen once you begin to look for them. Rejects of concrete sewer tiles, standing on end, can make a precise, tidy herb garden; bicycle baskets make smart hanging planters for a balcony. And don't forget that most-flattering-to-your-ego ploy of all, learning how to grow dozens of plants from a few cents worth of seeds, a handsome tall tree or a luxuriant shrub from a little cutting. And here are others:

Vivid geraniums in a contemporary asbestos planter for summer.

One exotic chartreuse coleus,
grown from a slip, in a fibre, less-than-three-dollars,
good looking pot.

Twenty-five feet of wintercreeper grown from a 6-inch
cutting. True there was a 3-foot hole
of goodies below it at planting time.

Preservative-treated railway ties
pick up a grade change from lawn to sunken patio;
they can often be bought second hand.

You can grow a swish border with inexpensive annual
flower seed — cleome, marigolds, zinnias,
daisies, nicotine, petunias.

One plant of chrysanthemums,
five plants of stunning flowering kale,
grown from half a packet of seeds,
in a simple, contemporary pot.

Nature's sculpture,
stones excavated at building time
and manoeuvred into a strong, bold group.

Gourmet's delight —
your own freshly picked vegetables grown from
a few packets of inexpensive seeds.

dendron, hedge laurel, ivy and other broad-leaved evergreens.

Trouble: Plants sicken and eventually die.

Control: Since this insect lives in the soil, best control is to stir insecticide into the planting hole at transplanting time, or, if plant already established, a soil or foliar spray can be used.

ROSE CHAFER affects roses, peony.

Trouble: Chewed leaves and flowers. Caused by fawn beetle, ½-inch long, with thin legs — particularly a nuisance in sandy soil.

Control: Spray with insecticide when seen.

SCALE Common.

Trouble: Branches and trunk dry up. Caused by scaly insects sucking sap. Can usually be seen on bark. San Jose scale is small grey lump with central nipple; Cottony Maple scale is flat oval with protruding cottony wad; Oystershell Scale is about ⅛-inch long and a miniature of an oyster shell; Lecanium is red-brown, conspicuously raised; Holly scales are round and flat, 1/16 inch across.

Control: Cut out and burn infected parts. Spray insecticide in short period between hatching of eggs and before young crawlers bed down. Approximate times are: for Oystershell Scale, June 1-10; Lecanium and Elm, July 10-20; Cottony Maple, July 20-30; San Jose, a dormant, spray before bud-break in spring, insecticide just after apple blossoms drop; Holly scale (west coast), late June and late July.

SAWFLIES Common on conifers.

Trouble: Chewed needles on spruce, balsam, pine, larch. Caused by yellow-green hairless larvae, ¾-inch long.

Control: Spray or dust with insecticide when larvae seen feeding.

MITES Common, especially on rose, azalea, fruits, arbor-vitae, juniper, spruce.

Trouble: Mottled yellow foliage, sometimes grey. Caused by tiny, almost invisible mites whose presence you can spot by fine silk webbing on foliage.

Control: When first seen spray with insecticide, especially formulated for mite control, and repeat in 10 days.

PINE SHOOT MOTH (**European**) affects pine, especially mugho, red and Scots.

Trouble: Lead shoots bend over and die, causing multiple head to develop instead of a single leader. Caused by ⅝-inch white caterpillar boring into buds and shoots in July.

Control: On isolated trees whose tip you can reach hand-pick and burn damaged shoots to prevent spread. On larger plantings, spray with insecticide last week of June and again 10 days later. On very large trees, use professional tree-spray services.

LEAF MINERS Common, especially birch, elm, lilac, holly, columbine.

Trouble: Large dead blotches or wiggly tunnels through leaves. Caused by small maggots or worms that tunnel between upper and lower surface of leaves.

Control: can vary. Check with your federal or state department of agriculture, or local tree service. For garden plants like columbine, spray with insecticide when seen and again 10 days later.

Birch: spray when miners first appear, when leaves well expanded. Repeat in 6 weeks.

Elm: same as birch, first spray only.

Lilac: when injury first seen. Repeat if necessary.

Holly: spray late April or early May and repeat 3 weeks later.

Some common diseases of flowers, ornamental trees and shrubs

POWDERY MILDEW: affects chrysanthemum, dahlia, delphinium, flowering cherry, hydrangea, lilac, pansy, phlox, privet, rose, snapdragon, others.

Trouble: White powdery growth usually appears on upper surface of leaves; stem and flower infections may occur on same plant, e.g. snapdragon. Badly infected leaves distort and fall. Most severe where plants crowded and humidity high.

Control: Avoid overcrowding plants, provide good air circulation by spacing. Destroy debris. Spray or dust fungicide every 10-14 days from mid-July to frost.

BOTRYTIS BLIGHT affects carnation, chrysanthemum, dahlia, geranium, lilac, marigold, peony, snapdragon, tulips, others. On the Northwest Coast, in a wet summer, botrytis can seriously disfigure aster, zinnia and Korean-type chrysanthemum.

Trouble: Light to dark brown water-soaked spots, later covered with grey fungus, occur especially on lower petals of flowers, on stems and leaves, which may also be curled and blighted, buds never open. Severe in humid weather and can spread rapidly.

Control: Destroy debris as soon as bloom over. With infected tulip bulbs, discard. Plant susceptible varieties

only in well-drained soil, rotating plantings. Dust or spray with fungicide if weather wet.

RUST affects carnation, cedar, chrysanthemum, holly-hock, pine, snapdragon, sweet william, others.

Trouble: Symptoms depend on affected plant. Mainly orange-red-brown rust pustules on under surfaces of leaves, but petioles and stems are susceptible in some species. Lower leaves may die and plants become unsightly. Galls form on twigs and branches of cedars and some pines.

Control: Eradicate weeds and remove alternate hosts. Destroy infected tissue. Grow resistant varieties if possible, e.g. snapdragon. When watering, soak soil at base without wetting upper parts of plants. Spray every 7-10 days with fungicide. Good coverage is essential for adequate control.

BLACK SPOT affects roses.

Trouble: Circular black spots with feathery margins occur on leaves, which turn prematurely yellow and drop, resulting in weakening of plants. Disease spread mainly by water splashing from diseased to healthy leaves. Fungus overwinters in canes and leaves.

Control: Prune canes of diseased plants, burn infected leaves before spring. Spray or dust plants, at first appearance of black spots on foliage, with fungicide at weekly intervals until hot, dry weather begins. Apply again within a day of rain, but not more than once within any week.

LEAFSPOT affects begonia, calendula, carnation, catalpa, chrysanthemum, hollyhock, iris, pansy, peony, phlox, rhododendron, sycamore, others.

Trouble: Spots progressively destroy leaves, size, shape and color depending on causal agent. Badly infected leaves fall prematurely. Fungi spread mainly by splashing water. More serious in wet seasons. Usually fungi overwinters on old leaves.

Control: Destroy fallen infected foliage. When weather wet, spray fungicide every 7-10 days from mid-June till dry weather.

ROOT ROT affects aster, calla lily, pansy, sweet pea, others.

Trouble: Symptoms vary depending on causing organisms, generally infected plants dwarfed and sick looking. Badly affected ones have little or no root, what is left is stubby and dark. In other cases, leaves suddenly wilt and plant collapses.

Control: Grow plants only in well-drained locations and water only enough to sustain growth. When transplanting, clean infected parts out thoroughly, allow to dry, and dust with fungicide before replanting. Rotate crops.

CANKER affects maple, peony, rose, spruce, others.

Trouble: Dead areas appear on canes and stems, bark and wood dies back from pruning cuts or flower stalk stubs, sometimes whole branches girdled and killed. Various types.

Control: No good practical control. Prune several inches back from canker and destroy piece you cut. Apply tree wound paint on all cuts, and try not to leave stubs. Sterilize shears after each cut by wiping with rubbing alcohol.

SOFT ROT affects calla lily, iris, narcissus, others.

Trouble: Soft, ill-smelling rot of rhizomes and bulbs and lower leaves. Infected plants wilt and often completely collapse. Infection generally enters through wounds made by insect borers, e.g. iris.

Control: When dividing rhizomes, cut out infected parts and destroy. In a non-metal container soak clean divisions in 1:1000 solution of corrosive sublimate for 10 minutes, then replant in new location.
Infected bulbs should be destroyed.
Plant both rhizomes and bulbs always in well-drained soil, not too close together nor in shady, constantly moist places. Remove all debris from established beds in fall.

WILT affects aster, calendula, carnation, chrysanthemum, dahlia, geranium, maple, others.

Trouble: Plants wilt or turn yellow and die before maturity. Two main types, fusarium wilt favored by hot weather, verticillium wilt by cool.

Control: Avoid planting in known infected soils. Take cuttings only from healthy plants. Destroy infected ones. Rotate crops.

VIRUS affects aster, chrysanthemum, peony, geranium, lily, others.

Trouble: Symptoms vary, foliage may be mottled, plants stunted, leaves twisted, distorted, curled, flowers blotchy with broken colors and of distorted shapes.

Control: Remove and destroy diseased plants. Control insects (particularly aphids) which can spread these diseases. Do not use bulbs and cuttings of infected stock. Destroy weeds that may contain viruses and sucking insects that can transfer them from one plant to another.

For special control measures for:
Vegetables, see CHAPTER 11.
Fruit, see CHAPTER 12.
Lawns, see CHAPTER 23.

PART III

THE FINE
POINTS
OF GROWING
GOOD
GARDEN PLANTS
WELL

20 TREES

Planting a tree is a gesture of faith in the future.
With it, you plant, inevitably, part of yourself—
it has always been so with people and trees.
Choose it carefully, plant it skillfully, care for it thoughtfully.

TO CHOOSE THE RIGHT TREE for you and your garden, know these things:

HARDINESS RATINGS

Trees you choose should be able to survive extremes of weather, grow well in the yearly rainfall, snow cover and wind gust of your garden. These factors have been measured by government horticultural experts and every well-known tree that will grow in our country has been given a hardiness rating indicating the zone in which it can reasonably be expected to live and grow well. Check the Plant Hardiness Map for your zone number, then match it to trees with a similar or lower zone number on our lists and in nursery catalogues. From these, make your choice.

Trees with higher zone numbers may grow successfully in your garden if you have places where more temperate conditions than the average prevail, but know when you choose them that you are taking a chance.

SIZES AT MATURITY AND RATE OF GROWTH

The eventual height and spread of any tree you plant is vital. Many an enthusiastic gardener, who planted a pair of small blue spruce to frame his front door 20 years ago, now scuttles up to it through a tunnel of chopped-back branches because he didn't check the mature base spread. With good growing conditions, this could be 10-12 feet in 20 years for blue spruce.

Don't plant a tall-growing tree directly under overhead wires, or a wide-spreading one where it may later block a good view. If you plan to grow grass under it know whether the tree's shade will be dense or light — you can't grow good grass in dense shade. Realize that a large tree with roots near the surface will absorb moisture and nourishment in fantastic amounts and make it virtually impossible to grow anything under it, unless you make special beds.

Check with your nurseryman on the rate of growth you may expect. For instance, the average maple, hornbeam, oak, linden and magnolia grow 10 inches in a year; birch, honey locust and flowering crab apple 18 inches; pine 8-10 inches; yew and spruce 8 inches.

Consider that, for your garden, a tree rated as small (25-35 feet at maturity) may be a better choice than a future forest giant. Although short-lived compared with big trees (25 years *vs.* 100 years), they are often a more complimentary size for a house; many are flowery, some are fragrant, many have bright fruit that attracts wild birds and cheers up the winter landscape.

FORM AND HABIT:

The future shape of a tree and its growth habit should influence your decision. Trees can be:

tall and spreading like a scarlet oak

tall and thin (listed in nursery catalogues as columnar or fastigiate) like the Lombardy poplar or Sentry sugar maple

conical or pyramidal like the white spruce or little leaf linden

globe headed (a round, circular head on a main stem) like the specially grown Globe Norway maple, or umbrella catalpa

weeping (graceful, pendulous branches) like weeping willow or weeping birch

dense, throwing heavy shade like a Norway maple

open and lacy throwing light shade like a honey locust

small at maturity like a flowering crab apple

large at maturity like a horse chestnut

slow growing like an oak or mountain ash

fast growing like a poplar, willow or false acacia

best grown in dry soil like a honey locust

best grown in moist soil like a willow or a white cedar

tolerant of city air like a tree of heaven or the London plane tree

full of character like a corkscrew willow, a ginkgo, a Camperdown elm, the Northwest Coast monkey puzzle.

Most important of all they can be:

deciduous, meaning that they lose their leaves every fall and remain bare all winter, like maples, birches, hawthorns: or

needled evergreen, meaning that for most of the

country they are cone-bearing, and green and lovely all year like pines, spruces, firs: or

broad-leaved evergreen, like the holly, arbutus and magnolia.

BRITTLENESS

Fast-growing trees like the Chinese or Siberian elm, false acacia, willow, although handy for quick screening, have the fault of being very brittle and subject to major breaking in ice storms. The branch structure of the silver maple puts it in this class too.

MAINTENANCE

If you have to budget carefully your time for gardening or the cost of having help, check what the care of different trees will be. Large, heavy-leafed trees need frequent raking in fall. The Norway maple, grown well, also sheds a thick crop of seeds in late spring. Lombardy poplars and weeping willows are noted for shedding twigs all season and Balm of Gilead for a large crop of catkins in spring. Some crab apples and mulberries have a fruit drop that can be a real nuisance on sidewalks and patios.

Some trees are more susceptible than others to pests and diseases. Birches are prone to leaf miner, crab apples to caterpillars, the London plane tree to mildew. Choose them knowing this means either a regular program of prevention and cure with dusts or sprays of insecticides and fungicides, or be prepared to take a chance on your tree surviving this kind of trouble if it occurs. A regular program of good care is the best insurance against pest and disease damage. Plant American elm or sweet chestnut knowing that both are susceptible to diseases for which there is at present no known prevention or cure.

COLOR

In foliage: Most deciduous trees are green in leaf and therefore add a serene coolness to the landscape in summer. Evergreens, being ever green, have the look of continuing life winter and summer. But some trees, other than green, are dramatic in the garden and should be deliberately placed for color accent. The Sunburst honey locust has yellow-tipped foliage that really does look as though the sun had burst on it. Crimson King maple, the purple and copper beeches, Pissard plum, Royalty crab apple all have foliage of bronze-purple red; Russian olive and sea buckthorn — also considered shrubs — are silvery grey and the white poplar turns its white-backed leaves over in the wind when it's going to rain. The harlequin maple, popular with many, has foliage of green bordered in white and pale green and is a knockout against a dark house. The whitebeam mountain ash, although susceptible to fire blight in some areas, is a most beautiful tree beginning the year with leaves of softest white-green velvet.

Among the evergreens, some are bluish — the blue Colorado spruce is the favorite; some silvery like the silver fir or Mountbatten juniper; some gold, like the golden western cedar.

In flowers: Clouds of white in spring — the shadbush and the May Day tree; later the spectacular flowering dogwoods of the Pacific Coast and the eastern states; the locusts and catalpa, yellowwood are all a delight. For pale to deepest pink and cerise there are dozens of cultivars of flowering crab apples, cherries, hawthorns; for golden yellow there is the graceful dripping beauty of laburnums.

In bark: It's the bare dormant tree of winter that shows fascinating color in bark. For grey bark, choose a red maple, red oak, Korean mountain ash, shadbush, yellowwood or — for its strong form and pointed, fat buds — the saucer magnolia.

For white-barked trees, nothing surpasses the white birch. When you see it against a turquoise late-day winter sky, with a red cardinal in it, everything stops. Lit on a dark summer night, it's equally a showstopper. Poplars can seem nearly as white-trunked as birches, but are not very satisfactory for home gardens — they grow too large and sucker all over the place.

When you come to red-brown barked trees, the red and Scots pines are

Shadbush.

182

excellent. (Gertrude Jekyll, the famous English landscape architect of the turn of the century, used to whack her Scots pines on frosty winter days to make them ring.) Three little known birches — the Chinese paper birch, the cherry birch and the western white birch — are colorful too.

For gold, nothing is so burnished as the golden weeping willow, or so sure a sign of spring when its bark glows against a late winter sunset.

For odd bark, nothing is stranger than a sycamore. The trunk is a lighter-than-elephant grey with great peeled patches showing pale yellow-green to orange — a photographer-of-texture's delight. The London plane tree, sturdy in city polluted air, has similar coloring but both these trees need a large space to grow well.

Cork trees have soft, deeply-grooved pale-grey bark and the moosewood of the northern forests is striped with lighter lines up and down its blue-green bark.

In autumn foliage: The soaring crescendos of trees in their fall color are familiar to every gardener — the scarlets of maple, oak and sumac; in the Northwest the dogwoods are the truly flaming ones. Less often noticed but just as lovely are the soft golds of birch and other maples, the burnt orange of Korean mountain ash, the muted burgundy-red of pear and shadbush and smoketree; the purple of white ash. All bring a dividend to your garden.

In autumn fruit: Flowering crab apples can be hung with fruit the size of an earring or little 2-inch apples in yellow, greenish, scarlet or dark red and all beloved by the birds, especially robins. Mountain ash, also bird fare, comes in pink, coral, orange or scarlet berries and hawthorns are scarlet-fruited too.

Where to get your trees

It is extremely difficult to transplant a wild tree to a garden successfully. Unless it is very small (2-4 feet), it is impossible to disentangle the roots from surrounding growth with sufficient soil to move it safely. It is wiser to go to nurseries that specialize in trees or send for catalogues. You will be surprised at the low cost and you will be sure of getting a tree true to name, correctly zoned, carefully grown, root and top pruned to move without loss and — from the most reliable nurseries — guaranteed to grow or be replaced. Some nurseries encourage their customers to visit their fields and tag a special tree when it is in leaf, bloom or fruit for delivery at the proper time.

Beware of advertisements for what seem to be beautiful trees with beautiful names at bargain prices. Track down their correct botanical name, check this against reputable lists for hardiness and suitability for *your* garden. Check the size of tree you are buying too — a tiny cutting could, by some unscrupulous characters, be called a "tree," but it will take years to look like one. A good but green

gardening friend of mine once sent away for six so-called fruit trees for the fancy sum of $1.98. She got notification from the railway express that her parcel had arrived and, having only a little car in her family, borrowed a large station wagon from a neighbor to collect her prospective orchard. You can guess the rest. The parcel contained six little rooted cuttings, 6 inches long — two apple, a pear, a plum, a cherry and a peach. She didn't even need a little car to take them home. The parcel fitted easily into her coat pocket.

WHEN TO PLANT

Deciduous trees in zones 1-5 are usually moved bare root in early spring before they leaf out — the two weeks after frost is out of the ground are the surest. In more temperate zones, there is also a good planting time in fall as soon as the leaves have dropped and while there are still some weeks for roots to become established before hard-freezing weather sets in.

Willow, birch, poplar and silver maple are exceptions. They should be planted *only* in spring; magnolia and flowering dogwood also in spring and they should be balled and burlapped. For exactly when, follow the same planting calendar as for other deciduous trees.

Nursery-grown trees in containers, if carefully handled, can be moved into your garden any time during the growing season.

Large-size trees, balled and burlapped, can be moved in by tree companies specializing in this highly technical task, at almost any time of the year, even in full leaf in midsummer, with the use of wax sprays on the foliage to reduce transpiration till the roots can take over. But you will need to have a flowing oil well handy — this is landscaping in style, money no object.

TREES ALREADY FULLY GROWN

Planting a small sapling that you hope will eventually be a big tree is certainly a gesture of faith in the future, but inheriting an already large tree is an immediate and visible legacy without price.

If you have bought new land for a new garden and it is heavily treed, read CHAPTER 16 on making a new garden. If you must pave, excavate, build, ditch or change grade close to an existing large tree you wish to keep, check information in CHAPTER 14. And do not forget that often the best way to handle a big tree in a vulnerable spot is to have professional tree men move it to another safer place in your garden.

Big trees of character whose age is beginning to tell on them are often worth professional repair. Decayed wood can be reamed out and cavities filled. Limbs at chancy angles can be braced. High pruning, spraying and fertilizing can bring an ailing tree back to health. To save a big tree is worth every penny it may cost for it will continue to add beauty to your garden, cool the air in summer, temper the frost and cold beneath it in winter, shelter a lively community of birds and small animals, provide a frame for a swing, a tree house or an exciting ladder to the sky for your small fry. And, inexplicably, it will always be something that you cherish.

For information on how to improve soil before planting trees, how to heel in to await planting, how to plant bare-root, balled, container trees, how to stake, protect, water, fertilize and prune trees, see

CHAPTER 18: Techniques and Tools. For how to control common pests and diseases, see CHAPTER 19; for the use of trees in the design of your garden, see CHAPTER 13. For the favorite trees for your part of the country, see Part V.

TREES FOR WINDBARRIERS

Planting trees in a pattern to slow and sift the gale is a familiar ploy of gardeners by the sea or other large windy sweeps of water, but it is in the northern plains that this has become a specialized art. For more than fifty years government forest and conservation services have been busy breeding and selecting the best trees for this purpose, studying the efficient management of windbarriers and making plant material and information available to those who ask for it.

The material is available to farmers for planting on farm land, which is interpreted to mean not only the fields given over to working crops, but also the gardens and land surrounding the homestead. Gardeners who don't qualify as bona fide farmers in northern plains states, but who may have similar problems with wind and the need for a barrier for their garden, can learn from the well-taught lessons of the forest services, then obtain their trees from other sources. (If you are windbarriering a large rural garden, inquire whether you are eligible for your local government tree services.)

The advantages of trees planted for this kind of protection have been proven. A farmstead thus sheltered is better able to maintain a garden, not only for the pleasure of growing flowers but for vegetables and fruit as well.

Preparation of a farmstead windbarrier

Plan to plant your windbarriers at least 100 feet from the nearest buildings, with the first, if you must do it in stages, where it will give the best protection from the prevailing wind.

One to twelve rows of trees may be planted, depending on space available — experts recommend six or more. Although each row should be of one kind, variety in the selection of the six kinds gives protection and insurance against crippling attacks of insects, disease or damaging weather.

Be sure to allow 12-20 feet between each row to provide for the proper development of proper density and protection. To conserve moisture and to remove established weeds and grass, summer-fallow the ground for one year prior to planting. Maintain two similar outside borders of summer fallow annually thereafter; otherwise weeds will take nourishment and moisture from the soil which your trees need for establishment and good growth.

AN EFFICIENT SIX-ROW WINDBARRIER FOR A DRY SITE

1st Row (the outside): Caragana, Lilac, Honeysuckle or Rocky Mountain Juniper or Ponderosa Pine

2nd Row: Siberian Crab Apple, Russian Olive, Amur Maple, Juniper or Pine

3rd Row: Green Ash, American Elm, Burr Oak

4th Row: Green Ash, American Elm, Burr Oak

5th Row: Green Ash, American Elm, Burr Oak

6th Row: Nanking Cherry (its tart fruit useful in preserves), Sand Cherry or any as recommended for the 1st Row.

FOR A MOIST SITE

Use: Poplar in the 4th Row
Willow in the 3rd, 4th or 5th Row
Juneberry or Dogwood in the 6th Row
Spruce (Colorado or Black Hills) in the 1st, 2nd or 6th Row

Recommended spacing between rows is 12-20 feet, and distances to plant individual trees and plants apart is approximately 8-10 feet for shrubs, 10-20 feet for trees.

Special situations

For maximum protection from snow and winter wind damage, especially on the north and west sides of the farmstead, plant a staggered row of evergreens 6-10 feet apart, 30-50 feet inside the windbarrier proper and at least 100 feet from the nearest building. These trees will also add greatly to the beauty of the garden.

Where space is limited, two rows — the first of caragana, the inside row of spruce or pine — will provide good shelter.

Do not vary the planting and design suggested. Evergreen trees, for instance, should not be planted in the same row with deciduous trees.

Order your trees from the nursery as early as possible in the summer or fall of the year before you intend to plant them.

Planting

Check district regulations for allowed distances of trees from highways and roads.

Plant in early spring as soon as frost is out of the ground. Seedlings are very perishable, so take delivery quickly when you are notified of their arrival.

If unable to plant immediately, cut open the packages — soak poplar and willows overnight if they appear at all dry, *not* other varieties — and heel in (see CHAPTER 18: Techniques and Tools). Backfill and water deeply. Plant in permanent location as quickly as you can.

To plant: use a tree-planting machine if possible. Otherwise plant by hand in furrows. Soil should be free of manure, fertilizer and herbicides. Keep roots moist and sheltered from sun and wind at all times. Plant at the same depth as tree was set in the nursery — this will show as a soil mark on the stem. Firm the soil after planting and water thoroughly.

Ongoing care

Weeds must be controlled for at least 3 years until subdued by foliage canopy. By then outside summer fallow strips can take over. During these early years, weeding is best done by shallow and clean cultivation of all rows or by the use of sprays of chemical herbicides.

For correct herbicide, strength and rate of application, consult your nearest government representative or tree nursery.

Keep your trees from drying out by extra watering when necessary: do this for at least 3 years if you possibly can — this is the critical time of their life.

Fence them from wandering farm animals. Prune only dead or diseased branches — the object of planting a windbarrier is to make the growth dense, not pruned out.

Be careful not to allow herbicides to drift onto the trees, and never use equipment for them that has previously been used for this type of chemical.

Replace any trees that die. Guard against fire damage.

Possible troubles

Rodents can girdle trunks and, if they chew all way round, kill the tree. To prevent this, set out poison bait in clay tiles under a forkful of straw

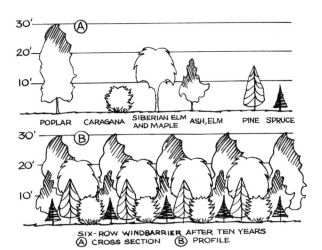

POPLAR CARAGANA SIBERIAN ELM AND MAPLE ASH, ELM PINE SPRUCE

SIX-ROW WINDBARRIER AFTER TEN YEARS
(A) CROSS SECTION (B) PROFILE

GARDEN PLANTS TO EXTEND WINDBARRIERS

Low and often decorative small trees and shrubs may be used for extra outside and inside rows and add to the beauty of the sheltered garden. Consider these:

Late lilacs, *Syringa villosa*, Zone 2
Honeysuckle, *Lonicera tatarica*, Zone 2
Buffaloberry, *Shepherdia*, Zone 2
Serviceberry, *Amelanchier alnifolia*, Zone 1
    or Choke cherry, *Prunus virginiana* 'Shubert', Zone 1
May Day Tree, *Prunus padus commutata*, Zone 2
Sea buckthorn, *Hippophae rhamnoides*, Zone 2
Hawthorn, *Crataegus*, selections, Zone 2
Dogwood, *Cornus*, selections, Zone 2
Flowering currant, *Ribes*, Zone 2
Hedge roses, *Rosa*, selections, Zone 1

at 10-12-foot intervals through the plantings or put a shield around the tree. (See CHAPTER 18.)

Wounds caused by insects may later become infected by disease carried by wind, causing cankers and killing bark. Cut out diseased areas and burn debris, then paint with special tree sealer.

Damage caused by storms should be mended by trimming off broken parts and dressing wounds with white lead paint with tree paint.

Trees that appear to be killed by drought are not always completely dead. Try cutting them back to the stump, then feed and water. With luck, they may shoot new growth from their surviving roots.

7 RECOMMENDED LARGE SHADE TREES

The average home garden can contain only one large shade tree — at the best two — but they are so important, so long living, they should be chosen with the greatest thought and care. Here are seven to choose from.

Beech, European: *Fagus sylvatica*; 80 feet; Zone 5

A mature beech is majestic, strong and handsome in leaf and out. Slow growing, it does best in rich, well-drained soil in an open, sunny spot, is tolerant of high winds and seashore salt spray. Dense of foliage — so dense in fact that you can grow nothing beneath it — round-headed, and low branching, it transplants fairly easily, always from the nursery, balled and burlapped.

It's long-lived. It should not be planted where earth will be packed down over its shallow roots or where fill will be needed to raise the grade over them. Foliage can be deep green, copper or purple-bronze, in familiar tree shape or weeping.

Branches of leaves cut in late August or early September and stood in ⅓ glycerine and ⅔ hot water become soft and glossy like well-polished leather and

last in bouquets in the house for many years. Branches cut in late winter and brought into the house for forcing have the most delicate beauty of pleated leaf.

Birch, White or Canoe: *Betula papyrifera*; 50-80 feet; Zone 2

The most popular shade tree in the whole country for home gardens. Its black-scarred white main trunk and rosy-brown side branches are a delight day and night, leafed and bare. You can plant one all by itself or a clump of as many as eleven. Narrowish and rounded at the top, the leaves have a light and open air. Easily transplanted, it grows fairly quickly, likes moist soil and full sun and turns golden yellow in autumn. Besides regular forms, there are weeping, cutleaf and columnar cultivars. Consider also the European birch, *B. verrucosa*; 60 feet; Zone 2; also a handsome tree.

Linden, Littleleaf: *Tilia cordata*; 40-50 feet; Zone 3

A favorite street tree with city planners because of its tolerance of polluted air, this is a well-disciplined, lovely-to-look-at tree. Symmetrical and narrow tipped, its leaves are heart shaped, its flowers pale yellow and wonderfully fragrant in the early evening. Two little-leaf lindens are a great joy to the blind in their Fragrant Garden in Toronto when they flower each July. Summer color of leaves is dark green above, pale green below, and in fall a not outstanding pale yellow. Easy to grow, very slow, likes moist earth. Sometimes a great favorite with aphids who pierce and suck the sap in the leaves, dropping a kind of sticky "honey-dew" on whatever is below; so do not plant where branches will be over your summer furniture or where cars will be parked.

Honey Locust: *Gleditsia triacanthos*; 30-50 feet; Zone 4

The most lightly feathery tree on our list and therefore it's easy to grow a lawn under it. The fern-like foliage is dark green above, yellow-green below and turns pale yellow in the fall. Moderately rapid as a grower, tolerant of city soot and seaside salt, drought resistant and broadheaded to a tip at the top. Many new cultivars are being selected by hybridists, one of the prettiest is 'Sunburst', with yellow-leafed tips on its branches all summer long; where I live (Zone 6b) there's a tendency for the twig tips to die back over winter, but this does not seem to seriously affect its growth.

Maple, Sugar: *Acer saccharum*; 40-90 feet; Zone 4

The best of the maples for home gardens for many reasons. It's a beautiful tree to look at — spectacular with its brilliant yellow, orange and scarlet fall colors — and fun, if your fancy runs this way, to tap for sap to make your own maple syrup in spring. It grows at a moderate rate, prefers sandy loam and good drain-

age (planting it on a mound is one way to ensure this), is easily transplanted, likes full sun. The main trunk is shaggy and grooved and the small side branches soft grey. It doesn't appreciate inner-city air. Cultivars come also in columnar shapes. Other maples available — Red, *A. rubrum*, Zone 3, which needs a very moist, acid site; Norway, *A. platanoides*, Zone 5, which, although positively magical in pale yellow-green bloom before its leaves come out, is a dreadful nuisance with dropped flowers, seeds and leaves that must be swept up; it is also so dense and shallow-rooted that it is impossible to grow grass under; Silver maple, *A. saccharinum*, hardy to Zone 2b, is a quick grower but unfortunately breaks easily in wind and ice storms.

Oak, White: *Quercus alba*; 50-90 feet; Zone 4

Wide spreading, muscled, massive, this oak gives, at maturity, the impression of tremendous strength — which in fact, it has. A deep taproot means that you can grow other plants beneath it. Its rate of growth is slow, the bark of the main trunk and branches is so deeply ridged small birds and animals climb easily all over it. Long-lived — some experts say up to 800 years. The leaves are deep green, indented around the edges and they make marvelous winter mulch for acid-loving azaleas and rhododendrons, for they stay crispy and dry. They take a long time to rot down if you want to compost them. Oak prefers dry, gravelly soil. Move only in small sizes. The best tree for hanging swings or building tree houses in.

Willow, Weeping (many kinds): *Salix*; 30-60 feet; Zone 4

I have included weeping willow in this list not because I feel I must, but because the popular vote would put it here. People seem to have a deep love for weeping

willows even though they are messy and drop bits of twiggy tresses all the time. Their leaves also fall in summer if there has been a prolonged dry spell. Their rapid growth makes for brittle wood which smashes down in a summer wind or winter ice storm, and their terrible thirst for water can clog weeping tiles and ruin plants trying to grow under them. But I must admit that their branches swaying in the wind are a graceful sight and their golden-turning bark and leafing out in early spring is a true tonic. They're also about the last trees to lose their leaves in fall. They transplant so easily you could almost grow a tree from a switch stuck in the ground and watered well. But if you want to be sure of getting one of the good special cultivars, consult your nurseryman's catalogue.

6 RECOMMENDED LARGE EVERGREENS

Evergreens, especially in the north, are cherished as much for their winter beauty as for their soft summer greenness. That they are also a beloved symbol of Christmas attracts us too. Lovely when tipped with new fresh green in spring, they are equally beautiful frosted with puffs of white snow in winter. Some are fragrant. They take a fairly long time to propagate and grow in nurseries, and because of their fibrous root system must always be moved balled and burlapped. This makes them more expensive than deciduous trees, so it's wise to take time to choose them carefully.

Cedar, White, selections: American Arborvitae; *Thuja occidentalis*; 15-45 feet; Zone 2b

This cedar is versatile as both a specimen tree and a formal or informal hedge. Thick and dense, the foliage is scaly and fan-shaped, the tiny cones like carved wood. It likes full sun, moist soil and if there has been light or no autumn rain it should be well watered before freeze-up. The tips take well to clipping, either to keep in bounds or to tidy the form. Cut branches last wonderfully indoors. Easily transplanted. Doesn't like city air. Cultivars with yellow tips are available besides the regular green.

Fir, Silver, White: *Abies concolor*; 100 feet; Zone 4

Soft, silvery, long needles make this the best of large evergreens for a specimen on the lawn or standing among other plants in the garden. Conical in shape, prefers full sun and free circulation of air all around it. Withstands heat and drought well. Cones greenish or purplish, standing up on the branches like candles.

Douglas Fir: *Pseudotsuga menziesii glauca*; 50-100 feet; Zone 3

The pride of the west, where in native stands it sometimes reaches 300 feet. Graceful because of its pendulous branchlets, easily transplanted, and adaptable to a wide range of soil conditions.

Pine, Austrian: *Pinus nigra austriaca*; 40-70 feet; Zone 4

A sturdy, rugged, needled evergreen that withstands city air, salt spray from street or sea and stays thick and green to the bottom, which most other pines do not. Pyramidal, compact and symmetrical, it grows fairly quickly. Should be deeply watered for at least two years after planting. Does well in poor dry soil. Other pines also good, but not so adaptable for the home garden, are: Scots, Jack, Norway or Red, Swiss Stone, Lodgepole.

Spruce, Colorado or Blue: *Picea pungens*; 40-60 feet; Zone 2

By all odds the favorite evergreen for home gardens, where it should be set out alone because of its stunning frosty blue color. A Christmas tree shape, branched well at the bottom for the first 25 years, after which the lower branches tend to die. Cones about 4 inches long, hang downward and make good-looking Christmas decorations. Stands up to dry conditions. Choose your tree at the nursery; even with the same name some trees will be bluer and more attractive than others. Other spruces with ratings as low as Zone 1, and of green rather than blue coloring, are available for gardens in colder parts of the country.

Hemlock: *Tsuga canadensis*; 60-75 feet; Zone 4

A delicately needled tree with outreaching branches and tiny cones. Extremely useful for planting in cities, in half shade, and where a semi-formal clipping is needed to keep it in bounds. Thrives in deep, moist soil and grows fairly quickly after it is established. Superb for screening winter and summer because it holds its foliage to the ground.

The best trees for your garden may well be some of those classified as small, meaning that they become, at maturity, about as high as a second-story window or maybe less. Advantages are that they will be in pleasing scale with your house, that they will take less food and light, less space than large trees and that often it's possible to have the fun of growing more than one in an average-sized garden. Also, unlike most large ones, small trees take only 3-10 years to come to flowering. Some, such as the saucer magnolia and flowering crab apple, will bloom even in the first few years if you buy well-developed stock. New ones are being introduced almost every year, so watch your nursery catalogues for them. Here are seven of the best.

Flowering Crab Apple (many): *Malus*; 15-30 feet high, 10-15 feet wide; some hardy to Zone 2b

Heads the list for beauty and long-term usefulness. Behaves like a small sister of a full size apple tree, with buds and leaves emerging in May then fruit — yellow, green or red — in fall. Flowers when they open can be white, pink or all shades of cerise and carmine; some are very fragrant; leaves are a tender green through to bronze, sometimes maturing later to green, sometimes, as in 'Royalty', staying a glossy purple-bronze all summer. Some are upright, some columnar and a boon for small narrow spaces; some dainty and roundheaded; at least one is weeping and an outstanding accent tree, another wider than it is tall and perfect for sheltering plants in a large rock garden. Many of these — and many others — are descendants of the famous 'Rosybloom' hybrids developed by Isabella Preston fifty years ago at the Central Experimental Farm in Ottawa. Working with these and other fine cultivars, horticultural stations in Canada and the northern United States are developing new and even more beautiful ones every year. Check with your local nursery for those best for your area and note your favorites on this list.

'**Almey**'; Zone 2b; 20 feet high; 8-15 feet wide; cherry red flowers, each blossom starred with white; orange-red fruit; leaves open purplish then turn green.

'**Crimson Brilliant**'; Zone 5; 20 feet high; 8-15 feet wide; crimson flowers, cherry-sized purple-red fruit; takes about 2 years from planting to first bloom, hardy.

'**Dorothea**'; Zone 4; 20 feet high; 8-15 feet wide; semi-double 2-inch, clear pink flowers, bright yellow fruit; blooms every year — not all crabs do.

'**Guiding Star**'; Zone 5; 20 feet high; 8-12 feet wide; a narrow tree; fragrant with white flowers, pink in bud; fruit small and yellow.

'**Hillieri**'; Zone 5; 10-15 feet high; 8-12 feet wide; a delight of pink and white flowers that completely cover the tree; small yellow fruit.

'**Radiant**'; Zone 3b; 25 feet high; 8-15 feet wide; red flowers, red fruit, red leaves in spring, hardy.

'**Red Jade**'; Zone 4; 15 feet high; 8-12 feet wide; outstanding; weeping shape; white flowers; bright red fruit.

'**Royalty**'; Zone 2b; 20 feet high; 8-15 feet wide; handsome shining purple-red leaves all summer; deep pink flowers; small dark red fruit; plant as an accent.

'**Sargent**'; Zone 4; 10 feet high; 10-11 feet wide; a delightful dwarf, wider than tall, white flowers, red fruit.

'**Van Eseltine**'; Zone 2b; 20 feet high; 8-10 feet wide; double rose flowes, red-blushed-yellow fruit; upright.

Flowering Dogwood: *Cornus florida*; 20-40 feet high; 15-20 feet wide; Zone 5. *C. nuttallii*; 20-40 feet high; 12-20 feet wide; Zone 7. *C. kousa*; 20 feet high; 10-15 feet wide; Zone 5

Surely the loveliest spring-flowering tree in the world. White or pink petal-like bracts like soft suede. *C. nuttallii*, a native of the Pacific coast, *C. florida* of the Atlantic, have been crossed to produce the spectacular 'Eddie's White Wonder', hardy in Ohio at −15° and flowering for a whole month in spring. *C. florida* 'White Cloud', 'Apple Blossom', light pink, and 'Spring Song', deep rose, are also beauties. Red-berried and leaved in fall. All need winter protection in early years and their trunks wrapped to prevent borer attack. Buy only in medium or small sizes. Plant, B & B, in well-drained, acid soil, in light shade, and water deeply if no rain. The Chinese dogwood, *C. kousa* chinensis 'Milky Way', blooms almost a month later and with starrier bracts and fruits for birds in fall. If space for two, plant one of each, and you'll have drifting bloom for two months every spring.

Magnolia: *Magnolia x soulangiana*; 15-25 feet high; 12-20 feet wide; Zone 5b

Porcelain pink and white flowers, uptilted on leafless stems, fragrant and bigger than a teacup, make this one of the loveliest trees of the springtime. Smooth grey bark the color of clouds on a rainy day, open shape with branches like spreading arms, leaves that are strong and of a good green the whole summer through. Even in winter this tree is fascinating, for its large buds are all formed in the fall, each with its own furry tippet. You order it for delivery and planting *first* thing in the spring, balled and burlapped. When you plant it, don't bump it around, loosen the burlap but leave under it until after tree is settled in its planting hole. Expensive compared to other small trees, but worth it.

Laburnum: *Laburnum x watereri* 'Vossii'; 25 feet high; 10-15 feet wide; Zone 5

The golden chain tree some people call it, and so it is. The blossoms are gracefully dripping panicles of bright yellow each like a tiny sweet pea. A gracefully shaped tree, too, with a green-barked bare trunk and a spreading umbrella of lacy leaves. There is magic in planting it on the south side of your house to break the north wind and where it will also be sheltered from the late afternoon northwest sun. Standards of laburnum are popular with florists for forcing at Easter, so you might have double the fun if you buy one at that time, feed and water it until frosts are over outside, then plant it out in your garden. If you live just beyond the normal range of hardiness for laburnums but yearn for one, try putting a cage of wire mesh around the trunk up to the first branches and pack it loosely with oak leaves. Leave the cage there for three years and then gradually take out the leaves over the next year. This has worked successfully for other tender trees outside their normal range and might for you.

Korean Mountain Ash: *Sorbus alnifolia*; 25-40 feet high; 15-20 feet wide; Zone 4b

A mildly pretty tree in flower and leaf, the mountain ash is a vivid and bountiful joy when it is covered with brilliant foliage and salmon-orange berries in fall. If you add a flock of acrobatic, black-masked cedar waxwings feasting on the berries, or robins eating till you'd think they would turn orange all over, your picture is lovely beyond belief. Simple leaves are carried high and you can grow almost anything under it if you make a good soil bed. Whatever plants you choose for this, they should repeat the vibrant orange of the ash berries if you want the full punch. Needs fertile soil. Cultivars are also available with coral pink berries and some are more red than orange.

European Bird Cherry or May Day Tree: *Prunus padus commutata*; 20-40 feet high; 12-20 feed wide; Zone 2

This is the favorite early early spring-flowering tree of the prairies and the north. A froth of white pendulous flowers is followed by black fruit; the tree adapts to almost any soil, any care and looks dreamy doing it.

Paul's Scarlet Hawthorn: *Crataegus oxyacanthoides* 'Paul's Scarlet'; Zone 5; 20 feet high; 10-14 feet wide
Double, bright scarlet flowers followed by scarlet fruit; easy to grow and an excellent specimen tree; birds love it because its thorns discourage nest raiders.

---

7 GOOD BUT NOT SO WELL-KNOWN SMALL FLOWERING TREES

Callery Pear: *Pyrus calleryana* 'Bradford'; Zone 4; 30-40 feet high; 15-20 feet wide; developed by the United States Department of Agriculture especially as a fine tree for residential street planting; masses of white flowers in spring; tiny russet fruit; leaves turn brilliant crimson in the fall.

Devil's-walkingstick: *Aralia spinosa*; Zone 5; 10-35 feet high; 6-10 feet wide.

A strange, stick-like, spiny-stemmed tree with a tuft of long exotic leaves like big feathers at the top; flowers in fall with foamy crests of creamy white or rose; a marvelous tree for contemporary design gardens.

Kelsey Locust: *Robinia kelseyi*; Zone 5; 9 feet high; about 6 feet wide; lacy foliage, rose-pink flowers in late spring.

Ohio Buckeye: *Aesculus glabra*; Zone 2b; 35 feet high; 15-20 feet wide; a hardy horse chestnut with greenish-yellow flowers and brilliant orange foliage in fall.

Serviceberry, Shadblow: *Amelanchier canadensis*; Zone 4; 25 feet tall, 12-15 feet wide; one of the loveliest and most useful native trees; lacy with white flowers in spring; inconspicuous fruit but bright yellow-orange foliage in fall; easy to grow.

Stockton Double Pin Cherry: *Prunus pensylvanica* 'Stockton'; Zone 2b; 30 feet high; 12-15 feet wide; double white flowers in spring, followed by small red fruit.

Weeping Cherry: *Prunus serrulata* 'Kiku-Shidare-sakura'; Zone 5; 20 feet high; 10-12 feet wide; double deep pink flowers that are particularly lovely to look up into; makes an excellent specimen.

As well as the familiar precise triangle of the spruces and firs and the relaxed pyramid of such trees as the lindens, there are other forms especially valuable to the home gardener. Weeping trees, used as major accents in the design, are rhythmic and graceful; narrow, columnar trees, also listed sometimes as fastigiate, are useful where you want a vertical line and space is limited. (For trees favored by gardeners in your part of the country, see PART V.)

Weeping — the most graceful of trees, the tips of the branches hang downward; many particularly lovely over water.

CAMPERDOWN ELM: *Ulmus glabra*; 'Camperdownii'; 40 feet; Zone 4b

FLOWERING CRAB APPLE, Red Jade: *Malus* 'Red Jade'; 15 feet; Zone 4

EUROPEAN MOUNTAIN ASH: *Sorbus aucuparia* 'Pendula'; 25 feet; Zone 3

HIGAN CHERRY: *Prunus subhirtella* 'Pendula'; 20 feet; Zone 5

Camperdown elm.   *Fastigiate ginkgo.*

JAPANESE PAGODA TREE: *Sophora japonica* 'Pendula'; 30 feet; Zone 6b

MULBERRY: *Morus alba* 'Pendula'; 15 feet; Zone 4

WEEPING BEECH: *Fagus sylvatica* 'Pendula' and 'Purpureo-Pendula' (purple-leaved); the first, 50-60 feet; Zone 5; the second, 15 feet; Zone 5

WEEPING BIRCH: *Betula verrucosa* 'Tristis' and 'Youngii' (more contorted); the first, 40 feet, Zone 2; the second, 30 feet; Zone 2b

WEEPING WILLOW:
Babylon: *Salix babylonica*: 30 feet; Zone 7b
Golden: *S. alba* 'Tristis'; 45-60 feet; Zone 4
Salamon: *S. x sepulcralis*; 60 feet; Zone 5
Thurlow: *S. x elegantissima*; 35 feet; Zone 4
Wisconsin: *S. x blanda*; 60 feet; Zone 4

Columnar — tall and thin, especially good for narrow spaces and where an exclamation mark is needed in the design.

AMANOGAWA JAPANESE CHERRY: *Prunus serrulata* 'Amanogawa'; 25 feet; Zone 5

COLUMNAR NORWAY MAPLE: *Acer platanoides* 'Columnare'; 40-50 feet; Zone 4

COLUMNAR RED MAPLE: *Acer rubrum* 'Columnare'; 40 feet; Zone 4

COLUMNAR SIBERIAN CRAB APPLE: *Malus baccata* 'Columnaris'; 20 feet; Zone 2b

FASTIGIATE GINKGO: *Ginkgo biloba* 'Fastigiata'; 50 feet; Zone 4

LOMBARDY POPLAR: *Populus nigra* 'Italica'; 70 feet; Zone 4

PYRAMIDAL EUROPEAN BEECH: *Fagus sylvatica* 'Fastigiata'; 30-40 feet; Zone 5

PYRAMIDAL EUROPEAN HORNBEAM: *Carpinus betulus* 'Fastigiata'; 30 feet; Zone 5b

PYRAMIDAL ENGLISH OAK: *Quercus robur* 'Fastigiata'; 40 feet; Zone 4

PYRAMIDAL WHITE BIRCH: *Betula verrucosa* 'Fastigiata'; 35-45 feet; Zone 2

SENTRY SUGAR MAPLE: *Acer saccharum* 'Newton Sentry'; 40 feet; Zone 4

SUTHERLAND CARAGANA: *C. arborescens* 'Sutherland'; 12-18 feet; Zone 2

SYCAMORE MAPLE: *Acer pseudoplatanus* 'Erectum'; 40 feet; Zone 5

TEMPLE'S UPRIGHT MAPLE: *Acer saccharum* 'Temple's Upright'; 40-50 feet; Zone 4

VAN ESELTINE FLOWERING CRAB APPLE: *Malus* 'Van Eseltine'; 20 feet; Zone 2b

TREES WITH CHARACTER

Corkscrew Hazel: *Corylus avellana* 'Contorta'; 15 feet; Zone 4

Corkscrew Willow: *Salix matsudana* 'Tortuosa'; 30 feet; Zone 4

These two bizarrely twisted corkscrews look as though a witch had played with their chromosomes.

Dawn-redwood: *Metasequoia glyptostroboides;* 60 feet; Zone 5

Ginkgo: *Ginkgo biloba*; 40-60 feet; Zone 4

Pacific Madrone: *Arbutus menziesii*; 30-45 feet; Zone 7

These three are full of history. The ginkgo and dawn-redwood are described as living fossils. Both have survived the years only because man made it possible. Both — and these are the only surviving species of their families — are considered to be over 200 million years old. According to fossil studies of the ginkgo, it was at one time common across the Arctic to Spitzbergen and as far south as England; then it was killed off by glaciers. The dawn-redwood, thought to be extinct, was dramatically discovered in China as recently as 1944. It looks like an evergreen, but drops its needles in the fall, like a bald-cypress, then bursts out fresh and green again in spring. Both trees should be planted in spring — the dawn-redwood is fairly fast growing, the ginkgo slow. Do not let either tree dry out. Be sure to specify a *male* ginkgo — the females produce evil-smelling fruit. The Pacific Madrone, a handsome tree of the west coast, has red-flaking bark and in fall bunches of red berries which look like strawberries. Folklore tells that it was brought from Spain by the conquistadors who were looking for a route to India. Evergreen, it grows best in well-drained soil with protection from the wind.

Larch in variety: *Larix*; 40-80 feet; Zone 1

A needled tree, but not evergreen; the bursting of its tufts of green needles in spring, its tiny cones like rosettes, first purple-pink then brown; and then its golden haze in fall would put this tree on anybody's character list.

Monkey Puzzle Tree: *Araucaria araucana*; 60 feet; Zone 7

White Pine: *Pinus strobus*; 60-100 feet; Zone 2b

One a symbol of Pacific coast gardens, one of the east, both trees are full of character because of their shape. The monkey puzzle tree looks as though it had been put together by a highly-organized snake charmer. It makes a fantastic ornament in some of the fine gardens of Victoria, B.C. The white pine comes into its own in windy sea and lake gardens where its gripping foothold on granite outcroppings is a miracle of perseverance and great strength.

The Tree of Heaven: *Ailanthus altissima*; 30-40 feet; Zone 5

There are many who would say that the only character this beautifully named tree really has is a bad one. A weed in many cities, it defies pavements and brick walls to get a toe hold, but it can still be an asset in a garden. Most particularly, I recommend it for city gardeners who want an inspired exotic conversation piece; plant a tree of heaven, prune it to the ground each winter, allow only one shoot to develop the following spring, cutting off all the others. Big tropical leaves develop — on one I saw they were almost 4 feet long — and they looked like an exotic plant from the deepest jungle.

TREES RECOMMENDED FOR SEASHORE GARDENS

AMERICAN ARBORVITAE, White-cedar: *Thuja occidentalis*; 15-45 feet; Zone 2b

AUSTRIAN PINE: *Pinus nigra*; 40-70 feet; Zone 4

BLACK CHERRY: *Prunus serotina*; 40-70 feet; Zone 2b

BLACK GUM, Sour gum: *Nyssa sylvatica*; 30-60 feet; Zone 5b

BLACK LOCUST: *Robinia pseudoacacia*; 30-50 feet; Zone 4

BLUE COLORADO SPRUCE, Koster's Spruce: *Picea pungens* 'Glauca'; 40-80 feet; Zone 2

COCKSPUR THORN: *Crataegus crus-galli*; 15-30 feet; Zone 2b

CRYPTOMERIA: *Cryptomeria japonica*; 30-100 feet; Zone 6b

EASTERN RED-CEDAR: *Juniperus virginiana*; 25-30 feet; Zone 3

ENGLISH HAWTHORN: *Crataegus oxyacanthoides*; 20 feet; Zone 5

GOLDEN WEEPING WILLOW: *Salix alba* 'Tristis'; 45-60 feet; Zone 4

HOLLY: *Ilex opaca*; 10-35 feet; Zone 7

HONEY LOCUST: *Gleditsia triacanthos*; 50-70 feet; Zone 4

HORSE-CHESTNUT: *Aesculus hippocastanum*; 75 feet; Zone 5b

JAPANESE PAGODA TREE: *Sophora japonica*; 25-60 feet; Zone 6b

JAPANESE PINE: *Pinus parviflora;* 80 feet; Zone 5

LITTLELEAF LINDEN: *Tilia cordata*; 40-50 feet; Zone 3

NORWAY MAPLE: *Acer platanoides*; 50-75 feet; Zone 5

PITCH PINE: *Pinus rigida*; 30 feet; Zone 5

RUSSIAN OLIVE: *Elaeagnus angustifolia*; 20-35 feet; Zone 2b

SCOTS PINE: *Pinus sylvestris*; 40-90 feet; Zone 2

SEA BUCKTHORN: *Hippophae rhamnoides*; 10-15 feet; Zone 2b

SERVICEBERRY: Shadblow: *Amelanchier canadensis*; 25 feet; Zone 4

SOUTHERN MAGNOLIA: *Magnolia grandiflora*; 20 feet; Zone 9a

SYCAMORE MAPLE: *Acer pseudoplatanus*; 40-70 feet; Zone 5b

TREE OF HEAVEN: *Ailanthus altissima*; 40-60 feet; Zone 5

WHITE OAK: *Quercus alba*; 50-90 feet; Zone 4

WHITE POPLAR: *Populus alba*; 50-80 feet; Zone 2

21 SHRUBS

Shrubs, of all plants of the garden, have a beauty of flower, an ease of care, a happy-go-lucky versatility that's outstanding. More than any other plant, they rate the highest recommendation to gardeners everywhere, whether by the salt-spraying sea, on the wind-ripped northern plains and prairies, on thin-soiled rocky shields, on slopes of high mountains, in the deeply fertile parts of our land or in the sandy lowlands of the far South. Everywhere, shrubs will grow and grow superbly.

FIRST OF ALL, WHAT IS A SHRUB?

Confusion reigns when you try to pin down exactly what a shrub is. All agree that it is a woody, multiple-stemmed plant and that a tree, which is very similar, is a woody, single-stemmed plant. But a woody, usually multiple-stemmed shrub is sometimes trained as a single-stem tree and a woody, single-stemmed tree often turns into a woody, multiple-stemmed plant which then looks like a shrub. So now you know what a shrub is.

They can be tall, medium or short; deciduous or evergreen; notable for flowers or foliage — sometimes both — be fragrant, bright barked or berried or of interest because of an intriguing winter silhouette. The variety is tremendous and choosing which to grow in your garden is tantalizingly difficult. Shrubs with special qualities for special gardens are mentioned in most of the chapters of PART I — to tolerate city air, CHAPTER 5; to do well in shade, CHAPTER 6; especially good for rock gardens, CHAPTER 7; native shrubs that transplant well, CHAPTER 8; fragrant shrubs, CHAPTER 9; berried and twiggy shrubs to attract wild birds, CHAPTER 10.

They have many other uses as well — for solo beauty standing alone in a conspicuous spot; dramatic as a group, or to set off a handsome feature such as a fine piece of sculpture; as a green wall, such as a hedge, or as ground cover, see CHAPTERS 22 and 24.

When you have analyzed your needs, look through our lists. You'll find six or a dozen that will give you what you want even if it's something as fey as a fuzzy weeper. You may not believe it, but there really is a shrub called the weeping fuzzy deutzia, *Deutzia crenata* 'Pendula'. It's hardy to Zone 6 and grows 3-6 feet tall.

HOW TO CHOOSE THE RIGHT SHRUB FOR YOUR GARDEN

Begin by measuring the space you want to plant in. You will find the space needs of various hedge shrubs in CHAPTER 22; of single plantings or groups in lists at the end of this chapter. Space needs are height and width at maturity, which will be a few years away from the day you buy and plant, but they should be considered. Many a 2-foot stick of beauty-bush has fountained into a plant 12 feet high and 12 feet wide in a space never intended for anything so big, and this is a common happening.

Next check your soil and drainage. Most shrubs are not fussy about soil, a few prefer it dry, a few moist, almost none wet. Some shrubs — rhododendrons, azaleas, pieris — need acid soil which can either occur naturally in your garden, be induced or substituted, (see CHAPTER 18.) Check the light your planting spot will have at all times of the day. All flowering shrubs and those with variegated leaves do best in full sunshine all day, but there are some which do pretty well in light, moving shade. For deep shade places, rather than for flower effect you might better plan for foliage, such as broad-leaved evergreen shrubs.

One of the best things about flowering shrubs is that you can have something in bloom, if you choose wisely, all the growing year. If this interests you, see Calendar, CHAPTER 1.

HOW TO BUY SHRUBS

First, choose shrubs recommended as hardy for your zone (see Plant Hardiness Map on endpapers, locate your zone number, then refer to the zones indicated with each shrub in our lists). You can expect to be able to grow all those with your zone number or lower; higher numbers call for more temperate climate than you have, except for odd places in your garden that are more sheltered. You might experiment in these spots with plants from one zone higher than yours.

Deciduous shrubs are, for the most part, sold bare-root for spring planting in Zones 1-5, for spring or fall planting in Zones 6-9 and in containers for planting in any zone at any time during the growing year. Evergreen and a few difficult-to-transplant deciduous shrubs — the saucer magnolia is one — are sold "B and B," which means with the roots balled in earth and tied tightly in burlap. (Broom should always be bought in a container.) These will be more expensive than bare-root shrubs because they cost more to grow and transport.

Preparation for Planting

Check the tilth of your soil, and if it's heavy clay or very light sand improve by adding humus and fertilizer as recommended in CHAPTER 18. Try to do this a whole season, or at least a few weeks before you intend to plant, to give the soil time to settle. Most shrubs require good drainage, so if you want to grow them in a wet place drain it by raising the level of the grade by 6-12 inches, or tile and drain the ground, or make a pool and plant your shrubs on its rim.

How to Plant

Shrubs are easy to plant. You need only follow regular garden practice as outlined in CHAPTER 18. Special techniques for individual recommended plants are explained in notes with each.

Ongoing Care

Special watering if the weather is dry needs to be done only for the first and possibly the second season; for how to do this see CHAPTER 18. Mulching for the same period is also a good idea. Extra fertilizer is seldom needed once shrubs are growing well — if they're not, put a handful of general purpose garden fertilizer around the base in early spring, not allowing any to touch the wood or leaves. Pruning is equally casual, except as noted in our lists. Cut out dead or diseased wood whenever you see it; all suckers from below any graft union; one or two of the oldest branches of multiple-stemmed shrubs at ground level once every 2-3 years, after flowering. Protection may be needed against nippers (rabbits) and nibblers (mice) and late winter sunburn for broad-leaved types. Directions for all these techniques are in CHAPTER 18. Control of pests and diseases is usually elementary, see CHAPTER 19.

HOW TO MAKE MORE SHRUBS FROM THOSE YOU HAVE

Getting something for nothing is always pleasant and many shrubs already in your garden can be induced to root branches, or bits of them, to make more. But the real payoff is in knowing how to propagate a slip from someone else's bush. I have seen great variation, for instance, in the depth of color of a beauty bush. Some are a washed-out grey pink, others a clear and beautiful rose. If you see an outstandingly lovely shrub in someone else's garden ask the owner if you may have a slip of it. (For how to propagate such material, see CHAPTER 18.)

---

14 OF THE BEST FLOWERING SHRUBS

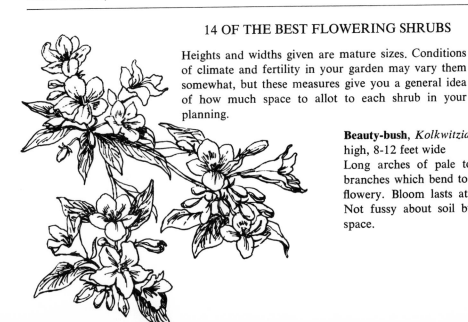

Heights and widths given are mature sizes. Conditions of climate and fertility in your garden may vary them somewhat, but these measures give you a general idea of how much space to allot to each shrub in your planning.

Beauty-bush, *Kolkwitzia amabilis*, Zone 5b, 10-12 feet high, 8-12 feet wide
Long arches of pale to rose-pink flowers cover the branches which bend to the ground, so that it's totally flowery. Bloom lasts at least 2 weeks in late spring. Not fussy about soil but needs full sun and lots of space.

Buddleia, *B. davidii*, Zone 5b; 5-8 feet high; 5 feet wide
Long wands of white, pink, rose or purple flowers in late summer. Showy, easy to care for, fragrant. Cut to the ground every fall, it grows 6 feet again every spring. What's especially dreamy about buddleia is that it dances with butterflies from the opening of the first flower till frost freezes the last.

Father Hugo's Rose, *Rosa hugonis*; Zone 5b; 7 feet high; 6 feet wide
A graceful bouquet of finely-leaved foliage, beautiful small single yellow gold roses in spring. They don't last very long but are most appealing while they do. A great favorite.

Forsythia, many, some hardy to Zone 5; from about 5-9 feet high, 8-10 feet wide
A true harbinger of spring. Golden stars of flowers all along its branches before any leaves, in the clearest, sunniest yellow. Easy to grow, even a branch touching the ground will root. Any soil. Glows its brightest in sunshine but will also bloom well in light shade. Lovely leaves all summer and fall. Prune by bringing branches indoors from Christmas till spring; standing in water they bloom in a few weeks into the floweriest tonic you could have. Some cultivars grow straight up, others bend gracefully down and look particularly lovely hanging over walls. My favorite is *F. x intermedia* 'Spring Glory', Zone 6, a fresh bouncy yellow, its branches completely tufted with flowers but I also grow six plants of the oldfashioned *F. x intermedia* 'Spectabilis', Zone 6, along an out-of-sight boundary just to have for winter cutting. *F. ovata* 'Tetragold', Zone 5, is early, hardier and has showy primrose yellow flowers.

Honeysuckle, many, *Lonicera*; some hardy to Zone 2; especially good and useful cultivars are *L. tatarica*, 'Arnold Red', 9 feet high, 6-7 feet wide; Zone 3, compact; dark red flowers and berries; grows well in either sun or shade and will take poor soil too; sweetberry, *L. coerulea edulis*, 4 feet tall, 2-3 feet wide; Zone 2; also compact, yellow-white flowers, dark blue, edible fruit; Zabel's honeysuckle, *L. korolkowii* 'Zabelii', 12 feet high, 7-8 feet wide; Zone 2; a graceful bush with blue green foliage, deep rose flowers and red berries.

Lilac, many, *Syringa*, some hardy to Zone 2, 15 feet high, 6-10 feet wide. Here we are again in the mix-up of the one-stemmed tree or the multiple-stemmed shrub. Lilacs can be either. What they all have is a spring flowering that moves people to rhapsodies and most have a fragrance so haunting it blows miles to catch your mind and heart, even when you can't see its source. All shades of lavender and violet, white, pinkish, dark red and a light creamy yellow. Some with single flowers, small or large, some crisply double. Some with flower heads that stand up, some hang gracefully down. Some with big leaves, some small, but all the shape of valentine hearts.

They came first to this country in the baggage of early colonists who, homesick for gardens they left behind, packed small slips in map cases. You can still see some of these old-fashioned lilacs throughout the countryside, often just clumps around an old stone cellar that was once part of a pioneer house. Today hybrids are much showier, not always more fragrant, but certainly more beautiful. Isabella Preston, working at the Central Experimental Farm in Ottawa many years ago, developed dozens of hardy hybrids and others have been bred from them. Some are still listed in nursery catalogues. 'Guinevere' has huge purple heads; 'Elinor', seen in froths of pink along the parkways of Ottawa in May, is very fragrant and bright pink; 'Donald Wyman', named for the famed horticulturist of the Arnold Arboretum in Boston, is very flowery and dark red-purple. Dr. Frank Skinner of Manitoba, working with prairie-hardy parents, developed his strain of American Hybrids, noted for being free from suckering — a frequent trouble with lilacs — and blooming two weeks earlier than the common lilac. 'Assessippi' is a pink mauve; 'Pocahontas' a red-purple; 'Sister Justina' a starched, crisp single white; 'Royal Purple' a strong purple, and his last one, 'Maiden's Blush', a beautiful clear pink double.

A little beauty, the Dwarf Korean lilac, *S. palibiniana*, Zone 4, is said by the Arnold Arboretum to be mature at a height of 3 feet. Dark, 6-inch panicles open to lavender-lilac. It's excellent in front of taller shrubs and lovely as an informal hedge. The leaves are small and clean, slightly downy on both sides.

You will find the so-called "French" hybrid lilacs listed in most catalogues and growing everywhere that good lilacs are grown. These are cultivars — many bred in North America — of the original beautiful French lilacs developed by Lemoine of France. Out of hundreds tested in the United States and in Canada the following are recommended:

SINGLE WHITE: 'Maud Notcutt', 'White Hyacinth', 'Mont Blanc'
DOUBLE WHITE: 'Prof. E. H. Wilson', 'Mme Lemoine'
SINGLE VIOLET: 'De Miribel'
DOUBLE VIOLET: 'Marechal Lannes'
SINGLE BLUE: 'Clark's Giant', 'Blue Hyacinth' 'Firmament', 'Crepuscule'
DOUBLE BLUE: 'Olivier des Serres', 'Ami Schott'
SINGLE LAVENDER: 'Christophe Colomb', 'Jacques Callot'
DOUBLE LAVENDER: 'Leon Gambetta', 'Victor Lemoine'
SINGLE PINK: 'Lucie Baltet'
DOUBLE PINK: 'Mme Antoine Buchner', 'Belle de Nancy'
SINGLE RED-PURPLE: 'Capitaine Baltet', 'Congo'
DOUBLE RED-PURPLE: 'Charles Joly', 'Mrs. Edward Harding'

196

SINGLE DEEP PURPLE: 'Ludwig Spaeth', 'Monge', 'Etna'

DOUBLE DEEP PURPLE: 'Adelaide Dunbar', 'Paul Therion'

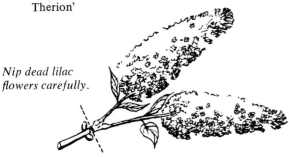

Nip dead lilac flowers carefully.

How to choose a lilac

There is no better way to choose the lilac you want than to see it in bloom in a nursery. If you can, visit these nurseries in spring when the lilacs are in bloom and tag the tree you want.

It should be growing on its own root (grafted cultivars can throw suckers from the less desirable root stock they are on and take over the whole shrub if not rigorously pruned out). Delivery will not be till fall, as soon as the plant can be safely moved. You might prepare the hole in the spring or early in the summer, so as to be ready for planting on arrival.

Where to plant, preparation of soil, ongoing care

To bloom well, lilacs must have full sun and their root run should not be crowded by too-near trees, other shrubs or a hedge. Drainage should be good. Plant as you would any shrub (see CHAPTER 18). Soil should be alkaline, but many gardeners still grow lilacs well without this by mixing a handful of agricultural lime into each bushel of soil when preparing the ground, and adding the same amount to the soil around the shrub each spring. Water deeply if no rain.

The first year, and again the second year if you can bear to do it, cut off the budding flower heads, to direct all possible strength into the growing of the shrub itself. After that, always cut off flower heads after blooming by nipping off *just the flower part*. If you go any farther you cut off the two buds on either side of the terminal part of the shoot and thus lose the flowering buds for next year.

Prune all suckers on grafted lilacs that break out below the union, right back to the main stem. With lilacs on their own roots, old enough to have four or more strong main stems, prune out the oldest one and let one new one grow each year. About every 10 years you will probably want to rejuvenate your lilacs completely by cutting out one third of the wood right to the ground in each of three successive years so that, at the end of that time, you have a whole new shrub.

Few pests and diseases bother lilacs. Borer and scale can be controlled with insecticide applied at the right time; mildew by fungicide and by improving air circulation in the area where they're growing. (For how-to and with what, see CHAPTER 19.)

If your lilacs don't bloom — and this is a fairly common complaint — either you are feeding them too much nitrogen, which pushes leaf growth at the expense of flowers (nitrogen is the first of the three numbers on every bag of chemical fertilizer); they are not getting enough sun (when first planted, they may have been in full sun, but some shadowy something you have not noticed has grown higher and cut this off); or they may not be old enough (some lilacs take a few years to reach blooming stage). The cure for the first is to change to feeding with a high phosphate fertilizer (the second number on the bag). The cure for the second is to prune out above your lilacs to let more sun get through, or transplant them to a sunnier place. The cure for the third is to go orchid hunting among the man-eating tribes of the Upper Amazon, or something equally absorbing, that will take your mind off your lilacs. You might also, as a drastic shock treatment, cut the roots by digging a trench one spade wide and about 18 inches deep, in a circle in line with the outermost branches. Mix the soil you take out with a good fat dollop of rotted manure and a handful of superphosphate per bushel, and replace. This is known as a Double Lilac Martini on the Rocks, with a twist.

Where to see famous lilac collections

THE UNITED STATES:

Des Moines, Iowa: Ewing Park
Jamaica Plains, Boston, Massachusetts: The Arnold Arboretum
Lisle, Illinois: The Morton Arboretum
Lombard, Illinois: Lilacia Park
Rochester, New York: Highland Park
Swarthmore, Pennsylvania: Swarthmore College

CANADA:

Hamilton, Ontario: The Katie Osborne Lilac Garden, The Royal Botanical Gardens
Ottawa, Ontario: Plant Research Institute Arboretum and Botanical Garden, Canada Department of Agriculture
Morden, Manitoba: Canada Department of Agriculture Research Station

Mock Orange, many, *Philadelphus*: some hardy to Zone 3; 4-9 feet high, 5-8 feet wide. The outstanding virtues of this shrub are its heavenly fragrance, its white flowers and its early summer blooming time when so many of the showiest shrubs have finished flowering. Also it is one of the few that blooms profusely in semi-shade, and does well in sun too. No special soil needed, but does like moisture. No special care except a little intelligent pruning once every few years. It has no particular graces except at flowering time but makes delightful hedges. My favorite of them all is *P. x virginalis* 'Minnesota Snowflake', Zone 5, an introduction of the University of Minnesota; double, pointed flowers, sweetly fragrant, long arching branches. For a little one, *P*. 'Manteau d'Hermine', Zone 4, is tiny-flowered and never grows more than 2½ feet high. Both of these are great favorites in the Fragrant Garden for the Blind in Toronto. Three especially bred for the prairies and northern plains of the Midwest, are *P*. 'Galahad', and *P*. 'Purity', both Zone 3; *P. lewisii* 'Waterton', Zone 2b.

Peegee Hydrangea, *Hydrangea paniculata* 'Grandiflora', Zone 3b; 5-8 feet high; 5-8 feet wide; a highly popular, late-summer flowering tree with huge conical heads of cream-to-pink-to-rose flowers. In early fall, or late summer if you like a paler color, they can be cut to bring indoors and they last all winter. Buy trained as a tree or multiple-stemmed. Not fussy as to care, prune back in spring. In very cold areas, top growth sometimes completely winterkills but sprouts again in spring. Trained as standards and used in a double file on either side of a driveway they move you into the Cadillac class.

Rhododendrons and Azaleas, both botanically called *Rhododendron*; Zone 5 and up depending on hardiness; different heights and widths. Spectacular is the only word that describes these shrubs in bloom except for the little ones — in their own miniature way, they're spectacular too. At their best in mild, humid climates and naturally acid soil. Certain hardy species and cultivars are being grown more and more in temperate ranges. New cultivars are also being bred to lengthen this list. With the right conditions, both rhododendrons and azaleas are easy to grow and some have lived and done well in New England gardens for more than 75 years.

Rhododendrons are broad-leaved evergreens with thick leathery leaves. They curl in cold weather, spread out again as the temperature warms. Flower heads are great tight bunches of white, pink, yellow, orange, red or purple, often with a contrasting blotch. They bloom in spring over a fairly long period.

Azaleas are more airy-fairy, some evergreen, but many deciduous, flowering in clustered heads of white, pink, orange, yellow, purple or red mostly before their leaves come out and for about the same span of time as rhododendrons. Some smell skunky, others pleasantly fragrant.

Rhododendrons and azaleas take approximately the same care. They are shallow rooters that demand sharp drainage, high in humus, natural or man-made acid soil, lots of moisture and a porous mulch to keep the roots cool and from drying out.

RECOMMENDED RHODODENDRONS

Lists are divided into those hardy to Zone 5 and those for higher zones. Hardiness is rated according to the system used by the American Rhododendron Society, as follows:

    H-1 hardy to —25° F
    H-2 hardy to —15° F
    H-3 hardy to —5° F
    H-4 hardy to plus 5° F
    H-5 hardy to plus 15° F
    H-6 hardy to plus 25° F
    H-7 hardy to plus 32° F

HARDY TO ZONE 5
(in order of blooming)

'Ramapo'; H-1; 2 feet; bright violet.
'P.J.M.' (P. J. Mezitt); H-1; not tested enough to state possible mature height; rose-purple; evergreen foliage turns purple in winter.
Carolina Rhododendron, *R. carolinianum*; H-1; 3-5 feet; delicate pink.
'America', H-1; 5 feet; rich, strong growing, dark red
'Catawbiense Album', H-1; 5-7 feet; the finest white, with a rich yellow fleck in the throat.

'Nova Zembla', H-2; 5 feet; dark red.
'Roseum Elegans', H-2; 5 feet; rose-pink to lilac.
'Van Weerden Poelman' H-2; 4 feet; rich crimson with darker blotch in throat.

ZONES 6 AND UP
Species in order of blooming

R. strigillosum; H-4; 12-20 feet; scarlet
R. fargesii; H-3; 10 feet; rose, pink
R. pemakoense; H-3; 6-18 feet; lilac pink.
R. augustinii; H-3; 15 feet; blue-lilac
R. campanulatum; var. aeruginosum; H-2; purple
R. wardii; H-3; 6-12 feet; creamy yellow.
R. fortunei; H-2; 6 feet; pink.
R. yakusimanum; H-3; 4 feet; white, rose.
R. decorum; H-3; 5-6 feet; white.

ZONES 6 AND UP
Cultivars (plants bred or selected for superior flower color, stamina, fragrance in order of blooming).

'Bric-a-brac'; H-3; 5 feet; pure white
'Avalanche'; H-3; 6-8 feet; white with red blotch.
'C. B. van Nes'; H-4; 4 feet; scarlet.
'Cilipnense'; H-4; 2 feet; pale shell-pink.
'David'; H-4; 3 feet; deep red.
'Elizabeth'; H-4; 3 feet; white.
'Alice Street'; H-4; 3 feet; deep yellow.
'Humming Bird'; H-3; 2 feet; red.
'Unique'; H-4; 3 feet; pale yellow, tinged peach.
'Unknown Warrior'; H-4; 6-8 feet; red.
'White Olympic Lady'; H-4; 3 feet; white.
'Anna Rose Whitney'; H-3; 6 feet; deep pink.
'Bow Bells'; H-3; 3 feet; pink.
'Cotton Candy'; H-4; 4 feet; pink.
'Jean Mary Montague'; H-3; 3 feet; bright red, frilled.
'Loderi King George' and all 'Loderi' group; H-4; 5 feet; blush-white, fragrant (for protected areas).
'Marcia'; H-3; 3 feet; very good, deep yellow.

'Mrs. A. T. de la Mare'; H-3; 5 feet; white, green blotch, fragrant.

'Mrs. Betty Robertson'; H-3; 3 feet; butter-yellow, red flare.

'Mrs. Furnival'; H-3; 3 feet; pink, crimson blotch.

'Naomi'; H-3; 4 feet; pink, shaded yellow and mauve, fragrant.

'Susan'; H-3; 3 feet; lavender-blue.

'Albatross'; H-3; 5 feet; white, fragrant.

'Angelo'; H-4; 5 feet; white to pink, green blotch.

'Britannia'; H-3; 3 feet; red.

'Day Dream'; H-4; 4 feet; biscuit-yellow.

'Lady Clementine Mitford'; H-3; 3 feet; peach-pink.

'Purple Splendour'; H-2; 4 feet; rich purple, dark blotch.

'Vulcan'; H-3; 3 feet; glowing red.

RECOMMENDED AZALEAS
SPECIES

Poukhan, *Rhododendron yedoense poukhanense;* 4-6 feet; Zone 6; red violet

R. luteum; 6-9 feet; Zone **7**; yellow, scented

Royal; *R. schlippenbachi;* 6-12 feet; Zone 5; rose pink, fragrant

Torch, *R. kaempferi;* 6-9 feet; Zone 6; orange red

Vasey's, *R. vaseyi;* 6-9 feet; Zone 6; light rose

CULTIVARS (Plants bred or selected for superior flower color, form, stamina, fragrance; mainly Zone 6)

Deciduous: Ghent (5-10 feet), Mollis (6 feet), Exbury and Knap Hill (7-8 feet) hybrids; bloom late spring

Coccinea speciosa, orange red
Narcissiflora, small yellow, double, fragrant
'Christopher Wren', large orange

'Dr. Oesthoek', deep orange red
'Gibraltar', spectacular orange
'Hortulanus H. Witte', yellow
'Homebush', double carmine rose
'Persil', white with yellow blotch
'Satan', deep red

In Zone 5 and up, investigate the Shammarello rhododendrons; zone 7 and up, the sometimes evergreen Gable, Kaempferi and Glenn Dale cultivars of azaleas.

Evergreen: recommended chiefly for the southeastern states and Northwest Coast, a few hardy in Zone 6b.

'Amoene', mauve
'Christmas Cheer', scarlet
Dewar's Pink', bright rose
'Elizabeth Gable', deep rose
'Gaiety', scarlet
'Hino-crimson', crimson
'Hinodegiri', scarlet
'Louise Gable', bright pink
'Palestrina', white
'Purple Triumph', deep violet purple
'Sea Shell', soft pink
'Sherwood Orchid', mauve
'Snow', pure white

How to buy, prepare for, plant and ongoing care

Visit named plantings and consult catalogues of nurseries specializing in these plants. Place your order for earliest possible spring delivery, plants will be shipped B and B. In the most temperate parts of the country fall planting can be successfully done too. Container-grown plants can be moved anytime during the growing season. If you can visit the nursery yourself, choose plants that are well branched at the bottom.

Prepare soil if possible some months ahead of planting to allow for settling and for building up a healthy chemical action. Rhododendrons and azaleas need an acid soil, with a pH of between 4 and 5.5. If your soil does not have this, see CHAPTER 18 for directions about ways to make it.

The best sites will have high shade, especially from late winter sun, be sharply drained (a northeast or east slope is ideal).

Plant rhododendrons 4 feet apart, azaleas 3 feet, and transplant if they become crowded.

Make the planting hole 6 inches wider than the root ball, and deep enough so that the plant has no more than 1 inch of soil *over* the root ball — this is *essential*. Water deeply if no rain, and continue weekly. Check the level of the plant often during its first season to be sure that it does not settle lower in the hole. If it does, pull it gently up to where it should be and push earth beneath it to hold it there.

Ongoing care:

do not allow to dry out at any time — rhododendrons like a top spray in hot dry weather as well as water at the roots. Mulches help, particularly of an acid material like oak leaves, shredded pine bark or pine needles. Experts warn not to use pure peat moss as a mulch: if it dries out, it pulls moisture up from the roots beneath, or blows away.

pick off flower heads after blooming by nipping the stem just below the bloom. Don't go as far down as the buds on the hard wood for this is where new ones will emerge next year.

feed with special formula acid fertilizer (you can buy this prepackaged) once in early spring.

do not mechanically cultivate or weed the ground around the roots, which are always near the surface and could be damaged. Instead, use mulches and weed by hand.

prune only for shape, which could be almost never.

for control of insects and disease see CHAPTER 19.

protect from sunburn by planting in a constantly high-shade site, shielding from sun in late winter with evergreen branches or a burlap screen. Spraying with anti-desiccant is also effective.

if you have had to make your soil acid, check it yearly to be sure it stays that way. If you find it does not, add 2 pounds ferrous sulphate per 100 square feet, or about 3 ounces per square foot, over the earth in spring, and water in.

If rhododendrons and azaleas are already, or could be, the sirens in your life, steer your bark to the Royal Horticultural Society's garden at Wisley in England and see Battleson Hill in rhodo time. You'll never, I promise — cross my heart and hope to die on acid soil — be the same again.

OTHER RECOMMENDED FLOWERING SHRUBS

Rose of Sharon in variety, *Hibiscus syriacus*: Zone 5; 8-12 feet high, 5-8 feet wide; late summer flowers — the singles look like tropical hibiscus, the doubles like camellias or double hollyhocks; white, pink, red, purple and a good clear blue with a dark eye — *H. syriacus* 'Blue Bird' with single flowers 5 inches in diameter. *H. syriacus* 'Red Heart' is a beauty too — white with a red heart. The shrub in bloom looks as though someone had been getting ready for a party and pinned each flower on its branch. Singularly elegant and controlled in a kind of ladylike way at a time when so much else in the garden is a careless exuberant tumble. Bush grows in narrow form and is therefore excellent beside a path or along the back of a flower bed. Prefers soil with plenty of humus, and water when dry. Unexpectedly gives great rewards in polluted city conditions and in salt-spray areas beside the sea.

Serviceberry, Saskatoon, *Amelanchier alnifolia*: Zone 1; 6-20 feet high, 5-10 feet wide.
A drifting white haze of a shrub in flower in very early spring. Looks particularly lovely planted among evergreens where its flowers seem even more fragile than they are, or on the edge of woodland. Bloom does not last long, especially if it pours rain, but nonetheless worthwhile. Edible fruit, but you'll have to have your running shoes on to get there before the birds.

Smoke tree, *Cotinus coggygria*: Zone 4; up to 12 feet high; 6-10 feet wide.
And by now you aren't even thinking about it being called a tree when it's a shrub. A feathery cloud of purple mist in late summer and more brilliant in the fall. Not fussy as to soil or care. Brilliant autumn yellow and orange foliage if in full sun. When it's smoky, you can hardly believe it is a plant and not something someone dreamed up for a mood painting.

Spirea, Bridalwreath, *Spiraea x vanhouttei*: 6 feet high; sometimes to 6 feet wide; Zone 4; the most popular shrub wherever it's hardy, which is most of the temperate part of the country. 'Snowhite': 4 feet high, 3 feet wide, Zone 2; similar to, but much hardier than the bridalwreath spirea, a great favorite in the Midwest. Both graceful, in spring the branches covered with tiny pure white flowers that make them look frosted. A good green in its summer leafing, fine-stemmed in winter and positively ethereal in quietly falling snow.

Viburnum, many: some hardy to Zone 2; many heights up to 12 feet; many widths up to 10 feet. The viburnums are so apt, so suitable in so many situations, and they grow in so many guises, you could choose one to fill almost any role in your garden. Intriguing shapes (the flat, outstretched arms of the Maries' doublefile viburnum, *V. plicatum* 'Mariesii' is especially lovely), delicate flowers, some cultivars with sparkling fruit or brilliant fall foliage. Easy to grow, tolerant of half-shade and, if you choose your cultivars carefully, you can have a season of bloom for 8 weeks. Some are

wonderfully fragrant. The most widely grown is the snowball bush, *V. opulus roseum*, Zone 2b; although its cousin, *V. plicatum*, Zone 5, is less likely to get those nasty little plant lice that sometimes curl the flowers and leaves of the more familiar one (these can be controlled with insecticide, see CHAPTER 19). One of the best is the fragrant viburnum, *V. farreri*, Zone 6b; it arches to one side of our south-facing living-room window (Zone 5) and in mid-December, when we're getting all scrunched up for winter snow and ice, it pops sweet tiny bouquets of pale pink flowers on a branch right outside the window pane. Then it goes into dormancy, but when it seems in late March and early April that spring will never come it does it again, and this time the whole shrub is covered with pink, before any leaves come out. If you bring a branch indoors anytime during the winter, the whole house is filled with the spicy fragrance of its flowers. Other popular fragrant ones are *V. x burkwoodii*, Zone 5, which is semi-evergreen in some zones, and the very showy and fragrant *V. x carlcephalum*, Zone 5. *V. x juddi*, Zone 4, is pale pink and also sweetly scented. The European highbush cranberry *V. opulus*, Zone 2b, with its ruby jewels of fruit hanging on all winter, is hardy, and the hobblebush, *V. lantanoides*, Zone 3, a native in the east, lays out the most exquisite flat clusters of white in the shadows of wild gardens in earliest spring. A hunting friend, who often travels through the woods with all his kit on his back (and sometimes the desirable parts of a deer) has a different and picturesque name for hobblebush but it's not printable. This shrub has a habit of rooting an arching branch at its very tip, leaving a loop sticking up like a croquet hoop, and many's the day my hunter has measured his length in the leaves because he caught his foot in the loop of a hobblebush. The glossy-leaved laurestinus, *V. tinus*, Zone 7, so popular for hedges on the west coast, is another in this family, and *V. davidii*, Zone 7b, is a dwarf, white-flowered, evergreen beauty. Especially recommended for the prairies and northern plains, the nannyberry, *V. lentago*, 10-20 feet high, 6-8 feet wide, Zone 2, is shapely with flat white flower heads and glossy leaves, blue-black fruit and purple red foliage in fall and the highbush cranberry, *V. trilobum*, 12 feet high, 6-8 wide, Zone 2, has similar flowers in spring, and edible red fruit.

A SELECTED LIST OF 16 NEEDLE AND BROAD-LEAVED EVERGREEN SHRUBS

(For others, consult nursery catalogues.)

These are the stars of the winter landscape, and a marvelous dividend all the rest of the year:

Box, *Buxus;* used most often as a tidy hedge, excellent also as a fine-leaved specimen shrub; Zone 4; height and width, 4-10 feet.

Cotoneaster, *C dammeri,* useful as a ground cover and in the rock garden; little bright red fruits. 'Skogholm', a rapid-growing cultivar, highly recommended; Zone 4; height up to 15 inches, feet wide.

Firethorn, many, *Pyracantha;* showy on a wall, as an independent shrub or as a hedge; generous bunches of bright orange berries in fall holding well into winter; some cultivars hardy to Zone 5; variable height and width.

Garland Flower, *Daphne cneorum;* a fragrant little pink-flowered shrub for low, warm well-drained places; Zone 2b; height 6-12 inches; variable width.

Heath, many, *Erica;* winter, spring and summer flowering low plants; white, pink and pink-red flowers which last a long time; some hardy to Zone 5, height 12 inches; spreading a variable distance.

Heather, many cultivars, *Calluna vulgaris;* the familiar, late-summer blooming British and Scottish heather; needs acid soil; must not dry out; full sun; height 6-12 inches, wide-spreading mats; shear flower heads after blooming.

Holly, *Ilex;* the evergreen hollies are grown mainly in temperate parts of the country, Zone 6 and up; most kinds need both a male and a female to produce the familiar and gay bright red berries. Grow in any well-drained good soil.

Juniper, many, many—one catalogue lists thirty-seven! *Juniperus;* hardy over a wide range—some to Zone 2b; different shapes that stand tall, stretch sideways or creep over the ground; many shades of green; various heights and widths; grows best in full sun.

Mahonia, many, the most familiar *M. aquifolium;* a lustrous holly-like native of the west coast; yellow flowers, blue-black fruit; grows well in shade; Zone 4; 3-6 feet tall; 2-3 feet wide. A creeping one, *M. repens,* hardy to Zone 3, and only 12 inches tall.

Mountain laurel, *Kalmia latifolia;* dainty, delicate little pink parachutes of flowers in spring; does well in shade; must have acid soil; Zone 5b; 5-10 feet high; 2-3 feet wide.

Pachistima, *P. canbyi,* a dwarf, low shrub, dandy for semishade ground covering; Zone 2b; *P. myrsinites,* the myrtle pachistima, a spreading native of the west coast; Zone 5, 4 feet high, and sometimes 3-4 feet wide, likes shade and a cool place.

Pieris, many, some hardy to Zone 5b; *P. japonica,* a particular beauty with pendulous flower clusters and new shoots of rich bronze foliage; likes full sun; can go to 9 feet, and be 3-5 feet wide.

Pine, *Pinus;* there are dwarf forms of both the white and Scots pine available but the best shrubby pine is the mugho, *P. mugo mughus;* hardy to Zone 1; height and width up to 8 feet; needs full sun.

Rhododendrons and azaleas, see pages 198-199.

Wintercreeper, many cultivars, *Euonymus fortunei,* some hardy to Zone 4; all superb when well grown; many uses—vine, hedge, creeper, bushy; needs north or east exposure to stay its best green all winter; variable heights and widths.

Yew, many, and all excellent, *Taxus;* by far the best evergreen shrub for cities; thrives in sun or partial shade; hardy to Zone 4; many shapes, heights and widths.

Planting container-grown evergreens.

Besides flowers and lush green leaves, shrubs can also bring the excitement of other colored foliage to your garden — yellow, red, green and white variegated, purple, grey or blue-green. And in fall, they can be a flaming scarlet or a more sophisticated red-purple, yellow or yellow-orange. Their bark, in winter, can seem painted — red or yellow as in dogwoods and willows, green as kerria is, grey as some honeysuckles and viburnums are. The first two are brighter if they are radically pruned in late winter to force new growth which will be a more vibrant color than the older bark would be.

There are special lists of shrubs that do well in moist, dry or acid soil, for growing well by the sea, others you would plant for their bright bonus of berries. An excellent book to guide you to these particularly favored shrubs is *Flowering Shrubs* by Frobel Zucker (New York: Van Nostrand Rheinhold Company, 1966).

22 HEDGES AND WINDBREAKS

HEDGES

A hedge is a closely-planted row of shrubs, small trees, or annual flowers that can be expected to grow to a height of from 6 inches to 10 feet at maturity. Anything planted similarly and growing taller than 10 feet I call a windbreak or shelterbelt.

Hedges can be evergreen or deciduous, formally clipped or informally guided, notable for their texture, color, flowers, foliage or fruit.

Taken literally, this means that almost every plant in your garden could be trained as a hedge if you planted it in a close-packed line. To further lead you into the maze — which was an 18th century you-chase-me-and-I'll-chase-you hedge version of a souped-up horticultural puzzle — I don't consider that a hedge, to be a hedge, must be planted in a *straight* line. It can wander a little, be curved, angled, a rectangular box, a circle: but two things it must be — closely set and all of one kind of plant.

In practice, certain plants over the years have proved themselves more amenable for use as hedges than others. They have thick, twiggy growth and take well to shearing, making new branches to fill gaps. (These are the plants you will find listed at the end of this chapter.) When I say "over the years," it's exactly that, for records of gardens in history tell of hedges used extensively in the gardens of Pompeii as early as 34 B.C. — particularly little low clipped ones in the way we use boxwood now. So we have tradition to draw from and further refine.

USES FOR HEDGES

Hedges are mainly used as boundary markers, as barriers to keep cut-acrossers out and our own small fry in — and to create a private world of our garden. Less often but sometimes, we plant them to hide an unattractive view, to divide parts of the garden from each other — vegetables from lawn, sandbox from patio, lawn from countryside — to guide a glance, or as a snow fence. (If for this, never plant to windward of a driveway or walk; this builds up drifts on the lee side where you're trying to avoid them.) As a secondary use, they serve as a flattering green background for flowers.

IF YOU'RE PLANNING A NEW HEDGE, CONSIDER THESE THINGS

Make sure that you have the space, sideways as well as up and down, to grow the hedge you want:

  small (6-12 inches), trimmed hedges need space for a basal
    width of 1-2 feet at maturity;
  medium (2-3 feet) ones need 3-4 feet;
  tall (4-8 feet) need 5-9 feet;
  small unclipped hedges need 3-4 feet clear for width;
  tall ones, up to 6-8 feet

If you cannot allocate this much space, you'd better think of an alternative, such as a fence, and green it with a vine.

If the hedge is to be a boundary marker, decide where best to plant it. You have two choices: *on* the line between you and your neighbor, when the decision about what plant, its cost and care are usually evenly shared with him; or *inside* your line when everything is your responsibility, although in the interests of goodwill, consultation about what plant you choose is thoughtful and fair.

If it is to be a shared expense with your neighbor, you will want to consult him about what to plant and who will look after it. Also it is only fair to warn him if he does not already know that hedges are greedy feeders and drinkers and will inevitably throw some shade. He should allow for this if he plants flowers or grass on his side near the hedge. In some cases, a fence might make more sense.

If the hedge is to border a sidewalk or road, find out what the municipal regulations are about this and also consider the closeness of people walking by in relation to the width your hedge will have. Also, plot where winter plowing could dump heavy salty snow that, if piled up on your hedge, could break and kill it.

Look up over the place where you intend to plant. If trees overhang any part of it, prune them up at least 8 feet and choose hedge materials that will withstand some shade.

If you want fast growth, realize that to keep a fast-growing hedge neat and in bounds takes 2-3 clippings a year, where slow-growing kinds usually need only one. Also fast-growing hedges are usually very brittle and break easily under snow and ice.

If you want an all-year screen, plan for evergreens rather than deciduous plants, which are leafless in winter; but know that they will be more expensive in the beginning and that, if you want to trim them to a flat top and you live

where heavy snowfall is normal, they will have to be protected with a sturdy shelter.

If you want to discourage people and pets from pushing through a hedge, grow a thorny one. Barberry has been recommended for this purpose in past years, but the extending list of barberries being banned because they are alternate hosts to cereal rust (which ruins thousands of acres of grain crops every year) makes it necessary to recommend other thorny hedge plants. Consider instead, buffalo berry, hawthorn, shrub roses.

The design should be one that will improve your total garden scene. Neatly clipped hedges are tidy, precise, their lines definite and surely drawn. Informal shrubby ones are more relaxed and can be planted to deliberately wander around a bit, throwing interesting shadows, giving greater depth of perspective. Small clipped hedges — boxwood is best for this — can be used to border a flower bed as a frame does a picture. A curved hedge, clipped or informal, can be a handsome backdrop for a fine piece of sculpture or be used to shelter a patio. Always anchor the ends of your hedge to something — your house, a wall, a large tree, a patio — don't leave it dangling in your design.

Stop a tall hedge short of the point where your driveway meets the street to leave a clear view of all oncoming traffic.

Hedges for small gardens should be chosen from the list of fine-leaved, close-textured plants. Large-leaved, rough-textured ones press boundaries in and make the garden appear smaller than it is. Consider the extra dividends of unclipped hedges — grace of flowers, brightness of winter bark and sometimes berries, their usefulness as nesting sites for desirable wild birds. Color of leaves can vary too — purple, grey, yellow, green variegated with white; but mainly you will be best pleased with plain green and the use of bright colors in flowers to contrast with it.

Recommended plants are listed at the end of this chapter. Also consult Part V for the favorite hedge plants of your area. Study nursery catalogues for new introductions and visit hedge demonstrations in parks, research stations and botanical gardens to help you decide what you like best. Always choose one hardy for your zone (see Plant Hardiness Maps on endpapers).

PREPARATION OF THE GROUND FOR PLANTING

Prepare soil in fall for spring planting, in spring for fall planting, if you possibly can. If you must do it the same season as you plant, prepare it at least 4 weeks before to allow for settling.

Decide on placement, and mark with stakes and a cord. Although you might think it a good idea, experts do not recommend a double hedge: the centre tends to die out for lack of light.

Make trench 2 feet deep and 1½-3 feet wide, depending on the size of material and its planned height. (For details on How to Dig, see CHAPTER 18.) Check drainage; if soil is wet, dig out to a depth of 30-32 inches and add a 6-8 inch layer of gravel below the 2 feet of soil to be prepared. Unless you have the perfect mix to start with, add extra humus, about one spadeful in three, and a general purpose garden fertilizer — 10-6-4 is a good one — at the rate of 6 pounds for 100 feet. Pile up the soil so that the finished level is a few inches higher than the surrounding ground to allow for settling. Water thoroughly.

Buy your stock from a reputable nursery; if possible, one in your climate range.

Choose small plants, well branched at the bottom, 2-3 years old for twiggy deciduous hedges, 3-5 years old for evergreen ones. Larger sizes of deciduous stock are not necessarily better because the small ones, well grown, will soon catch up with the slower-starting large ones; in the meantime, you will have been able to give them valuable early training. Larger sizes of evergreens are better if you want a quicker effect, but they will be more expensive.

Buy a few extra plants and set them in a holdover bed somewhere in the garden in case you need the odd replacement.

HOW TO PLANT

When stock arrives from the nursery, unwrap it immediately and examine it. If it looks at all dried out, soak it in water for 1-2 hours and plant immediately. If it looks dead — bark withered, branches dried and brittle to break — this is the time to claim replacement.

If you cannot plant right away, heel the plants in by laying the roots in a quickly dug trench in a shady spot in the garden, covering with earth and watering. This will hold them for 2-3 weeks, depending on the weather, but if it's spring, they should get into the ground before new growth begins and, if fall, as soon as possible because roots must become established before the ground freezes.

Recommended distances apart:

for trimmed hedges		**for untrimmed hedges**	
small,	6-8 inches;	small,	12-18 inches;
medium,	12 inches;	medium,	2-3 feet;
tall,	18-30 inches;	tall or wide,	3-6 feet;

for a tall screen conifers can be used 6 feet apart untrimmed.

In the final planting, set plants 1 inch deeper than in the nursery — you can see this mark on the main stem. Cover roots with earth. Jiggle plant gently up and down a couple of times to settle the soil around the roots, tamp firmly, water, then fill up trench with more prepared mix, scooping out a dip along the edge of each side to channel water (either rain or hose) to the roots.

Prune back new deciduous material one half the first year, and again at the beginning of the growing season of the second year. This makes for a thick, twiggy base. Prune new conifers only by nipping new growth in half — most will not branch out from radically cut back old wood as deciduous plants will. Prune broad-leaved evergreens as you would deciduous material, but more lightly.

ONGOING CARE OF HEDGES

A regular program of good garden care — watering deeply when the weather is dry, weeding and mulching (see CHAPTER 18) and controlling destructive pests and diseases (see CHAPTER 19) — helps to get your hedge off to a good start and keeps it growing with vigor.

Extra feeding is not necessary in the first year. Thereafter, early each spring use general purpose garden fertilizer according to manufacturer's directions until the hedge is as high as you want it. After that, feed only once every 2-3 years.

TRIMMING CLIPPED HEDGES:

correct time, and number of times, is determined by the habit of the plant you choose. Fast-growing ones such as Siberian (sometimes called Chinese) elm usually need at least two, sometimes three clippings a year — one in late spring, one in early summer, one in early fall. Slower-growing plants such as Alpine currant — one of the most satisfactory small-leaf hedges — need only one clipping per year, in early summer. Constantly precise hedges, with never a twig out of place, need to be trimmed every time you get your hair cut, providing you wear it short.

evergreen hedges should be clipped only once a year in early midsummer, during dull weather (to prevent sunburning). Where there is new sharply-defined growth, such as candles on pine trees, fresh tips on hemlocks and yews, cut this new growth in half only. Although hemlocks and yews will grow **again** from old wood, regrowth is often sparse. Pines, spruces, firs, never break from old wood.

boxwood, the ideal, small, clipped hedge plant, can be trimmed in straight level planes or, as it is in England and in the beautiful gardens of Virginia, in a billowing informal shape that best shows its fine shadings of green.

the final height of a clipped hedge in your front garden should be determined by its proportion to your house and whether you want an open design which allows passersby to look over it or a more private look which calls for a taller hedge. In the back garden, where privacy and screening are especially desirable, a mature height of 4 feet will hide you when you're sitting down and yet allow talk with your neighbors if you stand up; 6 feet and up cuts off all chat and, except for peeking from upstairs windows, all view of what you are up to, providing it's not something high up in the air like practising on your trapeze or sitting on your flagpole.

informal hedges — mostly grown for flowers, but occasionally, as the spindle tree is, for fall color — are clipped only to keep a graceful form and to cut out old skinny wood. This should be done right after flowering.

The shape your hedge is in — literally and colloquially — determines its continuing good health and beauty. You don't have to win a Prix de Rome at the Barber's School to be a good hedge-trimmer, but you do have to realize that hedges, to be thick and evenly dense to the ground, *must* be exposed to the sun or strong sky light *all over*. To accomplish this, you must trim so that the base is wider than the top, otherwise upper twigs and branches will shade and eventually thin lower growth.

This sounds and looks — see drawings, page 207 — surprisingly easy but when you take note of the number of incorrectly pruned, scrawny scraggly hedges in your neighborhood, you will know that, easy or not, most gardeners neglect this absolutely essential practice, *don't* you.

If you have a natural eye for line (many talents have more than one use), you can probably trim a hedge properly without further help. Failing this

Trim hedges so that base is wider than top.
Left is wrong, right is right.

ability (and some of us make up in mental appreciation what we lack in manual accuracy) make yourself a set of measured stakes and a string to stretch between them at the height you want to trim to. Set them level by checking the string with a spirit level, then cut along what you can now be sure is a straight line.

Protection for hedges: if dogs or people keep pushing through your hedge — a common trouble on corner lots — thread galvanized wire inconspicuously through the hedge a foot above the ground and about 6 inches below the top.

For winter protection against salt-spray from roads and burning in late winter sun, set up a screen of burlap, fibreglass sheets or heavy plastic, on the road side, as high as the hedge, but do *not* encase the whole hedge in plastic — this builds up heat inside that burns bark and buds.

In areas where broad-leaved evergreens are hardy but strong late winter sun can burn and damage foliage, a high burlap screen between the hedge and the middle-of-the-day sun is the best protection.

RENOVATING AN OLD HEDGE

Taking over an old garden, or having a fresh look at your own, frequently reveals a tired old hedge holding sway over too much space. Decide first whether you want a hedge there at all, then whether it should be that kind of a hedge. If the answer is yes, it's worth a try to renovate it.

Dig a trench 12 inches wide and one spade deep, 6-12 inches out from the main stems, down both sides. Mix the best of the soil you dig out with one third humus or rotted manure and about one handful of general purpose fertilizer to a bushel of soil. Replace and water then and thereafter if no rain, so that the earth is moist but not soaking wet.

Cut back all growth to 6-inch stubs — cutting only half or a third of the way back won't work.

The next season, cut new growth in half and keep this proportion until you have a twiggy dense hedge again. If in 3-4 years it still looks scruffy, dig it out and discard.

A trick with old hawthorn, pear and crab apple hedges, often successfully used in the plains, is to cut back the main trunk to 1½ feet, leaving the side shoots full length. Bend these sideways, half to each side, and lash them to the stubs. As they throw new vertical shoots, keep this growth trimmed as for a regular hedge.

Give all renovated hedges a continuing regular program of good garden care.

WINDBREAKS AND HIGH SCREENING

Some gardens adjoin a noisy, heavily-traveled highway or street, an industrial building or a busy parking lot. Some have extreme exposure to gale-force winds winter and summer. A happy solution for all is to plant screening trees with material that will have a height at maturity of 10 feet or over.

For years Lombardy poplars have been the favorite for this, but you will find other trees easier to live with. Although they grow quickly and with a narrow, tall habit, Lombardy poplars also die back easily and deadwood must be trimmed out often if they are to look well. If this happens when they are large, it can be expensive to cut them back or down. They are not the tree for an average home garden. They are greedy feeders and pop suckers up all through your and your neighbor's lawn — I have known them travel 40 feet. Their roots clog septic tank tile beds. Planting them on a boundary, if you have a neighbor who wants to grow fine flowers on his side, doesn't win you the nomination of Best Neighbor of the Year either.

I once heard a story about a man of great ingenuity who was faced with this problem. He was a champion rose grower and his beds ran right up to the back fence line. Much to his dismay, a new neighbor planted a close row of Lombardy poplars just a few inches inside his own line. The rose grower and his wife had a pair of Scottish terriers which one of them took for a walk in the garden every night. A few months after the poplars were planted the man said to his wife, "Florence, those poplars don't seem to be growing." "No Alf," said she, "they don't. But I'm not surprised." "Why not?" asked Alf. "Because," said his wife, "every night when I walk the dogs, I put my hand through the fence and give each tree a half turn." Her husband, bursting with laughter, said, "You'll never believe this. Every night *I* walk the dogs, I put my hand through the fence and give the trees a half turn." Whirling dervishes those poplars were, no chance of ever being trees.

Trees that are suitable as windbreaks and high screens you will find in the following sections:

> EVERGREENS, see CHAPTER 20
>
> DECIDUOUS, columnar and fastigiate, which means leafy, tall and narrow, in CHAPTER 20
>
> WINDBARRIER plantings in the Northern plains, CHAPTER 20

ANNUALS AS HEDGES

Annuals grown as hedges are fascinating for their form or flower. Inexpensive to the point of costing only a few cents for a whole hedge, they need little or no trimming and they have the distinct advantage of quietly dying every fall, which is handy if you have decided that you would like a different one.

A 3-foot hedge of clear yellow marigolds with their lovely ferny leaves is a knockout along a white board or picket fence; a row of sunflowers, although as a hedge they don't hide much, still give you a strong bold line and marvellous ready-made food for winter birds; cosmos makes a feathery dainty haze of a hedge, starred with daisy-like flowers; the puffy little kochia (banned in some parts — better check yours) makes a neat little front garden frame and turns a hot burgundy red in fall.

RECOMMENDED PLANTS FOR HEDGES

COMMON NAME	WILL CLIP	F: Fineleaved C: Coarse	B: Bloom Be: Berries Fr: Fruit	BOTANICAL NAME	ZONE
Short, 1-3 feet					
Box	C	F		*Buxus*	some hardy to 4
Caragana, Shortleaf	C	F		*Caragana brevifolia*	2
(especially good for dry areas on the plains)					
Cinquefoil, Shrubby	C	F	B	*Potentilla fruticosa*	1
Cotoneaster, Hedge	C	F	Be	*Cotoneaster lucida*	1
Peking	C	F	Be	*acutifolia*	2
Currant, Alpine	C	F		*Ribes alpinum*	2
Dogwood, selections	C	C		*Cornus*	2
Euonymus, Dwarf	C	F	Be	*Euonymus nana*	2
Winged	C	F	Be	*alata*	3
Sarcoxie	C	F		*fortunei* 'Sarcoxie'	5
(evergreen)					
Honeysuckle, Clavey's dwarf	C	F	B-Be	*Lonicera xylosteum* 'Claveyi'	2
Sakhalin's	C	F	B-Be	*maximowezii*	2
Juniper, Rocky mountain	C	F		*Juniperus scopulorum*	2
Ninebark, Dwarf	C	F	B	*Physocarpus opulifolius* 'Nanus'	2b
Peashrub, Pygmy	C	F		*Caragana aurantiaca*	2
Privet, many	C	F		*Ligustrum*	some to 4
Prinsepia, Cherry	C	F	Fr	*Prinsepia sinensis*	2b
Quince, Japanese	C	F	B-Fr	*Chaenomeles japonica*	5b
Spirea, many	C	F	B	*Spiraea x vanhouttei*	4
	C	F	B	'Snowhite'	2b
(The cultivars 'Bridalwreath' and 'Snowhite' are the most popular flowering hedges with all gardeners)					
Medium, 3-5 feet					
Arrowwood	C	C		*Viburnum dentatum*	4
Buffaloberry, Silver	C	F	Be	*Shepherdia argentea*	1
Bush-Cranberry,					
European High	C	C	B-Be	*Viburnum opulus*	2b
American (northern plains)		C		*rafinesquianum*	2
Cherry, Manchu	C	F	Fr	*Prunus tomentosa*	2
Chokecherry, Shubert	C	C		*virginiana* 'Shubert'	2
Crab apple, Van Eseltine		C	B-Fr	*Malus* 'Van Eseltine'	2b
Hawthorns, some		C	B-Be	*Crataegus*	2
Holly, Japanese	C	F	Be	*Ilex crenata*	5
Honeysuckle, Sweetberry		F	B-Be	*Lonicera coerulea edulis*	2
Inkberry	C	F	Be	*Ilex glabra*	6
Lilac, Dwarf Korean	C	C	B	*Syringa palibiniana*	
Mock Orange, some	C	C	B	*Philadelphus*	2b
Roses, Shrub, many		F	B	*Rosa*	3
(the Multiflora Rose frequently recommended is only useful for farm fields and even then is questionably desirable)					
Olive, Russian	C	F		*Elaeagnus angustifolia*	2b
Spirea, many		F	B	*Spiraea*	2b
(it will clip, but it is much more beautiful informally grown)					
Willows, many	C	F		*Salix*	1b
(if kept cut back)					
Tall, over 5 feet					
Abelia	C	F	B	*Abelia grandiflora*	5
Beech, European	C	C		*Fagus sylvatica* 'Fastigiata'	5
Caragana, Common	C	F		*Caragana arborescens*	2
(Siberian Peashrub)					
Cherry-laurel	C	C		*Prunus laurocerasus*	6

COMMON NAME	WILL CLIP	F: Fineleaved C: Coarse	B: Bloom Be: Berries Fr: Fruit	BOTANICAL NAME	ZONE
Crab apple, Siberian Columnar		C	Fr	*Malus baccata* 'Columnaris'	2b
Elm, Siberian (Chinese)	C	F		*Ulmus pumila*	3b
Hawthorn, some	C	F		*Crataegus*	2
Holly, English	C	C	Be	*Ilex aquifolium*	6
Honeysuckle, Tatarian	C	F	B-Be	*Lonicera tatarica*	2
Larch	C	F		*Larix*	2
Laurel	C	F		*Laurus nobilis*	9a
Lilacs, many		C	B	*Syringa*	2
(can be trimmed, but flowers best if left to grow informally)					
Maple, Amur	C	F		*Acer ginnala*	2
Oak, Shingle		C		*Quercus imbricaria*	2
Pear, Ussurian		C	B-Fr	*Pyrus ussuriensis*	2b
Saskatoon	C	C	B-Be	*Amelanchier alnifolia*	1
Serviceberry, Shadblow	C	C	B-Be	*Amelanchier canadensis*	4

Tall Evergreens

COMMON NAME	WILL CLIP	F: Fineleaved C: Coarse	B: Bloom Be: Berries Fr: Fruit	BOTANICAL NAME	ZONE
Cedar, White	C	F		*Thuja occidentalis*	2b
Cypress, Sawara False	C	F		*Chamaecyparis pisifera*	4b
Hemlock, Canadian	C	F		*Tsuga canadensis*	4
Western	C	F		*heterophylla*	4
Pine, many		F		*Pinus*	2
Spruce, many		F		*Picea*	1
Yew, Japanese	C	F	Be	*Taxus cuspidata*	4
(Hick's Yew, T. cuspidata 'Hicksii', is the most popular evergreen hedge in cities)					
Yew, English	C	F		*Taxus baccata*	6

ANNUALS FOR HEDGES (ALL ARE GROWN INFORMALLY)

COMMON NAME	BOTANICAL NAME	REMARKS
Castor-oil Bean	*Ricinus communis*	Huge, dramatic leaves, green or bronze; height 4-6 feet; seeds poisonous
Cosmos	*Cosmos*	Feathery foliage, daisy-like flowers excellent for cutting; blooms till frost; height 3-5 feet
Lavatera, Annual	*Lavatera trimestis*	Bushy, round-leaved; flowers pink and large; height 2-3 feet
Marigold, many especially good: 'First Lady' and the 'Jubilee' series	*Tagetes*	Easy, flowery, in yellow to orange; blooms to frost; foliage ferny; height 6 inches to 3 feet
Marvel-of-Peru, Four-o'Clock	*Mirabilis jalapa*	Red, yellow or white flowers; striped and mottled; opening in late afternoon; to 3 feet
Prince's-Feather	*Polygonum orientale*	Long plumy spikes of bright pink flowers all summer; height 3-4 feet
Summer Cypress Fire Bush, Belvedere (banned in some areas, check before planting)	*Kochia*	A fluff-ball of a bush; bright green in summer, bright red, including the stems, in fall; neat; height 2 feet
Summer Fir	*Artemisia sacrorum viridis*	Looks like its name—a small fir tree; rich green; height 3-6 feet
Sunflower, many	*Helianthus*	Tall or short; bright yellow flowers, the biggest provide a favorite food of wild, seed-eating birds; plant to the north if you want to see their faces, which turn to the sun; height 3-6 feet

23 LAWNS

Your lawn can be a lush green carpet, a jungle of weeds, or a batch of brown scalps; but it doesn't need to be either of the last two if you make it properly in the first place and take care of it thereafter.

Grass is, when you add everything up, one of the most satisfactory ground covers there is. There's no substitute for the feeling of vigor and life it gives you. Its color is both complimentary and complementary. When you consider its long life and the beautiful way it behaves itself, it's not expensive. If you choose to use sod rather than seed, you can have an instant lawn in a few hours. Of all garden chores, cutting grass is the easiest.

DESIGN OF YOUR LAWN

When you're planning the design of your garden put grass only where it will grow well, look well and wear well.

Some strains require full sun all day for good growth. Others will manage to produce healthy turf with as little as 6 hours of direct sunlight a day. But no strain of grass will grow thick and green in less. If less is what you have, plan instead to lay pavings, spread mulches or grow ground covers on these places.

And do not plant grass on steep slopes where it is difficult to grow and maintain, nor on heavy-traffic walkways. Although, when well-established, grass will take a certain amount of treading on, it will not take constant walking over without going bare. At the same time, I must confess that a bare scuffed spot under a swing never bothers me. I can always see, in my mind's

211

eye, the happy child who made it, dipping back and forth into the blue bowl of the sky. But rather than worn-thin patches of grass under the birdfeeder where the sunflower seed hulls pile up, where you step in front of the garbage box, or where two paths make a right angle but everybody cuts the corner, you might better have some form of hard surfacing.

In designing the shape and sweep of lawns, remember that a flowing line rather than an angled one adds grace and rhythm to your garden. If between your house and the street, you must pick up a grade, try to slope it down from the house to a gentle dip, then lift it back up to the street. This will both drain excess water away from your foundation and give a sense of distance and spaciousness that by actual measure is not there. If you use grass for the central part of your back garden, as most do, then carry it, if you can, around a tree, a screen or a group of shrubs out of sight, near the back line. Maybe it will only lead to your manure pile or compost heap, but a pleasurable sense of mystery is thus added to your design. (For further ideas on design, see CHAPTER 13.)

EASY MAINTENANCE

When you're planning a new lawn or renovating an old one, make it as easy to maintain as you can, for its care must be done regularly. Don't chop it up with plantings or flower beds — make it as generous an expanse as you can. Border it with specially planned mowing strips for easy cutting and be sure that its shape makes for convenient turning space for your mower. Don't take grass right up to a pool's edge. You will forever rue the day you did if you have to fish a bushelful of clippings out of the water every time the grass is cut. For changes of level, where you will have to take the mower up and down, plan ramps rather than steps.

(For other easy maintenance and economy ideas, see CHAPTER 15. For techniques to help you to do the job well, and good tools, see CHAPTER 18.)

MAKING A NEW LAWN

Preparation for a new lawn is so important, be prepared to take time to do it well. It will repay you for years and years.

Check the site, especially around the house, for buried debris and clear stones and sticks from the surface.

Stockpile topsoil from the whole site (not just the excavation) for use in making the bed for your new lawn. The reason for removing it all is that, if you did not, heavy construction equipment could move back and forth over it and compact the soil till it was of little use.

Check house plans to be sure that hose connections occur frequently enough so that you do not have to drag hoses and sprinkler heads more than 50 feet to water the grass in any part of the garden.

Consider installing an automatic watering system of buried pipes and sprinkler heads. (See CHAPTER 14: Permanent Features.)

Establish grades so that they slope away from the house on all sides and away from paths and driveways. Model the surface of the ground so that it is rolling and gentle, not abrupt and bumpy. Leave no low spots where water can stand for more than half a day. On large properties adjacent to heavily traveled streets or roads, built-up mounds of lawn are used to cut down noise and dust and to give greater privacy. Unfortunately, many look like Mother Earth with a dose of the hives rather than a well-planned landscape.

Build permanent features (such as patios and fences) first so that the resulting construction mess doesn't disturb the new lawn.

Cut low branches of large trees up at least 8 feet to allow air and light to reach the grass below. Selectively prune large dense trees all the way up to allow more light to get through. If you are planting new trees, make your selection from those that are best for grass to grow under (see CHAPTER 20).

Lay out the areas where you wish to put grass and bring the soil there to good tilth by adding humus (⅓ humus to ⅔ soil is average) in the form of peat or compost or any moisture-retentive material; chemical lawn fertilizer in dosage recommended by manufacturer and insecticide to kill harmful insects such as grubs, wireworms. Mix deeply (6 inches is minimum) with mechanical rototilling or by digging. Turf specialists recommend that this first chemical fertilizer be one with higher percentages of phosphorus and potash than nitrogen, such as 4-24-12. You will find a formula indicating this on every bag of fertilizer you buy. Fertilizer applied after the lawn is established and growing well should be higher in nitrogen than phosphorus and potash (10-6-4) because of its different needs at that time.

Rake, level, pick out stones and debris. A crumbly surface, rather than a pulverized one, makes the best seed or sod bed.

If topsoil is to be added other than your own, be sure to use clean material as free of weeds as possible. This is sometimes difficult to get, and can, if you have a large area, be costly. If possible, therefore, use your own material. Make this top layer 5-6 inches deep.

Roll with a light roller to find the uneven spots, then rake and level them. Common practice on the west coast is for two people with ropes to drag a weighted ladder, or two 8-foot lengths of 2-by-4s lashed together, across the ground. First drag parallel to the house, then at right angles and finally diagonally in both directions.

For seeding a lawn, the ideal time is late summer or very early fall when air and earth are warm during the day, nights are cool, and rainfall is usually enough to encourage best growth. Second best time to sow seed is very early in spring when the earth becomes dry enough to work. It should crumble in your hand. A spring-seeded lawn may need extra watering in early summer if weather is hot and dry. (See page 217 for recommended mixtures of seed.) Some turf specialists advise against mixing bent grass with other grasses, since the bent eventually takes over and, to be good, needs far more care than the average home gardener can give. The result, instead of being a lovely lawn, is a mess. For large areas, rent a mechanical seeder, otherwise do it by hand. Divide the total recommended quantity of seed into four, then divide the lawn in half, sowing one quarter of the seed on each. Next, moving at right angles to the first sowing, again divide the lawn in half and sow one quarter of the seed on each. In this way, the lawn is evenly covered and you don't, in your enthusiasm, put all you seed on the first section. Rake lightly and roll with an empty roller, just to press the seed into the ground. On slopes, mulch with clean straw if you have it, or use cheesecloth, coarse burlap or a special netting for this purpose, which is designed to disintegrate. This prevents soil and seedlings from washing out in heavy rains. Keep moist with a fine spray for 3 weeks and barricade against trespassers for 8 weeks.

For a sodded lawn, prepare the bed as you would if you were going to sow seed. Water and lay sod immediately after delivery. If you must hold it over, keep it cool and moist and shaded from hot sun. Pound the sod down well to give it firm contact with the soil beneath. Keep deeply watered if no rain, for the entire growing season.

Do first mowing of all new grass, seeded or sodded, when it is just over 2 inches high. Be sure that mower blades are very sharp so that the new roots will not be pulled out of the ground (reel mowers are better than rotary for this first clipping). Some experts recommend another rolling just to firm the roots into the soil, but this is not common practice.

RENOVATING AN OLD TIRED LAWN

Coldbloodedly diagnose the situation. If grades are wrong to the point that major renewal is needed; if soil is so compact that nothing growing in it looks at ease; if more than 50% is weeds, or if your plans for new garden construction will tear up much of the turf anyway, then rototill, mixing added humus and fertilizer to a depth of 6-12 inches, as for a new lawn.

If, on the other hand, only the turf looks sad it will be worth trying to improve it for at least a year with a shot-in-the-arm program. First, rent a machine that will vertically mow the grass, that is, pull up all the old accumulated, partially decomposed grass clippings that, through the years, have matted over the roots. Rake off this thatch and put it on your compost heap. Then in early spring aerate and feed; feed again in late spring and late summer. Never aerate during the high-temperature period of summer. Kill weeds when the days are warm enough (70°F and over) to make herbicides most effective. If no rain, water once a week thoroughly, never sprinkle.

CARE OF ESTABLISHED LAWNS

Feed with special lawn fertilizers (nitrogen, phosphorus and potash in the ratio of 2-1-1 are recommended) in quantities suggested by the manufacturer. Urea formaldehyde, though more expensive, is easy to use and safer because overgenerous application is less likely to burn the lawn. Also, they are longer-lasting. Give this treatment every year in very early and late spring, and again in late summer.

Many gardeners — and gardeners' helpers — consider that a good lawn-care program includes liming. Experts recommend that only acid soil needs lime added. Grass grows best in a soil with a pH between 5.9 and 6.9. If your soil pH is lower than this, you need lime and the average dose is 50 pounds per 1,000 square feet. To determine the acidity of your soil, either have it tested by your government laboratory (see lists of where, PART V), test it yourself, or ask a good-lawn neighbor what he does.

Moss in the lawn is another concern. Many gardeners think this indicates a need for lime, but more often than not it is a symptom of poor fertility and lack of sunshine. Where moss appears, feed and seed for one or two seasons.

If this does not correct it, then either change to paving, ground cover or a stone mulch, or go in for a garden of mosses.

Cut grass no shorter than 2 inches except on bent lawns, which should be cut often to keep them short. Be sure to make one last cut before freeze-up so that grass goes into winter no longer than 2 inches. This prevents matting and discourages fungus growth in conditions of wet snow and ice.

Pick up grass clippings. Although this can be a nuisance, especially on rotary-mowed lawns, the thatch that builds up when clippings are not picked up can become a major problem over the years.

Aerate your lawn with a spiker at least once a year just before feeding; oftener is better. Spikers can usually be rented or improvised from a few boards and spikes fastened on a broom handle.

Keep mower blades sharp — dull ones chew rather than cut the grass.

Roll, if at all, only lightly once in spring to press down air pockets caused by heaving frost. Do not attempt to correct low levels, permanent unevenness or poor grade by rolling. Instead lift sod, add or remove soil to bring it level, and replace.

Design your garden so that there is never constant steady traffic on any one part of the grass; discourage all traffic in winter and early spring, when the ground is frozen or soft. Wheedle paperboys, puppies and postmen into using the paths not shortcuts across the lawn. Don't build a skating rink on a lawn where you want good turf. To patch worn spots loosen the soil, mixing in fertilizer, then seed and cover with branches to keep people off it till it becomes established. A trick often used by golf courses as a spot remedy is to cover such an area after seeding with a piece of clear plastic stretched over wire hoops and weighted down on the sides. This forms a little greenhouse in which the new grass can catch on in ideal conditions. When it is well along, the tent is removed. If you are the impatient type, patch the damaged spot with new sod, first putting a 2-inch layer of fertilized garden soil below it to give it a good start.

Don't shovel salt-laced snow off walks onto grass: it will kill it. Don't let melted snow and salt from walks or drives run over the lawn either.

Summer furniture or sun mats lying on the grass should be moved around so that they do not stand in one place more than a day or so. The grass under them can become tender and will, when exposed, sunburn.

Rake up leaves in the fall, otherwise they could mat and damage the grass over winter.

See page 218 for information about lawn pests and diseases. Be sure of your diagnosis when you look for a pest or disease to blame for brown patches on your lawn in spring. They could be caused by a female dog or they could be just a young man's fancy lightly turning to thoughts of love. One spring, as the snow melted, our front lawn developed a great, queer pattern of brown. The trouble wasn't identified till we remembered that, on Valentine's Day, one of my daughter's gay Lotharios had painted a big red heart on the snow on the lawn as a symbol of his undying affection. There it was come spring — the outline of a big dead brown heart in the grass. Fortunately a close cut and a transfusion of quick-acting fertilizer brought it back.

Northwest Coast

Climate (mild winters, cool summers) in this area is practically ideal for good lawns. A regular program to maintain fertility is necessary because heavy winter rainfall (average: 60 inches) leaches out nitrates from the soil. Special feedings recommended: apply chemical lawn fertilizers in early and late spring, again in late summer, with the last feeding higher in percentage of phosphorus than nitrogen. Add an organic top dressing (screened soil or compost, peat) in spring or fall each year.

Common faults: not fertilizing often enough; shallow sprinkling, particularly in summer; liming of lawns in spring, which is seldom necessary and often burns the grass; not keeping bent grass lawns clipped short — they should be cut twice a week.

Northern Central

The hot dry periods of summer and sweeping winter winds make lawn-making a real challenge in the central and south parts of the plains. In the north, moderately warm days and cool nights make it easier. Both areas report the need for added humus in the soil — as much as 1 bushel of peat to every 5 bushels of soil. Experts also say that house builders too often fail to stockpile topsoil before beginning construction.

Special advice: do *deep* preparation of seed or sod bed to encourage grass roots to go well down, thus making summer droughts less damaging. Lay evergreen branches over the lawn after Christmas to hold snow for added moisture and protection. A custom in the heavy clay soils of some plains regions is to grow potatoes for one season before seeding in the area planned for lawn. The cultivation, weeding and fertilization of the ground for the potatoes help prepare a good seed bed for the future lawn.

Mid-America

Lawn making, although not as easy as on the west and east coasts, is still not difficult in these areas. In large centres, the relatively low cost of sod makes it more economical to use this method rather than seed. Sod farming has now developed into an industry with many thousand acres under cultivation, with highly technical programs of seed selection, fertilization, weed and insect control and cropping. Home gardeners who use sod must, however, still do proper and careful preparation of the bed and follow a regular program of ongoing care.

Northeast Coast

Good-to-excellent lawns are possible in east coast gardens when there is normal weather. The availability of local commercial peat at reasonable prices makes it possible to mix plenty of humus into the soil when preparing it to encourage deep rooting and moisture retention. Too many gardeners, experts report, still roll the daylights out of their lawns every spring, compacting the soil and inhibiting good growth.

(For grasses for other parts of the country, see Part V.)

All can be started from seed : some can be bought as sod. Do not skimp on good seed nor on the preparation of the soil bed. Lawn grasses are not zoned as other garden plants are—most strains do well even in the very low temperatures of the Far North, mainly because of the excellent insulation of snow cover. Bent grass lawns are grown more commonly on the northwest coast because weather conditions are favorable there. But even there, where climate is obliging, selected strains of Kentucky bluegrass are taking over, because of their much lower maintenance needs.

For an average, well-prepared lawn in sun, where watering is possible when weather is dry

80% 'Merion' Kentucky bluegrass (or other selected strain	rate : 3 pounds per 1,000 square feet
20% 'Norlea' ryegrass	
or :	
60% blend of 'Merion' and commercial Kentucky bluegrass	rate : 3 pounds per 1,000 square feet
30% creeping red fescue	
10% ryegrass	

For an average lawn with some shade, watering available when needed

65% creeping red fescue	rate : 4 pounds per 1,000 square feet
35% common Kentucky bluegrass	

For dry shade with watering available when needed

25% Kentucky bluegrass	rate : 4 pounds per 1,000 square feet
60% creeping red fescue	
15% common bluegrass	

For Northern plains where irrigation not possible

20% Kentucky bluegrass	rate : 4 pounds per 1,000 square feet
20% creeping red fescue	
60% Russian wild ryegrass (extremely durable)	

For very dry areas in the far west

100% crested wheat grass or Russian wild ryegrass or streambank wheat grass	rate : 6 pounds per 1,000 square feet

For bent grass lawns

Sandy soils :

60% creeping red fescue	rate : 3 pounds per 1,000 square feet
20% Kentucky bluegrass (selected strains)	
20% bent grass	

Heavy soils :

40% creeping red fescue	rate : 3 pounds per 1,000 square feet
30% Kentucky bluegrass	
30% bent grass, Colonial	

Weed Control on Lawns

A well-tended lawn seldom needs extensive weedkilling, so your first effort should be to set up a regular program of the best lawn care. However, onto every lawn some weeds may fall, so here are various ways to get rid of them.

Precautions for Applying Herbicides (Weedkillers)
Apply all spray herbicides when weather is calm and windless, to prevent damaging drift onto valuable garden plants. Also prevent runoff into garden beds. The most effective time is when the weather is warm (70°F) and weeds are growing vigorously. Apply when plants are dry, thoroughly soaking the leaves. Do not water for 24 hours nor cut for 3 days.

Spray and sprinkling equipment should be kept solely for this purpose — even a slight residue mixed with insecticide, fungicide or fertilizer could seriously damage a good plant. On bent grass and newly seeded lawns use specially recommended herbicide; check with your provincial or state department of agriculture for this.

For a broad-leaved weed (dandelion, plantain, etc.) here and there:
with a trusty old bread knife cut it out, or after a rain pull it out. In the hole, put a dab of good soil and fertilizer and some grass seed. Or, with a herbicide-filled plastic cane, spear the heart of the weed. Or, with a solution of herbicide or a mix containing it made up as directed by the manufacturer, sprinkle the offender.

For heavier crops of broad-leaved weeds
Draw over them a product available from your garden supplier — that is, a paraffin bar impregnated with herbicide; many gardeners fasten this to the bar of their mower and pull it behind them as they cut the grass. Or, with a solution of herbicide or a mix containing it, spray till they are thoroughly soaked.

For chickweeds, clovers, etc., resistant to some herbicides
Spray with a solution of herbicide especially for these plants.

For crabgrass, an annual that germinates only where there is lots of light — this is one of the important reasons for shading its roots by cutting your grass no shorter than 2 inches — control with the application of a chemical mixture in one of two ways. One, called a pre-emergent herbicide, is applied by itself or already mixed with fertilizer, in spring, to prevent germination. The other is a post-emergent chemical that kills young crabgrass plants and should be applied in late summer. The pre-emergent type is regarded as the more effective of the two. There are many products that do this so consult supplier for the best for you.

Control of Pests and Diseases on Lawns

PESTS: considered here to be insects, mites, slugs, grubs, millipedes, sowbugs, worms, etc.

DISEASE: covers disorders caused by fungi.

Chemicals recommended for control of garden pests and diseases change frequently as new products come onto the market and more experienced assessments of those already in use become available; so specific materials are not listed. For the correct spray or dust for your particular trouble, consult your government department of agriculture.

(For precautions, read CHAPTER 19, Pests and Diseases, including notes on the proper choice and use of equipment for spraying and dusting.)

High-nitrogen fertilizers, often the cause of trouble on lawns when used to excess, are those in which the first of the three numbers stating nitrogen, phosphorus and potash content (which all fertilizers must have printed on the bag) is the highest.

Lawn Pests

WHITE GRUBS

Trouble: dead patches of grass. Caused by 1-inch, root-feeding, fat white grubs found curled up in a stuffed stupor beneath the sod.

Control: spread dry insecticide evenly on lawn and thoroughly water in. This treatment will also kill earthworms and ants in the soil, so be sure you want to.

CHINCH BUGS

Trouble: Immature bugs, pinkish to brown, suck the sap from grass stems. Mature bugs (black, white wings) only 1/6″ long.

Control: Water lawn for an hour, then apply insecticide.

EARTHWORMS

Trouble: not really a pest of the worst order unless thinking about them bothers you. Castings can look untidy on a close-cut bent grass lawn.

Control: insecticide at double the strength recommended for grubs will eliminate, but robins and fishermen in your family won't love you if you do.

SOD WEBWORMS

LAWN MOTHS

Trouble: green, grass-gnawing caterpillars (small) make silk-lined tunnels at base of blades; later become moths. (You can hardly blame them for chewing your lawn — who wouldn't be a green, grass-gnawing caterpillar if you could live a life of luxury in a silk-lined tunnel?)

Control: Spray insecticide on lawn and water in.

Lawn Diseases

BROWN PATCH

Trouble: irregular, circular brown patches of grass, usually 1 inch to several feet in diameter. Look for during warm, humid weather when night temperatures above 70°F., following what you thought was the correct dose of a high-nitrogen fertilizer, but which was, in fact, too much. Most severe on bent grass, fescue, Kentucky bluegrass.

Control: Water lawn in early part of day so that it will dry before evening, when most fungi are out a-sporing. Skip using high-nitrogen fertilizers till trouble clears. Rake up clippings. Treat turf with fungicide repeating 2 or 3 times at 7-day intervals.

DOLLAR SPOT

Trouble: brown, later straw-colored spots about 2 inches wide, that may run together in irregular patches. Favored by cool, moist conditions. Damage most severe where soil lacks nitrogen and on bent grass.

Control: apply fungicide 2 or 3 times, one month apart, starting in June.

LEAF SPOT AND FOOT ROT (Helminthosporium)

Trouble: scattered circular to longish spots on blades of grass in early spring or late fall. Spots have noticeable red-brown to black borders, at first dark to light brown centres, later becoming straw-colored to white. Stems and crowns are often killed so that a slight tug will pull out rotted plant. More severe in cool rainy weather and on lawns that have been too closely clipped. Kentucky bluegrass is exceptionally susceptible.

Control: raise height of mower blades, skip high-nitrogen fertilizers. Spray with fungicide.

POWDERY MILDEW

Trouble: yellow, grey-white wefts of mildew appear on upper blade surfaces (often serious on Merion bluegrass). Common on shady, slow-drying lawns when nights cool, days warm.

Control: reasonable control with fungicide sprays.

SNOW MOLD

Trouble: webby growth varying in size from 1 inch to 1-2 feet in diameter covers patches of grass, appearing as snow melts. Occurs under near-freezing, moist conditions. As soil warms in spring, trouble vanishes. May be severe on bent grass.

Control: avoid late fall applications of high-nitrogen fertilizers. Treat lawn before first lasting snow with fungicide. Materials for this treatment are usualy highly poisonous, so best have professionals do it or wait for it to cure itself.

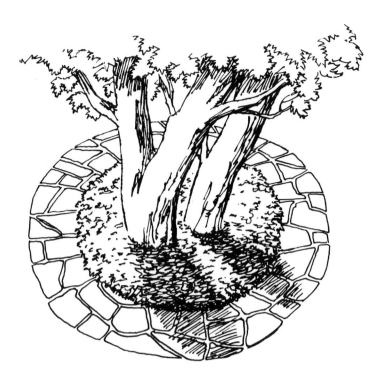

24 GROUND COVERS

Ground covers can be an integral part of your garden plan right from the beginning, or a very handsome help in time of trouble. They can be shrubs, perennials, annuals or vines; evergreen or deciduous; notable for their leaves or flowers, but always low and dense-growing, with a habit, when mass-planted, of attractively covering the ground.

They can add texture to a sophisticated garden, cover problem spots with vigorous greening, prevent washouts on sloping ground and steep banks, be a hiding place for untidy, ripening bulb foliage or a discouragement to weeds.

The plants you choose for this role should, in a relatively short time, be capable of completely covering the space you want them to. If they drag their heels, either because you have chosen the wrong plant or are not growing it properly, weeds and erosion take over and you have a new problem on your hands instead of a happy solution to an old one.

CONSIDER THESE THINGS FIRST

Ground cover plants are no substitute for lawn grass if the surface has 6 hours of sun daily, is to be walked on, sat on or played on. They are a welcome substitute for grass where there is not this much sun and traffic is light.

As a design element in your garden, know that they will add variation in greens, particularly in the side slanting, sparkling light that glances off plants below your line of vision. They will set off, by their uniformity and (if you've chosen well) their beauty, larger plants you place among them — a large needled Austrian pine, for instance, in a bed of sleek ivy; a pink flowering cherry tree with a white skirt of candytuft. Some have individual character all

219

their own, such as soft grey cushions of Silver Mound artemisia planted in a coral-red crushed tile mulch, or a gentle slant of rose daphne by a stone step at your front door. Some have lovely flowers, but mainly you choose ground covers not for bloom but for their habit, their leaves, their convenience and easy care.

Some can be mavericks — a wise choice only if you want a fast take-over, a headache if you don't control them right from the beginning. Violets are in this class in my garden.

Evergreens, both broad-leaved and needled, are best because they are good-looking all year, but many leafy plants, both shrubs and perennials, have their own special beauty, and annuals are a godsend when you need quick cover.

On an average it will take 2-3 years for perennial plants to really cover the ground (this partly depends on how closely you plant them in the first place); 4-5 years for shrubs; a third of a summer for annuals.

Think about the cost in relation to your own time and budget for gardening. Periwinkle, for instance, planted on 12-inch centers (that is, one plant in the middle of each square foot) will take 100 plants for 100 square feet. Planted on 8-inch centers, and therefore likely to make a close cover more quickly, will take more than double the number of plants at more than double the cost. But perhaps, for your situation, this is worth it. Then there is the possibility of increase by skillful handling. If you have time to do a little fine fingering yourself, you can train the runners of plants in the 12-inch squares to cover the ground just as quickly as untrained ones in 8-inch squares. This is not a difficult job, but you do have to be faithful about doing it whenever new growth reaches out.

And be comforted that although ground covers may take a while to settle in, once established, they are low-care, easy maintenance, economical, rich-reward plants for your garden.

WHERE TO USE

In a new garden: deliberately plan ground cover areas just as you plan lawn and flower beds. Make them generous in size, draw in their shape and form to fit the overall design of your garden; don't let them wander and spill over into other plantings, curb them and use this defined outline to add rhythm and grace to your whole plan.

Use shade-tolerant plants such as pachysandra under existing or newly planted trees, in heavy shade from buildings;

Use root-running ones such as fleece flower to hold a slippy bank or terrace;

If you have youngsters at the tricycle stage or bone-burying puppies, think of building wood-framed raised beds for your plantings; use ground covers to surface them and to set off some prima donna flowering plants within them — periwinkle interplanted with spring bulbs, and later bright annuals such as marigolds are just one version.

If you have a narrow but sunny patch between path and house, think of packing it with a ground cover of lettuce, strawberries, sage or flowering kale; if it's shady, with lily-of-the-valley; if it's overhung with a wide eave that makes the ground below dry, plant a neat vine out beyond the overhang where it will get the rain and the dewfall, and train its tendrils back over the dry ground below the eave. And don't forget to wash it off occasionally with the hose.

In an older garden: wherever there are bald patches, where plants are not doing well, consider using ground covers to improve the scene.

under large trees; euonymus, pachysandra or periwinkle

in heavy shade areas; goutweed, sweet woodruff or ivy

to take over a change of level — perhaps a rock garden which you now think takes too much work — one of the horizontal junipers or cotoneaster, or, if it's shady, dwarf yews

for underplanting some of the marvelous new daffodils and narcissus; pachistima or periwinkle; or some of the little early bulbs like crocus and scilla; the flatter bugleweed; or the miniature Kew euonymus.

ANALYZE THE QUALITIES OF YOUR SITE

Is the soil richly fertile? just fair? terrible? If the first, go ahead and plant; if fair or terrible, improve (see CHAPTER 18).

Is it dry? moist? soaking wet? (It can be just pleasantly moist most of the year but dangerously drowning in winter, especially in late winter when snow can melt and have nowhere to drain because of frozen ground.) If dry, add bashes of humus to make more moist; if moist, use a moisture-appreciating plant, if wet, arrange to drain — raising the level of the ground is the easiest way to do this.

Is it heavy clay or very light sand? A few ground covers will tolerate light, sandy soils — fleece flower, creeping phlox, snow-in-summer are some. Practically none grow well in heavy clay, so if this is what you have, improve it. (See CHAPTER 18.)

What would be the pleasing scale of a ground cover in relation to the other plants near it? to your whole garden? They can be tight-to-the-ground mats, as the bearberry cotoneaster or woolly thyme is; a little bouncy, as English ivy or periwinkle is; more so, as wintercreeper is, or really exuberant, as some of the junipers are.

What would be the most pleasing color? Most ground covers add a variety of green to the garden: shiny — pachysandra or periwinkle; leathery — ivy or oregon grape; feathery — the tamarix juniper; bluish — the Bar Harbor juniper; purple — the Andorra juniper; bronze-purple — bugleweed; variegations of white and green — the silver variegated plantain lily, goutweed, or Silver Gem euonymus. But some are themselves a distinct and sometimes distinguished color — the woolly, almost white of rabbit's ears; the metallic glint of Silver Mound artemisia; the autumn red of colorata euonymus.

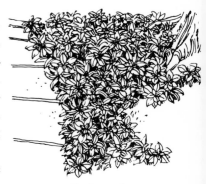

Pachysandra.

Do you want a dividend of bright berries or flowers? If so, think of the Hancock coralberry, mock strawberry, or cotoneaster for berries; lily-of-the-valley, rock cress, pinks, or forget-me-nots for flowers.

Do you live in a heavy-snowfall area? If you do, choose a flexible ground cover that will bend easily — any of the euonymus or junipers — or use a perennial plant that will disappear in winter, such as violets. And think of taking advantage of the insulation of deep snow cover to use the sometimes tender and temperamental little rose daphne which does so well in these conditions right to Zone 1.

HOW TO BUY GROUND COVER PLANTS

Check our lists and the catalogues of nurseries nearest you. Choose cultivars hardy for your zone and, if possible, those that have been grown under similar climate conditions to those in your garden. Order early. For the commoner ground covers such as periwinkle and pachysandra, there is often a special discount for quantity, so do a little shopping around if you need many. For annuals, buy prestarted plants or grow from seed.

Always buy a few more than the actual number you need and plant them in an out-of-the-way place in your garden; these can replace any that die.

If you want to take a chance with a possibly tender cultivar, buy only a few plants and try them in your garden before you plump for the whole bit. In the meantime, fill spaces with an annual such as the fragrant and easy sweet alyssum. If your tender ones survive a year, complete the planting.

HOW TO PLANT

If possible, prepare the soil at least 4 weeks beforehand to allow for settling, mixing in any needed humus and fertilizer at that time.

Plan to plant in early spring if you live in Zones 1-5; in early spring or early fall, in Zones 6-9.

Follow normal procedures for planting shrubs and perennials as outlined in CHAPTER 18. Do not mix two kinds together — one will always take over from the other.

If planting a bare, steep bank, press boards or galvanized iron strips crossways into the soil, about 18 inches apart, to hold the earth until the roots can take over, in about 3 years time.

If using plants that could run away with your garden, consider using a barrier around them — metal strips, wood frames treated with preservative, paving strips. Put them in place when you first plant.

If the site is under a large tree whose roots leave little food or moisture for other plants growing over them, consider building a raised bed, by first putting down over the area you want to plant, a layer of heavy polyethylene, pierced here and there to let excess water drain through. Frame it with stone or wood to whatever depth you want and backfill with prepared soil. For a comparatively shallow-rooting ground cover like periwinkle or pachysandra, this will need to be about 12 inches deep. Through the ground cover in such a bed you can plant blue scillas, some small daffodils or tulips, or a spurting of white crocuses to give you bright flowers in spring and a place to conceal their untidy foliage later on.

ONGOING CARE

A program of good garden care — watering deeply when dry, weeding (which you may have to do by hand at the beginning so as not to pull the ground cover plants out), mulching when the weather begins to get hot, replacing any that die — is all that is needed. (For details of these techniques, see CHAPTER 18.)

Once the plants are in place and as they grow closer together, fertilizing is tricky, for you must not spill any on stems or leaves. Best to foliar feed with liquid fertilizer or apply it in granular form when the plants are dry (even a spoonful on a wet leaf will dissolve into too strong a solution and burn it). Water in *immediately*. Another way is to apply liquid fertilizer through a metal wand feeder which you plunge into the ground near the roots.

To encourage plants to spread sideways as quickly as possible, keep growth down so that it is in direct contact with the ground, where it will very often root and establish a base for the next jump. Hairpins make good staples for fine plants. Stove wire, wire clothes line, cut-up wire hangers can be bent into sturdier holdfasts.

Winter protection is usually only needed for ground covers in the early years before they are fully established. The idea is to keep them cool and shaded in late winter when the sun is hot. Evergreen branches — cut-up Christmas trees are ideal — are the best for this and easy to take off when spring comes. You might also examine your new plants in the early spring for the first few years to see if they have heaved out of the ground. If they have, pull on your gumboots and tramp them back in again.

Knowing how to propagate successfully is a handy talent for the ground cover grower. This is one way to increase the number you may need at no cost. (See how to, CHAPTER 18.)

RECOMMENDED GROUNDCOVERING SHRUBS

Key to lists below

(a) are those that are dense and linking in habit, like Auld Lang Syne on New Year's Eve

(b) are those with spreading ground-rooting runners

(c) are those that root and spread underground

(d) are prostrate with a tendency for extending branches to root wherever they touch the ground.

---

4 FOR SHADE

Euonymus, selections; (b); broad-leaved evergreen; some hardy to Zone 4; 2-3 feet.

Ivy, *Hedera*; (b); Zone 5; broad-leaved and evergreen, a vine, excellent for a shady ground cover, but do not allow to reach valuable trees and shrubs for it will climb up anything in its path; can be kept low by clipping.

Pachysandra, Japanese spurge, *P. terminalis*; (c); Zone 3; evergreen, leathery; prefers cool, moist situations; plant close in the beginning; 8 inches.

Yew, selections; *Taxus*; (d); some to Zone 3; needled evergreen; especially good in cities and heavy shade.

---

10 FOR SUN

Broom, Prostrate; *Cytisus decumbens*; (a); Zone 2; yellow flowers in spring.

Coralberry, Hancock, *Symphoricarpos* 'Hancock'; (a); Zone 4; prostrate, graceful; sun or shade; 3 feet.

Cotoneaster, Bearberry; *C. dammeri*; (b); Zone 4 and the cultivar 'Skogholm', a little taller and more vigorous; both evergreen; red berries; 8-10 inches.

Cotoneaster 'Cranberry'; *C. apiculata*, Zone 4; fans out over the ground, red fruit, 2-3 feet. 'Autumn Fire';

C. salicifolia, Zone 4; fast-growing, bright green leaves, half shade or sun.

Heath, *Erica carnea*; **Heather**, *Calluna vulgaris*; (a); Zone 5; bushy and flowery; 12 inches.

Junipers, selections, *Juniperus*; (d); some to Zone 2; plumy evergreens in various shades of green; do best in full sun; light soil; some low, some medium, some tall.

Pachistima, Canby, *P. canbyi*; (d); Zone 2b; neat narrow-leaved evergreen; sun or shade; 12 inches.

Potentilla, selections; (a), Zone 2; especially 'Gold Drop', *P. Parviflora* 'Farrerii'; prefers dry, hot situations; flowers white to yellow all summer; 3-4 feet.

Salal, *Gaultheria shallon*; (c); Zone 6; broad-leaved; grows short and mats in full sun; taller in semishade.

RECOMMENDED PERENNIALS

(a) marks those that grow in clumps and have to be planted individually

(b) are overground spreaders

(c) are underground rooters

Low: up to 8 inches

Medium: up to 2 feet

Tall: over 2 feet

---

12 FOR SHADE

Barrenwort; many, *Epimedium*; (a); wiry-stemmed, delicate foliage, dainty flowers; medium.

Bugleweed, *Ajuga*; (b); flat, shining rosettes spreading over the ground; blue flowers; low.

Canada Blue Phlox, *Phlox divaricata canadensis*; (a); pale blue flowers in spring; excellent for woodland plantings; medium.

Creeping Jenny, Creeping Charlie; *Lysimachia nummularia*; (b); you may end up hating me for recommending this; polite nurserymen say it is "invasive," which means it goes all over the place, where you want it and where you don't; shade or sun; contain it and it can be Your Friend; low.

Ferns in variety; (a); many; low; medium; tall; all lovely.

Foamflower, *Tiarella cordifolia*; (c); white foamy flowers, leaves like a maple; likes rich, moist soil; medium.

Goutweed, *Aegopodium podagraria* 'Variegatum'; (c); put a barrier around this one unless your gout is so bad you need a constant supply of leaves and roots for a healing brew; yellowish and cream leaves, grows anywhere in anything; low.

Lily-of-the-valley, *Convallaria majalis*; (c); sweetly scented stalks of little white bells in spring; broad green leaves, red berries; likes moist soil; low.

Periwinkle, *Vinca minor*; (b); the most popular ground cover of all; glossy evergreen leaves; white, blue or purple flowers; needs fine, moist soil; low.

Plantain Lily, *Hosta*; (a); many, some broad-leaved, some narrow, some streaked with white or yellow; likes moist soil; late to leaf out in spring, so don't despair; medium to tall.

Sweet Woodruff, *Asperula odorata*; (c); popular; white flowered; leaves in dense whorls; needs moist soil; medium.

Violet, *Viola*; (c); a runaway plant if ever there was one, so contain; purple, pink, yellow, peach, white flowers in spring, some fragrant; low.

---

8 PERENNIALS FOR SUN

Candytuft; *Iberis sempervirens*; (b); evergreen; crisp white flowers in spring; moist, rich soil; cut back after flowering; low.

Crown Vetch, *Coronilla varia*; (c); for dry, poor soil, banks, looks like an exotic version of pink and white clover; flowers all summer; contain, for travels fast and far; low.

Mock Strawberry, *Duchesnea indica*; (b); a quick cover; leaves like a real strawberry, but flowers yellow, followed by red berries, not too tasty; biennial, so plant new runners from old plants every 2 years; low.

Moss Pink. *Phlox subulata*; (b); white, pink, lavender or blue flowers in spring; cut back after flowering and keep to small plantings — middle of large ones tend to die; low.

Rabbit's Ears, Lamb's Ears, *Stachys lanata*; (a); soft, silvery-white leaves, carmine flowers; low.

Reynoutria, Fleece Flower, *Polygonum cuspidatum* 'Compactum Femina'; (b); coral-rose flowers; excellent for banks, poor soil; restrain; low.

Thyme, many, *Thymus*; (b); the woolly grey-leaved thyme, *T. lanuginosus*, best to spread vigorously and remain thick; low.

Silver Mound, Angels-Hair, *Artemisia schmidtiana* 'Silver Mound'; (a); compact, fuzzy, silver-grey foliage in soft mounds; a showstopper; medium.

---

5 ANNUALS
THAT CAN DOUBLE AS GROUND COVERS

Almost any annual with a habit of spreading sideways will make an effective ground cover. Here are a few:

Iceland or California Poppy, *Papaver nudicaule, Eschscholzia californica*; tissue-paper thin flowers held well above the foliage; low.

Ivy Geranium, *Pelargonium peltatum*; not technically an annual, but grown as such outdoors; leathery green leaves; pink or white flowers; a trailer; low.

Patience Plant, *Impatiens*; a joy to gardeners with heavy shade; flowers all summer; be sure to plant dwarf, creeping kinds; low.

Petunia; petunias do just about everything, so think about using them to cover the ground too; buy spreading types; medium.

Portulaca; *P. grandiflora*; a flowery little plant that grows best in poor soil and hot dry places; flowers close in late day; low.

25 VINES AND CLIMBERS

Vines are the gay gymnasts of the garden. They climb, they creep, they twine and twirl. They twist blithely up into a tree, scale a wall, tumble over a fence. Their disdain for being earthbound, their exuberance for the sky add a light-hearted air to every garden they grow in. And many have other good points too:

honeysuckle can be both fragrant and graceful and the especially hardy 'Drop-more Scarlet Trumpet' flowers on and off all summer.

evergreen ivies and the glossy bigleaf wintercreeper, planted away from the scorch of late-winter sun, hold their broad green leaves all winter.

large-flowered clematis — a great favorite is the 5-7 inch flowered white 'Henryi' — is so exotic you cannot believe it's a northern-air plant.

wisteria can be trained to look like a Chinese print, a fragrant Chinese print if there is such a thing.

Dutchman's pipe can make a curtain so dense, the nosiest of neighbors will never get a glimpse of you.

a grape vine trained over a patio trellis will cast shadowy green coolness to sit beneath and gourmet jelly, juice and jam all year.

climbing roses give you more flowery return per square inch of ground than almost any other plant.

annual vines, all inexpensive and easy to grow — morning glories and sweet peas, scarlet runner beans, gourds, a dozen others — are quick delight.

SOME VERSATILE USES FOR VINES

Vines should enhance not upholster your house, adorn not entangle your garden. Their very vigor is a danger. Undisciplined, the strongest can take

over a view, strangle a tree, choke an eavestrough, yank down a rainspout and otherwise tie your garden in knots. Therefore, learn their habits before you make your choice and place them where control is easy.

Use them to hide an ugly feature such as a stained old wall of an adjoining building.

Or to add beauty to a good feature, such as a crest of foamy white silver lace vine over a dark, black-brown wood fence.

Where space is limited, as it may be, at the side paths of your house, consider a narrow-based vine on a fence rather than a wider-spreading hedge.

For early summer loveliness, twine arches of pink roses along a white picket fence or use a tumble of them to cover and hold a steep bare bank.

If you love the unexpected, lead a delicate fine vine like a pink-flowered clematis up into a sturdy thick blue spruce, or a climbing hydrangea into the skeleton of a dead apple tree.

For fun for children, grow gourds or have a race to see who can grow the tallest runner beans — they will even survive being dug up every day to see if they are sprouting.

To soften the lumpiness of a cobblestone fence in the country, festoon it with native Virginia creeper that will turn a gorgeous burgundy red in the fall.

CULTURE

For perennial vines, prepare a deep planting hole (2 x 2 feet for a vine the size of a clematis, up to 3 x 3 feet for one as large as a bigleaf wintercreeper), mixing in fertilizer and humus as needed. (For further instructions, see CHAPTER 18.)

For vines on wide-eaved houses where there will be a dry band at the foundation that gets neither rain, snow or dew, place planting holes well forward and train the vines over it before they start up the house. Otherwise they will never grow well.

Put supports in place before planting and be prepared to tie up first shoots until the plant itself takes over. (For details on setting good supports, see CHAPTER 14.)

Water deeply as needed; prune to the shape you want and especially to keep growth from invading wood cornices, window frames and sills, screens, chimney pots and eavestroughs. If the chatter of birds bothers you — sparrows seem always to be meeting in your vines just when you're going to have a catnap — keep growth clipped close to the wall and thus reduce the possibility of a gossipy gathering.

Fertilize as you would other garden plants, in early spring and early summer. Vines and climbers are rarely bothered with pests and diseases if they are healthy and growing well. (For what to do if something dire does appear, see CHAPTER 19.)

With rampant growers — English ivy is like this in some locations and Virginia creeper just about everywhere — keep them away from bases of valued trees and shrubs. Otherwise they will be off and up the tree, choking its growth.

The culture of annual vines is much like growing any other seed. For early bloom, start indoors about 6 weeks before the last frost and planting out time.

Most may also be sown directly in the ground. Alternatively, buy prestarted plants from your nursery.

SPECIAL NOTES ON CARE OF CLIMBING ROSES

Caring for climbing roses is a job for a knight in prickle-proof armor with his visor down. Sharp, scratchy, sometimes just plain mean thorns snatch and tear at you. You will need a pair of good heavy gloves and your arms and legs well clad when you work with them. In spite of all this, they're well worth every drop of blood you shed. (See CHAPTER 26 on general planting and care of roses.)

Special details for climbers mainly cover how to get them successfully through the winter. Some gardeners tie them together and bend them down as close to the ground as possible without breaking, then cover them with earth or weighted evergreen boughs. Others, where winters are not too harsh, leave them standing upright and wrap them snugly in burlap or waterproof paper (never plastic — it scorches) and tie them up tightly against their support. (For recommended cultivars of climbing roses to grow, see CHAPTER 26.)

Special Notes on Everybody's Favorite, the Large-Flowered Clematis

Buy, if you can, container-grown, named plants in a nursery. Be gentle in handling them: they break easily.

RECOMMENDED CULTIVARS OF CLEMATIS
(for others, check nursery catalogues)

LARGE-FLOWERED (all *Zone 5*, except *'Jackmanii' which is Zone 4*)
C. 'Duchess of Edinburgh': double, white, blooms in late spring and on and off all summer.
C. *lawsoniana* 'Henryi': huge, creamy white single, free flowering on old wood at beginning of summer, again on new wood at the end.
C. 'Jackmanii': single, small but prolific purple flowers; also red and white cultivars; summer flowering, a favorite for veranda trellises.
C. 'Nelly Moser': single, mauve with a carmine streak on each petal; free flowering, in spring on old wood, in fall on new.

C. 'Ramona': single, lovely hyacinth blue, blooms in late spring and off and on all summer.

SINGLE-FLOWERED:

C. *montana rubens*: Zone 5; single, rose-pink, very flowery, in size between the large and smallest-flowered.
C. *tangutica*: 'Golden Clematis'; Zone 2; bright yellow, hardy, summer flowering, silvery seed heads, grows well in shade or sun.
C. *paniculata*: 'Sweet Autumn Clematis': Zone 2; a lacy plant with scads of green-white fragrant flowers in late summer; hardy; fluffy seed heads.

Choose a site that will put the roots in shade but allow topgrowth a minimum of 5-6 hours of sun. If shade at the root does not happen naturally, create it by planting low shrubs or perennials in front or laying flat stones over the root after planting. Or set an ordinary clay weeping-tile about 6 inches into the earth and plant the vine so that it grows through the shady tunnel of tile. If your soil tends to be acid, a shovelful of broken-up plaster or a handful of agricultural lime mixed in the soil beneath the roots is good practice. Gardeners on the borderline of hardiness for this elegant plant sometimes have good luck placing it on a north or east wall warmed by the heat from inside.

Set in a deeply prepared hole — 2 x 2 feet is about right — so that the crown is 2-3 inches below the surface. Tie shoots carefully to the support, which is best set before planting.

Water well if weather dry — this is especially important near house foundations which are usually very sharply drained. Mulches help too — straw or evergreen branches, compost or rotted manure are good, but avoid acid materials such as some peat mosses or pine needles. (For details of these and other techniques, see CHAPTER 18.)

Fertilize in early spring and early summer with 5-10-5, according to manufacturer's directions.

Pruning of clematis is clouded in controversy with the experts giving conflicting advice about what is best to do. Most favor this plan:

those cultivars that bloom in late spring and early summer on old wood, and again in late summer on new wood, should be selectively pruned after the first flowering to reduce some of the old wood and to encourage new;

those vines that bloom in late summer — obviously on new wood — should be pruned back to within 2 feet of the ground in early spring as the buds break;

native clematis, grown in a wild garden, should be allowed to roam free, unpruned.

The Temperamental and Strong Willed Wisterias

"Temperamental" because they so often refuse to bloom; "strong willed" because they climb and clamber with almost overpowering strength. But withal, so handsome, hundreds of gardeners are willing to take a chance on growing them successfully.

Wisteria.

They look their best led up a strong wire to just below the roof line and eaves-trough, then trained along a horizontal wire at right angles to the first. With this scheme, the long, beautifully pendulous flowers drip downwards over the wall of the house and are at their most elegant as you look up. Supports must be very strong to carry their heavy weight and new growth threatening eavestroughs or roof shingles should be summarily pruned back.

The more commonly grown species — the Chinese wisteria, Zone 6 — has lilac or creamy white flowers and blooms, when it pleases to, in early spring. The Japanese cultivars, Zone 8b—*W. floribunda* 'Issai' is a beauty—sometimes with 3-4-foot purple panicles, are just plain spectacular. Foliage of both is open, lovely to look at and ferny.

Unfortunately, many well-cared-for wisterias never bloom and, as one gardener said sadly, "The only way to be sure of getting a bloomer is to dig up one you see flowering in somebody else's garden." Severely pruning the roots by digging a 2-foot deep trench closely around them and backfilling it with good earth mixed with superphosphate, or of scaring the plant into bloom by radically pruning the top growth, sometimes works. For the rest, a program of sensible garden care, especially in seeing that they are planted in full sun, not fed with high-nitrogen fertilizer, which could encourage leaf growth at the expense of flowers; being patient if winter kills the flower buds, and waiting for the vine to reach blooming maturity — sometimes 7 years — may win you the victory you will by then deserve.

6 PERENNIAL VINES FOR FINE FOLIAGE

Boston Ivy, *Parthenocissus tricuspidata*, Zone 5, deciduous; vigorous; self-supporting; does well in cities; brilliant scarlet in fall; can become rampant; not recommended for wood walls.

Dutchman's Pipe, *Aristolochia durior*, Zone 4, deciduous; huge, dense leaves, especially good for screening.

Engelmann's Virginia Creeper, *Parthenocissus quinquefolia* 'Engelmannii', Zone 2b, deciduous; a small-leaved version of the native Virginia creeper, self-supporting, brilliant red in fall.

English Ivy, *Hedera helix*, many, Zone 5, evergreen; glossy green; self-supporting; very strong; plant on north or east to avoid winter sunburn; not recommended for wood walls.

Fiveleaf Akebia, *Akebia quinata*, Zone 6b, deciduous; vigorous, fine-leaved; flowers small but fragrant; neat.

Wintercreeper, *Euonymus fortunei vegeta*, Zone 4, evergreen; handsome; vigorous; broad-leaved; one of the best; needs support.

3 PERENNIAL VINES FOR BRIGHT OR EDIBLE FRUIT

Chinese Bittersweet, *Celastrus loeseneri*, Zone 3, deciduous; rampant, twiny, fruit on leafless branches makes wonderful winter decorations indoors, need both a male and female vine for berries.

Firethorn, *Pyracantha coccinea*, many, Zone 5, semi-evergreen; handsome in winter with great bunches of bright orange berries through dark foliage, needs support.

Grape, *Vitis*, for recommended cultivars of commercial grapes, see Chapter 12; the wild riverbank grape, *Vitis riparia*, is grown in the North Central states; vigorous; fragrant; easy to grow; may need to net ripening grapes against marauding birds; no successful preventive known for marauding boys.

6 PERENNIAL VINES FOR FINE FLOWERS (all deciduous)

Climbing Hydrangea, *H. petiolaris*; Zone 4; great flat clusters of white lacy flowers in early summer; glossy leaves; a strong twisting shape; outstanding; slow to get started, but a thousand times worth the wait; sun or shade.

Honeysuckle, *Lonicera*

L. 'Dropmore Scarlet Trumpet', Zone 3b, masses of bright scarlet trumpets, from June till freeze-up, very hardy.

L. periclymenum 'Belgica', Early, Dutch honeysuckle, Zone 2b, pale yellow and pink, free flowering in June, very fragrant.

L. heckrotti, 'Goldflame', Zone 4, showy red and yellow all summer, fragrant.

L. japonica 'Halliana', Hall's Honeysuckle, Zone 5, semi-evergreen, white flowers changing to yellow, fragrant.

L. glaucescens, Zone 2, native of the Midwest, flowers yellow-tinged-red.

Jasmine, *Jasminum* (mainly grown on the west coast)

J. officinale, Summer-flowering Jasmine, Zone 8b, white, vigorous very fragrant, needs support, full sun.

J. nudiflorum, Winter Jasmine, Zone 8b, small yellow flowers in winter, prune after blooming.

Silver Lace Vine, *Polygonum aubertii*, Zone 6b, a joy in September with its froth of small flowers, rapid growing once established, excellent for an unhandsome fence.

Sweet Pea (Perennial), *Lathyrus latifolius*, Zone 2, a climber or rambler, hardy, bright cerise flowers in early summer, needs support, not fragrant.

Trumpet Vine, *Campsis radicans*, Zone 5, a heavy strong vine with masses of orange-scarlet flowers in summer, needs sturdy support and ruthless pruning as it gets old.

6 ANNUAL VINES FOR FLOWERS OR FUN (maybe both?)

For others, consult seed catalogues and do a little adventuring.

Cup and Saucer Vine, Cathedral Bells, *Cobaea scandens*, tendrilly and graceful, purple and green flowers; plant seed indoors, *on its edge*, 6 weeks before planting time outside, or buy prestarted.

Gourds, great fun for youngsters, buy mixed seed and sow directly in the ground when weather is frost free and warm, or prestart indoors. An amusing one is the dishcloth gourd, or luffa, whose fruit looks like a rolled-up sponge.

Morning Glory, *Ipomea*, favorites everywhere. Comes in the familiar Heavenly Blue, Super Giant Gentian Blue with flowers more than 5 inches across, Candy Pink, White Magic and the fabulously large-flowered Japanese strains with blooms 8 inches across if you pinch off side buds. All bloom earlier if started indoors in peat pots, which can be transplanted directly into the ground. Nick the side of each seed with a sharp knife and soak overnight before planting.

Scarlet Runner Beans, *Phaseolus coccinea*, and its purple sister, the hyacinth bean, *Dolichos lablab* produce both flowers and beans which, to be really tasty, must be picked from well-watered, well-fertilized vines when they are first ready: old ones are tough and tasteless.

Sweet Peas, *Lathyrus odoratus*; grow better in some parts than others. Check for cultivars best for you. I like the Royal Family and Cuthbertson strains which come in lovely colors. Plant in a deep ditch, 1 foot wide by 2 feet deep, in well-prepared soil, just as soon as you can work the ground in spring. When about 4-5 inches tall, tie gently up to a supported fish net or special plant net, or to twiggy brush pushed firmly into the ground. Fill in soil as they grow till it is level with the surrounding ground. Water deeply if no rain and feed regularly, but above all, to keep in bloom, pick off all flowers.

Black-eyed Susan Vine, *Thunbergia alata*, a dainty drooper or climber, covered all summer with white, yellow or orange flowers, looks smashing mixed with yellow marigolds, scarlet geraniums and white petunias in a brown wood window box.

229

26 ROSES

Beautiful but deceptive, roses are the sirens of the garden. Their thorns prick and scratch at you; their bushes have little or no design value in the landscape; their leaves are not as handsome as the thick glossy foliage of many other garden plants; for best growth, they need regular skillful attention and care; often, seemingly for no reason at all, they turn up their toes and die over winter.

But, in spite of all this woe and keening, they are still the undisputed queens of the garden. Their glorious flowers are, for many gardeners, the most beautiful in the world, their fragrance the most sweet and they move men to poetry, song, romance and bewitched admiration as no other flower ever has or probably ever will.

If you are one of this happy band (and the word "men" in the above sentence means the whole human race), it behooves you to read on.

THE THINKING TO DO BEFORE YOU CHOOSE ROSES FOR YOUR GARDEN

Do you live where there is a reasonable expectation that roses will grow well for you?

Roses are probably the most popular garden plant in all temperate parts of the country and, with some special care in selecting hardy cultivars and in providing successful winter protection, they grow in some of the intemperate parts too. In Flin Flon, northern Manitoba (Zone 1a), where they have early frost and temperatures drop to 50° below, a rose buff grows many beautiful roses. One year he had the fantastic good luck of cutting a perfect bloom of creamy Peace — the most dazzling hybrid tea rose of all time — on October 27. There is a generous list of shrub roses developed especially for the windswept, bitterly cold Northern plains of the United States and the Canadian prairies, and continued research is going on to develop new cultivars and successful growing techniques. If you wish special advice about growing roses where you live, consult your nearest government agent or nurseryman (see PART V, Where to Get Special Help).

Have you a place for them in your garden?

There are many kinds, some hardier than others:

hybrid teas: are the most familiar; bushy; some with single flowers like the thinnest fine china, more with doubled petals like silk velvet; many fragrant, especially in the early morning; dozens of colors. They look best in a specially placed rose bed, growing by themselves. For those who may need such vital information, these are the toss-one-with-a-kiss-to-your-lover roses. Need careful winter protection in most parts of the country.

floribundas: are also bushy, covered with clusters of flowers bunched like an old-fashioned nosegay. Easier to care for than hybrid teas and more useful for design, as they can make a flowery border to a walk or a low hedge.

grandifloras: are taller than hybrid teas but have similar flowers, though more of them, and are of about the same hardiness range. In a recent All-America poll of roses on the market for more than 5 years, rating flowers, foliage and general plant performance, 'Queen Elizabeth', a beautiful clear pink grandiflora scored 9.3 points out of a possible 10 and was beaten to the top only by the famous Peace, with 9.4 points.

standard roses: I'm going to have to eat my words about roses not contributing much to the design of a garden. As formal accents standing alone, these are superb. Basically they are a bush type rose grafted onto a long upright single stem. In bloom they look like a beauteous bouquet. Need special winter care in almost all parts of the country.

shrub roses: are the hardiest of all. Some stretch long arching canes upwards and mix well with other plants in borders. Individual flowers are not so showy as some other kinds, but total effect is delightful. Some are fragrant.

climbers and ramblers: one goes up, the other goes sideways or down. They clamber up a wall, arch a trellis, weave brilliant color along a fence, or cascade over a bank. Relatively hardy.

miniatures: the fairy queens of the rose world, tiny blossoms no bigger than your thumbnail on bushes no taller than the span of your hand. An endearing hobby plant that takes only a few square feet for a generous collection.

Space needs of the various kinds vary. Be sure to give them what they need to grow well. Hybrid teas, floribundas and grandifloras need 24 inches; shrub roses, climbers and ramblers should be planted 5-8 feet apart; standard roses need about 4-6 square feet and miniatures should be 9-12 inches apart.

Roses, to grow vigorously and bloom prolifically, need full sun but will do moderately well in 5-6 hours a day. It is often possible to increase sunniness in your garden by judicious pruning.

Is the soil well-drained?

They will not tolerate soggy soil, so choose a place where rain does not stand for more than an hour. There are two cures for a questionably damp situation, if it is your only possible site: dig out the earth to a depth of 2-3 feet, lay weeping tile through it, draining to a lower dry well; or, if conditions are slightly damp but not boggy, simply raise the level of the whole bed. Many gardeners do this as a precaution even when they do not have a serious drainage problem.

Is the soil fertile?

Any good garden soil will grow roses. If yours is too heavy or too sandy to be in this class, add, to a depth of 2 feet, peat moss, compost, leafmold, rotted manure. If regular barnyard manure is not available, use dried sheep or cow manure, bloodmeal, fish meal, tankage or urea formaldehyde. (See CHAPTER 18: How to Improve Soil, for recommended technique.) At the same time, mix in a complete fertilizer — 5-10-5 is a good one — at the rate of 2 pounds per 100 square feet. This preparation is best done in the fall for spring planting, to allow for settling and for a healthy chemical action to build up before you plant your roses in it. If you must do your digging and mixing in spring for spring planting, allow at least 4 weeks between preparation and planting.

Is there plenty of air circulation around the site?
Not too much wind?

Some of the common and most disfiguring troubles of roses stem from fungus disease which develops easily in still, moist air. Good circulation dries off the foliage and discourages this growth. Also, climbers should be fastened well out from walls so that air can move behind them and prevent excessively drying heat from bouncing back onto the canes.

Too much wind damages roses during the growing season by tearing at leaves and petals, but its greatest injury is during winter when gales can break canes and dry out bark.

Can you grow your roses
where their roots will not have to compete with nearby trees,
shrubs and hedges?

This is not as vital for shrub roses as for others, but all roses prefer a free root-run. If you must place them near invasive plants, you would be wise first to dig a narrow trench 2 feet deep between them and your new rose bed and in it set a piece of galvanized iron to block wandering roots.

Have you the time to give them regular care?

It takes minutes or hours, depending on how many bushes you have, but a rough idea of the care that will be needed is that 24 bushes, well planted and growing vigorously, take about an hour's regular care weekly, with a little more at pruning and feeding time, and again when you prepare them for winter and uncover them in spring. This includes time needed for spraying or dusting against pests and disease. You can skip a week or two at holiday time, if someone will come in and cut off the dead flowers for you and water the beds if the weather is dry; but roses are not flowers for people who take off for the north woods all summer.

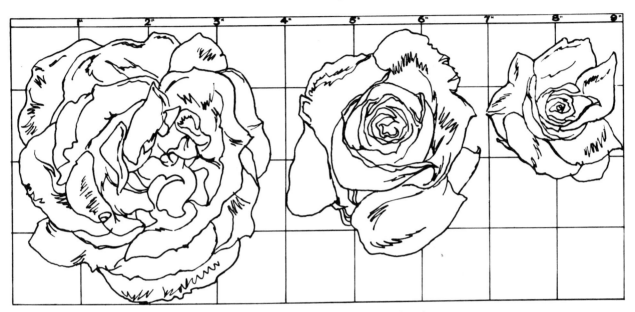

Relative sizes of three kinds of popular roses: grandiflora, hybrid tea, floribunda.

HOW TO BUY

Newcomers to roses would be wise to do a little research before plumping for a planting. Read the catalogues, especially of nurseries specializing in roses. Have a swoon or two over the gorgeous illustration. You will find any rose *you* grow endearing, but looking at a picture of a perfect rose obviously grown by an expert will spark your ambition. Visit rose gardens in public parks, at nurseries, in your neighbors' gardens. Join the American or Canadian Rose Society and get their excellent bulletins and annual handbooks. Send to your government department of agriculture for pamphlets.

If you plan to order by mail, get your list in early. Popular cultivars often sell out quickly. If you are on a snug budget, buy the older, tried-and-trues rather than the new more expensive cultivars.

If you are buying in a nursery or garden shop, the dime store or supermarket, know what to look for. Bare-root plants, usually wrapped with moss and heavy paper with a cheerful come-on picture on the package, can originate either in a local nursery where they will have been grown under conditions close to your own, or they may be obtained from growers in other regions whose conditions are a far cry from yours. The better buy for the long run is the stock from the local nursery. Choose a plant that shows a bud or two just emerging.

Container-grown roses, if they have been properly cared for since potting up, are an excellent buy. You don't have to hurry them into the ground for fear of drying up and transplanting from pot to plot causes a minimum of shock. Also, the move can be any time from spring to fall.

If, as most rose enthusiasts eventually do, you decide to import some roses from specialists in another country, it is well worth the extra cost to have them flown in by air. They are fresher and much more ready to begin growing in your garden right away.

Whatever you buy, the canes should be sturdy and green. Often they are waxed to reduce drying out. They should not be too twiggy or broken, or be scarred. With the bare-root ones you will be able to see if the roots are heavy enough to balance the top and are in good condition.

WHEN TO PLANT

Most gardeners prefer to plant in early spring, although in most temperate parts of the country (Zone 5 and up) it is also possible to plant in the fall and have your new roses established before winter. Container-grown roses can be planted any time during the growing season. Some gardeners buy their roses in the fall because they believe they are at their best at that time, then unwrap and bury them completely in the ground, to lift and plant them in the spring.

Preplanting know-how

If packaged plants, unwrap immediately and examine to be sure they are in good condition, not dried out or broken. If only the roots seem dry, soak them in water for 1-2 hours before planting. If the whole plant looks dry but not dead, put it all in water for a couple of hours and then cover it with moist soil for a day or two till it becomes turgid again. If it is dead, send it back.

If the plants look alright but you cannot plant right away, dig a hole or trench in moist ground in a shady place, lay the roots in it, cover them with soil and tramp it down firmly. Water. This will hold them safely for a week or two.

When you come to plant, never leave your bushes exposed to sun or wind. Keep them in the shade, covered with wet newspaper or burlap.

Go carefully over the whole plant and cut off any broken or bruised roots or canes.

HOW TO PLANT

Dig a hole about 18 inches wide, 14 inches deep and mound a half spadeful of prepared soil in the bottom.

Balance bush on the mound, spreading the roots downward — make a bigger hole if necessary, to prevent crowding roots. Set so that the graft union is 1 inch *below* the surface of the ground. (Most roses are grafted on tougher rootstock and the union of this and the bush above is an easily visible lumpy place on the main stem.) Backfill with prepared soil and jiggle the plant gently to settle the roots. When completely covered, tamp the earth down firmly and water deeply. Fill up the hole without further tamping or watering and mound soil 8-10 inches above the surface of the surrounding ground. If planting in spring, leave this for 10 days then remove. If fall planting, leave mounded earth in place till growth begins in spring. See next page.

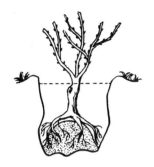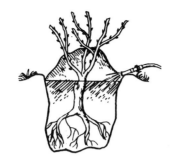

Planting roses: set bush in prepared hole with graft 1 inch below surface; mound soil 8-10 inches for 10 days in spring, overwinter if planting in fall.

ONGOING CARE

Fertilizing: You will not need to add extra fertilizer to your new bed the first year, but thereafter use a chemical fertilizer — 5-10-5 is good — or special rose food in early spring at the rate of 2 pounds to 100 square feet. In mid-spring add another pound at the same rate and another just before bloom begins. Water in. Don't let fertilizer touch the leaves or stems; it could burn them.

Watering: During dry spells, saturate the ground thoroughly by setting a special soaker on your hose nozzle or wrap in an old cloth so that water will run slowly over the surface of the beds. Be careful *not* to wet the foliage, but soak *deeply*. To encourage hardening of the wood before winter, reduce watering in the fall but water deeply once again just before freeze-up.

Mulches: Covering your rose beds with a 2-inch layer of moist peat moss, buckwheat hulls, shredded pine bark or other mulch material retains moisture in the soil and discourages weeds. Put it on as the weather gets hot and drying in early summer.

Spraying: Although many gardeners spray rose bushes weekly during the growing season with a combined insecticide and fungicide which they buy already mixed or make up themselves, recommended practice now is to use only a fungicide regularly to *prevent* disease and only to spray for insects when you find them invading your roses. This is to prevent the indiscriminate killing off of the Good Guys of the insect world, who may well be doing a better job of controlling the Bad Guys all over your garden than you are. (For recommended measures for pest and disease control, see CHAPTER 19).

Pruning: This is almost a skill in itself and I can promise you that a dozen expert rose gardeners will have a dozen different ideas about how it should be done. Basic ground rules are:

cut back winterkilled branches in the spring on all roses (these are not only the obviously dead ones but also any that may be green outside yet have a little dark pith in the centre, for they are on the way out and will be dead before summer cometh).

cut out twiggy crisscross growth on all roses in spring.

in the fall, when you prepare the bushes for winter, cut back any too-long canes that could whip around in winter wind.

except for shrubs, which you may want for their bright fruit in fall, cut off all dead flowers to the first or second eye at the base of a leaf with five leaflets (with young bushes, where you want to leave as much growth as possible, just snip the flower head off). Make this cut so that the eye at the top is on the outside of the bush.

cut out weaker canes in spring, leaving 3-4 of the strongest, for as long as possible. American Rose Society research reports that a developing shoot is dependent on food stored in the parent cane to sustain its growth until it is 12 inches long, so the longer such canes can be left the better the flowering shoot.

seek and cut out all suckers as close to the main stem as possible — these will be coming up from *below* the graft union. To do this, gently clear the soil away at the base — a hosing with water does this well — and expose the graft and any suckers. After cutting them off, leave the union exposed to the sun for 2-3 weeks, to encourage new canes to break above the union, then cover again with soil as the weather gets warm.

With shrub roses, which bloom on old wood, take out only one or two of the oldest branches at ground level after they have bloomed. If they have attractive hips you want to keep over winter, do it in spring.

With climbers, which bloom on new shoots on old wood, prune only weak and dead canes; shorten the laterals (the little side branches which flower) about two thirds and, as the bushes age, cut out at ground level enough of the toughest old canes to leave only four of the best.

With ramblers and those climbers which bloom well only on wood of the previous year, cut back after flowering to a half dozen of the strongest new canes.

With standard roses, take out any weak or winterkilled canes in spring and prune to a bouquet-shaped head, leaving 3-4 buds to a cane. Some further pruning may be needed in the fall to produce a head that can be given adequate winter protection.

With miniatures, prune as for hybrid teas but pretend you're Alice in Wonderland gone tiny.

Seal all fresh pruning cuts with a pruning paint bomb.

HOW TO PROTECT AGAINST WINTERKILL

First, grow healthy vigorous plants.

Second, do not feed after early summer, for this produces tender, easily damaged wood. Reduce watering during fall, but soak deeply once just before freeze-up.

Third, when ground is frozen, cut back any too-long canes on hybrid teas, floribundas, grandifloras, standards, miniatures. Burn the debris or wrap for the garbage — don't leave it around to breed trouble in your garden.

Fourth, spray or dust with all-purpose insecticide and fungicide, mound bush roses with earth or sawdust up 8-10 inches — collars can be bought to hold this in place — and on top of this pile straw or leaves. Some gardeners find it helps also to fence the whole bed with 14-16-inch wire and backfill the enclosed space with leaves, laying branches on top to prevent the leaves blowing away. Others are using, very successfully, the new plastic Igloo, a tent of three double plastic bags partially filled with water. The bags freeze and thaw as the weather dictates, but research has proved that the temperature inside never drops below 28°F, a survival temperature for roses. If mice are a problem with you, put mouse bait inside the Igloo and under any leaf or straw mulch. With standards and climbers, if you live in easy-winter areas, simply wrap in burlap or cornstalks and tie well to a sturdy support. In below-zero parts of the country, dig halfway round base of plant, approximately 2 feet from the stem, cutting the roots on that side. Tip rootball over and either mound all with earth or cover with heavy burlap weighted to keep it from blowing away.

EPILOGUE

These housekeeping details may well seem overpowering if you have read them all at once; spread over a year — some longer than that — the tasks will really be simple, and the reward well worth it. When you yourself have grown just one rose from its ugly-duckling beginning bit of thorny bush to its wondrous flowering, you have joined the worshipful company of dyed-in-the-wool rosarians and there is no rarer, happier breed.

236

PEST AND DISEASE CONTROL PROGRAM FOR ROSES

Buy only healthy stock in the first place, and give it good care.

Keep rose beds clean, rake up and destroy old leaves and prunings to reduce places where fungi could develop. This is especially important in the fall.

Apply, in early spring, a dormant spray of lime-sulphur (1 in 9 parts of water).

Apply a fungicide every 7-14 days mixed with ½ teaspoon household detergent per gallon to improve the spreading action — rose leaves are waxy and difficult to wet. In mid or late summer, when powdery mildew is likely to start, include a mildew control with above materials. Do not spray when weather very hot. Most effective spraying is done before a rain and to cover new leaves as they develop. Be sure to cover both the upper and lower surfaces of the leaves. Dusting may be substituted for spraying — it's easier to do — but spraying is more effective. Dust or spray only when the air is still.

Add spray insecticides and miticides to one or more of the fungicide applications only when insects appear (aphids, mites often known as red spiders, caterpillars, beetles and other leaf feeders.)

Commercial rose sprays and dusts contain all-purpose mixtures of fungicides, insecticides and miticides, and are especially useful when you need only small quantities. If you use them, read the label and follow manufacturer's directions implicitly.

Some gardeners who, with some reason, abhor the use of chemical sprays or dusts — and they are, after all, deadly poisons — swear by interplanting their hybrid tea roses with garlic or marigolds to prevent pests. If this appeals to you, be alert or you may find roses with the garlic in the salad dressing and garlic with roses in your party bouquets.

Popular Roses Recommended by the American Rose Society

Hybrid Teas

Chrysler Imperial, dark red	Eclipse, medium yellow
Fragrant Cloud, bright red	Pascali, white
Tropicana, orange-red	Garden Party, white
Charlotte Armstrong, light red and deep pink	Matterhorn, white
Mister Lincoln, medium red	Burnaby, white
Royal Highness, light pink	Peace, yellow blend
South Seas, medium pink	Tiffany, pink blend
King's Ransom, deep yellow	Confidence, pink blend

Floribundas

Spartan, orange-red	Iceberg, white
Europeana, dark red	Ivory Fashion, white
Frensham, dark red	Saratoga, white
Sarabande, orange-red	Little Darling, yellow blend
Betty Prior, medium pink	Roman Holiday, red blend
Gay Princess, light pink	Apricot Nectar, apricot blend

Grandifloras

Queen Elizabeth, medium pink	Camelot, medium pink
Montezuma, orange-red	John S. Armstrong, dark red
Carrousel, dark red	

Climbers

Aloha, medium pink

Blaze, medium red

Blossomtime, medium pink

Cadenza, dark red

Coralita, orange-red

Don Juan, dark red

Golden Showers, medium yellow

New Dawn, light pink

Paul's Scarlet Climber, medium red

Rhonda, medium pink

Shrub and Old-fashioned Roses

Austrian Copper, scarlet-orange

Roger Lambelin, red blend

Frau Karl Druschki, white

Harison's Yellow, deep yellow

Paul Neyron, medium pink

Sea Foam, white

Rugosa Roses

R. rugosa: 'F. J. GROOTENDORST'; double, red

'GROOTENDORST PINK'; double, pink } fringed; 3-6 feet; Zone 3

'GROOTENDORST WHITE'; double, white

'THERESE BUGNET'; double, soft pink; fragrant; 3-6 feet; Zone 2

'WASAGAMING'; double, lavender-pink, cabbage type; 3-6 feet; Zone 2

Miniature Roses

Small (10 inches high, with small flowers)

'BABY DARLING'; orange blend

'CINDERELLA'; white

'CORALIN'; medium red

'MIDGET'; medium red

'PERLA DE ALCANADA'; bright red

'PERLA DE MONTSERRAT'; pink

Larger (heavier bushes, larger flowers and foliage, yet an overall petite stature)

'BABY MASQUERADE'; red and yellow blend

'DWARFKING'; medium red

'EASTER MORNING'; white

'JUNE TIME'; light pink

'PEACHY'; apricot blend

'YELLOW DOLL'; medium yellow

Tree Roses

'ENA HARKNESS' (H.T.); crimson scarlet

'KORDES PERFECTA' (H.T.); cream flushed crimson

'MONTEZUMA' (Grand.); blend of red, orange and salmon

'PEACE' (H.T.); rich yellow, pink margins

'TROPICANA' (H.T.); vibrant orange-red

Fine Rose Gardens to Visit

California: Berkeley Municipal Rose Garden, Euclid Avenue at Bayview Place, Berkeley

Rose Hills Memorial Park, Pageant of Roses Garden, 3900 South Workman Mill Road, Whittier

Idaho: Municipal Rose Garden, Julia Davis Park, 512 South Fourth Avenue, Boise

Louisiana: New Orleans City Park Rose Garden, New Orleans

Minnesota: Minneapolis Municipal Rose Garden, Roseway Road, Minneapolis

Illinois: Grant Park Rose Garden, Balbo and Jackson, Lakeshore and Columbus Drive, Chicago

Missouri: Missouri Botanical Rose Garden, 2315 Tower Grove Avenue, St. Louis

New York: New York Botanical Garden, Bronx Park, Bronx, New York

Brooklyn Botanic Garden, 1000 Washington Avenue, Brooklyn, New York
Ohio: Columbus Park of Roses, 4000 North High Street, Columbus (the Garden of the American Rose Society, with 450 cultivars, 35,000 roses)
Oklahoma: Tulsa Municipal Rose Garden, 2435 South Peoria, Tulsa
Oregon: International Rose Test Garden, 400 S.W. Kingston Avenue, Portland
Lewis & Clark College Memorial Rose Garden, 0615 S.W. Palatine Road, Portland
Pennsylvania: Hershey Rose Gardens & Arboretum, Hershey
Mellon Park Rose Garden, 1047 Shady Avenue, Pittsburgh
Texas: Houston Municipal Rose Garden, Herman Drive, Houston
Municipal Park Rose Garden, West Front at Peach Street, Tyler

Canada: The Royal Botanical Gardens, Hamilton, Ontario
Little Mountain Park, West Thirty-third Avenue and Cambie Street, Vancouver
The Niagara Parks Commission, Niagara Falls, Ontario
The Central Experimental Farm, Canada Department of Agriculture, Ottawa, Ontario
Europe: Bagatelle, Paris, France
Baden-Baden, Baden-Baden, Germany
The National Rose Society, Chiswell Green Lane, St. Albans, Hertfordshire, England
City of Belfast International Rose Trials, Belfast, Ireland
Parque del Retiro, Madrid, Spain
Concours International des Roses Nouvelles, Geneva, Switzerland
International Rozen Concours, The Hague, Holland
Roseto di Roma, The Aventine, Rome, Italy

If You Want to Be a Real Rose Buff, Join a Rose Society

Membership in a special society of a flower you particularly treasure is money well and happily spent. The American Rose Society, with members all over the United States and Canada, has headquarters at 4048 Roselea Place, Columbus, Ohio 43214.

Benefits of belonging:
- publications, a monthly magazine and *The American Rose Annual*
- advice on rose problems from experts located in various parts of the country
- descriptions of all new roses being introduced in the United States and a national rating for all roses currently grown in the United States
- two national conventions and rose shows each year
- the loan of books by mail
- membership card that entitles you to attend rose shows and rose gardens and meet rose-growers all over the world
- list of all public rose gardens in the United States that you may visit

27 PERENNIALS AND BIENNIALS

PERENNIALS

These are the plants — some exotic, some startlingly beautiful, some just the faithful Marthas of the garden — that grow and flower in spring and summer, die down when winter comes, then (ideally) burst into bloom again next season. Some, such as the peonies, really do. Others, with timely rejuvenating by division, live a long time. Others are fine for a few years then turn up their toes and pass out, on or over, depending on which direction a perennial takes when it leaves this life. But even the short-span ones contribute a dazzle to the garden that is especially dramatic in the time between the great burst of flowers in spring and the brilliant summer blooming of the annuals. Others are the bright mainstays of late summer and fall right up to frost.

Their reasonable initial cost is also an asset and some simple green-fingering can easily increase them. Care is average and follows any good garden program, but for successful continuing growth must be given at certain times of the year. And let's face it, few perennials grow hammock-high.

The list of perennials is a long one — all colors of the rainbow and some you don't often see in a rainbow — and their habits diverse. The best way to decide which are the ones for your garden is to read this chapter through, consult nursery catalogues and visit gardens near you.

Send to your nearest Agricultural Extension Service for pamphlets (usually free or at a small charge). The Superintendent of Documents, Government Printing Office, Washington, D.C. 20402, also has excellent publications.

Everybody's favorites

When thousands of American gardeners grow millions of plants every year, some naturally become favorites. After querying experts in every area of the country, we know now what these are. Here, and in our other pictures, are some of the best beloved: graceful white birches and tall blue spruces; feathered junipers and sweetly-scented lilacs; the lovely rose; sprightly crocus and sleek tulips; handsome dahlias and silk-petaled peonies; red geraniums and white petunias (although pink geraniums and pink petunias run them a close second); for all gardens, the dashing 'Morden Pink' lythrum; where they're hardy, the enchanting flowering dogwood, dramatic rhododendrons and azaleas.

When you ask why they're favorites, you learn that they're easy to grow, long lived over the years or seasons, and all gardeners think they're beautiful. But even more valued is that each has an indefinable, endearing quality that makes it, without quibble or question, a favorite wherever it grows.

Sprightly crocus in the snow, pure and startling hocus-pocus.

*A flowery Maytime welcome
at a front door:
Hillier crab apple.*

A favorite for years, fragrant 'Festiva Maxima' peony.

Stars of Appalachian and Northwest Coast gardens, rhododendrons can also be grown well in many other parts of the country.

World famous 'Peace' rose, strong, tall and glossy green in leaf, handsome cream-brushed-with-pink blooms.

Flowers of the shade-loving impatience turn toward the light and bloom luxuriantly all summer.

'Frost and Flame', a lordly bearded iris standing tall above its arrowed leaves.

'Luxer', a handsome dahlia, pictured here in a seaside garden but growable everywhere.

'Landmark', a superb, award-winning gladiolus. Lovely in bouquets.

Lilacs top the polls everywhere.
Many are fragrant, some are double and all are lovely.

*The vibrant 'Morden Pink' lythrum,
favored everywhere for its dashing summer color.*

*Prized coast-to-coast
for its bouncy creamy blooms in May,
the familiar snowball bush (Zone 2).*

*A true Johnny Appleseedling,
found by chance almost 175 years ago
— the McIntosh apple.*

*My grandmother's junket bowl,
planted for all the year
with cheering green.*

Gardening indoors

A green and flowery bridge from
fall's first frost till spring's
greening is the best tonic in the
world and, happily for gardeners,
someone a long time ago invented
window glass and furnaces and,
more lately, fluorescent lights. Now
it's possible to grow glossy-leaved
beauties such as the tropical
philodendrons or a dainty miniature
ivy and dozens of flowers—from
the favorite African violet to the
glorious amaryllis—while the
mercury plummets to zero outside.
When you are sure that spring will
never come, you can have it right
on your windowsill, with daffodils,
hyacinths, tulips and pots of the
little violet-scented iris. If you have
a touch of sheikh in you, you can
make a miniature desert with
intriguing cactus. If you have a
streak of Scot, you can start seeds
indoors under an inexpensive light
unit two months before you could
sow them outdoors, and grow
dozens of new plants from cuttings
at almost no cost at all. Be a green
and flowery bridge-builder, you'll
enjoy it.

*Flowers from a greenhouse,
the florist or to grow yourself;
some of them are short-lived,
others bloom for years.*

A miniature desert scene with fascinating prickly cacti. It's even possible, with a little tender loving care, to coax them to bloom.

The best tonic in the world — a winter window garden all abloom with gaily flowering bulbs and plants, fascinating foliages.

Happy matchmates — African violets, ferns and ivy.

Everyone's Christmas favorite: the brilliant poinsettia with practically-no-care cultivars that bloom well for four to five months.

WHERE AND HOW TO USE PERENNIALS

Think of a Versatile Border

Perennials mix happily with spring and summer bulbs, small flowering shrubs and annuals added for quick color. Well planned, you can have something coming into bloom from earliest spring to latest fall (see Calendar, CHAPTER 1). Such a border can be as long or as wide as the space you have, but a good workable size would be about 25 feet long and no less than 7 feet wide. Ideally it should run east and west to get full sun.

Perennials, to be their best, must have lots of light, air and moisture, and should not have to compete with tree or shrub roots underground, nor overhanging heavy branches. It's possible to create a double-purpose break between a background hedge or shrub planting and your perennials by setting the border far enough forward to make a path of stepping stones, or wood chips, or a strip of grass just the width of your mower. Such access to the back of the border makes it far easier to care for the plants. It's also possible to keep roots of background trees and shrubs from invading the border by digging down and inserting a 2-3 foot wide barrier strip of galvanized iron as deep as you can reasonably go.

As Part of Other Plantings

If a whole border planned around perennials does not fit your scheme, think of using them here and there among other plantings. Clumps or masses of one kind in one color are more effective than a single plant spotted here and there. Be sure to consider the all-season look of the plants you choose — coming into bloom, in bloom, how long they stay in bloom, if there is an interesting aftermath like odd seed heads or fall color. Know the few shy ones, such as Virginia bluebells, poppies and bleeding heart which, after blooming, disappear leaving a blank space to be filled with shallow rooting annuals.

Let them Divert Your Glance

Tall perennials are particularly useful to hide something — try a row of raspberry pink delphiniums along an old garage wall; a patch of golden glow at the corner of a toolshed, some delicately blurry-flowered meadow rue along the edge of a ditch, a dozen brilliant cardinal flowers at the rim of a boggy place.

Use some of the medium height ones — iris, day lilies, lupines — to soften the sharp margin of a driveway or a walk; an underplanting of dainty astilbe, if you can provide moist shade under a big tree. Tall, spiky lythrum can make a brilliant summer meadow of a normally weedy place.

Low-height perennials — pinks, candytuft, rabbit's ears, the thymes, a dozen others — make tidy-textured ground covers, edgings to a bed or plantings beside a path.

Play up the Design of the Plant Itself

Visit gardens and nurseries where you can see perennials at their best, then visualize them in your own garden. Notice spike shapes like delphiniums, aconite; mass shapes, such as Michaelmas daisies and phlox; the bold beauty of poppies, peonies, hibiscus; feathery light flowers like coral bells, baby's breath, meadow rue; daisy-faced ones like painted and shasta daisies, 'mums and asters. Individually placed, all have value because of their special character.

HOW TO BUY

Both prestarted plants and seeds are available from nurseries. Send for catalogues — most list cultivars, colors, expected height at maturity and some also give hardiness indications. Seed can be imported by mail from anywhere in the world without plant inspection. Seed saved from your own plants, unless you're carrying on a controlled breeding program, is seldom satisfactory, mainly because the bees bumble things up. If you want to import plants you will need a government permit.

Order early to be sure to get what you want. Most perennials are shipped in spring for immediate planting. The few that are not (see General List and the Top Ten) are sent out at the appropriate time for planting.

HOW TO PLANT

(For preparation of the hole, improvement of soil and general planting instructions, see CHAPTER 18.)

Depth of planting is especially important for some perennials; too deep and your plants rot or refuse to bloom; too shallow and their roots become exposed to drying sun and wind. Generally, those with deep firm tap roots, such as Oriental poppy, anchusa, should be set 1 inch deeper than in the nursery; those with a mass of fibrous and fine-growing roots, like phlox, pink, painted daisy, yarrow, Michaelmas daisies, at the same level as in the nursery; those with crowns, like the Christmas rose, so that the centre of the plant is above the surrounding ground. Those that stem-root as they stretch along the surface, like arabis or rabbit's ears, should be planted at the same level as in the nursery.

Distance apart depends on how quickly you want your plants to fill the space and what your budget is. The most economical way to build up a good perennial collection is to buy a few plants, grow them well and increase them in a few years by dividing. In the meantime, empty spaces can be filled with less expensive annuals.

General guidelines for spacing: Large wide plants such as peonies, place 2-4 feet apart. Sizes similar to delphiniums, lupines (there are many like this) plant 3-5 to a square yard. Smaller plants — coral bells, doronicum, columbine — plant 7-9 per square yard. Allow double this space between clumps and as a distance from other plants.

ONGOING CARE

A regular program of good garden care is all that is needed to keep most perennials in top condition (see CHAPTER 18, Techniques and Tools, for this. For special techniques see under individual plant notes in our Top Ten and General List).

Very tall plants such as delphiniums and very heavy headed ones (especially in rain) such as peonies need early and careful staking. One simple and effective way is used in the famous perennial borders of the Royal Horticultural Society's gardens at Wisley in England. In early spring, twiggy brush cut from the woods is pushed into the ground around each plant, as tall as it is expected to grow. The perennials grow up through this, are supported by it and their leaves and flowers soon hide the brush. Another way is with bamboo stakes which are available at garden supply stores. For best effect they should be put in early, one to a stalk, and the plant tied up as it grows. A favorite peony support is a three-footed metal ring (about 18-24 inches high) put in place well before the leaves reach it. Bushy plants can often be held to a nonstaking height by pinching out lead shoots thus encouraging shorter sideshoot growth; or you can decide that you like your plants to grow naturally and not tie them up at all.

PROPAGATION

Some perennials, see Top Ten and General List, need to be divided frequently for continuing good growth. Others can go longer without dividing unless you want more plants. When they bloom or grow poorly, look crowded, skimpy or frail, it's time to dig them up, cut off the best parts, throw away the rest and, if possible, replant the good parts in a new place. This is to prevent a buildup of disease or a special pest. Most perennial plantings need a major overhaul every 3-4 years.

Fleshy-root perennials, such as poppies, iris, anchusa, Japanese anemone, are divided by digging up the whole plant, cutting the roots into pieces and replanting each separately, if possible in a different site.

Surface-layering plants, such as arabis and pinks, can be encouraged to make more plants by piling fine soil over the stems wherever they touch the ground. When rooted, cut the stem between this point and the main plant, water and feed it and leave it to become established. Then either grow it into a full-size plant where it is or move to another spot.

Ten Top Perennials

PEONY, *Paeonia*

At the top of the list in many gardens from Zone 3 to Zone 7. Unfortunately peonies do not withstand the long summers of the Deep South. Elsewhere these magnificent flowers, if early, mid- and late-season cultivars are chosen, can grace your garden for a good 6 weeks, the whole plant looking marvelous all season from the first reddish shoots in spring, through its flowering and leafing-out time to its luxuriant clean glossy foliage all summer, then purplush green in the fall: it's also easy to grow.

Many older cultivars are still high on the popular list, but newer and certainly fascinating cultivars are also about. As well as new shades of the familiar red, pink and white, they now come in creamy yellow, salmon pink, bright cerise and an almost-black, many developed by the late Dr. A. P. Saunders, whose reputation for fine peony-breeding is internationally recognized. He is said to have worked with more than 17,000 crosses, though he marketed only 165.

Earliest to bloom in spring is the dwarf fern-leaf *P. tenuifolia*, single and double, red and pink. A week later, the common peony, still to be seen in country dooryards (and many planted at least 50 years ago), comes into bloom, again double or single, white to red, but the most common is the double cerise red. Next to bloom are the newer hybrids, often not quite as tall as the later familiar Chinese peonies, but in many flower forms — single, semi-double, double, Japanese (single, wide petals, with bright modified stamens), rose, and the bomb-shaped double in white, pink and red and other more sophisticated colors.

VITAL STATISTICS:

Where to Plant: In full sun, with good drainage.

When and How to Plant: Fall is the best time, unless you buy plants already growing in containers which then can be moved into the garden without disturbing the roots. Peonies are deep rooters and heavy feeders and they're going to be where you plant them for a very long time, so prepare the planting hole well — 2 x 2 x 2 feet at least — use good soil mixed with a general purpose fertilizer, high in phosphorus, with plain soil on top. Set the root so that the buds are *no more* than 2 inches below the surface of the ground when it has finally settled; pack more soil carefully around the roots and over the top. Water, and mulch the first winter.

Height at Maturity: 2½-3 feet. Width: 3 feet

A good peony support: set in place as growth reaches 8-10 inches.

ONGOING CARE

Peonies most often fail to bloom because they're planted too deeply. The cure is to dig them up and replant more shallowly. A second reason could be

243

lack of sun, and this can be remedied by moving, or sometimes by pruning surrounding and overhanging plants. The third is allowing manure as a fertilizer to touch the crowns — this they abhor. Feed instead with a general purpose commercial fertilizer, high in phosphorus and potash, comparably low in nitrogen, once in spring and again after flowering. Staking is needed for heavy headers (see page 242). Disease is rare. About the only one that reaches do-something-about-it proportions is botrytis, which shrivels and blackens buds and the whole plant looks sick. Cure is to cut and burn immediately all foliage and stems, spray the stubs and ground with fungicide, and the following spring spray again before the shoots appear and every 10 days thereafter till early August. Be sure to cover both sides of leaves and stems and the ground around the plant.

Ants may seem to be a serious pest but really seldom hurt the plant. They are only collecting the sweet nectar on the buds; but if they make hills in the roots or you suspect them of carrying a virus because an unknown disease hits your plants, then spray with an insecticide.

To produce single large flower heads, take off side buds as soon as they form: for more but smaller flowers leave them all on.

If after doing well for some years, your peonies become small-flowered and skimpy, it is time to dig and divide them. This is done in fall. Lift roots carefully out of the ground, allow to sit for a couple of hours to soften and become less brittle, then cut the clump apart into sections, each with 5-6-inch healthy roots and no fewer than 5-7 eyes (fewer take too long to grow to good bloomsize, more than 7 seem to develop poor flowers). Dust open cuts with fungicide, prepare a new hole as you would for a new plant and follow the same program as for first planting.

RECOMMENDED CULTIVARS:

7 OLD FAVORITES:

'Festiva Maxima': white flecked with crimson, double, early, fragrant

'Hansina Brand': glistening pink with salmon reflex, double, mid-season

'Jules Elie': pink, double, early, fragrant; one of the top ones

'Kelway's Glorious': pink in bud, glistening white open, double, mid-season

'Le Cygne': creamy white, greenish centre, double, mid-season, fragrant, the highest rating in the American Peony Society list.

'Elizabeth Barrett Browning': large white, double, late, very fragrant

'Philip Rivoire': dark red with a blackish sheen, double, mid-season, very fragrant

11 NEWER HYBRIDS:

'Charles Mains': deep salmon pink, double

'Chocolate Soldier': almost black, single

'Claire de Lune': yellow with bright orange anthers, single

'Convoy': deep red, double

'Diana Parks': vivid scarlet, double, very early

'Illini Belle': black petals, red-tipped green carpels, semi-double

'Joyce Ellen': dark red, white centre, single

'Laura Magnuson': deep salmon, single

'Prairie Moon': yellow, single

'Red Charm': a sensation in all the shows, rich red, big petals, double; has won the coveted gold medal of the American Peony Society five times out of ten annual exhibitions.

'Yellow Moonrise': ivory yellow, single

4 SINGLES (*many gardeners like these better than the doubles, they have a wide outer row of petals and a central cluster of yellow stamens*)

'The Bride': white
'Sea Shell': pink
'President Lincoln': red
'Dawn Pink': pink

4 JAPANESE TYPES, (*these are exotic, exquisite, extra wide flowers, one or more circles of guard petals around a centre mound of modified stamens*)

'Isani Gidui': pure white, gold centre

'Mrs. Wilder Bancroft': red, red-tipped-with-gold centre

'Mrs. G. E. Hemerik': rosy pink with green gold, sunburst centre

'Tokio': large pink-petaled flowers with silvery reverse and central tuft of gold

TREE PEONY, *Paeonia suffruticosa*

More a shrub than a herbaceous plant as other peonies are, but one of the most glorious plants of the garden. Can grow to 6 feet when climate, location and the cultivar chosen are all working well together; 4-5 feet wide; woody stems, fernlike foliage which drops in fall; flowers outstanding — as big as tea plates sometimes, 4-8 inches across (the yellows are a little smaller); with the texture and sheen of oriental silk, in white, pink, rose, scarlet, crimson, lavender, purple, almost black, and yellow.

Although not widely grown, they are reported to be hardy to Zone 4 if given a sheltered site and special protection. Morden, Manitoba, reports a hardy Manchurian cultivar developed by Dr. Frank Skinner. They may take some time to mature when one plant can have as many as fifty flowers. They bloom about 1-2 weeks before the familiar Chinese cultivars.

Plant 4-6 feet apart, in light moving shade (they tend to wilt in hot sun). Make the planting hole at least 2 x 2 feet and 2 feet deep; if not already sharply drained, put gravel in the lower 6 inches, then good garden soil with a high percentage of humus, and mix in superphosphate, about a handful to a plant. Prepare this hole well ahead to allow for settling of the soil.

Buy plants that are at least 3 years old, older if you can get them, with roots balled and burlapped. Choose when in bloom in spring and tag for delivery in fall.

Planting is done in September or October; the graft

(all are grafted) set 5-6 inches below the surface (deeper than other peonies). Settle soil well around the roots, water deeply, mulch in winter and whenever summer weather is dry. The Montreal Botanical Garden grows thirty cultivars which they are able to keep for 7-8 years by covering in winter with wooden boxes filled with buckwheat hulls to about ⅓ the height of the peony. The boxes keep the buckwheat hulls from blowing away and protect the flower buds that formed the previous summer.

Care, disease prevention and cure is similar to that for other peonies.

RECOMMENDED CULTIVARS:

'Gessekai' or **'Renkaku'**: double white
'Tama-fuyo': pale pink, double
'Silver Sails': pale yellow, fragrant
'Higurashi': dark pink, double
'Kamata-fuji': pale lavender
'Uba-tama': dark maroon, semi-double

IRIS, Tall Bearded, *Iris germanica*; Dwarf and Median, *I. pumila* and *I. chamaeiris*; Siberian, *I. sibirica*; Japanese, *I. kaempferi*.

Iris are the most radiant flowers of the garden. The tall bearded cultivars fairly shimmer in the light, the smaller and, to some, lovelier Siberians give rhythm to the wind; the little dwarfs and medians are brilliant patches of color in the early spring garden. The striking Japanese cultivars are an absolute knockout wherever they will grow.

The Tall Beardeds, *I. germanica*.

Starting from a fleshy root called a rhizome, about as handsome as a wizened potato, these popular beauties spread fans of blue green swordlike leaves 1-2 feet high, sturdy branching stalks, often 3 feet tall, push up with a no-nonsense air through the fans to carry the gorgeous flower heads aloft. Newer cultivars have produced large flowers that each last 2-3 days, compared with the old-fashioned types that died each day, and there are several buds to each stalk, opening one after the other. Petals are often fluted or frilled and the best have marvelous substance and flare. Color is glorious — all the primaries and literally hundreds of variations: shining whites, all the blues and purples you could dream of, yellows from pale to deep gold and orange, pure pinks, sultry dark reds, brown and bronze, even an almost-black; solid, bicolored, stitched and often contrasting whiskered beards.

Place them so that the character of the whole plant can be fully seen. If in with other perennials, give them an island of light to themselves; if as a border to a path or a fence, make it all iris with only a small low-growing fringe of other flowering plants, perhaps sweet alyssum or yellow marigolds. You can, of course, become the complete iris fan and have marvelous large beds of nothing but iris, which will be breathtaking in bloom but pretty dull for the rest of the year. Certainly to see iris best, they should not be nudged at, crowded against or overhung with other plants.

General pattern of growth is to plant in July or August, expect the first flowering the following year, more and better bloom for 3-5 years, then dig up and divide; by then the extending rhizomes will be piling up over each other and growth and production of flowers will be slowed.

The Siberians, *I. sibirica*

Smaller in flower but more graceful than the tall beardeds, these iris take naturally to a streamside planting or any moist soil in a border, as a flowery divider between different parts of the garden, or in a clump by themselves. They're hardy, incredibly easy to grow, never need special care and are exquisite in bloom. Their colors are limited — bright blue, purple, sky blue and white — but breeding is going on to extend this range. Slender leaves make a grassy fountain and are pretty from spring to fall. Newer cultivars will have wider flaring falls and larger blooms than those now available, but I still like the older dainty ones, especially those developed by the late Isabella Preston in Ottawa and named for Canadian lakes and rivers.

The Dwarfs and Medians, *I. pumila* and *I. chamaeiris*

These little beauties are perfect companions for rock garden plants and for daffodils and tulips which bloom at the same time. One iris enthusiast I know plants a whole sunny slope with them as a ground cover and gets a smashing effect. There are two groups, dwarfs up to 15 inches high and medians from 15-26 inches. Colors follow almost the same range as the tall beardeds.

Japanese Iris, *I. kaempferi*

A showy large iris with flowers often 9 inches across; does best in wet areas but will grow in regular garden beds in the more temperate parts of the country if given acid soil and winter protection. Blooms in early summer for a fairly long period with striking colors and combinations of white, mauve and purple and blue, often beautifully marbled, striped and blotched, some single, some double. Look into the Marhigo cultivars — these are some of the best, not commonly available, but usually they can be ordered through a specialist iris supplier.

VITAL STATISTICS:

Height at Maturity: TBs, 2½ -4½ feet; Dwarfs, 10-15 inches; Medians, 15-26 inches; Siberians, 18-30 inches; Japanese, 2-4 feet.
Where to Plant: Tall beardeds, dwarfs and medians do best in full sun and good soil; the Siberians will take some shade and a moist soil; all need good drainage. The Japanese must have acid soil, a really wet place for best growth, and either sun or light shade.
When to Plant: TBs, dwarfs and medians are planted 6-8 weeks after blooming is over; Siberians and Japanese in early fall.
How to Plant: TBs, dwarfs and medians — prepare bed at least 2 weeks in advance, adding whatever is necessary to bring the soil to good tilth (see CHAPTER 18). Dig a hole deep enough so that rhizomes, when lying horizontally, can be covered with about 1 inch of soil

and will be level with surrounding ground. Make a small cone of soil in the middle of the hole. With the fans of leaves pointing away from each other, lay the rhizomes on the cone, spreading the roots carefully (see drawing above.) Fill hole with soil and press firmly around each rhizome. Soak thoroughly and continue to water deeply once a week, if no rain, until plants are well established and firmly set. Clumps of 3-5 rhizomes are average size; however, if you want a terrific show, plant more rhizomes per clump and be prepared to divide sooner. For easy care, treat the ground after planting with pre-emergent weed killer according to manufacturer's directions.

Siberians usually come as a clump of rhizomes rather than as singles. Specify when you order if you wish large clumps — they will be more expensive but will give you a good show sooner. They are planted as other iris but usually do not have to be divided before 8-10 years.

Distance Apart: TBs, dwarfs and medians should be planted with the rhizomes about 8 inches apart and clumps 18 inches apart; Siberians and Japanese 1-2 feet apart.

ONGOING CARE

Weeding during the early years should be done by hand so as not to dislodge the rhizomes, which are near the surface. Water to keep soil moist but not soggy. Snap off spent flowers as soon as they fade, to allow buds to come along. Fertilize with a 5-10-5 or similar commercial fertilizer according to manufacturer's directions, once before blooming and once after, to develop sturdy growth for next year. Some gardeners add, at digging time, 2 pounds of sulphate of potash to 25 pounds of bonemeal, about a cupful to a planting hole. This makes for sturdy stalks that do not break easily in high wind, a fault of some of the larger flowered cultivars.

Winter Care: cut fan of leaves back one third in fall. Where winter is severe and snow cover sparse, and for all new plantings, mulch with hay, straw or evergreen branches after the first hard frost. (All plantings, both new and established, in the famous iris garden of the Royal Botanical Gardens in Hamilton, Ontario, get a winter mulch of evergreen Christmas tree branches.) Remove mulch gradually as spring warms the ground and press back firmly any rhizomes which may have heaved.

Pests and Diseases: Iris are not plagued by many pests and diseases but those they do have can be messy, disfiguring and sometimes fatal. Keeping the plantings clean and free of old foliage and debris is highly impor-

tant. Remove dead material quickly and treat disease immediately.

Iris borer is the most serious pest. Its larvae hatch in spring from eggs laid the fall before in foliage on the ground, become about 1½ inches long and look like a pale pink caterpillar. It climbs to the tip of the fan, eats its way downwards, boring into and eating the rhizomes, leaving them open to bacterial soft rot disease. Chewed edges on the leaves are the first sign of trouble. Prevention and cure is to use either a spray or granular systemic insecticide when plant is 6 inches high and again before bloom, according to directions on the label.

(For control of aphids and soft rot and leaf spot diseases, see CHAPTER 19.)

A fairly rare disease, but unfortunately common to iris in some areas, is scorch, its cause as yet unknown. The whole plant turns yellow, the rhizome remains solid but the roots disintegrate. A worthy plant has a chance of being saved if you dig it up, cut off the dead roots, expose it to the sun for 3-4 hours and replant. If this doesn't work, dig it up, burn it, or wrap for garbage, disinfect the soil and do not plant iris again in that spot for 3-4 years.

SELECTED LISTS OF FINE GARDEN IRIS

Tall Bearded cultivars designated as DM are Dykes Medal winners, the highest award given to iris by experts. Award of Merit (AM) winners are—although not so fully proven— still outstanding cultivars and in the running for the Dykes. The Morgan Award is the highest given to Siberian iris. Membership in a national iris society (see list of Plant Societies, page 401) will bring you up-to-date information and the newest recommendations.

---

26 TALL BEARDED IRIS

White: 'Cup Race' (AM); 'Winter Olympics' (DM)
Pink and Rose: 'Esther Fay' (AM); 'One Desire' (AM); 'Cashmere' (AM)
Yellow: 'Kingdom' (AM); 'Ultrapoise' (AM)
Brown: 'Gingersnap'; 'Olympic Torch' (AM)
Blue: 'Music Maker' (AM); 'Skywatch' (DM); 'Allegiance' (DM)
Orchid: 'Rippling Waters' (DM); 'Pretty Carol' (AM)
Orange: 'Orange Parade' (AM)
Red: 'Jewel Tone' (AM); 'Jungle Fires' (AM)
Violet: 'Royal Touch' (AM); 'Indiglow' (AM)
Black: 'Dusky Dancer' (AM); 'Swahili' (AM)
Plicata: 'Stepping Out' (DM); 'Wild Ginger'
Bicolor: 'May Melody' (AM); 'Amigo's Guitar' (AM)
Blend: 'Commentary' (AM)

---

9 DWARF AND MEDIAN IRIS

'Blue Doll', 5": lavender-blue, very flowery
'Cherry Garden', 12": glowing red
'Drummer Boy', 16": light blue, etched darker
'Golden Fair', 10": medium yellow
'Lemon Flurry', 21": large ruffled lemon
'Lillipinkput', 12": bright apricot-pink

'Lilliwhite', 10": pure sparkling white
'Little Sapphire', 14': satiny sapphire blue
'Shine Boy', 12": nearly black-purple

---

5 SIBERIAN IRIS

'Blue Brilliant': bright blue (Morgan Award)
'Mountain Lake': medium blue
'Tropic Night': purple violet
'Tycoon': medium blue, large flower (Morgan Award)
'White Swirl': pure white, very wide flaring falls, cupped standards, very flowery (Morgan Award)

DELPHINIUM

Delphiniums, unsurpassed for color and form, their 4-6 foot spires of white, blue, purple, pink and the newest — crushed raspberry — are the exclamation points of the garden. Handle them always with a lavish hand, massing clumps midway or back in the border, clear of anything that might fuzz-up their stunning profiles.

Buy as nursery-started plants for flowering in a year, or start your own from seed. This is much cheaper but takes more know-how, more tender loving care and more time.

The 'Pacific Giants', well known and widely grown, often with individual florets as much as 3 inches across, come in elegant colors, stand firm against the wind and are resistant to mildew, one of the unsightly nuisances of some other cultivars. For truly showy production, most gardeners either divide old plants, buy new ones or grow from seed so that they have new plants every 2-3 years. Some divide 'Pacific Giants' every year. The European strains, on the other hand, are longer lasting, but not so striking. They must be grown from other plants, not from seed.

VITAL STATISTICS:

Height at Maturity: 4-8 feet. You may raise your eyebrows at the indicated possible maximum height, but, believe it or not, this is the height delphiniums can grow in the Far North.

Where to Plant: out of strong windstreams so they won't be blown over; where there is good air circulation for they like to be cool, and in skyshine or partial sun for the same reason.

How to Plant: dig the ground deeply — 18 inches is minimum — and add well-rotted manure if you can get it, or compost and 12-16-12 commercial fertilizer at the rate recommended on the label. Soil should be alkaline. If you're not sure that yours is, you can buy small testing kits (make sure that the material in them is fresh) and if adjustment is necessary, add garden lime in recommended doses while digging.

Set each plant at its natural level, piling a little of your choicest mix over the crown so that it is higher than the level of the surrounding ground, to allow for settling and good drainage. Delphiniums, like most garden plants, abhor sitting in wet earth summer or winter. If they do, they give up the ghost.

When to Plant: early spring, if plants; fresh first quality seed in midsummer if you can get it then because it is highly viable at that time, deteriorates quite rapidly for the next eight months then, surprisingly, viability rises again after a year. Deal with a highly qualified seed company to be sure you get the best. (For how to sow seed, transplant, see CHAPTER 18.) Grow over winter in cold frame or hotbed, then move to permanent location in spring.

Distance Apart: set plants 2 feet apart in groups of 3-5.

ONGOING CARE

A regular program of good garden care pays dividends (see CHAPTER 18). Fertilizing is seldom necessary in a well-prepared bed of new plants until after first bloom, but older plants benefit from a dose as they are coming up to it. Both should be fertilized (12-16-12) between the first bloom and the second late-summer flowering.

Because of their willowy height and the often sudden strike of summer storms, delphiniums should be staked. Do this as invisibly as you can. Some delphinium gardeners recommend a ¼-inch iron rod, 6 feet long as a stake. They consider it to be more pliable in the wind than the usual bamboo, but if bamboo is all you can get, use it. Put stake in place when the plant goes into the ground and tie the rising stalks to it as they grow — one to a stake — once at a height of 18 inches, again at 24 and every foot thereafter. When they get beyond where you can reach, use a stepladder with a banner tacked to the top reading "Hurray!" and be sure to get a picture of yourself beside them.

It's a good idea to reduce the number of shoots per plant to no more than five. A big healthy plant can sometimes produce as many as twelve, but to allow this many to come into bloom reduces the height of each spire and the size of the florets.

Mulch in summer (see CHAPTER 18) to keep the soil around the plants cool, but don't use acid peat as a material for this since delphiniums prefer alkaline conditions.

Pests and diseases are the ordinary ones (see CHAPTER 19).

Don't cultivate deeply to eliminate weeds, instead cut them off below the surface and let them wilt and decompose on top of the ground.

Pick off all dead flowers promptly, cut off and bend over stubs of all stalks after first blooming to encourage a second one.

Winter care involves cutting down and bending over all hollow stems (to keep rain from running into the crown) and cleaning away all foliage. Some growers have good success with putting a mound of sand and charcoal or ashes on the crowns over winter, others swear by no covering at all. Depth of snow is probably what determines the right method for you — leave your plants without a mulch if you usually have deep snow all winter, cover them if you don't. Evergreen branches are a practical cover for this.

To increase or improve old plants doing poorly lift the clump after blooming and gently pull it apart, discarding horny old pieces and replanting flourishing ones in renewed soil. An alternative method is to cut out the central, worn-out part of old plants with a sharp knife, backfill the hole with good soil and leave the ring of undisturbed, established young plants in place to grow on to full size.

A RECOMMENDED LIST OF CULTIVARS

Besides these well-known and loved colors, a breakthrough is expected in Dutch cultivars that, although not quite so statuesque, will put red, orange, yellow and bright pink on the list. Watch for these in your catalogues.

'Astolat': pale blush pink to deep raspberry rose
'Black Knight': tall, large and stiff; deep, dark violet
'Blue Jay': intense clear to dark blue, dark bee (the centre)
'Cameliard': clear mauve, exceptionally large florets
'Galahad': giant pure white with a white bee
'Guinevere': clear lavender pink with white bee
'King Arthur': rich deep blue with white bee
'Sir Percival': creamy white with dark bee

DAY LILIES, *Hemerocallis*

All the flattering words you can think of go naturally with today's day lilies. Hardy, popular, sturdy, lavish with bloom, free of diseases and pests, suitable for planting anywhere, great variety in color, as undemanding and permanent as peonies, choose your cultivars well and you'll have some in bloom for weeks and weeks, fragrant, appealing, wonderful facelifters for trouble spots, handsome and lovely to look at, foliage with interesting contours, even thrives in containers, which most perennials do not.

Also, just to gild the day lily, they do well in partial shade, need not be divided oftener than once in 5 years and they're inexpensive. Their only disadvantage is that each flower lasts but a day (night ones are being bred that are open in late afternoon and evening and others that have a second blooming period later in the summer, but most cultivars are so prolific the short life of any one bloom doesn't matter).

Place them as a one-plant green leafy fountain, or in a group, to frill along the top of a wall or the edge of a terrace, as foundation planting, a divider between lawn and vegetable garden, along a fence or boundary, or to cover a slope. You can naturalize them under high shade trees or choose a fragrant one or two for planting near windows.

Their colors are luminous yellows, mahogany and bright red, brownish, pink and rose, and some purples. Enthusiastic breeders introduce excellent new cultivars every year.

VITAL STATISTICS:

Height at Maturity: 2½-4 feet. Average width of clump: 3 feet.
Where to Plant: dry or damp, full sun or shade — they're versatile and good tempered anywhere.
When to Plant: mainly spring, but can also be planted in late summer, and will actually move from one place to another in your garden in full bloom.
How to Plant: in a well-prepared bed of loose friable garden soil (see CHAPTER 18) make a wide shallow hole and plant roots so that there is not more than 1 inch of soil above the crown and none above the white stem section which indicates the previous soil level in the nursery. Water well.
Distance Apart: 2-4 feet.

ONGOING CARE

A normal program of good garden care — watering deeply once a week if no rain, feeding with a high phosphorus garden fertilizer in spring, again a week before blooming and again 2 weeks after blooming — is all that is necessary.
Twist off the tattered, wispy dead flowers each day to allow the next ones to come on.
Pests and disease are rare — occasionally thrips will disfigure the flowers (see CHAPTER 19 for control).
Divide anytime by lifting clump, cutting or pulling apart and replanting as for new ones.

HOW TO CHOOSE CULTIVARS FOR YOUR GARDEN

Since there are over 3,000 named cultivars, and about 200 new ones coming on the market every year, your best plan is to read catalogues for color descriptions and blooming dates and make your choice this way. It is possible to have day lilies in bloom in your garden from July to frost if you choose a series of cultivars for sequence of bloom.

PHLOX, *P. paniculata*

Exuberant, easy to grow and flaunting great swashes of color over your summer garden, phlox fills a place no other plant does at this time of year (July-August). Except for mildew it is practically indestructible, although carelessness in not picking off wilted flower heads before they go to seed can end up in later years in a batch of dirty magenta plants, which are depressing to say the least, since uncontrolled crossing of seed does not come true to the original color. Unknowing gardeners often speak of their lovely colors of phlox "reverting" to this distressing magenta, but the plants are not at fault. What really reverts is the gardener's attention and care. If seedlings do get a head start, pull them out.

When you plan phlox for your garden picture, think of an artist using whole tubes of glorious colors, not dibs and dabs. Plant big clumps of it where you will be able to see it best. They come in white, light and rose pink, bright cherry red, splashy orange scarlet, frilly pale mauve, a royal purple that's lovely at night, and most have a contrasting wide-awake eye.

VITAL STATISTICS:

Height at Maturity: 2-3 feet.
Where to Plant: in sun or open shade; well-prepared garden soil high in humus (see CHAPTER 18).
How to Plant: set so that the growing point is no more than 1 inch below the surface. Water deeply.
When to Plant: early spring.
Distance Apart: 2-3 feet and keep generous clear space around them for free circulation of air.

ONGOING CARE

A regular program of feeding, watering deeply once a week if no rain, shallow cultivation to eliminate weeds, keeps them growing well. Phlox is both a heavy feeder and drinker.

Pests and disease can be unsightly. If leaves turn rusty and curl under, red spiders have taken up residence. Try first hosing them with a strong spray of water early in the day (so that it will dry before night). If this doesn't cure the trouble, use a miticide spray according to directions; if mildew appears, dust with a fungicide (for both see CHAPTER 19). If leaves at the base drop off — and this is not unusual — plant low-growing annuals in front.

Keep faded flower heads picked off both to prevent seed forming and to encourage secondary sideshoot bloom.

Phlox are at their showiest 2-4 years after planting. They will then probably need dividing. Dig up the clump in early fall, pull gently apart, discard the tough old bits and replant the vigorous new ones in a previously prepared new location in the garden.

---

15 RECOMMENDED CULTIVARS (all are 36 inches tall or over): for others see your nursery catalogues

'Blue Ice': pink-eyed white, compact heads, robust
'Charmaine': bright cherry-red with an ivory blaze
'Dodo Hanbury Forbes': huge clear pink
'Dramatic': salmon pink, very fragrant, cuts well
'Everest': dazzling white, faint rose eye, vigorous
'Fairy's Petticoat': pale pink, darker pink eye
'Gaiety': bright cherry-red suffused with orange
'Inspiration': bright wine red
'Lilac Time': clear lilac-blue
'Mount Fujiyama': white, strong and compact
'Olive Symons-Jeune': rich orange-rose
'Olive Wells Durant': light rose, carmine eye
'Royalty': imperial purple
'Starfire': brilliant red, early, strong
'Vintage Wine': rich claret red

CHRYSANTHEMUM

Whether you are the Emperor of Japan, the finest flower painter in China or just a gardener who loves exquisite flowers, you will admire and want to grow 'mums. Loved and grown extensively in Asia for over 2,000 years, outdoor garden 'mums are comparative newcomers to our western world — they've been with us only a scant 200 years.

They're the stars of the late summer and fall garden, a brilliant finale to the growing year, in all shades of yellow, orange, bronze, red, pink, mauve and purple; dwarf, medium and tall heights; flowers of different forms — pompon (small and stiff), single (like a daisy), double (like a double daisy), cushion (sometimes called 'azaleamums', early, low, bushy and reliably hardy), anemone (single with a rounded central crest), spoon (spoon-shaped petals) and quill (straight, tubular petals). There is also a race of big decorative cultivars grown mainly by specialists for exhibition.

All look well in the border, massed low towards the front, in the middle, or tall ones at the back. Most gardeners, instead of giving them valuable space in the main part of the garden during the summer, grow them in a separate bed, or in the vegetable garden, out of sight and move them in for a bright fall show. They can be lifted and moved in full bloom with no setback if they're firmed well into their new place and watered well. Alternatively if you do not have spare space or time to grow your own at this stage, local nurseries usually have container-grown, well-budded plants for sale in late summer and early fall and with them you can make a stunning flowery garden in minutes.

VITAL STATISTICS:

Height at Maturity: Tall, 2-3½ feet; cushion, 18 inches; others, 1½-2 feet.
Where to Plant: in fertile, well-drained soil; in full sun; with free air moving about them and not crowded by other plants.
When to Plant: divisions or cuttings in spring; full-grown plants any time.
How to Plant: dig a generous hole in well-prepared soil, set in place, press soil firmly around roots, water.
Distance Apart: low bushy cultivars, 1-1½-feet; others 2-2½ feet.

ONGOING CARE

Water deeply once a week if no rain. Weed by cultivating shallowly. Feed 4 weeks after planting in spring with 5-10-5 fertilizer and water in. Fertilize again just before blooming.
Mulch to a depth of 2 inches when weather gets hot (see CHAPTER 18).
Pinch all shoots of small-flowered cultivars when 6-8 inches high and when new growth is that high again until July 15 (but not after that). Pinch tall-flowered cultivars for bushy growth, or disbud for large single blooms.
Stake tall cultivars if you like them to stand up, or let them sprawl naturally. Cushion and low ones need no support.
Pests and diseases can be a real nuisance. Mildew, rust, bud rot, leaf spot, wilt, aphids, leafhoppers, tarnished plant bug, mites and thrips — in other words, the works. Best control is a home garden mixture of both fungicide and insecticide sprayed on when plants are 8 inches high and at 10-day intervals thereafter until bloom begins. Stunt, aster yellows and mosaic diseases — all sometimes affecting 'mums — cannot be cured

or controlled, so best dig out and either burn or wrap plant for garbage.

Winter Protection: tests in some of the coldest parts of the country have convinced horticulturalists that 'mums survive best if you leave them where they are growing in the garden, making sure that they are in a well-drained spot with their tops bent over but left on. Arch a few evergreen branches over them to catch and hold the snow.

RECOMMENDED CULTIVARS:

Since the adaptability and suitability of 'mums is a matter of local conditions and local supply, you do best to buy from a reputable nursery specializing in cultivars hardy for your region. Especially fine hardy 'mums have been developed in recent years at the United States Government Experimental Station at Cheyenne, Wyoming, and an excellent list of extra early cushion mums at the University of Minnesota. More will be released to the market over the next few years. If you would like to specialize in 'mums, join one of the national chrysanthemum societies (see page 401).

ORIENTAL POPPY, *Papaver orientale*

Great cups of iridescent gossamer, the texture of crinkled silk, are the exciting additions to your late-spring garden when you grow oriental poppies. Huge (5-8 inch) flowers in shell or deep pink, salmon, white, red or a blazing orange, some fringed or ruffled, single or double; ferny leaves, buds and stems as fascinating in their own way as the flowers, capturing with a thousand fine hairs every shaft of sunlight; they are just about the most dramatic perennial you can grow.

Grow them midway in a border, deliberately setting scene so that their great beauty can be fully appreciated, yet where, in midsummer, when all flowers and foliage disappear for a month, they will not leave a gaping hole. Clever camouflage is to grow something spreading like baby's breath near them, tie it together while the poppies are blooming, then release it to make its own fluffy cloud to fill the gap.

VITAL STATISTICS:

Height at Maturity: 18-42 inches; width 2-3 feet.
Where to Plant: in the border, full sun or part shade, deep rich soil with good drainage. Once planted, leave them be until scanty growth indicates time to divide.
When to Plant: time is critical — late summer or early fall — no other unless container grown, when you can move them into your garden at any time.
How to Plant: the root is set vertically in a hole about 3 inches below the surface. Roots 3 inches long should bloom in 2 years, larger pieces in 1 year. Water well after planting and until well established.
Distance Apart: 2 feet, and plant 3-5 of the same kind in a group for best effect.

ONGOING CARE:

Fertilize in early spring with 5-10-5 before blooming and again after. Leaves die down after blooming — don't cut them until they are quite brown. They reappear about 1 month later and make a pleasant green plant for late summer and fall.

Mulch the first winter by tucking dry leaves under and around the rosette of leaves, not over it.

Cut off dead flowers — do not allow them to go to seed.

Divide when crowded — probably every 3-4 years — in late August by digging up the root, cutting it into sections 3-5 inches long (it helps if you make the bottom cut slanting, the top straight across, then you can tell which end is up — always handy to know, in gardening, as in everything else). Replant where they are to grow, or in containers for moving in later; and be sure to mark the spot so that you will not dig them up again by mistake while they are doing their disappearing act.

Pests and disease control is average — spray or dust with a combined fungicide and insecticide when you are treating the rest of your garden. Put out bait if slugs are a nuisance.

---

10 RECOMMENDED CULTIVARS: for others, see your nursery catalogues

'Carmine': cardinal red, black splotches
'Curlilocks': deep rose-pink, sturdy, unusual
'Field Marshal van der Glotz': white, deep purple blend, with the pattern of an iron cross in the heart
'Helen Elizabeth': pink, crinkled
'Lavender Glory': lavender, very large
'Maiden's Blush': pink-banded white
'Pinnacle': white-centered pink, red ruffled edges
'Show Girl': blossom pink, white center, crinkled and ruffled; with luck does the cancan when the wind's in the right direction
'Victoria Dreyfus': silver-edged salmon, exceptional
'Watermelon': watermelon pink, delicious

PRIMROSE, *Primula*

Plants have personalities just as people do. Some, such as the pansies, are the pixie type. Some, such as the mints, are musclemen. But for frankness and freshness and a friendly appealing air, nothing can match primroses. They come in palest pink and deepest blue, reds both tile and ruby, sapphire, lavender, yellow from pale lemon to sulphur; single and double; an umbel of flowers on a single stalk: each little flower on its own; starred with white eyes or no eyes at all; flowers as big as a fifty-cent piece; flowers the shape of a lavender, bigger-than-golf ball; colors as clear as a summer day; colors as muddy as a palette at the end of a painting class and you don't have to have a green thumb to grow them well.

You do need a rich moist soil all the time except for the auriculas, which like it a little dry. Their enemy is not so much winter cold as summer drought, for if they dry out they are done for. With care in choosing the right growing location, selection in choosing the right planting medium and with deep soaking regularly if no rain, primroses can be grown and grown well in nearly everybody's garden.

Favorites are the polyanthus. The flowers stand in a cluster at the top of a sturdy stalk, 6-9 inches high, lifted well above the whorl of green leaves. Architecturally the whole plant is a delight of balance, design and scale. Earliest to bloom are the 3-6 inch 'Juliaea' hybrids, small cushions of flowers in jewel colors of purple, red and cerise. From Japan come the candelabra primroses, *P. japonica*, eventually 18 inches tall, throwing one parasol of bloom out of the one just finishing until they have had as many as five sets of flowers. They need very wet ground, but given the right conditions bloom for a long time in the spring. 'Sieboldii' is another Japanese one that flowers in late spring in lovely pink and rose shades and has an interesting crinkled leaf, which disappears when the weather gets hot. It too likes a moist root run.

Other favorites are the fragrant English primroses, *P. acaulis*, early, 6 inches high and with bright yellow flowers, each on its own stem, and the old-fashioned cowslip, *P. veris*, 8 inches, also with fragrant yellow flowers but in clusters.

From the Himalayas comes *P. denticulata* 'Cachemiriana'. From a base of mealy looking leaves, a stalk about 10 inches long shoots up to a ball of lavender-blue to rich magenta flowers, with yellow centres. It blooms in early spring and stands clear and bold among all the other small new growth, especially in the rock garden.

The muddy colored primroses I wrote about earlier are the auriculas of the European Alps, *P. auricula*. Their flowers are brown, plum purple, green faded pink, a lovely dirty saffron. Some are mottled and splotched. Their leaves are stone green and tough. You either put all your egg money into them or you don't give them houseroom. A little hard to grow, because they can't abide heat, they're truly a primrose collector's primrose. So too are many others — the family is a large one.

VITAL STATISTICS:

Height at Maturity: 3-18 inches depending on cultivar.
Where to Plant: in a cool, moist, shady place with deep rich soil. If you can't provide such a spot all year, it's possible to grow them in the open garden during their blooming time, then move them to an east or north shaded exposure for the warm summer months and winter; transplant them back into the open garden again before they bloom in spring.
How to Plant: as any garden plant (see CHAPTER 18).
When to Plant: prestarted nursery plants in spring. Seed either indoors under lights, or outdoors in a special seedbed when frost is out of the ground. It's very fine and not easy to grow. Most people buy plants.
Distance Apart: 8-10 inches.

ONGOING CARE

Water deeply if no rain. Give regular program of good garden care — fertilizing in early spring and again after blooming; control pests and diseases with home garden mixture of fungicide and insecticide — you may need bait for slugs too.

Divide by pulling clumps apart just after blooming — this usually needs to be done every 2-3 years, some do it every year — and replant.
Winter protection is best given by putting evergreen boughs over the plants after the first hard freeze to keep winter sun from burning and heaving them out of the ground. Crisp leaves, such as oak, make an equally good mulch and should be tucked in around the plant under its leaves, not over it.
Recommended cultivars: check with nursery catalogues for those hardy for your area. If making a special collection and learning the fine points of growing from seed intrigue you, join a national primrose society (see page 343).

HARDY ASTER, MICHAELMAS DAISY, ASTER HYBRIDA

Thousands of small daisies cover mounds or tall plants with pastel shades of solid bloom in late summer and fall and are affectionately known, in many parts of the country, as frost flowers. These are perennial asters and they often survive temperatures that kill most other fall flowers, even the hardy 'mums. More than 700 cultivars especially bred for use in the garden come in white, light and dark blue, lavender, purple, and light to deep pink. The form can be a mound of varying height, or a tall 4-foot flowery bouquet. Place tall ones in the back of the border, mounds midway or near the front.

VITAL STATISTICS:

Height at Maturity: mounds, 6-24 inches; talls, 4 feet.
Where to Plant: in full sun, with good drainage, well-prepared soil, free air circulation about them.
When to Plant: in spring. Unlike 'mums, they don't transplant well from one part of the garden to the other in bloom, so plant where they are to stay. If grown in containers, they can be moved in anytime.
How to Plant: as for other garden plants (see CHAPTER 18).
Distance Apart: moundy cultivars, 15-18 inches; tall ones, 2 feet.

ONGOING CARE:

Follow a program of good garden care (see CHAPTER 18).
Stake tall cultivars when shoots about 10 inches high.
Cut off flower heads before they can seed — with small bushy plants this is most easily done by shearing.
Pest and disease control is average: spray or dust with a combined fungicide and insecticide, according to manufacturer's recommendations, especially for mildew, aphids (see CHAPTER 19).
Divide when plants become crowded and are blooming less well — usually every 3 years although some gardeners divide every year. Dig up in spring when shoots are 1 inch above ground, divide clump into sections of 3-5 shoots, keeping and replanting the vigorous young ones, discarding the rest.

RECOMMENDED CULTIVARS:

See local nursery catalogues for cultivars best for you.

251

Be sure to consider the beautiful 'Oregon' series developed by Professor LeRoy Breithaupt of Corvallis, Oregon; 18 inches high, covered with bloom, pastel colors of mauve, pink, purple, blue and white.

DAISIES: Boltonia, Gaillardia, Helenium, Heliopsis, Rudbeckia and Shasta

Amenable, handy, hardy, easy to grow, a great show for the time and money, long season of bloom, smart colors — all these things daisies are. And their flowers have an entrancing wide-eyed and cheerful look.

Plant in spring, give good garden care, cut down after blooming and that's it. They make the Top Ten because they're wonderful as fillers in the border. Choose cultivars from your local catalogues.

Boltonia, *B. asteroides* (white); *B. latisquama* (pink): blooms in late summer and fall right up to frost, sometimes a little beyond. Small but profuse little flowers on a neat plant 4-6 feet tall.

Gaillardia, *G. aristata*: sometimes also called blanket flower: blooms all summer if flowers kept picked off, single or double, new cultivars in red, yellow, red-tipped gold, deep red, orange, crimson and brown flecked with yellow, with flowers 2-2½ inches across, plants 2 feet tall.

Helenium, *H. autumnale*, also called sneezeweed: strong, light green leaves, prolific 2-inch flowers in yellow, copper or dull red. Planted in spring makes large clumps by August. Divide at least every other year for best bloom.

Heliopsis, *H. scabra*: another all-summer yellow-to-gold flowering daisy, this one with 3-inch blooms, plants 3-4 feet tall. Non-fussy, will take poor soil, sun or part shade, survives drought well. 'Gold Greenheart', with double 3 inch chrome yellow flowers all summer; 'Golden Plume', similar but flowers feathery; 'Incomparabilis', semi-double, brilliant gold yellow, all recommended.

Painted Daisy, Pyrethrum, *Chrysanthemum coccineum*; a vivid, early summer daisy with finely cut leaves, single or double 3-4-inch flowers, in pink, lavender and rosy red; the plant about 2 feet tall. Especially free of pests and diseases, likes full sun, rich soil. Cut back first bloom for a second one later.

Rudbeckia; related to our native black-eyed susans, these big golden-yellow daisies sometimes behave as annuals, sometimes biennials, sometimes perennials. They bloom in late summer and fall. For a bold display, plant 3 or more, 15-18 inches apart. Tolerates drought. The Gloriosa Daisy, *R.* 'Tetraploid Giant' sometimes has flowers 5 inches across, in yellow with a maroon or green heart. *R. subtomentosa*, the sweet coneflower, grows to 5 feet or more, has toothed leaves and soft yellow daisies with a brown cone. *R. speciosa* 'Goldsturm' has 3-4-inch flowers of rich yellow.

Shasta Daisy, *Chrysanthemum maximum*: is clean, crisp white, dependable, hardy, a wonderful foil for other flowers in the summer border. Likes full sun, rich soil, sharp winter drainage. Long-blooming flowers, crested, sometimes yellow-centred, partially or fully double, and up to 4 inches across. Plant is 1-3 feet tall. Divide about every 3 years, in early fall.

NOTES ON 40 PERENNIALS LISTED BY SEASONS

SPRING FLOWERING:

Anemone, many; *Anemone patens*, 8-12 inches; the prairie crocus, Manitoba's floral emblem; lavender to blue-purple flowers centred with yellow; silky seed heads; full sun; plant in late summer. *A. pulsatilla*, the Pasque Flower, lilac to red flowers, fuzzy foliage; silky seed heads.

Aubrietia, Purple Rock Cress; *Aubretia*; 4 inches; brilliant purple, pink or lavender flowered mats; full sun; clip back after flowering and topdress with gritty soil and compost.

Basket-of-Gold, Gold Dust, Madwort; *Alyssum saxatile*, 8-15 inches; a golden bounty for your garden; free flowering; sun; average soil. A double form, *A. saxatile* 'Flore-pleno', and a less giddy gold, *A. saxatile* 'Luteum'.

Bleeding Heart, *Dicentra*; the beloved old-fashioned one, *D. spectabilis*; 3 feet; with beautiful leaves and arches of dripping cerise hearts grows best in moist shade, disappears in August, so mark well. *D. formosa*, the Western Bleeding Heart, 12 inches, is a delicate turquoise green with pale rose flowers. But the real showstopper is *D.* 'Bountiful', 18 inches, a silvery-green mound with flowers from spring into summer, then some on and off all season; hardy; full sun; good drainage.

Bluebell, Virginia; *Mertensia virginica*; 1-2 feet; blue-green leaves, nodding blue flowers; a perfect mate for daffodils; sun or shade; disappears after blooming, so mark well.

Candytuft, Perennial; *Iberis sempervirens*; 8-12 inches; evergreen; the whitest, crispest flowers you could imagine; shear after blooming and feed; full sun; good drainage; average soil. The cultivar 'Autumn Snow' blooms again in fall.

Christmas Rose, Lenten Rose: *Helleborus niger*; 6-12 inches; really a late-winter bloomer; where hardy a triumph to grow; white, sometimes flushed with pink flowers; must have good drainage all year; some shade from winter sun. The best clump I ever saw had forty-seven flowers on one plant and was kept under a bushel basket all winter, the planting bed set up 6 inches above the surrounding ground.

Columbine; *Aquilegia*; 10-30 inches; flower heads like tiny doves cooing at each other, held well above blue-green foliage; rich soil; semi-shade. The McKana hybrids in white, yellow, pink, red, blue and purple are especially beautiful.

Coral Bells; *Heuchera sanguinea*, 12-24 inches; hardy, excellent edging plant with tufts of good-looking leaves and stems of little bells in pink, scarlet or vermilion; blooms for a long time. Some fine new ones known as the Bressingham Hybrids.

Globe Flower; *Trollius*; 2 feet; fine-leaved, large yellow and gold double buttercups; moist semi-shade.

Leopard's Bane; *Doronicum*; 2-4 feet; one of the best spring garden plants; neat tufts of shiny green leaves and many-budded stalks of bright yellow daisies; moist semi-shade; blooms for three weeks in my garden.

Lily-of-the-Valley; *Convallaria majalis*; 9 inches; well known and widely loved; fragrant white bells; shade; spreads.

Lungwort; *Pulmonaria saccharata*; 1 foot; usually the first perennial to bloom; silver-spotted, hairy leaves; blue and rose flowers; sun or shade; any soil; a most dependable plant.

Lupine, Perennial; *Lupinus*; 1-4 feet; best are the Russell lupines with spikes of pea-shaped flowers in blue, pink, red, yellow or apricot; ornamental foliage. A measure of their hardiness is that the National Museum of Canada reports the finding of 10,000-year-old lupine seeds in the Yukon; they germinated in 48 hours when exposed to moist warmth, and later bloomed. This was, of course, the native blue Arctic lupine, not the fine hybrids recommended, but it's comforting to know they have a sturdy ancestor.

Moss Pink; *Phlox subulata*; 4-6 inches; white, pink, blue or red flowery mats; cut back after blooming to keep neat and to prevent formation of inferior seed.

Rock Cress; *Arabis*; 8 inches; pink, white, violet or rose, single or double flowers; one with variegated silver green foliage; average soil; full sun; tends to straggle so cut back after blooming and divide every 2 years.

SUMMER FLOWERING:

Astilbe, False Spirea; *Astilbe*; a 2½-foot beauty for moist shade; many reds, pink or lilac; beautiful foliage and delicate soft spikes of flowers; topdress yearly with compost or rotted manure.

Baby's Breath; *Gypsophila*; some creep (6 inches high), others form an airy cloud in the border (2-3 feet); any soil; any place. *G. paniculata* 'Bristol Fairy' is a double white; 'Pink Star', a New Zealander, pale pink and double.

Balloon Flower; *Platycodon grandiflora*; 2-3 feet; handsome violet-blue flowers — the buds are the balloons; mark where you plant it for it's late appearing; sandy loam; sun; has very long roots, so move only if you must.

Beardtongue, many; *Penstemon barbatus*; the cultivars 'Firebird' and 'Rose Elf' are large (1½-2 feet), the first a vivid crimson, the other rose.

Bee Balm, Oswego Tea, Bergamot; *Monarda didyma*; 2-4 feet; beloved by hummingbirds; sun or semi-shade; flowers white (a good one is 'Snow Queen'), red, pink, mahogany, or deep purple; hardy; easy to grow; leaves have a fresh bruising scent.

Bellflower, many; *Campanula*; the little ones (4-9 inches) come in clean colors of white, pale or deep blue, or dark purple. The 18-inch Dahurian bellflower, *C. glomerata* 'Dahurica', makes a fine border plant with narrow bells and clusters of flowers uptilted and facing outward, often 12 flowers to a cluster, hence its folk name "The Twelve Apostles"; rich, sandy loam; semi-shade.

Buttercup, Double; *Ranunculus acris* 'Flore-pleno'; 1-3 feet; hardy small golden-yellow buttercups; bloom all summer; any soil; sun.

Cardinal Flower; *Lobelia cardinalis*; 3-4 feet; brilliant red tall spikes in late summer; stunning at the edge of pools or streams; moist soil; semi-shade.

Cornflower, Perennial; *Centaurea*; 1-4 feet; thistlelike flowers in pink, blue or yellow, some with silvery foliage; full sun; easy to grow.

Evening Primrose, Sundrop; *Oenothera*; 1-3 feet; both prostrate and upright forms; wide-open yellow flowers; likes dry poor soil; easy to grow.

Gas Plant, Fraxinella; *Dictamnus albus*; 2-3 feet; dark green, glossy, aromatic leaves; neat; grows slowly; good soil; sun or shade; resents moving; spikes of white flowers; makes a great hit with young friends if you light the little whiff of gas that comes off them on a cool evening after a warm day.

Golden Glow; *Rudbeckia laciniata*; 7-8 feet; an old-timer that blooms no matter the weather, no matter where; double yellow flowers; cut-leaved foliage; spreads underground but can be controlled by driving a sharp spade into the ground around the plant; regular feeding and watering will prevent the common unsightly browning of lower leaves; to have bushy plants, shear back to half height in mid-June; sometimes needs staking.

Lythrum; 2-4 feet; brilliant Morden hybrids with tall spikes of pink or carmine; likes a damp place; spreads; flowers profusely.

Hibiscus, Rose Mallow; *Hibiscus palustris*; 3-5 feet; exotic big hybrids, some with flowers 6-8 inches across, in pink, red or white, very like the tropical hibiscus; likes moist, well-drained soil; full sun; spectacular.

Speedwell; *Veronica*; 6-15 inches; lovely blues and some pinks in small spires; sun or semi-shade; good drainage. There are many species and varieties. We might recommend 'Minuet', 12-15 inches with silvery pink flowers and a dense mat of grey-green foliage; 'Barcarolle', 12 inches, rose red; and the famous 'Crater Lake Blue'.

FALL FLOWERING:

Japanese Anemone; *A. japonica*; delicate and delightful, lifts it white, rose or lilac rose flowers up 2 feet; sun or light shade; protect from strong wind; rich soil; mulch in summer and give a cover of dry leaves or evergreen boughs in winter.

Monkshood; *Aconitum*; 3-6 feet; deep blue or blue and white flowers with hooded petals and glossy dark green leaves; rich, moist soil; does not move easily.

FOR A FINE EFFECT FROM SPRING TO FALL:

Artemisia, many — Southernwood, Wormwood, Old Man, Old Woman; *Artemisia*; all are aromatic; like full sun; dry soil. Two favorites are *A. albula* 'Silver King'; 3 feet; frosty silver leaves; a beautiful foil behind brilliant flowers, especially pink ones; and *A. schmidtiana* 'Silver Mound', 12 inches; compact; silvery, fern-foliaged; very soft to touch.

Bugleweed; *Ajuga*; 8-12 inches; glistening foliage in green, bronze or variegated green and white; deep blue spikes of flowers in spring; sun or shade.

Carnation, Pink, many; *Dianthus*; 4-18 inches; clean, fresh colors of flowers in white, pink, maroon or scarlet; full sun; most are easy to grow and vigorous. One of the best, *D. plumarius* 'Rosie', has grey-green foliage that looks lovely all season and spicily fragrant double rose-pink flowers in spring.

Hen and Chickens, Houseleek; many; *Sempervivum*; 1 foot; rubbery rosettes chiefly grown for their fascinating foliage and form; they die after blooming, but new ones develop around the edge; a dry site; full sun.

Lamb's Ears, Rabbit's Ears, Woolly Groundwort; *Stachys lanata*; 1 foot; incredibly soft white velvety leaves — the chief reason for growing it; flowers pink, in summer.

Plantain Lily, Funkia, Corfu Lily; *Hosta*; 18-24 inches; a truly handsome accent plant for the shady border or standing out by itself; grow for its foliage which can be all green or green marked with chartreuse or white; rich deep soil; plenty of moisture; flowers in early summer are white or mauve, and those of *H. plantaginea* a fragrant white in September.

Spurge, many; *Euphorbia*; 2-3 feet; the popular one is *E. polychroma*, attractive all season with soft green leaves and bright yellow bracts. The flowering spurge, *E. corollata*, with white star-shaped flowers in late summer, is useful in the border.

253

BIENNIALS

Because they take two years — which necessarily includes one winter — to grow large enough to flower and then die never to return, biennials have to be very special flowers to be worth the trouble of growing them. And they are. You can grow your own from seed, usually planted early one summer, grown on till fall, then either given the extra protection of a winter mulch (see CHAPTER 18) in the open garden or moved into a cold frame to be sure they will come through safely. Alternatively, you can buy year-old plants from a nursery. This is more expensive, but much easier, and what most people do. A couple — the silver-pennied honesty is one, forget-me-nots another — seed themselves so successfully that they will come through the winter without any help from you. In fact, in some gardens they seed themselves so successfully that the help they need from you is to be pulled out.

Let your eyes run down this list, and I defy you to resist at least two or three of them.

Canterbury Bells; *Campanula calycanthema*; 2½-3 feet; they ring out over the garden in late spring with tall stalks of single or double out-turned bells in white, pink, deep rose, blue and lavender purple; if you pinch off the flowers as they die, a secondary but smaller branchlet comes along; will grow in any soil, but do better in a rich one; plant about 1 foot apart in mid-border.

English Daisies; *Bellis perennis*; 4-8 inches; a little beauty for the front of a border or to mark an edging where weather is cool and soil moist; comes in pink, deep rose, white and a sort of peppermint candy-striped red, pink and white; my next-door neighbor once shared with me a flat of quilled little cerise ones that I grew very fond of and the two of us grew them for 10 years; one year he would lose all his and mine would come through, the next year I would lose mine and his would survive; but one very cold winter did them all in, and we both lost them all and had to begin again. Plant 4-6 inches apart.

Forget-me-not, Mountain; *Myosotis alpestris;* 6 inches; welcome in any garden, grows anywhere, the color of the bluest summer sky, seeds itself all over the place; sow where you want it to grow in summer and keep moist till germinated and growing well.

Foxglove, *Digitalis*; although 3-6 feet is its average height, I'm going to give 8 feet as its height because I once grew one that tall, and as the man who bred the famous 'Excelsior' strain — which mine was — said when he reported his spectacular introduction to the august Royal Horticultural Society of England, "Eight feet is really too tall for a foxglove"; may be, but it certainly bowls everybody over; my giant was pure white, the little gloves facing straight out instead of hanging down, as older cultivars do, and with flowers all around the stem; it grew at the base of a peaty old stump, in moving shade, in cool moist air — and that's what they like; they also come in pale pink or deep pink with fascinating purple

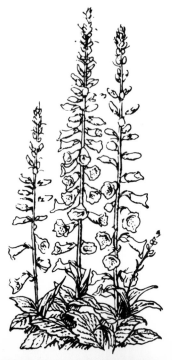

Foxglove.

freckles inside the throats; I sow mine in early summer, transplant some 6 weeks later into a nursery bed, some into a cold frame and some where they are to grow; this, I figure, covers all eventualities. (Once, in the hope of naturalizing a cross between the 'Excelsior' strain and the old strains that had escaped from an early settler's garden, I planted my seedlings all over a pasture where the older ones grew; the next year when the cows came down with a mysterious illness — I never dared ask if it was a fast pulse caused by too much digitalis — I felt so guilty I gave this project up.) Anyway, grow your foxgloves in rich fertile soil with lots of humus and don't ever let them dry out; if in the open garden, cover them with a winter mulch of crisp oak leaves tucked around and under the leaves, never *over* the crown.

Hollyhock; *Althaea rosea*; 5-6 feet; an old-fashioned plant in a new-fashioned dress; the cultivar 'Fire King' is double and red, 'Powderpuff', in mixed colors, looks as though someone had sown carnations all up and down a tall stem; there's also yellow and pink, all lovely; it's bold and needs generous spacing — about 3 feet between plants; blooms in midsummer, likes a light alkaline soil, and to be well-drained in winter; don't let it go to seed and be sure to pick off some of the large lower leaves to allow sun and air to get to the bottom of the plant; protect over winter.

Honesty, **Money Plant**; *Lunaria*; 3 feet; it does have purple flowers, but you really grow this one for its silver penny seed pods that make light-catching winter decorations; rub off the outer seed covering to reveal the silver membrane.

Iceland Poppy; *Papaver nudicaule*; 12-15 inches; delightful, dainty, delicate flowers with soft grey-green leaves and crinkled silky blossoms in white, pink, salmon, or yellow to orange, in spring; sow seed in summer where it is to grow.

Siberian Wallflower; *Erysimum asperum*; 12-18 inches; blooms with vivid orange flowers in spring, easy to grow in any good garden soil; can be moved in full flower; set 12 inches apart; Northwest coast custom plants them outdoors in fall then removes them after they bloom in the spring; in a normal winter, foliage stays green.

Sweet William, *Dianthus barbatus*; 6-12 inches; gorgeous velvet colors of white, pink, salmon, rose, cerise, red, scarlet and all combinations of these; blooms in spring and is wonderfully fragrant; set 9 inches apart in the garden.

Verbascum, Mullein, *V. phoeniceum*; little 2-foot plants with pink, white and purple flowers that bloom all summer; sow in summer where to grow, not fussy about where as long as it's full sun and well drained; allow to seed itself; V. 'Arctic Summer', growing 6 feet tall, make a fat rosette of woolly leaves which sparkles in the morning sun after a dewy night, and throw a tall spike of large bright yellow flowers which open in dull weather, close when it's sunny; they grew for me all over rocks in shallow soil quite simply by letting them go to seed, then twisting a bit off and poking it into an earth pocket here and there, in late summer; they have a long tap root so are almost impossible to start somewhere for moving later; another cultivar, 'Chaixii', is bright yellow with purple stamens, tall, very hardy and reliable too.

28 BULBS, CORMS AND TUBERS

You can count on bulbs, corms and tubers to be adroit performers in your garden. They come on with flair, hold centre stage while they flower and always bring out the best in the rest of the cast. Little spring bulbs spurt their fragile flowers through glassy snow just when you have begun to think that winter will never end. A few weeks later, when you're sure the world couldn't be more beautiful, the tulips and daffodils come on and make it so. Later again, when summer seems at its peak with spectacular perennials and annuals, lilies add elegant trumpets to the picture. And this is by no means the end of the bounty. There are still great tall spikes of gladiolus to come, exotic tuberous begonias and dahlias as little as the palm of your hand or as large as soup plates — all flowering till frost locks the world in winter again.

All spring bulbs are sure-success plants in your garden because within their brown skins — sometimes smooth and shiny, sometimes rough and bumpy — lies a whole new plant all ready to grow. Most are hardy in Zone 4 and up, and if planted a little deeper than normally recommended, in Zone 3 (North Dakota, northern Minnesota and extreme northern New England).

For gardeners in Zones 7, 8 and 9, many of the summer-flowering bulbs can be left in the ground the year round — Peruvian daffodils, Gloriosa, Hymenocallis, Lapeirousia, Ranunculus, Zephyranthes and others described on pages 273-275.

Figures for the number of bulbs shipped to North America by the Netherlands Flower-Bulb Institute in one year alone are astronomical — 21 million daffodils and narcissus, 25 million hyacinths, over 50 million crocus, 154 million tulips; nor does this include 43 million lesser-known Dutch bulbs, those imported from other countries and those grown on this continent.

In these tremendous totals there is also wide variety — approximately 100 different cultivars of hyacinths, over 300 cultivars of crocus and other small bulbs, more than 500 cultivars of daffodils or narcissus and at least 2,000 cultivars of tulips. Such figures are testimony to their initial appeal and to their continued importance in the garden scene. Obviously they perform superbly in all kinds of gardens.

HOW TO CHOOSE

Choose spring-flowering bulbs in late summer and early fall to get delivery in time to plant them before the ground freezes. No other time will do, for they need some weeks of steady cold for a good root system to form. The Dutch bulb industry is presently trying to find a way to cut down on this period, but results are not yet available to home gardeners. Watch for future news of this development.

To help you to make your choice, read lists in this chapter and check catalogues of bulb specialists and nurseries. Note particularly time of bloom, color and height. To classify all the available cultivars in an orderly fashion, official societies have set up agreed divisions for daffodils, tulips and hyacinths. These are listed in the notes on each of these bulbs.

Order your bulbs as soon as possible — stocks of the favorites sometimes sell out quickly and there is usually only one shipment each year. If you want something not carried by your local dealer, it's possible to import from another country but this requires a permit and inspection for clearance at both ends.

A calendar showing average sequence of bloom of twenty-four fine spring bulbs that flower over a period of 8-10 weeks is on page 260. You'll find this a handy guide if you would like a small smackerel of something in bloom over a long period. This can only be a guide: where you live, the weather in any one year, the climate of your garden, even the very spot the bulbs are growing in, may have bearing on the order and span of bloom. To say nothing of your own ingenuity. You can, for instance, deliberately snug a clump of snowdrops up against a big boulder that is warmed by the sun in late winter and stays warm well into the night, and thus have bloom a good two weeks earlier than if they were planted in the open garden. Conversely, you can plant daffodils, which grow best in cool air, where leafing-out trees will gradually shade them more and more and thus extend their blooming period by many days.

Beginning gardeners would be wise to buy cultivars that have been on the market for a few years — they will be less expensive and most certain of success to grow well. But don't overlook the real delight of trying one or two newer cultivars every year too.

Plan to plant early first-flowering little bulbs like crocus, aconite, snowdrops and all the daffodils in early fall; hyacinths in mid-fall, tulips any time till freeze-up.

Know that bulbs, even out of the ground, are living plants and for best results must be planted as soon as possible after delivery. If planting is delayed, open the bags and spread out the bulbs in an airy, cool (65°F) dark place till you can get them into the ground.

Prepare planting sites a few weeks ahead of time, if possible, to allow for settling and to lighten the job at the time of actual planting.

WHERE AND HOW TO PLANT

Early-flowering little bulbs are best planted where warm late-winter sun will bring them into bloom almost through the snow and, for the most tonic impact, where you can easily see them from indoors — this is seldom patio and iced-tea weather. They also do exceptionally well in rock gardens. Mid-season and late cultivars of daffodils, hyacinths and tulips can be set through all garden plantings, through foundation evergreens, shrub and perennial borders, rock gardens. Daffodils, scillas, wood hyacinths and English blue-bells look lovely naturalized in woodland, meadow or orchard.

From a design point of view, you'll be happiest if you plant small early bulbs in colonies of dozens or more; larger bulbs in clumps of not fewer than eight, twelve is better. And always plant all of one kind and one color to a clump; mixed bulb plantings are never as effective.

Special soil preparation for bulb plantings isn't necessary if your garden is already in good tilth, but one thing you must have is good drainage to prevent rotting and a build-up of disease. (For how to improve your soil if it needs it, and its drainage, see CHAPTER 18.)

Extra fertilizing for first year growth is usually unnecessary, but as you prepare the planting holes it's good practice to mix into the soil, *below* where the bulbs will sit, a slow-acting, high-phosphorus fertilizer, such as 5-12-5, to supply food for next year's bloom.

Planting can begin by digging out a large hole for each clump or individual holes for each bulb. A special bulb-planting tool is available which works like an apple corer, lifting out a straight-sided core of soil to the depth needed; or a regular trowel will do the job if you are careful to make the bottom of the hole wide enough for the bulb to sit firmly down on the soil with no air space beneath it. Be sure that there is no newly mixed-in fertilizer in direct contact with the bulb — some gardeners lay a layer of straight sand or unfertilized soil in the bottom of the hole to ensure this. Where you want to naturalize bulbs in drifts — "My heart with sudden laughter fills and dances with the daffodils" kind of a planting — toss your bulbs in a swinging sweep away from you, planting where they fall. Greenhouses sometimes sell spent bulbs (forced for florists' daffodils) at low prices for this use.

For depth to plant and distances apart, see chart, page 259. A general rule is to cover each bulb with soil to twice its depth. Exceptions to this are when you plan to leave plantings in place for a number of years or if you live in the far north. In both these cases you plant 4-6 inches deeper than the basic measure, depending on the size of the bulb. Also, if you want to do double-decker gardening and grow summer and fall-flowering annuals over bulbs that have finished flowering, it pays to plant the bulbs deeper than you normally would.

Water all bulbs after planting, even if at the time the ground seems moist enough. This encourages strong early root formation. If there are not ample rains through the fall, water deeply once a week.

1″	
2″	ACONITE
3″	GRAPE HYACINTH / SNOWDROP
4″	SCILLA SIBIRICA / BASE-ROOTING LILY
5″	TULIP
6″	STEM-ROOTING LILY
7″	CROCUS / DAFFODIL
8″	GLORY OF THE SNOW
9″	HYACINTH
10″	
11″	
12″	

Correct planting depth for bulbs.

If you like to know the name of what you're growing, this is the time to label your plantings or to make a small chart. The memory of an elephant you may have, even a bulb-loving elephant, but it's almost certain that you won't remember one of the names of your bulbs by spring, if they aren't marked when you plant them.

ONGOING CARE

First year plantings need little care till it's time to pick dead flowers off. This should be done promptly to prevent the strength of the bulb from going into seed-making rather than into building a strong new bulb for next year.

To build up flowering for future years (early small bulbs increase easily, daffodils are long-lived when planted in the right place, hyacinths and tulips grow really well in most gardens for only 3 years and then usually need replacing) it is absolutely necessary to leave the foliage to ripen. This takes several weeks and sometimes looks very messy. Several clever camouflages are possible. You can plant your bulbs — this works particularly well with the little early ones — under deciduous trees and shrubs, which will be bare when the bulbs bloom, and later will be thickly leafed, hiding the bulb foliage beneath. Or you can make your plantings beside perennials that will later grow up and conceal them — peonies are fine for this. You can interplant the bulbs with a later-flowering annual — ageratum, candytuft, forget-me-nots, petunias, alyssum, pansies are a few of the many good ones. Another way is to dig up your bulbs after they have bloomed, keeping the roots in soil and the leaves and stem intact, heel them in to ripen somewhere out of sight, then replant in fall.

Foliage is ready to be pulled from its bulb when it has become yellowish and limp and comes away with a gentle tug. Some gardeners tie up or braid ripening leaves for a tidier effect, but this cuts down the usefulness of the leaves which really need both air and sunlight to build the new bulb.

Established plantings benefit from a feeding of general purpose, high phosphorus fertilizer (5-10-5) or superphosphate, after flowering, to encourage robust new bulb growth.

Protection from squirrels, rabbits and mice, who consider bulbs to be the caviar of the rodent world, is sometimes necessary. See CHAPTER 18 for various trickeries.

Mulches, especially for new plantings, are effective in keeping the ground moist during the important root-forming period in the fall and in keeping it evenly cold, especially during late winter thaws and freezes. Contrary to usual garden practice, these are applied *before* the ground freezes. For what material to use and how to apply, see CHAPTER 18 under Mulches.

Most spring bulbs bloom before weeds become a problem, but later when foliage is ripening, they should be pulled so as not to deprive the bulb of the food it needs to grow to perfection.

Good garden practice puts new plantings where bulbs have not grown before to avoid a build-up of insects or disease.

You can have 8-10 weeks of spring bulbs in flower if you plant for sequence of bloom — choose from these

Snowdrop, *Galanthus*: fragile, porcelain white little drops that literally push their way through the last crystal snow to flower in late winter, 4-6 inches tall; a double form that's a charmer but you have to look up into it to see the extra frills; can be moved in full bloom.

Winter Aconite, *Eranthis*: a yellow buttercup of a flower with a ruff of fringed green leaves; blooms a few inches above the ground as soon as the snow goes and the flowers, like snowdrops and crocus, survive repeated freezings; tucked in near a south-facing garden door, aconites bloom before snowdrops in my garden.

The Tiny Daffodils, *Narcissus minimus* and *N. nanus* and a tiny narcissus, *N. watieri* (see Daffodils and Narcissus, this Chapter).

Crocus: comes through the ground in sprightly spurts of bright color, some the minute the snow melts, some as late as when the tulips bloom; striped or plain colors of blue, white, yellow, mauve and violet; if you want to plant them through your lawn, as they do for a broad landscape effect in many botanical gardens, then be prepared to go around their tufts of ripening leaves for six weeks when you cut the grass or cut right over them and plant new ones every fall; squirrels find them tasty, so take special precautions at planting time (see CHAPTER 18).

Glory-of-the-Snow, *Chionodoxa*: plant in drifts under trees and shrubs where its white-eyed, starry blue flowers will bloom when the ground is barely warm; 6 inches tall; hardy; leave in place for years and they will multiply into a broad blue carpet.

Iris species: *I. reticulata* is an exquisite miniature, 6-8 inches high, with the heavenly fragrance of violets, the flowers in dark purple, pale blue, sky blue with a yellow crest, red purple, dark blue or violet with an orange crest; *I. danfordiae*, golden yellow and very early; *I. histrioides major,* bright blue and thought by many to be the best; look in catalogues of bulb specialists for rare species — *I. susiana*, the Mourning Iris, with a huge flower in purple-veined grey-white; *I. Junonia* and *I. Regeliocyclus* are both unusual and worthwhile to grow; a hardy race of free-flowering hybrids also have veined flowers and three, 'Chione', 'Elvira' and 'Sylphide' are already award winners at flower shows in Europe and Britain.

Early daffodils (see notes, this Chapter, on Daffodils and Narcissus).

Tulip species, *Tulipa* (see notes this Chapter on Tulips).

Siberian Squill, *Scilla sibirica*: the very bluest of blue, vivid and in bloom for a long time if you plant them in light, moving shade; I use them in a crowd beneath a white birch beside a black pool and interplant them with white trilliums and bleeding heart, which hide their untidy ripening foliage when bloom is over and make a second lovely picture.

Dog's-Tooth Violet, *Erythronium dens-canis*: a first cousin — and a far handsomer one — of our wild dog's-tooth violet; larger, with many flowers to one stem, more vigorous and a bloom to every bulb; 6-8 inches tall; not hardy everywhere, but well worth trying; flowers in cream, deep rose, white, light purple pink and sulphur yellow, the leaves nearly always mottled.

Puschkinia, *P. scilloides*: a 4-inch, multiple-flowered little bulb; white, and white striped with grey-blue.

The Tazetta Daffodils (see notes on Daffodils and Narcissus, this Chapter).

Crown Imperial, *Fritillaria imperialis*: an absolute knockout of a plant; shoots up nearly 3 feet in early spring with glossy green leaves at the base, a bare stem with a tuft of green leaves at the top and right below it a crown of orange-red, orange-brown or sulphur yellow bell-like flowers hanging down; but don't plant it for a sweet fragrance. John Gerard, writing in 1597, politely called it "foxy." He also noted that "in the bottome of ech of its bels there is placed six drops of most cleere shining sweet water, in taste like sugar, resembling in shew faire orient pearls; the which drops if you take away, there doe immediately appear the like, as well in bigness as also in sweetness: notwithstanding if they may be suffered to stande still in the flower according to his own nature, they will never fall away, no not if you strike the plant, until it be broken." The bulb is large, and to prevent water collecting in and rotting its center it should be planted 6 inches deep, on its side.

Snakeshead Fritillary, *Fritillaria meleagris*: slender-stemmed nodding bells, 12 inches tall, in strange, moody, chequered and speckled colors of dark purple, purple-rose, pink and a large white, 'Aphrodite'.

Hyacinth, *Hyacinthus* (see notes on Hyacinths, this Chapter).

Mid-season Daffodils (see notes on Daffodils and Narcissus, this Chapter).

Mayflowering Tulips (see notes on Tulips, this Chapter).

Grape Hyacinth, *Muscari*: tiny steepled stalks of blue bells, and there's a white one too; plant them like a small stream, running through a rock garden or border, as they do so successfully in the famous Keukenhof Gardens in Holland.

Windflower, *Anemone blanda*: single flowers in blue, pink or white; 8 inches; hardy.

Camassia: a native of the Northwest; pale and deep blue, white, 20-36 inches tall, naturalizes well; plant in masses and be sure to mulch overwinter.

Allium, selections; these bulbs are of the onion family; many hardy and showy species in lilac, purple, white, bright yellow, carmine pink and violet-red; some pleasantly fragrant; 6-36 inches; the low ones are fine for rockeries, the tall ones in open beds.

Snowflake, *Leucojum vernum*: hardy; often mistaken for snowdrops but more vigorous and taller (12 inches); each white petal tipped with green.

Wood Hyacinth, Spanish Bluebell, *Scilla hispanica* and English Bluebell, *S. nonscripta*: 20-24 inches, nodding blue flowers, also white and pink; naturalizes well.

Ixiolirion, *I. montanum*: the last of the spring flowering bulbs; stems 12-18 inches with masses of deep blue tubular flowers; relatively inexpensive, rare and hardy.

THE THREE STARS OF THE SPRING BULBS

TULIPS

Nothing can touch the buoyant brilliance of tulips. Proof of their attraction for all gardeners is that more are sold every year than all other bulbs combined. Men have toasted their beauty, women have danced to them, chimney sweeps have traded in them: even the Wizard of Oz has tiptoed through them. More than 300 years ago, the Grand Turk of the Ottoman Empire, Sultan Mohammed III, planted thousands of tulips in the gardens of his palace on the Bosporus. In the spring, when he found himself bored with the current favorites of his 1,500-wife harem, he commanded new candidates to dance before vases of tulips; the most graceful and provocative then received his favor and an apartment of her own instead of having to bunk in with the rest of the girls. The sultan, obviously an ingenious and imaginative man, also designed one of the first night lighting features for a garden. He directed that candles be fastened to the backs of big turtles, which were then led through the paths of his gardens so that his guests could admire his tulips after dark even though they were partially closed.

The chimney sweeps who traded in tulips were only a small part of the passion that developed in Holland during the early 1600s. Men made and lost fortunes in tulip trading and, with the whole country in a frenzy of tulipomania, the Court of Holland finally had to step in to regulate trading by law. At one point, Anthony West writes, one hysterical man gave "two loads of wheat, four loads of rye, four fat oxen, eight fat pigs, twelve fat sheep, two hogsheads of wine, four barrels of beer, two barrels of butter, a thousand pounds of cheese, a bed with mattress, pillows and hangings, a suit of clothes and a silver jug" for one bulb of a cultivar named 'Viceroy', but there is no record of whether it was a truly beautiful tulip or just a rare one. Luckily, although they still cast a spell over gardeners, tulips change hands for much less today; who of us could give anyone a bed with hangings?

Acknowledging their popularity and proven hardiness over most of the country, the question then becomes, "Which are the tulips for you?" To start you off, here is the official classification of the Royal General Bulbgrowers Society of Haarlem, Holland.

EARLY:

Division 2: Single Early (these are brilliantly colored cultivars that finish early and therefore allow quick over-planting with annuals for the next bloom in your garden)
Division 3: Double Early (last well, look like full-blown roses)

MID-SEASON:

Division 4: Mendel (strong stems, resemble Darwins but bloom 2 weeks earlier)
Division 5: Triumph (Darwins crossed with Single Earlies; long stems)

MAY FLOWERING OR LATE:

Division 6: Darwins (popular, long strong stems)
Division 7: Darwin Hybrids (some of the most spectacular)
Division 8: Breeder (large, usually dark colors, unusual)
Division 9: Lily-flowered (graceful, reflexed, sprightly)
Division 10: Cottage (some multiflowered, all popular)
Division 11: Rembrandt (striped, feathered, blotched, red on white ground)
Division 12: Bizarre (striped, feathered, blotched)
Division 14: Parrot (strong-stemmed, feathered, fringed, the flower arranger's delight)
Division 15: Double Late or Peony-flowered (really do look like a peony)

Divisions 16-23: Species, Tulipas and their hybrids: (Included in these are the Fosteriana, Greigii and Kaufmanniana Hybrids, all a delight.)

You will note that Divisions 1 and 13 are omitted. These are tulips of historical interest only, covering obsolete types not now in commerce.

To start you off with a list of good cultivars to buy for your garden, The Netherlands Flower-Bulb Institute reports these as prime favorites either because they are present or predictable best sellers:

EARLY:

T. Fosteriana:	**'Galata'** (16 inches)	Orange red, yellow base
	'Red Emperor' (18 inches)	Immense, fiery red, very early, very popular
T. Greigii:	**'Red Riding Hood'** (8 inches)	Dwarf, bright scarlet, base black, exterior carmine red, leaves mottled
T. Kaufmanniana:	**'Heart's Delight'** (10 inches)	Pale rose, base gold with red blotches, exterior carmine red, edged pale rose, leaves mottled
	'Stresa' (10 inches)	Indian yellow, base blood red, exterior red edged with yellow, leaves mottled.
Single Early:	**'Princess Irene'** (12 inches)	Orange and purple, unique
	'Thule' (16 inches)	Red, edged yellow
Double Early	**'Monte Carlo'** (14 inches)	Sulphur yellow
Triumph:	**'Abbe Pierre'** (16 inches)	Blood red

MAY FLOWERING:

Darwin:	**'Aristocrat'** (28 inches)	Purple violet, enormous flower
	'Attila' (30 inches)	Light purple violet
	'Cantor' (30 inches)	Carmine red, base white
	'Gander' (26 inches)	Bright magenta pink
	'Pink Supreme' (22 inches)	Rich rose pink
	'Queen of Night' (30 inches)	Deep velvety maroon black
Darwin Hybrids:	**'Diplomate'** (20 inches)	Exterior vermilion, inside signal red, base green yellow
	'Golden Apeldoorn' (26 inches)	Golden yellow, base a black star
	'Gudoshnik' (27 inches)	Large flower of yellow spotted red, flamed rose, base bluish black, strong, early, fragrant
	'Jewel of Spring' (24 inches)	Sulphur yellow, small red edge, base greenish black

	'Oxford' (24 inches)	Brilliant red flushed with purple red, inside pepper red, base sulphur yellow	
	'Parade' (28 inches)	Signal red, black base, edged yellow	
	'Spring Song' (24 inches)	Strong, robust, bright red flushed with salmon, base white	
	'Yellow Dover' (26 inches)	Buttercup yellow, base black	
Cottage:	**'Asta Nielsen'** (26 inches)	Yellow, exterior sulphur yellow	
	'Balalaika' (26 inches)	Glowing turkey red, base yellow	
	'Bond Street' (24 inches)	Yellow and orange	
	'Golden Harvest' (28 inches)	Large lemon yellow	
	'Halcro' (26 inches)	Carmine red, base yellow edged green, lovely form long lasting	
	'Mrs. John T. Scheepers' (24 inches)	Clear golden yellow, thought by many to be the best yellow tulip	
	'Princess Margaret Rose' (21 inches)	Yellow, edged orange red	
	'Renown' (24 inches)	Light carmine red, edged paler, base yellow, very large	
Parrot:	**'Karel Doorman'** (22 inches)	Cherry red, edged yellow, very large	
Lily-flowered:	**'Aladdin** (22 inches)	Interior orange red, yellow base exterior scarlet with cream edge; long pointed petals	

'Mariette' (22 inches)	Gold Medal (Haarlem); deep, satin rose, tall strong stems, a true beauty
'Red Shine' (18 inches)	Deep ruby red, blue base

(*The above list is small for a flower with hundreds of cultivars and you may well find a now or future favorite of your own that's not on it.*)

Tulip cultivars tested and especially recommended for the cooler parts of the United States, Zone 3 through Zone 7.

TRIUMPH
'Arabian Mystery' (23 inches): Deep purple violet, edged white
'Grater' (18 inches): Bright carmine red, passing into vermilion at the edge; large, strong
'First Lady' (18 inches): Red violet, flushed purple
'Olaf' (18 inches): Scarlet
'Preludium' (18 inches): Rose, white base
'Rhineland' (18 inches): Yellow and red
'Topscore' (18 inches): Geranium red, yellow base
DOUBLE LATE
'Nizza' (16 inches): Sturdy; sulphur yellow, streaked red
DARWIN
'Golden Age' (22 inches): Deep yellow, edges turning orange
DARWIN HYBRID
'Gudoshnik' (27 inches): Blend of rose, cream, yellow; very large; early
'Oxford' (24 inches): Bright red, clear yellow base
LILY-FLOWERED
'Aladdin' (22 inches): Interior orange red, yellow base, exterior scarlet with narrow cream edge; long, pointed petals
COTTAGE
'Ivory Glory': Amber white
'Marshal Haig' (30 inches): Very tall; large; pointed petals; brilliant scarlet, clear yellow base

---

Special Culture and Care:

In the East, tulips are planted in mid-October to late November; in the North in September; on the West Coast in October to November. (For depth of planting and distance apart see drawing, page 259). Pick off dead flowers and destroy petals — don't let them fall on the garden for they could breed disease. Tulips are usually top quality for about 3 years only. In small gardens where every inch counts, you would be wise to plant new ones every year, lifting out and discarding the old ones. Rotate tulip plantings in your garden so that you plant them in the same place only once every 3 years. Tulips sometimes throw up one big leaf and have no flower. This indicates overcrowding of the bulbs in the ground because of new small ones forming around the old ones. If your tulips are doing this, dig them up and replant only the biggest bulbs in the conspicuous part of your garden; if you want to grow the small size bulbs on to blooming size — it is these that make the single big leaf — plant them in a hidden corner until they grow to flowering size.

DAFFODILS AND/OR NARCISSUS

These cheerful dancing flowers — all charmers in spring gardens — live under a certain amount of confusion about their names. Some people call all kinds "daffodil," some call all kinds "narcissus." For our purposes, trumpets, large cups, small cups and doubles will be daffodils; the triandrus, cyclamineus, jonquil, tazetta and poeticus divisions will be narcissus. And just so that no one will think we are taking sides, some of the miniatures will be daffodils, some will be narcissus.

Whatever they're called they're delightful, fragrant and pretty in your garden and, unlike tulips, given the right conditions they go on for years and years. I know one green grassy field beside a blue lake in northern Michigan that literally dances with them every May and the same bulbs have been there for well over fifty years. Although there is not extensive information on their hardiness range, the Peace River country reports them as suitable there and one adventuring gardener, in an area of the prairies where daffodils are usually only recommended for beside-foundation planting, has had great luck with a sizable clump of large-trumpeted yellow 'Dutch Master'.

Daffodils come mainly from Holland, but large breeding programs are also going on in England, Ireland, the United States and elsewhere, as well as being the hobby of many amateur hybridizers. This calls for true dedication for it takes at least 25 years from seedling to introduction to the trade.

Mainly yellow and white, there are some cultivars in delicate pink, some with cups frilled with giddy orange and scarlet, and a few boast green tingeing in the throat. They range in size from giants, 12-14 inches tall, with large flowers one to a stem, to the tiniest miniature, *N. minimum*, blooming a bare 3 inches above the ground with the littlest trumpet you have ever seen. Some — a favorite is 'Cheerfulness' — are many-flowered. All are fragrant, some with a more carrying scent than others.

Special Culture and Care:

Daffodils and narcissus are planted in September, if you can get delivery then. This is sometimes difficult because the import regulations now demand a washing of the bulbs between harvest and shipping, which is time-consuming because it must be done by hand. If yours arrive later than September, get them into the ground as soon as possible, water deeply, and mulch immediately to delay freezing of the ground.

Daffodils, unlike the one-bulb tulips, have more than one snout: this is why you often have a many-flowered clump from only a few bulbs.

Plant them in sun or semi-shade almost anywhere in the garden — they will last longest where it is cool. Where they are questionably hardy, plant next to the house foundation. They tend to face the light, so if you have a choice, plant where from indoors you will see their faces not the backs of their necks.

Daffodils root as deeply as 24 inches, so they need deeply prepared soil.

Latest information from bulb experts on the best feeding program recommends that fertilizer in the proportion of 3-18-18, at rates recommended by the manufacturer, be mixed into the soil when the holes are being prepared. If basal rot is a problem in your area, do not use organic fertilizers such as manure, bonemeal, cottonseed or compost of any kind. (If you are not sure about this, consult your nearest agricultural agent.)

Daffodils to be left in place for a number of years should be topdressed each spring with a 4-12-8 fertilizer at the rate of 2 pounds per 100 square feet, being careful not to let the fertilizer touch the foliage.

They prefer a slightly acid soil. If you are unsure about yours, have it tested in a soil laboratory (see PART V for the one nearest you); do it yourself with a home kit or consult an expert in your area. It's especially important to correct the pH if it is below 5.5. (For how to do this, see CHAPTER 18.)

A summer mulch (pine needles, buckwheat hulls, wood chips, ground corn cobs) helps to keep the soil cool and moist.

For depth to plant and distance apart, see drawing page 259.

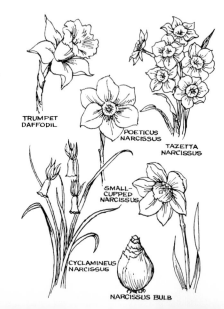

TRUMPET DAFFODIL

POETICUS NARCISSUS

TAZETTA NARCISSUS

SMALL-CUPPED NARCISSUS

CYCLAMINEUS NARCISSUS

NARCISSUS BULB

A delight of daffodils.

The Official Classification of Daffodils and Narcissus with Recommended Cultivars

Note: *The perianth is the pattern of petals at the back of the flower: The trumpet or cup extends forward from the centre of the perianth.*

DIVISION I: Trumpets (trumpet as long or longer than the perianth)
'Beersheba': Purest white; vigorous; early
'Dutch Master': Uniformly yellow; deeply serrated trumpet
'Golden Harvest': Large and sturdy; golden yellow; perianth sometimes 6 inches across
'Gold Medal': Short stemmed; large flowers
'Magnet': Strong stemmed, white perianth, yellow trumpet
'Magnificence': Very early; golden yellow
'Mrs. E. H. Krelage': Perianth snowy white, trumpet opens soft yellow turns white
'Mount Hood': Large, imposing; pure white; trumpet heavily frilled; tall
'Unsurpassable': Large; deep golden yellow
'William the Silent': This one is on the list because you couldn't believe that such a big bold trumpet would be called 'Silent'; golden yellow

DIVISION II: Large-cupped (the cup more than one third but less than the total length of the perianth)
'Belisana': Flowers 5 inches across; star-shaped, reflexed, perianth pure white, broad-rimmed orange cup
'Carlton': Five-inch flowers; soft yellow; frilled cup; early
'Golden Orchid': A novelty—a split trumpet attached to perianth; yellow
'Lady Luck': Deep yellow; large; orange cup
'Milk and Cream': Perianth is the milk, cup is the cream; large
'Missouri': Bright yellow perianth, orange cup; sunproof
'Salmon Trout': Considered the best of the pinks; pure white perianth, large deep salmon pink cup

DIVISION III: Small-cupped (cup not more than one third the length of the perianth)
'Apricot Distinction': Perianth red apricot, cup red orange

'Edward Buxton': Soft yellow perianth, orange cup; vigorous; early
'Jezebel': The nearest to an all-red daffodil; red gold perianth; intense red cup
'La Riante': Smooth white perianth, orange red cup

DIVISION IV: Double Daffodils (doubles from all divisions)
'Inglescombe': Lemon yellow; strong stemmed
'Mary Copeland': Large cream white, deep orange centre
'Texas': Large; yellow with orange intermixed; plant where protected from wind as heads heavy

DIVISION V: Triandrus Narcissus
'Horn of Plenty': Large flowered, 3-4 to a stem; pure white
'Silver Chimes': White perianth, yellow cup; 6 flowers to a stem; late
N. triandrus **'Thalia':** Glistening white nodding flowers 2-3 to a stem; delicate and graceful

DIVISION VI: Cyclamineus Hybrids
'February Gold': Slightly reflexed yellow perianth, trumpet gold; very early; blooms a long time
'Peeping Tom': Slender trumpet and reflexed perianth in golden yellow; lasts a long time

DIVISION VII: Jonquils and Jonquil Hybrids
'Cherie': Ivory white perianth, cup flushed shell pink
'Suzy': Bright yellow, red cup; many flowered, three to a bulb

DIVISION VIII: Tazetta Narcissus
'Cheerfulness': Double, white with buff centre

DIVISION IX: Poeticus Narcissus
'Actaea': Snow white perianth, dark red eye; large

DIVISION X: Species and Wild Forms
N. minimus: Smallest of the trumpets; 3 inches high, trumpet no more than an inch long; yellow; hardy
N. nanus: Excellent for rockery; 6 inches, yellow; early
N. triandrus **'Albus':** The Angel's Tears daffodil; creamy white flowers, 2-5 to a stem; not reliably hardy everywhere
N. watieri: Rare little narcissus from Morocco; starry up-facing white flowers; pure white; hardy and increases well

---

If of thy mortal goods thou art bereft,
And from thy slender store two loaves alone
To thee are left,
Sell one, and with the dole,
Buy hyacinths to feed thy soul.

SAADI

HYACINTHS

The two chief virtues of hyacinths in your garden are their wonderful fat spikes of bright flowers and their fragrance. Plant them near a door or a window, near a path where you can walk in early spring sunshine and enjoy their heavenly smell. In the coldest parts of the country they are practical only as forced plants for indoors: elsewhere they can be happily used to border a walk, as plantings through a border, or in the rock garden.

Officially, they are graded by size and listed by color. You'll be pleased to hear that bulb experts recommend that you do not buy the biggest and most expensive sizes for outdoors since they tend to fall over in rain and wind. Instead they recommend bulbs no more than 7 inches in circumference (this translates into 17-18 centimeters).

The Top Size, also known as Exhibition, is over 7½ inches in circumference; First Size is 7-7½ inches; Second Size is 6½-7 inches; Third Size is 5½-6 inches; Bedding, the most popular for outdoor gardens, is a little smaller; and a special class suitable for outdoors in protected plantings is Multiflora, a specially prepared bulb that produces eight or more stems.

Here is a list, by color, of some of the best. Consult your bulb dealer and nurseryman's catalogue for others.

BLUE:
'Bismarck': Sky blue; large
'King of the Blues': Dark blue, flowers late
'Ostara': Dark blue; a great favorite

PINK:
'Lady Derby': Light pink; loose belled
'Pink Pearl': Rose pink; large; very sweet scent
'Princess Irene': Light rose, silvery
'Queen of the Pinks': Bright rose; compact; late

WHITE:
'L'Innocence': White; loosely belled

RED:
'La Victoire': Brilliant red; large; full

YELLOW:
'City of Haarlem': Pale yellow; large

VIOLET:
'Hon. Mr. Balfour': Pinkish heliotrope

MULTIFLORA:
'Borah': Bright blue; 8 or more slender graceful spikes per bulb

Special Culture and Care

Plant in mid-fall in a well-drained, sunny place. For depth to plant and distance apart, see drawing page 259.

Where winters are cold but hyacinths hardy outdoors, mulch plantings with a loose covering of evergreen branches or straw and remove as soon as green tips appear.

Remove dead flowers by snicking off the little bells, leaving the green stems and foliage to ripen until it's brown and will pull away easily from the bulb.

Feed after blooming with a general purpose fertilizer (4-12-8).

Count on replacing bulbs every 2-4 years, and rotate where you plant.

SUMMER FLOWERING BULBS, CORMS AND TUBERS

These add a tropical air to your summertime garden. Nearly all are so tender you must bring them indoors in winter and store them in a cool though not freezing temperature; but in warm summer weather they grow like a charm.

From first growth to flower, their season is short, so they need more water and fertilizer than spring bulbs; some, if they are to bloom outdoors before frost, need an early start indoors in a flat of moist peat and sand, then a spell under fluorescent lights or on a sunny window sill before they can be planted outdoors when both weather and soil are reliably warm.

Some are readily available, others are rare and must be ordered from a bulb specialist. All are a joy to grow.

THE FOUR PRIMA DONNAS OF THE SUMMER SCENE
DAHLIAS, GLADIOLUS, LILIES, TUBEROUS BEGONIAS

DAHLIAS

Dahlia flowers come in cradling-in-your-hand sizes or great big beautiful bragging-size soup plates. The plants can be as high as your knee or, if you're medium-tall, look you smack in the eye with their wonderfully open-faced flowers. And all kinds

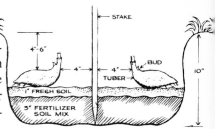

Correct planting for dahlias.

of glorious colors — well, nearly all: no blue yet. They're grown just about everywhere there are gardens. They bloom from late midsummer till frost wilts them down, are showy and handsome in borders, along walls, paths or fences, or in whole beds of their own kind. If you can give them the proper treatment and storage over winter, they increase from year to year. In other words, they're an absolutely marvelous garden plant and great favorites with gardeners all over the country.

Show-off sizes, known as Decoratives, sometimes have flower heads as large as 12 inches across. They're grown mainly for exhibition and competitive shows, but one floated on a big plate can look lovely as a table centre. This class is subdivided further as Formals — broad pointed or rounded and regularly set petals; and Informals, which are twisted and twirly and irregularly set. My favorites, the Cactus division, have rolled, quill-like petals, a subdivision called Incurved has petals that turn toward the centre; Semi Cactus are flat at the base, half quilled; Straight Cactus, the petals do not curve. Then there are Singles, like a daisy; Peony, with 2-5 rows of petals around a central disk; Anemone, with one ring of petals around a disk; Orchid, like the singles only with petals turning inward and somewhat tubular; Collarette with a single row around a disk and another row of smaller petals usually of a different color (these constantly dance with butterflies and darting hummingbirds). The Ball class are round with a spiral arrangement of petals, and Pompons are similar to Balls, but smaller. There is a class of small, short dahlias usually grown from seed that can be sown in spring and be in bloom the same year, making tubers which can be stored for future use. As well, there is a race of Dwarf Bedding Hybrids that is creating great interest, for they're just as beautiful as larger cultivars but shorter, the flowers are a shade smaller and they are often a better size for the average home garden and don't need to be staked.

They all like cool summer weather and are at their best in gardens by water where the air is gently moist all the time.

How to Choose: Decide the size of dahlia you would like to grow, then check catalogues for cultivars whose color and form appeal to you. Bulb specialists will carry more unusual ones. Order in late winter for spring delivery. Tubers should be plump and firm, each with a bit of stem, some will already have eyes showing. Don't accept weak, wizened ones.

How and Where to Plant: Dahlias like sun and cool air, which means that, if you live where sunny days are also hot, you should give them a place with some light shade at noon. Soil should be rich, with lots of humus and well drained. For how to make this if you do not have it see CHAPTER 18.

Dahlias are very susceptible to frost damage, and therefore should be planted where this is least likely to strike. Avoid low land where frost gathers early; favor slopes where it flows past and down. The Dwarf Bedding types are started similarly to other plants grown from seed (see CHAPTER 18).

Tubers of large kinds should be set 4 feet apart each way, medium sizes 3 feet, and miniatures 2 feet. In well-prepared ground, dig a hole 6 inches deep and about 12 inches wide. Set a sturdy stake 18 inches into the ground (a foot deeper than the bottom of the hole). Set two tubers of the same kind in each hole, horizontally, with the stem ends 3 inches from the stake and back to back. Cover with 2 inches of soil,

and water well, then as sprouts grow, fill in more and more soil till it's level with the ground or a little above it. Tie the growing stalk to the stake every 12 inches, see drawing above.

Water deeply if the weather is dry — they should never be allowed to dry out because growth then hardens and no eyes are produced. In light soil, this could mean watering every day — you will have to judge this for yourself.

Pinch the main leader when there are 3 sets of leaves so as to develop a bushy plant that will not be easily damaged by wind or heavy summer rain. With large sizes, let six stalks develop, then pinch out the two that would bump into the stake if allowed to grow. In this way, you grow four main stalks from each tuber and, in the experience of the champion dahlia grower who gave me these directions, each will flower as well as if you grew only one big stalk. With small sizes such as Pompons and Dwarfs, pinch the side shoots a second time. If you are entering Decoratives in exhibitions or shows, disbud the side buds when they are about as big as a pea, to throw all the strength into the main bud at the top.

Fertilize the ground initially when soil is being prepared (see CHAPTER 18) and again when flower buds are forming by spreading about ½ cup of high-phosphorus and potash garden fertilizer (5-10-10) around the plant, being careful not to touch stem or leaves; water it in. Some top dahlia growers also mix in 3 pounds of superphosphate per 100 square feet and grow a crop of perennial rye after the tubers are dug in the fall, turning it into the ground before planting in spring. Also once every three years they dig in a thick layer of rotted manure. It would be an understatement at this point to say that dahlias are heavy feeders.

Weed carefully so as not to damage feeder roots.

Spray with a combined insecticide and fungicide from the time the plants are 10 inches tall till flowers form. You may need a special miticide if you get red spiders on your plants (see CHAPTER 19 for controls).

Mulch with 3-4 inches of compost when plants are 18-24 inches high to keep the soil moist and cool and to discourage weeds. Scrape this mulch back when you put fertilizer on and then replace.

Cut off dead flower heads.

Dig up after first killing frost and turn upside down to dry for half a day outdoors (do this on a sunny day). Handle the tubers carefully for they bruise and break easily, particularly where the tuber meets the stem. At this point you have a choice of what to do next. Either clean the earth gently off the tubers and dust with a combined insecticide-fungicide; or leave the soil on the tubers till spring; or clean and cut them into growing sections for next year, then dust. Store in dry peat, sawdust, vermiculite or perlite, in or out of a perforated plastic bag. After the tubers are well dried, some gardeners dip them in barely-melting wax before storing, but I think that the perforated plastic bag does just as well and is easier. Be sure to label. Temperature for winter storage should be no more than 50°F., and it is a good idea to check the tubers once or twice during the winter, discarding any that are obviously not keeping well.

Rotate planting places if possible to prevent a build-up of diseases.

Specially successful techniques are used by some dahlia fans. One prestarts all his tubers in 4-6-inch flowerpots under fluorescent lights, then when shoots are 4 inches long, makes cuttings which he plants in perlite.

When they have rooted (10-20 days), he pots them up, keeps them at 50°F. under lights again until they can be planted out in the garden directly in the ground; with very precious cultivars, he leaves them in their pots, setting the rims an inch below the level of the ground, feeds and waters them inside the rim (sometimes every day) then digs them up and stores them over winter in the pots they grew in.

---

25 RECOMMENDED CULTIVARS

An—Anemone; Ba—Ball; Coll—Collarette; FD—Formal Decorative; IC—Incurved Cactus; ID—Informal Decorative; M—Miniature; Mig—Mignon; O—Orchid Flowering; P—Peony; Pom—Pompon; S—Single; SC—Semi-Cactus; StC—Straight Cactus

'Asahi Chohji': An; bicolor, red and white
'Billy': StC; yellow
'Bishop of Llandaff': P; red
'Bonne Esperance': Mig(dwf), S Min; dark pink
'Cha Cha': SC; blend of yellow and red
'Danny': IC; light pink
'Fandango': Coll; red, red, yellow and white collar
'Frontispiece': StC; white
'Giraffe': O; bronze
'Imp': O; yellow
'Joyce Seaburg': ID; variegated purple and white
'Juanita': StC; dark red
'Kidd's Climax': FD; blend of light pink and yellow
'Klankstad Kerkrade': StC; yellow
'Lion's International': FD; dark pink
'Little Robert': FD; blend of dark red and white
'Little Willo': Pom; white
'Moorplace': Pom; dark red
'Nita': StC; variegated lavender and red
'Purple Globe': Ba; purple
'Red Butterfly': S; bicolor of red and yellow
'Rothesay Superb': Ba; red
'Sterling Silver': FD; white
'Windlassie': ID; white
'Woody Woodpecker': Coll; dark red, red and yellow collar

GLADIOLUS

As hobby flowers to grow for competition and exhibition and as the most stunning and dependable material for flower arrangers, gladiolus are tops. It's possible to grow them effectively through other plants in your garden, particularly if you make a generous clump — say 10-20 corms of one cultivar — that will bloom all at the same time, in the same color; but mainly they will be most satisfactory if you grow them in a special site where, if they are going into competitive shows as either specimens or arrangements, you can grow them to perfection.

They come in five sizes of flowers. **Giants** are large tall spikes of florets, each at least 5½ inches across or larger, and, although they're mostly grown to show, they make handsome, imposing church and wedding flower arrangements. **Large** is a big glad with florets 4½-5½ inches across; **Medium** are 3½-4½ inches; **Small** are 2½-3½ inches and **Miniatures** are under 2½ inches across often with florets that look appealingly up rather than facing out. Growers and suppliers also classify glads by the size of their corms. Large are 1¼ inches; medium ¾-1¼ inches; small under ¾ inches. Catalogues usually indicate the size they supply.

Florets can be different shapes, their petals wavy, fluted, twisted, ruffled or plain, formally set along the spike in a double row or informally, however they please. The texture and finish of the flowers is something to rave about. Some are like velvet, some suede, some silky smooth. Others are ethereally transparent, some look carved and a rare one now and then seems to sparkle in the sun. The color range is fantastic — all the tints, tones and hues from white to black-red, some with a different colored throat, some feathered with a different color.

They're easy to grow, successful in the Far North, inexpensive, propagate well, are not fussy about soil or site and they're obviously beloved and enjoyed by thousands of gardeners all over the country for they're always on the best-seller list.

All-America Gladiolus Selections, with 35 test gardens in the United States and Canada, issue awards yearly to new glads which they judge have proved worthy in all parts of the country, under all kinds of conditions. Like other award flowers, they may or may not make the top of your list but they're always worth trying. The fact that, by the time they're introduced, they're in wide supply and therefore selling at a reasonable price, is in their favor too. Besides these selections, national societies rate the best cultivars and publish the list in their annual year books which are available through membership in the society. (See page 401 for how to join gladiolus societies.)

How to Choose: Deal with a reputable company and with a bulb specialist if you want special or unusual cultivars. The best stock will be plump, heavy, clean, with small basal scars on the corms. Many specialists in growing gladiolus advise that with giant, large and medium cultivars, it is wiser to choose a smaller corm than a large or giant size. It will bloom well the first year, but the chief advantage is that the corm it produces will make an even better and larger flower the following year, whereas large cultivars are likely to bloom well the first year but to produce a smaller corm the second year. If you do not have storage facilities and intend to grow the corm for one year and discard it, then the large or giant size will be the one for you. Avoid bargain discard stock, any corms that are large and flat with sunken bases, and damaged or obviously diseased corms. A few cultivars have naturally rough surfaced corms, but mainly they should be smooth and clean. Order in late winter for spring delivery.

When to Plant: You have a choice of ways to plant. Either set directly into well-prepared ground (see CHAPTER 18) when the leaves on the trees are just beginning to show green, or prestart indoors in peat pots, one to a pot, 4-6 weeks before planting-out time. In very cold areas, where growing seasons are short, research stations advise presprouting all corms by setting them, 10 days before planting-out time, on a ½-inch bed of damp vermiculite or peat, covering with another 3 inches of the same material, watering lightly and putting in a warm place until the sprout forms. Move the flats or pans out during the day and in at night until they can be safely planted out in the garden with no danger of frost. In all regions, for succession of bloom over the summer, make new plantings at 10-day intervals till 90 days before the first projected frost for your area. This is the length of time a gladiolus takes to bloom and to make a new corm for next year.

How to Plant: Choose a site in full sun, well drained, not too near other plants. Set 3-5 inches deep — the deeper measure is used if soil is light, to anchor well and prevent toppling of the flower spike — and 4-6 inches apart. If you aspire to win trophies, plant exhibition-size corms 10-15 inches apart and either stake each one individually or set wires at 2, 3 and 4 foot heights to which you can tie the developing flower stalk.

Water deeply (12 inches) weekly, if weather dry, especially when flower spikes are forming.

Weed shallowly so as not to harm roots.

Spray to control pests and diseases with a combined insecticide-fungicide when plants are 6 inches tall and weekly thereafter. Thrips are the most persistent pest, botrytis the most likely disease. (See CHAPTER 19 for how to control.)

If your soil is light, mulch to conserve moisture, but not on heavy soil because it would delay blooming. (See CHAPTER 18 for techniques and materials.) In very cold areas, clear polyethylene is successful as a mulch and gardeners in many areas have good luck in repulsing disease-carrying aphids with strips of aluminum foil laid on the ground along the rows and across both ends of plantings.

After bloom is finished and on a sunny, good-drying day before the ground freezes, but no later than the first two weeks in October even if you have a later frost-free season, dig corms. Cut stalk off flush with the corm, dry outdoors during that day, then move indoors to a well-ventilated place with a temperature, if possible, around 80°F. When the old corm will separate easily from the new one — about 1-2 weeks — pry them gently apart and discard the old one. Don't leave this job till later for the new and old corms will firmly fuse together making it almost impossible to get them apart. Clean off the outer loose skin but leave the last snug coat on the fleshy corm. Discard any scarred or diseased new corms by burning or wrapping for the garbage. Dust all you keep with a combined insecticide-fungicide, by shaking a few at a time in a paper bag with a few spoonfuls of the dust. Lay out and leave to dry further for about a week more at 80°F., then store for the winter in single layers on trays, a few in a paper bag with the top left open (you can mark the name on the bag) or in old nylon stockings hung from the ceiling, where the temperature will be about 40°F. This may seem like a complicated operation but it enables you to have sturdy healthy corms for next year's plantings at little expense. Check once in a while through the winter and discard any troubled corms.

A recommended list
of 11 medium, large and giant cultivars

New cultivars come on the market every year, but many of the most popular ones — the top on this list is one — have been in the Top Ten for many years. For information about new ones, check catalogues, garden columnists and broadcasters.

'Pink Prospector': On the list for many years but still tops; stands up well in all weather; a soft light pink; graceful, often with as many as 22-25 florets on one spike; midseason; large.

'Lavanesque': Blue lavender with a white throat; a beauty; good habit; easy to grow; early mid-season; medium.

'Marjorie Ann': White, fine for both exhibition and decoration; mid-season.

'Isle of Capri': A lively orange salmon; giant; early mid-season.

'Salmon Queen': Made its debut in 1955 and still the best salmon, a lovely deep color; never needs pampering; a consistent prizewinner; large; mid-season.

'Apricot Lustre': Large formal glad; late mid-season; rated highest of all in its color class.

'Aurora': Golden yellow of great substance with frilled petals; large; mid-season.

'Rainier': One of the best, a beautiful white, with, as glad buffs say, "great substance and stretch"; medium; mid-season.

'Angel Eyes': Blue-blushed white with a deeper blue throat; grows easily and well; marvelous form; medium; early mid-season.

'Lady Bountiful': A rich cream, thick ruffled petals; large; late mid-season. Tied with:

'Red Tornado': A bright red, wonderful performer; large; mid-season.

6 Fine All-America Selections

(*there are new ones each year*)

'Frostee Pink', large, pink and cream, ruffled, vigorous, tall, mid-season; 'Candy Doll', small, deep pink with a white throat, ruffled, mid-season; 'Grapejuice', rose purple, miniature, frilled, mid-season; 'Purity', ruffled white, mid-season; 'Royalty', rich deep rose red, mid-season; and 'Bluebird', white with blue throat, miniature, early.

10 Top Miniature and Small Sizes

'Parfait', early, salmon; 'Little Slam', early, red; 'Foxfire', mid-season, orange; 'Towhead', mid-season, yellow; 'Camelot', early, pink; 'Statuette', early, yellow; 'Elite', early mid-season, white; 'Blue Sapphire', early, violet; 'Domino', early, cream; 'Little Diamond', late mid-season, scarlet.

Butterfly Glads, part of the miniature group, are very popular, and rightly so, for they are gay and pretty, a versatile size, with lovely ruffled petals.

'Disneyland' is early mid-season, scarlet edged with yellow; 'Green Thumb', very early, a lively green yellow; 'Ivory Frills', white and mid-season; 'Mirth', a beautiful smooth pink with a creamy throat, very ruffled and very early; 'Orbit', deep pink with a yellow throat, early; 'Red Ribbon', rose red with a picotee edge, mid-season; 'Root Beer', brown and maroon with a leatherlike texture, mid-season.

LILIES

When you hold a lumpy lily bulb in your hand, you can hardly imagine the beauty it contains. Yet inside its dull brown scales lies the most stately and effective flower of the summer garden. Success is not an absolute certainty, but lilies grow superbly in many parts of the country — many showy and hardy cultivars are reported from gardens in northern parts of the country. Once you grow lilies, you'll agree that the reward is worth the gamble. They boast shining texture, pure color and aristocratic form. As well, the fragrance of some cultivars is one of the most lovely scents in the world.

Be clever about where you plant them — they're prima donnas and should have centre stage: not too close to roots of trees and shrubs, about midway in a border of good companions or, best of all, in a specially planned setting of their own. This could be, for white ones, against a flaming pink climbing rose with royal blue delphiniums and veined 'Blue Lace' petunias at their feet; for the yellows, a little cove of dark green hemlocks or yews, green 'Envy' zinnias, 'Limelight' nicotine and white dwarf sweet alyssum; for the unsurpassable fuchsia pink strains like 'Pink Perfection', a play of soft grey foliage — artemisia, rabbit's ears or dusty miller — around them and in front a repeat of the lily's color in cerise, pink and velvet red sweet william. For the reds and oranges, nothing is so handsome as a variety of greens behind, beside and before.

How to Choose: Both the United States and Canada have a world-wide reputation for fine lily-breeding. Excellent cultivars are widely available and new ones come on the market every year. Deal with a reputable bulb specialist or nursery; lists are issued in early summer. Buy virus-resistant cultivars.

When and Where to Plant: Lilies are usually delivered in late fall and should be planted immediately. Dealers sometimes expertly pack and store some cultivars at a temperature which keeps them in perfect condition and makes it possible to deliver them for spring planting. Nevertheless, experts prefer the fall, even very late fall when the ground is frozen. Since it is a good idea to prepare the soil some weeks before planting to allow it to settle, it's wise to pile branches, a bushel basket, a plastic or burlap bag over the planting hole to keep the soil unfrozen till the bulbs are delivered and you can plant them. The old-fashioned Madonna Lily, *L. candidum*, and *L. testaceum* are the exceptions: they ripen in early summer and are shipped in late August and early September for planting immediately. The Madonna lily produces a rosette of leaves which overwinter.

Choose places that are well drained — this is essential because at no time should water stand around the roots or at the base of the bulb. At the same time, the soil must have enough humus in it to be moist. If your flower beds are not naturally well drained, consider planting lilies somewhere on a slope or raise beds 12 inches above the surrounding ground. Don't crowd them with other planting, as they need good air circulation around them. Prepare soil to a depth of 18 inches, mixing in peat, leaf mold or vermiculite if it is too sandy or too heavy. The proportion of the final mix should be one part humus, two parts soil and one part sand. Mix all well, at the same time adding a high phosphorus and potash commercial fertilizer, according to manufacturer's recommendations. Do not add any fresh manure. If your lilies are delivered too late for you to get them into the ground — and even if it's frozen isn't too late for the bulbs if you can stand it — plant them one to a pot, keep moist and store in a cool (40°F) place till you can transplant them in spring to the garden outdoors; disturb them as lititle as possible when you do this.

How to Plant: Except for the Madonna Lily, which is planted with its tip only 1-2 inches below the surface, plant lilies 4-6 inches deep (a little deeper in sandy soil, a little shallower in clay); 6-12 inches apart, three or more to a clump. Water deeply then, and thereafter weekly if no rain. If summer is dry, mulch to keep cool, to discourage weeds and to retain moisture (see CHAPTER 18 for how to do this and what materials to use). Mark planting spots well for it is easy to chop off the emerging shoot in spring by mistake. Lay a winter mulch to prevent heaving of the ground after it's frozen.

After shoots appear, fertilize with a fertilizer high in phosphorus and potash; don't let it directly touch the stem or leaves. Large cultivars that sometimes stand 5-6 feet tall need staking (see CHAPTER 18).

Some gardeners never spray their lilies, but most experts recommend a multipurpose mixture every 10 days. This controls the worst lily pests — the virus-carrying aphids, and the worst lily disease, botrytis.

If you cut lilies for the house, take no more than one third of the stem, leaving the rest to nourish the bulb. Cut off all faded flowers. When the plant has turned yellow, cut it all back and burn the debris or wrap for garbage. A cluster of small shoots rather than large exuberant ones indicates that it's time to transplant, which should be done in early fall; separate the bulbs, and replant *immediately* — if possible, in a different place to prevent build-up of pests or disease.

RECOMMENDED LILIES TO GROW

Asiatic Hybrids

'Algoma': golden yellow, mid-July, 4-5 feet
'Connecticut Yankee': salmon-orange, July, 5-6 feet
'Destiny': lemon-yellow with brown spots, June, 3-4 feet
'Discovery': old rose and lilac blend, crimson-black spots, July, 3-4 feet
'Enchantment': nasturtium-red, up-facing, July, 2-3 feet
'Goldcrest': golden orange, late June, 3 feet
'Lemon Queen': lemon-yellow spotted brown, early July, 4-5 feet
'Mohawk': rich dark red, spotted, out-facing, June-July, 3-5 feet
'Nutmegger': lemon-yellow spotted black, late July, 6 feet
'Ruby': rich dark red, up-facing, June-July, 2 feet
'White Princess': apricot changing to white, July, 4 feet

Martagon Hybrids

'Black Prince': dark purple-red, early July, 5 feet
'Brocade': fuchsia-purple, lemon-yellow base, purple spots, June, 5 feet
'Mrs. R. O. Backhouse': pink and yellow blend, June, 4-5 feet
'Paisley Strain': colors of Paisley shawls, June, 6 feet

271

American Hybrids

'Bellingham Hybrids': yellow to orange, heavily spotted, long lasting, early July, 5 feet
'Shuksan': light orange, spotted maroon, July, 3-6 feet

Species

L. amabile: bright orange, dark brown spots, June-July, 2-3 feet
L. concolor: upright, star-shaped, brilliant scarlet, late May-June, 2 feet
L. martagon 'Album superbum': white with gold anthers, June-July, 4 feet
L. pumilum: lacquer-red, easy, May-June, 2 feet 'Golden Gleam' and 'Yellow Bunting', an orange and a yellow

Trumpets and Aurelian Hybrids

'Black Magic Strain': white with dark purple-brown reverse, July-August, 5-6 feet
'Damson': dark fuchsia-pink, silver overlay, July, 4-6 feet

'Golden Splendor Strain': rich yellow, maroon stripe on reverse, July, 6 feet
'Greatheart': creamy white, flame-orange center, late July, 5 feet
'Limelight': cool chartreuse-yellow, tall, vigorous, 5-6 feet
'Olympic Hybrids': white trumpets, July, 5-6 feet
'Regina': clear yellow, sunburst flaring flowers, late July, 6 feet
'Royal Gold Strain': shining gold, July, 5 feet
'Thunderbolt': apricot-orange, flaring flowers, July, 6 feet

Oriental Hybrids

'Allegra': pure white with green star in center, fragrant, August, 5-6 feet
'Empress of India': crimson-red spotted darker crimson, white border, August, 4-5 feet
'Imperial Silver Strain': silver-white spotted vermilion, requires slightly acid soil, August, 4-5 feet
'Magic Pink Strain': shell-pink, center dark green with reddish-yellow stripe, early July, 3-4 feet

---

TUBEROUS BEGONIAS

No more beguiling shady characters exist than the tuberous begonias. Flawless of flower, strong and bold of leaf, they are the perfect answer to what to plant in those tricky shaded places in your garden — north-facing doorways and flower beds, window boxes and containers that get no sun, borders under big trees, on the sky-shine side of fences.

One of my good gardening friends calls them copycats because they can look like a huge rose, a camellia, a carnation and have flowers sometimes 8 inches across. Smaller cultivars, marvelous for a shadowed rock garden or small shady planting of any kind, have flowers only an inch across but the plant is absolutely covered with them, and for weeks and weeks.

The colors are glistening whites; blush, peach and rose pink; salmon, scarlet, crimson, yellow and orange and the leaves huge and pointed. They're easy to grow and the tubers, if stored carefully over winter, live for years, even increasing. The one tricky bit about them is that, if you grow the giant ones really well, their flower heads become very heavy, especially in rain, and therefore they must be staked up or grown where you look up at them as they hang down — in a window box, for instance, a high planter, a hanging basket; or they can be picked and floated in a bowl for indoors. But there's no doubt that, wherever you put them, they'll make you feel a tingle in your green fingers.

The English Exhibition Doubles are a giant double rose form, with immense flowers and named cultivars. They're sturdy and strong and always prizewinners in competitions. The Pacific Giants, bred on the west coast of the United States, come in double rose forms; camellia; double and ruffled picotee (which means stitched with a different color); double ruffled (ballerina) and double carnation; and in named cultivars so that you can order a special color. The Belgian strains are less expensive and smaller than the English and Pacific Giants and often more suitable for places where their scale better fits the surroundings. They also come in different forms — double camellia (there's a handsome copper color in this); double carnation (also known as *B. fimbriata* or double frilled); single fringed (*B. crispa*) and *B. crispa marginata*, a beautiful two-toned fringed type with contrasting margin.

Flowers and leaves to highlight a shady garden —
begonias, clematis, coleus, caladium, ferns.

Know these better

Whether you're a novice wanting to begin with the best, or an old hand who can barely find room for one more, dollars to doughnuts there are plants you would enjoy knowing better. Some, such as the fresh-faced yellow doronicum, have a longer-than-usual blooming time. Some, such as the red osier dogwood, have brilliant color if you keep them cut back to encourage brighter new young shoots. Some, such as the hardy new lilies, the marvelous new peonies, iris and day lilies, are so good you should throw something out to make room for them. Some, such as the tasty 'Golden Beauty' corn, will ripen early enough to be successfully grown in cold northern areas, where till now, ripe corn was a sometime thing. Some, such as the 'Sunburst' locust, add the color of sunshine to the familiar green of trees. And some are just dandy plants to know well, for nothing is more exciting than a fine new plant superbly grown, unless it's an old one, newly known, superbly grown.

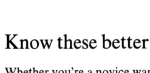

Only one of the marvelous new peonies,
'Donna Jean'.

The hardy serviceberry (Zone 1):
in spring, a drift of white flower
at the edge of woodlands;
come summer, tasty blue-black fruit.

The delicate narcissus
triandrus 'Thalia'.

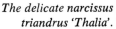

A hardy evergreen to know much,
much better — the weeping Nootka false-cypress,
graceful in storm or calm.

A hardy waterlily, 'Marliac Rosea',
easy to grow and can spend the winter in a pool
if it's deep enough not to freeze to the bottom.

A spreading lacy tree to
add the look of golden sunshine to the green of other
trees near it — the 'Sunburst' honey-locust.

Tulipa 'Tarda' —
an early spring darling everyone should grow —
opens on fine days, shuts if a cloud covers the sun.

Nothing prevents doronicum, a golden daisy, from blooming enthusiastically each spring for three to four weeks.

The dainty lily with the grace of a ballet dancer:
'White Princess'.

'Gatineau', a Siberian iris with flowers
like blue banners in the wind, grassy leaves; by Isabella Preston, Ottawa.

Of the small-flowered types, *B. multiflora* cultivars are as many-flowered as their name implies. Literally covered with bloom for weeks and weeks, each like a tiny miniature of the large camellia-flowered begonia, there are also named cultivars. *B. maxima* has flowers midway in size between the hybrid multifloras and the giant rose forms and *B. bertinii* 'Fireflame', a jazzy hot orange-scarlet, is strong and compact and dandy for places with some sun.

For high baskets, window boxes or planters where you need something gracefully hanging down, *B. pendula* is the answer. These too come in a Pacific strain, an English and a Belgian one and there is even a fragrant cultivar — 'Yellow Sweetie', delicate pale lemon yellow — and a double, two-toned picotee in pink and rose, red, salmon and apricot.

How to Choose: Decide on which of the kinds you want to grow by the space you can give them. The giants take a minimum of 2-2½ feet sideways and about the same in height; the smaller ones about half that. The pendulous cultivars imply an elevated container. Deal with a good nurseryman or bulb specialist, order early and expect delivery when frost will not damage the tubers in transit.

Where and How to Plant: Although it is possible to grow these beauties from seed or cuttings, most people begin with tubers, which are much easier and surer. And most start them indoors ahead of planting-out time or buy them already started from a greenhouse.

To start them yourself, fill 4-inch boxes, seed pans or pots with peatlite (see CHAPTER 18) or a moist mix of peat moss and vermiculite and press tubers into it with the concave, or depressed side up. Water well and set in a warm, light place — an indoor fluorescent light unit is just the ticket if you have it, but a bright windowsill will do. Keep moist and when the tubers have rooted well, pot each in a 4-5 inch pot using a fine mix of sandy loam, compost and vermiculite or perlite. Put them back in the light to grow until the weather is frost-free and warm, then plant outdoors either in their pots or directly in the ground. Set the plant in the garden so that the leaves are pointing where you want the flowers to face.

Site should be in shade, with a soil rich in humus, well drained but moist. Don't crowd your plants — air moving freely about them reduces chances of disfiguring mildew.

Ongoing Care: Water deeply if weather dry; if it's very hot, a fine spray on the leaves any time up till noon helps, but don't put water on the foliage in the late part of the day for this too encourages mildew. Feed, with a water-soluble fertilizer (20-20-20) once every 3 weeks from when buds form till just before frost. (For pest and disease control, see CHAPTER 19.) Pick off all dead flowers, and for longer-lasting bloom on the big doubles remove also the single female flowers which bloom on either side of the double. You can easily identify these by the three-winged seedpod forming just behind the flowers. Before frost, dig up the plant, leaving as much soil as possible around the tubers, and take it indoors (this is where leaving them in their pots comes in particularly handy), stop watering, and when the leaves have wilted cut them off, leaving a few inches of main stem on the tuber. A few

weeks later, take off the stem and soil and any roots adhering to the tuber and store in boxes or plastic bags, with peat moss or vermiculite (you never store begonias bare as you do glads) at a temperature of 50-60°F. Check once or twice during the winter, and if you find any disease or serious shrinking, discard the tuber.

24 exotic and unusual summer flowering bulbs

Acidanthera: 3-4 feet; much like a gladiolus; flowers white with a purple blotch, a spicy fragrance; plant in full sun when ground warm, 3 inches deep, 4-5 inches apart; water deeply once a week if no rain; fertilize every two weeks; mulch. Dig before frost and store as for glads.

Agapanthus africanus: Lily of the Nile: 3 feet; large loose head of bright blue or white flowers on long stems, also a dwarf form, 'Peter Pan' only 12 inches tall; a spectacular pot plant for patios; start indoors in March for late-summer bloom then transplant and move outdoors when weather warm and no chance of frost.

Allium giganteum: 5-6 feet; large heads of violet-blue flowers in July, sometimes as big as 9 inches in diameter; a true giant in the garden; plant in spring when ground warm, 24 inches apart, covering the bulb 2-3 times its own depth.

Anemone coronaria: believed to be the Biblical lily-of-the-field; 6-8 inches tall; flower 4 inches wide, in velvety blues, scarlet, pink, mauve, white; start indoors at end of March for early bloom, or for later, plant directly in the garden when ground is warm, in partial shade, sandy soil, 2 inches deep, 6 inches apart; keep well watered; dig plants in fall before frost and store in vermiculite or perlite in a cool place (45°-60°F.).

Caladium: tall 18 inches, dwarf 9 inches; showy, big, tissue-paper-thin leaves in pink, red and white, veined with green; a stunning plant with light behind it; start indoors in a warm place (70°F), 8-10 weeks before planting out, in a mixture of sand and peat, covering them 1 inch deep; water well; roots grow from top of tuber, so never let them dry out and always keep covered with peat; when sprouts are well up, transplant to 6-inch pots filled with equal parts good garden soil and peat; either set in garden beds right in their pots or use in a decorative container on patio; prefers shade; water every day and feed with a solution of 1 teaspoon of 20-20-20 fertilizer in 1 gallon of water, every second week; pick the flowers off if they start to bloom — they are not much to look at and detract from the beauty of the leaves; in the garden, shelter from heavy wind and rain; lift when leaves turn yellow and store in own soil at no less than 60°F.

There are over 50 cultivars, all handsome; here are some of the best:

'CANDIDUM'   White leaf with dark green ribs.
'IDA RED'   Christmas red, green veins and margins.
'MRS. W. B. HALDEMAN'   Watermelon-pink, green ribs and border.
'PEOCILE ANGLAIS'   Wavy crimson leaf, metallic border.
'KATHLEEN'   Dwarf rose pink, ruffled green edge.
'MISS CHICAGO'   Solid rose pink leaves with a little green.
'RED FLASH'   Vivid light red, dark veins and midriff, pink to white flakes all over.

Canna: tall 3-4 feet, dwarf 3 feet; large bold plants, useful as accents in a large garden; flowers pink, orange, scarlet, yellow speckled red, some with bronze foliage; should be started indoors by setting in flats of peat and sand, covering with 1 inch of peat, and watering, 8-10 weeks before planting out after last frost and when ground thoroughly warm; when shoots appear, replant in 4 inch pots; plant outdoors in full sun, just below the surface, 12-18 inches apart; water weekly if no rain and fertilize every two weeks; after first light frost, cut off stems, dig rhizomes and allow to dry with their own soil; store in flats of dried peat, at about 50°F.

Colchicum: sometimes also called Autumn Crocus; strange bulbs that will bloom on your desk or windowsill without water, soil, pot or leaves; must be ordered in early summer because of their short dormant period for shipping; flowers, single or double, are rose mauve or purple, leaves which disappear in summer, are untidy and floppy in spring, so plant where this will not matter, but where the spurt of flowers — very like a large crocus — can be well seen in the fall; either plant in August for September bloom, or buy and allow to bloom out of the ground, then after blooming plant immediately for future years; likes full sun or part shade, good soil; hardy except in the very coldest regions; a fully double rose mauve one of great size is 'Water Lily'.

Cyclamen, Hardy: *C. neapolitanum*: a little jewel for late summer and early fall in the rock garden; only 6 inches high with miniature cyclamen-like flowers in rose pink and a rarer white, marbled leaves; plant in early fall with the top of the corm just above the surface, 4-5 inches apart, in half shade, humus soil; for winter, protect with evergreen branches.

Eremurus: Foxtail Lily, Giant Asphodel, some call it the Gee Whiz plant, 4-12 feet high; from a cluster of swordlike leaves, a tall bare stem shoots way up and is hung with hundreds of white, golden yellow, pink or orange bells in early summer; plant only 3 inches deep, in September — handle the huge octopus-like bulbs gently for they're brittle and break easily; must have good drainage; don't be surprised if they don't bloom the first year, just leave undis-

turbed and be sure to mark where you have planted it or them; to prevent the early sprout from being killed by late spring frosts (these bulbs are hardy even in North Dakota) put a box or basket full of crispy leaves over it in very early spring and remove when weather is steadily warm; also, mulch with evergreen branches in late fall if you are in a no-snow-cover area.

Erythrina crista-gallii 'Compacta': Cockspur Coral Tree; 2 feet; not actually a bulb, but a thick root stock; a bushy plant with light green leaves, dazzling vermilion pea-shaped flowers; blooms in summer; plant in well-drained, rich soil, in full hot sun after the ground is warm; lift after first light frost and store like dahlias.

Eucomis comosa, Pineapple Lily or Flower: 2 feet; sturdy, ruffle-edged foliage; spike of star-shaped green flowers with tuft of leaves on top (hence "pineapple"); plant bulbs, which are large, close to the surface when the ground is warm; blooms in summer; dig and store as for glads, before frost; 'Pole-Evansi', a giant of 4-6 feet, has creamy flowers.

Galtonia candicans, Summer Hyacinth; 4-5 feet; plant this one in the back of the border for a group of stately spires in midsummer; white flowers are bell-shaped, fragrant and long lasting; plant 3 inches deep in rich friable soil when it has become thoroughly warm; lift before frost, dry and clean, store over winter at 60°F.

Gloriosa rothschildiana, Gloriosa Lily: a vine supported by tendrils at its leaf tips; flowers are red and gold, very odd and beautiful, with twisted petals; pot the tuber in March, pink tip up, in rich loose soil; when warm weather has come, plunge pot in soil outdoors in full sun, or transplant directly into the garden; water every week, deeply, if no rain, and fertilize every two weeks; dig after first frost, leaving in pot or store offsets in vermiculite or perlite in a cool place over winter.

Hymenocallis calathina, Ismene, Peruvian or Sea Daffodil; Basket Flower; 2-3 feet; large trumpet flowers, white, fragrant, delicately fringed, green striped; strap-like leaves; easy to grow; choose between potting indoors in May, planting out only when weather and soil are reliably warm, or plant directly in the garden then, for later bloom; sometimes flowers within a week of planting; if starting indoors, set in flat of vermiculite and peat, or sand and peat, where temperature is 70°F; move to 6-inch pot when roots have developed; if outdoors, plant 3 inches deep, 5 inches apart, in full sun; water weekly if no rain, and fertilize every 2 weeks with a solution of 1 teaspoon of 20-20-20 to 1 gallon of water; dig before frost when leaves turn yellow and store where temperature is above 60°F; 'Advance' is pure white and has a green-striped throat; *H. festalis* is pure white and spidery; 'Sulphur Queen' primrose yellow with light yellow throat and green stripes.

Incarvillea, Chinese Trumpet Flower: 8-16 inches; clusters of large gloxinia-like flowers in June, fine-cut foliage; easy to grow, plant in sun in light sandy soil; *I. delavayi* is lilac pink with a white throat; *I. grandiflora*, shorter (and therefore good for rockeries), with carmine red flowers.

Lapeirousia cruenta: 6-8 inches; bright scarlet flowers with crimson blotches in July-August; good in rock garden; plant 2-3 inches apart, 4 inches deep; start indoors for early bloom.

Lycoris squamigera, Hardy Amaryllis, Resurrection Lily, Spider Lily: 15-38 inches; half hardy; clusters of 6-9, pale lavender pink, fragrant flowers in August; large strap-like leaves appear in spring then die down in midsummer; because the plant has no leaves when it blooms, it's best to interplant it with a well-foliaged plant — short ferns that stay green all summer would be good; can be started early indoors in a 6-inch pot, or if outdoors, plant 4 inches deep, 8 inches apart in August, in deep sandy loam, sun or partial shade; leave undisturbed — they may not bloom for 1-2 years after first planting.

Montbretia, Tritonia, Crocosmia: 2-3 feet; spikes of red, orange or bronze 4-inch flowers in late summer, early fall; very like glads, only stems are arched; successive plantings are needed for continuous bloom; start early indoors in pots (they take a long time to sprout), or plant directly in the garden when weather and soil are both warm and no chance of frost; 4-7 inches deep, 6-8 inches apart; dig after first frost, spread in shade to dry for several weeks; keep only those 1 inch in diameter or more; store, like glads, at 35-45°F.

Ornithogalum thyrsoides, Chincherinchee: 2-3 feet; white flowers in clusters on stems last for weeks when cut; blooms in July, August; plant when ground warm, and no frost, 3-6 inches deep, 3-4 inches apart; each corm produces several spikes of bloom.

Ranunculus, Double Buttercup, Turban or Persian Buttercup: 1-2 feet; showy double flowers, some-times 2 inches across, in scarlet, golden yellow, orange, white, pink and blends of all; plant outdoors in early spring while weather cool and moist, in rich sandy soil; keep well watered; dig after foliage dies in late summer and store over winter in vermiculite or dry peat at 35-45°F; the hybrids 'Tecolete Giants' are large and vigorous and highly recommended.

Sprekelia formossisima, Jacobean or St. James Lily, Orchid Amaryllis: 18 inches; spidery crimson flowers in summer; plant when ground and weather warm; dig in fall and store in vermiculite at 50-60°F.

Sternbergia lutea: 5-6 inches; a bright yellow, 2-inch vase-shaped flower with a lovely sheen; leaves neat, excellent for rock gardens; plant as soon as you can get delivery (usually August), 4 inches deep, 4 inches apart; blooms in late fall, shelter and protect over winter, or take up just before frost and ripen and store indoors.

Polianthes tuberosa, Tuberose: 2 feet, probably the most fragrant of all garden flowers; in summer or fall has stalks of white waxy double flowers; looks well in border; buy large size bulbs; plant 2-3 inches deep, 8-12 inches apart in clumps of 6-8 tubers in full sun, in a well-drained site, in May; or in pots 6-8 weeks before that and transplant outdoors when ground and air are really warm; needs heat to grow best; water every day and fertilize every second week; dig after first light frost and store for winter in vermiculite at 40-50°F.

Zephyranthes candida, Zephyr Lily, Fairy Lily, Flower-of-the-West-Wind: 6-12 inches; prolific flowers, in white, pale yellow, violet pink, deep rose, funnel shaped; grassy foliage in August, September; plant outdoors, 3 inches deep, 2-6 inches apart when weather and soil are warm, or indoors in pots 6-8 weeks earlier and transplant outside; dig after first frost and store in their own soil kept barely moist, at 40-45°F.

29 ANNUALS

Annuals, more than any other plants, give your garden a flowers-flowers-everywhere look. Coming into peak of bloom when the glorious burst of spring blossoming is finished, when many of the showy perennials are over, they are an exciting mid-summer crescendo of color that continues well into fall. Some even survive light-fingered frosts, but all eventually die before winter.

This planned obsolescence of Mother Nature's is, in many ways, a blessing. You don't have to work out a program of long-term, over-the-years care; with each new season you have a chance to experiment with new colors, shapes and textures; each new year is a challenge to grow the best. Perhaps most comforting of all, your mistakes disappear forever with the first biting frost.

Annuals can play three important roles in your garden. They can be main-theme plantings of nothing but annuals; they can be a tonic for depressed areas, and they can be handy first aid for unexpected trouble.

As main-theme plantings
These are a particularly happy solution for gardens around newly-built, bare-ground houses or for temporary ones, such as a rented house or an apartment balcony.
For flower beds and borders in the new garden, choose tall growers for background, medium heights for the middle, low ones for the front and creeping carpeters for edging. Mix these heights back and forth in the beds for best effect and be sure to make them casual and lavish, never too precisely set.
For foundation plantings, apartment balconies and borders in limited spaces, as there are sometimes between a path and a house, choose plants with a scale and

mature habit of growth to fit the space. Use neat compact flowers around the house and choose their color to complement it. Balcony plantings, more than anything, need to be made with plants that will be showy in a small space, stand up well to high winds and in some cases limited sun (see CHAPTER 3: Balconies and Patios).

Containers of all kinds — pots, window boxes, hanging baskets — look best if you choose plants with a bold top line for the centre, lower bushy ones for the middle, then some to cascade over the rim (for lists, see CHAPTER 3).

Vines are, in many ways, the showiest of the annuals because they stretch themselves so quickly and easily into your view. They twine up a trellis, make a quick screen, garland a fence all in a few weeks. Most need support. If grown from seed, it's an advantage to start them early indoors to get a jump on the season or buy prestarted plants. (For recommended ones, see CHAPTER 25: Vines and Climbers.) Annual hedges are a marvelous answer for quick screening and to outline a design that you may decide to plant later with more permanent material. You can have low ones of 12-14 inches to frame a bed or border a walk; medium height, 2-4 feet, to suggest privacy or tall ones up to 6 feet to block out an unwanted view and make a handsome background for other plants. (For ideas of what plants to use, see CHAPTER 22: Hedges and Windbreaks.)

As a tonic for depressed areas

Annuals are the answer to flower up beds and borders that go into the doldrums when permanent plants have finished blooming. They're especially useful to hide ripening spring bulb foliage which can look like the dickens for 6-8 weeks while next year's flower is being built into the bulb underground. The best for this are those in flower when you buy them, or close to it — pansies and violas, fibrous begonias, geraniums, sweet alyssum, lobelia are some.

Also, by summer, even the most skillfully planned perennial border usually needs some bright-flowered annuals to fill gaps. Choose kinds that please you most and plant them in groups of no fewer than three; more will give you an even bigger splash of color. Check as they grow to be sure that moisture, air and light are not cut off from the perennials — a little careful trimming will usually do the trick — and feed and water the annuals regularly so they won't rob the perennials already growing near them.

Rock gardens are traditionally at their best in spring and are then over. Annuals can extend their flowery look into summer and fall. Choose those of small scale and side-spreading habit, although here and there a taller one is good for a vertical dramatic effect — some of the jewel-colored bushy snapdragons, for instance.

Annual ground covers are a boon in many a sticky situation. They can be grown as a holdover while you decide on a final plan for your garden — where to put the lawn, where to make permanent plantings, to hold a bank or steep slope and so on. (See CHAPTER 24: Ground Covers.)

As first aid for unexpected trouble

Annuals are a dandy pick-you-up for those trouble spots that suddenly develop in the best of gardens — some plant fails to grow or grows poorly; your pet dog buries a bone by digging up a pet plant and hasn't the grace to replace it; your own or your neighbor's misaim with the weed killer sears away a treasure.

To have fixings for these, plant some annuals that will move without a whimper and won't be missed if you do move them. Nearly all will transplant if you water them well a half day ahead and again after setting in place.

And, as a dividend, be a paint-in-a-plant artist

Using annuals that move easily and successfully in bloom — pansies, small marigolds and zinnias, silver-grey dusty miller, fibrous begonias are some — paint a picture with real flowers in some special spot, tucked in beside the steps, on either side of your front door, in a big sky-blue fibreglass pot on the patio, to rim a bird bath or what have you.

How to Choose

When you plan for annuals, decide which of three starting methods is the best for you. Growing from seed started early indoors, to be transplanted, hardened off and finally planted where they are to grow; growing from seed planted directly outdoors where they are to grow, or buying boxed plants which you will divide and plant directly in the garden. The last is by far the most popular and the business of producing these prestarted plants — known as bedding stock (nothing to do with sheets and mattresses) — has increased 94% in the past 5 years, proving its appeal to busy home gardeners.

Growing from Seed Started Indoors

If the pattern of your life fits their needs, nothing is so much fun as growing your own annuals from seed. This means, however, that you or someone else must give them almost daily care during the early stages. This is usually a period of 6-8 weeks, but some annuals require an even longer time between sowing and setting out, and after they're planted all seedlings need frequent care till they become established, usually 2-3 weeks. There is one exception for the first stage. If you have a built-in fluorescent light unit with automatic controls and the setup for growing seed, you can cut down considerably on the early personal attention seedlings need (see CHAPTER 31).

The advantages of growing your own are that you have the fun of reading the seed catalogues (if you collect superlatives, this is the place to find them); of deciding from a fantastically wide choice, what you will grow; of being able to order the newest, most improved strains, often in special colors not always carried by boxed-plant dealers. Realize though that you are going to have to provide certain facilities in your house and certain greenthumbery yourself to make this a success.

Growing from Seed Sown Directly Outdoors

Although the results are sometimes not as sure, sowing annuals directly in the garden has many advantages. Your growing medium is already there, you have ample light, hopefully some natural moisture and helpful temperatures day and night. You can put the seed where it is to grow, thin it out if too many plants appear in one spot, yet leave the ones you want without further transplanting.

A few can be sown outdoors either late in the fall or in very early spring just as soon as the ground can be worked. These stand a little frost without keeling over. Others cannot be sown outside until the ground is warm (55°-60°F.) and danger of frost is past.

Many gardeners do both indoor and outdoor seeding, getting early bloom from the first crop, later bloom from the second.

Buying Plants Already Started

Packaging for prestarted plants changes almost yearly, with each new one an improvement on the last. The most common method is to set transplants in a fibre box filled with soil, holding 6-8 seedlings. To plant, water well then knock out the whole chunk and either cut or pull the little plants gently apart leaving as much undisturbed root and soil with each as possible. Other packets are small pots, round or square, made of compressed peat, each holding one plant, which can be transferred directly into the ground. It is important to soak these in a starter solution of fertilizer and water for an hour before planting, then break the peat pot up with your hand so as not to disturb the roots, and set it in the ground with its rim pressed well below the surrounding surface so that moisture is not cut off. Another seed starter comes as a dried hard cookie which, when watered, suddenly expands into a little netted pot filled with peat and plant food. This holds one seedling and can be set, as is, in the ground. Another is a rack of spaces much like an ice-cube tray, with room for one plant in each, six to a set. Here the advantage is that you push each plant gently out of its space and pop it directly into the ground, keeping the rack for future use.

If you buy your plants packaged in any of these ways, there are some things you should know. First, most home gardeners buy and bring boxed plants home too soon. Nurseries display them, and everybody is hungry to buy as soon as the weather warms, but this is often 2-4 weeks before it is safe to plant many of them in the garden because of the possibility of killing frost. If you have a cold frame, or can put your plants out in bright light during the day and, when frost is predicted, bring them in at night, it's an advantage to buy early because you get the widest choice; but a shady veranda or a dark garage is not a substitute for bright light outdoors, and full sun is usually too hot and drying. If you cannot supply the right kind of care, then visit a good nursery early, choose your plants, and arrange to pick them up when your nurseryman says it's safe to plant them out.

If they have been properly hardened off before you buy them, a few very hardy ones — the bright-faced violas are one — can be planted out early because they will survive light frost.

HOW TO GROW

From Seed

Deal with a reputable dealer and be sure to buy fresh seed. Do not buy it more than 3 months before planting. Old seed can germinate much more slowly than fresh or not at all; and any plants that do grow from old seed tend to be weak and spindly.

Look for seed marked F_1 (available only for some annuals). It will cost more but is far superior because it's produced by the planned crossing of selected parents to produce a better plant. Don't be misled into buying F_2 because it sounds more improved than F_1. It isn't.

Keep seed dry and cool until it is planted and dust with seed disinfectant before planting, or water the seed bed with a soil disinfectant before planting.

Check directions on seed packet. Many first-time gardeners plant their seeds too soon and then have a difficult time keeping them growing properly before it's time to plant safely outdoors. Also if you start seed indoors, remember that the transplant stage takes up more room than first seeding.

PLANTING AND CARE OF ALL SEEDLINGS

Prepare the bed in the garden as for other plants. Remove seedlings from container and set each a little lower in the ground than it was in the box. Pinch out the leader to induce a side-branching bushy plant, allow it to develop if you want a tall one.

Water with starter solution. Except where noted, follow with general purpose fertilizer every 2 weeks, according to manufacturer's directions, and water it in well. Soak deeply only if no rain — most annuals are overwatered. Weed by hand until the plant takes over the space. Dust or spray for insects or diseases when necessary (see CHAPTER 19: Control of Common Pests and Diseases of Ornamental Plants).

Pick off or lightly shear dead flower heads where possible, both for continuing good looks and to keep the plant producing more flowers. This is especially important with ageratum, pot marigold, cosmos, geranium, marigold, pansy and viola, rudbeckia, pincushion flower, verbena, zinnia. For continuing bloom, make successive plantings of those with a limited flowering period — baby's breath, coreopsis, candytuft, cape marigold, bachelor's button, love-in-a-mist, love-lies-bleeding, mignonette, annual phlox, Swan River daisy.

Cut back vigorous growers in midsummer, and/or when you are going on vacation, to induce a second blooming.

Stake tall growers, or those with large flower heads, for instance, some cultivars of marigolds and zinnias, that can break if they get topheavy with rain.

Cover with newspaper or burlap if frost threatens. It your plants do get nipped, spray with a fine mist of cold water before the sun can hit them and continue until they are thoroughly thawed out.

TWELVE TOP ANNUALS

This list was chosen by present popularity. Many other fine ones, if they were better known, might have made it and there is always the possibility that inspired hybridizing will improve a so-so plant or produce a new beauty to go on such a list in the years ahead. Keep up with new introductions and have the fun of trying a couple of new ones every year.

Pansies, violas, fibrous begonias and geraniums are included here because, although not really annuals, most gardeners grow them as such.

PETUNIA, *Petunia*

By all odds, the head of the list. One grower, who sells more than a million boxes of annuals every year, reports that petunias account for 44% of this total; he also says that if people could have only one flower in their garden it would be a white petunia; seed can cost anywhere from $500 to $1,200 an ounce, a quantity equal to two little scoops of instant coffee and almost as fine; you can be sure that the people who package it are not easy sneezers. Hybridizers have produced more spectacular hybrids in petunias than any other annual. One of the easiest to grow, and one of the prettiest, they flower more continuously than almost any other summer bloom.

There are two kinds: *multifloras*, double and single, are compact, neat plants covered with flowers which stand up well after rain and are excellent for beds, rock gardens and tidy plantings; *grandifloras* are spreading, bigger plants with larger flowers, very showy, the edges sometimes ruffled or frilled and they also come single or double. These are the show-off petunias for window boxes, hanging baskets and containers. White, pink and red are the most popular colors, but some petunia fans think there's nothing lovelier than the blues veined with purple, the plain blues and purples; others prefer the pale yellow cultivars.

The fine seed is difficult to handle and you would be wise to buy prestarted plants. But if you do want to grow your own, buy only the superior F_1 seed.

VITAL STATISTICS:
Height at Maturity: 12-14 inches
Time to Sow Seed: indoors 10 weeks before planting out
Germination: 10 days
Distance Apart: 12-14 inches, plant cascade types only 6 inches apart to encourage them to stretch out and down
Remarks: Grows best in full sun. No need to pick off dead flower heads but the whole plant responds with new bloom if it is cut back in mid-season or at any time individual stems get too long. Cuts well for the house and plants can be dug from the garden before frost, trimmed back and potted for indoor bloom; slight perfume

MARIGOLD, *Tagetes*; these bright beauties fill your garden with sunshine; they grow equally well prestarted indoors or from seed planted directly outdoors; poor soil hastens their blooming, high fertility delays it; for earlier bloom, some gardeners recommend covering the plants with a black cloth for their first 6 weeks outdoors to allow only 9 hours of daylight to reach them; leaves are ferny, flowers neatly ruffled, some like carnations, some like 'mums. Colors range through the yellows — a few of the best have a greenish tinge — to orange and mixtures with rust-red and mahogany; many have a bruising scent which to some is strong

and unpleasant but to others attractive, others are odorless; there are cultivars ideal for flower beds, as middle filler for window boxes, baskets and pots; the tall ones make good hedges and I once saw a beautiful tiny city garden fairly glowing with the lemon-yellow 'Glitters', trained as four foot standards in pots, lining the paths; grows best in full sun and blooms from early summer till frost if dead flowers are picked off.

VITAL STATISTICS:
Height at Maturity: 6-30 inches
Time to Sow Seed: indoors 6-8 weeks before planting, outdoors after last frost
Germination: 5 days
Distance Apart: average sizes, 10-14 inches; large, 24 inches
Remarks: cut strong-smelling ones for indoors early in the day, arrange outdoors, put the vase in place and don't bump it after you bring it in.

GERANIUM, *Pelargonium*: the admired and beloved, and constantly improved favorite of thousands — probably if we counted Queen Victoria and the geranium fans of her reign, we should say millions; faithfully in flower all summer and into fall, their blooms held high above sturdy green leaves, they come in white, many pinks, cerise and many reds; florets can be single or double — the doubles stand up better in rain; favorites for flower beds, for containers of every kind; bought usually as potted plants but can also be grown from cuttings, and growers are looking for tremendous advances in cultivars to grow from seed; many kinds besides the well-known zonals; scenteds have a bruising fragrance of peppermint, apple, rose or lemon; variegated have leaves splashed or rimmed with white or bright color; ivy geraniums cascade, miniatures are only a few inches high; all need full sun, average soil.

VITAL STATISTICS:
Height at Maturity: miniatures 6-8 inches; pendulous ivies about 24-36 inches and the rest 12-24 inches.
Time to Sow Seed: until earlier-blooming cultivars come on the market, seed for early summer bloom must be sown indoors 3-4 months before planting out, after last frost; for later bloom, sow 8 weeks before planting out
Time to Take Cuttings: for the summer garden cuttings should be started in February
Germination: 20 days and could take longer
Distance Apart: 16-24 inches
Remarks: pick off dead flowers; can be potted up in fall for indoors or cuttings taken in August to start new plants; the latter produces a better plant. Everybody always wants to know if they can hang up their old geraniums by their toes in the basement and plant them out again the following spring. It's possible if you have a dry, very cool basement, but you will have far finer plants if you take August cuttings, grow them on and put those plants or February cuttings taken from them out in your garden

PANSIES, Violas, Johnny-Jump-Ups, *Viola*: heartsease is their folk name, and sweet ease for the heart they always are; children love the faces in their markings and a little bunch of pansies is a cherished present; they do well in shade and prefer moist soil and cool nights; they make ideal ground covers, edgings and bright accent for rock gardens; extended blooming time, as a result of skillful breeding, makes it possible to have pansies in flower from spring to fall and new cultivars of pansies have bigger and bigger blooms; this, to my mind, is not an advantage because at the same time they get floppier and more easily battered by rain and splashed with mud; I think a 2-2½-inch flower is just about right; gorgeous velvet colors; the smaller violas in blue, yellow, white, apricot, purple and ruby red are the first flowering plants to appear for sale in nurseries and make neater growth than pansies; Johnny-Jump-Ups are an even smaller type and they seed all over and really do jump up through the garden.

VITAL STATISTICS:
Height at Maturity: 6 inches
Time to Sow Seed: start seed in February indoors (buy F_1 hybrids), or the summer before, outdoors; most buy boxed plants
Germination: 10 days
Distance Apart: 8-10 inches
Remarks: pick off dead flowers and shear back any time the plant becomes leggy; regular feeding and watering helps

ZINNIA, *Zinnia*: coming up fast in popularity polls because of superior strains now available; very showy when planted in masses; blooms all summer and into fall in shades of red, salmon, yellow, lavender, creamy white; and there's a flower arrangers find intriguing — 'Envy' — a chartreuse green; the most popular are the giant double dahlia-flowered types and the giant cactus, with twisty petals; look in catalogues for those recommended as sturdy — some of the attractive large-flowered cultivars tend to blow over in storms if they get top heavy with rain; large-flowered cultivars are prettier planted so that you look down at them, because their sideways profile shows only the edge of the flower head; small cultivars, however, are mounds of bloom and pretty from any angle. *Z. linearis* unlike all the others, is a tiny, tiny single, excellent for miniature plantings.

VITAL STATISTICS:
Height at Maturity: 8-36 inches
Time to Sow Seed: outdoors when the ground is warm and danger of frost is over; indoors, 6-8 weeks before expected last frost.
Germination: 5 days
Distance Apart: 8-15 inches, depending on final size of plant.
Remarks: need full sun, except the green cultivars which hold their color best in semi-shade; tall cultivars are somewhat barelegged so best plant them behind or among something bushy at the bottom.

SNAPDRAGON, *Antirrhinum*: appealing spires in the summer and early fall garden; come in all sorts of beautiful clear colors and some mixtures; useful massed in beds, and the small and medium-branched

Pansies

ones are fine in rock gardens; wonderful fun for a small child to squeeze the jaws of the florets and make the dragon snap; great strides have been made in developing new strains that have more variety of size, more disease resistance and some of quite different form, such as the penstemon-flowered cultivars; most buy as boxed plants.

VITAL STATISTICS:
Height at Maturity: small 8 inches, medium 24 inches, tall 3 feet
Time to Sow Seed: indoors, 6-8 weeks before setting out after last frost; buy rust-resistant strains
Germination: 10 days
Distance Apart: 6-15 inches depending on eventual height
Remarks: a sweet fruity fragrance, especially pleasant in early fall; to keep flowering, pick off dead florets before they set seed and in midsummer shear the whole plant back and feed

SWEET ALYSSUM, *Lobularia maritima*: no plant is easier to grow nor so faithful in its lacy flowering; bloom hides leaves completely when well-grown; by far the favorite edging with all gardeners, also dandy for filling in gaps in rock garden and border and as a handy flower for tuck-ins; wonderfully improved strains available in white, rose and purple; can be sown directly in the garden in very early spring — some gardeners also have good luck sowing outdoors in fall for the following year's bloom; also available as boxed plants already in flower.

VITAL STATISTICS:
Height at Maturity: 2-8 inches
Time to Sow Seed: outdoors, very early spring
Germination: 5 days
Distance Apart: 10-12 inches
Remarks: prefers full sun but will do well in semi-shade, especially the deep colors; survives light frost; shear in midsummer before it can set seed and it will repay you with more bloom; its fragrance comes to meet you on a warm summer noonday.

SALVIA, Scarlet Sage, *Salvia splendens*: scarlet salvia has come flying up in lists of favorites like a fire engine charging up the street; more than any other annual, it is popular for front garden planting, perhaps because its flame red contrasts so handsomely with evergreens; it also makes a bright banner in back garden flower beds; besides the zinging scarlet, it comes in purple, pink and salmon; a quite different looking cousin, *S. farinacea*, with grey-green leaves and rich Wedgwood blue flowers, will bloom all summer and late on into fall; a lovely front-walk planting uses this blue salvia in the middle of each bed, white grandiflora petunias and salmon pink geraniums for middle height and crisp white alyssum as edging; most buy boxed plants.

VITAL STATISTICS:

Height at Maturity: from 6-30 inches
Time to Sow Seed: indoors, 12 weeks before planting out
Germination: 15 days or longer; warm moist conditions with bottom heat encourages sprouting, then move to 60°F for growing on; transplant only when two true leaves are showing.
Distance Apart: 12-15 inches
Remarks: plant in full sun; blooms all summer and takes a little frost in fall.

AGERATUM, Floss Flower, *A. houstonianum*: fluffy low mounds excellent for edging, in rock gardens and for massing in beds; blooms from early summer to frost and the best cultivars are so covered with flowers you can hardly see their leaves; familiar color is a misty blue, other cultivars in pink, white, a deeper blue, violet and hyacinth; being improved all the time; most buy boxed plants.

VITAL STATISTICS:

Height at Maturity: 8-12 inches
Time to Sow Seed: indoors, 6-8 weeks before planting out
Germination: 5 days; grow transplants at 60°F
Distance Apart: 10-12 inches
Remarks: prefers full sun, but will do well in semi-shade; shear flowers in midsummer for second bloom

ASTER, CHINA, *Callistephus chinensis*: the flower arranger's delight — lovely clear colors, lasts well, a dozen sizes and shapes, single or double; red, pink, lavender, purple, white; some kinds branch to make fairly bushy plants, others grow straight up, taller, and with longer stems for cutting; these sometimes need staking; early-flowering cultivars are available but the favorites bloom in late summer and early autumn; best in massed beds; since they need 4 months from seed to flower, most buy as boxed plants; for a continuous crop make successive plantings.

VITAL STATISTICS:

Height at Maturity: from 10-30 inches

Time to Sow Seed: indoors, 6-8 weeks before planting out; buy wilt-resistant seed
Germination: 8 days
Distance Apart: 10-12 inches
Remarks: Asters are susceptible to soil-borne disease so do not grow in the same place 2 years in a row; dig out and destroy any sick plant and spray with insecticide (see CHAPTER 19) to control leafhoppers which transmit disease; prefers full sun.

BEGONIA, Fibrous, *B. semperflorens*: these are the Tizzie-Lizzies of the flower world, by far the most popular bedding plant in America and Europe; improved cultivars in both singles and doubles, some with small waxy white, pink or red flowers, some with larger ones and an added color — soft apricot; leaves are shining green or bronze; stand up to rain and city conditions superbly; bloom all summer.

VITAL STATISTICS:

Height at Maturity: 8-12 inches
Time to Plant: Usually bought as plants from which you can take a continual supply of cuttings that root easily and grow well indoors or out; or sow seed 8-10 weeks before planting out after last frost
Distance Apart: 8-10 inches
Remarks: they grow best in rich, moist soil with plenty of humus and should not be allowed to dry out; through the blooming season pinch off largest leaves to develop more flowers and to discourage mildew.

IMPATIENCE, Patience Plant, *Impatiens sultanii*: the favorite shady garden flower; easy to grow; lovely clear colors of white, rose, salmon, cerise, orange, red and some splashed with another color; foliage usually green, but there is a lovely one 'Red Herald' with red flowers and bronze-green foliage; blooms all summer; lovely as a ground cover under trees if grown in rich, moist soil with plenty of humus and not allowed to dry out.

VITAL STATISTICS:

Height at Maturity: 1-2 feet
Time to Plant: difficult for the average gardener to grow from seed, so best buy as plants and take cuttings each year
Distance Apart: 10-12 inches

To these twelve, I would add two annual vines you will find in CHAPTER 25 — morning glories and sweet peas.

A LIST OF 52 ANNUALS TO TICKLE YOUR FANCY

(For others, consult seed catalogues and for the rare or unusual, look to world seed specialists. Improved cultivars are introduced every year, notably those that have won All America Awards, and these are widely available. Visit trial gardens to see what can be grown and to help you make your choice.)

General directions for growing annuals from seed are given in CHAPTER 18. Specific details and times to start seed indoors and outdoors are indicated with each plant as follows:

A. plant outdoors in early spring as soon as the ground can be worked

B. plant outdoors where to grow, after soil is warm in spring (55°-60°F)

C. start indoors 6-8 weeks before last average frost date in your area (see PART V for this information)

D. buy as boxed plants if possible. Many annuals are sold as boxed plants and, if you cannot grow your own from seed, are a good buy. The list indicates only those it is wise not to grow from seed yourself but to buy boxed.

To get early bloom, many gardeners start tender seeds indoors 6-8 weeks before planting-out time and for a later crop make a second planting outdoors when frosts are over.

Angel's Trumpet, *Datura meteloides:* 3-5 feet; a bold, exotic plant with down-hung fragrant white trumpets in summer; use as an accent plant; B, C.

Baby Blue-eyes, *Nemophila menziesii;* 3-12 inches; white with blue, or all blue eyes; prolific; grow in moist soil, full sun; excellent for edging; A.

Baby's-breath, *Gypsophila elegans;* 1-2 feet; a fine thread-stemmed, white cloud of a plant; blooms all summer if successive plantings are made; A.

Bachelor's - button; Cornflower; *Centaurea cyanus;* 1-3 feet; blue, pink or white flowers; easy to grow in semi-shade; excellent for cutting; A.

Bellflower (annual), *Campanula macrostyla;* 12-18 inches; *C. ramosissima;* 12 inches; both are belled, purple-blue, dainty and attractive; excellent for rock garden; B, C.

Blue-eyed African Daisy, *Arctotis stoechadifolia;* 15-18 inches; woolly grey-green foliage and pearl-white daisies with blue or yellow centres; sandy soil; B, C.

Blue Lace-flower, *Trachymene caerulea;* 24 inches; a lovely blue, excellent for cutting; B, C.

Candytuft (annual), *Iberis affinis;* 16 inches; crisp white flowers in late spring; grows in shade or sun; rich soil; rock garden or edging; cut off dead flowers for continuing bloom; A.

Cape Marigold, *Dimorphotheca aurantiaca;* 18 inches; gay daisies in cream, lemon and orange; grows quickly in full sun, sandy loam; blooms all summer if dead flowers picked off; although a native of Africa where it's perennial, it grows well as an annual in Alaska even surviving some frost; B.

Carnation (annual), many kinds; *Dianthus;* up to 12 inches; most are biennials or perennials that bloom the first year from seed sown in very early spring; full sun, slightly alkaline or neutral soil; single or double flowers in white, pink, rose, red and mixtures, not fragrant; pick off dead flowers for longer bloom; useful as edgings; A.

Castor bean, *Ricinus communis;* 4-6 feet; the most spectacular of foliage annuals; a handsome accent plant for contemporary houses and a boon to the new homeowner with a bare garden; big, pointed leaves in glossy green or bronze; the flowers nothing to write home about and seeds poisonous, so remove if you have small children; plant 4 feet apart; B, C.

Clarkia, *C. elegans;* 2-2½ feet; a graceful bending spray of pink or white flowers; grows best where nights cool and soil rich and moist; B, C.

Cockscomb, *Celosia argentea* and Plume Plant, *C. argentea plumosa;* 1-1½ feet; the first is the shape of a cock's comb, the second a spire; both are plushy in texture; red, mustard yellow, chartreuse, beige pink; grow in full sun; B, C.

Coleus, *C. blumei;* 2-2½ feet; grow for its brilliant foliage in red, cerise, plum, chartreuse, green and white; ideal for edging or in beds, window boxes, rock gardens; finest color develops in full sun but will take semi-shade; pinch off insignificant flowers; grow in rich, deep, moist soil, feed regularly; grow from cuttings; or C

Cupflower, *Nierembergia caerulea;* 6-12 inches; lavender blue, cup-shaped flowers with a yellow eye, on thin stems; sun or shade; light sandy soil; tops for rock gardens or as edging; seed must be sown 10-12 weeks before planting out after last average frost date; or D.

Dusty Miller, *Centaurea cineraria* and *C. gymnocarpa;* 1 foot; soft, velvety grey-white foliage, much indented; a marvelous foil for other plants; B, D.

Forget-me-not, *Myosotis,* and Chinese Forget-me-not, *Cynoglossum;* 6-8 inches; easy to grow, self-seeds; grow as ground cover, edging, beside water, in shade; B.

Fountain Plant, *Amaranthus tricolor salicifolius;* up to 3 feet; a large, coarse-leaved plant, its chief value is its striking bronze-red leaves; grow in full sun as a hedge or at back of border; B, C.

Foxglove (annual), *Digitalis;* 2 feet; usually a biennial but annual seed now available, that, if planted early (10 weeks before last frost), will bloom the same year; grow in shade, deep moist soil; comes in white, pink or rose; C, D.

Gazania, *G. splendens;* 18 inches; a South African perennial that grows as an annual in America; prostrate stems, silky white leaves, large yellow and orange flowers with a black and white spot at the base; grow in full sun, dry soil; blooms all summer; C.

Globe Amaranth, *Gomphrena globosa;* 1-1½ feet; cloverlike flowers of creamy white, pink or cerise; dries like a charm; C.

Gloriosa Daisy, *Rudbeckia bicolor;* 2-3 feet; a big-flowered, orange daisy with dark brown or green centre; very easy to grow; full sun; any soil; sometimes a perennial; B.

Hollyhock (annual), *Althaea rosea;* up to 6 feet; a lovely spire of a plant; rainbow colors; grow in full sun as a hedge or by itself in the background; B, C.

Larkspur, *Delphinium ajacis;* 2-3 feet; white, pink, rose, red, lavender, purple spires of flowers like dainty delphiniums; lovely in masses; A.

Lobelia, *L. erinus;* 6-12 inches; a little plant covered with the brightest blue, white or pink flowers; excellent for edging, window boxes and rock gardens; can be loose or compact; pinch when transplanting and shear after first bloom; seed sometimes hard to grow, should be sown indoors 8-10 weeks before planting out after last frost; D.

Love-in-a-mist, *Nigella damascena;* 12-18 inches; fluffy blue or white flowers with interesting seed heads for winter bouquets; easy to grow; in full sun; blooming season short, so make successive plantings if you would like bloom all summer; A.

Love-lies-bleeding; *Amaranthus caudatus;* up to 5 feet; a strong, well-branched plant with long droops of crimson flowers which look like fringe for old-fashioned plush curtains; use as background, specimen or hedges; B, C.

Madagascar Periwinkle, *Vinca rosea;* 18 inches; really a perennial, but can be grown as an annual; useful as a ground cover; rose or white flowers, very glossy leaves; D.

Mignonette, *Reseda odorata;* 1-2 feet; a favorite fragrant flower especially in evening air; fuzzy bloom in a mixture of green, red, white and yellow; grow in semi-shade or sun; A.

Nasturtium, *Tropaeolum majus;* 6-12 inches; yellow, orange or red flowers, a favorite of hummingbirds and fun as bright flecking for a salad; grows best in poor soil, full sun; pick off dead flowers for continuing bloom; spray with insecticide if little black aphids a nuisance; B.

Nicotine, *Nicotiana alata;* 2-2½ feet; a flowering tobacco; the favorite night-time fragrance; flowers in white, rose, lime green or dark red; older cultivars tend to close or droop downwards during the day, newer ones stay open; B, C, D.

Night-scented Stock, *Mathiola bicornis;* 18-24 inches; an insignificant flower but an exciting fragrance at night; B, C.

Phlox, (annual); Texas Pride; *P. drummondii;* 8-12 inches; clear, lovely colors of white, buff, pink, light and dark red, crimson, mauve or purple in mats; easy to grow; full sun, rich soil; shear dead flowers for more bloom but for the best show in late summer make a second planting; B, C.

Pincushion Flower, *Scabiosa atropurpurea;* 2½ feet; flowers in lavender, blue, pink, rose, maroon or white really do look like little pincushions; keep dead ones picked off; grow in full sun; B, C.

Poppy, California; *Eschscholzia californica* and the **Shirley Poppy,** *Pap-*

aver rhoeas; 6-12 inches; look-alikes and grown alike for their fragile, tissue-thin flowers in white, yellow, orange and red; grow in full sun, gravelly soil; A.

Portulaca, *P. grandiflora;* 6 inches; a delightful creeping ground cover; single and double flowers in white, pink, cerise, red, yellow and orange; that close in late day or dull weather; grow in full sun, sandy soil; B.

Pot Marigold, *Calendula officinalis;* 8-12 inches; the old-fashioned marigold which grows easily and well; hardy and self-sows all over the place; improved cultivars with double smaller flowers but more of them; grow in sun or semi-shade, any soil; best where nights cool; orange, also cream, primrose and gold; B, C.

Snow-on-the-mountain; *Euphorbia marginata;* 2 feet; a find for a sketchy rock garden; grey-green leaves margined with white are its chief beauty; grow in semi-shade; B, C.

Spider Flower, *Cleome spinosa;* 3 feet; a big bold plant that fills space quickly; use in masses or as background for borders; most popular cultivar is pink and white but an all-white one, 'Helen Campbell', introduced by a Canadian grower, is also available and I saw it growing to perfection against a background of a snowy mountain in Switzerland; grow in full sun; 15 inches apart; A, C.

Statice, Sea Lavender, *Limonium;* 2 feet; some kinds are a dry airy plant; others have flowers of purple, lavender, white, yellow or cerise; not outstanding in the garden, but well worth growing for decoration indoors; full sun, sandy soil; C.

Stock, *Mathiola incana;* 24 inches; spires of single or double flowers in white, buff, pink, rose, crimson, lavender, purple; one of the most fragrant of garden flowers; buy early-flowering cultivars and discard seedlings that are dark green and spindly if you want all-double florets; rotate crops by planting in different ground each year; B, C.

Strawflower, *Helichrysum bracteatum;* 2 feet; not much in the garden but tops for winter bouquets; shiny stiff flowers in white, orange, pink, cerise or maroon; cut in tight flower while center still closed; full sun, good soil; B, C.

Summer Cypress, Burning Bush, Belvedere; *Kochia scoparia;* 2-2½

feet; a dandy little fine-leaved plant for a hedge; green in summer, startling red—even the stems—in the fall. Grow in full sun; banned as a noxious weed in some places, so best check with your department of agriculture; B, C.

Summer Fir, *Artemisia sacrorum viridis;* 3-6 feet; like a little, bright green fir tree; useful as a hedge or a small specimen; B, C.

Sunflower, *Helianthus;* some are huge-headed and tall, 5-10 feet; others shorter, smaller and flowerier; grow in full sun; dry soil; plant the large ones at the back of the border or along a fence and—if you want to see their faces—to your north for they face the south and the sun; B.

Swan River Daisy, *Brachycome iberidifolia;* 8-12 inches; white, pink or blue daisies, 1-1½ inches across, fine-cut foliage; grow in full sun; for longer blooming time, sow successive plantings; fine for edgings, rock gardens; cuts well; B, C.

Sweet Sultan, *Centaurea moschata;* 2 feet; thistlelike fragrant flowers in white, blue, lavender, purple and yellow; semi-shade; A.

Sweet William Catchfly, *Silene armeria;* 2 feet; William takes a while to get steam up, but when he does he is covered with deep rose or small white star-shaped flowers in late summer; foliage grey-green; grow in full sun; A.

Tithonia, Mexican Sunflower, *T. rotundifolia;* 3-4 feet; a showy plant with soft blue-green leaves, flowers like a bright orange single dahlia; use for a tall hedge or at the back of a border; grows in full sun; good soil; B, C.

Toadflax, *Linaria maroccana,* 1 foot; first cousin to the wild butter-and-eggs of summertime roadsides, but much more beautiful; flowers in combinations of pink, purple, yellow and white like tiny snapdragons; grows best in full sun; A.

Verbena, *V. hortensis;* 1-1½ feet; a beauty as a side-spreading carpeter; flowers in white, pink, cerise, scarlet, some with a white eye; if dead flowers kept cut, will bloom till frost; very fragrant; grow in full sun; B, C.

Wishbone Flower, *Torenia fournieri;* 6-8 inches; a sweet little flower as an edging or low planting; tubular flowers in yellow, lavender or deep purple, rosy red leaves in the fall; grow in moist, cool soil, semi-shade; B, C.

PART IV

THE FUN
OF GARDENING
INDOORS

30 PLANTS FOR YOUR HOUSE

House plants are the flourish that gives fine character to a house. They can be a glorious windowful of gay bulbs, an interesting old china vegetable dish planted with ivies and green glossy-leaved plants, a graceful twirl of philodendron on a mantel, or an absorbing collection of African violets or cacti and succulents.

There's no hocus-pocus about being able to grow them well — it's simply a matter of choosing the right plants for the right places and providing their basic needs as best you can. If one kind does poorly for you — and I know one topflight gardener who grows everything superbly but who can't keep an African violet even half alive for a month — then switch to something else. The world is full of fascinating indoor plants to grow and to enjoy in the growing.

How to choose: Most begin with plants already started by a florist or greenhouse. The wise thing here is to deal with someone you can trust to provide healthy, disease-free material. If you can't be sure of this, then spray your new plants with insecticide and isolate them for a month before you put them with others.

With flowering plants, choose those just coming into bloom and well-budded so that you will have the longest possible pleasure from them. With foliage plants, choose those of vibrant color, well covered with leaves. Small sizes will be cheaper, but it's easier to keep a full- or nearly full-grown plant pruned and trained than to wait months for it to grow to good size. Bargain plants in dime stores and supermarkets are seldom a good long-term buy unless you enjoy nursemaiding.

With bulbs and corms, if you're growing your own, again buy from a reputable dealer and be guided by his recommendations of cultivars that force well indoors: all don't. If you buy your bulbs already started, choose those in bud so that you'll see their opening beauty — what happens for instance when an amaryllis bursts into bloom is nothing short of pure magic.

Decorating with house plants: Sunny windows filled with bright flowers are the best cure in the world for the winter doldrums. South and west exposures are ideal. It's also possible to have luxuriant leafy growth in north or east windows but the list of plants that will *flower* well in them is much shorter (see page 293-294).

Collections of plants look best grouped together in one unit: plant-keeping is easier and, with the pots fairly close together, healthy humidity levels are easier to maintain. A simple setup is to have your local tinsmith make a 3-4-inch galvanized iron tray, paint it to match your room, set on a windowsill, half fill with pea gravel and pieces of charcoal (to keep the water sweet), pour in enough water to barely show through the stones and set your plants on this. Put tall varieties at the back and cascaders such as ivy or philodendron tipped forward along the front to hide the clay pots of those behind. Plant a succession of paper-white narcissus bulbs right in the gravel to come up through the plants and to add a heavenly fragrance to your whole house. If your sills are narrow you can still use a generous width of metal box by letting it project forward and fastening the sides to the window frame with bathtub chain. One small disadvantage with this kind of indoor garden is that you can't open the window behind it in winter. Don't make the mistake of making the pans 5-6 inches deep, thinking that you will hide large pots by setting them deeper. They'll just look strangled. (For a drawing of the right way, see page 286.)

A wheeled tea wagon that can be moved to a bright window during the day and near a lamp in the evening is also a good idea. It can be fitted with metal trays too and a little garden built on both shelves.

In large groupings of many plants, keep them in their pots, then you can change them, if they get gangly or die, without disturbing the whole garden. With groupings in small containers, plants grow best if they're knocked out of their pots and planted directly in soil. In containers without drainage holes, be sure to put an inch or two of gravel or broken pot and a few pieces of charcoal in the bottom, and over that a slice of foam rubber to keep the soil from washing down into the gravel, then add soil and plants. Once a month brace such an undrained pot on its side for a few hours so that the soil will take up any excess water that may have collected in the bottom.

Flowering plants with a limited life are best left in their own pots and either grouped with good-looking foliage plants or set off by themselves in eye-catching containers. Most are best discarded after they bloom unless you have facilities to carry them over successfully. Bulbs, except paperwhite narcissus, can be ripened and held till they can be planted in the garden for bloom outdoors in the following years.

In houses with a contemporary air and lots of light, there's nothing more exciting that the sun-and-shadow patterns thrown across wall and floor by a big bold plant. Here again, it's best to buy in an almost final size if you want

Paperwhite narcissus.

immediate effect. Leave the plant in its pot, but slip it into a handsome container with an inch or two of gravel and charcoal in the bottom and damp peat moss packed between the clay pot and the outside one.

Cactus collections are most decorative if you can plant them in a shallow, earth-toned container, building a desert scene. Terrariums to reproduce the little-plant-look of the forest floor are best made in large fishbowls, aquariums or brandy snifters — something big enough and wide enough to allow a miniature landscape at various levels and with a top that can be partially closed to contain the moist air these plants need. A pad of moss is laid in first, upside down against the glass, then peaty soil, (two peat, one soil, one sand) mixed with finely broken charcoal. A tree-shaped plant or a piece of driftwood to look like a small stump is next set in place, then the lower plants placed around it. Last of all the creepers, such as a bit of snowberry or twin flower, mosses and lichens. Wildlings for this kind of garden are best gathered in the fall: cultivated plants can be used any time, but be sure to choose those that do well in high humidity — small ferns, miniature tropicals, see list page 294. Plants should be watered lightly after being put in the soil — doing it with a spray is good — then a piece of glass or plastic wrap placed *partially* over the opening and the garden set in a light but never sunny place. If you close the top completely, mold forms. If strong sun shines on so tender a little garden it burns. Watering is usually needed only once a month or less, and then it can be done with a spray that washes the plants at the same time.

SIX KEYS TO SUCCESS

All house plants, to grow well, need light and warmth, water and humidity, food and cleaning. And these must be provided regularly. Plants not getting enough light are weak and lanky, have a wishy-washy color and generally look sick. Plants getting too much light and warmth wilt easily and look sunburned: with some of the very tender ones, flower buds drop off. Plants kept too cool just don't grow. Plants not watered enough wilt and the edges of the leaves turn brown. Plants watered too much rot. Plants not fed properly look runty: overfed their growth is rank or they die mysteriously of unseen fertilizer-burned roots. Plants not kept clean get buggy and look messy. Here are the simple dos and don'ts to prevent such sad-sack situations.

Light: most flowering plants, cacti especially, need strong sunlight or its equivalent most of the day as they come up to bloom. This does not need to be direct-through-the-window sunshine, it can be some sunshine and some artificial light, or even all artificial light. (For the special equipment and techniques of gardening under lights, see CHAPTER 31.)

Plants grown only for elegant leaves will be happy with little or no actual sunlight, but to be really luxuriant they still need strong clear light during the day, and in the short days of winter some artificial light for a couple of hours every evening.

Warmth: long-lived foliage plants — many of them from tropical climates — grow well in the temperatures of our winter houses (65°F-75°F during the day, 10°F cooler at night). Most popular flowering plants, however, are grown up to blooming time in cool greenhouses and when moved to house temperatures have a fairly short life. Such plants as cyclamen, 'mums, hydrangeas, azaleas, begonias, cinerarias and geraniums do best if put in a night temperature of 40°-50°F. If you don't have this, curtains can be drawn over a windowsill with the plant next the glass. Be careful, though, not to do this when the weather is bitterly cold outside for you could freeze your plants. On very cold nights, put a piece of cardboard or paper between plant and glass.

Although not a matter of adjusting temperature, plants thrive in winter if you open a nearby door or window for a few minutes to allow fresh air to come into the house.

Water: watering house plants sensibly is a matter of touch. They must have water to live but they must also have air in the soil around their roots to provide the oxygen they need. Soil will feel dry and the pots light if plants need water, moist and heavy if they don't. Let them get a little on the dry side before you water again.

To water effectively, be sure to include good drainage when you're potting up plants. Put a humped piece of pot, then an inch of gravel or a slice of sponge rubber over the drainage hole. Next add soil, leaving about an inch clear at the top to hold the water. Alternate methods of watering — one day pour it in from the top, next time set the pot in deep water up to its rim and let it absorb all it needs. When the top is moist, lift out and drain, pouring away any surplus sitting in the container an hour later.

Wick-fed pots suitable for small and medium-sized plants can be bought from garden suppliers; or you can rig your own from an ordinary flower pot with a drainage hole, a wick made of a piece of nylon stocking pulled into a tube, a reservoir to hold water beneath and the plant set firmly above it. The pot must fit snugly into the rim of the reservoir so that water does not evaporate nor the wick dry out, and be sure to wet the wick before inserting it in the pot. Wick-fed plants are also easy to feed for you simply put water-soluble fertilizer into the water in the reservoir.

Plants coming into bloom and plants with large heavy leaves, such as hydrangeas and cinerarias, take a lot of water. To prevent rot, cacti and succulents should be allowed to dry between waterings. An odd few, such as the umbrella plant and Chinese evergreen will grow right in water.

Humidity: in winter, do everything possible to increase humidity around your plants for air in heated houses is bound to be abnormally dry. Set them on trays or saucers of gravel, sand or peat moss that is kept wet, keep tricky ones in moist places, such as a sill near your kitchen sink and install supplementary humidifiers in your house — you'll feel better too with more moisture in the air. Keep a mist sprayer filled with water at room temperature and top spray plants every day, except the woolly or hairy ones such as African violets.

Fertilizer: house plants bought from greenhouses or florists have enough nourishment in their soil to keep them growing for at least 3 months. From that time on, regular feeding with some form of house-plant fertilizer will continue healthy growth. The handiest of many kinds can be dissolved in the regular water for the plants. Never feed a dry plant. Never fertilize newly potted or dormant plants. Never fertilize an obviously ailing plant: get it back to good health first with frequent water-spraying, change of light and perhaps repotting with fresh soil.

When potting up rooted cuttings or bulbs, or repotting root-bound older plants, either buy specially prepared soil with fertilizer already in it or mix your own. For this, make up a bushel at a time of one part good garden soil, one part coarse sand and one part leaf mold or peat moss. Mix well and into each 6-inch potful mix 1 teaspoon of superphosphate. Old plants need repotting when, on knocking them out of the pot, you find the root ball completely entangled. Move only to a one-size-larger pot, packing new soil under, around and over the old root ball.

Cleanliness: carry plants to the kitchen sink for spraying once a week, or if they are too heavy to move wash both sides of the leaves lightly with a soft, water-dampened cloth, holding your hand behind each leaf as you press. About once a month, give the movable ones a bath or shower in sink or tub, fastening a piece of plastic over the soil of the pot so that it will not wash out. Swish them in lukewarm, mild soapy water, let stand overnight, then repeat the swish in clear water. This is also a marvellous preventive for pests.

Even with the best of care, house plants sometimes get buggy or develop fungus disease. Inspect any new plant before you buy it to be sure it has no visible troubles. If bugs or blights do appear, here is how to identify the enemy.

undersized leaves and flowers and white woolly globs in axils of leaves is mealy bug. Pick the bugs off with a toothpick and pop them into a bath of rubbing alcohol to kill them.

streaked leaves, flower petals that turn brown and wilt and deformed buds is thrips. Spray with house-plant insecticide bomb.

sticky, shiny, deformed leaves and a weak plant is aphids. Spray weekly with house plant bomb for 3 weeks, then watch closely to see if needed again.

rusty mottled leaves and little webs is red spider. Wash, spray: they hate water.

leaves, particularly new ones, that crinkle and turn brown and deformed buds is cyclamen mites. Throw out the plant.

clouds of little white flies when you move the plant, leaves pale and dropping off and unsightly sooty fungus on upper sides of leaves: get rid of the flies by spraying with a bomb at night once a week for a month.

a sickly plant with hard scales on undersides of leaves is scale insects. Rub off scales and spray with bomb.

ragged holes in leaves is slugs or snails. Lay commercial bait or mount a safari to hunt individually, squash. They roam at night.

Be sure to read all directions on house-plant sprays carefully — they are poisons and some are specifically not recommended for certain plants.

GROWING BULBS INDOORS

A few bulbs and corms will grow into gloriously flowering plants by just being potted and cared for with no special treatment. Amaryllis are certainly the most spectacular, with huge, trumpet-shaped flowers and in bloom, if you make successive plantings, from Christmas to May. Orange, scarlet, dark red, white, pink and white stitched with pink, they come into flower in 6-8 weeks and with as many as four huge flowers belling out on a stalk at one time. Buy bulbs in fall and pot up with the top quarter of the bulb above the soil. Place on a warm windowsill and water generously but don't let the soil be sopping wet. After bloom is over, keep in a cool airy place, watering only to keep from completely drying out. When frost is over and the weather warm, plant out in the garden with the rim of the pot below soil level and do not allow to dry out. When fall comes, bring them indoors and grow on again for more bloom. When the sprout begins to show for the second and successive years, fertilize.

Paperwhite narcissus are also easy to grow. Anchor the bulbs in a bowl with pebbles or gravel and some bits of charcoal to keep the water sweet and water up to but not over their necks. With regular room temperature and light and successive plantings they will shoot fragrant white stars all winter.

The gloriosa lily, a superb flowering vine with exotic blossoms of scarlet and yellow, will bloom in 3-4 months from planting. Set the tuber in a 6-inch pot of fairly sandy soil, laying it on its side and covering it with a few inches of soil. Soak, then water lightly till top growth starts, and water more generously while it's growing and blooming.

Hardy bulbs from the Netherlands, England, Ireland and the west coast of North America — daffodils, tulips, hyacinths — should be chosen from recommended cultivars for forcing. Plant them in pots of good soil, their noses poking out just below the rim of the pot, water well and bury outdoors when cool weather sets in. This is best done in a trench — near the house if possible and right against the foundation is ideal — deep enough to hold 1-2 inches of gravel, then 6-8 inches of leaves or shredded styrofoam, the pots of bulbs and another 6-8 inches of leaves or styrofoam on top. Put a piece of 1-inch chicken wire snugly over the top to prevent the mulch from blowing away and the invasion of mice or squirrels. After a minimum of 12 weeks outdoors, bring pots in to a 60°F. storeroom or basement till buds show, then move them into the house for their full flowering. The Dutch bulb industry hopes to eliminate the need for this pre-cooling period outdoors. Watch for news of this.

Because different cultivars bloom at different times, be sure to plant only one kind to a pot, label and bring them into the house a few days apart. After flowering, hardy bulbs can be held over to put in the garden outdoors — slide them, pot, leaves and all into a plastic bag with a few holes in it and tie it up. When the ground is warm and thawed out, knock them from their pot and plant in the garden. After a year, you'll have bloom again outside but they will not force well again indoors.

AFRICAN VIOLETS: DELIGHT OR DESPAIR?

African violets, without any doubt, are the most popular house plant in America today. The delight of devoted thousands, the despair of an untutored few, they have an appeal and a challenge unmatched by any other flowering plant. What's the secret of their popularity?

First of all, it's because they grow best in the same temperatures that we keep our houses in winter — 65°-75°F in the daytime, 10°F cooler at night. They do require higher humidity than most houses register in winter, see how to increase this in the "Six Keys to Success" section of this chapter. These dainty little plants are also in pleasing proportion to our rooms, they never look untidy if they're properly cared for and they're so easy to propagate that many fans use ordinary mail to send each other leaves to grow into new plants.

They grow best in bright light, but not hot burning sun, and respond particularly to the controlled conditions you can set up with a fluorescent light unit. (See CHAPTER 31 for how to do this.) Their leaves are brittle and the pots should be set so they don't bump against each other — this improves needed air circulation too. Watering can be either from bottom or top — alternating is a good idea — but be sure that when feeding a liquid fertilizer you do it from the top. Many experts advise watering plants thoroughly — really soaking them — three times in one day about once every three months to wash out fertilizer residues and salts; all experts agree that all violets benefit from a gentle upside-down bath in lukewarm water when the foliage becomes dusty.

Ernest Fisher, one of America's best hybridizers and growers, recommends, for mature plants, a feeding of liquid fish emulsion at the rate of ½ teaspoon to a gallon once a week for 3 weeks, then in the fourth week a solution of a high-phosphorus and potash liquid and fish emulsion in the proportion of 1:2, ½ teaspoon to a gallon, every 7-10 days. Soil should always be moist when fertilizer is added. (For pest and disease control, see "Six Keys to Success" earlier in this chapter.)

Propagating African violets is amazingly easy. Begin with a medium-sized leaf from a young vigorous plant. Make a clean cut, leaving about 1-1½ inches of stem, insert almost up to the base of the leaf, in a plastic pot filled with tamped down coarse vermiculite. Thoroughly water and keep damp. Set in a bright but not sunny window, or under fluorescent lights. Cuttings should root in 10 days to 3 weeks. To test for this, gently pull on the cutting — if it resists you'll know it has rooted and you can begin with fertilizing. If it has not rooted, leave for a further period. In 3-5 weeks, small plants should be showing. When they're 3 inches high, divide, one to a pot, using a porous soil mix. You can buy this at your garden supplier, or if you wish to make your own here is Ernest Fisher's formula:

2 quarts sterilized clay loam; 2 quarts perlite; 2 quarts coarse vermiculite; 2 quarts fine chip charcoal; 8 quarts screened sphagnum peat moss. Mix separately 1 cup bone meal, 1 cup calcium carbonate (ground limestone), 1 tablespoon of fungicide. Combine all ingredients and add ½ gallon of water to which ½ teaspoon of soil disinfectant is added. Store in a plastic bag — this should yield about half a bushel.

As bloom begins, repot to the 3-inch size, then as your plants become crowded — usually at 6-month intervals — repot again into one size larger. (For recommended book on the fine points of African violet culture, see BIBLIOGRAPHY.)

THIRTEEN OF THE BEST

Azalea: does best in cool air (60°F); keep moist and, because they grow in acid soil, give a deep soak once a week with a solution of ¼ teaspoon aluminum sulphate or 1 teaspoon cider vinegar to 1 quart of water. Pick off dead flowers, wash by spraying once a week. To keep for another year, set outdoors in a garden bed in semi-shade for the summer, do not allow to dry out, bring in before frost, feed and give regular care and your azalea can be a flowery pleasure for years.

Bromeliads: a race of spectacular and bizarre plants. Some grow in soil, others on trees from which they take no nourishment. For a handsome decoration, wrap the roots of the tree-growing types with osmunda fibre and tie them to a twist of driftwood. Water by filling the cup formed by the leaves, keeping it full at all times. These leaves can be striped or banded, sometimes tipped with scarlet; the flowers are sturdy and waxy and last for months. Once flowered, the central plant dies, leaving side shoots to grow on. Very dramatic and dashing, these beauties.

Cactus and succulents are easy-care, favorite plants. Collecting them is brightened with some lovely nutsy names—the Horse Crippler, Jelly Beans and Owl's Eyes, Fragrant Moondrops, Chilean Old Lady and the Red Headed Irishman are only a few. They thrive in dry air and like periods of drought, normally from December to March. When you water them regularly again—usually early spring—they bloom with the most exotic little flowers. A good soil mix is 3 parts good garden soil, 1 part leaf mold, ½ part sand, ½ part crushed limestone, ½ part crushed brick. Indoors they should have the sunniest window possible. For a good book on the fine points of growing these intriguing plants, see Bibliography.

Chrysanthemum: the best value in a gift plant for its flowers last for weeks. Ordinary house-plant care keeps it healthy, and when bloom is over cut stems back to 3 inches, feed and water and you may get a second bloom. To keep over, plunge pot in the garden when summer comes, in a sunny place, feed and water, nip shoots, and it may bloom again outdoors. To bloom again indoors, they have to be kept in the dark for 14-16 hours a day.

Cyclamen: the most decorative of house plants with their lovely butterfly flowers held high above veined, heart-shaped leaves. Likes cool air (60°F), to be kept moist, although your must be careful not to pour on so much water the corm rots. Difficult to hold over.

Easter Lily: Buy in bud and have the fun of watching the bells burst open. Care is average. With your thumbnail, nick off the yellow pollen on the stamens as soon as the flower opens to prolong the bloom and to keep the throat clean. Cut off dead flowers and, when frost is over, bury pot outdoors in the garden for a second bloom in early fall.

Gloxinia: a first cousin of the African Violet and likes the same care; wonderful velvet colors. Pick off dead flowers carefully to allow buds behind to develop. Bloom is usually in spring and summer, the plant then goes dormant, leaves fall off and it looks dead. But if you can store it for the winter in a dry warm place, it's possible to water and feed when growth begins again and produce a second season of bloom.

Hydrangea: these are the big show-stoppers of spring. They need a daily soak in deep water. Pink ones hold their color if fertilizing is done with a mix high in superphosphate; blue ones, to hold their color, need acid watering similar to azaleas. Not hardy outdoors in most of the country but can be held over for another year's bloom indoors if you bury the pot in semi-shade in the garden for the summer, bring in before frost, hold at 40°-50°F for 6 weeks, then at 60°F with average care till blooming time.

Jerusalem Cherry: Christmas Pepper: bright red-fruited little plants that like moist soil and moist air. To prevent leaf drop, spray daily and give ordinary care. To hold over, keep pruned to encourage new growth.

Kalanchoe: orange or golden stars above rubbery leaves; take average care, pick off dead flowers, set out in the garden for the summer, bring in before frost, feed and water for second bloom.

Orchids: these exotic jewels of flowers may be successfuly grown in your house if you choose the right kinds, give them the right light and the humidity of a tropical forest. This isn't as difficult as it sounds—a good fluorescent light unit and a space enclosed by glass or fold-up plastic curtains make it possible to create and maintain the necessary conditions. A few will even grow on open windowsills with bright light. For details of culture see recommended book in Bibliography, and for special orchid societies to join see List of Plant Societies.

Orange, Lemon Trees: these are often disappointing as gift plants. They're so pretty and so fragrant that one tiny flower fills the house, some even produce real oranges and lemons. But they must have a bright, sunny window, high humidity, regular watering and feeding and cool air. Top spraying a couple of times a day helps. To hold over, set in the ground outdoors for the summer and bring in before frost.

Poinsettia: one of the longest blooming plants of the winter, the flowers often lasting 3-4 months. Average care in a sunny window. Can be held over if you set the pot in the garden for the summer, water and feed and bring in before frost. But to produce another season of bloom, they must have 16 hours of complete darkness daily—the kind they would have if you shut them up in a cupboard from 4 p.m. to 8 a.m. every day from October to Christmas.

HOUSE PLANTS TO TRY—WHERE

(Suggested varieties for beginners are starred)

For the Brightest Sunniest Windows
Annuals, such as nasturtiums, morning glories, petunias, etc.
Azaleas
Browallia, blue and white
Bulbs: spring flowering daffodils, tulips, hyacinths; corms and exotics such as amaryllis, * cape hyacinths, calla and Easter lilies, * clivia, cyclamen, gloriosa lily
Cacti * and most Succulents *
Christmas Cactus: Thanksgiving Cactus
Cineraria
Crown-of-thorns
Jerusalem Cherry: Christmas Pepper
Kalanchoe *
Chrysanthemum *
Poinsettia *

For Light But Not Sunny Windows
African Violet *
Begonia, Fibrous *
Bulbs: spring flowering and exotic, if they are in bud when you move them in *
Caladium
Ferns, * many
Foliage Plants: ivy, * nephthytis, * philodendron, * pothos, * grape ivy, * kangaroo vine, * German ivy, * pilea, pick-a-back plant
Gloxinia

For Fragrance
Daffodils * and Hyacinths *
Easter lily *
Exacum (smells like lily-of-the-valley)
For Pinching Fragrance: scented geraniums—apple, mint, peppermint, rose, lemon; lemon verbena
Gardenia (need a cool air and daily top spray)
Genista
Heliotrope

Iris reticulata
Paperwhite Narcissus *

For Hanging Pedestals and Baskets
Asparagus * and Boston Fern *
Campanula isophylla (needs a cool,
  sunny window)
Christmas Cactus : Thanksgiving Cactus
Columnea
Episcia
Fuchsia
Ivy Geranium
Spider Plant *
Wandering Jew *

For Bold Accent
Aralia
Aspidistra *
Azalea
Bromeliads
Clivia
Dieffenbachia
Dracaena
Fatsia *
Fiddleaf Fig

Hydrangea
Kangaroo Vine *
Large Varieties of Philodendron *
Mexican Breadfruit
Norfolk Island Pine
Pandanus
Rubber Plant *
Schefflera *

For Desert Gardens
Cacti, * Succulents, * Sedums * in variety : buy the ones that tickle your fancy

For Woodsy Terrariums*
(*Be thoughtful about collecting wild-
lings: always get permission from the
owner of the land where they are
growing and take only a small growing
piece*)
Goldthread
Mosses and lichens
Partridge Berry
Pipsissewa
Seedling Ferns and Evergreens
Snowberry

Starflower
Sundew (needs a lot of moisture)
Twinflower
Wintergreen

For Terrariums of Cultivated Plants
Bottle Gardens
Babies' Tears *
Coleus
Fittonia
Maranta
Miniature African Violets, Ferns * such
  as Pteris ; Ivies *
Small Begonias *

For Bowls Planted with Foliages
Chinese Evergreen
Dracaena
Maranta
Nephthytis *
Peperomia, * (variegated and all green)
Pothos *
Pilea
Watermelon Begonia

31 GARDENING UNDER LIGHTS

Flick a switch and make a garden? Impossible, you'll say. Not at all — the new world of artificial light and research into plants that will grow happily under it make it possible now to flick a switch and have flowers and glowing green foliage all year. It is even possible to put an electric timer on that switch and have it flick on and off without you even being there.

Gardening like this is easy; plants are pretty and healthy and it has intriguing sidepaths too — rooting cuttings or growing seedlings for your outdoor garden or to sell; growing herbs for your cooking, even in midwinter; making collections of interesting close-up-lovely plants such as miniature roses, cacti or dwarf geraniums.

CHOOSE WHERE YOU ARE GOING TO PUT YOUR INDOOR GARDEN

Ideally, two indoor gardens are best. One is a working production centre out of sight in basement or attic, even in a roomy closet. The other is a display garden in your living or dining room, as a divider between the two; in a hall or stair well; on a kitchen or bathroom shelf. You can even have an intimate little garden under a lamp on your desk where you will really see every leaf and budding blossom up close. If you can't manage two gardens it's still possible to have one that will both produce and display.

Versatile light fixtures for table top, wall shelves and basement units are widely available. A two-level cart on castors makes it possible to roll your garden around to different parts of the house — into the living room for showing off, out to the kitchen for cleaning up, into a cool sunroom for the night. A desk lamp with a circular fluorescent tube has a shelf for plants.

Eighty-watt, 12-inch square fluorescent panels, 1½ inches thick are especially useful for square spaces. Or you can also rig your own trays and lights.

INSTALLATION

Have a licensed electrician check your house wiring to be sure that it will carry the load, then have him wire all necessary connections. Units you will be using are 100 volts, single phase and they can be connected to regular wall outlets.

The most useful basic unit is two 48-inch, 40-watt, cool-white fluorescent tubes (preheat is better than rapid start: you will have less trouble with moisture collecting on this type and a longer life) and one 25-watt incandescent bulb in a porcelain socket. Special horticultural tubes which throw a rosy lavender glow over the plants, enhancing pinks and reds, are on the market but the less expensive cool-white, combined with incandescent, is rated just as effective for good growth.

Don't consider a fixture with just one tube, it isn't big enough to throw the light you'll need. Don't install two 24-inch tubes to get 48 inches, for fluorescent lights are less intense at the ends of the tube than in the middle and the smaller size increases the number of ends you have. All electrical connections should be in metal junction boxes. Ballasts can be mounted with the tubes or behind, on asbestos, where they will be out of sight and throw less heat on the plants.

You will want an independent switch for each unit, also a timer with a three-pronged plug that connects to a three-aperture grounded outlet. Exact control of the number of hours that lights are on each day is the main secret of success. Install extra outlets near the "working" garden, for you may decide to add equipment such as a cool-vapor humidifier (the type that runs for approximately 8-10 hours on one filling and shuts off automatically) or a fan to improve ventilation. A guide to measure both temperature and humidity is useful too, and water outlets and a sink nearby are handy if you have many plants to care for.

Metal reflectors for both fluorescent tubes and incandescent bulbs can be bought from electrical suppliers. Wherever possible, the lighting unit should be hung from pulleys in the ceiling on sashcord or chains so that it can be raised or lowered according to the intensity of light needed. If the lights have to be permanently fixed — as they would be over a shelf garden set into the wall, for instance — paint the top sides and bottom of the niche a glossy white to reflect as much light as possible. For easy working, be sure to make the space 2-6 inches wider than the lights at each end.

The most convenient base for plant pots to sit on is a galvanized metal tray 3-4 inches deep. For display, this can be painted to match the room or faced with plywood, painted or stained. For the 2-tube, 48-inch fixture, a good tray would be 30 inches wide, 48 inches long. Half fill it with gravel, stone chips, crushed tile or finely broken oyster shells, pushing in small pieces of charcoal about 12 inches apart to keep the water sweet. At all times, keep the level of the water where you can just see it, but not above the stones because then pots would be standing in it and roots would get waterlogged. To bring short plants or seed pans closer to the lights, set them on bricks or upside-down clay pots on the gravel. Some light gardeners, to prevent their pots rooting into the stones, put a screen of hardware cloth above the gravel and set the pots on that. All materials used in these installations should be rustproof since the air around the garden will be very moist.

THE GROWING OPERATION

Plants for your indoor garden can come from florist, greenhouse or supermarket, slips or cuttings from friends, bits and pieces from your outdoor garden, wildlings, or seeds (see suggestions, page 299).

To acclimatize new plants, begin with fixtures 50 percent higher above the tops of the plants than the distance recommended for their final position, then move them gradually nearer to the plants. Group together plants needing similar light — those needing most in the centre and those needing least at the end. High-intensity-light plants should have 6-12 inches between their tops and the lights; medium-intensity 12-18 inches, and low ones can be up to 36 inches away. Do not put small plants any closer to the tubes than 2 inches, large ones 6 inches. If plants grow too tall, they're not getting enough light. If their leaves are abnormally light-colored and are growing downwards they're getting too much light. If they're growing well but not flowering, experiment with different lengths of darkness — this is the factor that most strongly influences blooming.

Ideal temperatures for night are 60°-65°F (this is very important for best growth); day, when the lights are on, 70°-75°F for plants, 75°-85°F for seed germination. (To hasten the rooting of cuttings in quantity, use a deeper pan, then connect and bury a lead-covered heating cable, such as is used in greenhouses, in the lower 2 inches of the pan and add 4 inches of growing medium to hold the cuttings above it.)

Ventilation should be good but neither breezy nor drafty. A successful African violet grower sets a small fan to direct airflow at the ceiling, thus moving the air but not blowing it directly on the plants. In working gardens, plants should be set far enough apart not to touch each other; this helps to prevent leggy growth and foliage diseases. In display units, most plants will look lovelier set a little closer so that you don't see the pots. Trailing ivies, spider plant, episcias are especially decorative at the front, helping to hide pots behind and, at the same time, breaking the harsh line of the edge of the tray.

Watering should be done in the morning when the temperature is rising. One handy way is to push a funnel gently into the soil at the top of the pot, fill with water till no more disappears, then plug the spout with your finger and remove it. Always water thoroughly, then wait for the leaves to show signs of wilting before watering again. Too frequent watering waterlogs roots. Try not to spill water on the leaves. Although some growers recommend top-spraying leaves to increase humidity, others prefer a humidifier or a plastic sheet dropped down around the garden at night. Wick-watering is good, especially for hairy-leaved plants like African violets. All plants should be doused in lukewarm water in the sink whenever they get dusty.

Potting soil, bagged and sterile, is available in most garden supply stores and, if you need only a small amount, is more convenient than making your own. But here is a good recipe: 3 parts of garden loam, 1 part of either leaf mold, vermiculite, perlite or peat moss, 1 part of sand. To each bushel, add one tablespoon of superphosphate and 1 tablespoon of ground limestone, both available from your garden supplier. Sterilize the soil first (see CHAPTER 19) so that you don't introduce any disease or pests with it.

Humidity should be 50-60 percent for normal growth. This is fairly easy to achieve if the gravel base is kept moist at all times and automatic humidifying added when necessary.

Fertilize with water-soluble solutions only when plants are actively growing. Do this every time you water by adding one twentieth of the recommended dose, or apply the full dose once every two weeks after watering. Never fertilize a dry or sick plant. If a white crust forms on top of the soil after a few months, scrape it off and replace with fresh sterile soil.

Insects and diseases are not hard to control. If you're at all uncertain about the state of a plant's health, quarantine it for a week away from the rest of your garden. Learn to identify the signs of trouble early (see "Six Keys to Success," CHAPTER 30).

Plant pots should be new or scrubbed clay, or plastic (dark colors are best for they absorb heat). Plastic pots don't need watering as often as clay for they are not porous.

Replacement of fluorescent tubes is usually necessary at the end of a year if they have been burning 14-16 hours daily. By then the intensity of light is reduced by 20 percent and it's better to replace them even if they're not totally burned out. When tubes age beyond their full usefulness, dark rings appear at the ends. A good idea is to write the installation date and the calculated replacement date on the glass of each lamp with a grease pencil when you install it. Keep tubes and bulbs dusted and clean at all times.

LIGHT NEEDS OF SOME FAVORITE PLANTS FOR INDOOR GARDENS

Plants fall into three light-need groups:

those needing a short day, long night (approximately 10-13 hours of light)

those needing a long day, short night (from 14-18 hours of light)

those easy going ones that don't seem to mind as long as the lights are on 12-18 hours.

For plants to flower properly the dark period must be solid and uninterrupted. If you wish to grow short-day plants in a spot where house or street lighting interrupts the dark period, rig up a shield of black plastic cloth or building paper, or lower a cardboard carton over them. A commercial grower once lost a crop of 25,000 poinsettias he was growing for the Christmas trade because a new nightwatchman, contrary to instructions, turned on a light bulb every night in the end of the greenhouse to eat his lunch by and thus interrupted the critical period of darkness.

You can delay flowering in short-day plants by timing the lights to come on ten minutes of each hour and this same timing will hasten flowering of long-day plants by interrupting the dark.

Short-day, long-night plants (lights on 10-13 hours): chrysanthemums, poinsettias, gardenias, kalanchoe, Christmas cactus, subtropical foliages and ferns.

Long-day, short-night plants (lights on 14-18 hours): geraniums (especially the scented cultivars), tuberous begonias — which, by the way, can be grown continuously under lights, or started, put out in the garden and then brought back under lights — calceolaria, cineraria, bouvardia, nasturtium, heather, clarkia, centaurea, primroses.

Easy going plants (lights on 12-14-16-18 hours): African violets — large thick-leaved cultivars need all the light they can get; dark, thin-leaved ones need more than pink-and-white-flowering, light-leaved cultivars — gloxinias, miniature roses, cacti, fibrous begonias, pinks and coleus.

Growing your own outdoor plants from seed indoors is economical, good fun and you can choose your colors by buying seed in individual colors. Vegetable plants too can be ready to set outside as soon as the ground is warm and danger of frost is over.

Sow 8-10 weeks before time to plant out. Prepare pots or flats with sterilized soil; water; plant seeds; cover with glass or plastic or slide the whole thing into a plastic bag and tie. Set about 6 inches below tubes. Small plastic greenhouses for seed-sowing and pre-planted boxes are also on the market. Remove cover when seeds germinate and increase distance from light as seedlings grow. Transplant when two pairs of true leaves are showing. Harden outdoors before planting out permanently.

For compact bushy plants, light 10 hours daily and keep at temperatures of 50°-65°F. For quicker growth, give light up to 16 hours and temperatures of 70°-75°F. Experts recommend that you turn off the incandescent bulbs in your fixtures for seedlings.

Annuals to try: cosmos, marigold, salvia, zinnia, China aster, bachelor's buttons, coreopsis, rudbeckia, petunia, snapdragon, salpiglossis, scabiosa, verbena, nasturtium, globe amaranth.

Vegetables to start: lettuce, beets, broccoli, cauliflower, cucumber, eggplant, peppers and, the most popular of all, tomatoes.

Biennials and Perennials: if you have the space to house the last size of these plants just before they are moved outdoors, seeds sown in early summer can be grown under lights which will shorten the usual time from planting to flower by at least one whole season. Favorite biennials: Canterbury bells, English daisies, foxgloves and sweet william. Favorite perennials are almost anything you want to grow — delphinium, primroses, day lilies, lilies, lupines, columbines are only a few.

Bulbs and Corms: the best loved of the spring bulbs — crocus, snowdrops, tulips, hyacinths, daffodils — must have 10-12 weeks planted in their pots, stored in the dark, at 40°F. (See CHAPTER 30 for the best way to do this.) They are then transferred to a cool basement at 50°-60°F. till active leaf and bud growth starts. Only then can they be brought under lights for flowering. Amaryllis, on the other hand, can be put directly under lights as soon as it is potted up. Summer bulbs and corms — gladiolus, dahlia, tuberous begonia and caladiums — can be started into early growth under lights by being set shallowly on moist peat or vermiculite and later moved to the garden when soil is warm and there is no danger of frost.

Herbs: grow at 60°-70°F temperatures and easy-going light lengths: parsley, chives, watercress, sweet basil, rosemary, borage, chervil, marjoram and sage. All will do well and give flavory snippings for treats all year.

GUIDES
TO GARDENING
IN ELEVEN REGIONS
OF THE UNITED STATES

32 HOW TO USE THIS SECTION

Part V is for beginning gardeners everywhere in the United States. Gardening, all along the way, is discovery learning; therefore the more you learn of what others have discovered, the more curious you become about plants and practices. As you gather more information, the more delightful your own gardening experience becomes.

The summaries of climate, soils and special characteristics of each region have been provided by eleven experts—associates of government departments of agriculture, professors in university departments of horticulture, directors of botanical gardens or arboreta, and well-known garden consultants and lecturers. Each has also contributed information on places of special interest and lists of some favorite plants grown in his region. Included in these lists are large trees, small flowering trees, large and small evergreens, broad-leaved evergreens, shrubs, hedges and windbreaks, ground covers, lawn grasses, native plants useful in gardens, and named varieties of roses. Perennials, biennials, annuals and bulbs have not generally been listed, inasmuch as these are virtually the same for any part of the country. Some special comment regarding them is offered where relevant to certain regions. In the lists "in variety" refers to both species and cultivars and indicates that the buyer will have a wide choice.

Be sure to check, in the case of trees and shrubs, the plant-hardiness ratings indicated by zone numbers. You can locate the zone your garden is in by referring to the "Plant Hardiness Map" on the endpapers. Plants with your zone number or a lower one can reasonably be expected to grow well for you, except that in Zone 9, and more extensively in Zone 10, the heat, the long growing season and other factors are unsuitable, if not intolerable, to some northern plants.

The designation of a zone as 3a or 3b indicates that the plant is hardy in the (a) generally cooler or more mountainous parts of that zone or (b) in the warmer and less elevated parts. These qualifications can only be approximate and suggestive, as local conditions within any zone vary. The U.S. Department of Agriculture publishes a large and highly detailed map showing these variations *a* and *b,* but it is far too elaborate to be useful in the necessarily reduced scale of the endpapers.

Places and plantings of interest are in most cases necessarily brief, but there are two excellent publications that offer a great deal of information in considerable detail: The American Horticultural Society's *1971 Directory of American Horticulture,* available from the society at 901 N. Washington Street, Alexandria, Virginia 22314, and the Brooklyn Botanic Garden Handbook, *American Gardens—A Traveler's Guide,* Brooklyn Botanic Garden, 1000 Washington Avenue, Brooklyn, New York 11225.

The presentation and emphasis of material in this section reflects the preferences of the various contributors.

33 NORTHEAST

Maine through Connecticut and part of New York
Zones 3, 4, 5, 6

by Dr. Gordon P. DeWolf, Jr., *Horticulturist,*
The Arnold Arboretum of Harvard University,
Jamaica Plain, Massachusetts

In spite of densely populous cities and suburbs and the consequent network of highways, New England still keeps some of its traditional reputation as one of the most beautiful and most livable parts of the nation. The overall landscape is a combination of pastoral valleys and wooded hills, which rise into mountains in New Hampshire and Vermont. Tall-growing white pines, Norway pines, many oaks, red maples, sugar maples and surviving American elms are found not only in the forests but in farmland and along country and small-town roads. The autumnal pageant of flaming foliage is unmatched in any part of the world. The old villages of predominantly white-painted houses under massive trees with gardens behind white picket fences are a reminder of one way of life that greatly helped to fashion this country.

One type of garden still seen was derived from the early colonists, who brought seeds and a few plants from England and cultivated them in small plots enclosed against wandering cows and sheep. This led to the tidy patterned garden of bordered beds, often of vegetables and flowers and herbs together. Later on, the paths might be paved with bricks or flat stones, a sundial placed at the central axis, and in larger gardens a dovecote or water tank or hive of bees. Sometimes the pattern was elaborated by interlacing edgings of herbs and developed into the fragrant knot garden entirely of herbs. There are delightful modern examples of these, the interest in herbs having a vigorous revival.

Toward the end of the nineteenth century, under the influence of William Robinson and Gertrude Jekyll, the hardy perennial border became prominent, often backed by a curving line of flowering shrubs and fronted by ample stretches of lawn. This type of garden also still exists, but it demands far more care and continuous labor than most homeowners can give or afford. The current emphasis is upon simplified gardens of minimum and low-cost maintenance, with paved terrace or patio, a few shrubs, flowers in large containers and a pool.

In this relatively small Northeast region there is both a wide range of temperature from winter to summer and an almost continuous fluctuation between fair weather and rainy or snowy. The influence of the ocean makes a narrow strip all along the coast — and the greater part of Connecticut and Rhode Island — sufficiently mild to become a part of Hardiness Zone 6 and affects Cape Cod and extreme southwestern Connecticut to a greater degree, admitting these areas into Zone 7 (associated with Long Island and southeastern New Jersey).

Only the very northern parts of Vermont, New Hampshire and Maine are in Zone 3. Here and in central Maine, average midsummer temperatures are 64° to 66°, and the growing season is 120 days or less. In parts of central Massachusetts, Rhode Island and Connecticut the summer temperature averages 70° to 72°, and the growing season is 160 to 200 days. Northern New England has the reputation for being clear and cool, though some precipitation may be expected one day in three. Southern New England is subject to periods of hot sultry weather at any time through the summer.

The easternmost part of New York State — from New York City up the Hudson River Valley and to Lake Champlain — corresponds closely to this hardiness-zonal pattern of New England, having much the same types of trees, shrubs and herbs. Being farther inland and west of the Taconic and Berkshire hills, the Hudson Valley is apt to be warm in the summer with a long growing season and spells of humid weather. A few plants, such as the empress-tree, the beach plum and certain hybrid azaleas, considered reliably hardy only in Zone 7, do grow for a few miles up the Hudson; and there are many fine gardens in this area.

Most of the familiar temperate-climate hardy perennials, biennials and annuals will grow well in the Northeast, and a few that enjoy cool summers will do unusually well, particularly in Zones 4 and 5. In this group are *Delphinium grandiflorum* cultivars and the Connecticut Yankee strain; also the annual larkspur, *D. ajacis,* and nasturtiums, lupines, peonies and sweet peas. A hardy and most useful vine, characteristic of New England, is the American woodbine (*Parthenocissus quinquefolia*).

Most New England soils are shallow, acid and poor in nutrients. In general they benefit from liberal additions of organic matter and fertilizer. Leaves, lawn clippings and kitchen garbage should be composted. Sawdust, wood-chips, leaves or hay may be used for mulching — but be sure to add extra nitrogenous fertilizer. Sewage sludge, where available, is an excellent soil amender.

New England's coastline is popular for vacationers. However, gardening near the sea poses special problems. Many plants are intolerant of salt. Coastal soils tend to be particularly barren and sandy. The on-shore winds produce problems not usually found farther inland. On the other hand, temperatures are less extreme, and growing seasons are long.

WHERE TO GET SPECIAL HELP

Nearly every county has one or more county agents who can supply information based on local conditions. Look in the telephone book under your County Extension Service, or write to your State Extension Service.

Connecticut: Agricultural Experiment Station, University of Connecticut, Storrs, Connecticut 06268.

Maine: Extension Information Specialist, Department of Public Information and Central Services, University of Maine, Orono, Maine 04473.

Massachusetts: College of Agriculture, Agricultural Experiment Station, University of Massachusetts, Amherst, Massachusetts 01002.

New Hampshire: Agricultural Extension Service, University of New Hampshire, Durham, New Hampshire 03824.

Rhode Island: Agricultural Experiment Station, University of Rhode Island, Kingston, Rhode Island 02881.

Vermont: Agricultural Extension Service, University of Vermont, Burlington, Vermont 05401.

Also: The Arnold Arboretum of Harvard University, The Arborway, Jamaica Plain, Massachusetts 02130.

Free publications for home gardeners are available through the State Experiment Stations and from the county agents. Contact the Experiment Stations for directions for having soils tested. The Arnold Arboretum will provide identification of plant material.

PLACES AND PLANTINGS OF INTEREST

Connecticut: CONNECTICUT ARBORETUM, Connecticut College, New London. Plantings of native woody plants spread about the grounds of the college.
BARTLETT ARBORETUM, University of Connecticut, Stamford. Formerly the demonstration plantings of the Bartlett Tree Experts, featuring mature specimens of many cultivated trees and shrubs.

Mountain-Laurel is the state flower; White Oak, the state tree.

Maine: BOTANICAL PLANTATIONS OF THE UNIVERSITY OF MAINE, Orono. Demonstration plantings for university classes, featuring trees and shrubs; also hardiness tests of exotics.

Pine Cone and Tassel is the state flower; White Pine, the state tree.

Massachusetts: ARNOLD ARBORETUM OF HARVARD UNIVERSITY, Jamaica Plain. Approximately 265 acres of landscaped parkland. Famous for displays of azaleas, lilacs and crabapples, but also exhibiting representatives of about 5,500 kinds of hardy, woody plants. Open dawn to dusk every day of the year.
BOSTON PUBLIC GARDEN, Boston. An oasis of green in the midst of the city, featuring specimen trees, broad sweeps of lawn and elaborate annual bedding.
BOTANIC GARDEN OF SMITH COLLEGE, Northampton. Outstanding for its rock gardens, perennial beds and display greenhouses.
HERITAGE PLANTATION AND GARDEN, Sandwich. The home of the Dexter rhododendrons, with extensive ornamental plantings and nature trails.
GARDEN IN THE WOODS, South Sudbury. Extensive displays of native American wild flowers grown naturalistically.
BERKSHIRE GARDEN CENTER, Stockbridge. Demonstration plantings of annuals, perennials, shrubs and trees, and featuring iris, hemerocallis, roses, phlox and herbs.
ALEXANDRA BOTANIC GARDEN AND HUNNEWELL ARBORETUM, Wellesley College, Wellesley. The arboretum has one of the oldest collections of conifers in the East, as well as an especially fine collection of rhododendrons. The botanic garden has a series of five display greenhouses with a large collection of tender exotics.

Mayflower (arbutus) is the state flower; American Elm, the state tree.

New Hampshire: LILAC ARBORETUM, University of New Hampshire, Durham. Collection of lilacs for New Hampshire conditions. Used as a basis for breeding new varieties.

WENTWORTH-COOLIDGE MANSION, Portsmouth. House dating from 1690; garden includes display of old lilacs.

Purple Lilac is the state flower; Paper Birch, the state tree.

Rhode Island: SMITH'S CASTLE GARDENS, Cocumscussoc. Re-created eighteenth-century garden. Includes displays of spring bulbs, old roses and herbs.

BROWNELL MEMORIAL ROSE GARDENS, Little Compton. Display of roses, including those especially bred for New England conditions.

THE ELMS, Newport, features a formal French garden.

Violet is the state flower; Red Maple, the state tree.

Vermont: STONE CHIMNEY GARDENS, Reading. Displays of pimroses, herbs and perennials.

Red Clover is the state flower; Sugar Maple, the state tree.

SOME FAVORITE GARDEN PLANTS OF NEW ENGLAND

LARGE TREES

COMMON NAME	BOTANICAL NAME	HEIGHT	ZONE
Ash, White	Fraxinus americana	120'	4
Not for coastal planting.			
Basswood	Tilia americana	120'	3
Beech, European	Fagus sylvatica	90'	5
Birch, Canoe	Betula papyrifera	90'-120'	3
European	pendula	60'	3
Honey-Locust	Gleditsia triacanthos	130'	5
Linden, Littleleaf	Tilia cordata	90'	4
Maple, Norway	Acer platanoides	90'	4
Sugar	saccharum	120'	4
Not for roadside or coastal planting.			
Oak, Bur	Quercus macrocarpa	75'-150'	3
Pin	palustris	75'-120'	5
Scarlet	coccinea	75'	5
White	alba	100'	0
Sycamore	Platanus occidentalis	120'-150'	5
Willow, Weeping	Salix alba 'Tristis'	75'	3

SMALL DECIDUOUS FLOWERING TREES

COMMON NAME	BOTANICAL NAME	HEIGHT	ZONE
Cherry, Korean	Prunus maackii	45'	3
Crabapple, in variety	Malus	15'-45'	4,5
Bechtel's	ioensis 'Plena'	30'	3
Cherry	x robusta	45'	4
Siberian	baccata 'Jackii'	40'	3
	'Flame'	15'-20'	3
Dogwood, Flowering	Cornus florida	45'	5
Japanese Pagoda-Tree	Sophora japonica	75'	5
Mountain-Ash, European	Sorbus aucuparia	45'-60'	4
Redbud, American	Cercis canadensis	30'-45'	5
Sourwood	Oxydendrum arboreum	75'	5
Yellow-Wood	Cladrastis lutea	45'-60'	4

Brick-paved and bordered paths frame the geometrically laid out beds of this New England herb garden—a traditional design well worth keeping. (*George Taloumis photo*)

LARGE EVERGREENS

COMMON NAME	BOTANICAL NAME	HEIGHT	ZONE
Arborvitae, American	*Thuja occidentalis*	60'	3
Fir, Nikko	*Abies homolepis*	90'	5
White	*concolor*	120'	5
Hemlock, Canadian	*Tsuga canadensis*	90'	4
Pine, Red (Norway)	*Pinus resinosa*	75'-150'	3
White	*strobus*	90'-150'	4
Red-Cedar	*Juniperus virginiana*	90'	3
Spruce, Blue	*Picea pungens* 'Glauca'	90'-150'	3
Engelmann	*engelmannii*	150'	3
Norway	*abies*	150'	3
White	*glauca*	90'	3

SMALL, NEEDLE-LEAVED EVERGREENS

COMMON NAME	BOTANICAL NAME	HEIGHT	ZONE
Arborvitae, American	*Thuja occidentalis*	low	2
False-Cypress, Hinoki	*Chamaecyparis obtusa*	low	4
Sawara	*pisifera*	low	4
Heather	*Calluna vulgaris*	10-18"	5
Hemlock	*Tsuga canadensis*	low	5
Juniper, Chinese	*Juniperus chinensis*	6-15"	5
Common	*communis*	12-36"	2
Creeping	*horizontalis*	6-12"	2
Pine, Mugho	*Pinus mugo mughus*	8'	2
Japanese Stone	*pumila*	8'	4
Yew, Hybrid	*Taxus* x *media*	low	5
Japanese	*cuspidata*	low	5

BROAD-LEAVED EVERGREENS

COMMON NAME	BOTANICAL NAME	HEIGHT	ZONE
Box, Korean	*Buxus microphylla koreana*	3'-6'	5
Leucothoe, Drooping	*Leucothoe fontanesiana (catesbaei)*	6'	5
Mountain-Laurel	*Kalmia latifolia*	6'-30'	5
Rhododendron, Carolina	*Rhododendron carolinianum*	6'	6
Catawba	*catawbiense* cults.	6'-18'	5
Rosebay	*maximum*	12'-35'	4
Sheep-Laurel	*Kalmia angustifolia*	3'	3

FLOWERING DECIDUOUS SHRUBS

COMMON NAME	BOTANICAL NAME	HEIGHT	ZONE
Azaleas, Ghent	*Rhododendron* x *gandavense* cults.	6'-9'	5
Mollis Hybrids	x *kosterianum* cults.	3'-6'	6
Royal	*schlippenbachii*	15'	5
Forsythia, Early	*Forsythia ovata*	6'-9'	5
Showy Border	x *intermedia* 'Spectabilis'	1'	6
Lilac, Common	*Syringa vulgaris* cults.	18'	4
Preston Hybrids	x *prestoniae* cults.	9'	3
Rhododendron, Korean	*Rhododendron mucronulatum*	6'	5
Rose, Rugosa	*Rosa rugosa* cults.	6'	3
Witch-Hazel	*Hamamelis* x *intermedia* 'Arnold Promise'	15'	5

HEDGES AND WINDBREAKS

(T—tall, 10' and up; M—medium, 5'-9'; L—low, 1'-4')

COMMON NAME	BOTANICAL NAME	HEIGHT	ZONE
Arborvitae, American	*Thuja occidentalis*	T	3
Hemlock, Eastern	*Tsuga canadensis*	T	4
Honeysuckle, Amur	*Lonicera maackii*	T	3
Pine, White	*Pinus strobus*	T	4
Privet, Amur	*Ligustrum amurense*	M-T	4
Common	*vulgare*	M-T	5
Rose, Japanese	*Rosa multiflora*	M	6
Rugosa	*rugosa* cults.	L-M	3
Yew, Hybrid	*Taxus* x *media* cults.	L-T	5
Japanese	*cuspidata* cults.	M-T	5

TREES AND SHRUBS FOR SEASIDE PLANTING

COMMON NAME	BOTANICAL NAME	HEIGHT	ZONE
Bayberry	*Myrica pensylvanica*	9'	3
Honey-Locust	*Gleditsia triacanthos*	120'	5
Juniper, Creeping	*Juniperus horizontalis* cults.	1'-2'	3
Linden, Littleleaf	*Tilia cordata*	90'	4
Oak, Red	*Quercus borealis*	75'	4
Pine, Japanese Black	*Pinus thunbergii*	90'	6
Red-Cedar	*Juniperus virginiana*	90'	3
Rose, Rugosa	*Rosa rugosa* cults.	6'	3
Rose-of-Sharon	*Hibiscus syriacus*	15'	6
Spruce, Dragon	*Picea asperata*	75'	5
Summersweet	*Clethra alnifolia*	9'	4
Winterberry	*Ilex verticillata*	9'	4

GROUND COVERS

COMMON NAME	BOTANICAL NAME	HEIGHT	ZONE
Bearberry	*Arctostaphyllos uva-ursi*	6"-12"	3
Juniper, Shore	*Juniperus horizontalis* cults.	1'-2'	3
Pachysandra	*Pachysandra terminalis*	6"	6
Rockspray	*Cotoneaster horizontalis*	3'	5
Sumac, Fragrant	*Rhus aromatica*	3'	4
Wintercreeper, Bigleaf	*Euonymus fortunei* cults.	1'-2'	6

LAWN GRASSES

COMMON NAME	BOTANICAL NAME
Bentgrass, Colonial	*Agrostis tenuis*
Bluegrass, Kentucky Merion	*Poa pratensis*
Clover, White Dutch	*Trifolium repens*
Fescue, Creeping Red Pennlawn	*Festuca rubra*
Redtop	*Agrostis alba*
Ryegrass, Perennial	*Lolium perenne*

NATIVE PLANTS USEFUL FOR THE GARDEN

COMMON NAME	BOTANICAL NAME
False-Indigo	*Baptisia australis*
Gayfeather	*Liatris spicata*
Lily, Canada Turk's-Cap	*Lilium canadense superbum*
Loosestrife	*Lythrum salicaria*
Lupine	*Lupinus perennis*
Milkweed, Swamp	*Asclepias incarnata*
Rhodora	*Rhododendron canadense*
Shadbush, Dwarf	*Amelanchier stolonifera*
Swamp-Honeysuckle	*Rhododendron viscosum*
Sweetfern	*Comptonia peregrina*
Violet, Bird's-Foot	*Viola pedata*

RECOMMENDED ROSES

George J. Jung, a knowledgeable rosarian
in the New England area
(See also Chapter 26.)

HYBRID TEAS

Charlotte Armstrong, light red and deep pink
Chrysler Imperial, dark red
Confidence, pink blend
Eclipse, medium yellow
Fragrant Cloud, orange-red
Garden Party, white
Mister Lincoln, medium red
Pascali, white
Peace, yellow blend
Tiffany, pink blend
Tropicana, orange-red

FLORIBUNDAS

Apricot Nectar, apricot blend
Betty Prior, medium pink
Europeana, dark red
Iceberg, white
Roman Holiday, red blend
Saratoga, white
Spartan, orange-red

GRANDIFLORAS

Camelot, medium pink
Carrousel, dark red
Montezuma, orange-red
Queen Elizabeth, medium pink

CLIMBERS

Blaze, medium red
Blossomtime, medium pink
Golden Showers, medium yellow
Paul's Scarlet, medium red

SHRUB AND OLD-FASHIONED ROSES

Austrian Copper, scarlet-orange
Frau Karl Druschki, white
Harison's Yellow, deep yellow
Paul Neyron, medium pink
Roger Lambelin, red blend
Sea Foam, white

311

34 MID-ATLANTIC

New York, Pennsylvania, New Jersey, Maryland,
Delaware, District of Columbia
Zones 5, 6, 7

by Barbara H. Emerson, *Consulting Horticulturist,*
Gwynedd Valley, Pennsylvania

The Mid-Atlantic states constitute a region of cool-temperate, rather humid climate with moderate rainfall, where an exceptionally wide range of desirable plants can be grown. The area north of Albany, New York, has restricting growth conditions like those of neighboring New England states, but Wilmington, Baltimore, and Washington, D.C., are almost southern. The southernmost locations for such typically northern native species as balsam fir and paper birch and the northern reaches of flowering dogwood, Eastern redbud and others are found within this region.

The southeastern triangle (southern New Jersey, Delaware and eastern Maryland) constitutes the main eastern vegetable-growing area. The long, comparatively hot summers encourage tomatoes, lima beans, melons, peppers and eggplant. The less cold winters permit growing hybrid tea roses without protection, peaches, true cedars, English holly and boxwood and camellias. Some shade from the drying winter sun prevents leafburn of broad-leaved evergreens. With little or no snow cover winter mulching with light material, which does not pack down into a wet mass, helps keep the soil temperature uniformly low. Frost action, which can heave poorly anchored young or surface-rooted plants out of the ground, is thus held to a minimum. Mulches should be taken off when plants show signs of resuming active growth in the spring.

With a growing season of two hundred days or longer development of woody plants in this triangle is more extensive than farther north. Long-season plants are able to mature satisfactorily. The longer mild fall also permits growing a second crop of cool-preference lettuce, broccoli and spinach.

Certain plants, such as delphinium and foxglove, are often killed by disease following the ground's alternate freezing and thawing. They grow better where winters are continuously cold and afford a cover of snow, as in central and northern Pennsylvania, northernmost New Jersey and nearly all of New York State. The correspondingly lower summer temperatures are also preferred by such cool-season plants as tuberous begonias, fuchsias, lupines, garden and sweet peas and many members of the cabbage family. Lawn grasses also grow better here. Shorter growing seasons (eighty-five to one hundred days) may limit the development of such long-season plants as sweet corn and chrysanthemums. Here, it is helpful to start slow-growing vegetables early, indoors.

Besides latitude, two major factors modify the climate of the Mid-Atlantic states — huge bodies of water and land elevation. The low-lying Philadelphia corner of Pennsylvania, eastern Maryland, Delaware and southern New Jersey near the Atlantic Ocean, or cities like Erie and Rochester in parts of Pennsylvania and New York along the Great Lakes, have a much more moderate climate than that generally found inland and at higher elevations in Pennsylvania, northern New Jersey and most of New York State, although Buffalo is notorious for its long cold winters.

Average annual temperatures vary from 60° in Delaware to 45° in the New York mountains, where the area's minimum winter temperatures of 25° below zero occur. Summer temperatures seldom go above 90° to 100°. The last killing frost in spring may be experienced in late March (Maryland and Delaware) or mid-May (Adirondack Mountain Region and northwestern Pennsylvania). First killing frosts in fall in these same regions are expected early in November and by late September respectively.

Rain, averaging thirty to forty-five inches per year, follows an irregular pattern with usually greater amounts in spring and fall and occasional drought periods not uncommon in late summer. There is considerable variation from season to season and also from year to year. Predictions are difficult because of fluctuating movements of warm moist air from the Gulf of Mexico or cool dry Arctic air from the West, as well as occasional tropical storms originating in the Caribbean area.

Many of the soils in the Mid-Atlantic region are derived from worn mountain peaks as sedimentary deposits or as glacial till and form a comparatively thin layer. Much of the natural woodland and its litter have been removed, and there has too often been further depletion by misuse. These soils, which are generally acid (pH 6.2 is common), usually need large amounts of additional humus and fertilizer and often of lime. Soil analysis by the State Agricultural Extension Service (see below) can provide accurate guidelines for improvement. Soils along the Atlantic Coast are mainly sandy and are easier to garden, being light and extremely well drained. However, these same characteristics mean that nutrients can easily be lost. Adding a good deal of humus-making material supplies nutrients and increases the soil's ability to hold water.

Most sections of the Mid-Atlantic region offer excellent opportunities for many kinds of satisfying gardens.

WHERE TO GET SPECIAL HELP

Each state agricultural college offers publications, information, soil testing and other services through its Agricultural Extension Service. Address inquiries to the service in your state.

Delaware: University of Delaware, Newark, Delaware 19711.

Maryland: University of Maryland, College Park, Maryland 20742.

New Jersey: Rutgers – The State University, New Brunswick, New Jersey 08903.

New York: New York State College of Agriculture, Ithaca, New York 14850.

Pennsylvania: Pennsylvania State University, University Park, Pennsylvania 16802.

There are horticultural societies that help their members and often unaffiliated gardeners, too. Mid-Atlantic ones include the American Horticultural Society, 901 North Washington Street, Alexandria, Virginia 22314; Horticultural Society of New York, 128 West Fifty-eighth Street, New York, New York 10019; and Pennsylvania Horticultural Society, 325 Walnut Street, Philadelphia, Pennsylvania 19106. Also, staff members of botanical gardens and arboretums, such as those described in the next section, can often help gardeners with problems.

PLACES AND PLANTINGS OF INTEREST

Delaware: THE WINTERTHUR GARDENS, Winterthur (on Route 52, six miles northwest of Wilmington). Ninety-nine acres of naturalized plantings of over a thousand flowers, shrubs and trees; the personal gardens of the late Henry Francis Du Pont; uniquely harmonious arrangements of color and form. Masses of azaleas and rhododendrons; pinetum of mature conifers. Garden Pavilion with cafeteria. Open from mid-April to late May and during October. Garden tickets $1.00.

Peach Blossom is the state flower; American Holly, the state tree.

District of Columbia: THE BISHOP'S GARDEN, Washington Cathedral, Massachusetts and Wisconsin Avenues N.W. An enclosed garden of Old World tranquillity and charm; ancient boxwoods and yews; rose and medieval herb gardens; carved stonework, architectural features dating back to Charlemagne. Open to the public daily 9:00-5:00.

DUMBARTON OAKS, 1703 Thirty-second Street N.W. Sixteen acres. Imaginative formal country garden adjoining the Georgian Robert Woods Bliss home, now a museum of Byzantine and pre-Columbian art. Terraces, lawns and winding paths lead into natural woodland; herbaceous borders; roses; flowering shrubs and trees. Library. Open daily 2:00-5:00 from July to Labor Day.

KENILWORTH AQUATIC GARDENS, Douglas Street N.E. Fourteen acres of ponds. Night- and day-blooming hardy and tropical waterlilies, best seen before noon. Open daily.

U.S. BOTANIC GARDEN, Maryland Avenue between First and Second Streets S.W. Conservatory with tropical and subtropical plants including orchids, cacti, ferns, bromeliads. Open daily 9:00-4:00.

U.S. NATIONAL ARBORETUM, Bladensburg Road and M Street N.E. Approximately four hundred acres of woodland ravines and open rolling fields administered by the U.S. Department of Agriculture for research and education. Plant breeding and testing programs include many plants. Morrison Hill azalea display; Fern Valley native plants; Gotelli collection of naturally dwarf conifers; Cryptomeria Valley Oriental plantings; Cedrus and Himalayan Pine Valleys. Library; herbarium. Open daily during daylight.

American Beauty Rose is the District of Columbia's flower; Scarlet Oak, its tree.

Maryland: CLYBURN WILDFLOWER PRESERVE AND GARDEN CENTER, 4915 Greenspring Avenue, Baltimore. One-hundred-seventy-six-acre park for horticultural study. Wildflower Preserve, plant collections, formal garden, herb garden and greenhouse. Educational programs, nature walks, garden seminars. Park open daily 6 A.M. to midnight; buildings by appointment. Guided tours by appointment.

U.S.D.A. AGRICULTURAL RESEARCH CENTER, U.S. Route 1, Beltsville. Eleven thousand acres. Extensive facilities for research including garden, orchard, nursery and florists' problems of soil, pest control and plant breeding. Open weekdays. Guided tours for large groups by appointment.

Black-eyed Susan is the state flower; White Oak, the state tree.

New Jersey: CEDAR BROOK PARK, Plainfield. One hundred acres. Notable collections of dogwoods, irises, daffodils, daylilies and peonies. Shakespearean garden. Open daily.

DUKE GARDENS FOUNDATION, INC., Route 206 South, Somerville. Eight and a half acres. Italian, Colonial, Edwardian, French, English, Chinese, Japanese, Indo-Persian gardens under glass. Separate houses with desert and tropical plants, tree ferns and orchids. Open 1:00-5:00 in summer, 12:00-4:00 in winter, Admission charge.

RUTGERS DISPLAY GARDENS, The State University, New Brunswick. One hundred twenty-three acres. Collections of small trees, azaleas, hollies, pyracanthas, primarily for students. Open daily 9:00 until dusk.

WILLOWWOOD ARBORETUM OF RUTGERS, The State University, Gladstone. Collection of trees begun in 1908 when Willowwood was a farm; American hollies, native pines and other conifers, oaks, maples, willows, crabapples and lilacs. Use by students encouraged; open to interested groups by advance arrangement.

Purple Violet is the state flower; Red Oak, the state tree.

New York: BROOKLYN BOTANIC GARDEN, 1000 Washington Avenue, Brooklyn. "Fifty acres of beauty only twelve minutes from Wall Street." Japanese Hill-and-Pond garden; replica of the five-hundred-year-old Ryoanji temple garden of Kyoto, Japan; the Cranford Memorial Rose Garden; a Garden of Fragrance; an Elizabethan knot garden of kitchen herbs; waterlilies in reflecting pools; rock garden; irises; Tallman Memorial Garden of naturally dwarf conifers; and a Shakespearean garden; superb collections of Japanese and other flowering cherries, bonsai, orchids, succulents, cycads, begonias and bromeliads; ten thousand kinds of shrubs, trees and other plants growing on the grounds. Conservatories of desert plants and a tropical forest. Extensive library and herbarium. Information service. Open weekdays 8:00 until sunset; until 11:00 on Saturdays, Sundays and holidays.

THE CLOISTERS, Northern Avenue and Cabrini Circle, Fort Tryon Park, New York City. Replicas of three twelfth-to-fourteenth-century monastery cloister gardens. Open Tuesday to Saturday 10:00-5:00; Sunday 1:00-5:00 (1:00-6:00 from May to September).

CORNELL PLANTATIONS, 100 Judd Falls Road, Ithaca. Fifteen hundred acres. The gardens and arboretum of Cornell University. The Minns Memorial Garden of annuals and perennials, scree-type rock garden, a patio garden on campus. Beyond are the American Rose Society rose-test demonstration, experimental hedge plantings, many collections. Open daily during daylight.

THOMAS C. DESMOND ARBORETUM, R.D. 1, Newburgh. Forty-nine acres. Planted during time of Andrew Jackson Downing, whose work and books on landscape architecture were the most influential in America. Superb old trees; wide range of shrubs and woody vines. Open weekdays 10:00-4:00.

DURAND-EASTMAN AND HIGHLAND PARKS, 375 Westfall Road, Rochester. Six hundred acres. In Durand-Eastman Park on Lake Ontario impressive hillside plantings of conifers. Highland Park is famous for its lilacs, crabapples, rhododendrons and azaleas and magnolias. In Lamberton Conservatory permanent plantings of desert and mixed tropical species.

GEORGE LANDIS ARBORETUM, Esperance. One hundred acres. Located on former farmland between the Catskill and the Adirondack mountains with dramatic views of the Schoharie and the Mohawk valleys. Small botanical garden used as a test ground for climatic factors determining northern limits of tender species, such as magnolias and rhododendrons, and for developing winter-hardy strains of plants. Collections of Asian, European, American conifers and native deciduous trees. Bonsai, spring-flowering bulbs, gardens of roses, irises, annuals and perennials and native plants. Sun pit for propagating. Open daylight hours April to October.

NEW YORK BOTANICAL GARDEN, Southern Boulevard, Bronx. Two hundred thirty acres. One of the world's leading botanical institutions patterned after the Royal Botanic Gardens at Kew, England. In the Museum Building plant exhibits, the internationally known library of seventy thousand volumes, and about three million herbarium specimens; in the eleven greenhouses displays from mosses and ferns to plants of economic importance. Waterlilies, a Tudor knot of herbs, a border of plants *as families.* Pools and waterfalls on the Bronx River; wild flowers and a rock garden in the surrounding oak-hemlock-ash forest. Rhododendron Slope, Daffodil Hill, Azalea Glen, the Montgomery Conifer Collection, a formal rose garden, the Havermeyer Lilac Collection, Magnolia Dell and the forty-acre Hemlock Forest, kept as Indians once knew New York. Open daily 10:00 to one-half hour after sunset. $1.00 parking fee for cars.

STERLING FOREST GARDENS, Tuxedo. One hundred twenty-five acres. A horticultural showplace in a wooded valley of the Ramapo Mountains. Elaborate displays of spring bulbs patterned after those of Keukenhof in Holland. Numerous special gardens. Admission charge.

Rose is the state flower; Sugar Maple, the state tree.

Pennsylvania: THE ARBORETUM OF THE BARNES FOUNDATION, 300 Latches Lane, Merion Station. Twelve acres. Trees planted from 1880, special plant collections. Mature specimens of species not usually hardy in this region. Educational program. Open by appointment.

BOWMAN'S HILL STATE WILDFLOWER PRESERVE, Washington Crossing State Park, Route 32, River Road, Washington Crossing. One hundred acres. Collection of Pennsylvania's native flora for plant identification, botany, ecology and conservation. Displays include special habitats along twenty-three named walking trails and in three larger wooded areas. Classes, nature walks, lectures. Open daily throughout the year. Guided tours by appointment.

HERSHEY ROSE GARDENS AND ARBORETUM, Hershey. Thirty-two acres. Twelve hundred varieties of roses; hollies; daylilies; dwarf evergreens; azaleas; spring bulbs; chrysanthemums. Open daily April 15 to December 1.

LONGWOOD GARDENS, Kennett Square. One thousand acres. Estate of the late Pierre S. Du Pont, with old trees on land granted by William Penn in 1702. Blue-tiled Italian water garden and other formal gardens; rock and wild-flower gardens; waterlily pools; Perception Center; topiary, flower, vegetable and herb demonstrations; arboretum. Extensive greenhouses. Rotating orchid, acacia, and seasonal shows in the great conservatory. Cultural and plant-breeding techniques research. Outdoor theater; daytime and lighted nighttime fountain displays. Information service. Adult education, student trainee and cooperative graduate student programs. Gardens open daily 8:00 until sunset; conservatories 11:00-5:00.

MORRIS ARBORETUM OF THE UNIVERSITY OF PENNSYLVANIA, 9414 Meadowbrook Avenue, Chestnut Hill, Philadelphia. One hundred seventy acres. Eastern Asiatic and other unique species. Fine shrub collections; rhododendrons, and rose, rock, wall, bog and medicinal plant gardens. Educational courses. Open Monday to Friday 9:00-4:00; Saturday and Sunday 9:00-5:00.

PHIPPS CONSERVATORY, Schenley Park, Pittsburgh. Thirteen-room conservatory, eight outdoor growing houses. Four seasonal flower shows in landscaped garden settings. Palms, cacti, ferns, orchids, bromeliads and other tropicals. Herbaceous and azalea gardens outdoors. Open daily 9:00-5:00.

ARTHUR HOYT SCOTT FOUNDATION, Swarthmore College, Swarthmore. Two hundred fifty acres. "Established to grow and show to amateur gardeners the finest ornamental plants in eastern Pennsylvania." Trees, shrubs and flowers on college campus and woods. Always open.

SWISS PINES PARK, Charlestown Road, Malvern. Ten acres. Japanese, Polynesian, rose, herb and heather gardens; wild-flower plantings. Open Monday to Friday 10:00-4:00 and Saturday morning. Admission and parking fee. Guided tours by appointment.

JOHN J. TYLER (PAINTER) ARBORETUM, 515 Painter Road, Lima. Seven hundred eleven acres with magnificent old trees, probably dating from 1825. Giant redwood, cedar of Lebanon, Chinese ginkgo, bald cypress with "knees" and a thirty-one-inch sassafras. Old boxwoods and yews; rhododendrons, lilacs, dogwoods, conifers, fragrance garden, woodland trails, Pink Hill serpentine barren. Nature walks. Open daily during daylight.

Mountain-Laurel is the state flower; Eastern Hemlock, the state tree.

Mounding textures of superbly grown boxwood frame the patio of a herring-boned brick Pennsylvania terrace. *(George Taloumis photo)*

SOME FAVORITE GARDEN PLANTS OF THE MID-ATLANTIC
(N means native to eastern North America.)

LARGE TREES FOR SHADE

COMMON NAME	BOTANICAL NAME	HEIGHT	ZONE
Ash, European, in variety	*Fraxinus excelsior*	90'	4
White (N)	*americana*	80'	4
Beech, European, in variety	*Fagus sylvatica*	80'	5
Birch, Paper (N)	*Betula papyrifera*	75-90'	2-5
Buttonwood (N)	*Platanus occidentalis*	80-100'	6
Elm, Siberian	*Ulmus pumila*	50'	4
Honey-Locust (N)	*Gleditsia triacanthos*	70-100'	5
Japanese Pagoda-Tree	*Sophora japonica*	70'	4
Larch, European	*Larix decidua*	70-80'	3
Linden, American (N)	*Tilia americana*	100'	4
Littleleaf	*cordata*	60'	4
Locust, Black (N)	*Robinia pseudoacacia*	60-70'	4
Maple, Norway	*Acer platanoides*	50-90'	4
Red (N)	*rubrum*	50-70'	3
Sugar (N)	*saccharum*	60-100'	3
Oak, Pin (N)	*Quercus palustris*	75-80'	5
Red (N)	*borealis*	60'	5
Scarlet (N)	*coccinea*	70-80'	5
Sweet Gum (N)	*Liquidambar styraciflua*	60-100'	5

SMALL TREES FOR BLOSSOMS AND FRUIT

COMMON NAME	BOTANICAL NAME	HEIGHT	ZONE
Carolina Silverbell	*Halesia carolina*	20'	5
Cherry, Asian, in variety	*Prunus*	15-40'	3
Crabapple, Flowering, in variety	*Malus*	10-30'	3-5
Crape-Myrtle	*Lagerstroemia indica*	15-25'	7
Dogwood, Flowering (N)	*Cornus florida*	15-30'	5
Japanese	*kousa chinensis*	20'	5
Fringetree (N)	*Chionanthus virginicus*	30'	5
Goldenchain-Tree	*Laburnum* x *watereri*	30'	6
Hawthorn, Washington (N)	*Crataegus phaenopyrum*	25-30'	5
Japanese Snowbell	*Styrax japonica*	30'	6
Korean Stewartia	*Stewartia koreana*	20-30'	6
Magnolia, Saucer	*Magnolia soulangiana*	20-30'	6
Star	*stellata*	20'	6
Maple, Japanese	*Acer palmatum*	15-20'	6
Mountain-Ash, American (N)	*Sorbus americana*	30'	3
Redbud (N)	*Cercis canadensis*	30'	5
Silktree	*Albizia julibrissin* 'Ernest Wilson'	15-30'	6
Sorrel-Tree (N)	*Oxydendrum arboreum*	20-40'	5
Witch-Hazel, Chinese	*Hamamelis mollis*	30'	6

EVERGREEN TREES

COMMON NAME	BOTANICAL NAME	HEIGHT	ZONE
Arborvitae, American (N)	*Thuja occidentalis*	60'	3
Cedar, Blue Atlas	*Cedrus atlantica* 'Glauca'	100'	6
Douglas-Fir	*Pseudotsuga menziesi*	100-150'	4
False-Cypress, Lawson	*Chamaecyparis lawsoniana*	50-100'	6
Fir, Colorado	*Abies concolor*	50'	4-7

COMMON NAME	BOTANICAL NAME	HEIGHT	ZONE
Hemlock, Common (N)	*Tsuga canadensis*	90'	3
Holly, American, in variety (N)	*Ilex opaca*	20-35'	6
English, in variety	*aquifolium*	30-50'	6
Incense-Cedar	*Calocedrus decurrens*	40-100'	7
Magnolia, Southern (N)	*Magnolia grandiflora*	90-100'	7
Pine, Austrian	*Pinus nigra*	60-80'	4
Himalayan	*wallichiana*	60-100'	6
Japanese Black	*thunbergii*	60-70'	6
White (N)	*strobus*	60-100'	3
Spruce, Colorado	*Picea pungens*	50'	3
Norway	*abies*	100'	2

SMALL NEEDLE-LEAVED EVERGREENS

COMMON NAME	BOTANICAL NAME	HEIGHT	ZONE
Juniper, Spreading	*Juniperus chinensis* 'Pfitzeriana'	8'	5
Tamarisk	*sabina tamariscifolia*	2'	5
Pine, Mugho	*Pinus mugo mughus*	5'	3
Yew, English, in variety	*Taxus baccata*	30'	5-6
Japanese, in variety	*cuspidata*	1-50'	5

Fine design using ivies, heathers, hemlocks and bamboos around a well-laid patio makes maximum use of a small space. (*M. E. Warren photo*)

BROAD-LEAVED EVERGREEN SHRUBS

COMMON NAME	BOTANICAL NAME	HEIGHT	ZONE
Andromeda, Japanese	*Pieris japonica*	10'	6
Boxwood, Common	*Buxus sempervirens*	20'	6
Firethorn, Laland	*Pyracantha coccinea* 'Lalandi'	8-20'	6
Grape-Holly, Oregon	*Mahonia aquifolium*	5'	5
Holly, Burford	*Ilex cornuta* 'Burfordii'	10'	6
Japanese	*crenata*	4-10'	6
Inkberry (N)	*glabra*	6-10'	4
Leucothoe, Drooping (N)	*Leucothoe fontanesiana*	6'	5
Mountain-Laurel, (N)	*Kalmia latifolia*	6-10'	5
Pachistima, Canby (N)	*Pachistima canbyi*	1'	5
Rhododendron (including Azaleas), in wide variety	*Rhododendron*	4-20'	5-7

FLOWERING SHRUBS

COMMON NAME	BOTANICAL NAME	HEIGHT	ZONE
Abelia, Glossy	*Abelia grandiflora*	4-5'	6
Barberry	*Berberis thunbergii*	6'	5
Beauty Bush	*Kolkwitzia amabilis*	8-10'	6
Butterfly Bush, Orange-eye	*Buddleia davidii*	8'	6
Cotoneaster, in variety	*Cotoneaster*	3-6'	6
Forsythia, in variety	*Forsythia*	7-12'	5
Honeysuckle, in variety	*Lonicera*	6-12'	6
Lilac, French, in variety	*Syringa vulgaris* hybrids	10'	3
Mock Orange	*Philadelphus*	10'	4
Quince, Flowering	*Chaenomeles speciosa*	6'	5
Redvein Enkianthus	*Enkianthus campanulatus*	15-30'	5
Rose, Shrub, in variety	*Rosa* species	5-7'	5-7
St. Johnswort	*Hypericum patulum* 'Hidcote'	2-3'	6
Sweet Pepperbush (N)	*Clethra alnifolia*	9'	3
Viburnum, in variety	*Viburnum*	6-10'	5-6
Weigela, in variety	*Weigela* hybrids	7'	5

HEDGES
(T—tall, 10' and up; M—medium, 5'-9'; L—low, 1'-4')

COMMON NAME	BOTANICAL NAME	HEIGHT	ZONE
Arborvitae, American (N)	*Thuja occidentalis*	T	2
Barberry, Japanese	*Berberis thunbergii*	M	5
Boxwood, Common	*Buxus sempervirens*	M	6
Burning Bush	*Euonymus alatus*	M	4
Hemlock	*Tsuga canadensis*	T	4
Holly, Japanese	*Ilex crenata* 'Convexa'	L	6
Honeysuckle, Tatarian	*Lonicera tatarica*	M	3
Juniper, Keteleer	*Juniperus chinensis* 'Keteleeri'	M	4
Lilac, Common	*Syringa vulgaris*	M	3
Privet, California	*Ligustrum ovalifolium*	T	6
Russian-Olive	*Elaeagnus angustifolia*	T	3
Yew, Hicks	*Taxus* x *media* 'Hicksii'	T	5

WOODY VINES

COMMON NAME	BOTANICAL NAME	HEIGHT	ZONE
Ampelopsis, Porcelain	*Ampelopsis brevipedunculata*	10'	5
Bittersweet (N)	*Celastrus scandens*	10-20'	3

COMMON NAME	BOTANICAL NAME	HEIGHT	ZONE
Clematis, in variety	*Clematis*	6-25'	5-7
Dutchman's-Pipe (N)	*Aristolochia durior*	30'	5
Grape, in variety	*Vitis*	8'	5-7
Honeysuckle, Hall's	*Lonicera japonica 'Halliana'*	20'	5
Trumpet	*sempervirens*	20'	4
Hydrangea, Climbing	*Hydrangea petiolaris*	40'	5
Ivy, Boston	*Parthenocissus tricuspidata*	40'	5
English	*Hedera helix*	90'	6
Rose, Climbing, in variety	*Rosa*	8-20'	6
Silver-Lace-Vine	*Polygonum aubertii*	25'	5
Trumpet-Vine (N)	*Campsis radicans*	20'	6
Virginia-Creeper (N)	*Parthenocissus quinquefolia*	75'	4
Wintercreeper	*Euonymus fortunei*	30'	5
Wisteria, Chinese	*Wisteria sinensis*	25'	5

GROUND COVERS

COMMON NAME	BOTANICAL NAME	HEIGHT	ZONE
Bearberry (N)	*Arctostaphylos uva-ursi*	8"	2
Bugleweed	*Ajuga reptans*	8"	6
Canby Pachistima	*Pachistima canbyi*	12"	5
Cotoneaster, Bearberry	*Cotoneaster dammeri*	12"	6
Crown Vetch	*Coronilla varia*	12-24"	3
Honeysuckle, Japanese	*Lonicera japonica 'Halliana'*	18"	5
Ivy, Baltic	*Hedera helix baltica*	6"	5
Juniper, Creeping, in variety	*Juniperus horizontalis*	10"	3
Lily-of-the-Valley	*Convallaria majalis*	9"	5
Moss-Pink (N)	*Phlox subulata*	6"	5
Pachysandra	*Pachysandra terminalis*	8"	5
Partridgeberry (N)	*Mitchella repens*	2"	4
Periwinkle	*Vinca minor*	6"	5
Rockspray	*Cotoneaster horizontalis*	12"	5

LAWN GRASSES

COMMON NAME	BOTANICAL NAME	ZONE
Bentgrass, Colonial	*Agrostis*	5-6
Creeping		
Highland		
Penncross		
Bermuda Grass, U-3	*Cynodon dactylon*	7
Bluegrass, Kentucky	*Poa pratensis*	5-7
Merion		
Fescue, Chewings	*Festuca rubra*	5-7
Creeping Red		
Illahee		
Pennlawn		
Tall	*elatior arundinacea*	5-7
Zoysia, Manila Grass	*Zoysia matrella*	7

VEGETABLES

(F means good for freezing.)

COMMON NAME	VARIETY NAME
Asparagus	Waltham Washington (F)
Bean	Executive Pencil Pod Wax, Fordhook 242, Kentucky Wonder (F)
Beet	Ruby Queen, Detroit
Broccoli	Spartan Early (F)
Brussels Sprout	Jade Cross (F)
Carrot	Nantes (F)
Cauliflower	Snowball (F)
Corn, sweet	Seneca Chief (F)
Cucumber	Triumph Hybrid
Eggplant	Burpee Hybrid (F)
Lettuce	Buttercrunch, Oak Leaf
Parsnip	Harris Model
Pea	Little Marvel (F)
Pepper	Peter Piper (F)
Radish	Burpee's White
Spinach	America (F)
Squash	Chefini, Butternut (F)
Tomato	Burpee's Big Boy, Rutgers

PERENNIALS AND ANNUALS

As in New England, the Mid-Atlantic area is a gratifying place to grow herbaceous perennials (plants that die back to the ground in winter but produce new growth spring after spring) because the range of suitable ones is so very wide. There are few exceptions to what can be grown in these states. After determining such elements as degree of sun or shade; sandy, clayey or other unusual soil characteristics; and sheltered or windy exposure, the exciting possibilities are limited only by space and a gardener's imagination, energy or pocketbook.

Among the six or eight dozen different sorts and their multitude of varieties from which to choose, almost any color, height, texture, time of bloom and degree of adaptability can be found. However, there is an even half-dozen whose dependability and other virtues form the foundation of most good perennial gardens: irises (the rainbow of tall beardeds, more slender Siberians or picturesque Japanese), peonies (familiar Chinese doubles or the silky singles and Japanese types), trouble-free daylilies in an increasing variety of colors and shapes, stately phlox as midsummer companions, and throughout the fall the glory of chrysanthemums from the Orient and sturdy asters or Michaelmas daisies developed from ancestors that purpled American fields.

Annuals live for only one growing season, but what radiance they add to the months of their blooming! Whether for masses of color in beds, for adding sparkle to the briefer show of perennial bloom or for cut flowers to enjoy indoors, annuals offer "the mostest for the leastest." The big three are petunias in ever-wider variety, lacey-leaved Irish marigolds and pert French or bold African ones and zinnias with dozens of forms and colors and as many uses. After that, selection will depend largely on what strikes your fancy in seed catalogues or garden-supply centers: spires of snapdragons for cutting, flowering tobacco to scent the evening air, saucy-faced pansies, dramatic cockscombs, nasturtiums for poor sandy soil, sweet peas and lobelia for cool summers, velvety verbenas and sweet alyssum for hot ones. Again, the possibilities are almost without end, with new ones to be tried each year.

RECOMMENDED ROSES
(See also Chapter 26.)

All varieties listed below are eminently suitable for the entire Mid-Atlantic area; *** means highest all-around merit, ** means almost as meritorious, * means outstanding merit.

HYBRID TEAS

Charlotte Armstrong, light red and deep pink
Chrysler Imperial, dark red**
Confidence, pink blend
Eclipse, medium yellow
Fragrant Cloud, orange-red
Garden Party, white
King's Ransom, deep yellow

Mister Lincoln, medium red***
Pascali, white*
Peace, yellow blend**
Royal Highness, light pink
South Seas, medium pink
Tiffany, pink blend
Tropicana, orange-red***

FLORIBUNDAS

Betty Prior, medium pink***
Europeana, dark red***
Fashion, coral*
Fire King, bright orange-red
Gay Princess, light pink

Ivory Fashion, white
Roman Holiday, red blend
Sarabande, orange-red
Saratoga, white
Spartan, orange-red*

GRANDIFLORAS

Camelot, medium pink
Golden Girl, yellow
John S. Armstrong, dark red

Montezuma, orange-red*
Queen Elizabeth, medium pink**

CLIMBERS

Aloha, medium pink
Blaze, medium red
Blossomtime, medium pink*
Coralita, orange-red
Don Juan, dark red**

Golden Showers, medium yellow*
New Dawn, light pink*
Rhonda, medium pink*

MISCELLANEOUS TYPES

Austrian Copper, scarlet orange
Chipper, apricot-orange
Cinderella, white
Frau Karl Druschki, white*
Harison's Yellow, deep yellow

Paul Neyron, medium pink
Roger Lambelin, red blend
Scarlet Gem, red*
Sea Foam, white*
The Fairy, pink*

35 UPPER SOUTH

Tennessee, Georgia, South Carolina, North Carolina,
Virginia, West Virginia
Zones 6, 7, 8

by Sam L. Fairchild, *Garden Consultant,*
Reidsville, North Carolina

The area of the Upper South is well adapted to the growing of many plants, including the acid-loving rhododendrons of the mountain area, the famous azaleas of the coastal area, live oaks, crape-myrtle and the majestic southern magnolia. Wide climatic conditions vary from subtropical on the outer banks of North Carolina and the sea islands of South Carolina and Georgia to northern conditions of almost an alpine flora in the mountains of North Carolina, Tennessee and Virginia. The length of the growing season varies from 170 days in the mountain regions to 310 days in the southern coastal plains.

The average last-frost date and first-frost date for Atlanta, Georgia, are March 23 and November 9, and those of Memphis, Tennessee, are March 17 and November 10. Richmond, Virginia, has an average of the first fall frost on November 2, and the last average spring frost on March 29; those in Charleston, South Carolina, are December 5 and February 23.

Rainfall is usually abundant with a general average of fifty inches, but more than one hundred inches of rainfall in one year has been reported in Highlands, North Carolina, and parts of the Alabama coast, where the yearly average is eighty inches. Rainfall is usually well distributed with the driest periods occurring during the summer.

Soils of the whole region are generally acid with some isolated alkaline areas and approaching the neutral on the western edge. Soils vary from sands and fine sandy loams of the coast to Cecil clay and heavy clay of the Piedmont to clay loams of the Porter series in the mountains. Most of these soils are rather low in nutrients and humus, which are broken down rapidly and leached out by the summer heat and high annual rainfall.

Gardening is a well-organized and favorite pastime in the Upper South. The varied climate of the area permits the use of a great diversity of ornamental and garden plants. Fortunate indeed are those who live in the Piedmont and lower mountain areas where the finest plants from both the South and the North can be grown. Numerous and active garden clubs throughout the region and civic beautification groups encourage all phases of gardening and landscape improvement. Both flower- and vegetable-gardening are popular, and the long growing season in many places permits two crops a year of most vegetables.

In the Coastal Plains and the Sandhills favorite plants include the famed azaleas — Indicas, Kurumes, Pericats, Glenn Dales — gardenias, camellias and a wide variety of the less hardy broad-leaved evergreens, such as aucuba, feijoa, viburnum, tea-olive and both American and Oriental hollies. Tulips can be grown only with artificial cold treatment, and daffodils do only moderately well. Magnolia, dogwood, willow and live oak, along with longleaf and slash pine, are favorite trees. Roses do well in early spring and fall but poorly during the high humidity and heat of the summer months.

In the Piedmont, Kurume, Kaempferi and Glenn Dale azaleas attain their perfection and are perhaps the most widely planted shrubs. Camellias, especially the hardier types, are increasingly popular, as are the newer rhododendron hybrids, which have been developed to withstand heat. Daffodils are a favorite in this section, and tulips are widely used but must be replaced each year. A wide variety of broad-leaved evergreens is grown, including all types of hollies, aucuba, leucothoe, eurya, nandina and various photinias. Many flowering shrubs are popular, including lilacs, which about reach their southern limit here. Roses are at their best in September and October. Favorite trees are willow-oak, dogwood, maple, sweet gum and white pine. This, too, is the most northerly part of the country where the magnificent southern magnolia is extensively planted.

In the mountain area the deciduous azaleas and rhododendrons reach their perfection, as do daffodils, tulips and many lilies. Only the hardier broad-leaved shrubs are used, but arborvitae, junipers and yews are widely planted. Most popular trees are maple, pin oak and Northern red oak, fir, hemlock and white pine. Roses do exceptionally well.

The long growing season of 210 to 270 frost-free days and the abundant rainfall make growing a large variety of plant material, both edible and ornamental, successful. The same conditions also create problems associated with warm humid conditions. Nutrients must be constantly replaced by ample fertilizing, and the addition of lime is essential. Breakdown and leaching out of humus is rapid, and additional humus must be applied periodically. High humidity and heat are conducive to pest and disease, and a continual preventive-control program is essential. Although rainfall is usually ample, watering is necessary during periods of extreme heat and drought. Mulches to conserve water and lower soil temperatures are an absolute must, and these mulches, disintegrating, supply the additional needed humus.

Roses are an all-time favorite everywhere in the Upper South but are at their best in the mountain and upper Piedmont regions. High heat and humidity give sparse and poor-quality blooms during July and August in the lower Piedmont and coastal areas, where constant insect and disease prevention is necessary. In these areas it is advisable to cut roses back heavily (fifteen to eighteen inches) in early August and to fertilize liberally then. This will induce new growth and an abundance of bloom in the fall.

Most annuals do well in the Upper South, but many will be subject to fungus diseases in periods of high humidity and heat. Only perennials that will stand long periods of heat do well. Delphinium and peonies can be successfully grown only in the mountain area. Dahlias are popular in all sections. Chrysanthemums of all types are widely grown. Hemerocallis, an old summer favorite, has been revived in recent years through the introduction of many new varieties in a wider range of colors and blooming periods. Bearded iris, candytuft and columbine all do well.

WHERE TO GET SPECIAL HELP

Many fine publications are available through the Agricultural Extension Service of the U.S.D.A. located in each state. Free soil-testing is available from each of the state laboratories. For individual help contact your local County Extension Service Agent, or write directly to The Director, Extension Service, at address given below for your state.

Georgia: College of Agriculture, University of Georgia, Athens, Georgia 30601.

North Carolina: North Carolina State University, State College Station, Raleigh, North Carolina 27607.

South Carolina: Clemson University, Clemson, South Carolina 29631.

Tennessee: College of Agriculture, University of Tennessee, Knoxville, Tennessee 37901.

Virginia: Virginia Polytechnic Institute, Blacksburg, Virginia 24061.

West Virginia: Evansdale Campus, West Virginia University, Morgantown, West Virginia 26506.

PLACES AND PLANTINGS OF INTEREST

Georgia: FOUNDERS MEMORIAL GARDEN AND LIVING ARBORETUM, Athens. An outstanding display of ornamental plants for the Piedmont section of the South.

IDA CASON CALLAWAY GARDENS, Pine Mountain. Twenty-five hundred acres with several miles of walking trails. One of the country's best collections of hollies, native azaleas, crabapples, magnolias and rhododendrons. Good recreation facilities. Open to public all year.

THE SPRING HOUSE AND GARDEN PILGRIMAGE OF SAVANNAH offer many displays of azaleas and camellias.

Cherokee Rose is the state flower; Live Oak, the state tree.

North Carolina: BILTMORE, the former Vanderbilt estate, near Asheville, has fine gardens of azaleas, rhododendrons, roses and native plants; also ten thousand square feet of display greenhouses.

SARAH P. DUKE MEMORIAL GARDEN, Duke University, Durham. Formal terraced gardens featuring spring-flowering plants.

TRYON PALACE, New Bern, has a beautiful restored formal garden. Tryon is the governor's palace.

NORTH CAROLINA BOTANICAL GARDENS, Chapel Hill. Three hundred sixty acres of native plants with several miles of walking trails.

Dogwood is the state flower; Pine, the state tree.

South Carolina: BROOKGREEN GARDENS, Georgetown. Collection of native flora; display of American sculpture in formal settings of pools and vistas. Open year round except Christmas and Mondays.

CYPRESS GARDENS, MAGNOLIA GARDENS, AND MIDDLETON GARDENS, Charleston, open from mid-February through May, are famous for displays of azaleas and camellias.

EDISTO GARDENS, Orangeburg. A municipal park featuring azaleas, camellias, dogwood, wisteria, roses, and daylilies.

Yellow Jessamine is the state flower; Palmetto, the state tree.

Tennessee: GREAT SMOKY MOUNTAINS NATIONAL PARK. Headquarters at Gatlinburg. Wildflower pilgrimage in late April is outstanding. Flame azaleas and rhododendron in mid-June. Spectacular foliage color in September and October.

THE TENNESSEE BOTANICAL GARDENS AND FINE ARTS CENTER, Nashville. Boxwood gardens, terraced gardens, pools, rock gardens, flowering shrubs and trees.

KETCHUM MEMORIAL IRIS GARDEN, Memphis. Collection of iris including 'Dykes Row', planted with winners of the Dykes Medal AIS.

Iris is the state flower; Tulip-Popular (*Liriodendron*), the state tree.

Virginia: ARBORETUM OF THE VIRGINIA POLYTECHNIC INSTITUTE, Blacksburg. Excellent collection of dwarf plant material and flame azaleas. A general collection of 2,400 species of 35 plant families.

NORFOLK BOTANIC GARDENS, Norfolk. Canals, virgin timber, open vistas, good collection of broad-leaved evergreens, azaleas, perennials and bulbs.

WILLIAMSBURG. The restored gardens of Colonial Williamsburg are outstanding.

Dogwood is the state flower and tree.

West Virginia: MONONGAHELA NATIONAL FOREST. Twenty-nine state parks and forests. White Sulphur Springs. Berkeley Springs. Harpers Ferry restoration.

Rhododendron maximum is the state flower; Sugar Maple, the state tree.

SOME FAVORITE GARDEN PLANTS OF THE UPPER SOUTH

LARGE TREES

COMMON NAME	BOTANICAL NAME	HEIGHT	ZONE
Ash, White	*Fraxinus americana*	80'	6
Beech, American	*Fagus grandifolia*	70'	6
European	*sylvatica*	80'	6
Birch, European White	*Betula pendula*	60'	6
River	*nigra*	70'	6
Chestnut, Chinese	*Castanea mollissima*	60'	6
Elm, Chinese	*Ulmus pumila*	50'	6
Empress-Tree	*Paulownia tomentosa*	50'	6
Ginkgo	*Ginkgo biloba*	80'	6
Hornbeam, European	*Carpinus betulus*	60'	6
Horse-Chestnut, Red	*Aesculus* x *carnea*	60'	6
Japanese Pagoda-Tree	*Sophora japonica*	60'	6
Locust, Black	*Robinia pseudoacacia*	100'	6
Maple, Norway	*Acer platanoides*	90'	6
Red	*rubrum*	100'	6
Sugar	*saccharum*	100'	6

COMMON NAME	BOTANICAL NAME	HEIGHT	ZONE
Oak, Darlington	*Quercus laurifolia* 'Darlington'	60'	6
Live	*virginiana*	70'	7
Pin	*palustris*	90'	6
Southern Red	*rubra*	70'	6
Water	*nigra*	80'	6
White	*alba*	100'	6
Willow	*phellos*	60'	6
Poplar, Lombardy	*Populus nigra* 'Italica'	100'	6
Silver	*alba nivea*	80'	6
Sassafras	*Sassafras albidum*	80'	6
Silverbell	*Halesia monticola*	60'	6
Sweet Gum	*Liquidambar styraciflua*	120'	6
Sycamore, American	*Platanus occidentalis*	120'	6
London Plane	*x hybrida*	100'	6
Walnut, Black	*Juglans nigra*	100'	6
Willow, Weeping	*Salix babylonica*	50'	6
Yellow-Poplar (Tulip-Tree)	*Liriodendron tulipifera*	100'	6

SMALL FLOWERING TREES

COMMON NAME	BOTANICAL NAME	HEIGHT	ZONE
Cherry, Flowering, in variety	*Prunus sargentii*	20'-50'	6
Crabapple, Flowering, in variety	*Malus*	10'-20'	6
Crape-Myrtle	*Lagerstroemia indica*	20'	7
Dogwood, Flowering	*Cornus florida*	25'	6
Japanese	*kousa*	20'	6
Franklin-Tree	*Franklinia alatamaha*	20'	6
Fringetree	*Chionanthus virginicus*	20'	6
Goldenchain-Tree	*Laburnum x watereri*	25'	6
Goldenrain-Tree	*Koelreuteria paniculata*	20'	6
Hawthorn, English	*Crataegus oxyacantha*	15'	6
Magnolia, Saucer	*Magnolia soulangiana*	30'	6
Star	*stellata*	30'	6
Peach, Flowering	*Prunus (Amygdalus) persica*	20'	6
Plum, Flowering	*Prunus x blireiana*	15'	6
Redbud, Chinese	*Cercis chinensis*	15'	6
Eastern	*canadensis*	30'	6
Shadblow	*Amelanchier canadensis*	30'	6
Sourwood	*Oxydendrum arboreum*	40'	6
Stewartia	*Stewartia ovata grandiflora*	20'	6

LARGE EVERGREENS

COMMON NAME	BOTANICAL NAME	HEIGHT	ZONE
Arborvitae, American	*Thuja occidentalis*	60'	6
Cedar, Deodar	*Cedrus deodara*	70'	7-8
False-Cypress, Sawara	*Chamaecyparis pisifera*	70'	6-7
Fir	*Abies fraseri*	70'	6-7
	nordmanniana	100'	6-7
	veitchii	60'	6,7, part 8
Hemlock, Carolina	*Tsuga caroliniana*	75'	6
Holly, American	*Ilex opaca*	60'	6
Japanese Evergreen	*Cryptomeria japonica*	70'	6
Magnolia, Southern	*Magnolia grandifolia*	100'	7
Pine, Austrian	*Pinus nigra*	90'	6
Japanese Black	*thunbergii*	75'	6
Longleaf	*palustris*	100'	6
White	*strobus*	100'	6

COMMON NAME	BOTANICAL NAME	HEIGHT	ZONE
Red-Cedar	*Juniperus virginiana*	80'	6
Spruce, Colorado	*Picea pungens*	50'	6

SMALL NEEDLE-LEAVED EVERGREENS

COMMON NAME	BOTANICAL NAME	HEIGHT	ZONE
Arborvitae	*Thuja occidentalis* 'Douglas Pyramidal'	8'-20'	6
Globe	*globosa* and forms	3'-6'	6
Golden	'Rheingold'	6'	6
False-Cypress, Dwarf Hinoki	*Chamaecyparis obtusa* 'Nana Gracilis'	6'-10'	6
Sawara	*pisifera* 'Cyanoviridis'	5'-8'	6
Hemlock, Globe	*Tsuga canadensis globosa*	6'-8'	6
Sargent's Weeping	'Pendula'	3'-4'	6
Junipers, in variety	*Juniperus*	1'-20'	6
Mugho Pine	*Pinus mugo mugo*	2'-6'	6
Yew, Brown's	*Taxus* x *media* 'Brownii'	6'	6
English Dwarf	*baccata* 'Adpressa'	4'-6'	6
Hatfield	x *media* 'Hatfieldii'	10'	6
Hicks	'Hicksii'	6'	6
Japanese	*cuspidata capitata*	10'-15'	6
Spreading	*baccata* 'Repandens'	2'-4'	6

BROAD-LEAVED EVERGREENS

COMMON NAME	BOTANICAL NAME	HEIGHT	ZONE
Abelia	*Abelia grandiflora*	6'-8'	6
Andromeda, Mountain	*Pieris floribunda*	5'	6
Japanese	*japonica*	6'	6
Aucuba	*Aucuba japonica*	6'-10'	6
Azalea, in variety	*Rhododendron-Azalea*	2'-10'	6
Barberry, Mentor	*Berberis* x *mentorensis*	5'-7'	6
Wintergreen	*julianae*	5'-7'	6
Boxwood, Common	*Buxus sempervirens*	15'-20'	6
Dwarf	'Suffruticosa'	5'-6'	6
Littleleaf	*microphylla*	4'	6
Camellia	*Camellia japonica*	to 25'	7
Sasanqua	*sasanqua*	to 15'	6
Cotoneaster, Bearberry	*Cotoneaster dammeri*	1'	6
Littleleaf	*microphylla*	3'	6
Rockspray	*conspicua*	6'	6
Daphne, Rose	*Daphne cneorum*	1'	6
Winter	*odora*	4'	7
Euonymus, Bigleaf Wintercreeper	*Euonymus fortunei vegetus*	4'	6
Evergreen	*japonicus*	3'-8'	6
Purpleleaf	'Coloratus'	1'	6
Firethorn	*Pyracantha coccinea*	6"-12"	6
Grape-Holly, Oregon	*Mahonia aquifolium*	4'	6
Heath, Spring	*Erica carnea*	1'	6
Heavenly-Bamboo	*Nandina domestica*	6'	6
Holly, Burford	*Ilex cornuta* 'Burfordii'	10'	6
Chinese	*cornuta*	10'	6
English	*aquifolium*	to 40'	7
Japanese	*crenata*	2'-10'	6
Yaupon	*vomitoria*	to 15'	7

COMMON NAME	BOTANICAL NAME	HEIGHT	ZONE
Leucothoe, Drooping	*Leucothoe fontanesiana*	6'	6
Mountain-Laurel	*Kalmia latifolia*	8'	6
Osmanthus, Fortune's	*Osmanthus fortunei*	7'	7
Privet, California	*Ligustrum ovalifolium*	5'-15'	6
Glossy	*lucidum*	to 25'	6
Skimmia, Japanese	*Skimmia japonica*	3'-5'	7
Sweet-Olive	*Osmanthus fragrans*	7'	7
Viburnum, Leatherleaf	*Viburnum rhytidophyllum*	7'-10'	6

DECIDUOUS SHRUBS

COMMON NAME	BOTANICAL NAME	HEIGHT	ZONE
Almond, Flowering	*Prunus glandulosa*	4'	6
Althea	*Hibiscus syriacus*	10'	6
Azalea	*Rhododendron*	2'-10'	6
Bridalwreath	*Spiraea prunifolia*	4'-6'	6
Butterfly Bush, Fountain	*Buddleia alternifilia*	10'-12'	6
Chastetree	*Vitex agnus-castus*	8'-10'	6
Cotoneaster, Cranberry	*Cotoneaster apiculata*	2'-6'	6
Deutzia, Slender	*Deutzia gracilis*	3'-5'	6
Goldenbells	*Forsythia intermedia*	6'-10'	6
Honeysuckle, Winter	*Lonicera fragrantissima*	6'-8'	6
Hydrangea	*Hydrangea macrophylla*	6'	6
Indian-Currant	*Symphoricarpos orbiculatus*	5'-7'	6
Japanese-Quince	*Chaenomeles japonica*	2'-8'	6
Jetbead	*Rhodotypos scandens*	5'	6
Lilac	*Syringa vulgaris* hybrids	8'	6
Chinese	*x chinensis*	8'-10'	6
Mock Orange	*Philadelphus coronarius*	10'	6
Rose-Acacia	*Robinia hispida*	4'-8'	6
Snowball, Japanese	*Viburnum plicatum*	8'-12'	6
Snowberry	*Symphoricarpos albus*	3'	6
Spirea, Red	*Spiraea* x *billiardii*	4'-6'	6
Sweetshrub	*Calycanthus floridus*	6'-8'	6
Weigela	*Weigela* hybrids	6'-8'	6

HEDGES AND WINDBREAKS
(H—hedge; W—windbreak; T—tall, 10' and up; M—medium 5'-9')

COMMON NAME	BOTANICAL NAME	HEIGHT AND USE	ZONE
Barberry, Mentor	*Berberis mentorensis*	H,M	6
Boxwood, Common	*Buxus sempervirens*	W,H,T	6
Camellia	*Camellia sasanqua*	H,M	6
Cotoneaster, Franchet	*Cotoneaster franchetii*	H,M	6
Euonymus, Spreading	*Euonymus patens*	H,M	6
Holly, Burford	*Ilex cornuta* 'Burfordii'	H,W,T	6
Juniper, Canaert	*Juniperus virginiana* 'Canaertii'	H,M	6
Osmanthus, Fortune's	*Osmanthus fortunei*	H,M	6
Viburnum, Leatherleaf	*Viburnum rhytidophyllum*	H,W,T	6
Yew, Hatfield	*Taxus* x *media* 'Hatfieldii'	H,M	6

GROUND COVERS

COMMON NAME	BOTANICAL NAME	HEIGHT	ZONE
Bugleweed	*Ajuga reptans*	8″	6
Cotoneaster	*Cotoneaster horizontalis*	1′	6
English Ivy	*Hedera helix*	6″	6
Galax	*Galax aphylla*	6″	6
Heath, Spring	*Erica carnea*	1′	6
Japanese-Spurge	*Pachysandra terminalis*	6″	6
Juniper, Creeping	*Juniperus horizontalis*	to 18″	6
Lily-Turf	*Liriope spicata*	8″-10″	6
Mother-of-Thyme	*Thymus serpyllum*	2″	6
Pachistima	*Pachistima canbyi*	1′	6
Phlox, Creeping	*Phlox subulata*	6″	6
Rose, Memorial	*Rose wichuraiana*	3′	6

LAWN GRASSES

COMMON NAME	BOTANICAL NAME	ZONE	REMARKS
Bentgrass	*Agrostis capillaris*	6	Usually for golf courses, requires much care.
Redtop	*palustris*	6	Short-lived "nurse" grass used in mixtures with other grasses.
Bermuda Grass	*Cynodon dactylon*	6	Fine-bladed creeping grass for Zones 7 and 8. Must be sprigged. Drought-resistant. Browns with frost. Overplant with ryegrass in winter.
Bluegrass, Kentucky Merion	*Poa pratensis*	6	Favorite for cooler regions of Zone 6 and parts of 7. Not for Zone 8.
Carpet Grass	*Axonopus furcatus*	7	Coarse, light-green grass only for wet places in Zone 8.
Centipede Grass	*Eremochloa ophiuroides*	7	For coastal areas, a low-growing dense mat. Overplant with ryegrass in winter.
Fescue, Chewings, Creeping Red	*Festuca rubra*	6	One of the better lawn grasses, used with bluegrass in Zones 6 and parts of 7.
Tall	*elatior arundinacea*	7,8	Tall-growing coarse grass for any soil, takes abuse, heat, and drought.
Ryegrass, Italian	*Lolium multiflorum*	6	Annual ryegrass used to overplant Bermuda, Centipede, and Carpet Grass. Gives a quick temporary cover.
Perennial		6	Another quick cover for a temporary lawn.
Zoysia, Manila Grass	*Zoysia matrella*	6	Low-growing, dark-green ruglike turf, green longer than Bermuda. Must be sprigged or plugged. Dense growth crowds out weeds. Turns brown with frost.

NATIVE PLANTS USEFUL FOR THE GARDEN

COMMON NAME	BOTANICAL NAME	ZONE
Adam's-Needle	*Yucca filamentosa*	**6,7,8**
Andromeda, Mountain	*Pieris floribunda*	**6,7**
Azalea, Flame	*Rhododendron calendulaceum*	**6,7**
Beautyberry	*Callicarpa americana*	**7,8**
Birch, River	*Betula nigra*	**6,7,8**
Butterfly-Weed	*Asclepias tuberosa*	**6,7,8**
Chinquapin	*Castanea pumila*	**6,7,8**
Clammy-Honeysuckle	*Rhododendron viscosum*	**6,7,8**
Dogwood, Flowering	*Cornus florida*	**6,7,8**
Loblolly Bay	*Gordonia lasianthus*	**8**
Maple	*Acer rubrum, saccharum, spicata*	**6,7,8**
Mountain-Laurel	*Kalmia latifolia*	**6,7**
Red Buckeye	*Aesculus pavia*	**7,8**
Redbud, Eastern	*Cercis canadensis*	**6,7,8**
Sassafras	*Sassafras albidum*	**6,7,8**
Silky-Camellia	*Stewartia malacodendron*	**6,7,8**
Sweetbay	*Magnolia virginiana*	**6**
Sweet-Pepperbush	*Clethra alnifolia*	**7,8**
Sweetshrub	*Calycanthus floridus*	**6,7,8**
Tulip-Poplar	*Liriodendron tulipifera*	**6,7,8**
Umbrella-Tree	*Magnolia tripetala*	**6,7,8**
Virgin's-Bower	*Clematis virginiana*	**6,7,8**

RECOMMENDED ROSES
(See also Chapter 26.)

HYBRID TEAS

Charlotte Armstrong, light red
Chrysler Imperial, dark red
Eclipse, medium yellow
Mister Lincoln, medium red
Pascali, white
Peace, yellow blend
Royal Highness, light pink
Tiffany, pink blend
Tropicana, orange-red

FLORIBUNDAS

Europeana, dark red
Gay Princess, light pink
Roman Holiday, red blend
Sarabande, orange-red
Saratoga, white
Spartan, orange-red

GRANDIFLORAS

John S. Armstrong, dark red
Queen Elizabeth, medium pink

CLIMBERS

Blaze, medium red
Blossomtime, medium pink
Don Juan, dark red
New Dawn, light pink

SHRUB AND OLD-FASHIONED ROSES

Frau Karl Druschki, white
Paul Neyron, medium pink
Sea Foam, white

36 GULF COAST

Southern Texas, Arkansas, Louisiana, Mississippi,
Southern Alabama, Florida
Zones 8, 9, 10

by F. A. C. McCulla, *Editor,* The Yardner,
Men's Garden Club of Houston, Texas

Gardening along the Gulf Coast, which extends for well over fifteen hundred miles, is a ten-to-twelve-month pleasure and problem, for the weather is extremely variable. The old saying "Just stand still and the weather will change" could well have originated in Southern Texas. January and February will have temperatures of 60° to 80°, but there may be drops of 20° to 30° for short spells. Lack of dormancy causes special problems, and the consequent long growing season tends to reduce the size of blooms. In the larger towns air pollution is becoming an increasing problem, as elsewhere in the nation. The Gulf Coast's special hazard is hurricanes. Every year one or more hurricanes devastate some stretch of the long coastline. In spite of these conditions, however, gardening has become the leading hobby throughout most of the region.

For the greater part the soils contain much sand or sandy loam. The loam, of course, retains moisture and is usually better for all gardening purposes.

In Southern Texas surface soils are generally sandy loam. Timber country frequently has a subsoil of crumbly or heavy clay. The coastal areas and Rio Grande Valley are sandy, and irrigation is necessary for the large crops of vegetables and fruits, which include onions, tomatoes, blackberries, dewberries, strawberries, watermelons and figs. In the Rio Grande Valley the famous ruby-red grapefruit is grown, as well as oranges. Pecans are a valuable crop. Tyler, Texas, is one of the rose capitals of the world; from it hundreds of thousands of old and new varieties of roses are distributed to gardeners every year.

Arkansas, although situated many miles north of the actual coast, is predominantly influenced by the Gulf. More than half of the state is part of the coastal plain, having long summers and up to fifty-five inches of rain each year. The fertile alluvial soil produces great quantities of cotton, soybeans, rice, peaches, melons and other crops. The northwestern half of the state is hilly or mountainous with rich forests of oak, hickory, tupelo, red gum and pine. Cypresses and shortleaf pine and loblolly pine thrive on the plain.

Louisiana delta soils are rich and tend to be alkaline, but this is not true everywhere. Sandy loam is found along stretches of coast, and back from the streams a heavy black soil is still very productive. This state is known for its fine old mansions and gardens. It has magnificent oak trees and in the lowlands great stands of bald cypress and unique species of wild iris. Many broad-leaved and needle-leaved evergreens can be grown here. Sweet potatoes are a major crop; sugar cane, strawberries and rice are others. Gardens are apt to display azaleas, camellias, gardenias, magnolias and the Creole Easter lily (*Lilium nobilissimum*). Old plantations along the bayous with water-hyacinths in bloom are a nostalgic sight.

The soils of Mississippi, particularly along the coast, are of fine silt or sandy loam, low in organic matter and requiring enrichment. Here pecans are grown extensively, as are tung-oil trees, and the longleaf pine for lumber. Wild azaleas and dogwood are scattered throughout the countryside. Beautiful old houses and gardens are open in season, and women's garden clubs are very active.

Southern Alabama has a greater diversity of soils, including those derived from granite and along the coast sandy to clayey soil. Quantities of azaleas and camellias are grown. Peaches are the main fruit crop. As in the other Gulf Coast states, there are two crops of vegetables each year.

In Florida most soils are very sandy and either neutral or acid. Around the Everglades and some rivers there is organic peat and muck that are most fertile. Unfortunately government and private engineers have been draining many swamps, most destructive to plant and animal life, and changing the constituency of the soil. The Sunshine State still has a good deal of rain in the summer, and many kinds of fruits and vegetables thrive there. Citrus fruits are grown throughout the state but only certain varieties in the northern counties. The far southern region furnishes subtropical fruits and nuts. The ornamental flowering plants featured in Florida are mostly acid-loving.

Along the entire Gulf Coast roses are a conspicuous feature of gardens. Evergreen trees and shrubs and colorful masses of herbaceous annuals are also widely planted. The use of vegetables — beets, carrots, parsley and others — as edging plants is becoming popular.

In such a climate, with frequent cool winds from the Gulf, people naturally spend a good deal of time out of doors, and many become keen gardeners. For extremely warm midsummer weather, glassed-in and air-conditioned patios, with plants in raised beds or in containers, are being built here and there. In spring the Gulf Coast states are a world of beauty. Country places and woods are strewn with a great variety of wild flowers.

Most of the familiar perennials long grown in the Atlantic states and the Middle West will thrive in Zone 8 and some in Zone 9. Others cannot withstand the heat of Zone 9; gardeners here must go without bearded iris, forget-me-nots, peonies and Oriental poppies. In the warmest parts of that zone bleeding-heart, columbine, coralbells, fall anemones, foxglove, hosta, speedwell and a few others will not thrive. In Zone 10 only a handful of the northern perennials are found — among them beebalm, butterfly-weed, chrysanthemum, coreopsis, daylily, mist-flower, evening-primrose, liatris and yarrow.

To compensate are some perennials virtually unknown as garden plants farther north, such as air-plant, angelonia, bird-of-paradise, century-plant, gerbera, jacobinia, lobster-claw and night-blooming cereus.

A shady path through the Florida sunshine. This lovely walled garden features palms, ferns and split-leaf monsteras as a frothy ground cover under tall trees; the tailored look of the precisely cut stone and trap-rock mulch makes an excellent foil for the plants. *(Rudi Rada photo)*

The golden-yellow flowers of an allamanda vine festoon the roof between a Florida house and its carport. *(George Taloumis photo)*

WHERE TO GET SPECIAL HELP

Write to State Extension Editor, Agricultural Extension Service, at the address for your state:

Alabama: Auburn University, Auburn, Alabama 36830.

Arkansas: University of Arkansas, P.O. Box 391, Little Rock, Arkansas 72203.

Florida: University of Florida, Gainesville, Florida 32603.

Louisiana: Louisiana State University, University Station, Baton Rouge, Louisiana 70803.

Mississippi: Mississippi State University, State College, Mississippi 39762.

Texas: Texas A & M University, College Station, Texas 77841.

PLACES AND PLANTINGS OF INTEREST

Alabama: BELLINGRATH GARDENS near Mobile, and the many stately old homes on the Azalea Trails.

Camellia is the state flower; Southern Pine, the state tree.

Arkansas: HOT SPRINGS NATIONAL PARK, Garland County.
OUAHITA NATIONAL FOREST in the west-central part of the state.
OZARK NATIONAL FOREST in the northwest. There are also numerous state parks totaling over seventeen thousand square miles.
TERRITORIAL CAPITAL RESTORATION at Little Rock.

Apple Blossom is the state flower; Pine, the state tree.

Florida: CYPRESS GARDENS near Winter Haven. Native shrubs and other plants.
EVERGLADES NATIONAL PARK, Miami.
BOTANICAL GARDEN AND ARBORETUM, Sebring.
FAIRCHILD TROPICAL GARDEN, Coconut Grove. Exotic and unusual plants.
MCKEE JUNGLE GARDENS, Vero Beach. Hibiscus, orchids and other tropical flowers.

Orange Blossom is the state flower; Cabbage Palmetto, the state tree.

Louisiana: HODGES GARDENS at Many. Camellias, azaleas, roses, particularly the old ones; also a native wild area to explore.
AVERY ISLAND JUNGLE GARDENS.
ROSEDOWN at St. Francisville. An antebellum house with gardens fully restored.
LOUISIANA DUTCH GARDENS, Newellton.

Magnolia is the state flower; Bald Cypress, the state tree.

Mississippi: The Delta country with fertile silt loams is ideal for gardens and flowers. The forty-mile Gulfside drive through Biloxi, Gulfport and Pass Christian is beautiful, featuring old homes and gardens. The women's garden clubs are very active around Jackson and at Belzoni; the Wister Gardens is a delightful place to rest. Wild azaleas, dogwoods and early spring flowers brighten the countryside.

Southern Magnolia is the state flower and tree.

Southern Texas: Rio Grande Valley known for its "ruby-red" grapefruit. New arboretum at Houston. Fine rose garden at Garden Center. State parks on the Gulf Coast are numerous and well maintained.

Blue Bonnet is the state flower; Pecan, the state tree.

SOME FAVORITE GARDEN PLANTS OF THE GULF COAST

LARGE TREES

COMMON NAME	BOTANICAL NAME	HEIGHT	ZONE
Ash, European	*Fraxinus excelsior*	60'-140'	8
Red	*pennsylvanica*	40'-60'	8
White	*americana*	60'-120'	8
Cottonwood	*Populus deltoides*	50'-90'	8
Elm, American	*Ulmus americana*	60'-120'	8
Cedar	*crassifolia*	30'-60'	8
Chinese	*parvifolia*	30'-60'	8
Maple, Box-Elder	*Acer negundo*	30'-70'	8
Oak, Laurel	*Quercus laurifolia*	30'-60'	8
Overcup	*lyrata*	50'-100'	8
Spanish Red	*falcata*	40'-80'	8
Willow	*phellos*	40'-60'	8
Pecan	*Carya pecan*	60'-150'	8
Sycamore	*Platanus occidentalis*	70'-140'	8
Willow, Weeping	*Salix babylonica*	20'-30'	8
White	*alba*	30'-75'	8

SMALL FLOWERING TREES

COMMON NAME	BOTANICAL NAME	HEIGHT	ZONE
Cherry, Flowering	*Prunus* species	15'-30'	8
Crape-Myrtle	*Lagerstroemia indica*	10'-20'	8
Dogwood, Flowering	*Cornus florida*	20'-40'	8
Magnolia, Saucer	*Magnolia soulangiana*	20'-50'	8
Peach, Flowering	*Prunus persica*	10'-15'	8
Redbud, American	*Cercis canadensis*	20'-40'	8
Chinese	*chinensis*	20'-50'	8
Silktree	*Albizia julibrissin*	30'-40'	8

LARGE EVERGREENS

COMMON NAME	BOTANICAL NAME	HEIGHT	ZONE
Holly, American	*Ilex opaca*	35'-60'	8
Magnolia, Southern	*Magnolia grandiflora*	40'-100'	8
Oak, Live	*Quercus virginiana*	to 60'	8
Pine, Loblolly	*Pinus taeda*	50'-120'	8
Longleaf	*palustris*	50'-120'	8
Slash	*caribaea*	60'-150'	8

SMALL NEEDLE-LEAVED EVERGREENS

COMMON NAME	BOTANICAL NAME	HEIGHT	ZONE
Arborvitae, in variety	*Thuja occidentalis*	3'-10'	8
Juniper, in variety	*Juniperus*	3'-20'	8
Podocarpus	*Podocarpus macrophylla maki*	3'-8'	8
Yew, in variety	*Taxus baccata, cuspidata* and varieties	3'-15'	8

BROAD-LEAVED EVERGREENS

COMMON NAME	BOTANICAL NAME	HEIGHT	ZONE
Azalea, in variety	*Rhododendron*	2'-6'	8
Box, Common	*Buxus sempervirens*	2'-15'	8
Littleleaf	*microphylla*	to 3'	8
Camellia	*Camellia japonica*	3'-10'	9
Sasanqua	*sasanqua*	3'-10'	9
Cape-Jasmine	*Gardenia jasminoides*	2'-6'	9
Euonymus, Evergreen	*Euonymus japonicus*	2'-15'	8
Firethorn, in variety	*Pyracantha*	to 15'	8
Gold-Dust Shrub, in variety	*Aucuba japonica*	to 15'	8
Jasmine	*Jasminum humile*	to 20'	8
Loquat	*Eriobotrya japonica*	to 20'	9
Nandina	*Nandina domestica*	to 8'	8
Oleander	*Nerium oleander*	to 15'	9
Oregon-Grape	*Mahonia aquifolium*	to 3'	8
Pittosporum	*Pittosporum tobira*	to 10'	9

DECIDUOUS SHRUBS

COMMON NAME	BOTANICAL NAME	HEIGHT	ZONE
Cestrum, in variety	*Cestrum*	2'-12'	9,10
Cotoneaster, in variety	*Cotoneaster*	1'-8'	8
Flowering Almond	*Prunus glandulosa*	3'-5'	8
Flowering-Quince	*Chaenomeles lagenaria*	5'-10'	8
Honeysuckle, in variety	*Lonicera tatarica*	5'-10'	8
Jasmine, Winter	*Jasminum nudiflorum*	to 15'	8
Pomegranate	*Punica granatum*	to 20'	9
Rose-of-China	*Hibiscus rosa-sinensis*	10'-20'	10
Rose-of-Sharon	*syriacus*	6'-12'	8
Spirea, in variety	*Spiraea*	3'-5'	8
Viburnum, in variety	*Viburnun*	4'-12'	8
Weigela, in variety	*Weigela*	4'-6'	8

HEDGES AND WINDBREAKS
(T—tall, 10' and up; M—medium, 5'-9'; L—low, 1'-4')

COMMON NAME	BOTANICAL NAME	HEIGHT	ZONE
Arborvitae, in variety	*Thuja occidentalis*	M-T	8
Bamboo species	*Bambusa* and *Arundinaria*	M-T	9
Box, in variety	*Buxus*	L	8
Holly, in variety	*Ilex*	M-T	8
Honeysuckle, Bush	*Lonicera tatarica*	T	8
Juniper, in variety	*Juniperus*	M-T	8
Privet, in variety	*Ligustrum*	M-T	8
Yew, in variety	*Taxus*	M-T	8

GROUND COVERS
(All are hardy in Zone 8.)

COMMON NAME	BOTANICAL NAME	HEIGHT
Bugleweed	*Ajuga reptans*	8"
Honeysuckle	*Lonicera henryi; L. japonica*	8"
Ivy, English	*Hedera helix*	12"
Juniper, Chinese	*Juniperus chinensis* 'Pfitzeriana' and 'Pfitzeriana glauca'	2'
Creeping	*horizontalis,*	
Waukegan	and *horizontalis* 'Douglasii'	2'
Lantana, Trailing	*Lantana montevidensis*	18"
Lily-Turf	*Liriope spicata*	12"
Mondo	*Ophiopogon japonicus*	10"
Periwinkle	*Vinca minor*	8"
Sedum	*Sedum ewersii, pilosum, sempervivoides, spurium* are not too invasive	low

LAWN GRASSES

COMMON NAME	BOTANICAL NAME
Bermuda Grass	*Cynodon dactylon*
Korean Grass	*Zoysia japonica*
Manila Grass	*Zoysia matrella*
St. Augustine Grass	*Stenotaphrum secundatum*

SOME EXOTIC FLOWERING PLANTS GROWN IN SOUTHERN FLORIDA (ZONE 10)

COMMON NAME	BOTANICAL NAME	COMMENT
Allamanda	*Allamanda cathartica*	Climber to 15 feet; large fragrant yellow flowers
Ashanti Blood	*Mussaenda erythrophylla*	African shrub with fantastic red flowers
Bottlebrush	*Callistemon lanceolatus*	Small tree with pendent spikes of petal-less red-stamened flowers
Bougainvillea	*Bougainvillea spectabilis*	Well-known magenta-, purple- or red-flowered vine
Chalice-Vine	*Solandra grandiflora*	Evergreen climber. In winter huge creamy-white fragrant flowers
Flame-Vine	*Pyrostegia ignea*	Masses of blazing trumpets from January through April
Frangipani	*Plumeria rubra*	Intensely fragrant clusters of white or pink waxy flowers
Fringed Hibiscus	*Hibiscus schizopetalous*	Shrub with dangling lacy red flowers, April to September
Geiger-Tree	*Cordia sebestena*	Dense clusters of vermilion, frilled, crepe-textured flowers
Glory-Bower	*Clerodendron thomsoniae*	Twining shrub, flowers crimson with white calyx, in summer and fall

COMMON NAME	BOTANICAL NAME	COMMENT
Gold Coast Jasmine	*Jasminum dichotomum*	Vine or clambering shrub with evergreen leaves and loose clusters of very fragrant white nocturnal flowers in late winter-early spring
Golden Shower	*Cassia fistula*	Medium-size tree, spectacular in spring
Mango	*Mangifera indica*	Tropical tree to ninety feet bearing delicate much-cherished fruit
Mountain-Ebony	*Bauhinia variegata*	Small tree with broad-lobed leaves and profuse rose-purple flowers
Purple Wreath	*Petrea volubilis*	Woody vine; long racemes of lavender flowers
Rangoon-Creeper	*Quisqualis indica*	Clambering shrub; flowers fragrant, white changing to red, on long slender green calyx tube
Royal Poinciana	*Delonix regia*	Wide-spreading tree, in summer covered with orange-scarlet flowers
Shower-of-Orchids	*Congea tomentosa*	Climbing shrub; wands of white and reddish-mauve flowers
Sky-Vine	*Thunbergia grandiflora*	Woody twiner with long leaves and blue flowers three inches wide in racemes

NATIVE PLANTS USEFUL FOR THE GARDEN

COMMON NAME	BOTANICAL NAME
Bluebell	*Eustoma russellianum*
Coralberry	*Symphoricarpos orbiculatus*
Dogwood	*Cornus florida*
French-Mulberry	*Callicarpa americana*
Indian Blanket	*Gaillardia pulchella* and hybrids
Louisiana Iris	*Iris fulva, foliosa, hexagona*
Penstemon	*Penstemon* species
Texas Blue Bonnet	*Lupinus subcarnosus*
Violet	*Viola* species

Also Agave, Cactus and Yucca species and various Ferns.

RECOMMENDED ROSES
(See also Chapter 26.)

The first hybrid tea rose was 'La France', and today this rose, which dates back to 1867, is still found in many old gardens. Along with it, of course, are grown some of the superb roses that have been developed in the past forty years or so. A selection of these is listed below. Roses in the Deep South do best in medium heavy soil that is also well drained. Along the Gulf Coast raised beds are desirable because of high rainfall. Roses need plenty of nourishment; fertilize them when new growth appears and again after first prolific bloom. Decayed manure and bonemeal should be applied in the fall. Container-grown roses are available in late fall, spring or summer.

Rose troubles most common along the Gulf Coast are black spot, powdery mildew and, in early spring, aphids. All can be properly controlled by sprays and dusts. Good air circulation avoids some black spot and mildew.

Here is a list of roses found suitable for the Gulf Coast states. Because of the long growing period, severe pruning is necessary.

HYBRID TEAS

American Heritage,
    ivory-salmon
Christian Dior, crimson
Chrysler Imperial, dark red
Fragrant Cloud, orange-red

Helen Traubel, pink-apricot
Pink Peace, deep pink
Swarthmore, rose-red
Tropicana, orange-red

POLYANTHAS

Cecile Brunner, pink
China Doll, pink-yellow
    blend

Gloria Mundi, orange-scarlet
Margo Koster, salmon-pink

FLORIBUNDAS

Crimson Rosette, crimson
Europeana, dark red
Fancy Talk, salmon-pink;
    other Talk varieties

Gene Boerner, pink
Summer Snow, white

GRANDIFLORAS

Camelot, medium pink
Granada, scarlet blend
Montezuma, orange-red

Queen Elizabeth, medium pink
Roundelay, red
Tickled Pink, pink

CLIMBERS

Margo Koster, salmon-pink
Peace, yellow blend

Queen Elizabeth, medium pink
Summer Snow, white

OLD ROSES

Old-time roses require plenty of room, and they do best on their own roots. Only small amounts of fertilizer are needed, but regular watering is essential. Mildew and black spot are in general less bothersome than on modern roses, but excessive damp weather causes blooms to ball or rot and upsets the regular blooming schedule. In pruning take only the dead wood at any time and the tips after the blooming period. The one disadvantage of these roses is that most of them bloom only once a year. A few will have occasional later flowers. Of the many old rose varieties here are some that do well along the Gulf Coast:

Archduke Charles (China,
    pink to red)
Catherine Mermet (Tea,
    pink, 1869)
Duchesse de Brabant (Tea,
    pink, 1857)
Frau Karl Druschki
    (Hybrid Perpetual, white,
    1900)
Kathleen (Hybrid Musk,
    pale pink, 1922)
Kathleen Harrop (Bourbon,
    shell pink, 1919)

Louis Philippe (China,
    pink to red)
Mme. Scipion Cochet
    (Bourbon, pink, 1900)
Maiden's Blush (Alba, blush
    pink, 1797)
Maréchal Niel (Noisette,
    pale yellow, 1864)
Paul Neyron (Hybrid
    Perpetual, pink, 1869)
Rosa banksiae 'Lutea'
    (Climber, yellow)
Salet (Moss, pink, 1854)

37 MID-AMERICA EAST

Illinois, Indiana, Kentucky, Ohio, Southern Michigan
Zones 5, 6, 7

by Victor H. Ries, *Professor Emeritus, Horticulture,*
Ohio State University, Columbus, Ohio

There is virtually no limit to the types of north-temperature-latitude gardens possible in Mid-America East. Many kinds of herbaceous and woody plants may be grown: annuals, perennials, flowering shrubs, coniferous trees, hardwood trees and vines. Roses, with knowledgeable care, do particularly well. Rhododendrons, including azaleas, are grown and enjoyed, although they are actually not so well suited to this region as to the East and Northwest.

All the standard northern fruits do well — except that peaches and most flowering cherries are a little too tender for the farthest north areas. So, too, are wisteria and magnolias. But in the southern part of Kentucky some fine plants too tender to survive in most of this area can be grown, such as heavenly-bamboo (*Nandina domestica*), spider-lilies (*Crinum longifolium, C. moorei* and *C. powellii*), alstroemerias, the *Rhododendron fortunei* hybrids, the evergreen Kurume azaleas, including the famous white *R.* x *loderi* 'King George', the long-leaved magnolia tree (*Magnolia macrophylla*) and in sheltered places *M. grandiflora.*

Most of the familiar perennials and annuals can be grown to perfection in these states if adequately watered and protected, when needed, against aphids, red-spiders and other pests that come with spells of hot and dry weather. The northern regions are better for delphiniums, larkspurs, lupines, nasturtiums, primroses and sweet peas that require cool summer nights. The longer growing season along the Ohio River and southward enables gardeners to have cardinal climbers, daturas, moonflowers, tithonias and other delightful plants that do not as a rule do very well in the Northeast or North Central states.

Some perennials that put on a fine show throughout this part of

Mid-America are Japanese anemones, columbines, daylilies in great variety, bearded iris, globe-thistles, Shasta daisies, clove pinks and the beautiful blue *Salvia pitcheri.* Among annuals, or plants grown as annuals, *Dianthus chinensis, Salvia farinacea* and snapdragons do excellently. Of bulbous plants many species and modern hybrids of *Lilium* are recommended, and for woodland or light-shade places the enchanting *Lycoris squamigera* with its pure pink amaryllislike trumpets in late summer.

The weather is extremely variable. In northern sections the ground is usually snow-covered in winter, so the root systems of plants are protected from the many freezings and thawings somewhat farther south. In the middle area the winters are often open, with only occasional snow, and many plants suffer. Even woody plants are damaged by alternate freezing and thawing. Mulches for winter protection help a lot. In southern areas the winters are less severe, so less damage is caused.

Late frosts in valleys and bottomlands often injure early-flowering plants such as *Magnolia soulangiana.* Do not set out any tender plants until all danger of frost is past, which may be four to six weeks after the last killing frost.

Summers are frequently hot, nights as well as days. This affects a number of flowering plants that prefer cooler weather and should therefore be situated where they get some light shade for part of the day, though actually it is not shade so much as cooler nights that are desired. Cool air drainage from nearby hills helps this situation at times. Among the plants affected are stocks, clarkia, schizanthus, monkshood and many lupines.

Winter sun is often a problem. Its warming effect when the ground is frozen can dry out or burn woody plants. Afternoon sun is the most damaging. Where practical, the provision of winter shade and protection from strong, drying winds may be helpful, especially if broad-leaved evergreens are attempted. Screens, fences and natural windbreaks are examples of this kind of winter protection.

Soils vary greatly in composition, texture and degree of acidity (pH reading). Some areas, like western Ohio, are almost entirely alkaline; others are acid. Consult your local agricultural agent as to the need for liming. It is often not necessary.

Most soils here do require additional organic matter, and some heavy soils need sand to loosen and aerate them. Very few natural soils are rich enough or friable enough for gardening. Incorporate at least an inch of organic matter — peatmoss, sawdust or rotted leaves — with the top twelve inches of soil, or plow under a green-manure crop of winter wheat or rye.

Fertilizing is necessary. Apply a complete commercial fertilizer, such as 5-10-5, 4-12-4, 10-6-4, or a farm fertilizer, as 12-12-12 or 15-15-15. Follow directions on the package as to the amount to use. Do this each spring with additional applications in late summer.

A few soils may be deficient in minor elements — magnesium, manganese, iron. The county agent can have soil tested for you and tell you how to remedy it if desired. In many parts of this region, even on hillsides, soil drainage is rather poor and should be improved by installing lines of agricultural drain tile.

WHERE TO GET SPECIAL HELP

The Agricultural Extension Agent in each county will usually have bulletins available. His office is in the county seat. Additional information may be obtained by writing to Agricultural Extension Service at the proper address for your state.

Illinois: College of Agriculture, University of Illinois, Urbana, Illinois 61801.

Indiana: Purdue University, West Lafayette, Indiana 47906.

Kentucky: University of Kentucky, Lexington, Kentucky 40505.

Michigan: Michigan State University, East Lansing, Michigan 48823.

Ohio: Ohio State University, 2120 Fyffe Road, Columbus, Ohio 43210.

PLACES AND PLANTINGS OF INTEREST

Illinois: GARFIELD PARK CONSERVATORY, Chicago.
BOTANIC GARDEN, Chicago.
MORTON ARBORETUM, Lisle.
UNIVERSITY OF ILLINOIS FLOWER TRAILS, Urbana.

Violet is the state flower; Bur Oak, the state tree.

Indiana: BUTLER UNIVERSITY BOTANIC GARDEN, Indianapolis.

Zinnia is the state flower; Tulip-tree, the state tree.

Kentucky: GENERAL ELECTRIC APPLIANCE PARK, Louisville.
LOCUST GROVE, home of George Rogers Clark, and FARMINGTON, designed by Jefferson, both at Louisville.
FORTY STATE AND NATIONAL PARKS.

Goldenrod is the state flower; Tulip-tree the state tree.

Michigan: UNIVERSITY OF MICHIGAN BOTANIC GARDEN, Ann Arbor.
MICHIGAN STATE UNIVERSITY BOTANIC GARDEN, East Lansing.
HILLSDALE COLLEGE ARBORETUM, Hillsdale.

Apple Blossom is the state flower; White Pine, the state tree.

Ohio: EDEN PARK CONSERVATORY, Cincinnati.
MT. AIRY ARBORETUM, Cincinnati.
KINGWOOD CENTER, Mansfield.
HOLDEN ARBORETUM, Mentor.
DAWES ARBORETUM, Newark.
SECRIST ARBORETUM, Wooster.

Red Carnation is the state flower; Buckeye, the state tree.

SOME FAVORITE GARDEN PLANTS OF MID-AMERICA EAST

LARGE TREES

COMMON NAME	BOTANICAL NAME	HEIGHT	ZONE
Birch, River	*Betula nigra*	75'	5
Corktree, Amur	*Phellodendron amurense*	40'	5
Ginkgo	*Ginkgo biloba*	100'	5
Honey-Locust	*Gleditsia triacanthos*	100'	5
Linden, Littleleaf	*Tilia cordata*	75'	5

COMMON NAME	BOTANICAL NAME	HEIGHT	ZONE
Maple, Red	*Acer rubrum*	75'	5
Sugar	*saccharum*	100'	5
Oak, Pin	*Quercus palustris*	75'	5
Scarlet	*coccinea*	75'	5
Sweet Gum	*Liquidambar styraciflua*	100'	6

SMALL FLOWERING TREES

COMMON NAME	BOTANICAL NAME	HEIGHT	ZONE
Cherry, Higan	*Prunus subhirtella*	30'	5
Oriental	*serrulata*	25'	5
Crabapple, Flowering, in variety	*Malus*	8'-25'	5
Dogwood, Flowering	*Cornus florida*	25'	5
Goldenrain-Tree	*Koelreuteria paniculata*	30'	6
Hawthorn, Paul's Scarlet	*Crataegus oxyacantha* variety	15'	5
Washington	*phaenopyrum*	25'	5
Magnolia, Sweetbay	*Magnolia virginiana*	35'	6
Redbud, Eastern	*Cercis canadensis*	30'	5

LARGE EVERGREENS

COMMON NAME	BOTANICAL NAME	HEIGHT	ZONE
Arborvitae, Giant	*Thuja plicata*	40'	6
Douglas-Fir	*Pseudotsuga menziesii*	100'	5
Hemlock, Canadian	*Tsuga canadensis*	100'	5
Pine, Red	*Pinus resinosa*	75'	5
Scots	*sylvestris*	75'	5
White	*strobus*	100'	5
Spruce, Norway	*Picea abies*	100'	5

SMALL NEEDLE-LEAVED EVERGREENS

COMMON NAME	BOTANICAL NAME	HEIGHT	ZONE
Arborvitae, American	*Thuja occidentalis*	2'-30'	5

Use dwarf forms. Best in more northern areas; subject to infestation of spider mites in hot dry locations.

False-Cypress, Hinoki	*Chamaecyparis obtusa*	3'-40'	5

Use dwarf forms.

Juniper, Chinese, in variety	*Juniperus chinensis*	1'-6'	5
Creeping, in variety	*horizontalis*	1'-2'	5
Yew, Dwarf English	*Taxus baccata* 'Repandens'	3'	6
Japanese, in variety	*cuspidata*	3'-20'	5

BROAD-LEAVED EVERGREENS

COMMON NAME	BOTANICAL NAME	HEIGHT	ZONE
Box, Common, in variety	*Buxus sempervirens*	1'-15'	5
Korean Hybrids	*microphylla* hybrids	2'-6'	5-7
Cherry-Laurel	*Prunus laurocerasus*	3'-10'	6-7
Firethorn	*Pyracantha*	6'-10'	5-7

COMMON NAME	BOTANICAL NAME	HEIGHT	ZONE
Holly, American	*Ilex opaca*	25'-40'	5
English	*aquifolium*	25'-50'	6-7
Japanese	*crenata*	2'-15'	5
Mountain-Laurel	*Kalmia latifolia*	4'-10'	
Rhododendron	*Rhododendron catawbiense*	1'-15'	
	and some modern hybrids		

SHRUBS

COMMON NAME	BOTANICAL NAME	HEIGHT	ZONE
Azalea, Mollis Hybrids	*Rhododendron* x *kosterianum*	3'-8'	5
Cotoneaster, Cranberry	*Cotoneaster apiculata*	3'	5
Spreading	*divaricata*	6'	5
Deutzia, Lemoine	*Deutzia* x *lemoinei*	4'	5
Slender	*gracilis*	3'	5
Euonymus, Dwarf Winged	*Euonymus alatus* 'Compactus'	6'	5
Forsythia, in variety	*Forsythia*	3'-8'	5
Spirea, Froebel	*Spiraea* x *bumalda* 'Froebelii'	3'	5
Garland	x *arguta*	4'-5'	5
Viburnum, Fragrant	*Viburnum carlesii*	5'	5
Japanese Snowball	*plicatum*	8'	5
Nannyberry	*lentago*	20'	5
Tea	*setigerum*	12'	5
Weigela, in variety	*Weigela*	4'-8'	5

HEDGES AND WINDBREAKS

(H — hedge; W — windbreak; T — tall, 10' and up; M — medium, 5'-9'; L — low, 1'-4')

COMMON NAME	BOTANICAL NAME	HEIGHT AND USE	ZONE
Arborvitae, Giant	*Thuja plicata*	H,W,T	6
Box	*Buxus*	H,M	5-7
Buckthorn	*Rhamnus frangula* 'Tallhedge'	H,T	5
Cornelian-Cherry	*Cornus mas*	H,W,T	5
Honeysuckle, Winter	*Lonicera fragrantissima*	H,M	5
Maple, Amur	*Acer ginnala*	H,W,T	5
Privet, Regel	*Ligustrum obtusifolium*		
	regelianum	H,L	5
Spirea, Froebel	*Spiraea bumalda* 'Froebelii'	H,L	5
Wintercreeper	*Euonymus fortunei vegetus*	H,L	5
Yew, Low-growing, Spreading and	*Taxus*	H,M	5
Upright varieties		H,W,M-T	5

GROUND COVERS

COMMON NAME	BOTANICAL NAME	HEIGHT	ZONE
Bellflower, Serbian	*Campanula poscharskyana*	8"	5
Bugleweed	*Ajuga reptans*	6"	5
Ivy, English	*Hedera helix*	vine	5
Japanese-Spurge	*Pachysandra terminalis*	8"-12"	5
Periwinkle	*Vinca minor*	6"	5
Saxifrage, Strawberry	*Saxifraga sarmentosa*	6"	5
Stonecrop, in variety	*Sedum*	3"-6"	5-6
Wintercreeper, in variety	*Euonymus fortunei*	vine	5
Woodruff, Sweet	*Asperula odorata*	8"	5

LAWN GRASSES

COMMON NAME	BOTANICAL NAME
Kentucky Bluegrass, esp. Merion	*Poa pratensis* vars.
Chewings Red Fescue	*Festuca rubra* vars.
Creeping Fescue (for shade)	

(Not Zoysia in this area; however good it may be farther south, here, it is brown eight months of the year and spreads rampantly where not wanted.)

NATIVE PLANTS USEFUL FOR THE GARDEN
(All hardy in Zone 5.)

COMMON NAME	BOTANICAL NAME	HEIGHT
Bloodroot	*Sanguinaria canadensis*	6"
Columbine, American	*Aquilegia canadensis*	1'-2'
Fern, Christmas	*Polystichum acrostichoides*	1'-2'
Cinnamon	*Osmunda cinnamomea*	2'-6'
Marginal Shield	*Dryopteris marginalis*	1'-2'
Goatsbeard	*Aruncus sylvester*	4'-6'
Hepatica	*Hepatica triloba*	6"
Lady's-Slipper, Yellow	*Cypripedium calceolus pubescens*	2'
Phlox, Blue	*Phlox divaricata*	6"-12"
Snakeroot	*Cimicifuga racemosa*	6'

RECOMMENDED ROSES
(See also Chapter 26.)

So many different-named roses are well grown and popular in this part of America that any meaningful listing would run into hundreds. It is not the specific variety that counts in this region but rather good drainage and winter protection. The frequently cold winters tend to rule out standard or tree forms unless they are heeled in and covered over each fall. Of other types, a few out of many that have been top-rated and proved popular are:

HYBRID TEAS

Butterscotch, yellow   Mister Lincoln, medium red
Chicago Peace, yellow to
    pink

POLYANTHAS

Happy, red   Snow White, white
Margot Koster, salmon-   The Fairy, pink
    pink

FLORIBUNDAS

Betty Prior, medium pink   Gene Boerner, pink
Fashion, coral   Sandringham, yellow
Frensham, dark red

GRANDIFLORAS

Carrousel, dark red   Queen Elizabeth, medium pink
Montezuma, orange-red

CLIMBERS

Dorothea, medium red   Gold Rush, gold
    flushed with yellow   White Dawn, white
Dream girl, salmon-pink

SHRUB AND OLD-FASHIONED ROSES

Frau Dagmar Hastrup,   Schneezwerg, purest white
    silvery pink

38 MID-AMERICA WEST

Southern Nebraska, Southern Iowa, Kansas, Missouri,
Western Illinois
Zones 4, 5, 6

by Dr. John Philip Baumgardt, *Garden Consultant,
Kansas City, Missouri*

Middle West gardeners learn to count on extremes: the air is still, or the wind blows a gale; it is hot, or it is cold. Though the total annual rainfall is a fairly satisfactory plus or minus forty-three inches, rain comes over a flooding period of torrential downpour — followed by drought. When Canadian air pours southward between October and April, the temperature may plummet to below zero, and hours later when a high-pressure center develops in the Gulf of Mexico, the thermometer zooms upward. Snowfall may be heavy for a week or two, but all too often when sub-zero temperatures come, there is no snow cover, the sun shines bright and the wind blows and desiccates plants and gardens. Over a fifty-five-year period the number of frost-free days has averaged 185, the last killing frost of spring occurring about April 10, and the first killing frost of fall about October 20. Considerable variation on both sides of these dates makes early planting or dependence on a late crop risky business.

In the Middle West you soon learn how to create and utilize microclimates and wind shelters. You have to develop a well-drained garden with plenty of hose outlets for the dry spells. You learn that while prairie soils may be deep and fertile, they are poorly drained and crack like a drained-lake bottom during dry weather. You learn that plants that fail in high heat, wind or very cold weather are not worth the effort. Sweet peas, lupines, cauliflower, Iceberg lettuce, many species of primrose and meconopsis are examples of plants that can be counted on to fail. Still, here and there, a dedicated gardener accepts the challenge and raises a specimen of an "impossible" plant.

At the turn of the century common lilacs, *Spiraea vanhouttei,* jetbead, kerria, Pfitzer juniper, Norway spruce and an occasional bush-honeysuckle (plus native trees) made up the usual landscape planting. Today gardeners have acidified the neutral to limy soils to grow many evergreen and deciduous azaleas and rhododendrons. Most gardens south of the Missouri River enjoy dogwood, American and Japanese hollies and the new hybrid lilies. Crape-myrtle, a true Southerner, is field-grown by southwestern Iowa nurseries (low strains that are cut to the ground each winter and bloom on new wood). *Amaryllis belladonna,* once listed as tender, is left in the ground, quite hardy, at Des Moines.

With the advent of new species of ornamentals, unfamiliar pests and diseases have appeared. Dutch elm disease destroyed the widely planted American elms, and the so-called hybrid selections are apt to be uncouth-appearing — shallow-rooted affairs of little merit. The sterile selections of honey-locust promised to be a fine shade-tree group, but widespread use of the Japanese silktree, *Albizia julibrissin,* brought in the clay-colored beetle and mimosa webworm, so now honey-locusts must be sprayed throughout the summer. Some of the most promising new woody plants are the selected green ash and white ash cultivars, the low-growing species and hybrid lilacs, broad-leaved evergreens chosen for both winter and summer hardiness and, of course, annuals and perennials tolerant of extreme conditions.

WHERE TO GET SPECIAL HELP

Gardening advice is hard to come by in Mid-America. The state universities all have horticulture departments, but none have trial gardens and test plots, much less botanic gardens. The Missouri Botanic Garden offers considerable assistance; and for certain groups of plants assistance may be had from the Arie Den Boer Arboretum and the Ewing Park Lilac Arboretum, both in Des Moines, Iowa. County Horticultural Agents in the metropolitan areas have felt the paucity of reliable data from the state, and most keep careful tabs of good gardens in their areas and use them as a source of information to pass on to tyro gardeners. Still, your best bet is to move next door to a friendly, dedicated home gardener. Addresses of the Agricultural Extension Service for these states are:

Illinois: College of Agriculture, University of Illinois, Urbana, Illinois 61801.

Iowa: Iowa State University, Ames, Iowa 50010.

Kansas: Kansas State University, Manhattan, Kansas 66502.

Missouri: University of Missouri, Columbia, Missouri 65201.

Nebraska: College of Agriculture, University of Nebraska, Lincoln, Nebraska 68503.

PLACES AND PLANTINGS OF INTEREST

Illinois: LINCOLN PARK CONSERVATORY, Chicago.

Violet is the state flower; Bur Oak, the state tree.

Iowa: LILAC ARBORETUM, Ewing Park, Des Moines.

Wild Rose is the state flower; Oak, the state tree.

Kansas: INDIAN HILL ARBORETUM, Topeka.

Sunflower is the state flower; Cottonwood, the state tree.

Missouri: MISSOURI BOTANICAL GARDEN, St. Louis.

Hawthorn is the state flower; Dogwood, the state tree.

Nebraska: ARBOR LODGE STATE PARK ARBORETUM, Nebraska City.

Goldenrod is the state flower; American Elm, the state tree.

SOME FAVORITE GARDEN PLANTS OF MID-AMERICA WEST

LARGE TREES

COMMON NAME	BOTANICAL NAME	HEIGHT	ZONE
Ash, Green sterile cult.	*Fraxinus pennsylvanica lanceolata*	60'	4
Rose Hill, patented White Ash cult.	*F. americana* 'Rose Hill'	80'	4
Linden	*Tilia* species and cults.	40'-85'	4
Maidenhair-Tree	*Ginkgo biloba*	60'	4
Maple, Norway	*Acer platanoides* cults.	65'	4
Red	*rubrum* cults.	45'-75'	4
Oak, Pin	*Quercus palustris*	50'-100'	4
Scarlet	*coccinea*	50'-100'	4
Shingle	*imbricaria*	50'-100'	4
Shumard	*shumardii*	50'-100'	4
White	*alba*	50'-100'	4
Sweet Gum	*Liquidambar styraciflua*	to 140'	5
Sycamore	*Platanus* species and hybrids		
London Plane	x *hybrida*	to 120'	4
American Plane	*occidentalis*	to 150'	4
Oriental Plane	*orientalis*	to 100'	4

SMALL ORNAMENTAL TREES

COMMON NAME	BOTANICAL NAME	HEIGHT	ZONE
Crabapple, Flowering	*Malus* species and hybrids	15'-35'	4
Dogwood, Chinese	*Cornus kousa chinensis*	20'	5
Flowering	*florida* vars.	30'	5
Goldenrain-Tree	*Koelreuteria paniculata*	50'	5
Japanese Pagoda-Tree	*Sophora japonica*	65'	4
Magnolia	*Magnolia* species and hybrids	10'-45'	4
Oriental Maples	*Acer palmatum* and *A. japonicum* vars.	10'-35'	4
Redbud	*Cercis canadensis* vars.	30'	4

LARGE EVERGREENS (CONIFERS)

COMMON NAME	BOTANICAL NAME	HEIGHT	ZONE
Douglas-Fir	*Pseudotsuga menziesii*	75'	4
Fir, White and Balsam	*Abies concolor* and *A. balsamea*	40'	4
Hemlock, Canadian	*Tsuga canadensis*	35'	4
Pines, White, Scotch, Austrian	*Pinus strobus, sylvestris, nigra*	50'-85'	4
Spruce, Norway, Black Hills, White and Colorado selections	*Picea abies, glauca* var. *densata, glauca, pungens* cults.	40'-85'	4

LOW-GROWING EVERGREENS

COMMON NAME	BOTANICAL NAME	HEIGHT	ZONE
Juniper, in variety	*Juniperus*	1'-20'	4
Yews, in variety	*Taxus*	3'-15'	4

BROAD-LEAVED EVERGREENS

COMMON NAME	BOTANICAL NAME	HEIGHT	ZONE
Azalea	*Rhododendron* cults.	4'-8'	5
Bull Bay	*Magnolia grandiflora*	50'	5
Euonymus	*Euonymus* species and cults.	6'-10'	4-5
Holly, American	*Ilex opaca* cults.	12'-40'	5
Japanese	*crenata* cults.	1'-10'	5
Leucothoe	*Leucothoe fontanesiana*	5'	5-6
Pieris	*Pieris japonica*	6'	5-6
Rhododendron	*Rhododendron* species and cults.	4'-8'	4-5

DECIDUOUS FLOWERING SHRUBS

COMMON NAME	BOTANICAL NAME	HEIGHT	ZONE
Buddleia	*Buddleia* cults.	4'-8'	4
Caryopteris	*Caryopteris* cults.	2'-5'	4
Euonymus	*Euonymus* species	6'-12'	4
Flowering-Quince	*Chaenomeles* species and cults.	4'-8'	4
Forsythia	*Forsythia* cults.	3'-12'	4
Lilac	*Syringa* species and cults.	4'-10'	4
Spirea	*Spiraea* species and cults.	1'-10'	4
Viburnum	*Viburnum* species and vars.	5'-10'	4
Weigela	*Weigela* species and cults.	5'-8'	4

Note: Recently introduced selections of lilac, spirea, caryopteris and the like are available from local and mail-order sources; many of these shrubs are low-growing, topping out at five feet or less; ideal for city-lot gardening.

HEDGES

DECIDUOUS, SHEARED

COMMON NAME	BOTANICAL NAME	HEIGHT	ZONE
Barberry, Japanese	*Berberis thunbergii*	2'-5'	4
Mentor	x *mentorensis*	3'-5'	4
Buckthorn	*Rhamnus frangula* 'Tallhedge'	4'-8'	4
Honeysuckle, Zabel	*Lonicera korolkowii* 'Zabelii'	5'-8'	4
Privet, Amur	*Ligustrum amurense*	3'-6'	5
Lodense	*vulgare* 'Lodense'	1'-3'	4

DECIDUOUS, UNSHEARED

All of the above; also most flowering shrubs.

EVERGREEN, SHEARED OR ALLOWED TO GROW NATURALLY

COMMON NAME	BOTANICAL NAME	HEIGHT SHEARED	ZONE
Arborvitae, American	*Thuja occidentalis* vars.	4'-10'	4
Barberry, Julian	*Berberis julianae*	3'-6'	6
Boxwood, Korean	*Buxus microphylla koreana*	1'-3'	4
Euonymus	*Euonymus kiautschovicus*	1'-6'	5
Holly, Japanese	*Ilex crenata* vars. and cults.	1'-4'	4
Juniper, Hetz	*Juniperus chinensis* 'Hetzi'	2'-6'	4
Keteleer	'Keteleeri'	3'-12'	4
Pfitzer	'Pfitzeriana'	2'-8'	4
Yews	*Taxus* in variety	1'-10'	4

GROUND COVERS

COMMON NAME	BOTANICAL NAME	HEIGHT	ZONE
Bishop's-Goutweed	*Aegopodium podagraria*	1'	4
Bugleweed	*Ajuga* species and cults.	6"-15"	4
English Ivy	*Hedera helix* cults.	6"	4
Juniper, Andorra	*Juniperus horizontalis* 'Plumosa'	15"	4
Wilton	'Wiltonii'	12"	4
Lily-of-the-Valley	*Convallaria majalis*	10"	4
Wintercreeper	*Euonymus fortunei* cults.	6"-8"	4

LAWN GRASSES

COMMON NAME	BOTANICAL NAME	SEASON	CUT AT
Bent, select strains	*Agrostis maritima* cults.	Apr.-Nov.	3"
Bermuda, select strains	*Cynodon dactylon*	Apr.-Oct.	1"
Bluegrass, select strains	*Poa pratensis* cults.	Apr.-Nov.	3"
Zoysia, select strains	*Zoysia japonica* cults.	May-Sept.	1"

Note: Bluegrass, especially domestic or Canadian Kentucky bluegrass, is the common grass for the Middle West; hot-weather grasses, such as Zoysia and Bermuda, have a very short season and are invasive. Bentgrass is suitable for golf greens but difficult for home-owners, though it is used on manicured private properties.

VEGETABLES

Almost all vegetables found in mail-order catalogues will grow well in Mid-America, but timing is all-important. Cool-weather crops such as peas, spinach, lettuce and most of the cabbage family must be started early to mature before the onset of late June heat. Often second crops of these can be brought on during the prolonged fall growing season. Hot-weather crops such as peppers, sweet corn, tomatoes, eggplant, squash and lima beans grow to perfection in Mid-America.

PERENNIALS AND ANNUALS

Most perennial flowers hardy through Zone 4 perform well in the Mid-America region with a few notable exceptions. Some species and cultivars originating in or developed in northern, mild climates, such as England or the Pacific Northwest, do not tolerate the extreme summer heat of the Missouri basin. These include the tall sorts of delphiniums, lupines, eremurus and some campanulas, though examples of all of these can be found in the gardens of experts.

Long-lived perennials include anchusa, bergamot, bleeding-heart, coreopsis, gaillardia, daylily, plantain-lily, iris, lythrum and Michaelmas daisy.

Among annuals, sorts susceptible to heat damage, such as arctotis, lobelia, dimorpho-theca, tuberous begonias and bedding fuchsia, are to be avoided. Again, experts titillate these into growth and bloom, but they are not for the average garden.

Such hardy annuals as bachelor's-buttons, California poppies, larkspur and Shirley poppies may be sown in November in the Middle West; February sowing is also successful, but plants will be smaller. Winter-grown plants provide late-spring bloom with lasting quality. These may also be sown in spring, but plants are weaker and bloom in early summer.

NATIVE PLANTS USEFUL FOR THE GARDEN

Asclepias tuberosa
Aster species
Baptisia species
Cimicifuga racemosa
Eupatorium ageratoides
Geranium maculatum
Iris cristata
Liatris species
Mertensia virginica

Phlox divaricata
Polemonium reptans
Polygonatum biflorum
Smilacina species
Thalictrum species
Tradescantia species
Trillium species
Viola species

RECOMMENDED ROSES

by The May Seed and Nursery Company, Shenandoah, Iowa
(See also Chapter 26.)

HYBRID TEAS

Charlotte Armstrong, light red and deep pink
Countless Vandal, salmon and yellow
Forty-Niner, red with yellow reverse

Helen Traubel, pink to apricot
Mirandy, garnet red
Sutter's Gold, golden orange

GRANDIFLORAS

Aquarius, pink
Golden Girl, yellow

Queen Elizabeth, medium pink
Scarlet Knight, red

FLORIBUNDAS

Angel Face, lavender
Betty Prior, medium pink
Fashion, coral

Gene Boerner, pink
Independence, scarlet
Red Pinocchio, red

CLIMBERS

Blaze, Improved, medium red
Chrysler Imperial, dark red
Golden Showers, medium yellow

Joseph's Coat, red-yellow
Peace, yellow blend
White Dawn, white

Stunning 'Green Dragon' lilies, hot pink 'Morden' lythrum and purple cone-flowers make a summery border to this sunny Iowa garden. *(Gretchen Harsh-barger photo)*

39 NORTH CENTRAL

North Dakota, South Dakota, Northern Nebraska,
Minnesota, Northern Iowa, Wisconsin, Northern Michigan
Zones 3, 4, 5

by Dr. Edward R. Hasselkus, *Associate Professor,*
College of Agriculture and Life Sciences,
University of Wisconsin, Madison, Wisconsin

The North Central region is the meeting ground of the western prairie, the southern hardwood forest, the northern conifer-hardwood forest and the far northern spruce-fir or boreal forest. Temperature extremes range from a record of −20° to 104° in southwestern Michigan to a record of −60° to 112° for Montrail County, North Dakota. Plant-hardiness-zone designations are based on these *extremes* of temperature, not on *mean* temperature.

In the Great Lakes area annual precipitation averages about thirty inches in contrast to less than twenty inches in the western prairie area. The use of mulches to help retain soil moisture and watering of new tree and shrub plantings during the first one to three years is especially important in areas where rainfall is inadequate. Not only are the prairies drier, but strong winds, drifting snow and seasonal temperature extremes make gardening more of a challenge in the western part of the region. Experienced gardeners utilize shelterbelt plantings to temper the prevailing winds and to help direct snow accumulation where it will insulate tender plants.

Soils throughout the region are generally alkaline except for the areas where pines or spruce are common native trees in parts of Michigan, Wisconsin and Minnesota. In the extreme western part of the region soils may be more alkaline than is desirable for optimum growth of many kinds of plants. Under these conditions elements, such as iron, that are essential to plant growth may be present in the soil in an unavailable form. As a result of the lack of iron in the plant, the foliage becomes yellowish. Such unnatural lack of green color in the leaves is known as chlorosis. The addition of acidifying materials such as ammonium sulfate at one pound per one hundred square feet or powdered sulfur at one to three pounds per one hundred square feet of soil may correct iron chlorosis symptoms. If this treatment is not completely effective, the addition of iron in the form of a ferrous-sulfate solution or chelated iron may be required.

The most practical solution to the problem of iron chlorosis is to select lime-tolerant plants.

SOME PLANTS RESISTANT TO CHLOROSIS IN ALKALINE SOILS

Buckthorn	Lilac
Buffaloberry	Pea Shrub
Chokecherry	Rocky Mountain Juniper
Clematis	Russian-Olive
Fragrant Sumac	Shrubby Cinquefoil
Harison's Yellow Rose	Spruce

Atmospheric moisture is much higher in the Great Lakes area. Plant diseases favored by high-humidity conditions, such as juniper blight and apple scab, are consequently more serious in the eastern part of the region.

Plant-hardiness-zone designations suggested for this region are necessarily rather general. At a particular planting location consideration of cold hardiness may be less important than factors such as soil pH, soil-drainage conditions, available moisture, snow cover and wind protection.

Most of the well-known flowering perennials. biennials and annuals of the temperate climes will thrive in the North Central States. Exceptions are obviously those that require a long growing season, such as many of the composites from South Africa, Mexico and the southern United States. The same thing is true of certain mints, borages, legumes and others of Mediterranean origin that will grow in Zones 6 and 7. On the other hand, the herbaceous plants that enjoy cool summers often do especially well in the northerly and lakeside parts of these northern states—among them coralbells, delphinium, several campanulas, Siberian and Japanese iris, lythrum, forget-me-nots, peonies and summer phlox. Most of the modern hybrid lilies do well here; and there are two native lilies of special charm: *Lilium philadelphicum andinum* and *L. michiganense,* sometimes seen in gardens although not readily grown without knowledgeable care.

Several other native prairie plants, along with their improved varieties, including wild-indigo, gayfeather (*Liatris*) and the coneflowers, are reliable additions to the perennial gardens of the region.

WHERE TO GET SPECIAL HELP

Publications and assistance with gardening problems are available from county Cooperative Extension offices, which are usually located in the county courthouse. The State Land Grant Universities also have state extension horticultural specialists on their campuses. Questions and requests may be directed to the Agricultural Extension Service and these locations:

Iowa: Iowa State University, Ames, Iowa 50010.

Michigan: Michigan State University, East Lansing, Michigan 48823.

Minnesota: University of Minnesota, St. Paul, Minnesota 55101.

Nebraska: University of Nebraska, Lincoln, Nebraska 68503.

North Dakota: North Dakota State University, State University Station, Fargo, North Dakota 58103.

South Dakota: South Dakota State University, Brookings, South Dakota 57006.

Wisconsin: University of Wisconsin, Madison, Wisconsin 53706.

Arboreta, botanical gardens and the park departments of some larger municipalities offer gardening information services.

PLACES AND PLANTINGS OF INTEREST

Iowa: HORTICULTURAL DEPARTMENT TRIAL GARDENS, Iowa State University Campus, Ames.
WATER WORKS PARK, Des Moines.

Wild Rose is the state flower; Oak, the state tree.

Michigan: NICHOLS ARBORETUM AND MATTHAEI BOTANICAL GARDEN, University of Michigan Campus, Ann Arbor.
THE GARDENS OF CRANBROOK HOUSE, Bloomfield Hills.
FORD MOTOR COMPANY'S MICHIGAN ARBORETUM, Dearborn.
BEAL-GARFIELD BOTANICAL GARDEN AND MSU ARBORETUM, Campus of Michigan State University, East Lansing.
HIDDEN LAKE GARDENS, Tipton (near Dearborn).

Apple Blossom is the state flower; White Pine, the state tree.

Minnesota: MINNESOTA LANDSCAPE ARBORETUM, Chaska.
MUNICIPAL ROSE GARDEN AND LYNDALE GARDEN CENTER, Minneapolis.

Showy Lady's-Slipper is the state flower; Red Pine, the state tree.

Nebraska: ARBOR LODGE STATE PARK ARBORETUM, Nebraska City.

Goldenrod is the state flower; American Elm, the state tree.

North Dakota: INTERNATIONAL PEACE GARDEN, Dunseith.

Prairie Rose is the state flower; American Elm, the state tree.

South Dakota: HORTICULTURE DEPARTMENTAL GARDENS, South Dakota State University Campus, Brookings.

American Pasque-flower is the state flower; Black Hills Spruce, the state tree.

Wisconsin: UNIVERSITY OF WISCONSIN ARBORETUM, Madison.
ALFRED L. BOERNER BOTANICAL GARDEN, Hales Corners.
PAINE ART CENTER AND ARBORETUM, Oshkosh.

Wood Violet is the state flower; Sugar Maple, the state tree.

SOME FAVORITE GARDEN PLANTS OF THE NORTH CENTRAL REGION
(A "b" following the zone number indicates the more southerly part.)

LARGE TREES

COMMON NAME	BOTANICAL NAME	HEIGHT	ZONE
Ash, Green	*Fraxinus pennsylvanica lanceolata* 'Marshall's Seedless'	30'-60'	3
White	*americana*	50'-80'	3
Birch, Cutleaf Weeping	*Betula pendula* 'Gracilis'	40'-50'	3
Paper	*papyrifera*	40'-60'	3
River	*nigra*	40'-80'	3
Ginkgo	*Gingko biloba*	60'-80'	4b
Hackberry	*Celtis occidentalis*	30'-50'	3
Honey-Locust	*Gleditsia triacanthos* 'Imperial'	40'-60'	4
	'Skyline'	60'-80'	4
	'Sunburst'	60'	4b
Larch, European	*Larix decidua*	60'-80'	3
Linden, Greenspire	*Tilia cordata* 'Greenspire'	30'-50'	3
Redmond	x *euchlora* 'Redmond'	40'-70'	4
Maple, Norway	*Acer platanoides*	40'-50'	3b
Red	*rubrum*	50'-60'	3
Royal Red	'Royal Red'	40'-50'	4
Schwedler	'Schwedleri'	40'-50'	4
Sugar	*saccharum*	50'-80'	3
Oak, Pin	*Quercus palustris*	40'-75'	4
Red	*rubra (borealis)*	40'-75'	3
Poplar, Bolleana	*Populus alba* 'Pyramidalis'	40'-60'	3
Willow, Niobe Weeping	*Salix alba* 'Tristis'	45'-60'	3

SMALL FLOWERING TREES

COMMON NAME	BOTANICAL NAME	HEIGHT	ZONE
Chokecherry, Shubert	*Prunus virginiana* 'Shubert'	15'	3
Crabapple, Flowering	*Malus,* 'Red Splendor', 'Radiant',	8'-35'	3-4b
Hawthorn, Cockspur	'Beverly', 'Bob White'	20'-30'	4
Washington	*Crataegus crus-galli phaenopyrum (cordata)*	25'-30'	4
Lilac, Japanese Tree	*Syringa amurensis japonica*	20'-25'	3
Magnolia, Saucer	*Magnolia soulangiana*	25'	5
Maple, Amur	*Acer ginnala*	15'-20'	3
Mountain-Ash, European	*Sorbus aucuparia*	20'-40'	3
Korean	*alnifolia*	20'-25'	3
Plum	*Prunus cerasifera* 'Newport'	10'-15'	4
Russian-Olive	*Elaeagnus angustifolia*	15'-30'	3
Serviceberry, Apple	*Amelanchier* x *grandiflora*	20'-25'	3
Viburnum, Blackhaw	*Viburnum prunifolium*	10'-15'	3

357

LARGE EVERGREENS

COMMON NAME	BOTANICAL NAME	HEIGHT	ZONE
Arborvitae, American	*Thuja occidentalis*	15'-45'	3
Techny Dark Green	'Techny'	15'-45'	3
Douglas-Fir	*Pseudotsuga menziesii*	50'-70'	4
Fir, White	*Abies concolor*	70'	4
Hemlock, Canada	*Tsuga canadensis*	60'-75'	3
Pine, Austrian	*Pinus nigra*	40'-50'	4
Eastern White	*strobus*	60'-75'	3
Ponderosa	*ponderosa*	50'-60'	3
Red	*resinosa*	50'	3
Scotch	*sylvestris*	40'-50'	3
Spruce, Black Hills White	*Picea glauca* 'Densata'	20'	3
Blue Colorado	*pungens* 'Glauca'	60'-80'	3
Colorado	*pungens*	60'-80'	3
Norway	*abies*	60'-80'	3
Serbian	*omorika*	50'-70'	3b
Silver Colorado	*pungens* 'Argentea'	40'-60'	3
White	*glauca*	50'-60'	3

SMALL EVERGREENS

COMMON NAME	BOTANICAL NAME	HEIGHT	ZONE
Arborvitae, American, in variety	*Thuja occidentalis*	many	3
Juniper, in variety	*Juniperus*	1'-30'	3
Pine, Mugho	*Pinus mugo mughus*	5'	3
Spruce, Dwarf Alberta	*Picea glauca* 'Conica'	7'	3
Yew, in variety	*Taxus*	4'-15'	4

BROAD-LEAVED EVERGREENS

Success with broad-leaved evergreens depends largely on their planting location. Plants should not receive exposure to wind or direct winter sun. Planting sites on the north or east side of buildings or shelterbelts or beneath the branches of deciduous plants are possibilities. All of these plants may be grown in zones colder than those indicated where a generous winter snow cover is assured. Rhododendrons require an acid soil.

COMMON NAME	BOTANICAL NAME	HEIGHT	ZONE
Boxwood, Korean	*Buxus microphylla koreana*	3'-5'	4b
Daphne, Rose	*Daphne cneorum*	1'	3
Euonymus, Bigleaf Wintercreeper	*Euonymus fortunei vegetus*	2'	4b
Purpleleaf Wintercreeper	'Coloratus'	2'	4b
Ivy, Bulgarian	*Hedera helix* 'Bulgaria'	6"-8"	5
Oregon-Grape	*Mahonia aquifolium*	2'-3'	5
Pachistima	*Pachistima canbyi*	6"-12"	5
Rhododendron	*Rhododendron* 'PJM' Hybrids	2'-6'	4

SHRUBS

COMMON NAME	BOTANICAL NAME	HEIGHT	ZONE
Almond, Double Flowering	*Prunus triloba*	8'	3
Azalea, Mollis Hybrids	*Rhododendron* x *molle*	3'-5'	4b
Barberry, Japanese	*Berberis thunbergii*	2'-5'	3-4
Beauty Bush	*Kolkwitzia amabilis*	6'-8'	4b
Cherry, Manchu	*Prunus tomentosa*	6'-8'	3
Purpleleaf Sand	x *cistena*	5'-6'	3
Chokeberry, Black	*Aronia melanocarpa*	4'-6'	3
Brilliant	*arbutifolia* 'Brilliantissima'	8'	4b
Cinquefoil, in variety	*Potentilla*	2'-4'	3
Cotoneaster, Cranberry	*Cotoneaster, apiculata*	2'-3'	5
Many-flowered	*multiflora*	10'-12'	3b
Dogwood, Bailey	*Cornus baileyi*	8'-9'	3
Creamedge	*alba* 'Argenteo-marginata'	6'	3
Gray	*racemosa*	6'-10'	3
Euonymus, Winged	*Euonymus alatus*	8'-10'	3b
Dwarf Winged	'Compactus'	4'-5'	4b
Forsythia, in variety	*Forsythia*	2'-8'	4-5
Honeysuckle, Clavey's Dwarf	*Lonicera xylosteum* 'Claveyi'	3'-5'	3
Zabel	*tatarica* 'Zabelii'	8'-10'	3
Hydrangea	*Hydrangea arborescens* 'Annabelle'	3'-5'	3
Lilac, in variety	*Syringa*	5'-15'	3
Mock Orange, in variety	*Philadelphus*	2'-10'	3-5
Ninebark, Dwarf Common	*Physocarpus opulifolius* 'Nanus'	2'-4'	3
Pea Shrub, in variety	*Caragana*	3'-8'	3
Rose, Shrub, in variety	*Rosa rugosa*	3'-5'	3-5
Spirea	*Spiraea*	2'-6'	3-5
Sumac, Cutleaf Staghorn	*Rhus typhina* 'Laciniata'	10'-12'	3
Fragrant	*aromatica*	3'-5'	3
Viburnum, in variety	*Viburnum*	2'-20'	3-5
Weigela, in variety	*Weigela*	5'-7'	3-5

HEDGES AND WINDBREAKS

(H — hedge; W — windbreak; T — tall, 10' and up; M — medium, 5'-9'; L — low, 1'-4')

COMMON NAME	BOTANICAL NAME	HEIGHT	ZONE
Arborvitae, American, in variety	*Thuja occidentalis*	W,H,M-T	3
Barberry, Japanese, in variety	*Berberis thunbergii*	H,L	3-4
Boxwood, Korean	*Buxus microphylla koreana*	H,L	4b
Buckthorn, Tallhedge	*Rhamnus frangula* 'Columnaris'	W,H,T	4
Buffaloberry, Silver	*Shepherdia argentea*	W,T	3
Cotoneaster, Peking	*Cotoneaster acutifolia*	H,M	3
Currant, Alpine	*Ribes alpinum*	H,L	3
Elm, Siberian	*Ulmus pumila*	W,H,T	3b
Euonymus, Winged	*Euonymus, alatus*	H,M	3b
Hawthorn, Cockspur	*Crataegus crus-galli*	W,H,T	4
Washington	*phaenopyrum*	W,H,T	4
Honeysuckle, Clavey's Dwarf	*Lonicera xylosteum* 'Claveyi'	H,L	3
Zabel	*korolkowii* 'Zabelii	H,M	3
Junipers, in variety	*Juniperus*	W,H,T	3
Lilac, Chinese	*Syringa* x *chinensis*	W,H,M	3
Maple, Amur	*Acer ginnala*	H,T	3
Pea-Shrub, Siberian	*Caragana arborescens*	W,T	3
Pine, in variety	*Pinus*	W,T	3-4
Privet, in variety	*Ligustrum*	H,L-M	4
Rose, Shrub	*Rosa rugosa*	H,L-M	3-5
Russian-Olive	*Elaeagnus angustifolia*	W,T	3
Spruce, in variety	*Picea*	W,T	3
Willow, Dwarf Purple	*Salix purpurea* 'Gracilis'	H,L-M	3
Yew, Japanese	*Taxus cuspidata*	H,L-T	4

GROUND COVERS

COMMON NAME	BOTANICAL NAME	HEIGHT	ZONE
Candytuft	*Iberis sempervirens*	12"	3
Carpetbugle	*Ajuga reptans*	8"	3
Cotoneaster, Cranberry	*Cotoneaster apiculata*	18"-24"	5
Creeper, Virginia	*Parthenocissus quinquefolia*	1'-2'	3
Euonymus, Purpleleaf Wintercreeper	*Euonymus fortunei* 'Coloratus'	18"-24"	4-5
Fleece-Flower	*Polygonum reynoutria*	18"	4
Ginger, Wild	*Asarum canadense*	8"	3
Goutweed, Silveredge	*Aegopodium podagraria variegatum*	6"-14"	3
Honeysuckle, Everblooming	*Lonicera* x *heckrottii*	vine	4
Juniper, Blue Rug	*Juniperus horizontalis* 'Wiltonii'	8"	3
Compact Andorra	'Plumosa Compacta'	12"-18"	4b
Japgarden	*procumbens*	18"-24"	4
Sargent	*chinensis sargentii*	12"-18"	3
Tamarix Savin	*sabina tamariscifolia*	18"-24"	3
Lily-of-the-Valley	*Convallaria majalis*	8"	3
Pachistima	*Pachistima canbyi*	8"-12"	5
Pachysandra, Japanese	*Pachysandra terminalis*	8"	5
Periwinkle	*Vinca minor*	6"	4
Phlox, Moss	*Phlox subulata*	6"	3
Plantain-Lily, in variety	*Hosta*	18"-36"	3
Rockcress	*Arabis alpina*	4"-6"	3
Stonecrop, in variety	*Sedum*	2"-6"	3-5
Thyme	*Thymus serpyllum*	3"-6"	3
Violet, in variety	*Viola*	6"	3-5

LAWN GRASSES

COMMON NAME	BOTANICAL NAME
Bentgrass	*Agrostis*
Highland, Penncross, Seaside	
Bluegrass, Kentucky	*Poa pratensis*
Delta, Fylking, Kenblue, Merion, Newport, Park, Pennstar, Prato, South Dakota certified, Windsor	
Fescue, Red	*Festuca rubra*
Chewings, Illahee, Pennlawn, Ruby	
Redtop	*Agrostis alba*
Ryegrass, Italian	*Lolium multiflorum*
Perennial	*perenne*

NATIVE PLANTS USEFUL FOR THE GARDEN

COMMON NAME	BOTANICAL NAME	ZONE
Birch, Paper	*Betula papyrifera*	3
River	*nigra*	3
Bittersweet, American	*Celastrus scandens*	3
Bloodroot	*Sanguinaria canadensis*	3
Bluebells, Northern	*Mertensia paniculata*	3
Butterfly-Weed	*Asclepias tuberosa*	3
Columbine	*Aquilegia canadensis*	3
Crabapple, Prairie	*Malus ioensis*	3
Dogwood, Pagoda	*Cornus alternifolia*	3b
Ferns, Native	Species of *Asplenium, Athyrium, Dryopteris, Osmunda,* and others	3
Gayfeather	*Liatris,* in variety	3
Hepatica	*Hepatica americana*	4
Jack-in-the-Pulpit	*Arisaema triphyllum*	4
Lily, Canada or Meadow	*Lilium canadense*	3
Ninebark	*Physocarpus opulifolius*	3
Phlox, Blue	*Phlox divaricata*	3
Shadblow, Serviceberry	*Amelanchier canadensis, laevis*	3
Trillium	*Trillium grandiflorum*	4
Viburnum, Highbush Cranberry	*Viburnum trilobum*	3
Violet, in variety	*Viola*	3,4,5
Winterberry	*Ilex verticillata*	3

RECOMMENDED ROSES
by John Voight, of the Boerner Botanical Garden,
Hales Corners, Wisconsin
(See also Chapter 26.)

HYBRID TEAS

Charlotte Armstrong, light
red and deep pink
Chrysler Imperial, dark red
Eclipse, medium yellow
Fragrant Cloud, orange-red
Mister Lincoln, medium red

Pascali, white
Peace, yellow blend
Royal Highness, light pink
Tiffany, pink blend
Tropicana, orange-red

FLORIBUNDAS

Apricot Nectar, apricot blend
Betty Prior, medium pink
Europeana, dark red

Frensham, dark red
Iceberg, white
Roman Holiday, red blend

GRANDIFLORAS

Camelot, medium pink
Carrousel, dark red
John S. Armstrong, dark red

Queen Elizabeth, medium
pink
Montezuma, orange-red

CLIMBERS

Blaze, medium red
New Dawn, light pink

Paul's Scarlet, medium
red

SHRUB AND OLD-FASHIONED ROSES

Austrian Copper, scarlet-orange
Harison's Yellow, deep yellow

Paul Neyron, medium pink
Roger Lambelin, red blend

40 SOUTHWEST

New Mexico, Texas, Oklahoma
Zones 4, 5, 6, 7, 8, 9

by Dr. Fred B. Widmoyer, *Professor and Head,*
Department of Horticulture,
New Mexico State University, Las Cruces, New Mexico

The Southwest is well known for its diversity of climate, topography, soils and ecology. The lowest rainfall probably occurs in New Mexico, with an average of only a few inches; the highest is somewhat over sixty inches in the extreme southern part of Texas. Climatically, the area ranges from frost-free growing conditions to temperatures of 35° below zero. As a general observation, this area is not densely populated and is industrialized only in and around the larger centers of population.

The higher elevations in the western part of the region assure diurnal variations in temperature — sometimes as much as 40°. This is also the less humid area. From the central part of Texas eastward higher temperatures and higher humidity exist, increasing disease incidence in plants.

Most of the irrigated soils of the region are alkaline. These soils are lowest in organic matter and deficient in one or more plant nutrients. In the nonirrigated areas there are zones of limestone accumulations. This layer is deeper where higher rainfall prevails. Phosphate, iron, zinc, manganese and in some areas boron are common deficiencies. From central Texas and Oklahoma eastward soil reaction is neutral to acid, but variations are found locally.

The most serious problem of gardeners in all of this region may well be the extreme variation in temperature. In New Mexico too much light may be detrimental. In the Houston area smog may be damaging. It is wise to collect those plants known to be tolerant of these conditions.

Pests can be controlled by proper selection of plants or the safe use of other controls. Check with your county agent for specific troubles and remedies. Wherever possible, choose plants known to be resistant to the insects and diseases apt to exist in your locality. Root-knot nematodes frequently cause unthrifty plants. Disease control and proper soil management are two essential factors of good horticulture.

Gardening endeavors in this region vary. Some gardeners are most concerned over low maintenance. Others prefer to concentrate on growing only flowers or vegetables or fruit; and some to specialize in only one or two genera of plants. A potpourri gardener is probably the most common type among amateurs.

Among favorite perennials that thrive in the Southwest are alyssum, Shasta and Michaelmas daisy, gaillardia, columbine, Oriental poppy, phlox, santolina, iris and chrysanthemum. The best method of selecting perennials in any location is by visiting with your gardening neighbors. Many will be willing to share their successes with you. Geraniums perform best in semishade and frequently overwinter in the warmer regions. Santolina will be more attractive here if the plants are pruned. It will also usually regrow from the roots if the top is winter-killed. Delphinium does not do well in the warmer areas of these regions, though some success has been obtained by planting on the north side of a house.

The sensitive use of foliages makes this Texas garden noteworthy; mowing strips to edge the grass, soldier strips to contain the beds, and the use of ground cover under the tree all make for easy maintenance. (*Gretchen Harshbarger photo*)

WHERE TO GET SPECIAL HELP

Write to the County Agricultural Extension Service in your state.

New Mexico: New Mexico State University, Las Cruces, New Mexico 88001.

Oklahoma: Oklahoma State University, Stillwater, Oklahoma 74074.

Texas: Texas A & M University, Department of Plant and Soil Science, College Station, Texas 77843.

PLACES AND PLANTINGS OF INTEREST

New Mexico: BOTANICAL-ZOOLOGICAL GARDENS, Carlsbad. Desert flora and fauna.
HORTICULTURE FARM, New Mexico State University, Las Cruces. Bedding-plant display — best from mid-May to July 1.
CACTUS GARDEN, New Mexico State University, Las Cruces.
STAHMANN FARMS, four miles south of Las Cruces on State Highway 28. World's largest producing pecan orchard.

Yucca is the state flower; Pinon or Nut Pine, the state tree.

Oklahoma: HONOR HEIGHTS PARK, Fortieth Street and Park Boulevard, Muskogee. One hundred acres of beautiful gardens, lakes and picnic grounds. Azaleas in mid-April.
OKLAHOMA STATE UNIVERSITY, Stillwater. A well-landscaped and well-maintained campus.

Mistletoe is the state flower; Redbud, the state tree.

Texas: AMARILLO GARDEN CENTER, Amarillo, on U.S. 66. Noted for floral displays by garden clubs; special shows throughout the year.
TEXAS A & M UNIVERSITY EDUCATION AND RESEARCH CENTER, Bryan-College Station. Displays of interests to professional and amateur horticulturists.
DALLAS GARDEN CENTER. Tropical plants in natural surroundings.
EL PASO. Small rose garden open five days a week, also on Sundays at height of bloom (generally mid-April to mid-May).
FORT WORTH. Botanic Gardens adjoin Trinity Park, one mile west of town center. Lily pools and rose garden.
TEXAS TECH UNIVERSITY, Lubbock. Excellent landscapes, noted for garden trials of annuals and chrysanthemums.
TYLER. One of the rose capitals of the world; Texas Rose Festival held here every October. Municipal rose garden on West Front Street.

Blue Bonnet is the state flower; Pecan, the state tree.

SOME FAVORITE GARDEN PLANTS OF THE SOUTHWEST
(An "a" following the zone number indicates northern areas; "b" indicates southern areas.)

LARGE TREES

COMMON NAME	BOTANICAL NAME	HEIGHT	ZONE
American Plane	*Platanus occidentalis*	30'-60'	**6a**
Ash, Arizona	*Fraxinus velutina*	40'-60'	**6a**
Honey-Locust	*Gleditsia triacanthos* 'Inermis', 'Rubylace', 'Moraine', 'Shademaster', 'Skyline', 'Sunburst'	35'-70'	**4b**
Mulberry, White	*Morus alba,* varieties: 'Fruitless', 'Kingan', 'Stribling', 'Mapleleaf'	50'-60'	**4b**
Pecan	*Carya illinoensis* (*C. pecan*)	40'-70'	**5**
	'Western', 'Wichita', 'San Saba Improved'		**6b**
	'Success', 'Stuart', 'Schley'		**7b**
Sweet Gum	*Liquidambar styraciflua*	60'-80'	**5b**
Willow, Globe	*Salix matsudana* 'Navajo'	30'-50'	**4b**

SMALL FLOWERING TREES

COMMON NAME	BOTANICAL NAME	HEIGHT	ZONE
Ash, Modesto	*Fraxinus velutina glabra*	30'-40'	**6a**
Crabapple, Flowering, in variety	*Malus*	10'-40'	**4b**
Goldenrain-Tree	*Koelreuteria paniculata*	20'-25'	**4b**
Japanese Pagoda-Tree	*Sophora japonica*	25'-35'	**4b**
Jujube	*Zizyphus jujuba*	20'-30'	**7b**
Mimosa (Silktree)	*Albizia julibrissin*	20'-40'	**6b**
Pear, Bradford	*Pyrus calleryana* 'Bradford'	20'-30'	**4b**
Redbud, American	*Cercis canadensis*	20'-25'	**4b**
Russian-Olive	*Elaeagnus angustifolia*	10'-25'	**4b**

LARGE EVERGREENS

COMMON NAME	BOTANICAL NAME	HEIGHT	ZONE
Cedar, Atlas	*Cedrus atlantica*	25'-50'	**6b**
Deodar	*deodara*	50'-60'	**6b**
Cypress, Arizona	*Cupressus arizonica*	30'-45'	**7a**
Fan Palm, Mexican	*Washingtonia robusta*	25'-60'	**8a**
Pine, Aleppo	*Pinus halepensis*	40'-50'	**7b**
Austrian	*nigra*	25'-40'	**4a**
Western Yellow	*ponderosa*	50'-75'	**4b**

SMALL EVERGREENS

COMMON NAME	BOTANICAL NAME	HEIGHT	ZONE
Arborvitae	*Thuja occidentalis*	1'-25'	**4b**
Juniper in variety	*Juniperus*	various	**4b**

BROAD-LEAVED EVERGREENS

COMMON NAME	BOTANICAL NAME	HEIGHT	ZONE
Boxwood, Common	*Buxus sempervirens*	3'-10'	**5a**
Euonymus, Evergreen	*Euonymus japonicus*	8'-10'	**7b**
Firethorn	*Pyracantha coccinea*	8'-10'	**5b**
Holly, Chinese	*Ilex cornuta*	8'-10'	**6b**
Yaupon	*vomitoria*	15'-20'	**5b**
Nandina	*Nandina domestica*	3'-17'	**7b**
Oregon-Grape	*Mahonia aquifolium*	2'-6'	**5a**
Photinia	*Photinia serrulata*	5'-20'	**6b**

SHRUBS

COMMON NAME	BOTANICAL NAME	HEIGHT	ZONE
Barberry	*Berberis thunbergii*	4'-6'	**4b**
Chaste-Tree	*Vitex agnus-castus*	6'-25'	**6b**
Cotoneaster, in variety	*Cotoneaster*	2'-10'	**5a**
Crape-Myrtle	*Lagerstroemia indica*	8'-10'	**7b**
Flowering-Quince	*Chaenomeles japonica*	3'-6'	**4b**
Honeysuckle, Bush	*Lonicera tatarica*	6'-10'	**4b**
Jasmine, Winter	*Jasminum nudiflorum*	2'-4'	**6a**
Oleander	*Nerium oleander*	to 12'	**7b**
Pea-Shrub, Siberian	*Caragana arborescens*	5'-10'	**4b**
Pomegranate	*Punica granatum*	8'-10'	**7a**
Rose-of-Sharon	*Hibiscus syriacus*	5'-8'	**5a**
Smoketree	*Cotinus coggygria*	12'-15'	**5a**

HEDGES AND WINDBREAKS
(H — hedge; W — windbreak; T — tall, 10' and up; M — medium, 5'-9'; L — low, 1'-4')

COMMON NAME	BOTANICAL NAME	HEIGHT AND USE	ZONE
Arborvitae	*Thuja occidentalis*	W,H,T	**4b**
Boxwood	*Buxus sempervirens*	H,L	**5a**
Firethorn	*Pyracantha coccinea*	H,M	**5b**
Juniper, in variety	*Juniperus*	W,H,T	**4b**
Privet, Amur	*Ligustrum amurense*	H,M	**4b**
Rose	*Rosa rugosa*	H,L	**4b**
Russian-Olive	*Elaeagnus angustifolia*	W,H,T	**4b**

GROUND COVERS

COMMON NAME	BOTANICAL NAME	HEIGHT	ZONE
Cotoneaster, in variety	*Cotoneaster*	1'-6'	**5a**
English Ivy, in variety	*Hedera helix*	low	**5b**
Juniper, Blue Rug	*Juniperus horizontalis* 'Wiltonii'	4"	**4b**
Rosemary	*Rosmarinus officinalis*	2'-5'	**6b**
Stonecrop, English	*Sedum anglicum*	2"-4"	**4b**
	lineare	4"	**4b**
Wintercreeper	*Euonymus fortunei*	low	**5b**

LAWN GRASSES

COMMON NAME	BOTANICAL NAME
Bentgrass, Creeping	*Agrostis palustris*
Bermuda Grass	*Cynodon dactylon*
Bluegrass, Kentucky	*Poa pratensis*
Fescue	*Festuca rubra*
St. Augustine Grass	*Stenotaphrum secundatum*
Zoysia (Manila Grass)	*Zoysia matrella*

NATIVE PLANTS USEFUL FOR THE GARDEN

COMMON NAME	BOTANICAL NAME
Algerita	*Mahonia haematocarpa*
Apache Plume	*Fallugia paradoxa*
Big Sagebrush	*Artemisia tridentata*
Blazing Star or Gayfeather	*Liatris punctata*
Cactus	Various genera and species
Chamiza or Four-winged Saltbush	*Atriplex canescens*
Cliff-Rose	*Cowania mexicana*
Creosotebush	*Larrea divaricata*
Desert-Willow	*Chilopsis linearis*
Greasewood or Chico	*Sarcobatus vermiculatus*
Mountain-Mahogany	*Cercocarpus* species
Ocotillo or Candlewood	*Fouquieria splendens*
Shrubby Cinquefoil	*Potentilla fruticosa*
Sotol	*Dasylirion* species
Squawbrush or Skunkbrush	*Rhus trilobata*
Verbena	*Verbena wrightii*

RECOMMENDED ROSES
(See also Chapter 26.)

HYBRID TEAS

Chicago Peace, yellow to pink   Matterhorn, white
Eclipse, medium yellow   Mister Lincoln, medium red
First Prize, pink   Mrs. Pierre S. DuPont, yellow
Fragrant Cloud, orange-red   Tropicana, orange-red

FLORIBUNDAS

Apricot Nectar, apricot blend   Roman Holiday, red blend
Europeana, dark red   Saratoga, white
Gene Boerner, pink   Spartan, orange-red

GRANDIFLORAS

Camelot, medium pink   Queen Elizabeth, medium
Carrousel, dark red   pink

CLIMBERS

Blaze, medium red   Paul's Scarlet, medium red

SHRUB AND OLD-FASHIONED ROSES

Frau Karl Druschki, white   Sea Foam, white

41 MOUNTAIN STATES

Idaho, Montana, Wyoming, Colorado, Utah
Zones 3, 4, 5, 6, 7

by Dr. F. L. Steve O'Rourke, *Associate Professor of
Horticulture, Colorado State University,
Fort Collins, Colorado*

The Mountain States are so diversified in soils, climate, topography, altitude and type of vegetation that any statement made for any one locality might not be true even a few miles distant. The only region somewhat homogeneous in topography and vegetation is that east of the continental divide, which bisects Montana, Wyoming and Colorado in a northwest-southeastward direction.

High Plains. This eastward area ranges from less than three thousand to more than six thousand feet in elevation, but the slopes are rather gentle and incline mostly to the east. It has a typical continental climate, which is characterized by hot summers, cold winters, rough winds, low humidity and meager rainfall. It is known as short-grass country and is excellent for grazing. But woody plants are sparse or nonexistent except for the hardy cottonwoods, willows and box-elders in the water courses.

In this region of sparse snowfall and strong drying winds landscape plants often suffer from drought in winter. Both the aboveground and the belowground parts are affected. Windbreaks and winter watering, while not absolutely essential, are excellent practices to assure survival and vigor.

The physical texture of the soils of the High Plains varies widely. Many tend toward compact clay and have an abundance of calcium and potash salts. Because of the high alkalinity, phosphorus is often unavailable. The addition of nitrogen is generally needed for satisfactory plant growth. The organic-matter content is usually low, and garden soils are greatly improved by the addition of humus either tilled into the soil or used as a mulch.

The sculptured use of well-laid rock, softened with evergreens and backed with a hand-split fence, is typical of the best Colorado gardens. Note also the fine use of pebbles in the paved terrace. *(Gretchen Harshbarger photo)*

Landscape and garden plants thrive best when planted in the very early spring and watered at regular intervals throughout the year. The soil should be allowed to drain well between waterings, and care should be taken not to overwater plants in compact soil during the growing season.

In spite of the harsh conditions, many attractive plants thrive in the gardens and grounds of the High Plains. Those listed for the U.S.D.A. Hardiness Zone of the section involved — 3, 4 or 5 — should be chosen. At the higher elevations and particularly in the areas close to the mountains there are hazards due to late-spring and early-fall storms and freezes. It is always advisable to check with local plantsmen before making extensive plantings.

Mountain Country. Westward from the continental divide the land is usually broken into valleys and canyons, which may slope in any direction. Here and there are relatively level "parks" and "mesas," usually at high elevations, and long stretches of desert in the more southern regions, but overall the long deep valleys predominate.

In this region *the elevation and the degree and direction of slope determine the type of vegetation.* A cool moist north slope may bear an excellent stand of native spruce, and its counterpart sloping to the south or west may be given over to pines or junipers. There are often microclimatic areas within the valleys which are well sheltered from dry northern winds and have abundant soil moisture. Here, some plants listed for hardiness zones well to the south may be grown in perfect safety, even a few from Zone 7, as the immediate lists show.

PLANTS FOR SHELTERED, MOIST VALLEYS

DECIDUOUS TREES

COMMON NAME	BOTANICAL NAME	ZONE
Ash, European	Fraxinus excelsior	4
Beech, European	Fagus sylvatica	4
Cherry, Japanese	Prunus serrulata	5
Dogwood, Flowering	Cornus florida	4
Empress-Tree	Pauiownia tomentosa	5
Ginkgo	Ginkgo biloba	4
Magnolia, Saucer	Magnolia soulangiana	5
Maple, Japanese	Acer palmatum	5
Mulberry, White	Morus alba	4
Pear, Callery	Pyrus calleryana	5
Plane, London	Platanus x hybrida	5
Redbud	Cercis canadensis	4
Snowbell, Japanese	Styrax japonica	5
Sweet Gum	Liquidambar styraciflua	4
Waltnut, Persian	Juglans regia	5
Yellow-Wood	Cladrastis lutea	4

DECIDUOUS SHRUBS

COMMON NAME	BOTANICAL NAME	ZONE
Abelia, Glossy	Abelia grandiflora	5
Butterfly Bush	Buddleia davidii	5
Crape-Myrtle	Lagerstroemia indica	7
Firethorn, Scarlet	Pyracantha coccinea	6
Magnolia, Star	Magnolia stellata	5

SMALL NEEDLE-LEAVED EVERGREENS

COMMON NAME	BOTANICAL NAME	ZONE
Arborvitae, American	Thuja occidentalis	3
Oriental	orientalis	6
Crytomeria	Crytomeria japonica	6
False-Cypress, Hinoki	Chamaecyparis obtusa	3
Lawson	lawsoniana	5

BROAD-LEAVED EVERGREENS

COMMON NAME	BOTANICAL NAME	ZONE
Boxwood, Common	Buxus sempervirens	6
Littleleaf	microphylla	5
Holly, Chinese	Ilex cornuta	7
Japanese	crenata	6
Nandina	Nandina domestica	7
Osmanthus, Holly	Osmanthus heterophyllus	6
Photinia, Chinese	Photinia serrulata	7
Viburnum, Leatherleaf	Viburnum rhytidophyllum	5

Almost all areas in the Mountain States have an abundance of sunshine. Not only are there more sunny days in the year than in many areas, but the high altitudes allow a much greater light intensity than in lower regions. Therefore junipers and other sun-loving plants often grow well on the north side of buildings, where they receive sufficient reflected light to meet their requirements.

The higher elevations receive a greater amount of snow and rainfall, and since temperatures are cooler, the moisture stress is less than in the valleys and plains. These areas are particularly adapted to evergreens and perennials. Though the growing season is short, the light intensity during the long days of spring and summer stimulates plant growth and flowering. During the winter the deep snow-cover protects the roots and lower parts of the plants from desiccation and deep freezing. It is therefore often possible to grow certain species at high elevations which would not survive at lower altitudes.

SOME HIGH-ALTITUDE PLANTS

COMMON NAME	BOTANICAL NAME
Cherry, Pin	*Prunus pensylvanica*
Currant, Alpine	*Ribes alpinum*
Wax	*cereum*
Elder, Red-berried	*Sambucus microbotrys*
Hazel, Beaked	*Corylus cornuta*
Kinnikinnick (Bearberry)	*Arctostaphyllos uva-ursi*
Maple, Rocky Mountain	*Acer glabrum*
Mountain-Mahogany	*Cercocarpus montanus*
Ninebark	*Physocarpus opulifolius*
Oregon-Grape	*Mahonia aquifolium*
Creeping	*repens*
Raspberry, Rocky Mountain	*Rubus deliciosus*
Serviceberry (Saskatoon)	*Amelanchier alnifolia*
Willow, Arctic	*Salix purpurea*

Many of the native plants of the mountain country are attractive and have a high potential for landscape use but are often not obtainable from either local or mail-order nurseries. These plants seldom transplant well if dug from their habitat. They should be nursery-grown from seeds, cuttings or grafts in order to develop a satisfactory root system that will enable them to survive and flourish after transplanting. When these species become better known and their desirable features more widely appreciated, it is probable that nurserymen will add them to their production list. At the present time the nursery of Western Evergreens, Inc., 14201 West Forty-fourth Avenue, Route 1, Golden, Colorado 80401, is growing native plants from seed collected in the mountains and testing them for climatic response on the plains just east of the foothills. They do some shipping.

Much of the joy and enthusiasm derived from gardening in the Mountain States is due both to the diversity of the terrain and to the unpredictability of the climate. After a long, warm, sunny winter a late-spring freeze may shatter the hopes not only of bloom but of the very life of the plant itself. A heavy snowfall in early fall may break many foliage-laden branches and wreck an impending spectacle of autumn color. However, compensating factors include the excellent growth and color of many tender plants in microclimatic surroundings and the response of the usual run of garden plants under the clear blue skies to a little tender loving care, such as the right amount of water throughout the year, soil aeration, addition of humus-building materials and a little fertilizer lightly applied when needed.

WHERE TO GET SPECIAL HELP

The local County Agricultural Extension Agent in each county seat will be glad to advise on all gardening problems and to distribute both federal and state publications. You may also call or write to the State Agricultural Extension Service of each state.

Colorado: Colorado State University, Fort Collins, Colorado 80521.

Idaho: University of Idaho, Moscow, Idaho 83843.

Montana: Montana State University, Bozeman, Montana 59715.

Utah: Utah State University, Logan, Utah 84321.

Wyoming: University of Wyoming, Laramie, Wyoming 82076.

PLACES AND PLANTINGS OF INTEREST

Colorado: THE GLENMORE ARBORETUM, Buffalo Creek.
DENVER BOTANIC GARDENS, 909 York Street, Denver.

Colorado Columbine is the state flower; Blue Spruce, the state tree.

Idaho: THE CHARLES HOUSTON SHATTUCK ARBORETUM, College of Forestry, University of Idaho, Moscow.

Lewis Mock-Orange is the state flower; Western White Pine, the state tree.

Montana: THOMPSON PARK, Butte.

Bitterroot is the state flower; Ponderosa Pine, the state tree.

Utah: BOTANICAL GARDEN, Brigham Young University, Provo.
CITY AND COUNTY PARK, Ogden.
UNIVERSITY OF UTAH ARBORETUM, Salt Lake City.

Sego-Lily is the state flower; Blue Spruce, the state tree.

Wyoming: U.S.D.A. HORTICULTURAL FIELD STATION, Cheyenne.

Wyoming Paintbrush is the state flower; Balsam Poplar, the state tree.

SOME FAVORITE GARDEN PLANTS OF THE MOUNTAIN STATES
(M following the name indicates that the species is marginal in the designated
zone but may survive at lower elevations and in protected sites.)

LARGE TREES

COMMON NAME	BOTANICAL NAME	HEIGHT	ZONE
Alder, Mountain	*Alnus tenuifolia*	35'	3
Ash, Green	*Fraxinus pennsylvanica lanceolata*		
	'Marshall's Seedless'	50'	3
Aspen, Trembling	*Populus tremuloides*	80'	3
Birch, European	*Betula pendula*	45'	3
Cottonwood, Siouxland	*Populus sargentii* 'Siouxland'	120'	3
Hackberry	*Celtis occidentalis*	60'	3
Honey-Locust	*Gleditsia triacanthos*	80'	4
Linden, American	*Tilia americana*	70'	3
Maple, Norway	*Acer platanoides*	70'	3
Schwedler	'Schwedleri'	80'	3
Silver	*saccharinum*	80'	3
Oak, Bur	*Quercus macrocarpa*	90'	3
Walnut, Black	*Juglans nigra*	100'	4
Willow, Laurel	*Salix pentandra*	50'	4

SMALL FLOWERING TREES

COMMON NAME	BOTANICAL NAME	HEIGHT	ZONE
Buckeye, Ohio	*Aesculus glabra*	30'	3
Cherry, Choke	*Prunus virginiana melanocarpa*	25'	3
European Bird	*padus*	40'	3
Shubert Choke	*virginiana* 'Shubertii'	25'	3
Crabapple	*Malus* species and hybrids	15'-30'	4
Goldenchain-Tree (M)	*Laburnum* x *watereri*	25'	5
Goldenrain-Tree (M)	*Koelreuteria paniculata*	30'	5
Hawthorn, Cockspur	*Crataegus crus-galli*	25'	4
Downy	*mollis*	25'	4
Lilac, Japanese Tree	*Syringa amurensis japonica*	30'	4
Mountain-Ash	*Sorbus aucuparia*	40'	3
Plum, American	*Prunus americana*	15'	3
Newport	x 'Newport'	20'	3
Russian-Olive	*Elaeagnus angustifolia*	20'	3
Serviceberry (Saskatoon)	*Amelanchier alnifolia*	15'	3
Smoketree, American	*Cotinus obovatus*	30'	5

LARGE EVERGREENS

COMMON NAME	BOTANICAL NAME	HEIGHT	ZONE
Douglas-Fir	*Pseudotsuga menziesii*	150'	4
Fir, Alpine	*Abies lasiocarpa*	90'	3
White	*concolor*	100'	4
Juniper, Rocky Mountain selected clones	*Juniperus scopulorum*	35'	5
Pine, Austrian	*Pinus nigra*	80'	4
Bristlecone	*aristata*	60'	5
Pinyon	*cembroides* 'Edulis'	50'	5
Ponderosa	*ponderosa*	80'	5
Spruce, Black Hills	*Picea glauca* 'Densata'	40'	3
Colorado	*pungens*	100'	3
Engelmann	*engelmannii*	100'	3
White	*glauca*	80'	3

SMALL EVERGREENS

COMMON NAME	BOTANICAL NAME	HEIGHT	ZONE
Juniper, Chinese, in variety	*Juniperus chinensis*	1'	4
Common, in variety	*communis*	2'	3
Creeping, in variety	*horizontalis*	1'	3
Savin, in variety	*sabina*	4'	4
Pine, Mugho	*Pinus mugo mughus*	3'	3
Spruce, Alberta	*Picea glauca* 'Conica'	12'	3

BROAD-LEAVED EVERGREENS

COMMON NAME	BOTANICAL NAME	HEIGHT	ZONE
Boxwood, Korean (M)	*Buxus microphylla koreana*	2'	5
Euonymus (M)	*Euonymus fortunei* 'Coloratus'	1'	5
	radicans	1'	5
Mountain-Mahogany	*Cercocarpus ledifolius*	5'	3
Oregon-Grape	*Mahonia aquifolium*	3'	5

DECIDUOUS SHRUBS

COMMON NAME	BOTANICAL NAME	HEIGHT	ZONE
Almond, Dwarf Flowering	*Prunus glandulosa*	4'	4
Bluebeard (Blue Mist-Flower)	*Caryopteris incana*	4'	5
Burning Bush	*Euonymus alatus*	9'	3
Dwarf	'Compactus'	4'	3
Cherry, Manchu	*Prunus tomentosa*	8'	3
Purpleleaf Sand	x *cistena*	7'	3
Cinquefoil, Bush	*Potentilla fruticosa*	3'	3
Cotoneaster, Cranberry	*Cotoneaster apiculata*	3'	4
Creeping	*adpressa*	1'	4
Hedge	*acutifolia*	9'	4
Large-flowering	*multiflora calocarpa*	8'	5
Rockspray	*horizontalis*	3'	4
Currant, Alpine	*Ribes alpinum*	5'	3
Clove	*odoratum*	6'	4
Wax	*cereum*	4'	4
Dogwood, Redtwig	*Cornus stolonifera coloradensis*	6'	3
European Cranberry-Bush	*Viburnum opulus*	12'	3
Honeysuckle, Tatarian	*Lonicera tatarica*	9'	3
Hydrangea, Hills-of-Snow	*Hydrangea arborescens* 'Grandiflora'	3'	4
Lilac, Common	*Syringa vulgaris*	15'	3
Late	*villosa*	9'	3
Mock Orange, Sweet	*Philadelphus coronarius*	8'	4
Pea-Shrub, Siberian	*Caragana arborescens*	15'	3
Salt-Tree	*Halimodendron halodendron*	6'	3
Spirea, Bridalwreath	*Spiraea* x *vanhouttei*	6'	4
Squawbush	*Rhus trilobata*	3'	3
Sumac, Staghorn	*typhina*	20'	3
Wayfaring-Tree	*Viburnum lantana*	12'	3
Weigela, Vanicek	*Weigela florida* 'Vanicek'	8'	5

HEDGES AND WINDBREAKS
(H — hedge; W — windbreak; T — tall, 10' and up; M — medium, 5'-9'; L — low, 1'-4')

COMMON NAME	BOTANICAL NAME	HEIGHT AND USE	ZONE
Buffaloberry	*Shepherdia argentea*	W,H,T	3
Cotoneaster, Hedge	*Cotoneaster acutifolia*	H,M	4
Currant, Alpine	*Ribes alpinum*	H,L	3
Wax	*cereum*	H,M	4
Elaeagnus, Autumn	*Elaeagnus umbellata*	W,H,M	3
Honeysuckle, Tatarian	*Lonicera tatarica*	W,H,M	3
Juniper, Pfitzer	*Juniperus chinensis* 'Pfitzeriana'	H,M	4
Rocky Mountain	*scopulorum*	W,T	3
Lilac, Common	*Syringa vulgaris*	W,H,T	3
Late	*villosa*	W,H,M	3
Maple, Amur	*Acer ginnala*	W,H,T	3
Rocky Mountain	*glabrum*	H,M	3
Mock Orange, Sweet	*Philadelphus coronarius*	W,H,T	4
Pea-Shrub, Siberian	*Caragana arborescens*	W,H,T	3
Pine, Mugho	*Pinus mugo mughus*	H,L	4
Pinyon	*cembroides* 'Edulis'	W,H,T	4
Western Yellow	*ponderosa*	W,T	4
Poplar, Bolleana	*Populus alba* 'Bolleana'	W,T	4
Privet, Amur	*Ligustrum amurensis*	H,M	5
Sagebrush	*Artemisia tridentata*	W,H,M	5
Spirea, Vanhouttei	*Spiraea* x *vanhouttei*	H,M	4
Spruce, Colorado	*Picea pungens*	W,T	4
Wayfaring-Tree	*Viburnum lantana*	H,M	3
Willow, Laurel	*Salix pentandra*	W,T	3

GROUND COVERS

COMMON NAME	BOTANICAL NAME	HEIGHT	ZONE
Bishop's-Weed	*Aegopodium podagraria*	1'	3
Bugleweed	*Ajuga reptans*	4"	4
Coralberry	*Symphoricarpos orbiculatus*	3'	3
Cotoneaster, Bearberry (M)	*Cotoneaster dammeri*	1'	5
Euonymus	*Euonymus fortunei* 'Coloratus'	1'	5
	radicans	1'	5
	vegetus	2'	5
Juniper, Chinese	*Juniperus chinensis sargentii*	1'	4
Common	*communis* 'Compressa'	2'	3
Creeping	*horizontalis* 'Andorra'	1'	3
Tamarix Savin	*sabina tamariscifolia*	2'	4
Lily-of-the-Valley	*Convallaria majalis*	10"	4
Periwinkle (Myrtle)	*Vinca minor*	8"	4
Sedum	*Sedum* species	2"	4-6
Strawberry, Mountain	*Fragaria ovalis*	2"	5
Thyme, Creeping	*Thymus serpyllum*	1"	3

LAWN GRASSES

COMMON NAME	BOTANICAL NAME	ZONE
Bentgrass	*Agrostis palustris*	4,5
Bluegrass, Kentucky	*Poa pratensis*	4,5
also Merion, Windsor	(Straight Kentucky needs less maintenance.)	
Fescue, Red	*Festuca rubra*	4,5

DRYLAND TURF GRASSES

COMMON NAME	BOTANICAL NAME	ZONE
Bermuda Grass	*Cynodon dactylon*	5
Buffalo Grass	*Buchloe dactyloides*	3
Crested Wheatgrass	*Agropyron cristatum*	3

NATIVE PLANTS USEFUL FOR THE GARDEN

Alder, Mountain	*Alnus tenuifolia*	Maple, Rocky Mountain	*Acer glabrum*
Aspen, Quaking	*Populus tremuloides*	Mountain-Mahogany	*Cercocarpus montanus*
Birch, Water	*Betula fontinalis*	Pasque-Flower	*Anemone patens*
Cherry, Choke	*Prunus virginiana melanocarpa*	Pine, Bristlecone	*Pinus aristata*
Cinquefoil, Bush	*Potentilla fruticosa*	Pinyon	*cembroides* 'Edulis'
Columbine, Blue	*Aquilegia coerulea*	Western Yellow	*ponderosa*
Currant, Golden	*Ribes aureum*	Rabbitbrush	*Chrysothamnus nauseosus*
Elder	*Sambucus pubens*	Sagebrush	*Artemisia tridentata*
Hawthorn, Red-stemmed	*Crataegus erythropoda*	Saskatoon (Shadbush)	*Amelanchier alnifolia*
Juniper, Common	*Juniperus communis*	Spruce, Colorado	*Picea pungens*
Rocky Mountain	*scopulorum*	Engelmann	*engelmannii*
Kinnikinnick	*Arctostaphylos uva-ursi*	Squawbush	*Rhus trilobata*
Mahonia, Creeping	*Mahonia repens*	Thimbleberry	*Rubus parviflorus*

RECOMMENDED ROSES
(See also Chapter 26.)

Hybrid teas, polyanthas, floribundas, grandifloras and rugosas that do well in the North Central States are generally reliable here, given winter protection in the colder localities. Climbers are always vulnerable, but we have found these varieties relatively hardy: Blaze (Improved), Coral Dawn, Don Juan, Joseph's Coat, New Dawn, Paul's Scarlet, and Royal Gold.

Of Shrub and old-fashioned roses Austrian Copper, Harison's Yellow, Paul Neyron and Roger Lambelin are usually good; of the grandifloras, Carrousel, Camelot, John S. Armstrong.

42 PACIFIC NORTHWEST

Coastal Washington, Coastal Oregon, Northern California
Zones 5, 6, 7, 8, 9, 10

by Joseph A. Witt, *Associate Director,*
University of Washington Arboretum,
Seattle, Washington

Because of the relatively mild climate, the fertile soils and at least to the present time the lack of serious air pollution except in a very few urban areas, the portions of the Pacific Coast west of the Cascade and Sierra ranges have gained the reputation of being an easy place in which to garden, and to a large extent this is true. This area, which includes Zone 7 in the north and east through Zones 8 and 9 to Zone 10 along the California coast and in the San Francisco Bay region, has weather that is generally maritime.

The growing season varies from an average of 356 frost-free days in San Francisco to 307 in Sacramento, 205 in Eugene, 263 in Portland and 255 in the Seattle-Tacoma area. Rainfall ranges from heavy along the northwest coast, where it may reach over 120 inches a year, to moderate in the inland valleys and light in the south. San Francisco has an average annual precipitation of 20.5 inches, and Seattle and Portland have nearly double that amount. One feature that the entire region has in common is its rainfall distribution pattern. Most precipitation falls in the winter months, November through February, accounting for more than half of the year's total, whereas June, July and August receive only minimal amounts. This wet-winter, dry-summer precipitation pattern influences gardening activities. Summer irrigation is a must except in gardens featuring native plant materials.

Northern California is rarely plagued with one problem faced by its more northerly neighbors — periodically recurring cold spells that can wreak havoc with tender plants. These cold waves, which occur about every five to ten years, can drop winter temperatures to near zero and are usually accompanied by a dry north wind that desiccates broad-leaved evergreens. Despite this, most gardeners in western Washington and western Oregon are optimists and continue planting species that may be killed or cut back by these cold winters.

As might be expected, soil conditions are widely varied, ranging from acid glacial till in the north to sticky clays in the central valley of California. The river valleys often have a fertile silt loam soil that is wonderful for gardening, as in the Willamette Valley of Oregon. Most of the coastal area has soils that are either acid or neutral, the exception again being the interior valley of California, where alkaline conditions sometimes prevail. Because of this, and because of the moist warm winters, a great range of acid-loving plants are popular, with rhododendrons, many other ericaceous plants and camellias doing extremely well.

Low maintenance is a key phrase, and many gardens rely extensively on broad-leaved evergreen ground covers in addition to trees and shrubs. The Oriental style of garden is popular and seems especially suited to the environment. In the north the cooler moister climate allows the gardener to indulge in an almost English style featuring naturalistic plantings. Container gardening is more common in the southern half of the region, where conditions are warmer and drier. Gardens designed for outdoor living are common throughout the whole area.

The coastal area is suited to many fruits and nuts, ranging from lemons and limes in favored sections of the Bay region to blueberries and cranberries in the acid soils of Oregon and Washington. Filberts, cherries, almonds, peaches, raspberries and strawberries are commonly grown. Vegetable-gardening is sometimes frustrating in the Puget Sound and San Francisco areas, for tomatoes and corn are slow to ripen because of lack of summer heat. On the other hand, many vegetables, such as peas, thrive in the cool summers.

The kinds of herbaceous garden plants that grow readily in the Pacific Northwest are those that grow generally throughout the United States; and it would be superfluous to list them. However, frequently grown in the Northwest as perennials are a number of plants not reliably hardy in the Central and Northeastern states. Among them are blue-poppy, cineraria, dahlia, gazania, Martha Washington geranium, red-hot poker and Transvaal daisy. Because of the cool and moist climate, delphiniums, lupines and sweet peas are often very successful here.

Washington and Oregon, east of the Cascade Mountains (Zones 5 and 6), have an entirely different climate from that of the coastal strip. Gardening conditions here are similar to those of the intermountain regions of the West. Because it is in the rain shadow of the Cascades, the east side is hotter in the summer, colder in the winter and receives much less total precipitation than does the warmer, more lush west side. Spokane, Washington, for instance, receives a yearly precipitation of slightly over seventeen inches and has a growing season of 184 days. The soils east of the Cascades are generally more alkaline than those of the west side and are often rich agricultural lands, famous for wheat and fruit. The very dry climatic conditions are offset, so far as the gardener is concerned, by the availability of ample irrigation water. The rich soils and warm sunny summers allow a wide range of annuals, perennials and vegetable crops to thrive. Most of the common deciduous trees and shrubs and needle-leaved evergreens grow well here, but only the very hardiest broad-leaved evergreens will survive the hot summers, cold winters and dry winds.

WHERE TO GET SPECIAL HELP

All three Pacific Coast states have an agricultural extension service operating in conjunction with their state universities and planned, in part, to provide advice and help to gardeners. The county agent's office is the place to apply. He has a wide selection of pamphlets and publications from state and federal sources covering nearly all phases of gardening from planting lawns to controlling pests. He can also make arrangements for soil-testing. If some problem should arise that he or his staff cannot handle, he will call on the resources of the various experiment stations in his area. Or you may write to the Agricultural Extension Service that serves your state.

California: University of California, 2200 University Avenue, Berkeley, California 94720.

Oregon: 206 Waldo Hall, Oregon State University, Corvallis, Oregon 97331.

Washington: 115 Wilson Hall, Washington State University, Pullman, Washington 99163.

PLACES AND PLANTINGS OF INTEREST

Northern California: TILDEN PARK, Berkeley, has a twenty-acre garden devoted to native plants of California.

THE UNIVERSITY OF CALIFORNIA BOTANIC GARDENS, Berkeley, contain a wide range of species and cultivars of plants that thrive in the mild Bay region.

THE UNIVERSITY OF CALIFORNIA ARBORETUM, Davis, is redeveloping after major rearrangement. It features ornamental trees and shrubs suitable for interior northern California.

THE STRYBING ARBORETUM, Golden Gate Park, San Francisco, displays ornamental trees and shrubs from the temperate world and is one of the most successful of small arboretums. It includes the demonstration garden of *Sunset Magazine*. Golden Gate Park is also the home of San Francisco's famous Japanese Garden and has excellent collections of flowering trees, shrubs and herbaceous plants.

MUIR WOODS, beyond Sausalito, is a national monument devoted to the great redwoods.

California Poppy is the state flower; Redwood, the state tree.

Oregon: PORTLAND has three gardens of interest — at Washington Park the famous Rose Test and Demonstration Garden, one of the finest in the world, with at least ten thousand cultivars; nearby Hoyte Arboretum, featuring a very complete collection of conifers; and the Japanese Garden, now maturing into a real gem of Oriental style and technique.

THE AMERICAN RHODODENDRON SOCIETY'S TEST GARDEN at Crystal Springs Island is one of the finest in America, with flowering displays from March through June.

HENDRICKS PARK, Eugene, has a very large collection of rhododendrons and magnolias.

LAMBERT GARDENS, Portland, has a rose garden with many climbers; pool; Italian garden, Spanish garden.

COOLEY'S GARDENS, Silverton, features extensive iris displays.

OREGON BULB FARMS, Gresham, is known for its lilies.

Oregon-grape is the state flower; Douglas-Fir, the state tree.

Washington: THE PEACE PARK at Blaine, a park jointly operated by the State of Washington and the Province of British Columbia, includes a formal garden with bedding plants.

THE UNIVERSITY OF WASHINGTON ARBORETUM, Seattle, contains within its two hundred acres a very wide selection of labeled trees and shrubs.

THE HIRAM CHITTENDEN LOCKS GARDEN, Seattle, is a beautifully landscaped garden containing many rare plants which surround the Locks operated by the U.S. Army Corps of Engineers.

WOODLAND PARK ROSE GARDEN, Seattle, is a test garden for the American Rose Society.

POINT DEFIANCE PARK, Tacoma, contains numerous display gardens, including an ecologically oriented planting of Northwest native plants.

THE FINCH ARBORETUM, Spokane, has a good collection of trees and shrubs, and MANITO PARK has an excellent display of annuals and perennials useful in the Inland Empire.

OHME GARDENS, Wenatchee, Washington, is a privately owned garden open to the public, famous for its displays of creeping phlox and other spring bloomers in rock-garden setting. A small admission fee is charged.

Coast Rhododendron is the state flower; Western Hemlock, the state tree.

SOME FAVORITE GARDEN PLANTS OF THE PACIFIC NORTHWEST

The north coastal region of the three Pacific States has such a wide diversity of climate within its boundaries that it would be safe to say that nearly any plant from the temperate world can be cultivated somewhere here. Therefore these lists are woefully incomplete and merely give an inkling of the wealth of plants that thrive in Washington, Oregon and northern California. Since broad-leaved evergreens are a salient element of the landscape, this category has been eliminated and its members included in the tree and shrub lists.

LARGE TREES

COMMON NAME	BOTANICAL NAME	HEIGHT	ZONE
Beech, European	*Fagus sylvatica*	80'-100'	5-8
Birch, in variety	*Betula*	30'-60'	5-9
Eucalyptus, in variety	*Eucalyptus*	50'-150'	7-10
Ginkgo	*Ginkgo biloba*	60'	5-9
Honey-Locust, in variety	*Gleditsia triacanthos*	40'	5-10
Horse-Chestnut, European	*Aesculus hippocastaneum*	80'	5-9
Magnolia, Southern	*Magnolia grandiflora*	60'	7-9
Maple, in variety	*Acer*	30'-90'	5-7
Oak, in variety	*Quercus*	40'-80'	5-8
Palm, Fan	*Washingtonia robusta*	60'-100'	9-10
Pepper-Tree, California	*Schinus molle*	30'-40'	9-10
Pistachio, Chinese	*Pistacia chinensis*	60'	8-10
Plane-Tree, London	*Platanus x hybrida*	80'	5-10
Sweet Gum	*Liquidambar styraciflua*	60'-80'	7-10

SMALL FLOWERING TREES

COMMON NAME	BOTANICAL NAME	HEIGHT	ZONE
Acacia, in variety	*Acacia*	15'-30'	8-10
Cherry, Flowering	*Prunus*	20'-35'	5-10
Crabapple, Flowering, in variety	*Malus*	20'-30'	5-9
Crape-Myrtle	*Lagerstroemia indica*	10'-30'	7-10
Dogwood, in variety	*Cornus*	20'-40'	5-9
Goldenchain-Tree	*Laburnum* x *watereri*	25'	6-9
Hawthorn, in variety	*Crataegus*	20'-40'	5-7
Jacaranda	*Jacaranda acutifolia*	10'	10
Magnolia, in variety	*Magnolia*	15'-40'	6-10
Melaleuca, in variety	*Melaleuca*	15'-30'	9,10
Mountain-Ash, European	*Sorbus aucuparia*	40'	5-9
Plum, Flowering	*Prunus*	30'	5

LARGE EVERGREENS (CONIFERS)

COMMON NAME	BOTANICAL NAME	HEIGHT	ZONE
Arborvitae, Giant	*Thuja plicata*	200'	5-9
Bunya-Bunya	*Araucaria bidwillii*	80'	9-10
Cedar, True	*Cedrus atlantica; libani*	60'-100'	5-9
Douglas-Fir	*Pseudotsuga menziesii*	150'	5-10
False-Cypress, in variety	*Chamaecyparis*	30'-90'	5-9
Fir, in variety	*Abies*	50'-100'	5-8
Hemlock, in variety	*Tsuga*	40'-150'	5-8
Japanese-Redwood	*Cryptomeria japonica*	150'	6-10
Monkey-Puzzle	*Araucaria araucana*	50'-70'	8-10
Pine, in variety	*Pinus*	30'-90'	5-7
Redwood, Coast	*Sequoia sempervirens*	200'	8
Giant	*Sequoiadendron giganteum*	150'	7
Spruce, in variety	*Picea*	40'-80'	5,6

SMALL EVERGREENS

COMMON NAME	BOTANICAL NAME	HEIGHT	ZONE
False-Cypress, dwarf forms	*Chamaecyparis*	3'-20'	5-7
Holly, English	*Ilex aquifolium*	10'-20'	7
Juniper, in variety	*Juniperus*	to 20'	5
Pine, Mugho	*Pinus mugo mughus*	10'	5
Plum-Yew	*Cephalotaxus harringtonia*	15'	6
Spruce, Dwarf	*Picea*	2'-10'	5
Yew, in variety	*Taxus*	5'-40'	5-6

SHRUBS

COMMON NAME	BOTANICAL NAME	HEIGHT	ZONE
Acacia, in variety	*Acacia*	6'-15'	**9,10**
Andromeda, Japanese	*Pieris japonica*	10'	**6**
Aucuba	*Aucuba japonica*	10'	**7**
Azalea, in variety	*Rhododendron*	2'-10'	**6-9**
Bamboo, Golden	*Phyllostachys aurea*	10'-20'	**7**
California-Lilac, in variety	*Ceanothus*	1'-10'	**7-10**
Camellia, in variety	*Camellia*	6'-20'	**7-9**
Cotoneaster, in variety	*Cotoneaster*	1'-20'	**5-8**
Daphne, in variety	*Daphne*	1'-5'	**5-9**
Forsythia, in variety	*Forsythia*	5'-15'	**5,8**
Hebe, in variety	*Hebe*	1'-6'	**7-9**
Hydrangea, Common	*Hydrangea macrophylla*	4'-8'	**6-8**
Lilac, in variety	*Syringa*	10'-15'	**5-10**
Mahonia, in variety	*Mahonia*	4'-10'	**6-10**
Manzanita, in variety	*Arctostaphylos*	1'-15'	**5-10**
New-Zealand-Tea	*Leptospermum scoparium*	1'-10'	**9-10**
Pyracantha, in variety	*Pyracantha*	6'-10'	**6-10**
Rhododendron, in variety	*Rhododendron*	1'-20'	**5-9**
Spirea, in variety	*Spiraea*	3'-10'	**5,6**
Viburnum, in variety	*Viburnum*	3'-25'	**5-10**

HEDGES AND WINDBREAKS

(H — hedge; W — windbreak; T — tall, 10' and up; M — medium, 5'-9')

COMMON NAME	BOTANICAL NAME	HEIGHT AND USE	ZONE
Box, Common	*Buxus sempervirens*	T,H,M-T	**6-10**
Cherry-Laurel	*Prunus laurocerasus*	T,H,M-T	**8-9**
Escallonia, in variety	*Escallonia*	T,H,W,M-T	**7-9**
Hemlock, Canadian	*Tsuga canadensis*	H,T	**5-9**
Holly, English	*Ilex aquifolium*	H,W,T	**7-10**
Japanese	*crenata*	H,M	**7-10**
Huckleberry, Evergreen	*Vaccinium ovatum*	H,M	**7-9**
New-Zealand-Tea	*Leptospermum scoparium*	W,M-T	**9-10**
Photinia, in variety	*Photinia*	W,M-T	**6-8**
Pittosporum, in variety	*Pittosporum*	W,H,M-T	**8-9**
Privet, Common	*Ligustrum vulgare*	H,M	**6-9**
Texas	*japonicum* 'Lusterleaf'	W,H,M-T	**8-10**
Yew, in variety	*Taxus*	W,H,T	**5-8**

GROUND COVERS

COMMON NAME	BOTANICAL NAME	HEIGHT	ZONE
Carpet-Bugle	*Ajuga reptans*	6"-8"	**5-10**
Ceanothus, prostrate forms	*Ceanothus*	low	**7-10**
Chilean Strawberry	*Fragaria chiloensis*	6"	**7-10**
Epimedium, in variety	*Epimedium*	6"-15"	**6-9**
Heather, in variety	*Erica* and *Calluna*	6"-2'	**6-8**
Ice-Plant, in variety	*Mesembryanthemum*	low	**7-10**
Ivy, in variety	*Hedera helix*	low	**6-10**
Juniper, in variety	*Juniperus*	1'-3'	**5,10**
Lily-of-the-Valley	*Convallaria majalis*	9"	**6-8**
London Pride	*Saxifraga umbrosa*	10"	**8-10**
Manzanita (Bearberry)	*Arctostaphylos uva-ursi*	low	**5-8**
Periwinkle, in variety	*Vinca minor, major*	10"-12"	**5-10**
St. Johnswort, Creeping	*Hypericum calycinum*	1'	**6-10**

COMMON NAME	BOTANICAL NAME	HEIGHT	ZONE
Sedum	*Sedum spathulifolium*	4"	6-10
Spurge, Japanese	*Pachysandra terminalis*	1'	5-9
Wintercreeper, in variety	*Euonymus fortunei*	6"-3'	6-10

VINES

COMMON NAME	BOTANICAL NAME	ZONE
Actinidia	*Actinidia kolomikta*	5-10
Akebia, Five-Leaf	*Akebia quinata*	6-10
Boston-Ivy	*Parthenocissus tricuspidata*	5-10
Bougainvillea, in variety	*Bougainvillea*	10
Cape-Honeysuckle	*Tecomaria capensis*	9-10
Clematis, in variety	*Clematis*	5-10
Climbing Hydrangea	*Hydrangea anomala petiolaris*	5-10
Honeysuckle, in variety	*Lonicera*	5-10
Jasmine, in variety	*Jasminum*	9-10
Star-Jasmine	*Trachelospermum jasminoides*	9-10
Virginia-Creeper	*Parthenocissus quinquefolia*	5-10
Wisteria, in variety	*Wisteria*	5-10

LAWN GRASSES

COMMON NAME	BOTANICAL NAME
Bentgrass Astoria, Exeter, Highland	*Agrostis tenuis*

Bluegrass
    Delta, Merion, Newport,
    Prado, Windsor
	Poa pratensis

Red Fescue
    Chewings, Illahee, Pennlawn,
    Rainier
	Festuca rubra

ROCK-GARDEN PLANTS

COMMON NAME	BOTANICAL NAME	ZONE
Aster, Dwarf	*Aster* hybrids	5-8
Avens, in variety	*Geum*	5-10
Basket-of-Gold	*Alyssum saxatile*	5-10
Beard-Tongue, in variety	*Penstemon*	5-10
Bellflower, in variety	*Campanula*	5-10
Candytuft	*Iberis sempervirens*	5-10
English Daisy	*Bellis perennis*	5-10
Heather, in variety	*Erica* and *Calluna*	6-9
Houseleek	*Sempervivum*	5-10
Iris, Crested	*Iris cristata*	6-9
Dwarf Bearded	*Iris* hybrids: Miniature and Standard Dwarf	5-10
Phlox, Creeping	*Phlox subulata*	5-10
Pinks, in variety	*Dianthus*	5-10

COMMON NAME	BOTANICAL NAME	ZONE
Rockcress	*Arabis*	**5-10**
Rockcress, Purple	*Aubrieta*	**5-8**
Rock-Jasmine	*Androsace*	**5-10**
Sedum, in variety	*Sedum*	**5-10**
Stonecress	*Aethionema*	**5-10**

NATIVE PLANTS USEFUL FOR THE GARDEN

COMMON NAME	BOTANICAL NAME	ZONE
Beard-Tongue	*Penstemon,* many species	**5-10**
Bunchberry	*Cornus canadensis*	**5-9**
Ceanothus	*Ceanothus,* several species	**5-10**
Currant, Red-flowering	*Ribes sanguineum*	**5-9**
Dogwood, Pacific	*Cornus nuttallii*	**5-9**
Fern, Deer	*Blechnum spicant*	**5-10**
Sword	*Polystichum munitum*	**5-9**
Huckleberry, Evergreen	*Vaccinium ovatum*	**5-9**
Iris	*Iris,* many species	**5-10**
Lupine	*Lupinus,* several species	**5-10**
Manzanita	*Arctostaphylos,* many species	**5-10**
Maple, Vine	*Acer circinatum* (actually a tree)	**5-9**
Matilija-Poppy	*Romneya coulteri*	**8-10**
Oak	*Quercus,* many species	**5-10**
Oregon-Grape	*Mahonia aquifolium; M. nervosa*	**6-10**
Salal	*Gaultheria shallon*	**7-9**
Silk-Tassel	*Garrya,* several species	**7-9**
Trillium	*Trillium,* several species	**5-9**

RECOMMENDED ROSES
(See also Chapter 26.)

Roses suitable for eastern Washington and eastern Oregon are much the same as those suggested for the Mountain States.

HYBRID TEAS

Charlotte Armstrong, light
   red and deep pink
Garden Party, white
King's Ransom, deep yellow

Matterhorn, white
Mister Lincoln, medium red
Peace, yellow blend
Tropicana, orange-red

FLORIBUNDAS

Apricot Nectar, apricot blend
Betty Prior, medium pink
Europeana, dark red
Frensham, dark red
Ivory Fashion, white

Little Darling, yellow blend
Sarabande, orange-red
Saratoga, white
Spartan, orange-red

GRANDIFLORAS

John S. Armstrong, dark red
Montezuma, orange-red

Queen Elizabeth, medium
   pink

CLIMBERS

Blaze, medium red
Golden Showers, medium
   yellow
Joseph's Coat, yellow and red

New Dawn, light pink
Paul's Scarlet, medium
   red

SHRUB AND OLD-FASHIONED ROSES

Austrian Copper, scarlet-orange
Buccaneer, yellow
Frau Karl Druschki, white

Harison's Yellow, deep
   yellow

43 PACIFIC SOUTHWEST

Southern California, Arizona, Nevada
Zones 5, 6, 7, 8, 9, 10, 10C

by Dr. R. B. Streets, Sr., *Plant Pathologist Emeritus,
University of Arizona, Tucson, Arizona*

The climate and soil conditions in the Southwest present unique problems. High temperatures and low humidities for long periods and alkaline soils low in organic matter are typical in the more settled areas. These are challenging even to persons quite experienced in gardening in the midwestern, eastern and northern states. Also the numerous and widely various plants adapted to these environmental conditions differ from those found in other parts of the country.

Because of the many large mountain ranges and high plateaus in the Southwest, this region includes six hardiness zones (5 to 10), but Zones 5, 6 and 7 are sparsely populated, and gardening practices there will follow those in the adjoining regions 8 and 9.

Zone 10 is practically frost-free (Southern California Coast and Imperial Valley), and very tender plants can be grown. Zone 9, covering most of central California and the coast north of the Bay region, and the low desert in Arizona, grows citrus, dates, cotton, winter vegetables and many relatively tender ornamentals. Zone 8 includes the intermediate desert in Arizona and in California the coast ranges and the foothill regions of the Sierras. A few cold winter nights in Zone 8 limit the use of tender plants to the warmest protected spots.

It is necessary to designate the coastal area of California, where rainfall, fog, humidity and soil conditions are different, by a special Zone 10C, because many plants that thrive there will not thrive farther inland.

CLIMATIC FEATURES—GOOD AND BAD—OF ZONES 8, 9, 10 and 10C

Good: The long growing season: The high number of sunny days and warm days permits the growing of many tender exotic plants.
Bad: Plants from cool or temperate climates are often not adapted.

Good: The low humidity and long rainless periods limit or prevent occurrence of numerous foliage, blossom and fruit diseases.
Bad: In the warm and dry areas year-round irrigation is a *must.*

Bad: Most soils are alkaline and very low in organic matter and nitrogen.
Good: These soils can be made very fertile and productive by the addition of organic matter, nitrogen and minor elements.

Bad: The summer season is a succession of long, hot days.
Good: The humidity is so low that you don't feel the heat.

Good: The heat is quickly lost to the sky, and evenings and nights are cool and pleasant.
Also Good: The California Coast, influenced by the ocean, is much cooler than inland.

POPULAR TYPES OF GARDENS

Gardens are usually made to harmonize with the general architecture of the house. The most frequently seen types of houses are: (1) Pueblo or Mission, based on adobe walls and flat roofs; (2) Mediterranean, white or tinted plastered walls and tiled roofs; (3) Modern, with bold lines; (4) Territorial, unplastered brick or tan adobe with arches.

Desert homesites are usually landscaped with native and/or exotic desert plants entirely or with desert planting outside a patio wall and lush semitropical planting inside.

The landscaping of city lots may be of either style, but it tends more to the semitropical effect, either traditional or modern. Swimming pools are very common in middle-size or larger home grounds. Fountains or pools are often used as garden features, most welcome in dry areas. Residents of retirement communities and of subdivisions generally have more leisure for gardening and have created some very interesting gardens.

The ranch house, a low rambling structure, calls for a spacious setting and is very popular in suburban areas with generous-size lots. Large oaks or other old trees usually dominate the scene.

New and modern apartment houses (including high-rise) and condominiums accompany the rapid growth of southwestern cities. The landscaping is often quite intelligently done and maintained by professional gardeners.

Flower gardens brighten the landscape most of the year. Annuals predominate: petunias, violas, snapdragons, African daisies, stocks and Iceland poppies in winter and early spring; zinnias, marigolds and cosmos in summer and fall. A few perennials are especially adapted and widely used: iris (various types are superb) and Shasta daisies in spring, and hardy and exhibition chrysanthemums in fall. Roses thrive in all zones. They have a heavy spring bloom in April and May and a similar fall bloom in October and November, with more continuous bloom along the coast.

Vegetables can be grown winter and summer, but home vegetable gardens are not often seen, as vegetables are plentiful and good in the markets. Vegetables grown by hobby gardeners, however, are well worth the effort.

Patio gardening is characteristic of southwestern homes. It may be formal or informal, creating the outdoor living room enclosed by a wall or fence for privacy and much used for lounging and barbecue meals. Unless the patio is large, there is a minimum of lawn and considerable pavement of flagstones, brick or tile, with evergreen or flowering plants in beds and planters. Annuals (petunias, geraniums, etc.) or shrubs (camellias, gardenias, hibiscus, roses) are grown in large pots or redwood tubs, often on wheeled platforms and moved to a salient spot when in peak of bloom. A colorful scene can be created in this way with very little well-chosen plant material.

Hobby gardens thrive where the weather is good and people have ample time to indulge their special interest — which may be a garden of roses or of iris, chrysanthemums, dahlias, camellias, rhododendrons, fuchsias or vegetables. Automatic heating, cooling and humidity-control guarantee favorable weather within greenhouses, and many enthusiasts in this way grow orchids, brilliantly colored bromeliads or other tropical plants.

Clusters of long pointed blue flowers, followed by fernlike leaves, make the jacaranda a favorite lawn tree in southern California. *(George Taloumis photo)*

WHERE TO GET SPECIAL HELP

The Pacific Southwest is composed of a great many local areas or microclimates, differing so markedly in weather conditions and suitability to specific plants that you may well need special information. The State Agricultural Extension Services are designed to help the home gardener as well as the farmer. Consult your County Agricultural Agent, whose office is usually in the county seat, or write to Agricultural Extension Service for your state.

Arizona: College of Agriculture, University of Arizona, Tucson, Arizona 85721.

California: Agricultural Extension Service, 2200 University Avenue, Berkeley, California 94720.

Nevada: University of Nevada, Reno, Nevada 89507.

PLACES AND PLANTINGS OF INTEREST

Arizona: SAHUARO NATIONAL MONUMENT, Tucson.
ARIZONA-SONORA DESERT MUSEUM, Tucson.
ROSE TEST GARDEN, Randolph Park, Tucson.
SOUTHWEST DESERT ARBORETUM, Superior.
DESERT BOTANICAL GARDEN, Phoenix.

Giant Cactus is the state flower; Palo Verde, the state tree.

California: BOTANICAL GARDEN, Santa Barbara.
GOLDEN GATE PARK, San Francisco. Rhododendrons, Japanese and Rose gardens.
EXPOSITION PARK, San Diego.
CAPITOL PARK ROSE GARDEN (also trees), Sacramento.
EXPOSITION PARK, Rose Garden, Los Angeles.
CARMEL MISSION GARDEN. One of the many formal mission gardens of native trees, wild flowers, etc.
LEISURE WORLD, Los Angeles.
HEARST CASTLE AND GARDEN, San Simeon. An extensive elegant formal garden.
STRYBING ARBORETUM, Los Angeles.
HUNTINGTON BOTANICAL GARDENS, San Marino. Cactus to deciduous trees and shrubs; also Oriental Garden.
DESCANSO GARDENS, La Canada.
ROSE GARDENS in Berkeley and Oakland.
LOS ANGELES COUNTY ARBORETUM, Arcadia.

California Poppy is the state flower; Coast Redwood, the state tree.

Nevada: MUNICIPAL ROSE GARDEN, Reno.

Sagebrush is the state flower; Single-leaf Pinon, the state tree.

SOME FAVORITE GARDEN PLANTS OF THE PACIFIC SOUTHWEST

SELECTED PLANT MATERIALS

Oaks: Deciduous oaks are seldom grown in the desert areas, but three live (evergreen) oaks do well there: Cork oak (*Quercus suber*) from Spain, Coast live oak (*Q. agrifolia*) from California, and Southern live oak (*Q. virginiana*) from the Gulf States and the Southeast. Several other oaks will thrive in the less arid parts of California. Most prized are the large stately natives, especially the valley white oak (*Quercus lobata*), deciduous; the interior live oak (*Q. wislizenii*) and Canyon live oak (*Q. chrysolepis*), both evergreen; and California live oak (*Q. agrifolia*), mentioned above. These are often saved when land is cleared for building.

Mulberries: Shade is greatly prized in desert country, and the wide-spreading mulberries are the best adapted and fastest-growing deciduous trees for this situation. The fruitless 'Kingan' and the newer Maple-leaved or 'Stribling' cultivars become shapely trees without any help of pruning.

Some Choice Natives: These tolerate cold, heat and drought in Zones 8, 9 and 10. Regular watering is necessary for rapid growth. Arizona ash (*Fraxinus toumeya*), California sycamore (*Platanus racemosa*), Arizona cypress (*Cupressus arizonica*), Blue palo verde (*Cercidium torreyanum*) and Mexican palo verde (*C. Parkinsonia aculeata*) are all excellent.

Trees for Ranch and Desert Homes: This group of trees has wide-ranging roots, and most of them grow to a size too awkward for city lots. These trees withstand cold, heat and irregular watering: Fremont cottonwood (*Populus fremonti*), Arizona cypress, mesquite (*Prosopis glandulosa*) and Chilean mesquite (*P. pubescens*), a more shapely tree. These are useful for windbreaks as well as shade. The robust evergreen tamarisk (*Tamarix aphylla*), hardy to 10°, imported from the oases of the Sahara, grows to thirty feet with a trunk diameter of two to four feet. It tolerates heat, drought and alkali and is a dominant tree for windbreaks and shade around desert farms, ranches and homes, where its size and rootspread are acceptable. Ten other smaller species of tamarisk have deciduous branchlets and are more tolerant of cold.

Flowering Shrubs and Trees: Gardenias, camellias, azaleas, rhododendrons, magnolias and species of manzanita (*Arctostaphyllos*), which require a highly organic soil, thrive along the coast, along with magnolias, coast redwood and scarlet-flowering gum (*Eucalyptus ficifolia*). The last two are not happy inland.

Coniferous Evergreens: Like the redwood, spruce and fir, a number of pines, cypresses and arborvitaes enjoy the moist air and coolness of the coast. The Aleppo pine does best in dry inland country.

Palms: Both feather palms and fan palms come in a variety of sizes and are widely used to give a tropical effect to landscape plantings. They tolerate heat and drought, but a few species are susceptible to cold. Among the most attractive and best adapted to Zone 10C are the queen palm (*Arecastrum romanzoffianum,* formerly *Cocos plumosa*) and the Sonora fan palm (*Washingtonia robusta*), whose slender trunks are a conspicuous feature of the Southern California landscape. In the interior, Zone 9, the dominant palms are the heavy-trunked California fan palm (*Washingtonia filifera*) and the Carnary Island date palm (*Phoenix canariensis*). Where smaller palms are needed, the slow-growing blue fan palm (*Erythea armata*) and the small windmill palm (*Trachycarpus fortunei*) can be planted. All these thrive in Zone 10C also.

Flamboyant Exotics are popular in the warmest areas — crimson or magenta bougainvillea, hibiscus in many colors, two kinds of bird-of-paradise (*Strelitzia* and *Caesalpina*) and bignonia vines. At Los Angeles and southward jacaranda trees display their large clusters of violet flowers in early summer. Just as showy is the desert palo verde, a mass of gold in late April.

A Great Variety of Fruits can be raised if the particular varieties recommended for any given microclimate are chosen. Virtually all kinds of citrus fruits are grown in Zones 9 and 10; apples, pears and stone fruits in Zones 8 and 9; grapes (8, 9 and 10); and cane fruits (8 and 9). Avocado and date (10), loquat, quince, pomegranate (8 and 9) and passion fruit (10) have been cultivated and improved for generations.

Cacti and Succulents: Adapted to an open, well-drained soil and scant moisture, these plants are most appropriate landscape material in the drier areas and thrive with a minimum of care. It is best not to mix them with plants requiring regular watering.

Column Cacti: Sahuaro (*Carnegia gigantea*), ten to thirty feet; organ-pipe cactus (*Lemaireocereus* species), six to twenty feet, with many vertical branches.

The Common Barrel Cactus (*Ferocactus wislizenii*), three to six feet, has a curious habit of leaning to the southwest. The golden-spined barrel (*Echinocactus grusonii*), eventually three feet high, is a most attractive Mexican species.

The much-branched chollas so abundant in the desert are not so much cultivated as the prickly-pear types with flat fleshy joints. The most striking and much cultivated is 'Burbank's Spineless', a variety of *Opuntia ficus-indica,* treelike to fifteen feet with edible orange fruits. *O. santa-rita* is unique in having reddish-purple pads instead of the usual green and lends color to the desert plantings. *O. engelmannii,* three to four feet with lemon-yellow flowers, and the beavertail (*O. basilaris*) are frequently grown.

Other cacti of special interest are the night-blooming *Peniocereus greggii* and the South American *Hylocereus* and *Nyctocereus* species and hybrids.

Agaves come in assorted sizes, including the century-plant, which produces a twenty-foot flower stalk after twenty to thirty (not one hundred) years.

Aloes are somewhat smaller and bear clusters or spikes of long-lasting brilliant orange, coral-colored or red flowers.

Yuccas all have huge panicles of waxy white flowers. One species is the curious Joshua-tree. Another, the Lord's-candle (*Y. whipplei*), produces thousands of fragrant flowers on a ten-foot stalk. Another is the decorative Spanish-bayonet (*Y. aloifolia*).

PERENNIALS AND ANNUALS

Many of the cherished perennials and annuals of eastern and midwestern gardens cannot stand the heat and dryness of the Southwest. However, the summer annuals of the East and North are the winter annuals, being planted in September-October to bloom (some starting in December-January) in March-April-May. Among these are petunias in variety,

The heat-tolerant species planted in May for summer and fall bloom include zinnias in variety, marigolds — French, African and their dwarfs — and cosmos.

Flowering bulbs grow readily and bloom early (February-March) but do not naturalize and multiply well in this climate. They are often treated as annuals and discarded after blooming. Exceptions are bulbous iris and amaryllis. Rhizomatous plants (iris in variety, cannas, etc.) thrive and multiply.

LAWN GRASSES

Today lawns are a conspicuous feature of the cultivated landscape of the Pacific Southwest, in spite of the heat and long rainless periods. Common Bermuda Grass is by far the most tolerant to heat and drought, hence it is most often employed. It does bleach to straw color in a frost but regains its bright green in early May. At that time an application by a grass seeder of ammonium sulfate (1 pound to 100 square feet) and a subsequent good hosing spray will greatly improve the color and texture of the lawn. A repetition in September will keep the grass green for several weeks longer than otherwise.

Hybrid Bermudas and Zoysia produce lawns of finer texture but require rather more care. *Dichondra repens,* a cloverlike creeping plant of the morning-glory family, sometimes substitutes for grass in Zone 10 or where temperatures do not fall much below 25°. A dichondra lawn demands as much care as a grass lawn.

A winter lawn can be made with Annual Rye Grass. Seeded from August 20 to October 1, this grass grows fast and is usually tall enough to mow in ten to fourteen days. After seeding, apply 1/4 inch of sifted, composted manure to cover the seed; keep it moist by daily sprinkling until the stand of grass is secured. At the first mowing cut close and remove the clippings. In early May, if water is withheld for two weeks, the winter lawn will die out.

Unfortunately there seems to be no special grass for all of this region that will produce a really good turf in shade.

EFFECTIVE AND SATISFACTORY PLANTS FOR ZONES 8 and 9
(Evergreen unless otherwise specified)

Pyracanthas, many cultivars, most vigorous six to ten feet, some new ones low and spreading. Red berries fall and winter.

Xylosma senticosa, glossy bright-green leaves; shrub, hedge or small tree.

Pyracanthas and Xylosmas are excellent espaliered on walls, especially pyracanthas with their bright red berries all winter.

Japanese Privet (*Ligustrum japonicum*), large shrub, tall hedge or small tree. Widely planted.

Oleander (*Nerium oleander*), abundant bloom in May and June. Large shrub, tall hedge or small tree.

Cocculus (*Cocculus laurifolius*), vigorous shrub to fifteen feet, four-to-5-inch glossy green leaves (Zone 9 only).

Myrtles. Roman Myrtle (*Myrtus communis*) and its small-leaved variety (*M.c. microphylla*).

Japanese Pittosporum (*Pittosporum tobira*), a broad, compact shrub, eventually six to eight feet. Glossy leaves.

Photinia serrulata, an erect shrub, six to eight feet. Old leaves turn red in cold weather. *P. Arbutifolia,* the toyon of California, shrub to fifteen feet with large flat clusters of red berries.

Cotoneaster dielsiana, whose dark green arching branches make a graceful accent.

Chinese Jasmine (*Jasminum mesnyi*), first to bloom in spring, the long stems most effective as a "waterfall."

Texas Ranger (*Leucophyllum texanum*), silvery foliage, intermittent showers of violet "snapdragons."

Junipers, many cultivars. 'Pfitzeriana' and 'Blue Vase' are vigorous and tend to get large.

Viburnums (*Virburnum tinus, V. suspensum, V. robustum*), well adapted to shade but not to afternoon sun. Bloom in early spring.

Waxleaf Privet (*Ligustrum lucidum*), a glossy-leaved plant for shade.

Crape-Myrtle (*Lagerstroemia indica*), deciduous. Blooms through the summer. Mildews. 'Watermelon Red' is an especially good variety.

Oriental Redbud (*Cercis orientalis*), deciduous. Purple-red blooms before the leaves.

PLANTS FOR THE CALIFORNIA COAST

The Southern California Coast for some distance inland gets from ten to twenty inches of rain in the winter months; with irrigation during the dry months, it supports a lush vegetation. This is Zone 9, except for the narrow coastal strip warmed by the Pacific Ocean (10C).

Pelargoniums are grown as hedges and sometimes as vines to ten feet, and ivy geraniums are a most colorful ground cover on slopes. Hydrangeas flaunt their large flower clusters, and fuchsias are three-to-six-foot shrubs blooming all summer.

Blue Lily-of-the-Nile (*Agapanthus*) is used en masse, contrasting with cannas and tritomas to furnish bold yellow-orange, pink and red.

Delphiniums with four-to-six-foot spikes of white and all shades of blue join with the yellow-pink and red spectrum of hollyhocks to furnish a colorful background.

Dahlias really thrive, encompassing the full gamut of color except blue, and many sizes of plants and types of bloom.

Tuberous Begonias are choice but more demanding, requiring a high humus soil, at least part shade and cool, moist air. The flowers are spectacular. They are often grown in pots or hanging baskets and are placed about for color accents.

Vining species of *Mesembryanthemum* (ice-plant) hold sand on banks and dunes, subsisting mostly on dew.

RECOMMENDED ROSES
(See also Chapter 26.)

Roses grow readily in the Southwest, even in the hottest parts. Because of the long growing season there are two periods of heavy bloom — April-May in the spring and October-November in autumn. In the cooler coastal area, roses bloom continuously. The following are among the best of the tested varieties. Selections are based on twenty years of "baby-sitting" with more than two thousand roses in our test gardens, plus visits to all the major Pacific Coast rose gardens.

HYBRID TEAS

Bewitched, medium pink
Charlotte Armstrong, light red and deep pink
Christian Dior, Crimson
Chrysler Imperial, dark red
Columbus Queen, medium pink
Countess Vandal, salmon-yellow
First Prize, pink blend
Garden Party, white

Hawaii, orange-red
Matterhorn, white
Peace, yellow blend
Picture, light pink
Red American Beauty, medium red
Summer Sunshine, deep yellow
Sutter's Gold, golden orange
Tropicana, orange-red

FLORIBUNDAS

Apricot Nectar, apricot blend
Else Poulsen, medium pink
Fusilier, orange-red
Garnette, dark red
Gay Princess, light pink

Ivory Fashion, white
Lilac Dawn, mauve
Redgold, yellow blend
Sarabande, orange-red

GRANDIFLORAS

Duet, medium pink
El Capitan, medium red
Golden Scepter, deep yellow

Granada, red blend
Polynesian Sunset, orange-red
Queen Elizabeth, medium pink

CLIMBERS

Charlotte Armstrong, light red and deep pink
Chrysler Imperial, dark red
Golden Showers, medium gold
Improved Blaze, medium red

Peace, yellow blend
Picture, light pink
Showgirl, medium pink
Sutter's Gold, golden orange

AVERAGE ANNUAL DURATION OF FROST-FREE WEATHER
IN VARIOUS LOCALITIES OF FORTY-EIGHT STATES

(Reprinted from *Climate and Man*, 1941 Yearbook of Agriculture,
United States Department of Agriculture)

STATE	KILLING FROST AVERAGE DATES		Growing Season, Number of Days
	Last in Spring	First in Fall	
Alabama			
Birmingham	Mar. 16	Nov. 11	240
Florence	Apr. 5	Oct. 29	207
Mobile	Feb. 17	Dec. 12	298
Montgomery	Mar. 3	Nov. 19	261
Ozark	Mar. 7	Nov. 19	257
Scottsboro	Apr. 8	Oct. 30	205
Arizona			
Flagstaff	June 3	Sept. 29	118
Kingman	Apr. 12	Nov. 16	212
Phoenix	Feb. 5	Dec. 6	304
Prescott	May 17	Oct. 7	143
Tucson	Mar. 19	Nov. 19	245
Yuma	Jan. 12	Dec. 26	348
Arkansas			
Camden	Mar. 25	Nov. 4	224
Fort Smith	Mar. 21	Nov. 10	234
Jonesboro	Apr. 1	Nov. 4	217
Little Rock	Mar. 17	Nov. 13	241
Mountain Home	Apr. 8	Oct. 23	198
Warren	Mar. 27	Nov. 7	225
California, Northern			
Eureka	Jan. 26	Dec. 20	328
Oakland	Jan. 11	Dec. 28	351
Red Bluff	Mar. 6	Dec. 5	274
Sacramento	Feb. 6	Dec. 10	307
San Francisco	Jan. 7	Dec. 29	356
Sonora	Mar. 29	Nov. 22	238
California, Southern			
Bakersfield	Feb. 21	Nov. 25	277
Brawley	Feb. 5	Dec. 5	303
Hanford	Mar. 3	Nov. 14	256
Pasadena	Feb. 3	Dec. 13	313
San Diego	None	None	365
San Luis Obispo	Jan. 30	Dec. 16	320
Colorado			
Del Norte	May 30	Sept. 25	118
Denver	Apr. 26	Oct. 14	171
Idaho Springs	May 23	Sept. 25	125
Pueblo	Apr. 23	Oct. 14	174
Steamboat Springs	June 28	Aug. 24	57
Wray	May 7	Oct. 3	149
Connecticut			
Bridgeport	Apr. 26	Oct. 10	173
Greene	May 28	Sept. 18	113
Hartford	Apr. 19	Oct. 18	182
New Haven	Apr. 11	Oct. 23	195
Storrs	May 5	Oct. 7	155
Torrington	May 11	Sept. 30	142
Waterbury	May 1	Oct. 11	163

STATE	KILLING FROST AVERAGE DATES		Growing Season, Number of Days
	Last in Spring	First in Fall	
Delaware			
Dover	Apr. 19	Oct. 24	188
Millsboro	Apr. 21	Oct. 21	183
Wilmington	Apr. 17	Oct. 28	194
Florida			
Daytona Beach	Jan. 21	Dec. 24	337
Homestead	Very rare	Very rare	365
Jacksonville	Feb. 15	Dec. 11	299
Key West	None	None	365
Miami	Very rare	Very rare	365
Orlando	Feb. 3	Dec. 14	314
Pensacola	Feb. 16	Dec. 13	300
Quincy	Mar. 10	Nov. 21	256
Tallahassee	Feb. 25	Dec. 4	282
Tampa	Jan. 13	Dec. 27	348
Georgia			
Athens	Apr. 2	Nov. 5	217
Atlanta	Mar. 23	Nov. 9	231
Augusta	Mar. 16	Nov. 13	242
Bainbridge	Mar. 10	Nov. 15	250
Blue Ridge	Apr. 19	Oct. 20	184
Moultrie	Mar. 1	Nov. 24	268
Rome	Mar. 31	Nov. 3	217
Savannah	Feb. 28	Nov. 28	273
Idaho			
Boise	Apr. 23	Oct. 17	177
Challis	May 29	Sept. 17	111
Idaho Falls	May 15	Sept. 19	127
Lakeview	May 10	Oct. 8	151
Moscow	May 6	Oct. 6	153
Pocatello	Apr. 28	Oct. 6	161
Illinois			
Chicago	Apr. 13	Oct. 26	196
Harrisburg	Apr. 13	Oct. 22	192
Joliet	May 3	Oct. 12	162
Macomb	Apr. 26	Oct. 17	174
Rockford	May 6	Oct. 10	157
Springfield	Apr. 11	Oct. 22	194
Urbana	Apr. 21	Oct. 18	180
Indiana			
Evansville	Apr. 2	Oct. 30	211
Fort Wayne	Apr. 23	Oct. 16	176
Indianapolis	Apr. 15	Oct. 24	192
Kokomo	Apr. 29	Oct. 11	165
La Porte	May 7	Oct. 11	157
Madison	Apr. 22	Oct. 21	182
Terre Haute	Apr. 13	Oct. 24	194
Iowa			
Burlington	Apr. 20	Oct. 16	179
Des Moines	Apr. 19	Oct. 11	175
Dubuque	Apr. 19	Oct. 18	182
Fort Madison	Apr. 25	Oct. 9	167
Keokuk	Apr. 15	Oct. 19	187
Mason City	May 8	Oct. 3	148
Sioux City	Apr. 25	Oct. 7	165

STATE	KILLING FROST AVERAGE DATES		Growing Season, Number of Days
	Last in Spring	First in Fall	
Kansas			
Atchison	Apr. 14	Oct. 18	187
Cimarron	Apr. 24	Oct. 16	175
Dodge City	Apr. 15	Oct. 25	193
Independence	Apr. 15	Oct. 22	190
St. Francis	May 3	Oct. 8	158
Sublette	Apr. 24	Oct. 20	179
Topeka	Apr. 8	Oct. 20	195
Kentucky			
Ashland	Apr. 20	Oct. 17	180
Beaver Dam	Apr. 14	Oct. 21	190
Frankfort	Apr. 15	Oct. 20	188
Louisville	Apr. 9	Oct. 24	198
Paducah	Apr. 7	Oct. 24	200
Williamstown	Apr. 21	Oct. 20	182
Louisiana			
Baton Rouge	Feb. 24	Nov. 20	269
Lafayette	Mar. 3	Nov. 14	256
Lake Charles	Mar. 3	Nov. 23	265
Monroe	Mar. 11	Nov. 13	247
Natchitoches	Mar. 21	Nov. 8	232
New Orleans	Feb. 20	Dec. 9	292
Shreveport	Mar. 8	Nov. 15	252
Tallulah	Mar. 20	Oct. 27	221
Maine			
Ashland	June 7	Sept. 22	107
Bangor	May 9	Oct. 6	150
Bar Harbor	May 13	Oct. 5	145
Eastport	Apr. 29	Oct. 22	176
Lewiston	May 2	Oct. 8	159
Millinocket	May 27	Sept. 18	114
Portland	Apr. 27	Oct. 17	173
Maryland			
Annapolis	Apr. 10	Nov. 1	205
Baltimore	Apr. 8	Nov. 2	208
Chestertown	Apr. 17	Oct. 27	193
Clear Spring	Apr. 24	Oct. 16	175
Cumberland	Apr. 27	Oct. 14	170
Frederick	Apr. 21	Oct. 17	179
La Plata	Apr. 18	Oct. 22	187
Massachusetts			
Boston	Apr. 13	Oct. 29	199
Provincetown	Apr. 17	Nov. 3	200
Springfield	Apr. 27	Oct. 15	171
Williamstown	May 6	Oct. 5	152
Worcester	Apr. 28	Oct. 14	169
Michigan			
Atlanta	May 29	Sept. 21	115
Detroit	Apr. 24	Oct. 18	177
Escanaba	May 12	Oct. 5	146
Flint	May 8	Oct. 8	153
Grand Rapids	May 1	Oct. 17	169
Lansing	May 5	Oct. 10	158

STATE	KILLING FROST AVERAGE DATES		Growing Season, Number of Days
	Last in Spring	First in Fall	
Minnesota			
Baudette	May 25	Sept. 17	115
Caledonia	May 1	Oct. 3	155
Duluth	May 10	Oct. 5	148
Minneapolis	Apr. 25	Oct. 13	171
Pipestone	May 13	Sept. 25	135
St. Paul	Apr. 23	Oct. 10	170
Mississippi			
Biloxi	Feb. 26	Nov. 29	276
Jackson	Mar. 19	Nov. 8	234
Meridian	Mar. 17	Nov. 11	239
Tunica	Mar. 25	Nov. 2	225
Tupelo	Mar. 30	Nov. 1	216
Missouri			
Caruthersville	Mar. 28	Nov. 1	218
Jefferson City	Apr. 15	Oct. 20	188
Kansas City	Apr. 7	Oct. 28	204
St. Joseph	Apr. 12	Oct. 15	186
St. Louis	Apr. 2	Oct. 29	210
Springfield	Apr. 8	Oct. 28	203
Versailles	Apr. 22	Oct. 14	175
Montana			
Billings	May 15	Sept. 25	133
Havre	May 11	Sept. 22	134
Helena	May 2	Oct. 2	153
Kalispell	May 5	Oct. 1	149
Miles City	Apr. 30	Oct. 5	158
Poplar	May 16	Sept. 18	125
Nebraska			
Ainsworth	May 8	Oct. 4	149
Lincoln	Apr. 18	Oct. 15	180
Norfolk	May 3	Oct. 4	155
North Platte	Apr. 29	Oct. 10	164
Omaha	Apr. 14	Oct. 20	189
Scottsbluff	May 11	Sept. 26	138
Nevada			
Carson City	May 25	Sept. 19	117
Elko	June 1	Sept. 18	105
Las Vegas	Mar. 16	Nov. 10	239
Reno	May 8	Oct. 10	155
Wells	June 11	Sept. 13	94
New Hampshire			
Berlin	May 30	Sept. 16	109
Concord	May 3	Oct. 3	153
Durham	May 17	Sept. 28	134
Nashua	May 18	Sept. 26	133
New Jersey			
Atlantic City	Apr. 6	Nov. 7	215
Cape May	Apr. 8	Nov. 12	218
Moorestown	Apr. 24	Oct. 19	178
New Brunswick	Apr. 22	Oct. 20	181
Newark	Apr. 14	Oct. 28	197
Newton	Apr. 27	Oct. 12	168
Paterson	Apr. 18	Oct. 19	184
Trenton	Apr. 13	Oct. 27	197

STATE	KILLING FROST AVERAGE DATES		Growing Season,
	Last in Spring	First in Fall	Number of Days
New Mexico			
Albuquerque	Apr. 13	Oct. 28	198
Aztec	May 5	Oct. 7	155
Deming	Apr. 2	Nov. 1	213
Elephant Butte	Apr. 2	Nov. 11	223
Roswell	Apr. 7	Oct. 31	207
Santa Fe	Apr. 24	Oct. 19	178
New York			
Albany	Apr. 23	Oct. 14	174
Chazy	May 13	Sept. 30	140
Jamestown	May 15	Oct. 6	144
New York	Apr. 9	Nov. 6	211
Scarsdale	Apr. 21	Oct. 21	183
Southampton	Apr. 21	Oct. 25	187
Syracuse	Apr. 23	Oct. 22	182
Watertown	May 6	Oct. 9	156
Westfield	May 3	Oct. 23	173
North Carolina			
Asheville	Apr. 11	Oct. 22	194
New Bern	Mar. 28	Nov. 10	227
Pinehurst	Apr. 2	Nov. 2	214
Raleigh	Mar. 23	Nov. 9	231
Tarboro	Apr. 6	Oct. 31	208
Winston Salem	Apr. 11	Oct. 25	197
North Dakota			
Bismark	May 10	Sept. 27	140
Devils Lake	May 15	Sept. 23	131
Grand Forks	May 16	Sept. 26	132
Willton	May 15	Sept. 25	133
Ohio			
Cincinnati	Apr. 12	Oct. 25	196
Cleveland	Apr. 16	Nov. 5	203
Columbus	Apr. 19	Oct. 23	187
Marietta	Apr. 23	Oct. 21	181
Toledo	Apr. 20	Oct. 22	185
Youngstown	Apr. 25	Oct. 17	175
Oklahoma			
Enid	Mar. 30	Oct. 24	208
Lawton	Mar. 31	Nov. 6	220
Oklahoma City	Mar. 28	Nov. 7	224
Tulsa	Mar. 25	Nov. 1	221
Oregon			
Astoria	Mar. 8	Dec. 6	273
Eugene	Apr. 13	Nov. 4	205
Medford	May 6	Oct. 14	161
Portland	Mar. 6	Nov. 24	263
Salem	Apr. 1	Oct. 31	213
Pennsylvania			
Allentown	Apr. 20	Oct. 18	181
Clearfield	May 16	Oct. 2	139
Erie	Apr. 20	Oct. 31	194
Harrisburg	Apr. 9	Oct. 30	204
Philadelphia	Apr. 5	Nov. 2	211
Pittsburgh	Apr. 20	Oct. 20	183
Towanda	May 16	Oct. 2	139
West Chester	Apr. 16	Oct. 22	189

STATE	KILLING FROST AVERAGE DATES		
	Last in Spring	First in Fall	Growing Season, Number of Days
Rhode Island			
Block Island	Apr. 10	Nov. 14	218
Greene	May 28	Sept. 18	113
Kingston	May 8	Oct. 8	153
Providence	Apr. 17	Oct. 26	192
South Carolina			
Aiken	Mar. 17	Nov. 19	247
Charleston	Feb. 23	Dec. 5	285
Columbia	Mar. 15	Nov. 18	248
Conway	Mar. 14	Nov. 13	244
Greenville	Mar 27	Nov. 10	228
South Dakota			
Mobridge	May 10	Sept. 28	141
Pierre	Apr. 30	Oct. 8	161
Rapid City	May 1	Oct. 4	156
Sioux Falls	May 6	Oct. 3	150
Watertown	May 16	Sept. 27	134
Tennessee			
Chattanooga	Mar. 21	Nov. 11	235
Johnson City	Apr. 16	Oct. 23	190
Knoxville	Mar. 30	Nov. 2	217
Memphis	Mar. 17	Nov. 10	238
Nashville	Mar. 30	Oct. 30	214
Texas			
Amarillo	Apr. 11	Oct. 2	205
Austin	Mar. 6	Nov. 25	264
Corpus Christi	Jan. 26	Dec. 27	335
Dallas	Mar. 18	Nov. 17	244
El Paso	Mar. 21	Nov. 14	238
Fort Worth	Mar. 11	Nov. 17	251
Galveston	Jan. 21	Dec. 28	341
Houston	Feb. 10	Dec. 8	301
Lubbock	Apr. 12	Nov. 3	205
San Angelo	Mar. 25	Nov. 9	229
San Antonio	Feb. 24	Dec. 3	282
Waco	Mar. 10	Nov. 15	250
Wichita Falls	Mar. 22	Nov. 14	237
Utah			
Logan	May 7	Oct. 11	157
Manti	May 25	Sept. 26	124
Moab	Apr. 24	Oct. 10	169
St. George	Apr. 10	Oct. 23	196
Salt Lake City	Apr. 13	Oct. 22	192
Vernal	May 26	Sept. 21	118
Vermont			
Bennington	May 16	Sept. 29	136
Burlington	May 4	Oct. 10	159
Northfield	May 21	Sept. 25	127
Rutland	May 16	Oct. 4	141
St. Johnsburg	May 22	Sept. 26	127
Woodstock	May 28	Sept. 21	116

STATE	KILLING FROST AVERAGE DATES		Growing Season,
	Last in Spring	First in Fall	Number of Days
Virginia			
Charlottesville	Apr. 6	Nov. 5	213
Danville	Apr. 2	Oct. 30	211
Fredericksburg	Apr. 15	Oct. 25	193
Norfolk	Mar. 19	Nov. 16	242
Richmond	Mar. 29	Nov. 2	218
Tazewell	May 8	Oct. 5	150
Williamsburg	Apr. 9	Oct. 31	205
Winchester	Apr. 17	Oct. 27	193
Washington			
Bellingham	Apr. 20	Oct. 23	186
Centralia	Apr. 27	Oct. 17	173
Olympia	Apr. 20	Oct. 28	191
Seattle	Mar. 14	Nov. 24	255
Spokane	Apr. 12	Oct. 13	184
Walla Walla	Mar. 31	Nov. 5	219
Wenatchee	Apr. 24	Oct. 14	173
West Virginia			
Charleston	Apr. 20	Oct. 23	186
Hinton	Apr. 24	Oct. 23	182
Morgantown	May 1	Oct. 13	165
Parkersburg	Apr. 18	Oct. 19	184
White Sulphur Springs	May 15	Oct. 6	144
Wisconsin			
Eau Claire	May 4	Oct. 1	150
Green Bay	May 5	Oct. 9	157
Madison	Apr. 29	Oct. 9	166
Milwaukee	Apr. 22	Oct. 23	184
Superior	May 11	Oct. 2	144
Wausau	May 22	Sept. 29	130
Wyoming			
Casper	May 19	Sept. 29	133
Cheyenne	May 4	Oct. 2	141
Cody	May 17	Sept. 19	125
Green River	June 3	Sept. 11	100
Lander	May 18	Sept. 20	125
Lusk	May 26	Sept. 18	115

SPECIAL PLANT AND HORTICULTURAL SOCIETIES OF THE UNITED STATES, CANADA AND GREAT BRITAIN

To belong to a special plant or national horticultural society is a fascinating learning source for many gardeners.

For a few dollars you may become a member of The American Horticultural Society, receiving their quarterly magazine and information on special plant and supply sources; for a further fee, you may participate in their annual Congress, which features lectures, panels, a film festival, a rare-plant auction and supplementary tours to famous gardens in the area where the Congress is held. Write to: The Executive Director, The American Horticultural Society, 2401 Calvert St. N.W., Washington, D.C., 20008.

For a few pounds you may become an Overseas Fellow of The Royal Horticultural Society of England and receive their monthly *Journal,* free seed through their annual seed exchanges, information on special plant and supply sources and, if you should be lucky enough to be in England at the proper time, free tickets for Fellow's Day at the famous Chelsea Flower Show, for the delightful, more intimate small shows in their halls all year and to visit the magnificent trial gardens of the Society at Wisley near London. Write to: The Secretary, The Royal Horticultural Society, Vincent Square, London, S.W.1, England.

As well, there are botanical gardens, horticultural societies, garden clubs and garden centers in all parts of North America that are a marvelous help and pleasure with their programs of meetings, exhibitions and shows, demonstrations of practical gardening, libraries, and advisory services; many publish excellent bulletins. Ask your government department of agriculture to put you in touch with the one nearest you.

The surest way to become an expert in one kind of plant is to belong to a society that specializes in the study of that plant. Such societies issue bulletins, answer members' questions, usually stage shows in some part of the country every year, organize round robins and frequently carry on seed and plant exchanges.

SPECIAL PLANT SOCIETIES

UNITED STATES

Write to: The Executive Director, The American Horticultural Society, Inc., 2401 Calvert St. N.W., Washington, D.C., 20008, for the name and address of the secretary of the society you are interested in.

THE AFRICAN VIOLET SOCIETY OF AMERICA, INC.

THE AMERICAN ASSOCIATION OF BOTANICAL GARDENS AND ARBORETA

THE AMERICAN ASSOCIATION OF HORTICULTURAL SCIENCE

THE AMERICAN BEGONIA SOCIETY, INC.

THE AMERICAN BONSAI SOCIETY

THE AMERICAN BOXWOOD SOCIETY

THE AMERICAN CAMELLIA SOCIETY

THE AMERICAN DAFFODIL SOCIETY, INC.

THE AMERICAN DAHLIA SOCIETY, INC.

THE AMERICAN DELPHINIUM SOCIETY

THE AMERICAN FERN SOCIETY

THE AMERICAN FUCHSIA SOCIETY

THE AMERICAN GERANIUM SOCIETY

THE AMERICAN GESNERIA SOCIETY

THE AMERICAN GLOXINIA AND GESNERIAD SOCIETY

THE AMERICAN HEMEROCALLIS SOCIETY

THE AMERICAN HIBISCUS SOCIETY

THE AMERICAN HORTICULTURAL SOCIETY

THE AMERICAN HOSTA SOCIETY

THE AMERICAN IRIS SOCIETY

THE AMERICAN LILY SOCIETY

THE AMERICAN MAGNOLIA SOCIETY

THE AMERICAN ORCHID SOCIETY

THE AMERICAN PENSTEMON SOCIETY

THE AMERICAN PEONY SOCIETY

THE AMERICAN PLANT LIFE SOCIETY (has a committee:
THE AMERICAN AMARYLLIS SOCIETY)
THE AMERICAN POINSETTIA SOCIETY
THE AMERICAN POMOLOGICAL SOCIETY
THE AMERICAN PRIMROSE SOCIETY
THE AMERICAN RHODODENDRON SOCIETY
THE AMERICAN ROCK GARDEN SOCIETY
THE AMERICAN ROSE SOCIETY
THE BROMELIAD SOCIETY
THE CACTUS AND SUCCULENT SOCIETY OF AMERICA
THE CALIFORNIA NATIONAL FUCHSIA SOCIETY
THE CYMBIDIUM SOCIETY OF AMERICA
THE EPIPHYLLUM SOCIETY OF AMERICA
THE GOURD SOCIETY OF AMERICA
THE HERB SOCIETY OF AMERICA
THE HOLLY SOCIETY OF AMERICA, INC.
THE INDOOR LIGHT GARDENING SOCIETY OF
AMERICA, INC.
THE INTERNATIONAL GERANIUM SOCIETY
THE INTERNATIONAL SHADE TREE CONFERENCE
THE NATIONAL ASSOCIATION OF PROFESSIONAL
GARDENERS
THE NATIONAL CHRYSANTHEMUM SOCIETY, INC.
THE NATIONAL TULIP SOCIETY
THE NORTH AMERICAN GLADIOLUS COUNCIL
THE NORTH AMERICAN LILY SOCIETY, INC.
THE PALM SOCIETY
SAINTPAULIA INTERNATIONAL
THE SOCIETY FOR HORTICULTURAL SCIENCE
THE WILDFLOWER PRESERVATION SOCIETY OF
NEW ENGLAND, INC.

CANADA

Write to: The Director, Royal Botanical Gardens, Box
399, Hamilton, Ontario, for the name and address of
the secretary of the society you are interested in.
THE AFRICAN VIOLET SOCIETY OF CANADA
CACTUS AND SUCCULENT INFORMATION EXCHANGE
THE CANADIAN CHRYSANTHEMUM SOCIETY
THE CANADIAN GLADIOLUS SOCIETY
THE CANADIAN IRIS SOCIETY

Canadian Sections of THE NORTH AMERICAN LILY
SOCIETY
CANADIAN CHAPTER OF THE AMERICAN RHODODENDRON
SOCIETY
SOUTHERN ONTARIO CHAPTER OF THE AMERICAN
ORCHID SOCIETY
THE CANADIAN ROSE SOCIETY

GREAT BRITAIN

Address your inquiry to the secretary of the society
your are interested in, care of The Secretary, The
Royal Horticultural Society, Vincent Square, London,
S.W. 1, England. It will be forwarded.
THE AFRICAN SUCCULENT PLANT SOCIETY
THE ALPINE GARDEN SOCIETY
THE BRITISH FUCHSIA SOCIETY
THE BRITISH GLADIOLUS SOCIETY
THE BRITISH IRIS SOCIETY
THE BRITISH PANSY AND VIOLA FLORAL SOCIETY
THE BRITISH PELARGONIUM'AND GERANIUM SOCIETY
THE BRITISH PTERIDOLOGICAL (FERN) SOCIETY
THE CACTUS AND SUCCULENT SOCIETY OF GREAT
BRITAIN
THE DAFFODIL SOCIETY OF GREAT BRITAIN
THE DELPHINIUM SOCIETY OF GREAT BRITAIN
THE HEATHER SOCIETY OF GREAT BRITAIN
THE INTERNATIONAL CAMELLIA SOCIETY
THE JAPAN SOCIETY OF LONDON (BONSAI)
THE LILY GROUP OF THE ROYAL HORTICULTURAL
SOCIETY
THE NATIONAL AURICULA AND PRIMULA SOCIETY
THE NATIONAL BEGONIA SOCIETY
THE NATIONAL CACTUS AND SUCCULENT SOCIETY
THE NATIONAL CHRYSANTHEMUM SOCIETY
THE NATIONAL DAHLIA SOCIETY
THE NATIONAL SWEET PEA SOCIETY
THE NATIONAL VIOLA AND PANSY SOCIETY
THE ORCHID SOCIETY OF GREAT BRITAIN
THE ROYAL NATIONAL ROSE SOCIETY
THE SAINTPAULIA AND HOUSEPLANT SOCIETY
THE RHODODENDRON GROUP OF THE ROYAL
HORTICULTURAL SOCIETY

African-Violets:
Wilson, Helen Van Pelt. *Helen Van Pelt Wilson's African-Violet Book.* New York: Hawthorn Books, Inc., 1970.

Annuals:
Nehrling, Arno and Irene. *The Picture Book of Annuals.* New York: Hearthside Press, Inc., 1966.

Artificial Light Gardening:
Cherry, Elaine C. *Fluorescent Light Gardening.* New York: Van Nostrand Reinhold Company, 1965.

Azaleas:
Lee, Frederic P. *The Azalea Book,* 2d ed. Washington, D.C.: The American Horticultural Society, 1965.

Begonias:
Kramer, Jack. *Begonias, Indoors and Out.* New York: E. P. Dutton & Co., Inc., 1967.

Bonsai:
Behme, Robert Lee. *Bonsai, Saikei, and Bonkei.* New York: William Morrow and Company, Inc., 1969.
Pipe, Anne. *Bonsai, The Art of Dwarfing Trees.* New York: Hawthorn Books, Inc., 1964.

Bulbs:
Baumgardt, John P. *Bulbs for Summer Bloom.* New York: Hawthorn Books, Inc., 1970.
Miles, Bebe. *The Wonderful World of Bulbs.* New York: Van Nostrand Reinhold Company, 1963.
Reynold, Marc, and Meacham, W. L. *The Garden Bulbs of Spring.* New York: Funk & Wagnalls Company, Inc., 1967.

Cacti:
Chidamian, Claude. *The Book of Cacti and Other Succulents.* New York: Doubleday & Company, Inc., 1958.

Chrysanthemums:
Cumming, Roderick W. *The Chrysanthemum Book.* New York: Van Nostrand Reinhold Company, 1964.

City Gardens:
Truex, Philip. *The City Gardener.* New York: Alfred A. Knopf, Inc., 1964.

Climbing and Hanging Plants:
Baumgardt, John P. *Hanging Plants for Home, Garden, and Greenhouse.* New York: Simon & Schuster, Inc., 1972.
Wyman, Donald. *Shrubs and Vines for American Gardens,* rev. ed. New York: The Macmillan Company, 1969.

Container Gardening:
Taloumis, George. *Gardening in Containers.* New York: Simon & Schuster, Inc., 1972.

Design:
Ireys, Alice Recknagel. *How to Plan and Plant Your Own Property.* New York: Barrows & Co., Inc., 1967.
Roberts, Irving. *Home Landscaping You Can Do Yourself.* New York: Hawthorn Books, Inc., 1972.
Smith, Alice Upham. *Patios, Terraces, Decks, and Roof Gardens.* New York: Hawthorn Books, Inc., 1969.

Espaliers:
Perkins, Harold O. *Espaliers and Vines for the Home Gardener.* New York: Van Nostrand Reinhold Company, 1964.

Ferns:
Foster, F. Gordon. *Ferns to Know and Grow.* New York: Hawthorn Books, Inc., 1971.

Fragrant Gardens:
Wilson, Helen Van Pelt, and Bell, Léonie. *The Fragrant Year.* New York: Bonanza, 1967.

Fruit:
Kraft, Ken and Pat. *Fruits for the Home Garden.* New York: William Morrow and Company, Inc., 1968.

Gesneriads:
Wilson, Helen Van Pelt, ed. *African Violet and Gesneriad Questions Answered by 20 Experts.* New York: Van Nostrand Reinhold Company, 1966.

Greenhouses:
Blake, Claire L. *Greenhouse Gardening for Fun.* New York: Barrows and Co., Inc., 1967.

Herbs:
Simmons, Adelma Grenier. *Herb Gardening in Five Seasons.* New York: Van Nostrand Reinhold Company, 1964.
————. *Herbs to Grow Indoors.* New York: Hawthorn Books, Inc., 1969.

House Plants:
Ballard, Ernesta D. *Garden in Your House.* New York: Harper & Row, 1971.
Fitch, Charles Marden. *The Complete Book of Houseplants.* New York: Hawthorn Books, Inc., 1972.
Kramer, Jack. *1000 Beautiful House Plants and How to Grow Them.* New York: William Morrow and Company, Inc., 1969.
McDonald, Elvin. *The World Book of House Plants.* Cleveland: The World Publishing Company, 1963.

Lilies:
De Graaff, Jan, and Hyams, Edward. *Lilies.* New York: Funk & Wagnalls Company, Inc., 1968.

Orchids:
Kramer, Jack. *Growing Orchids at Your Window.* New York: Hawthorn Books, Inc., 1972.
Logan, Harry B. *Orchids You Can Grow.* New York: Hawthorn Books, Inc., 1971.
Northen, Rebecca T. *Home Orchid Growing.* New York: Van Nostrand Reinhold Company, 1969.

Peonies:
Nehrling, Arno and Irene. *Peonies Outdoors and In.* New York: Hearthside Press, Inc., 1960.

Perennials:
Nehrling, Arno and Irene. *The Picture Book of Perennials.* New York: Hearthside Press, Inc., 1964.

Rhododendrons:
Clarke, J. Harold. *Getting Started with Rhododendrons and Azaleas.* New York: Doubleday & Company, Inc., 1960.
Leach, David G. *Rhododendrons of the World.* New York: Charles Scribner's Sons, 1961.

Rock Gardens:

Foster, Lincoln H. *Rock Gardening, A Guide to Growing Alpines and Other Wild Flowers in the American Garden.* Boston: Houghton Mifflin Company, 1968.

Kolaga, Walter A. *All about Rock Gardens and Plants.* New York: Doubleday & Company, Inc., 1966.

Roses:

Bassity, Mathew A. R. *The Magic World of Roses.* New York: Hearthside Press, Inc., 1966.

Seeds:

Haring, Elda. *The Complete Book of Growing Plants from Seed.* New York: Hawthorn Books, Inc., 1967.

Shrubs:

Zucker, Isabel. *Flowering Shrubs.* New York: Van Nostrand Reinhold Company, 1966.

Trees:

Wyman, Donald. *Trees for American Gardens,* rev. ed. New York: The Macmillan Company, 1965.

Vegetables:

Carlton, R. Milton. *Vegetables for Today's Gardens.* New York: Van Nostrand Reinhold Company, 1967.

Hériteau, Jacqueline. *The How to Grow and Cook It Book of Vegetables, Herbs, Fruits, and Nuts.* New York: Hawthorn Books, Inc., 1970.

Water Gardens:

Thomas, G. L., Jr. *Goldfish Pools, Water-Lilies and Tropical Fishes.* New York: T. F. H. Sterling, 1965.

Wild Flowers:

Aiken, Senator George D. *Pioneering in Wild Flowers.* Englewood Cliffs, N.J.: Prentice-Hall, Inc., 1968.

Kieran, John. *An Introduction to Wild Flowers.* New York: Doubleday & Company, Inc., 1965.

Rickett, H. W. *Wild Flowers of the United States.* Vol. 1, *Northeastern.* Vol. 2, *Southeastern.* New York: McGraw-Hill Book Company, 1966, 1967.

Taylor, K. S., and Hamblin, Stephen. *Handbook of Wildflower Cultivation.* New York: The Macmillan Company, 1962.

GENERAL:

Haring, Elda. *Color for Your Yard and Garden.* New York: Hawthorn Books, Inc., 1971.

McDonald, Elvin, and Power, Lawrence, *The Low-Upkeep Book of Lawns and Landscape.* New York: Hawthorn Books, Inc., 1971.

Tarantino, Rhoda. *Small Gardens Are More Fun.* New York: Simon & Schuster, Inc., 1971.

REFERENCE BOOKS:

Bailey, L. H. *Hortus Second.* New York: The Macmillan Company, 1941. *Hortus Third* is in preparation.

The Royal Horticultural Society Dictionary of Gardening. Four volumes and Supplement. Oxford, England: Clarendon Press.

SERIES:

Handbooks of The Brooklyn Botanic Garden, Brooklyn, New York 11225.

INDEX

If you want to be happy for an hour,
                    get Drunk;
If you want to be happy for three days,
                    get Married;
If you want to be happy for eight days,
                    kill Your Pig and eat it;
If you want to be happy for Ever,
                    Make a Garden.

AN
OLD
CHINESE
PROVERB

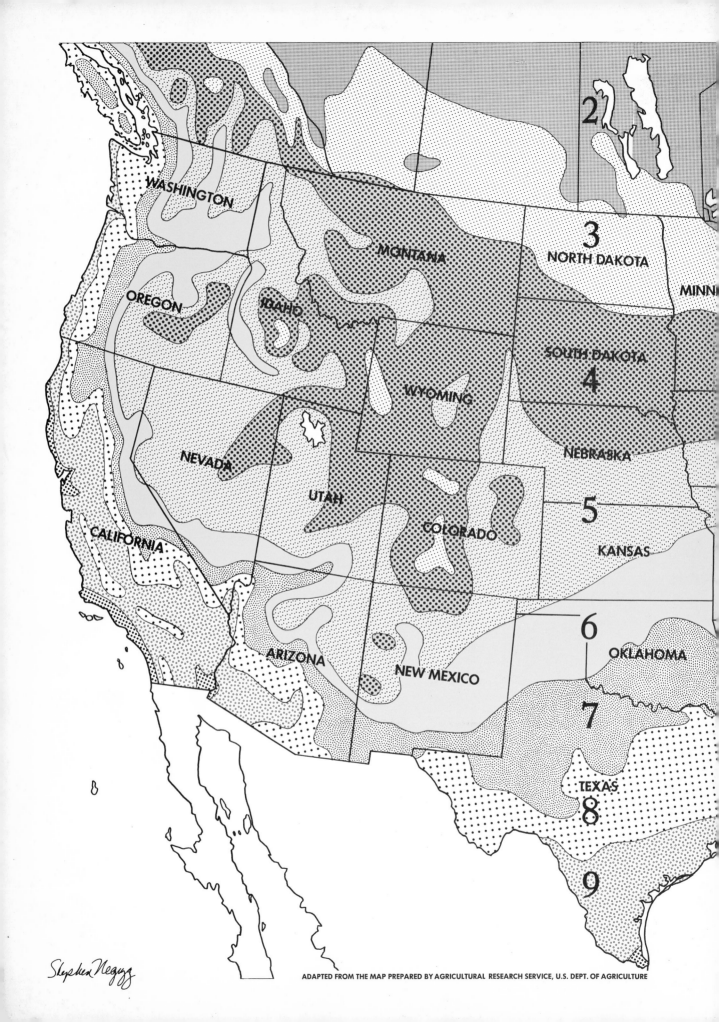

ADAPTED FROM THE MAP PREPARED BY AGRICULTURAL RESEARCH SERVICE, U.S. DEPT. OF AGRICULTURE